UNIX® SYSTEM V RELEASE 4

INCLUDES MULTIPROCESSING

User's Reference Manual / System Administrator's Reference Manual

(Commands a-l)

⸻ ◇ ⸻
Intel Processors
⸻ ◇ ⸻

UNIX
PRESS
A Prentice Hall Title

P R E N T I C E   H A L L

ORDERING INFORMATION

UNIX® SYSTEM V RELEASE 4 DOCUMENTATION

To order single copies of UNIX® SYSTEM V Release 4 documentation, please call (201) 767-5937.

ATTENTION DOCUMENTATION MANAGERS AND TRAINING DIRECTORS:

For bulk purchases in excess of 30 copies, please write to:

Corporate Sales
Prentice Hall
Englewood Cliffs, N.J. 07632

Or call: (201) 461-8441.

ATTENTION GOVERNMENT CUSTOMERS:

For GSA and other pricing information, please call (201) 767-5994.

Prentice-Hall International (UK) Limited, *London*
Prentice-Hall of Australia Pty. Limited, *Sydney*
Prentice-Hall Canada Inc., *Toronto*
Prentice-Hall Hispanoamericana, S.A., *Mexico*
Prentice-Hall of India Private Limited, *New Delhi*
Prentice-Hall of Japan, Inc., *Tokyo*
Simon & Schuster Asia Pte. Ltd., *Singapore*
Editora Prentice-Hall do Brasil, Ltda., *Rio de Janeiro*

Preface

UNIX System V Reference Manuals describe the interfaces and execution behavior of each System V component. The components of UNIX System V include the graphical user interface (GUI), Shell command line interface, application program interface (API) and Device Driver Interface / Driver Kernel Interface (DDI/DKI), as well as device special files, header files and other system files. The following table summarizes the general categories of manual pages:

Table 1: Manual Page Categories

Description	Section Reference
Shell & Command Line Interface	
— General Purpose Utilities	1
— Maintenance Utilities	1M
Application Program Interface (API)	
— UNIX System Calls	2
— C Language Libraries	3
System Files & Devices	
— System File Formats	4
— Miscellaneous Facilities	5
— Special Files (Devices)	7
Device Driver Interface/Driver Kernel Interface (DDI/DKI)	
— DDI/DKI Driver Data Definitions	D1
— DDI/DKI Driver Entry Point Routines	D2
— DDI/DKI Kernel Utility Routines	D3
— DDI/DKI Kernel Data Structures	D4
— DDI/DKI Kernel Defines	D5

Reference Manuals supply technical reference information that describes the source-code interfaces and run-time behavior of each component of System V on a component by component basis. As concise reference material, manual pages assume some familiarity with the information.

Organization of the Reference Manuals

Each section in a Reference Manual consists of a number of independent entries called "manual pages." A "Table of Contents" precedes each manual page section. Within each section, manual pages are arranged in alphabetical order based on the name of the component described by that manual page. Some manual pages may describe several commands, functions, or other type of system facility. In such cases, the manual page appears only once in a table of contents, alphabetized under its "primary" name, the name that appears at the upper corners of each manual page. For each Reference Manual, a "Permuted Index" of all manual pages for that manual is provided at the back of the book.

This latest edition of the UNIX System V Release 4 Reference Manuals has reorganized the reference manuals to make it easier to identify which manual contains a given manual page, and to locate the manual page within that manual. The new organization of the UNIX System V Reference Manuals

- includes all reference manual pages found in various Programmer's Guides in the Reference Manuals

- makes each manual page unique, rather than repeating it in different Reference Manuals

- sorts each section together, rather than breaking it out by subsection, for example, all of Section 1, including subsections 1C, 1F, 1M, and 1N

- precedes each section with its own table of contents

The set of UNIX System V Reference Manuals organizes the manual pages into volumes aligned with the different types of interfaces that make up UNIX System V Release 4. Manual pages for the same type of components are found in the same volume, and components of different types are found in separate volumes. For example, you will no longer find programming commands (cc, make, and so on) in the *Programmer's Reference Manual*. Those commands have been moved to join Section 1 commands in the *User's Reference Manual/System Administrator's Reference Manual*. At the same time, all Section 4, 5 and 7 manual pages, which describe various system files and special files (devices) and were previously located in the *Programmer's Reference Manual* or the *System Administrator's Reference Manual*, have been consolidated in a new, separate volume entitled *System Files and Devices Reference Manual*. The table on the following page lists the contents of the new complete set of Reference Manuals:

Table 2: The UNIX System V Release 4 Reference Manual Set

Reference Manual	Description	Sections
User's Reference Manual/ *System Administrator's* *Reference Manual* *(Commands* a – l *and* m – z*)*	General-Purpose User Commands Basic Networking Commands Form and Menu Language Interpreter System Maintenance Commands Enhanced Networking Commands	1 1C 1F 1M 1N
Programmer's Reference *Manual: Operating* *System API*	System Calls BSD System Compatibility Library Standard C Library Executable and Linking Format Library General-Purpose Library Math Library Networking Library Standard I/O Library Specialized Library	2 3 3C 3E 3G 3M 3N 3S 3X
Programmer's Reference *Manual: Windowing* *System API*	X Window System Library X Window System Toolkit OPEN LOOK Intrinsics Toolkit	3X11 3Xt 3W
System Files and Devices *Reference Manual*	System File Formats Miscellaneous Facilities Special Files (Devices)	4 5 7
Device Driver Interface/ *Driver Kernel Interface* *Reference Manual*	DDI/DKI Driver Data Definitions DDI/DKI Driver Entry Point Routines DDI/DKI Kernel Utility Routines DDI/DKI Kernel Data Structures DDI/DKI Kernel Defines	D1 D2 D3 D4 D5

Reference Manual Index

A "Permuted Index" for this reference manual is provided at the back. The Permuted Index is a list of keywords, alphabetized in the second of three columns, together with the context in which each keyword is found. The manual page that produced an entry is listed in the right column.

Entries are identified with their section numbers shown in parentheses. This is important because there is considerable duplication of names among the sections, arising principally from commands and functions that exist only to exercise a particular system call.

The index is produced by rotating the NAME section of each manual page to alphabetize each keyword in it. Words that cannot fit in the middle column are rotated into the left column. If the entry is still too long, some words are omitted, and their omission is indicated with a slash ("/").

Here is an example of some of the entries produced for the manual pages rand(3C), sleep(1), sleep(3), and sleep(3C):

Figure 1: Sample of a Permuted Index

generator	rand, srand simple random number	rand(3C)
srand simple	random number generator rand, ...	rand(3C)
rand, srand	simple random number generator	rand(3C)
interval	sleep suspend execution for an	sleep(1)
interval	sleep suspend execution for an	sleep(3)
interval	sleep suspend execution for an	sleep(3C)
generator rand,	srand simple random number	rand(3C)

Table of Contents

Introduction to the User's Reference Manual/System Administrator's Reference Manual

Section 1 – Commands a – l

Table of Contents

Table of Contents _____

Table of Contents

Table of Contents

Section 1 – Commands m – z

Table of Contents

Table of Contents

Table of Contents

Table of Contents

Section 4 – File Formats

Table of Contents

Section 5 – Miscellaneous Facilities

Section 7 – Special Files

Permuted Index

Introduction

This reference manual describes the commands of the UNIX system. It contains individual manual pages that describe user and administrative commands. (For a general overview of the UNIX system, see the *Product Overview*.)

Note that not all commands described in this manual are available in every UNIX system. Some of the features require additional utilities that may not exist on your system.

Organization of this Reference Manual

This manual contains the following sections (sorted together, alphabetically):

Section	Component Type
1	Commands (User)
1C	Commands (Basic Networking)
1F	Commands (Form & Menu Language Interpreter (FMLI))
1M	Commands (Administration)
1N	Commands (Enhanced Networking)

Section 1 (*Commands, user*) describes programs intended to be invoked directly by the user or by command language procedures, as opposed to subroutines that are called by the user's programs. Commands usually are in the **/usr/bin** and **/usr/sbin** directories. In addition, some commands are in **/sbin**. These directories are searched automatically by the command interpreter called the *shell*. Also, UNIX systems often have a directory called **/usr/lbin** that contains local commands.

Section 1C (*Commands, basic networking*) contains commands that are used when files are exchanged with another computer system.

Section 1F (*Commands, forms and menus*) contains commands and programs that are used by the Form & Menu Interpreter (FMLI).

Section 1M (*Commands, system maintenance*) contains commands and programs that are used in administering a UNIX system.

Section 1N (*Commands, enhanced networking*) contains commands and programs that are used for enhanced networking.

Manual Page Format

All manual page entries use a common format, not all of whose parts always appear:

- The **NAME** section gives the name(s) of the entry and briefly states its purpose.

- The **SYNOPSIS** section summarizes the use of the command, program or function. A few conventions are used:

  - `Constant width typeface` strings are literals and are to be typed just as they appear.

  - *Italic* strings usually represent substitutable argument prototypes and functions.

  - Square brackets [ ] around an argument prototype indicate that the argument is optional. When an argument prototype is given as *name* or *file*, it typically refers to a file name.

  - Ellipses **. . .** are used to show that the previous argument prototype may be repeated.

  - For commands, an argument beginning with a minus − or plus + sign is often taken to be a flag argument, even if it appears in a position where a file name could appear. Therefore, it is unwise to have files whose names begin with − or +.

- The **DESCRIPTION** section describes the utility.

- The **EXAMPLE** section gives example(s) of usage, where appropriate.

- The **FILES** section gives the file names that are built into the program.

- The **SEE ALSO** section gives pointers to related information. Reference to manual pages with section numbers other than those in this book can be found in other reference manuals, as listed above.

- The **DIAGNOSTICS** section discusses the diagnostic indications that may be produced. Messages that are intended to be self-explanatory are not listed.

■ The **NOTES** section gives generally helpful hints about the use of the utility.

How to Get Started

This discussion provides the basic information you need to get started on the UNIX system: how to log in and log out, how to communicate through your terminal, and how to run a program. (See the *User's Guide* for a more complete introduction to the system.)

Logging In

You must connect to the UNIX system from a full-duplex ASCII terminal or the console monitor (on a PC). You must also have a valid login ID, which may be obtained (together with how to access your UNIX system) from the administrator of your system. Common terminal speeds are 1200, 2400, 4800 and 9600 baud. Some UNIX systems have different ways of accessing each available terminal speed, while other systems offer several speeds through a common access method. In the latter case, there is one "preferred" speed; if you access it from a terminal set to a different speed, you will be greeted by a string of meaningless characters. Keep hitting the BREAK, INTERRUPT, or ATTENTION key until the `login:` prompt appears.

Most terminals have a speed switch that should be set to the appropriate speed and a half-/full-duplex switch that should be set to full-duplex. When a connection has been established, the system displays `login:`. You respond by typing your login ID followed by the RETURN key. If you have a password, the system asks for it but will not print, or "echo," it on the screen. After you have logged in, the ENTER, RETURN, NEW-LINE, and LINE-FEED keys all have equivalent meanings.

Make sure you type your login name in lower-case letters. Typing upper-case letters causes the UNIX system to assume that your terminal can generate only upper-case letters, and it will treat all letters as upper-case for the remainder of your login session. The shell will print a `$` on your screen when you have logged in successfully.

When you log in, a message-of-the-day may greet you before you receive your prompt. For more information, consult the **login**(1) manual page, which discusses the login sequence in more detail, and the **stty**(1) manual page, which tells you how to describe your terminal to the system. The **profile**(4) manual page explains how to accomplish this last task automatically every time you log in.

Logging Out

To log out of your system type an end-of-file indication (ASCII EOT character, usually typed as CTRL-d) to the shell. The shell will terminate, and the **login:** message will appear again.

How to Communicate Through Your Terminal

When you type on your keyboard, your individual characters are being gathered and temporarily saved. Although they are echoed back to you (displayed on the screen), these characters will not be "seen" by a program until you press ENTER (or RETURN or NEW-LINE) as described above in "Logging In."

UNIX system terminal input/output is full duplex. It has full read-ahead, which means that you can type at any time, even while a program is displaying characters on the screen. Of course, if you type during output, your input characters will have output characters interspersed among them. In any case, whatever you type will be saved and interpreted in the correct sequence. There is a limit to the amount of read-ahead, but it is not likely to be exceeded.

The character @ cancels all the characters typed before it on a line, effectively deleting the line. (@ is called the "line kill" character.) The character # erases the last character typed. Successive uses of # will erase characters back to, but not beyond, the beginning of the line; @ and # can be typed as themselves by preceding them with \ (thus, to erase a \, you need two #s). These default erase and line kill characters can be changed; see the **stty**(1) manual page.

CTRL-s (also known as the ASCII DC3 character) is entered by pressing the CONTROL key and the alphabetic **s** simultaneously; it is used to stop temporarily screen output. It is useful with CRT terminals to prevent output from disappearing before it can be read. Output is resumed when a CTRL-q (also known as DC1) is pressed. Thus, if you had typed **cat** *yourfile* and the contents of *yourfile* were passing by on the screen more rapidly than you could read it, you would enter CTRL-s to freeze the output. Entering CTRL-q would allow the output to resume. The CTRL-s and CTRL-q characters are not passed to any other program when used in this manner. Also, there may be a scroll lock key on your keyboard that can be used to stop temporarily screen output.

The ASCII DEL (also called "rubout") character is not passed to programs but instead generates an interrupt signal, just like the BREAK, INTERRUPT, or ATTENTION signal. This signal generally causes whatever program you are running to terminate. It is typically used to stop a long printout to the screen that you do not want. Programs, however, can arrange either to ignore this signal altogether or to be notified and take a specific action when it happens (instead of being terminated). The editor **ed**(1), for example, catches interrupts and stops what it's doing, instead of terminating, so an interrupt can be used to halt an editor printout without losing the file being edited.

Besides adapting to the speed of the terminal, the UNIX system tries to be intelligent about whether you have a terminal with the NEW-LINE function, or whether it must be simulated with a CARRIAGE-RETURN and LINE-FEED pair. In the latter case, all *input* CARRIAGE-RETURN characters are changed to LINE-FEED characters (the standard line delimiter), and a CARRIAGE-RETURN and LINE-FEED pair is echoed to the terminal. If you get into the wrong mode, the **stty**(1) command will rescue you.

Tab characters are used freely in UNIX system source programs. If your terminal does not have the tab function, you can arrange to have tab characters changed into spaces during output, and echoed as spaces during input. Again, the **stty**(1) command will set or reset this mode. The system assumes that tabs are set every eight character positions. The **tabs**(1) command will set tab stops on your terminal, if that is possible.

How to Run a Program

When you have successfully logged into the UNIX system, a program called the shell is communicating with your terminal. The shell reads each line you type, splits the line into a command name and its arguments, and executes the command. A command is simply an executable program. Normally, the shell looks first in your current directory (see "The Current Directory" below) for the named program and, if none is there, then in system directories, such as **/usr/bin**. There is nothing special about system-provided commands except that they are kept in directories where the shell can find them. You can also keep commands in your own directories and instruct the shell to find them there. See the manual entry for **sh**(1), under the sub-heading "Parameter

Substitution,'' for the discussion of the **PATH** shell environmental variable.

The command name is the first word on an input line to the shell; the command and its arguments are separated from one another by space or tab characters.

When a program terminates, the shell will ordinarily regain control and give you back your prompt to show that it is ready for another command. The shell has many other capabilities, which are described in detail on the **sh**(1) manual page.

The Current Directory

The UNIX system has a file system arranged in a hierarchy of directories. When you received your login ID, the system administrator also created a directory for you (ordinarily with the same name as your login ID, and known as your login or home directory). When you log in, that directory becomes your current or working directory, and any file name you type is, by default, assumed to be in that directory. Because you are the owner of this directory, you have full permissions to read, write, alter, or remove its contents. Permissions to enter or change other directories and files will have been granted or denied to you by their respective owners or by the system administrator. To change the current directory, use the **cd** command (see the **cd**(1) manual page.

Pathnames

To refer to files or directories not in the current directory, you must use a pathname. Full pathnames begin with **/**, which is the name of the root directory of the whole file system. After the slash comes the name of each directory containing the next subdirectory (followed by a **/**), until finally the file or directory name is reached (for example, **/usr/ae/filex** refers to file **filex** in directory **ae**, while **ae** is itself a subdirectory of **usr**, and **usr** is a subdirectory of the root directory). Use the **pwd** command (see the **pwd**(1) manual page) to print the full pathname of the directory you are working in. See the introduction to section 2 in the *Programmer's Reference Manual: Operating System API* for a formal definition of *pathname*.

If your current directory contains subdirectories, the pathnames of their respective files begin with the name of the corresponding subdirectory (without a prefixed /). A pathname may be used anywhere a file name is required.

Important commands that affect files are **cp**, **mv**, and **rm**, which respectively copy, move (that is, rename), and remove files (see the **cp**(1), **mv**(1) and **rm**(1) manual pages). To find out the status of files or directories, use **ls** (see the **ls**(1) manual page). Use **mkdir** for making directories and **rmdir** for removing them (see the **mkdir**(1) and **rm**(1) manual pages).

Text Entry and Display

Almost all text is entered through an editor. Common examples of UNIX system editors are **ed**(1) and **vi**(1). The commands most often used to print text on a terminal are **cat**, **pr**, and **pg** (see the **cat**(1), **pr**(1) and **pg**(1) manual pages). The **cat** command displays the contents of ASCII text files on the screen, with no processing at all. The **pr** command paginates the text, supplies headings, and has a facility for multi-column output. The **pg** command displays text in successive portions no larger than your screen.

Writing a Program

Once you have entered the text of your program into a file with an editor, you are ready to give the file to the appropriate language processor. The processor will accept only files observing the correct naming conventions: all C programs must end with the suffix **.c**, and Fortran programs must end with **.f**. The output of the language processor will be left in a file named **a.out** in the current directory, unless you have invoked an option to save it in another file. (Use **mv** to rename **a.out**.) If the program is written in assembly language, you will probably need to load library subroutines with it (see the **ld**(1) manual page).

When you have completed this process without provoking any diagnostics, you may run the program by giving its name to the shell in response to the **$** prompt. Your programs can receive arguments from the command line just as system programs do; see the **exec**(2) manual page. For more information on writing and running programs, see the *Programmer's Guide: ANSI C and Programming Support Tools.*

Communicating with Others

Certain commands provide inter-user communication. Even if you do not plan to use them, it's helpful to learn something about them because someone else may try to contact you. **mail** or **mailx** (see the **mail**(1) and **mailx**(1) manual pages) will leave a message whose presence will be announced to another user when they next log in and at periodic intervals during the session. To communicate with another user currently logged in, use **write** (see the **write**(1) manual page). The corresponding entries in this manual also suggest how to respond to these commands if you are their target.

See the tutorials in the *User's Guide* for more information on communicating with others.

Section 1 – Commands a – l

NAME

intro – introduction to commands and application programs

DESCRIPTION

This section describes, in alphabetical order, commands, including user commands, programming commands and commands used chiefly for maintenance and administration (1M commands).

Because of command restructuring for the Virtual File System architecture, there are several instances of multiple manual pages with the same name. For example, there are four manual pages called **mount**(1M). In each such case the first of the multiple pages describes the syntax and options of the generic command, that is, those options applicable to all FSTypes (file system types). The succeeding pages describe the functionality of the FSType-specific modules of the command. These pages all display the name of the FSType to which they pertain centered and in parentheses at the top of the page. Note that the administrator should not attempt to call these modules directly. The generic command provides a common interface to all of them. Thus the FSType-specific manual pages should not be viewed as describing distinct commands, but rather as detailing those aspects of a command that are specific to a particular FSType.

Manual Page Command Syntax

Unless otherwise noted, commands described in the **SYNOPSIS** section of a manual page accept options and other arguments according to the following syntax and should be interpreted as explained below.

name [*–option*...] [*cmdarg*...]
where:

[ ]	Surround an *option* or *cmdarg* that is not required.
...	Indicates multiple occurrences of the *option* or *cmdarg*.
name	The name of an executable file.
option	(Always preceded by a "–".) *noargletter*... or, *argletter optarg*[,...]
noargletter	A single letter representing an option without an option-argument. Note that more than one *noargletter* option can be grouped after one "–" (Rule 5, below).
argletter	A single letter representing an option requiring an option-argument.
optarg	An option-argument (character string) satisfying a preceding *argletter*. Note that groups of *optargs* following an *argletter* must be separated by commas, or separated by white space and quoted (Rule 8, below).
cmdarg	Path name (or other command argument) *not* beginning with "–", or "–" by itself indicating the standard input.

Command Syntax Standard: Rules

These command syntax rules are not followed by all current commands, but all new commands will obey them. **getopts**(1) should be used by all shell procedures to parse positional parameters and to check for legal options. It supports Rules 3-10 below. The enforcement of the other rules must be done by the command itself.

1. Command names (*name* above) must be between two and nine characters long.

2. Command names must include only lower-case letters and digits.

3. Option names (*option* above) must be one character long.

4. All options must be preceded by "–".

5. Options with no arguments may be grouped after a single "–".

6. The first option-argument (*optarg* above) following an option must be preceded by white space.

7. Option-arguments cannot be optional.

8. Groups of option-arguments following an option must either be separated by commas or separated by white space and quoted (e.g., **–o xxx,z,yy** or **–o "xxx z yy"**).

9. All options must precede operands (*cmdarg* above) on the command line.

10. "––" may be used to indicate the end of the options.

11. The order of the options relative to one another should not matter.

12. The relative order of the operands (*cmdarg* above) may affect their significance in ways determined by the command with which they appear.

13. "–" preceded and followed by white space should only be used to mean standard input.

SEE ALSO

getopts(1)

exit(2), wait(2), getopt(3C) in the *Programmer's Reference Manual*

How to Get Started in the "Introduction" to this document

DIAGNOSTICS

Upon termination, each command returns two bytes of status, one supplied by the system and giving the cause for termination, and (in the case of "normal" termination) one supplied by the program [see **wait**(2) and **exit**(2)]. The former byte is 0 for normal termination; the latter is customarily 0 for successful execution and non-zero to indicate troubles such as erroneous parameters, or bad or inaccessible data. It is called variously "exit code", "exit status", or "return code", and is described only where special conventions are involved.

NOTES

Throughout the manual pages there are references to *TMPDIR, BINDIR, INCDIR,* and *LIBDIR.* These represent directory names whose value is specified on each manual page as necessary. For example, *TMPDIR* might refer to **/var/tmp**. These are not environment variables and cannot be set. [There is an environment variable called **TMPDIR** which can be set. See **tmpnam**(3S).] There are also references to *LIBPATH,* the default search path of the link editor and other tools.

Some commands produce unexpected results when processing files containing null characters. These commands often treat text input lines as strings and therefore become confused upon encountering a null character (the string terminator) within a line.

NAME

accept, **reject** – accept or reject print requests

SYNOPSIS

accept *destinations*

reject [–**r** *reason*] *destinations*

DESCRIPTION

accept allows the queueing of print requests for the named *destinations*. A *destination* can be either a printer or a class of printers. Run **lpstat** –**a** to find the status of *destinations*.

reject prevents queueing of print requests for the named *destinations*. A *destination* can be either a printer or a class of printers. (Run **lpstat** –**a** to find the status of *destinations*.) The following option is useful with **reject**.

–**r** *reason*   Assign a *reason* for rejection of requests. This *reason* applies to all *destinations* specified. *Reason* is reported by **lpstat** –**a**. It must be enclosed in quotes if it contains blanks. The default reason is **unknown reason** for existing destinations, and **new destination** for destinations just added to the system but not yet accepting requests.

FILES

/var/spool/lp/*

SEE ALSO

lpadmin(1M), lpsched(1M)

enable(1), lp(1), lpstat(1) in the *User's Reference Manual*

NAME

acct: acctdisk, acctdusg, accton, acctwtmp closewtmp, utmp2wtmp – overview of accounting and miscellaneous accounting commands

SYNOPSIS

/usr/lib/acct/acctdisk

/usr/lib/acct/acctdusg [–u *file*] [–p *file*]

/usr/lib/acct/accton [*file*]

/usr/lib/acct/acctwtmp *"reason"*

/usr/lib/acct/closewtmp

/usr/lib/acct/utmp2wtmp

DESCRIPTION

Accounting software is structured as a set of tools (consisting of both C programs
and shell procedures) that can be used to build accounting systems. **acctsh**(1M)
describes the set of shell procedures built on top of the C programs.

Connect time accounting is handled by various programs that write records into
/var/adm/wtmp, as described in **utmp**(4). The programs described in
acctcon(1M) convert this file into session and charging records, which are then
summarized by **acctmerg**(1M).

Process accounting is performed by the UNIX system kernel. Upon termination of
a process, one record per process is written to a file (normally **/var/adm/pacct**).
The programs in **acctprc**(1M) summarize this data for charging purposes;
acctcms(1M) is used to summarize command usage. Current process data may
be examined using **acctcom**(1).

Process accounting and connect time accounting (or any accounting records in the
tacct format described in **acct**(4)) can be merged and summarized into total
accounting records by **acctmerg** (see **tacct** format in **acct**(4)). **prtacct** (see
acctsh(1M)) is used to format any or all accounting records.

acctdisk reads lines that contain user ID, login name, and number of disk blocks
and converts them to total accounting records that can be merged with other
accounting records.

acctdusg reads its standard input (usually from **find / –print**) and computes
disk resource consumption (including indirect blocks) by login. If **–u** is given,
records consisting of those filenames for which **acctdusg** charges no one are
placed in *file* (a potential source for finding users trying to avoid disk charges). If
–p is given, *file* is the name of the password file. This option is not needed if the
password file is **/etc/passwd**. (See **diskusg**(1M) for more details.)

accton alone turns process accounting off. If *file* is given, it must be the name of
an existing file, to which the kernel appends process accounting records (see
acct(2) and **acct**(4)).

acctwtmp writes a **utmp**(4) record to its standard output. The record contains the
current time and a string of characters that describe the *reason*. A record type of
ACCOUNTING is assigned (see **utmp**(4)). *reason* must be a string of 11 or fewer
characters, numbers, **$**, or spaces. For example, the following are suggestions for
use in reboot and shutdown procedures, respectively:

```
acctwtmp "acctg on" >> /var/adm/wtmp
acctwtmp "acctg off" >> /var/adm/wtmp
```

For each user currently logged on, **closewtmp** puts a false **DEAD_PROCESS** record in the **/var/adm/wtmp** file. **runacct** (see **runacct(1M)**) uses this false **DEAD_PROCESS** record so that the connect accounting procedures can track the time used by users logged on before **runacct** was invoked.

For each user currently logged on, **runacct** uses **utmp2wtmp** to create an entry in the file **/var/adm/wtmp**, created by **runacct**. Entries in **/var/adm/wtmp** enable subsequent invocations of **runacct** to account for connect times of users currently logged in.

FILES

/etc/passwd	used for login name to user ID conversions
/usr/lib/acct	holds all accounting commands listed in sub-class 1M of this manual
/var/adm/pacct	current process accounting file
/var/adm/wtmp	login/logoff history file

SEE ALSO

acctcms(1M), acctcon(1M), acctmerg(1M), acctprc(1M), acctsh(1M), diskusg(1M), fwtmp(1M), runacct(1M), acct(4), utmp(4)
acctcom(1) in the *User's Reference Manual*
acct(2) in the *Programmer's Reference Manual*

NAME

acctcms – command summary from per-process accounting records

SYNOPSIS

/usr/lib/acct/acctcms [-a [-p] [-o]] [-c] [-j] [-n] [-s] [-t] *files*

DESCRIPTION

acctcms reads one or more *files*, normally in the form described in acct(4). It adds all records for processes that executed identically-named commands, sorts them, and writes them to the standard output, normally using an internal summary format. The options are:

-a   Print output in ASCII rather than in the internal summary format. The output includes command name, number of times executed, total kcore-minutes, total CPU minutes, total real minutes, mean size (in K), mean CPU minutes per invocation, "hog factor", characters transferred, and blocks read and written, as in acctcom(1). Output is normally sorted by total kcore-minutes.

-c   Sort by total CPU time, rather than total kcore-minutes.

-j   Combine all commands invoked only once under "***other".

-n   Sort by number of command invocations.

-s   Any filenames encountered hereafter are already in internal summary format.

-t   Process all records as total accounting records. The default internal summary format splits each field into prime and non-prime time parts. This option combines the prime and non-prime time parts into a single field that is the total of both, and provides upward compatibility with old (that is, pre-UNIX System V Release 4.0) style acctcms internal summary format records.

The following options may be used only with the -a option.

-p   Output a prime-time-only command summary.

-o   Output a non-prime (offshift) time only command summary.

When -p and -o are used together, a combination prime and non-prime time report is produced. All the output summaries will be total usage except number of times executed, CPU minutes, and real minutes, which will be split into prime and non-prime.

A typical sequence for performing daily command accounting and for maintaining a running total is:

```
acctcms file ... > today
cp total previoustotal
acctcms -s today previoustotal > total
acctcms -a -s today
```

SEE ALSO

acct(1M), acctcon(1M), acctmerg(1M), acctprc(1M), acctsh(1M), fwtmp(1M), runacct(1M), acct(4), utmp(4)
acctcom(1) in the *User's Reference Manual*
acct(2) in the *Programmer's Reference Manual*

NOTES

Unpredictable output results if **-t** is used on new style internal summary format files, or if it is not used with old style internal summary format files.

NAME

acctcom – search and print process accounting file(s)

SYNOPSIS

acctcom [options] [file . . .]

DESCRIPTION

acctcom reads *file*, the standard input, or **/var/adm/pacct**, in the form described by **acct**(4) and writes selected records to the standard output. Each record represents the execution of one process. The output shows the **COMMAND NAME, USER, TTYNAME, START TIME, END TIME, REAL (SEC), CPU (SEC), MEAN SIZE (K)**, and optionally, **F** (the **fork/exec** flag: 1 for **fork** without **exec**), **STAT** (the system exit status), **HOG FACTOR, KCORE MIN, CPU FACTOR, CHARS TRNSFD**, and **BLOCKS READ** (total blocks read and written).

A **#** is prepended to the command name if the command was executed with superuser privileges. If a process is not associated with a known terminal, a **?** is printed in the **TTYNAME** field.

If no *files* are specified, and if the standard input is associated with a terminal or **/dev/null** (as is the case when using **&** in the shell), **/var/adm/pacct** is read; otherwise, the standard input is read.

If any *file* arguments are given, they are read in their respective order. Each file is normally read forward, i.e., in chronological order by process completion time. The file **/var/adm/pacct** is usually the current file to be examined; a busy system may need several such files of which all but the current file are found in **/var/adm/pacct***incr*.

The *options* are:

-a   Show some average statistics about the processes selected. The statistics will be printed after the output records.

-b   Read backwards, showing latest commands first. This option has no effect when the standard input is read.

-f   Print the **fork/exec** flag and system exit status columns in the output. The numeric output for this option will be in octal.

-h   Instead of mean memory size, show the fraction of total available CPU time consumed by the process during its execution. This ''hog factor'' is computed as (total CPU time)/(elapsed time).

-i   Print columns containing the I/O counts in the output.

-k   Instead of memory size, show total kcore-minutes.

-m   Show mean core size (the default).

-r   Show CPU factor (user-time/(system-time + user-time)).

-t   Show separate system and user CPU times.

-v   Exclude column headings from the output.

-l *line*   Show only processes belonging to terminal **/dev/term/***line*.

-u *user*   Show only processes belonging to *user* that may be specified by: a user ID, a login name that is then converted to a user ID, a **#**, which designates only those processes executed with superuser privileges, or **?**, which designates only those processes associated with unknown user IDs.

-g *group*	Show only processes belonging to *group*. The *group* may be designated by either the group ID or group name.
-s *time*	Select processes existing at or after *time*, given in the format *hr* [: *min* [: *sec*]].
-e *time*	Select processes existing at or before *time*.
-S *time*	Select processes starting at or after *time*.
-E *time*	Select processes ending at or before *time*. Using the same *time* for both **-S** and **-E** shows the processes that existed at *time*.
-n *pattern*	Show only commands matching *pattern* that may be a regular expression as in **regcmp**(3G), except + means one or more occurrences.
-q	Do not print any output records, just print the average statistics as with the **-a** option.
-o *ofile*	Copy selected process records in the input data format to *ofile*; suppress printing to standard output.
-H *factor*	Show only processes that exceed *factor*, where factor is the "hog factor" as explained in option **-h** above.
-O *sec*	Show only processes with CPU system time exceeding *sec* seconds.
-C *sec*	Show only processes with total CPU time (system-time + user-time) exceeding *sec* seconds.
-I *chars*	Show only processes transferring more characters than the cutoff number given by *chars*.

FILES

```
/etc/passwd
/var/adm/pacctincr
/etc/group
```

SEE ALSO

ps(1), **su**(1)

acct(2), **regcmp**(3G) in the *Programmer's Reference Manual*

acct(1M), **acctcms**(1M), **acctcon**(1M), **acctmerg**(1M), **acctprc**(1M), **acctsh**(1M), **fwtmp**(1M), **runacct**(1M), **acct**(4), **utmp**(4) in the *System Administrator's Reference Manual*

NOTES

acctcom reports only on processes that have terminated; use **ps**(1) for active processes.

If *time* exceeds the present time, then *time* is interpreted as occurring on the previous day.

NAME

acctcon, acctcon1, acctcon2 – connect-time accounting

SYNOPSIS

/usr/lib/acct/acctcon [*options*]

/usr/lib/acct/acctcon1 [*options*]

/usr/lib/acct/acctcon2

DESCRIPTION

acctcon converts a sequence of login/logoff records to total accounting records (see the tacct format in acct(4)). login/logoff records are read from standard input. The file **/var/adm/wtmp** is usually the source of the login/logoff records, however, because it may contain corrupted records or system date changes, it should first be fixed using **wtmpfix**. The fixed version of file **/var/adm/wtmp** can then be redirected to acctcon. The tacct records are written to standard output. Here are the options for acctcon:

-l *file*   *file* is created to contain a summary of line usage showing line name, number of minutes used, percentage of total elapsed time used, number of sessions charged, number of logins, and number of logoffs. This file helps track line usage, identify bad lines, and find software and hardware oddities. Hangup, termination of **login**(1) and termination of the login shell each generate logoff records, so that the number of logoffs is often three to four times the number of sessions. See **init**(1M) and **utmp**(4).

-o *file*   *file* is filled with an overall record for the accounting period, giving starting time, ending time, number of reboots, and number of date changes.

acctcon is a combination of the programs acctcon1 and acctcon2. acctcon1 converts login/logoff records, taken from the fixed **/var/adm/wtmp** file, to ASCII output. acctcon2 reads the ASCII records produced by acctcon1 and converts them to tacct records. acctcon1 can be used with the −l and −o options, described above, as well as with the following options:

-p   Print input only, showing line name, login name, and time (in both numeric and date/time formats).

-t   acctcon1 maintains a list of lines on which users are logged in. When it reaches the end of its input, it emits a session record for each line that still appears to be active. It normally assumes that its input is a current file, so that it uses the current time as the ending time for each session still in progress. The −t flag causes it to use, instead, the last time found in its input, thus assuring reasonable and repeatable numbers for non-current files.

EXAMPLES

The acctcon command is typically used as follows:

```
acctcon -l lineuse -o reboots < tmpwtmp > ctacct
```

The acctcon1 and acctcon2 commands are typically used as follows:

```
acctcon1 -l lineuse -o reboots < tmpwtmp | sort +1n +2 > ctmp
acctcon2 < ctmp > ctacct
```

FILES

　　`/var/adm/wtmp`

SEE ALSO

　　acct(1M), acctcms(1M), acctmerg(1M), acctprc(1M), acctsh(1M), fwtmp(1M),
　　init(1M), runacct(1M), acct(4), utmp(4)
　　acctcom(1), login(1) in the *User's Reference Manual*
　　acct(2) in the *Programmer's Reference Manual*

NOTES

　　The line usage report is confused by date changes. Use **wtmpfix** (see **fwtmp**(1M)),
　　with the **/var/adm/wtmp** file as an argument, to correct this situation.

NAME

acctmerg – merge or add total accounting files

SYNOPSIS

/usr/lib/acct/acctmerg [-a] [-i] [-p] [-t] [-u] [-v] [*file*] . . .

DESCRIPTION

acctmerg reads its standard input and up to nine additional files, all in the tacct format (see acct(4)) or an ASCII version thereof. It merges these inputs by adding records whose keys (normally user ID and name) are identical, and expects the inputs to be sorted on those keys. Options are:

-a   Produce output in ASCII version of tacct.
-i   Input files are in ASCII version of tacct.
-p   Print input with no processing.
-t   Produce a single record that totals all input.
-u   Summarize by user ID, rather than user ID and name.
-v   Produce output in verbose ASCII format, with more precise notation for floating–point numbers.

EXAMPLES

The following sequence is useful for making "repairs" to any file kept in this format:

acctmerg −v <*file1* > *file2*

Edit *file2* as desired . . .

acctmerg −i <*file2* > *file1*

SEE ALSO

acct(1M), acctcms(1M), acctcon(1M), acctprc(1M), acctsh(1M), fwtmp(1M), runacct(1M), acct(4), utmp(4)
acctcom(1) in the *User's Reference Manual*
acct(2) in the *Programmer's Reference Manual*

NAME

acctprc, acctprc1, acctprc2 – process accounting

SYNOPSIS

/usr/lib/acct/acctprc

/usr/lib/acct/acctprc1 [*ctmp*]

/usr/lib/acct/acctprc2

DESCRIPTION

acctprc reads standard input, in the form described by acct(4), and converts it to total accounting records (see the tacct record in acct(4)). acctprc divides CPU time into prime time and non-prime time and determines mean memory size (in memory segment units). acctprc then summarizes the tacct records, according to user IDs, and adds login names corresponding to the user IDs. The summarized records are then written to standard output. acctprc1 reads input in the form described by acct(4), adds login names corresponding to user IDs, then writes for each process an ASCII line giving user ID, login name, prime CPU time (tics), non-prime CPU time (tics), and mean memory size (in memory segment units). If *ctmp* is given, it is expected to contain a list of login sessions sorted by user ID and login name. If this file is not supplied, it obtains login names from the password file, just as acctprc does. The information in *ctmp* helps it distinguish between different login names sharing the same user ID.

From standard input, acctprc2 reads records in the form written by acctprc1, summarizes them according to user ID and name, then writes the sorted summaries to the standard output as total accounting records.

EXAMPLES

The acctprc command is typically used as shown below:

    acctprc < /var/adm/pacct > ptacct

The acctprc1 and acctprc2 commands are typically used as shown below:

    acctprc1 ctmp </var/adm/pacct | acctprc2 >ptacct

FILES

/etc/passwd

SEE ALSO

acct(1M), acctcms(1M), acctcon(1M), acctmerg(1M), acctsh(1M), cron(1M), fwtmp(1M), runacct(1M), acct(4), utmp(4)

acctcom(1) in the *User's Reference Manual*

acct(2) in the *Programmer's Reference Manual*

NOTES

Although it is possible for acctprc1 to distinguish among login names that share user IDs for commands run normally, it is difficult to do this for those commands run from cron(1M), for example. A more precise conversion can be done using the acctwtmp program in acct(1M). acctprc does not distinguish between users with identical user IDs.

A memory segment of the mean memory size is a unit of measure for the number of bytes in a logical memory segment on a particular processor.

NAME

chargefee, ckpacct, dodisk, lastlogin, monacct, nulladm, prctmp, prdaily, prtacct, runacct, shutacct, startup, turnacct – shell procedures for accounting

SYNOPSIS

/usr/lib/acct/chargefee *login-name number*

/usr/lib/acct/ckpacct [*blocks*]

/usr/lib/acct/dodisk [-o] [*files ...*]

/usr/lib/acct/lastlogin

/usr/lib/acct/monacct *number*

/usr/lib/acct/nulladm *file*

/usr/lib/acct/prctmp

/usr/lib/acct/prdaily [-l] [-c] [*mmdd*]

/usr/lib/acct/prtacct *file* [*"heading"*]

/usr/lib/acct/runacct [*mmdd*] [*mmdd state*]

/usr/lib/acct/shutacct [*"reason"*]

/usr/lib/acct/startup

/usr/lib/acct/turnacct on | off | switch

DESCRIPTION

chargefee can be invoked to charge a *number* of units to *login-name*. A record is written to **/var/adm/fee**, to be merged with other accounting records by **runacct**.

ckpacct should be initiated via **cron**(1M) to periodically check the size of **/var/adm/pacct**. If the size exceeds *blocks*, 1000 by default, **turnacct** will be invoked with argument *switch*. If the number of free disk blocks in the **/var** file system falls below 500, **ckpacct** will automatically turn off the collection of process accounting records via the *off* argument to **turnacct**. When at least 500 blocks are restored, the accounting will be activated again on the next invocation of **ckpacct**. This feature is sensitive to the frequency at which **ckpacct** is executed, usually by **cron**.

dodisk should be invoked by **cron** to perform the disk accounting functions. By default, it will use **diskusg** (see **diskusg**(1M)) to do disk accounting on the s5 file system in **/etc/vfstab** and **acctdusg** [see **acct**(1M)] on non-s5 file systems. If the –o flag is used, it will use **acctdusg** (see **acct**(1M)) to do a slower version of disk accounting by login directory for all file systems. *files* specifies the one or more filesystem names where disk accounting will be done. If *files* are used, disk accounting will be done on these filesystems only. If the –o flag is used, *files* should be mount points of mounted filesystems. If the –o option is omitted, *files* should be the special file names of mountable filesystems.

lastlogin is invoked by **runacct** to update /var/adm/acct/sum/loginlog, which shows the last date on which each person logged in.

monacct should be invoked once each month or each accounting period. *number* indicates which month or period it is. If *number* is not given, it defaults to the current month (01–12). This default is useful if **monacct** is to executed via **cron**(1M) on the first day of each month. **monacct** creates summary files in /var/adm/acct/fiscal and restarts the summary files in /var/adm/acct/sum.

nulladm creates *file* with mode 664 and ensures that owner and group are **adm**. It is called by various accounting shell procedures.

prctmp can be used to print the session record file (normally /var/adm/acct/nite/ctmp created by **acctcon1** (see **acctcon**(1M)).

prdaily is invoked by **runacct** to format a report of the previous day's accounting data. The report resides in /var/adm/acct/sum/rprt/mmdd where *mmdd* is the month and day of the report. The current daily accounting reports may be printed by typing **prdaily**. Previous days' accounting reports can be printed by using the *mmdd* option and specifying the exact report date desired. The –1 flag prints a report of exceptional usage by login id for the specified date. Previous daily reports are cleaned up and therefore inaccessible after each invocation of **monacct**. The –c flag prints a report of exceptional resource usage by command, and may be used on current day's accounting data only.

prtacct can be used to format and print any total accounting (**tacct**) file.

runacct performs the accumulation of connect, process, fee, and disk accounting on a daily basis. It also creates summaries of command usage. For more information, see **runacct**(1M).

shutacct is invoked during a system shutdown to turn process accounting off and append a "reason" record to /var/adm/wtmp.

startup can be invoked when the system is brought to a multi-user state to turn process accounting on.

turnacct is an interface to **accton** (see **acct**(1M)) to turn process accounting **on** or **off**. The **switch** argument moves the current /var/adm/pacct to the next free name in /var/adm/pacct*incr* (where *incr* is a number starting with 1 and incrementing by one for each additional **pacct** file), then turns accounting back on again. This procedure is called by **ckpacct** and thus can be taken care of by the **cron** and used to keep **pacct** to a reasonable size. **shutacct** uses **turnacct** to stop process accounting. **startup** uses **turnacct** to start process accounting.

FILES

/var/adm/fee	accumulator for fees
/var/adm/pacct	current file for per-process accounting
/var/adm/pacct*incr*	used if **pacct** gets large and during execution of daily accounting procedure
/var/adm/wtmp	login/logoff summary

`/usr/lib/acct/ptelus.awk`	contains the limits for exceptional usage by login ID
`/usr/lib/acct/ptecms.awk`	contains the limits for exceptional usage by command name
`/var/adm/acct/nite`	working directory
`/usr/lib/acct`	holds all accounting commands listed in section 1M of this manual
`/var/adm/acct/sum`	summary directory contains information for `monacct`
`var/adm/acct/fiscal`	fiscal reports directory

SEE ALSO

acct(1M), acctcms(1M), acctcon(1M), acctmerg(1M), acctprc(1M), cron(1M), diskusg(1M), fwtmp(1M), runacct(1M), acct(4), utmp(4)
acctcom(1) in the *User's Reference Manual*
acct(2) in the *Programmer's Reference Manual*

NAME
     addbib – create or extend a bibliographic database

SYNOPSIS
     /usr/ucb/addbib [–a] [–p *promptfile*] *database*

DESCRIPTION
     When **addbib** starts up, answering **y** to the initial **Instructions?** prompt yields
     directions; typing **n** or RETURN skips them. **addbib** then prompts for various
     bibliographic fields, reads responses from the terminal, and sends output records
     to *database*. A null response (RETURN) means to leave out that field. A '–' (minus
     sign) means to go back to the previous field. A trailing backslash allows a field
     to be continued on the next line. The repeating **Continue?** prompt allows the
     user either to resume by typing **y** or RETURN, to quit the current session by typ-
     ing **n** or **q**, or to edit *database* with any system editor (**vi**, **ex**, **ed**).

     The following options are available:

     –a   Suppress prompting for an abstract; asking for an abstract is the default.
             Abstracts are ended with a CTRL–D.

     –p *promptfile*
             Use a new prompting skeleton, defined in *promptfile*. This file should con-
             tain prompt strings, a TAB, and the key-letters to be written to the *data-
             base*.

USAGE
  Bibliography Key Letters
     The most common key-letters and their meanings are given below. **addbib** insu-
     lates you from these key-letters, since it gives you prompts in English, but if you
     edit the bibliography file later on, you will need to know this information.

             %A   Author's name

             %B   Book containing article referenced

             %C   City (place of publication)

             %D   Date of publication

             %E   Editor of book containing article referenced

             %F   Footnote number or label (supplied by **refer**(1))

             %G   Government order number

             %H   Header commentary, printed before reference

             %I   Issuer (publisher)

             %J   Journal containing article

             %K   Keywords to use in locating reference

             %L   Label field used by **–k** option of **refer**(1)

             %M   Bell Labs Memorandum (undefined)

%N	Number within volume
%O	Other commentary, printed at end of reference
%P	Page number(s)
%Q	Corporate or Foreign Author (unreversed)
%R	Report, paper, or thesis (unpublished)
%S	Series title
%T	Title of article or book
%V	Volume number
%X	Abstract — used by **roffbib**, not by **refer**
%Y,Z	Ignored by **refer**

SEE ALSO

indxbib(1), **lookbib**(1), **refer**(1), **roffbib**(1), **sortbib**(1)

ed(1), **ex**(1), **vi**(1) in the *User's Reference Manual*

NAME

admin – create and administer SCCS files

SYNOPSIS

admin [–n] [–i[*name*]] [–r*rel*] [–t[*name*]] [–f*flag*[*flag-val*]] [–d*flag*[*flag-val*]] [–a*login*]
[–e*login*] [–m[*mrlist*]] [–y[*comment*]] [–h] [–z] *files*

DESCRIPTION

admin is used to create new SCCS files and change parameters of existing ones. Arguments to admin, which may appear in any order, consist of keyletter arguments (that begin with –) and named files (note that SCCS file names must begin with the characters **s.**). If a named file does not exist, it is created and its parameters are initialized according to the specified keyletter arguments. Parameters not initialized by a keyletter argument are assigned a default value. If a named file does exist, parameters corresponding to specified keyletter arguments are changed, and other parameters are left unchanged.

If a directory is named, admin behaves as though each file in the directory were specified as a named file, except that non-SCCS files (last component of the path name does not begin with **s.**) and unreadable files are silently ignored. If a name of – is given, the standard input is read; each line of the standard input is taken to be the name of an SCCS file to be processed. Again, non-SCCS files and unreadable files are silently ignored.

The keyletter arguments are listed below. Each argument is explained as if only one named file were to be processed because the effect of each argument applies independently to each named file.

–n   This keyletter indicates that a new SCCS file is to be created.

–i[*name*]   The *name* of a file from which the text for a new SCCS file is to be taken. The text constitutes the first delta of the file (see –r keyletter for delta numbering scheme). If the –i keyletter is used, but the file name is omitted, the text is obtained by reading the standard input until an end-of-file is encountered. If this keyletter is omitted, then the SCCS file is created empty. Only one SCCS file may be created by an admin command on which the i keyletter is supplied. Using a single admin to create two or more SCCS files requires that they be created empty (no –i keyletter). Note that the –i keyletter implies the –n keyletter.

–r*rel*   The *rel*ease into which the initial delta is inserted. This keyletter may be used only if the –i keyletter is also used. If the –r keyletter is not used, the initial delta is inserted into release 1. The level of the initial delta is always 1 (by default initial deltas are named 1.1).

–t[*name*]   The *name* of a file from which descriptive text for the SCCS file is to be taken. If the –t keyletter is used and admin is creating a new SCCS file (the –n and/or –i keyletters also used), the descriptive text file name must also be supplied. In the case of existing SCCS files: (1) a –t keyletter without a file name causes removal of the descriptive text (if any) that is currently in the SCCS file, and (2) a –t keyletter with a file name causes text (if any) in the named file to replace the descriptive text (if any) that is currently in the SCCS file.

−f*flag*   This keyletter specifies a *flag*, and, possibly, a value for the *flag*, to be placed in the SCCS file. Several −f keyletters may be supplied on a single **admin** command line. The allowable *flag*s and their values are:

b   Allows use of the −b keyletter on a **get** command to create branch deltas.

c*ceil*   The highest release (that is, ceiling): a number greater than 0 but less than or equal to 9999 that may be retrieved by a **get** command for editing. The default value for an unspecified **c** flag is 9999.

f*floor*   The lowest release (that is, floor): a number greater than 0 but less than 9999 that may be retrieved by a **get** command for editing. The default value for an unspecified **f** flag is 1.

d*SID*   The default delta number (SID) to be used by a **get** command.

i[*str*]   Causes the **No id keywords (ge6)** message issued by **get** or **delta** to be treated as a fatal error. In the absence of this flag, the message is only a warning. The message is issued if no SCCS identification keywords [see **get**(1)] are found in the text retrieved or stored in the SCCS file. If a value is supplied, the keywords must exactly match the given string. The string must contain a keyword, and no embedded newlines.

j   Allows concurrent **get** commands for editing on the same SID of an SCCS file. This flag allows multiple concurrent updates to the same version of the SCCS file.

l*list*   A *list* of releases to which deltas can no longer be made (**get −e** against one of these "locked" releases fails). The *list* has the following syntax:

                      <list> ::= <range> | <list> , <range>
                      <range> ::= RELEASE NUMBER | **a**

        The character **a** in the *list* is equivalent to specifying all releases for the named SCCS file.

n   Causes **delta** to create a null delta in each of those releases (if any) being skipped when a delta is made in a new release (for example, in making delta 5.1 after delta 2.7, releases 3 and 4 are skipped). These null deltas serve as anchor points so that branch deltas may later be created from them. The absence of this flag causes skipped releases to be non-existent in the SCCS file, preventing branch deltas from being created from them in the future.

q*text*   User-definable text substituted for all occurrences of the %Q% keyword in SCCS file text retrieved by **get**.

      m*mod*   *mod*ule name of the SCCS file substituted for all occurrences of the %M% keyword in SCCS file text retrieved by get. If the m flag is not specified, the value assigned is the name of the SCCS file with the leading s. removed.

      t*type*   *type* of module in the SCCS file substituted for all occurrences of %Y% keyword in SCCS file text retrieved by get.

      v[*pgm*]   Causes delta to prompt for Modification Request (MR) numbers as the reason for creating a delta. The optional value specifies the name of an MR number validity checking program [see delta(1)]. This program will receive as arguments the module name, the value of the type flag (see t*type* above), and the *mrlist*. (If this flag is set when creating an SCCS file, the m keyletter must also be used even if its value is null).

−d*flag*   Causes removal (deletion) of the specified *flag* from an SCCS file. The −d keyletter may be specified only when processing existing SCCS files. Several −d keyletters may be supplied in a single admin command. See the −f keyletter for allowable *flag* names.

           (l*list* used with −d indicates a *list* of releases to be unlocked. See the −f keyletter for a description of the l flag and the syntax of a *list*.)

−a*login*   A login name, or numerical UNIX System group ID, to be added to the list of users who may make deltas (changes) to the SCCS file. A group ID is equivalent to specifying all login names common to that group ID. Several a keyletters may be used on a single admin command line. As many logins or numerical group IDs as desired may be on the list simultaneously. If the list of users is empty, then anyone may add deltas. If login or group ID is preceded by a ! they are to be denied permission to make deltas.

−e*login*   A login name, or numerical group ID, to be erased from the list of users allowed to make deltas (changes) to the SCCS file. Specifying a group ID is equivalent to specifying all login names common to that group ID. Several −e keyletters may be used on a single admin command line.

−m[*mrlist*]   The list of Modification Requests (MR) numbers is inserted into the SCCS file as the reason for creating the initial delta in a manner identical to delta. The v flag must be set and the MR numbers are validated if the v flag has a value (the name of an MR number validation program). Diagnostics will occur if the v flag is not set or MR validation fails.

−y[*comment*]

           The *comment* text is inserted into the SCCS file as a comment for the initial delta in a manner identical to that of delta. Omission of the −y keyletter results in a default comment line being inserted.

The **-y** keyletter is valid only if the **-i** and/or **-n** keyletters are specified (that is, a new SCCS file is being created).

-h   Causes **admin** to check the structure of the SCCS file [see **sccsfile**(4)], and to compare a newly computed check-sum (the sum of all the characters in the SCCS file except those in the first line) with the check-sum that is stored in the first line of the SCCS file. Appropriate error diagnostics are produced. This keyletter inhibits writing to the file, nullifying the effect of any other keyletters supplied; therefore, it is only meaningful when processing existing files.

-z   The SCCS file check-sum is recomputed and stored in the first line of the SCCS file (see **-h**, above). Note that use of this keyletter on a truly corrupted file may prevent future detection of the corruption.

The last component of all SCCS file names must be of the form **s**.*file*. New SCCS files are given mode 444 [see **chmod**(1)]. Write permission in the pertinent directory is, of course, required to create a file. All writing done by **admin** is to a temporary x-file, called **x**.*file*, [see **get**(1)], created with mode 444 if the **admin** command is creating a new SCCS file, or with the same mode as the SCCS file if it exists. After successful execution of **admin**, the SCCS file is removed (if it exists), and the x-file is renamed with the name of the SCCS file. This renaming process ensures that changes are made to the SCCS file only if no errors occurred.

It is recommended that directories containing SCCS files be mode 755 and that SCCS files themselves be mode 444. The mode of the directories allows only the owner to modify SCCS files contained in the directories. The mode of the SCCS files prevents any modification at all except by SCCS commands.

admin also makes use of a transient lock file (called **z**.*file*), which is used to prevent simultaneous updates to the SCCS file by different users. See **get**(1) for further information.

FILES

x-file	[see **delta**(1)]
z-file	[see **delta**(1)]
bdiff	Program to compute differences between the "gotten" file and the g-file [see **get**(1)].

SEE ALSO

bdiff(1), **ed**(1), **delta**(1), **get**(1), **help**(1), **prs**(1), **what**(1), **sccsfile**(4)

DIAGNOSTICS

Use the **help** command for explanations.

NOTES

If it is necessary to patch an SCCS file for any reason, the mode may be changed to 644 by the owner allowing use of a text editor. You must run **admin -h** on the edited file to check for corruption followed by an **admin -z** to generate a proper check-sum. Another **admin -h** is recommended to ensure the SCCS file is valid.

NAME
apropos – locate commands by keyword lookup

SYNOPSIS
/usr/ucb/apropos *keyword* . . .

DESCRIPTION
apropos shows which manual sections contain instances of any of the given key-words in their title. Each word is considered separately and the case of letters is ignored. Words which are part of other words are considered; thus, when look-ing for 'compile', **apropos** will find all instances of 'compiler' also.

Try

        apropos password

and

        apropos editor

If the line starts '*filename*(*section*) . . .' you can do '**man** *section filename*' to get the documentation for it. Try

        apropos format

and then

        man 3s printf

to get the manual page on the subroutine **printf**.

apropos is actually just the **−k** option to the **man**(1) command.

FILES
/usr/share/man/whatis   data base

SEE ALSO
man(1), whatis(1), catman(1M)

NAME
    ar – maintain portable archive or library

SYNOPSIS
    ar [-v] – *key* [*arg*] [*posname*] *afile* [*name*. . .]

DESCRIPTION
    The **ar** command maintains groups of files combined into a single archive file. Its main use is to create and update library files. However, it can be used for any similar purpose. The magic string and the file headers used by **ar** consist of printable ASCII characters. If an archive is composed of printable files, the entire archive is printable.

    When **ar** creates an archive, it creates headers in a format that is portable across all machines. The portable archive format and structure are described in detail in **ar**(4). The archive symbol table [described in **ar**(4)] is used by the link editor **ld** to effect multiple passes over libraries of object files in an efficient manner. An archive symbol table is only created and maintained by **ar** when there is at least one object file in the archive. The archive symbol table is in a specially named file that is always the first file in the archive. This file is never mentioned or accessible to the user. Whenever the **ar** command is used to create or update the contents of such an archive, the symbol table is rebuilt. The **s** option described below will force the symbol table to be rebuilt.

    The –**v** option causes **ar** to print its version number on standard error.

    Unlike command options, the *key* is a required part of the **ar** command line. The *key* is formed with one of the following letters: **drqtpmx**. Arguments to the *key*, alternatively, are made with one of more of the following set: **vuaibcls**. *posname* is an archive member name used as a reference point in positioning other files in the archive. *afile* is the archive file. The *name*s are constituent files in the archive file. The meanings of the *key* characters are as follows:

    d   Delete the named files from the archive file.

    r   Replace the named files in the archive file. If the optional character **u** is used with **r**, then only those files with dates of modification later than the archive files are replaced. If an optional positioning character from the set **abi** is used, then the *posname* argument must be present and specifies that new files are to be placed after (**a**) or before (**b** or **i**) *posname*. Otherwise new files are placed at the end.

    q   Quickly append the named files to the end of the archive file. Optional positioning characters are invalid. The command does not check whether the added members are already in the archive. This option is useful to avoid quadratic behavior when creating a large archive piece-by-piece.

    t   Print a table of contents of the archive file. If no names are given, all files in the archive are listed. If names are given, only those files are listed.

    p   Print the named files in the archive.

    m   Move the named files to the end of the archive. If a positioning character is present, then the *posname* argument must be present and, as in **r**, specifies where the files are to be moved.

x   Extract the named files. If no names are given, all files in the archive are extracted. In neither case does **x** alter the archive file.

The meanings of the other key arguments are as follows:

v   Give a verbose file-by-file description of the making of a new archive file from the old archive and the constituent files. When used with **t**, give a long listing of all information about the files. When used with **x**, print the filename preceding each extraction.

c   Suppress the message that is produced by default when *afile* is created.

1   This option is obsolete. It is recognized, but ignored, and will be removed in the next release.

s   Force the regeneration of the archive symbol table even if **ar**(1) is not invoked with a command which will modify the archive contents. This command is useful to restore the archive symbol table after the **strip**(1) command has been used on the archive.

SEE ALSO

    ld(1), **lorder**(1), **strip**(1), **a.out**(4), **ar**(4)

NOTES

    If the same file is mentioned twice in an argument list, it may be put in the archive twice.

    Since the archiver no longer uses temporary files, the **-1** option is obsolete and will be removed in the next release.

    By convention, archives are suffixed with the characters **.a**.

NAME

    arch – display the architecture of the current host

SYNOPSIS

    /usr/ucb/arch

DESCRIPTION

    The **arch** command displays the architecture of the current host system.

SEE ALSO

    mach(1)

    uname(1) in the *User's Reference Manual*

NAME
>   arp – address resolution display and control

SYNOPSIS
>   arp *hostname*
>
>   arp **-a** [*unix* [*kmem*]]
>
>   arp **-d** *hostname*
>
>   arp **-s** *hostname ether_address* [**temp**] [**pub**] [**trail**]
>
>   arp **-f** *filename*

DESCRIPTION
>   The **arp** program displays and modifies the Internet-to-Ethernet address transla-
>   tion tables used by the address resolution protocol [**arp**(7)].
>
>   With no flags, the program displays the current ARP entry for *hostname*. The host
>   may be specified by name or by number, using Internet dot notation.
>
>   The following options are available:
>
>   -a   Display all of the current ARP entries by reading the table from the file
>   *kmem* (default **/dev/kmem**) based on the kernel file *unix* (default
>   **/stand/unix**).
>
>   -d   Delete an entry for the host called *hostname*. This option may only be
>   used by the super-user.
>
>   -s   Create an ARP entry for the host called *hostname* with the Ethernet address
>   *ether_address*. The Ethernet address is given as six hexadecimal bytes
>   separated by colons. The entry will be permanent unless the word **temp** is
>   given in the command. If the word **pub** is given, the entry will be pub-
>   lished, for instance, this system will respond to ARP requests for *hostname*
>   even though the hostname is not its own. The word **trail** indicates that
>   trailer encapsulations may be sent to this host.
>
>   -f   Read the file named *filename* and set multiple entries in the ARP tables.
>   Entries in the file should be of the form
>
>   *hostname ether_address* [**temp**] [**pub**] [**trail**]
>
>   with argument meanings as given above.

SEE ALSO
>   ifconfig(1M), **arp**(7)

NAME

as – assembler

SYNOPSIS

as [*options*] *file*

DESCRIPTION

The **as** command creates object files from assembly language source *files*. The following flags may be specified in any order:

−o *objfile* Put the output of the assembly in *objfile*. By default, the output file name is formed by removing the **.s** suffix, if there is one, from the input file name and appending a **.o** suffix.

−n Turn off long/short address optimization. By default, address optimization takes place.

−m Run the **m4** macro processor on the input to the assembler.

−R Remove (unlink) the input file after assembly is completed.

−dl Obsolete. Assembler issues a warning saying that it is ignoring the −dl option.

−T Accept obsolete assembler directives.

−V Write the version number of the assembler being run on the standard error output.

−Q{y| n} If −Qy is specified, place the version number of the assembler being run in the object file. The default is −Qn.

−Y [md],*dir* Find the **m4** preprocessor (**m**) and/or the file of predefined macros (**d**) in directory *dir* instead of in the customary place.

FILES

By default, **as** creates its temporary files in **/var/tmp**. This location can be changed by setting the environment variable **TMPDIR** [see **tempnam** in **tmpnam**(3S)].

SEE ALSO

cc(1), ld(1), m4(1), nm(1), strip(1), tmpnam(3S), a.out(4)

NOTES

If the −m (m4 macro processor invocation) option is used, keywords for **m4** [see m4(1)] cannot be used as symbols (variables, functions, labels) in the input file since **m4** cannot determine which keywords are assembler symbols and which keywords are real **m4** macros.

The **.align** assembler directive may not work in the **.text** section when long/short address optimization is performed.

Arithmetic expressions may only have one forward referenced symbol per expression.

Whenever possible, you should access the assembler through a compilation system interface program such as **cc**.

NAME

at, batch – execute commands at a later time

SYNOPSIS

at [-f *script*] [-m] *time* [*date*] [+ *increment*]

at -l [*job* ...]

at -r *job* ...

batch

DESCRIPTION

at and batch read commands from standard input to be executed at a later time. at allows you to specify when the commands should be executed, while jobs queued with batch will execute when system load level permits. at may be used with the following options:

-f *script*   Reads commands to be executed from the named *script* file.

-l [*job*]   Reports all jobs scheduled for the invoking user, or just the *job*s specified.

-m   Sends mail to the user after the job has been completed, indicating that the job is finished, even if the job produces no output. Mail is sent only if the job has not already generated a mail message.

-r *job*   Removes specified *job*s previously scheduled using at.

Standard output and standard error output are mailed to the user unless they are redirected elsewhere. The shell environment variables, current directory, umask, and ulimit are retained when the commands are executed. Open file descriptors, traps, and priority are lost.

Users are permitted to use at if their name appears in the file /usr/sbin/cron.d/at.allow. If that file does not exist, the file /usr/sbin/cron.d/at.deny is checked to determine if the user should be denied access to *at*. If neither file exists, only root is allowed to submit a job. If only at.deny exists and is empty, global usage is permitted. The allow/deny files consist of one user name per line. These files can only be modified by the privileged user.

If the DATEMSK environment variable is set, it points to a template file that at will use to determine the valid *time* and *date* values instead of the values described below. For more information about using DATEMSK, see the last paragraph of the DESCRIPTION section.

time may be specified as follows, where *h* is hours and *m* is minutes: *h*, *hh*, *hhmm*, *h*:*m*, *h*:*mm*, *hh*:*m*, *hh*:*mm*. A 24-hour clock is assumed, unless am or pm is appended to *time*. If zulu is appended to *time*, it means Greenwich Mean Time (GMT). *time* can also take on the values: noon, midnight, and now. at now responds with the error message too late; use now with the *increment* argument, such as: at now + 1 minute.

An optional *date* may be specified as either a month name followed by a day number (and possibly a year number preceded by a comma) or a day of the week. (Both the month name and the day of the week may be spelled out or abbreviated to three characters.) Two special "days", today and tomorrow are recognized. If no *date* is given, **today** is assumed if the given hour is greater than the current hour and **tomorrow** is assumed if it is less. If the given month is less than the current month (and no year is given), next year is assumed.

The optional *increment* is simply a number suffixed by one of the following: **minutes, hours, days, weeks, months,** or **years.** (The singular form is also accepted.) The modifier **next** may precede the *increment;* it means "+ 1."

Thus valid commands include:

```
at 0815am Jan 24
at 8:15am Jan 24
at now + 1 day
at now next day
at 5 pm Friday
```

at and **batch** write the job number and schedule time to standard error.

at -r removes jobs previously scheduled by **at** or **batch.** The job number is the number returned to you previously by the **at** or **batch** command. You can also get job numbers by typing **at -l.** You can only remove your own jobs unless you are the privileged user.

If the environment variable **DATEMSK** is set, **at** will use its value as the full path name of a template file containing format strings. The strings consist of field descriptors and text characters and are used to provide a richer set of allowable date formats in different languages by appropriate settings of the environment variable **LANG** or **LC_TIME** (see *environ*(5)). (See *getdate*(3C) for the allowable list of field descriptors; this list is a subset of the descriptors allowed by **calendar**(1) that are listed on the *date*(1) manual page.) The formats described above for the *time* and *date* arguments, the special names **noon, midnight, now, next, today, tomorrow,** and the *increment* argument are not recognized when **DATEMSK** is set.

EXAMPLES

The **at** and **batch** commands read from standard input the commands to be executed at a later time. **sh**(1) provides different ways of specifying standard input. Within your commands, it may be useful to redirect standard output.

This sequence can be used at a terminal:

```
batch
sort filename > outfile
CTRL-d (hold down 'control' and depress 'd')
```

This sequence, which shows redirecting standard error to a pipe, is useful in a shell procedure (the sequence of output redirection specifications is significant):

```
batch <<!
sort filename 2>&1 > outfile | mail loginid
!
```

To have a job reschedule itself, invoke **at** from within the shell procedure, by including code similar to the following within the shell file:

echo "sh *shellfile*" | at 1900 thursday next week

The following example shows the possible contents of a template file **AT.TEMPL** in /var/tmp.

```
%I %p, the %est of %B of the year %Y run the following job
%I %p, the %end of %B of the year %Y run the following job
%I %p, the %erd of %B of the year %Y run the following job
%I %p, the %eth of %B of the year %Y run the following job
%d/%m/%y
%H:%M:%S
%I:%M%p
```

The following are examples of valid invocations if the environment variable **DATEMSK** is set to /var/tmp/AT.TEMPL.

```
at 2 PM, the 3rd of July of the year 2000 run the following job
at 3/4/99
at 10:30:30
at 2:30PM
```

FILES

/usr/sbin/cron.d	main cron directory
/usr/sbin/cron.d/at.allow	list of allowed users
/usr/sbin/cron.d/at.deny	list of denied users
/usr/sbin/cron.d/queuedefs	scheduling information
/var/spool/cron/atjobs	spool area

SEE ALSO

atq(1), atrm(1), calendar(1), crontab(1), date(1), kill(1), mail(1), nice(1), ps(1), sh(1), sort(1)

cron(1M), environ(5), in the *System Administrator's Reference Manual*

getdate(3C) in the *Programmer's Reference Manual*

DIAGNOSTICS

Complains about various syntax errors and times out of range.

NAME

atq – display the jobs queued to run at specified times

SYNOPSIS

atq [-c] [-n] [*username...*]

DESCRIPTION

atq displays the current user's queue of jobs submitted with **at** to be run at a later date. If invoked by the privileged user, atq will display all jobs in the queue.

If no options are given, the jobs are displayed in chronological order of execution.

When a privileged user invokes atq without specifying *username*, the entire queue is displayed; when a *username* is specified, only those jobs belonging to the named user are displayed.

The atq command can be used with the following options:

-c   Display the queued jobs in the order they were created (that is, the time that the **at** command was given).

-n   Display only the total number of jobs currently in the queue.

FILES

/var/spool/cron   spool area

SEE ALSO

at(1), atrm(1)

cron(1M) in the *System Administrator's Reference Manual*

NAME

atrm – remove jobs spooled by at or batch

SYNOPSIS

atrm [-a f i] *arg* . . .

DESCRIPTION

atrm removes delayed-execution jobs that were created with the at(1) command, but not yet executed. The list of these jobs and associated job numbers can be displayed by using atq(1).

arg a user name or job-number. atrm removes each job-number you specify, and/or all jobs belonging to the user you specify, provided that you own the indicated jobs.

Jobs belonging to other users can only be removed by the privileged user.

The atrm command can be used with the following options:

-a   All. Remove all unexecuted jobs that were created by the current user. If invoked by the privileged user, the entire queue will be flushed.

-f   Force. All information regarding the removal of the specified jobs is suppressed.

-i   Interactive. atrm asks if a job should be removed. If you respond with a y, the job will be removed.

FILES

/var/spool/cron   spool area

SEE ALSO

at(1), atq(1).

cron(1M) in the *System Administrator's Reference Manual*.

NAME

`automount` – automatically mount NFS file systems

SYNOPSIS

`automount` [`-mnTv`] [`-D` *name=value*] [`-M` *mount-directory*] [`-f` *master-file*]
[`-t` *sub-options*] [*directory   map* [`-`*mount-options*]] . . .

DESCRIPTION

`automount` is a daemon that automatically and transparently mounts an NFS file system as needed. It monitors attempts to access directories that are associated with an `automount` map, along with any directories or files that reside under them. When a file is to be accessed, the daemon mounts the appropriate NFS file system. You can assign a map to a directory using an entry in a direct `automount` map, or by specifying an indirect map on the command line. The `automount` daemon resides in `/usr/lib/nfs` directory.

`automount` uses a map to locate an appropriate NFS file server, exported file system, and mount options. It then mounts the file system in a temporary location, and replaces the file system entry for the directory or subdirectory with a symbolic link to the temporary location. If the file system is not accessed within an appropriate interval (five minutes by default), the daemon unmounts the file system and removes the symbolic link. If the indicated directory has not already been created, the daemon creates it, and then removes it upon exiting.

Since the name-to-location binding is dynamic, updates to an `automount` map are transparent to the user. This obviates the need to pre-mount shared file systems for applications that have hard coded references to files.

If you specify the dummy directory /–, `automount` treats the *map* argument that follows as the name of a direct map. In a direct map, each entry associates the full pathname of a mount point with a remote file system to mount.

If the **directory** argument is a pathname, the *map* argument points to a file called an indirect map. An indirect map contains a list of the subdirectories contained within the indicated **directory**. With an indirect map, it is these subdirectories that are mounted automatically. The *map* argument must be a full pathname.

The *–mount-options* argument, when supplied, is a comma-separated list of `mount`(1M) options, preceded by a hyphen (–). If mount options are specified in the indicated map, however, those in the map take precedence.

Only a privileged user can execute this command.

The following options are available:

-m   Disable the search of the Network Interface Services map file. (See "The NIS" chapter of the *Programmer's Guide: Networking Interfaces*.) This option can only be used in conjunction with the **-f** option.

-n   Disable dynamic mounts. With this option, references through the `automount` daemon only succeed when the target file system has been previously mounted. This can be used to prevent NFS servers from cross-mounting each other.

-T   Trace. Expand each NFS call and display it on the standard output.

-v   Verbose. Log status messages to the console.

-D *name=value*
      Assign *value* to the indicated **automount** (environment) variable.

-f *master-file*
      Specify all arguments in *master-file* and instruct the daemon to look in it
      for instructions.

-M *mount-directory*
      Mount temporary file systems in the named directory, instead of
      /tmp_mnt.

-t *sub-options*
      Specify *sub-options* as a comma-separated list that contains any combina-
      tion of the following:

      l *duration*
            Specify a *duration*, in seconds, that a file system is to remain
            mounted when not in use. The default is 5 minutes.

      m *interval*
            Specify an *interval*, in seconds, between attempts to mount a file
            system. The default is 30 seconds.

      w *interval*
            Specify an *interval*, in seconds, between attempts to unmount file
            systems that have exceeded their cached times. The default is 1
            minute.

ENVIRONMENT

Environment variables can be used within an **automount** map. For instance, if
$HOME appeared within a map, **automount** would expand it to its current value
for the HOME variable.

If a reference needs to be protected from affixed characters, enclose the variable
name within braces.

USAGE

Direct/Indirect Map Entry Format

A simple map entry (mapping) takes the form:

      directory [*-mount-options*] *location* ...

where **directory** is the full pathname of the directory to mount when used in a
direct map, or the basename of a subdirectory in an indirect map. *mount-options*
is a comma-separated list of **mount** options, and *location* specifies a remote file
system from which the directory may be mounted. In the simple case, *location*
takes the form:

      host:*pathname*

Multiple *location* fields can be specified, in which case **automount** sends multiple
mount requests; **automount** mounts the file system from the first host that replies
to the **mount** request. This request is first made to the local net or subnet. If
there is no response, any connected server may respond.

If *location* is specified in the form:

    host:path:subdir

host is the name of the host from which to mount the file system, *path* is the pathname of the directory to mount, and *subdir*, when supplied, is the name of a subdirectory to which the symbolic link is made. This can be used to prevent duplicate mounts when multiple directories in the same remote file system may be accessed. With a map for **/home** such as:

    able homebody:/home/homebody:able
    baker homebody:/home/homebody:baker

and a user attempting to access a file in **/home/able**, **automount** mounts **homebody:/home/homebody**, but creates a symbolic link called **/home/able** to the **able** subdirectory in the temporarily mounted file system. If a user immediately tries to access a file in **/home/baker**, **automount** needs only to create a symbolic link that points to the **baker** subdirectory; **/home/homebody** is already mounted. With the following map:

    able homebody:/home/homebody/able
    baker homebody:/home/homebody/baker

automount would have to mount the file system twice.

A mapping can be continued across input lines by escaping the NEWLINE with a backslash. Comments begin with a **#** and end at the subsequent NEWLINE.

Directory Pattern Matching

The **&** character is expanded to the value of the **directory** field for the entry in which it occurs. In this case:

    able homebody:/home/homebody:&

the **&** expands to **able**.

The ***** character, when supplied as the **directory** field, is recognized as the catch-all entry. Such an entry resolves to any entry not previously matched. For instance, if the following entry appeared in the indirect map for **/home**:

    *   &:/home/&

this would allow automatic mounts in **/home** of any remote file system whose location could be specified as:

    hostname:/home/hostname

Hierarchical Mappings

A hierarchical mapping takes the form:

    directory [/ [subdirectory]]] [–mount-options] location. . .
         [/ [subdirectory] [–mount-options] location. . .] . . .

The initial **/**[*subdirectory*] is optional for the first location list and mandatory for all subsequent lists. The optional *subdirectory* is taken as a filename relative to the **directory**. If *subdirectory* is omitted in the first occurrence, the **/** refers to the directory itself.

Given the direct map entry:

```
/arch/src    \
/           -ro,intr  arch:/arch/src          alt:/arch/src   \
/1.0        -ro,intr  alt:/arch/src/1.0       arch:/arch/src/1.0    \
/1.0/man    -ro,intr  arch:/arch/src/1.0/man  alt:/arch/src/1.0/man
```

automount would automatically mount **/arch/src**, **/arch/src/1.0** and **/arch/src/1.0/man**, as needed, from either **arch** or **alt**, whichever host responded first.

Direct Maps
A direct map contains mappings for any number of directories. Each directory listed in the map is automatically mounted as needed. The direct map as a whole is not associated with any single directory.

Indirect Maps
An indirect map allows you to specify mappings for the subdirectories you wish to mount under the **directory** indicated on the command line. It also obscures local subdirectories for which no mapping is specified. In an indirect map, each **directory** field consists of the basename of a subdirectory to be mounted as needed.

Included Maps
The contents of another map can be included within a map with an entry of the form

> **+***mapname*

where *mapname* is a filename.

Special Maps
The **-null** map is the only special map currently available. The **-null** map, when indicated on the command line, cancels a previous map for the directory indicated.

FILES
/tmp_mnt   parent directory for dynamically mounted file systems

SEE ALSO
df(1M), **mount**(1M), **passwd**(4)

NOTES
Mount points used by **automount** are not recorded in **/etc/mnttab**. **mount**(1M) on such mount points will fail, saying mount point busy, although the mount point is not in **/etc/mnttab**.

Shell filename expansion does not apply to objects not currently mounted.

Since **automount** is single-threaded, any request that is delayed by a slow or non-responding NFS server will delay all subsequent automatic mount requests until it completes.

NAME

autopush – configure lists of automatically pushed STREAMS modules

SYNOPSIS

autopush -f *file*
autopush -r -M *major* -m *minor*
autopush -g -M *major* -m *minor*

DESCRIPTION

This command allows one to configure the list of modules to be automatically pushed onto the stream when a device is opened. It can also be used to remove a previous setting or get information on a setting.

The following options apply to autopush:

-f   This option sets up the autopush configuration for each driver according to the information stored in the specified file. An autopush file consists of lines of at least four fields each where the fields are separated by a space as shown below:

        maj_ min_ last_min_ mod1 mod2 ... modn

The first three fields are integers that specify the major device number, minor device number, and last minor device number. The fields following represent the names of modules. If *min_* is -1, then all minor devices of a major driver specified by *maj_* are configured and the value for *last_min_* is ignored. If *last_min_* is 0, then only a single minor device is configured. To configure a range of minor devices for a particular major, *min_* must be less than *last_min_*.

The last fields of a line in the autopush file represent the list of module names where each is separated by a space. The maximum number of modules that can be automatically pushed on a stream is defined to be eight. The modules are pushed in the order they are specified. Comment lines start with a # sign.

-r   This option removes the previous configuration setting of the particular *major* and *minor* device number specified with the -M and -m options respectively. If the values of *major* and *minor* correspond to a setting of a range of minor devices, where *minor* matches the first minor device number in the range, the configuration would be removed for the entire range.

-g   This option gets the current configuration setting of a particular *major* and *minor* device number specified with the -M and -m options respectively. It will also return the starting minor device number if the request corresponds to a setting of a range (as described with the -f option).

SEE ALSO

streamio(7)
Programmer's Guide: STREAMS

NAME

awk – pattern scanning and processing language

SYNOPSIS

awk [**-F**c] [*prog*] [*parameters*] [*files*]

DESCRIPTION

awk scans each input *file* for lines that match any of a set of patterns specified in *prog*. With each pattern in *prog* there can be an associated action that will be performed when a line of a *file* matches the pattern. The set of patterns may appear literally as *prog*, or in a file specified as **-f** *file*. The *prog* string should be enclosed in single quotes (') to protect it from the shell.

Parameters, in the form x=... y=... etc., may be passed to *awk.*

Files are read in order; if there are no files, the standard input is read. The file name – means the standard input. Each line is matched against the pattern portion of every pattern-action statement; the associated action is performed for each matched pattern.

An input line is made up of fields separated by white space. (This default can be changed by using FS; see below). The fields are denoted **$1, $2,** ...; **$0** refers to the entire line.

A pattern-action statement has the form:

pattern { *action* }

A missing action means print the line; a missing pattern always matches. An action is a sequence of statements. A statement can be one of the following:

```
if ( conditional ) statement [ else statement ]
while ( conditional ) statement
for ( expression ; conditional4; expression ) statement
break
continue
{ [ statement ] ... }
variable = expression
print [ expression-list ] [ >expression ]
printf format [ , expression-list ] [ >expression ]
next # skip remaining patterns on this input line
exit # skip the rest of the input
```

Statements are terminated by semicolons, new-lines, or right braces. An empty expression-list stands for the whole line. Expressions take on string or numeric values as appropriate, and are built using the operators **+, -, *, /, %,** and concatenation (indicated by a blank). The **C** operators **++, --, +=, -=, *=, /=,** and **%=** are also available in expressions. Variables may be scalars, array elements (denoted x[i]) or fields. Variables are initialized to the null string. Array subscripts may be any string, not necessarily numeric; this allows for a form of associative memory. String constants are quoted (").

The *print* statement prints its arguments on the standard output (or on a file if >*expr* is present), separated by the current output field separator, and terminated by the output record separator. The **printf** statement formats its expression list according to the format [see *printf*(3S) in the *Programmer's Reference Manual*].

The built-in function *length* returns the length of its argument taken as a string, or of the whole line if no argument. There are also built-in functions **exp**, **log**, **sqrt**, and *int*. The last truncates its argument to an integer; *substr*(*s*, *m*, *n*) returns the *n*-character substring of *s* that begins at position *m*. The function **sprintf**(fmt , expr , *expr*, ...) formats the expressions according to the **printf**(3S) format given by *fmt* and returns the resulting string.

Patterns are arbitrary Boolean combinations (**!**, **| |**, **&&**, and parentheses) of regular expressions and relational expressions. Regular expressions must be surrounded by slashes and are as in **egrep**(1). Isolated regular expressions in a pattern apply to the entire line. Regular expressions may also occur in relational expressions. A pattern may consist of two patterns separated by a comma; in this case, the action is performed for all lines between an occurrence of the first pattern and the next occurrence of the second.

A relational expression is one of the following:

> *expression matchop regular-expression*
> *expression relop expression*

where a relop is any of the six relational operators in C, and a matchop is either ~ (for *contains*) or !~ (for *does not contain*). A conditional is an arithmetic expression, a relational expression, or a Boolean combination of these.

The special patterns BEGIN and END may be used to capture control before the first input line is read and after the last. BEGIN must be the first pattern, END the last.

A single character *c* may be used to separate the fields by starting the program with:

> **BEGIN** { FS = *c* }

or by using the **−F***c* option.

Other variable names with special meanings include NF, the number of fields in the current record; NR, the ordinal number of the current record; FILENAME, the name of the current input file; OFS, the output field separator (default blank); ORS, the output record separator (default new-line); and OFMT, the output format for numbers (default **%.6g**).

EXAMPLES

Print lines longer than 72 characters:

> ```
> ```

Print first two fields in opposite order:

> ```
> { print $2, $1 }
> ```

Add up first column, print sum and average:

```
    { s += $1 }
END   { print "sum is", s, " average is", s/NR }
```

Print fields in reverse order:

```
{ for (i = NF; i > 0; --i) print $i }
```

Print all lines between start/stop pairs:

```
/start/, /stop/
```

Print all lines whose first field is different from previous one:

```
$1 != prev { print; prev = $1 }
```

Print file, filling in page numbers starting at 5:

```
/Page/ { $2 = n++; }
       { print }
```

command line: **awk −f** *program* **n=5** *input*

SEE ALSO

grep(1), **nawk**(1), **sed**(1)
lex(1), **printf**(3S) in the *Programmer's Reference Manual*

NOTES

Input white space is not preserved on output if fields are involved.
There are no explicit conversions between numbers and strings. To force an expression to be treated as a number add 0 to it; to force it to be treated as a string concatenate the null string (" ") to it.

NAME

backup – initiate or control a system backup session

SYNOPSIS

backup **-i** [**-t** *table*] [**-o** *name*] [**-m** *user*] [**-ne**] [**-s** | **-v**] [**-c** *week:day* | **demand**]

backup [**-t** *table*] [**-o** *name*] [**-m** *user*] [**-ne**] [**-c** *week:day*| **demand**]

backup **-S** | **-R** | **-C** [**-u** *user* | **-A** | **-j** *jobid*]

DESCRIPTION

Without options, the **backup** command performs all backup operations specified for the current day and week of the backup rotation in the backup register. This set of backup operations is considered a single job and is assigned a **backup** job ID which can be used to control the progress of the session. As backup operations are processed, their status is tracked [See **bkstatus**(1M)]. As backup operations are completed, they are recorded in the backup history log.

backup may only be executed by a privileged user.

A backup job can be controlled in three ways. It can be canceled, suspended or resumed (after being suspended).

Modes of Operator Intervention

Backup operations may require operator intervention to perform such tasks as inserting volumes into devices or confirming proper volume labels. **backup** provides three modes of operator interaction.

backup with no options assumes that an operator is present, but not at the terminal where the **backup** command was issued. This mode sends a **mail** message to the operator. The mail identifies the device requiring service and the volume required. The operator reads the mail message, invokes the **bkoper** command, responds to the prompts, and the backup operation continues.

backup **-i** establishes interactive mode, which assumes that an operator is present at the terminal where the **backup** command was issued. In this mode, **bkoper** is automatically invoked at the terminal where the **backup** command was entered. The operator responds to the prompts as they arrive.

Register Validations

A number of backup service databases must be consistent before the backups listed in a backup register can be performed. These consistencies can only be validated at the time **backup** is initiated. If any of them fail, **backup** will terminate. Invoking **backup** **-ne** performs the validation checks in addition to displaying the set of backup operations to be performed. The validations are:

1. The backup method must be a default method or be an executable file in **/bkup/method** .

2. The dependencies for an entry are all defined in the register. Circular dependencies (eg., entry **abc** depends on entry **def;** entry **def** depends on entry **abc**) are allowed.

3. The device group for a destination must be defined in the device group table, **/etc/dgroup.tab** (For more information, see the section on devices in the *System Administrator's Guide*.)

Options

-c *week:day*| **demand**
> Selects from the backup register only those backup operations for the specified week and day of the backup rotation, instead of the current day and week of the rotation. If **demand** is specified, selects only those backup operations scheduled to be performed on demand.

-e
> This option displays an estimate of the number of volumes required to perform each backup operation.

-i
> Selects interactive operation

-j *jobid*
> Controls only the backup job identified by *jobid*. *jobid* is a **backup** job ID.

-m *user*
> Sends mail to the named *user* when all backup operations for the backup job are complete.

-n
> Displays the set of backup operations that would be performed but does not actually perform the backup operations. The display is ordered according to the dependencies and priorities specified in the backup register.

-o *name*
> Initiates backup operations only on the named originating object. *name* may be a device name or the name of a file system beginning with a slash (/).

-s
> Displays a "." for each 100 (512-byte) blocks transferred to the destination device. The dots are displayed while each backup operation is progressing.

-t *table*
> Initiates backup operations described in the specified backup register instead of the default register, **etc/bkup/bkreg.tab**. *table* is a backup register.

-u *user*
> Controls backup jobs started by the named *user* instead of those started by the user invoking the command. *user* is a valid login ID.

-v
> While each backup operation is progressing, display the name of each file or directory as soon as it has been transferred to the destination device.

-A
> Controls backup jobs for all users instead of those started by the user invoking the command.

-C
> Cancels backup jobs.

-R
> Resumes suspended backup jobs.

-S
> Suspends backup jobs.

DIAGNOSTICS

> The exit codes for the **backup** command are the following:

> 0 = successful completion of the task
> 1 = one or more parameters to **backup** are invalid.
> 2 = an error has occurred which caused **backup** to fail to
> complete *all* portions of its task.

EXAMPLES
>Example 1:
>
>>`backup -i -v -c 2:1 -m admin3`
>
>initiates those backups scheduled for Monday of the second week in the rotation period instead of backups for the current day and week. Performs the backup in interactive mode and displays on standard output the name of each file, directory, file system partition, or data partition as soon as it is transferred to the destination device. When all backups are completed, sends mail notification to the user with login ID **admin3**.
>
>Example 2:
>
>>`backup -o /usr`
>
>initiates only those backups from the **usr** file system.
>
>Example 3:
>
>>`backup -S`
>
>Suspends the backup jobs requested by the invoking user.
>
>Example 4:
>
>>`backup -R -j back-359`
>
>resumes the backup operations included in backup job ID **back-359**.

FILES
>`/etc/bkup/method/*`
>`/etc/bkup/bkreg.tab`
>`/etc/device.tab`
>`/etc/dgroup.tab`

SEE ALSO
>bkhistory(1M), bkoper(1M), bkreg(1M), bkstatus(1M)

NAME

backup – perform backup functions

SYNOPSIS

backup [-t] [-p | -c | -f <*files*> | -u "<*user1*> [*user2*]"] -d <*device*>
backup -h

DESCRIPTION

-h produces a history of backups. Tells the user when the last complete and incremental/partial backups were done.

-c complete backup. All files changed since the system was installed are backed up. If an incremental/partial backup was done, all files modified since that time are backed up, otherwise all files modified since the last complete backup are backed up. A complete backup must be done before a partial backup.

-f backup files specified by the *files* argument. file names may contain characters to be expanded (that is, *, .) by the shell. The argument must be in quotes.

-u backup a user's home directory. All files in the user's home directory will be backed up. At least one user must be specified but it can be more. The argument must be in quotes if more than one user is specified. If the user name is "all", then all the user's home directories will be backed up.

-d used to specify the device to be used. It defaults to **/dev/SA/diskette**.

-t used when the device is a tape. This option must be used with the **-d** option when the tape device is specified.

A complete backup must be done before a partial backup can be done. Raw devices rather than block devices should always be used. The program can handle multi-volume backups. The program will prompt the user when it is ready for the next medium. The program will give you an estimated number of floppies/tapes that will be needed to do the backup. Floppies must be formatted before the backup is done. Tapes do not need to be formatted. If backup is done to tape, the tape must be rewound.

NAME

    banner – make posters

SYNOPSIS

    banner *strings*

DESCRIPTION

    banner prints its arguments (each up to 10 characters long) in large letters on the
    standard output.

SEE ALSO

    echo(1)

NAME

basename, dirname – deliver portions of path names

SYNOPSIS

basename *string* [*suffix*]

dirname *string*

DESCRIPTION

basename deletes any prefix ending in / and the *suffix* (if present in *string*) from *string*, and prints the result on the standard output. It is normally used inside substitution marks (` ` `) within shell procedures. The *suffix* is a pattern as defined on the **ed**(1) manual page.

dirname delivers all but the last level of the path name in *string*.

EXAMPLES

The following example, invoked with the argument **/home/sms/personal/mail** sets the environment variable **NAME** to the file named **mail** and the environment variable **MYMAILPATH** to the string **/home/sms/personal**.

```
NAME=` basename $HOME/personal/mail `
MYMAILPATH=` dirname $HOME/personal/mail `
```

This shell procedure, invoked with the argument **/usr/src/bin/cat.c**, compiles the named file and moves the output to **cat** in the current directory:

```
cc $1
mv a.out `basename $1 .c`
```

SEE ALSO

ed(1), sh(1)

NAME

basename – display portions of pathnames

SYNOPSIS

/usr/ucb/basename *string* [*suffix*]

DESCRIPTION

basename deletes any prefix ending in '/' and the *suffix*, if present in *string*. It directs the result to the standard output, and is normally used inside substitution marks (` `) within shell procedures. The *suffix* is a pattern as defined on the ed(1) manual page.

EXAMPLE

This shell procedure invoked with the argument **/usr/src/bin/cat.c** compiles the named file and moves the output to **cat** in the current directory:

```
cc $1
mv a.out `basename $1 .c`
```

SEE ALSO

ed(1), sh(1) in the *User's Reference Manual*

NAME

bc – arbitrary-precision arithmetic language

SYNOPSIS

bc [−c] [−1] [*file* . . .]

DESCRIPTION

bc is an interactive processor for a language that resembles C but provides unlimited precision arithmetic. It takes input from any files given, then reads the standard input. **bc** is actually a preprocessor for the desk calculator program **dc**, which it invokes automatically unless the −c option is present. In this case the **dc** input is sent to the standard output instead. The options are as follows:

−c   Compile only. The output is sent to the standard output.

−1   Argument stands for the name of an arbitrary precision math library.

The syntax for **bc** programs is as follows: *L* means letter **a**−**z**, *E* means expression, *S* means statement.

Comments

are enclosed in /* and */.

Names

simple variables: *L*
array elements: *L* [*E*]
the words **ibase**, **obase**,and **scale**

Other operands

arbitrarily long numbers with optional sign and decimal point
(*E*)
sqrt (*E*)
length (*E*)   number of significant decimal digits
scale (*E*)   number of digits right of decimal point
L (*E* , . . . , *E*)

Operators

```
+      −      *      /      %      ^
```
(% is remainder; ^ is power)
```
++     −−     (prefix and postfix; apply to names)
==     <=     >=     !=     <      >
=      =+     =−     =*     =/ =%     =^
```

Statements

E
{ *S* ; . . . ; *S* }
if (*E*) *S*
while (*E*) *S*
for (*E* ; *E* ; *E*) *S*
null statement
break
quit

Function definitions
```
     define L ( L , ... , L ) {
          auto L , ... , L
    "     S" ; ... S
          return ( E )
     }
```

Functions in **-1** math library

s(x)	sine
c(x)	cosine
e(x)	exponential
l(x)	log
a(x)	arctangent
j(n,x)	Bessel function

All function arguments are passed by value.

The value of a statement that is an expression is printed unless the main operator is an assignment. Either semicolons or new-lines may separate statements. Assignment to **scale** influences the number of digits to be retained on arithmetic operations in the manner of **dc**. Assignments to **ibase** or **obase** set the input and output number radix respectively.

The same letter may be used as an array, a function, and a simple variable simultaneously. All variables are global to the program. **auto** variables are pushed down during function calls. When using arrays as function arguments or defining them as automatic variables, empty square brackets must follow the array name.

EXAMPLE
```
          scale = 20
          define e(x){
               auto a, b, c, i, s
               a = 1
               b = 1
               s = 1
               for(i=1; 1==1; i++){
                    a = a*x
                    b = b*i
                    c = a/b
                    if(c == 0) return(s)
                    s = s+c
               }
          }
```
defines a function to compute an approximate value of the exponential function and
```
          for(i=1; i<=10; i++) e(i)
```
prints approximate values of the exponential function of the first ten integers.

FILES

    `/usr/lib/lib.b`   mathematical library
    `/usr/bin/dc`   desk calculator proper

SEE ALSO

    dc(1)

NOTES

    The **bc** command does not recognize the logical operators **&&** and | |.

    The **for** statement must have all three expressions (E's).

    The **quit** statement is interpreted when read, not when executed.

NAME
bdiff – big diff

SYNOPSIS
bdiff *file1* *file2* [*n*] [-s]

DESCRIPTION
bdiff is used in a manner analogous to diff to find which lines in *file1* and *file2* must be changed to bring the files into agreement. Its purpose is to allow processing of files too large for diff. If *file1* *(file2)* is –, the standard input is read.

Valid options to bdiff are:

n   The number of line segments. The value of *n* is 3500 by default. If the optional third argument is given and it is numeric, it is used as the value for *n*. This is useful in those cases in which 3500-line segments are too large for diff, causing it to fail.

-s   Specifies that no diagnostics are to be printed by bdiff (silent option). Note, however, that this does not suppress possible diagnostic messages from diff, which bdiff calls.

bdiff ignores lines common to the beginning of both files, splits the remainder of each file into *n*-line segments, and invokes diff on corresponding segments. If both optional arguments are specified, they must appear in the order indicated above.

The output of bdiff is exactly that of diff, with line numbers adjusted to account for the segmenting of the files (that is, to make it look as if the files had been processed whole). Note that because of the segmenting of the files, bdiff does not necessarily find a smallest sufficient set of file differences.

FILES
/tmp/bd?????

SEE ALSO
diff(1)

NAME

bfs – big file scanner

SYNOPSIS

bfs [–] *file*

DESCRIPTION

The **bfs** command is similar to **ed** except that it is read-only and processes much larger files. Files can be up to 1024K bytes and 32K lines, with up to 512 characters, including new-line, per line (255 for 16-bit machines). **bfs** is usually more efficient than **ed** for scanning a file, since the file is not copied to a buffer. It is most useful for identifying sections of a large file where the **csplit** command can be used to divide it into more manageable pieces for editing.

Normally, the size of the file being scanned is printed, as is the size of any file written with the **w** command. The optional – suppresses printing of sizes. Input is prompted with * if **P** and a carriage return are typed, as in **ed**. Prompting can be turned off again by inputting another **P** and carriage return. Messages are given in response to errors if prompting is turned on.

All address expressions described under **ed** are supported. In addition, regular expressions may be surrounded with two symbols besides **/** and **?**: **>** indicates downward search without wrap-around, and **<** indicates upward search without wrap-around. There is a slight difference in mark names: only the letters **a** through **z** may be used, and all 26 marks are remembered.

The **e, g, v, k, p, q, w, =, !** and null commands operate as described under **ed**. Commands such as **–––, +++–, +++=, –12**, and **+4p** are accepted. Note that **1,10p** and **1,10** both print the first ten lines. The **f** command only prints the name of the file being scanned; there is no remembered file name. The **w** command is independent of output diversion, truncation, or crunching (see the **xo, xt,** and **xc** commands, below). The following additional commands are available:

xf *file*
> Further commands are taken from the named *file*. When an end-of-file is reached, an interrupt signal is received or an error occurs, reading resumes with the file containing the **xf**. The **xf** commands may be nested to a depth of 10.

xn List the marks currently in use (marks are set by the **k** command).

xo [*file*]
> Further output from the **p** and null commands is diverted to the named *file*, which, if necessary, is created mode 666 (readable and writable by everyone), unless your **umask** setting dictates otherwise; see **umask**(1). If *file* is missing, output is diverted to the standard output. Note that each diversion causes truncation or creation of the file.

: *label*
> This positions a *label* in a command file. The *label* is terminated by new-line, and blanks between the **:** and the start of the *label* are ignored. This command may also be used to insert comments into a command file, since labels need not be referenced.

(. , .)**xb**/*regular expression*/*label*
> A jump (either upward or downward) is made to *label* if the command succeeds. It fails under any of the following conditions:
>
>> 1. Either address is not between **1** and **$**.
>> 2. The second address is less than the first.
>> 3. The regular expression does not match at least one line in the specified range, including the first and last lines.
>
> On success, **.** is set to the line matched and a jump is made to *label*. This command is the only one that does not issue an error message on bad addresses, so it may be used to test whether addresses are bad before other commands are executed. Note that the command
>
>> ```
>> xb/^/ label
>> ```
>
> is an unconditional jump.
>
> The **xb** command is allowed only if it is read from someplace other than a terminal. If it is read from a pipe only a downward jump is possible.

xt *number*
> Output from the **p** and null commands is truncated to at most *number* characters. The initial number is 255.

xv[*digit*] [*spaces*] [*value*]
> The variable name is the specified *digit* following the **xv**. The commands **xv5100** or **xv5 100** both assign the value **100** to the variable **5**. The command **xv61,100p** assigns the value **1,100p** to the variable **6**. To reference a variable, put a **%** in front of the variable name. For example, using the above assignments for variables **5** and **6**:
>
>> ```
>> 1,%5p
>> 1,%5
>> %6
>> ```
>
> all print the first 100 lines.
>
>> ```
>> g/%5/p
>> ```
>
> globally searches for the characters **100** and prints each line containing a match. To escape the special meaning of **%**, a \ must precede it.
>
>> ```
>> g/".*\%[cds]/p
>> ```
>
> could be used to match and list lines containing a **printf** of characters, decimal integers, or strings.
>
> Another feature of the **xv** command is that the first line of output from a UNIX system command can be stored into a variable. The only requirement is that the first character of *value* be an **!**. For example:

```
.w junk
xv5!cat junk
!rm junk
!echo "%5"
xv6!expr %6 + 1
```

puts the current line into variable **5**, prints it, and increments the
variable **6** by one. To escape the special meaning of **!** as the first
character of *value*, precede it with a **\ **.

    xv7\!date

stores the value **!date** into variable **7**.

xbz *label*

xbn *label*

These two commands test the last saved *return code* from the execution of a UNIX system command (**!***command*) or nonzero value,
respectively, to the specified label. The two examples below both
search for the next five lines containing the string **size**.

```
xv55
: 1
/size/
xv5!expr %5 - 1
!if 0%5 != 0 exit 2
xbn 1
xv45
: 1
/size/
xv4!expr %4 - 1
!if 0%4 = 0 exit 2
xbz 1
```

xc [*switch*]

If *switch* is **1**, output from the **p** and null commands is crunched; if
switch is **0** it is not. Without an argument, **xc** reverses *switch*. Initially *switch* is set for no crunching. Crunched output has strings of
tabs and blanks reduced to one blank and blank lines suppressed.

SEE ALSO

    csplit(1), ed(1), umask(1)

DIAGNOSTICS

    ? for errors in commands, if prompting is turned off. Self-explanatory error
messages when prompting is on.

NAME

> **biff** – give notice of incoming mail messages

SYNOPSIS

> /usr/ucb/biff [**y** | n]

DESCRIPTION

> **biff** turns mail notification on or off for the terminal session. With no arguments, **biff** displays the current notification status for the terminal.

> The **y** option allows mail notification for the terminal. The **n** option disables notification for the terminal.

> If notification is allowed, the terminal rings the bell and displays the header and the first few lines of each arriving mail message. **biff** operates asynchronously. For synchronized notices, use the **MAIL** variable of **sh**(1) or the **mail** variable of **csh**(1).

> A 'biff y' command can be included in your ~/.login or ~/.profile file for execution when you log in.

FILES

> ~/.login
> ~/.profile

SEE ALSO

> csh(1), mail(1), sh(1) in the *User's Reference Manual*

NAME
    biod – NFS daemon

SYNOPSIS
    biod [*nservers*]

DESCRIPTION
    biod starts *nservers* asynchronous block I/O daemons. This command is used on an NFS client to buffer read-ahead and write-behind. Four is the usual number for *nservers*.

    The **biod** daemons are automatically invoked in run level 3.

SEE ALSO
    mountd(1M), nfsd(1M), sharetab(4)

NAME

bkexcept – change or display an exception list for incremental backups

SYNOPSIS

bkexcept [-t *file*] [-d *patterns*]
bkexcept [-t *file*] -a | -r *patterns*
bkexcept -C [*files*]

DESCRIPTION

The **bkexcept** command displays a list of patterns describing files that are to be excluded when backup operations occur using **incfile**. The list is known as the "exception list."

bkexcept may be executed only by a user with superuser privilege.

bkexcept -a adds patterns to the list.

bkexcept -d displays patterns from the list.

bkexcept -r removes patterns from the list.

Patterns

Patterns describe individual pathnames or sets of pathnames. Patterns must conform to pathname naming conventions specified under **DEFINITIONS** on the **intro**(2) page. A pattern is taken as a filename and is interpreted in the manner of **cpio**. A pattern can include the shell special characters *, ?, and []. Asterisk (*) and question mark (?) will match period (.) and slash(/). Because these are shell special characters, they must be escaped on the command line.

There are three general methods of specifying entries to the exception list:

- To specify all files under a particular directory, specify the directory name (and any desired subdirectories) followed by an asterisk:

    /*directory*/*subdirectories*/*

- To specify all instances of a filename regardless of its location, specify the filename preceded by an asterisk:

    */*filename*

- To specify one instance of a particular file, specify the entire pathname to the file:

    /*directory*/*subdirectories*/*filename*

If *pattern* is a dash (–), standard input is read for a list of patterns (one per line until EOF) to be added or deleted.

Compatibility

Prior versions of the backup service created exception lists using **ed** syntax. **bkexcept** -C provides a translation facility for exception lists created by **ed**. The translation is not perfect; not all **ed** patterns have equivalents in **cpio**. For those patterns that have no automatic translation, an attempt at translation is made, and the translated version is flagged with the word **QUESTIONABLE**. The exception list translation is directed to standard output. Redirect the standard output to a translation file, review the contents of the translation file (correcting entries that were not translated properly and deleting the **QUESTIONABLE** flags), and then use the resulting file as input to a subsequent **bkexcept** **-a**. For example, if the translated file was named **checkfile** the **-a** option would appear as follows:

```
bkexcept -a - < checkfile
```

Options

-t *file*　The filename used in place of the default file.

-a *pattern. . .*

Adds *pattern* to the exception list where *pattern* is one or more patterns (comma-separated or blank-separated and enclosed in quotes) describing sets of paths.

-d *pattern. . .*

Displays entries in the exception list. If *pattern* begins with a slash (/), **-d** displays all entries whose names begin with *pattern*. If *pattern* does not begin with a slash, **-d** displays all entries that include *pattern* anywhere in the entry. If *pattern* is a dash (-), input is taken from standard input. *pattern* is not a pattern -- it matches patterns. *pattern* **a∗b** matches **/a∗b** but does not match **/adb**. For files containing a carriage return, a null exception list is returned. For files of zero length (no characters), an error is returned (search of table failed).

The entries are displayed in ASCII collating sequence order (special characters, numbers, then alphabetical order).

-r *pattern. . .*

Removes *pattern* from the exception list. *pattern* is one or a list of patterns (comma-separated or blank-separated and enclosed in quotes) describing sets of paths. *pattern* must be an exact match of an entry in the exception list for *pattern* to be removed. Patterns that are removed are echoed to standard output, **stdout**.

-C [*files*]

Displays on standard output the translation of each *file* (a prior version's exception list) to the new syntax. Each *file* contains **ed** patterns, one per line.

If *file* is omitted, the default UNIX exception list, **/etc/save.d/except**, is translated. If *file* is a dash (–), input is taken from standard input, one per line.

DIAGNOSTICS

The exit codes for the **bkexcept** command are the following:

0 = the task completed successfully
1 = one or more parameters to **bkexcept** are invalid
2 = an error has occurred, causing **bkexcept** to fail to
　　complete all portions of its task

EXAMPLES

Example 1:

```
bkexcept -a /tmp/*,/var/tmp/*,/usr/rje/*,*/trash,
```

adds the four sets of files to the exception list, (all files under **/tmp**, all files under **/var/tmp**, all files under **/usr/rje**, and any file on the system named **trash**).

Example 2:

        `bkexcept -d /tmp`

displays the following patterns from those added to the exception list in Example 1.

        `/tmp/*`

        `bkexcept -d tmp`

displays the following patterns from those added to the exception list in Example 1.

        `/tmp/*, /var/tmp/*`

displays one per line, with a heading.

Example 3:

        `bkexcept -r /var/tmp/*,/usr/rje/*`

removes the two patterns from the exception list.

Example 4:

        `bkexcept -C /save.d/old.except > trans.except`

translates the file **/save.d/old.except** from its **ed** format to **cpio** format and sends the translations to the file **trans.except**. The translations of **/save.d/old.except** may be added to the current exception list by using **bkexcept -a** as follows:

        `bkexcept -a - < trans.except`

FILES

/etc/bkup/bkexcept.tab   the default exception list for UNIX System V Release 4.

/etc/save.d/except   the default exception list for pre-UNIX System V Release 4.

SEE ALSO

        backup(1M), incfile(1M)
        cpio(1), ed(1), sh(1) in the *User's Reference Manual*
        intro(2) in the *Programmer's Reference Manual*
        "The Backup Service"chapter in the *System Administrator's Guide*

NAME

bkhistory – report on completed backup operations

SYNOPSIS

bkhistory [–hl] [–f *field_separator*] [–d *dates*] [–o *names*] [–t *tags*]
bkhistory –p *period*

DESCRIPTION

bkhistory without options reports a summary of the contents of the backup history log, bkhist.tab. Backup operations are sorted alphabetically by tag. For
each tag, operations are listed from most to least recent. backup(1M) updates
this log after each successful backup operation.

bkhistory may be executed only by a user with the superuser privilege.

bkhistory –p assigns a rotation *period* (in weeks) for the history log; all entries
older than the specified number of weeks are deleted from the log. The default
rotation period is one (1) week.

Options

–d *dates*

Restricts the report to backup operations performed on the specified dates.
dates are in the **date** format. *day, hour, minute,* and *year,* are optional and
will be ignored. The list of *dates* is either comma-separated or blank-
separated and surrounded by quotes.

–f *field_separator*

Suppresses field wrap on the display and specifies an output field separator to be used. The value of *c* is the character that will appear as the field
separator on the display output. For clarity of output, do not use a
separator character that is likely to occur in a field. For example, do not
use the colon as a field separator character if the display will contain dates
that use a colon to separate hours from minutes. To use the default field
separator (tab), specify the null character ("") for *c*.

–h   Suppresses header for the reports.

–l   Displays a long form of the report. This produces an ls –1 listing of the
files included in the backup archive (if backup tables of contents are available on-line).

–o *names*

Restricts the report to the specified originating objects (file systems or data
partitions). *names* is a list of *onames* and/or *odevices*. [See bkreg(1M)].

The list of names is either comma-separated or blank-separated and surrounded by quotes.

–p *period*

Sets the number of weeks of information that will be saved in the backup
history table. The minimum value of *period* is 1, which is also the default
value. the size of int. By default, *period* is 1.

-t *tags*

    Restricts the report to backups with the specified *tags*. *tags* is a list of tag values as specified in the backup register. The list of *tags* is either comma-separated or blank-separated and surrounded by quotes.

DIAGNOSTICS

The exit codes for the **bkhistory** command are the following:

0 =	the task completed successfully
1 =	one or more parameters to **bkhistory** are invalid
2 =	an error has occurred, causing **bkhistory** to fail to complete all portions of its task

EXAMPLES

Example 1:

    bkhistory -p 3

sets the rotation period for the history log to three weeks. Entries older than three weeks are deleted from the log.

Example 2:

    bkhistory -t SpoolDai,UsrDaily,TPubsWed

displays a report of completed backup operations for the three tags listed.

Example 3:

    bkhistory -l -o /usr

Displays an **ls -l** listing of the files that were backed up from **/usr** (the originating object) if there is a table of contents.

FILES

/etc/bkup/bkhist.tab	the backup history log that contains information about successfully completed backup operations
/etc/bkup/bkreg.tab	description of the backup policy established by the administrator
/var/sadm/bkup/toc	list of directories with on-line tables of contents

SEE ALSO

backup(1M), bkreg(1M)
date(1), ls(1) in the *User's Reference Manual*

NAME

bkoper – interact with backup operations to service media insertion prompts

SYNOPSIS

bkoper [–u *users*]

DESCRIPTION

Backup operations may require an operator to insert media and to confirm proper volume labels. The **bkoper** command provides a **mailx**-like interface for these operator interactions. It begins by printing a list of headers. Each header describes a backup operation requiring interaction, the device requiring attention including the media type and label of the volume to be inserted (see EXAMPLE). The system displays prompts and the operator issues commands to resolve the backup operation. Typing a carriage return invokes the current header. If no headers have been serviced, the current header is the first header on the list. If a header has been selected and serviced, the current header is the next one following.

bkoper may be executed only by a user with superuser privilege. By default, the operator may interact only with backup operations that were started by the same user ID .

If the **–u** *users* option is given, the operator interacts only with backup operations started by the specified *user*(s).

Commands

!*shell-command*
           Escapes to the shell. The remainder of the line after the ! is sent to the UNIX system shell (**sh**) to be interpreted as a command.

=   Prints the current backup operation number.

?   Prints this summary of commands.

[p|t] [*n*]   Both the **p** and **t** options operate in the same way. Either option will interact with the backup operation described by the *n*'th header. *n* defaults to the current header number.

h   Prints the list of backup operations.

q   Quits from **bkoper**.

DIAGNOSTICS

The exit codes for **bkoper** are the following:

0 = successful completion of the task
1 = one or more parameters to **bkoper** are invalid.
2 = an error has occurred which caused **bkoper** to fail to
    complete *all* portions of its task.

EXAMPLE

A sample header is shown below. Items appearing in the header are listed in the following order: header number, job-ID, tag, originating device, destination group, destination device, destination volume labels. [See **bkreg**(1M) for descriptions of items.] Not every header contains values for all these fields; if a destination group is not specified in **/etc/bkup/bkreg.tab**, then no value for "destination group" appears in the header.

```
1 back-111 usrsun /dev/dsk/c1d0s1 disk /dev/dsk/c2d1s9 usrsave
2 back-112 fs2daily /dev/dsk/c1d0s8 ctape /dev/ctape/c4d0s2 -
```

Backup headers are numbered on the basis of arrival; the oldest header has the lowest number. If the destination device does not have a volume label, a dash is displayed in the header.

SEE ALSO

bkreg(1M), bkstatus(1M), getvol(1M), mailx(1)

NAME

bkreg – change or display the contents of a backup register

SYNOPSIS

bkreg   **-p** *period* [**-w** *cweek*] [**-t** *table*]

bkreg   **-a** *tag* **-o** *orig* **-c** *weeks:days*| **demand** **-d** *ddev* **-m** *method*| **migration**
          [**-b** *moptions*] [**-t** *table*] [**-D** *depend*] [**-P** *prio*]

bkreg   **-e** *tag* [**-o** *orig*] [**-c** *weeks:days*| **demand**] [**-m** *method*| **migration**]
          [**-d** *ddev*] [**-t** *table*] [**-b** *moptions*] [**-D** *depend*] [**-P** *prio*]

bkreg   **-r** *tag* [**-t** *table*]

bkreg   [**-A**|**-O**|**-R**] [**-hsv**] [**-t** *table*] [**-c** *weeks*[:*days*]| **demand**]

bkreg   **-C** *fields* [**-hv**] [**-t** *table*] [**-c** *weeks*[:*days*]| **demand**] [**-f** *c*]

DESCRIPTION

A backup register is a file containing descriptions of backup operations to be performed on a UNIX system.   The default backup register is located in
/etc/bkup/bkreg.tab. Other backup registers may be created.

The **bkreg** command may be executed only by a user with superuser privilege.

Each entry in a backup register describes backup operations to be performed on a
given disk object (called the originating object) for some set of days and weeks
during a rotation period.   There may be several register entries for an object, but
only one entry may specify backup operations for an object on a specific day and
week of the rotation period.   The entry describes the object, the backup method
to be used to archive the object, and the destination volumes to be used to store
the archive.   Each entry has a unique *tag* that identifies it. *Tag*s must conform to
file naming conventions.

Rotation Period

Backups are performed in a rotation period specified in weeks.   When the end of
a rotation period is reached, a new period begins.   Rotation periods begin on
Sundays.   The default rotation period is one week.

Originating Objects

An originating object is either a raw data partition or a filesystem.   An originating object is described by its originating object name, its device name, and
optional volume labels.

Several backup operations for different originating objects may be active concurrently by specifying priorities and dependencies.   During a backup session,
higher priority backup operations are attempted before lower priority backup
operations.   All backup operations of a given priority may proceed concurrently
unless dependencies are specified.   If one backup is declared to be dependent on
others, it will not be started until all of its antecedents have completed successfully.

Destination Devices

Each backup archive is written to a set of storage volumes inserted into a destination device.   A destination device can have destination device group, a destination device name, media characteristics, and volume labels.   Default characteris-

tics for a medium (as specified in the device table) may be overridden (see the "Device Management" chapter in the *System Administrator's Guide*).

Backup Methods

An originating object is backed up to a destination device archive using a method. The method determines the amount of information backed up and the representation of that information. Different methods may be used for a given originating object on different days of the rotation. Each method accepts a set of options that are specific to the method.

Several default methods are provided with the Backup service. Others methods may be added by a UNIX system site. For descriptions of the default methods, see **incfile**(1M), **ffile**(1M), **fdisk**(1M), **fimage**(1M), and **fdp**(1M).

A backup archive may be migrated to a different destination by specifying **migration** as the backup method. The device name of the originating object for a migration must have been the destination device for a previously successful backup operation. This form of backup does not re-archive the originating object. It copies an archive from one destination to another, updating the backup service's databases so that restores can still be done automatically.

Register Validations

There are items in a single backup register entry and items across register entries that must be consistent for the backup service to conduct a backup session correctly. Some of these consistencies are checked at the time the backup register is created or changed. Others can be checked only at the time the backup register is used by **backup**(1M). See **backup**(1M) for a complete list of validations.

Modes

The **bkreg** command has two modes: changing the contents of a backup register and displaying the contents of a backup register.

Changing Contents

bkreg −p	changes the rotation period for a backup register. The default rotation period is one week.
bkreg −a	adds an entry to a backup register. This option requires other options to be specified. These are listed below under **Options**.
bkreg −e	edits an existing entry in a backup register.
bkreg −r	removes an existing entry from a backup register.

Displaying Contents

bkreg −C	produces a customized display of the contents of a backup register.

bkreg [−A|−R|−O]
produces a summary display of the contents of a backup register.

Options

−a   Adds a new entry to the default backup register. Options required with −a are: *tag, originating device, weeks:days, destination device*, and *method*. If other options are not specified, the following defaults are used: the default backup register is used, no method options are specified, the priority is 0, and no dependencies exist between entries.

−b *moptions*

Each backup method supports a specific set of options that modify its behavior. *moptions* is specified as a list of options that are blank-separated and enclosed in quotes. The argument string provided here is passed to the method exactly as entered, without modification. For lists of valid options, see "The Backup Service" chapter in the *System Administrator's Guide* and the following entries in this book: **fdisk**(1M), **fdp**(1M), **ffile**(1M), **fimage**(1M), and **incfile**(1M).

−c *weeks:days*| **demand**

Sets the week(s) and day(s) of the rotation period during which a backup entry should be performed or for which a display should be generated. *weeks* is a set of numbers including 1 and 52. The value of *weeks* cannot be greater than the value of **−p***period*. *weeks* is specified as a combination of lists or ranges (either comma-separated or blank-separated and enclosed in quotes). An example set of weeks is

    ''1 3-10,13''

indicating the first week, each of the third through tenth weeks, and the thirteenth week of the rotation period.

days is a set of numbers between 0 (Sunday) and 6 (Saturday). In addition, *days* are specified as a combination of lists or ranges (either comma-separated or blank-separated and enclosed in quotes).

demand indicates that an entry is used only when explicitly requested by

    backup −c demand

−d *ddev*

Specifies *ddev* as the destination device for the backup operation. *ddev* is of the form:

    [*dgroup*] [: [*ddevice*] [:*dchar*] [:*dmname*]]

where either *dgroup* or *ddevice* must be specified and *dchar* and *dmname* are optional. (Both *dgroup* and *ddev* may be specified together.) Colons delineate field boundaries and must be included as indicated above.

dgroup is the device group for the destination device. [See **devgroup.tab**(4).] If omitted, *ddevice* must be specified.

ddevice is the device name of a specific destination device. [See **device.tab**(4).] If omitted, *dgroup* must be specified and any available device in *dgroup* may be used.

dchar describes media characteristics. If specified, they override the default characteristics for the device and group. *dchar* is of the form:

    keyword=*value*

where **keyword** is a valid device characteristic keyword (as it appears in the device table.) *dchar* entries may be separated by commas or blanks. If separated by blanks, the entire string of arguments to *ddev* must be enclosed in quotes.

dlabels is a list of volume names of the destination volumes. The list of *dlabels* must be either comma-separated or blank-separated. If blank-separated, the entire *ddev* argument must be surrounded by quotes. Each *dlabel* corresponds to a *volumename* specified on the `labelit` command. If *dlabels* is omitted, `backup` and `restore` do not validate the volume labels on this entry.

-e   Edits an existing entry. If any of the options –b, –c, –d, –m, –o, –D, or –P are present, they replace the current settings for the specified entry in the register.

–f *c*   Overrides the default output field separator. *c* is the character that will appear as the field separator on the display output. The default output field separator is colon (:).

–h   Suppresses headers when generating displays.

–m *method*| `migration`
          Performs the backup using the specified *method.* Default methods are: `incfile`, `ffile`, `fdisk`, `fimage`, and `fdp`. If the method to be used is not a default method, it must appear as the executable file in the standard method directory `/etc/bkup/method`. `migration` indicates that the value of *orig* (following the -o option) matches the value of *ddev* during a prior backup operation. The originating object is not rearchived; it is simply copied to the location specified by *ddev* (following the -d option). The backup history (if any) and tables of contents (if any) are updated to reflect the changed destination for the original archive.

–o *orig*
          Specifies *orig* as the originating object for the backup operation. *orig* is specified in the following format:

              oname:*odevice*[:*omname*]

where *oname* is the name of an originating object. For file system partitions, it is the nodename on which the file system is usually mounted, `mount`. For data partitions, it is any valid path name. This value is provided to the backup method and validated by `backup`. The default data partition backup methods, `fdp` and `fdisk`, do not validate this name.

odevice is the device name for the originating object. In all cases, it is a raw disk partition device name. For AT&T 3B2 computers, this name is specified in the following format: `/dev/rdsk/c?d?s?`.

olabel is the volume label for the originating object. For file system partitions, it corresponds to the *volumename* displayed by the `labelit` command. A data partition may have an associated volume name that appears nowhere except on the outside of the volume (where it is taped); `getvol` may be used to have an operator validate the name.

On AT&T 3B2 computers, the special data partition `/dev/rdsk/c?d?s6` names an entire disk and is used when disk formatting or repartitioning is done to reference the disk's volume table of contents (VTOC). [See `fmthard`(1M) and `prtvtoc`(1M).] `backup` validates this special full disk partition with the disk volume name specified when the disk was partitioned. [See **fmthard**(1M).] If the disk volume name is omitted, **backup** does not validate the volume labels for this originating object.

-p *period*
: Sets the rotation period (in weeks) for the backup register to *period*. The minimum value is 1; the maximum value is 52. By default the current week of the rotation is set to 1.

-r
: Removes the specified entries from the register.

-s
: Suppresses wrap-around behavior when generating displays. Normal behavior is to wrap long values within each field.

-t *table*
: Uses *table* instead of the default register, **bkreg.tab**.

-v
: Generates displays using (vertical) columns instead of (horizontal) rows. This allows more information to be displayed without encountering problems displaying long lines.

-w *cweek*
: Overrides the default behavior by setting the current week of the rotation period to *cweek*. *cweek* is an integer between 1 and the value of *period*. The default is **1**.

-A
: Displays a report describing all fields in the register. The display produced by this option is best suited as input to a filter, since in horizontal mode it produces extremely long lines.

-C *fields*
: Generates a display of the contents of a backup register, limiting the display to the specified fields. The output is a set of lines, one per register entry. Each line consists of the desired fields, separated by a field separator character. *fields* is a list of field names (either comma-separated or blank-separated and enclosed in quotes) for the fields desired. The valid field names are **period**, **cweek**, **tag**, **oname**, **odevice**, **olabel**, **weeks**, **days**, **method**, **moptions**, **prio**, **depend**, **dgroup**, **ddevice**, **dchar**, and **dlabel**.

-D *depend*
: Specifies a set of backup operations that must be completed successfully before this operation may begin. *depend* is a list of *tag*(s) (either comma-separated or blank-separated and enclosed in quotes) naming the antecedent backup operations.

-f *c*
: Overrides the default output field separator. *c* is the character that will appear as the field separator on the display output. The default output field separator is colon (":").

-O
: Displays a summary of all originating objects with entries in the register.

-P *prio*
: Sets a priority of *prio* for this backup operation. The default priority is 0; the highest priority is 100. All backup operations with the same priority may run simultaneously, unless the priority is 0. All backups with priority 0 run sequentially in an unspecified order.

-R   Displays a summary of all destination devices with entries in the register.

DIAGNOSTICS

The exit codes for **bkreg** are the following:

0 = the task completed successfully
1 = one or more parameters to **bkreg** are invalid
2 = an error has occurred, causing **bkreg** to fail to
    complete *all* portions of its task

Errors are reported on standard error if any of the following occurs:

1. The **tag** specified in **bkreg** −e or **bkreg** −r does not exist in the backup register.

2. The tag specified in **bkreg** −a already exists in the register.

EXAMPLES

Example 1:

```
bkreg -p 15 -w 3
```

establishes a 15-week rotation period in the default backup register and sets the current week to the 3rd week of the rotation period.

Example 2:

```
bkreg -a acct5 -t wklybu.tab \
-o /usr:/dev/rdsk/c1d0s2:usr -c "2 4-6 8 10:0,2,5" \
-m incfile -b -txE \
-d diskette:capacity=1404:acctwkly1,acctwkly2,acctwkly3 \
```

adds an entry named *acct5* to the backup register named **wklybu.tab**. If **wklybu.tab** does not already exist, it will be created. The originating object to be backed up is the **/usr** file system on the **/dev/rdsk/c1d0s2** device which is known as **usr**. The backup will be performed each Sunday, Tuesday, and Friday of the second, fourth through sixth, eighth, and tenth weeks of the rotation period using the **incfile** (incremental file) method. The method options specify that a table of contents will be created on additional media instead of in the backup history log, the exception list is to be ignored, and an estimate of the number of volumes for the archive is to be provided before performing the backup. The backup will be done to the next available diskette device using the three diskette volumes **acctwkly1, acctwkly2,** and **acctwkly3**. These volumes have a capacity of 1404 blocks each.

Example 3:

```
bkreg -e services2 -t wklybu.tab \
-o /back:/dev/rdsk/c1d0s8:back -m migration \
-c demand -d ctape:/dev/rdsk/c4d0s3 \
```

changes the specifications for the backup operation named **services2** on the backup table **wklybu.tab** so that whenever the command **backup −c demand** is executed, the backup that was performed to the destination device **back:dev/rdsk/c1d0s2:back** will be migrated from that device (now serving as the originating device) to a cartridge tape.

Example 4:

```
bkreg -e pubsfri -P 10 -D develfri,marketfri,acctfri
```

changes the priority level for the backup operation named **pubsfri** to 10 and makes this backup operation dependent on the three backup operations **devel-fri, marketfri,** and **acctfri**. The **pubsfri** operation will be done only after all backup operations with priorities greater than 10 have begun and after the **develfri, marketfri,** and **acctfri** operations have been completed successfully.

Example 5:

```
bkreg -c 1-8:0-6
```

provides the default display of the contents of the default backup register, for all weekdays for the first through eighth weeks of the rotation period. The information in the register will be displayed in the following format:

```
Rotation Period = 10    Current Week = 4
```

```
Originating Device: / /dev/root
```

Tag	Weeks	Days	Method	Options	Pri	Dgroup
rootdai	1-8	1-6	incfile			diskette
rootsp	1-8	0	ffile	-bxt	20	ctape

```
Originating Device:  /usr /dev/dsk/c1d0s2
```

Tag	Weeks	Days	Method	Options	Pri	Dgroup
usrdai	1-8	1-5	incfile			diskette
usrsp	1-8	0	ffile	-bxt	15	ctape

FILES

```
/etc/bkup/method/*
/etc/bkup/bkreg.tab     describes the backup policy established by the adminis-
                        trator
/etc/dgroup.tab         lists logical groupings of devices as determined by the
                        administrator
/etc/device.tab         describes specific devices and their attributes
```

SEE ALSO

backup(1M), fdisk(1M), fdp(1M), incfile(1M), ffile(1M), fimage(1M), fmthard(1M), getvol(1M), labelit(1M), mkfs(1M), mount(1M), prtvtoc(1M), restore(1M)

NAME

bkstatus – display the status of backup operations

SYNOPSIS

bkstatus [–h] [–f *field_separator*] [–j *jobids*] [–s *states* | –a] [–u *users*]

bkstatus –p *period*

DESCRIPTION

Without options, the **bkstatus** command displays the status of backup operations that are in progress: either **active, pending, waiting** or **suspended**. When
used with the –a option, the **backup** command includes **failed** and **completed**
backup operations in the display.

bkstatus –p defines the amount of status information that is saved for display.

bkstatus may only be executed by a user with superuser privilege.

Each backup operation goes through a number of states as described below. The
keyletters listed in parentheses after each state are used with the –s option and
also appear on the display.

pending(p)

> **backup** has been invoked and the operations in the backup register for
> the specified day are scheduled to occur.

active(a)

> The backup operation has been assigned a destination device and
> archiving is currently underway; or a suspended backup has been
> resumed.

waiting(w)

> The backup operation is waiting for operator interaction, such as
> inserting the correct volume.

suspended(s)

> The backup operation has been suspended by an invocation of **backup**
> –S.

failed(f)

> The backup operation failed or has been cancelled.

completed(c)

> The backup operation has completed successfully.

The –a and –s options are mutually exclusive.

Options

–a

> Include **failed** and **completed** backup operations in the display. All
> backup operations that have occurred within the rotation period are
> displayed.

–f *field_separator*

> Suppresses field wrap on the display and specifies an output field
> separator to be used. The value of *c* is the character that will appear
> as the field separator on the display output. For clarity of output, do
> not use a separator character that is likely to occur in a field. For
> example, do not use the colon as a field separator character if the

display will contain dates that use a colon to separate hours from minutes. To use the default field separator (tab), specify the null character ("") for *c*.

−**h**   Suppress header on the display.

−**j** *jobids*   Restrict the display to the specified list of **backup** job ids (either comma-separated or blank-separated and enclosed in quotes). [See **backup**(1M)].

−**p** *period*   Define the amount of backup status information that is saved and made available for display as *period*. *period* is the number of weeks that information is saved in **/bkup/bkstatus.tab**. Status information that is older than the number of weeks specified in *period* is deleted from the status table. The minimum valid entry is 1. The maximum valid entry is 52. The default is 1 week.

−**s** *states*   Restrict the report to backup operations with the specified *states*. *states* is a list of state key-letters (concatenated, comma-separated or blank-separated and surrounded by quotes). For example,

         apf
         a,p,f
         "a p f"

all specify that the report should only include backup operations that are **active, pending** or **failed**.

−**u** *users*   Restrict the display to backup operations started by the specified list of *users* (either comma-separated or blank-separated and enclosed in quotes). *users* must be in the **passwd** file.

DIAGNOSTICS

The exit codes for the **bkstatus** command are the following:

0 = successful completion of the task
1 = one or more parameters to **bkstatus** are invalid.
2 = an error has occurred which caused **bkstatus** to fail to
     complete *all* portions of its task.

EXAMPLES

Example 1:

     bkstatus −p 4

specifies that backup status information is to be saved for four weeks. Any status information older than four weeks is deleted from the system.

Example 2:

     bkstatus −a −j back-459,back-395

produces a display that shows status for the two backup jobs specified, even if they have **completed** or **failed**.

Example 3:

```
bkstatus -s a,c -u "oper3 oper4"
```

produces a display that shows only those backup jobs issued by users **oper3** and **oper4** that have a status of either **active** or **completed**.

FILES

`/etc/bkup/bkstatus.tab`	lists the current status of backups that have occurred or are still in progress
`/etc/bkup/bkreg.tab`	describes the backup policy decided on by the System Administrator

SEE ALSO

backup(1M), bkhist(1M), bkreg(1M)

NAME

boot – UNIX system boot program

DESCRIPTION

The **boot** program interactively loads and executes stand-alone UNIX programs. While **boot** is used primarily for loading and executing the UNIX system kernel, it can load and execute any other programs that are linked for stand-alone execution. The **boot** program is a required part of the UNIX Base Operating System software set and must be present in the root file system to ensure successful loading of the UNIX System kernel. Note that during installation of the UNIX operating system, a custom **masterboot** is placed on the hard disk. The **masterboot** program resides on sector 0 of the hard disk and is the default boot program for hard-disk boot procedures.

The system invokes the **boot** program each time the computer is started. It tries to locate the **boot** program on the floppy disk drive first; if the floppy disk drive is empty, the system invokes the hard-disk boot procedure. The boot procedure depends on whether you are booting from a floppy disk or hard disk, as described below.

The floppy-disk boot procedure has two stages:

1. The boot block in sector 0 of the file system loads **boot**.

2. **boot** executes and prompts the user.

The hard-disk boot procedure has three stages:

1. The ROMs load in the **masterboot** block from sector 0 on the hard disk.

2. The **masterboot** boot block then loads the partition boot block from sector 0 of the active partition [see **fdisk**(1M)].

3. The remainder of **boot** is loaded from the next 29 sectors of the hard disk.

When first invoked, **boot** displays the following status message:

    Booting the UNIX System ...

To instruct **boot** to use the default kernel and values specified in the boot default file, **/stand/boot**, press **RETURN**. If you press any key other than **RETURN**, **boot** pauses and prompts you for custom information. If you have just loaded the **boot** program from the distribution diskette, press RETURN so **boot** will use the default values.

To load a program that is not the default program, press any key to interrupt **boot**. The **boot** program pauses and prompts you with the following message for the name of the program you want to load:

    Enter the name of a kernel to boot:

The system waits at this point for you to type the name of the program you want to load and press RETURN. The length of the pause is the number of seconds specified with the **TIMEOUT** option in **/stand/boot** (see "**boot Options**"). If you have not typed something after the specified number of seconds and **AUTOBOOT** is set to **YES** in **/stand/boot**, **boot** times out and behaves as though you pressed

RETURN. The **boot** program proceeds through the boot process, and **init**(1M) is passed an **-a** flag with no *prompt* argument.

If you are booting from a program other than the **boot** program on the distribution diskette, you must specify the location of the program by providing a filename (if the program you want to load is on the default boot device). The filename must include the full pathname of the file containing the stand-alone program. To indicate a program other than the **boot** program on the distribution diskette, use the following format:

> *filename*

where *filename* is the standard UNIX system pathname. If *filename* is the only argument typed at the boot prompt, **boot** looks for the *filename* on the default boot device and tries to boot from it.

boot Options

Options for the **boot** program can be set or changed with keywords in **/stand/boot** The following keywords are recognized by **boot**:

AUTOBOOT=YES or **NO**	Indicates whether or not **boot** starts loading the kernel immediately or displays a boot prompt first.
BOOTMSG=*string*	The default boot message is changed to *string*.
BOOTPROMPT=*string*	The default boot prompt is changed to *string*.
DEFBOOTSTR=bootstring	Sets default bootstring to **bootstring**. This is the string used by **boot** when the user presses RETURN only to the boot prompt or when **boot** times out.
INITPROG=*path*	Specifies an initialization program to be loaded and run before **boot** sizes memory.
MEMRANGE=*range*[,*range*. . .]	Tells **boot** where to look when sizing memory. A *range* is a pair of decimal addresses, separated by a dash (such as 1M–4M), followed by a one-byte set of flags. This set of flags should be encoded as an integer in the range of 0–255. Use a colon (:) to separate addresses from flags. Note that only two values are currently defined: 0 (indicates no special properties) and 1 (indicates memory for which DMA is not allowed). All other flags are currently undefined and reserved for future use. Both upward (such as 15M–16M) and downward (such as 16M–15M) address ranges are supported. The first address in the pair is inclusive; the last address is exclusive.
MEMREQ=*size*	Tells **boot** to enforce a minimum memory size of *size*. If **boot** doesn't find at least *size* bytes of

	memory, it will print a message and halt. *size* is given in the same format as addresses for **MEMRANGE**.
MREQMSG1=*string*	This sets the message printed when the **MEMREQ** memory requirement is not met.
MREQMSG2=*string*	Specifies an optional second line for the **MREQMSG1** message.
TIMEOUT=*number*	If **boot** is waiting for a boot line from the user and **TIMEOUT** is set, **boot** will wait for *number* seconds, then use the default boot line defined by **DEFBOOTSTR**.

Customizing the Boot Process

You can set the boot process up to be automatic. To set up **boot** to run automatically, using the default configuration information in the **/stand/boot** file, set **AUTOBOOT** to **YES** in the **/stand/boot** file. This causes **boot** to display the default boot message and load the program. If an error occurs or a key is pressed during this automatic boot process, **boot** returns to the boot prompt and tries to load the program again. The **boot** program on the UNIX operating system installation diskette performs this automatic boot procedure.

If **AUTOBOOT** is set to **NO** in the **/stand/boot** file, **boot** gives you an opportunity to type a bootstring before **boot** begins loading the program. If you do not type a bootstring at the prompt, **boot** assumes the user wants the default configuration. At this point, **boot** behaves as though **AUTOBOOT** is set to **YES** in the **/stand/boot** file. The **boot** program reads the configuration in the **/stand/boot** file then displays the default boot message (**BOOTMSG**) and begins loading the program.

the filesystem type of the root file system can also be specified, as follows:

```
rootfstype=fstype
```

where **fstype** is the filesystem type, probably either **s5** or **ufs**.

Kernel Configuration

The **boot** program passes any boot string typed at the boot prompt to the kernel except for the *prompt* string. The kernel reads the boot string to determine which peripherals are the **root**, **pipe**, **swap**, and **dump** devices. If no devices are specified in either the **/stand/boot** description or on the command line, the default devices compiled into the kernel are used. Additional arguments in the boot string can override the default. These additional arguments have the following form:

dev=xx(m,o)

where

- *dev* is the desired system device (**root[dev]**, **pipe[dev]**, **swap[dev]**, or **dumpdev**).

- *xx* is the device name ("hd" for the hard disk or "fd" for floppy diskette device).

- *m* is the minor device number.

- *o* is the offset in the partition (usually 0).

If any combination of **root**, **pipe**, **swap**, or **dumpdev** is specified, those system devices will reside on that device with the unspecified system devices using the defaults compiled in the kernel. Setting one device does not affect the default values for the other system devices.

FILES

/stand/boot

SEE ALSO

fdisk(1M), init(1M), fd(7), hd(7)

DIAGNOSTICS

The **masterboot** and **boot** programs have different error messages. The **masterboot** program displays an error message and locks the system. The following is a list of the most common **masterboot** messages and their meanings:

IO ERR　　　An error occurred when trying to read in the partition boot of the active operating system.

BAD TBL　　The bootable partition indicator of at least one of the operating systems in the **fdisk** table contains an unrecognizable code.

NO OS　　　There was an unrecoverable error after trying to execute the active operating system's partition boot.

The **boot** program displays an error message, then returns to its prompt. Some **boot** messages indicate fatal errors that cause the system to halt and require rebooting. Other **boot** messages are not fatal but indicate that the **boot** program is not running properly.

The following four messages indicate fatal errors. When one of these messages occurs, you will need to correct the problem described in the message and reboot the system:

Error reading bootstrap

The **boot** program could not locate the bootstrap, or the bootstrap is not readable. Make sure that the bootstrap is properly located on the specified boot device and is compatible with the kernel you are booting. Then reboot the system.

No active partition on hard disk

There is currently no active partition from which to run the **boot** program. Activate an appropriate partition and reboot the system.

No file system to boot

The **boot** program could not locate a **/stand** or root file system on the specified boot device. Make sure the boot device has a **/stand** or root file system and reboot the system.

The following list describes **boot** warning messages. When one of these messages occurs, you will need to correct the problem described in the message and restart the **boot** program:

Cannot load initprog
> The **boot** program cannot locate the initialization program specified with the **INITPROG** option, or the initialization program is not set up properly for execution. Make sure that the *path* argument to **INITPROG** is a valid path and the file is executable. Then restart **boot**.

Cannot open defaults file
> The **boot** program cannot locate the **/stand/boot** file on the boot device, or the file is not readable. Make sure that the **/stand/boot** file exists on the boot device and that the file is readable. Then restart **boot**.

command **argument missing or incorrect**
> The **boot** program received a command with no argument or with an invalid argument. Make sure that *command* in **/stand/boot** has the correct number of arguments and that all the arguments are valid, then restart **boot**.

Cannot load *file*; **file not opened**
> The **boot** program cannot locate *file* on the specified device, or *file* is not set up properly for execution. Check that *file* exists on the specified device and restart **boot**.

Cannot load *file*; **cannot read COFF header**
> The specified Common Object File Format (COFF) file contains no file header, or the file header is not readable. Make sure that *file* contains a readable file header, then restart **boot**.

Cannot load *file*; **not an 80386 ELF or COFF binary**
> The specified file is not an 80386 ELF or COFF binary. Check that the file you want to load is a valid COFF binary that is compatible with 80386 systems and restart **boot**.

Cannot load *file*; **cannot read segment/sections**
> The specified file does not contain a section header, or the section header is not readable. Check that *file* contains a readable section header and restart **boot**.

Cannot load *file*; **cannot read BKI section**
> The specified file does not include the bootstrap-kernel interface (BKI) section, or the BKI section is not readable. Make sure the BKI section of *file* is accurate for your version of the kernel and bootstrap, then restart **boot**.

Cannot load *file*; **BKI too old**
> The BKI of the current bootstrap is not compatible with the BKI of the program (*file*) you are loading. Make sure that the BKI of the bootstrap and *file* are compatible and restart **boot**.

Cannot load *file*; **BKI too new**
> The BKI of the current bootstrap is not compatible with the BKI of the program (*file*) you are loading. Make sure that the BKI of the bootstrap and *file* are compatible and restart **boot**.

Cannot load *file*; **missing text or data segment**
> The specified file does not contain a necessary text or data segment. Check that *file* contains the proper text and data segments, then restart **boot**.

Cannot load *file*; **missing BKI segment**
> The specified file does not contain the BKI segment. Make sure that the BKI segment in *file* exists and is compatible with the BKI of the bootstrap.

Cannot load *file*
> not present The amount of memory available for the kernel is not present or is inadequate. Make sure you have allocated enough memory for the kernel you want to load, then restart **boot**.

Too many lines in defaults file; extra lines ignored
> The **file/stand/boot** contains too many lines. All extra lines will be ignored.

NOTES

The computer always tries to boot from any diskette in the floppy diskette drive first. If the diskette does not contain a valid bootstrap program, errors occur.

The **boot** program cannot be used to load programs that have not been linked for standalone execution. To create stand-alone programs, use the option of the UNIX system linker [**ld** (1)] and special stand-alone libraries.

Although stand-alone programs can operate in real or protected mode, they must not be large or huge model programs. Programs in real mode can use the input/output routines of the computer's startup ROM.

NAME
    bootparamd – boot parameter server

SYNOPSIS
    bootparamd [–d]

DESCRIPTION
    bootparamd is a server process that provides information to diskless clients necessary for booting. It obtains its information from the **/etc/bootparams** file.

    bootparamd can be invoked either by inetd(1M) or by the user.

    The –d option displays the debugging information.

FILES
    /etc/bootparams

SEE ALSO
    inetd(1M)

NAME

brc, bcheckrc – system initialization procedures

SYNOPSIS

/sbin/brc

/sbin/bcheckrc

DESCRIPTION

These shell procedures are executed via entries in **/etc/inittab** by **init** whenever the system is booted.

First, the **bcheckrc** procedure checks the status of the root file system. If the root file system is found to be bad, **bcheckrc** repairs it.

Then, **bckeckrc** mounts the **/stand**, **/proc**, and **/var** (if it exists) file systems (**/var** may exist as a directory in the root file system, or as a separate file system).

The **brc** script performs administrative tasks related to file sharing.

After these two procedures have executed, **init** checks for the **initdefault** value in **/etc/inittab**. This tells **init** in which run level to place the system. If, for example, **initdefault** is set to **2**, the system will be placed in the multi-user state via the **rc2** procedure.

Note that **bcheckrc** should always be executed before **brc**. Also, these shell procedures may be used for several run-level states.

SEE ALSO

fsck(1M), init(1M), rc2(1M), shutdown(1M), inittab(4), mnttab(4)

NAME

cal – print calendar

SYNOPSIS

cal [[*month*] *year*]

DESCRIPTION

cal prints a calendar for the specified year. If a month is also specified, a calendar just for that month is printed. If neither is specified, a calendar for the present month is printed. The *month* is a number between 1 and 12. The *year* can be between 1 and 9999. The calendar produced is that for England and the United States.

NOTES

An unusual calendar is printed for September 1752. That is the month 11 days were skipped to make up for lack of leap year adjustments. To see this calendar, type: cal 9 1752

The command cal 83 refers to the year 83, not 1983.

The year is always considered to start in January even though this is historically naive.

NAME

calendar – reminder service

SYNOPSIS

calendar [–]

DESCRIPTION

calendar consults the file calendar in the current directory and prints out lines that contain today's or tomorrow's date anywhere in the line. Most reasonable month-day dates such as Aug. 24, august 24, 8/24, and so on, are recognized, but not 24 August or 24/8. On weekends "tomorrow" extends through Monday. calendar can be invoked regularly by using the crontab(1) or at(1) commands.

When an argument is present, calendar does its job for every user who has a file calendar in his or her login directory and sends them any positive results by mail(1). Normally this is done daily by facilities in the UNIX operating system (see cron(1M)).

If the environment variable DATEMSK is set, calendar will use its value as the full path name of a template file containing format strings. The strings consist of field descriptors and text characters and are used to provide a richer set of allowable date formats in different languages by appropriate settings of the environment variable LANG or LC_TIME (see environ(5)). (See date(1) for the allowable list of field descriptors.)

EXAMPLES

The following example shows the possible contents of a template:

    %B %eth of the year %Y

%B represents the full month name, %e the day of month and %Y the year (4 digits).

If DATEMSK is set to this template, the following calendar file would be valid:

    March 7th of the year 1989 < Reminder>

FILES

/usr/lib/calprog   program used to figure out today's and tomorrow's dates
/etc/passwd
/tmp/cal*

SEE ALSO

at(1), date(1), crontab(1), mail(1)
cron(1M), environ(5) in the *System Administrator's Reference Manual*

NOTES

Appropriate lines beginning with white space will not be printed.
Your calendar must be public information for you to get reminder service.
calendar's extended idea of "tomorrow" does not account for holidays.

NAME

  `captoinfo` — convert a *termcap* description into a *terminfo* description

SYNOPSIS

  `captoinfo [-v . . .] [-V] [-1] [-w` *width*`]` *file* `. . .`

DESCRIPTION

  `captoinfo` looks in *file* for `termcap` descriptions. For each one found, an equivalent `terminfo` description is written to standard output, along with any comments found. A description which is expressed as relative to another description (as specified in the `termcap tc = field`) will be reduced to the minimum superset before being output.

  If no *file* is given, then the environment variable `TERMCAP` is used for the filename or entry. If `TERMCAP` is a full pathname to a file, only the terminal whose name is specified in the environment variable `TERM` is extracted from that file. If the environment variable `TERMCAP` is not set, then the file `/usr/share/lib/termcap` is read.

  `-v` print out tracing information on standard error as the program runs. Specifying additional `-v` options will cause more detailed information to be printed.

  `-V` print out the version of the program in use on standard error and exit.

  `-1` cause the fields to print out one to a line. Otherwise, the fields will be printed several to a line to a maximum width of 60 characters.

  `-w` change the output to *width* characters.

FILES

  `/usr/share/lib/terminfo/?/*` Compiled terminal description database.

NOTES

  `captoinfo` should be used to convert `termcap` entries to `terminfo` entries because the `termcap` database (from earlier versions of UNIX System V) may not be supplied in future releases.

SEE ALSO

  `curses`(3X), `infocmp`(1M), `terminfo`(4)

NAME

cat – concatenate and print files

SYNOPSIS

cat [−u] [−s] [−v [−t] [−e]] *file*...

DESCRIPTION

cat reads each *file* in sequence and writes it on the standard output. Thus:

        cat file

prints file on your terminal, and:

        cat file1 file2 >file3

concatenates file1 and file2, and writes the results in file3.

If no input file is given, or if the argument − is encountered, cat reads from the standard input file.

The following options apply to cat:

−u   The output is not buffered. (The default is buffered output.)

−s   cat is silent about non-existent files.

−v   Causes non-printing characters (with the exception of tabs, new-lines and form-feeds) to be printed visibly. ASCII control characters (octal 000 – 037) are printed as ^n, where n is the corresponding ASCII character in the range octal 100 – 137 (@, A, B, C, . . ., X, Y, Z, [, \ ], ^, and _); the DEL character (octal 0177) is printed ^?. Other non-printable characters are printed as M-x, where x is the ASCII character specified by the low-order seven bits.

When used with the −v option, the following options may be used:

−t   Causes tabs to be printed as ^I's and formfeeds to be printed as ^L's.

−e   Causes a $ character to be printed at the end of each line (prior to the new-line).

The −t and −e options are ignored if the −v option is not specified.

SEE ALSO

cp(1), pg(1), pr(1)

NOTES

Redirecting the output of cat onto one of the files being read will cause the loss of the data originally in the file being read. For example,

        cat file1 file2 >file1

causes the original data in file1 to be lost.

NAME

catman – create the cat files for the manual

SYNOPSIS

/usr/ucb/catman [–nptw] [–M *directory*] [–T *tmac.an*] [*sections*]

DESCRIPTION

The **catman** commands creates the preformatted versions of the on-line manual from the **nroff**(1) input files. Each manual page is examined and those whose preformatted versions are missing or out of date are recreated. If any changes are made, **catman** recreates the **whatis** database.

If there is one parameter not starting with a '–', it is taken to be a list of manual sections to look in. For example

        catman 123

only updates manual sections **1**, **2**, and **3**.

The following options are available:

–n   Do not (re)create the **whatis** database.

–p   Print what would be done instead of doing it.

–t   Create **troff**ed entries in the appropriate **fmt** subdirectories instead of **nroff**ing into the **cat** subdirectories.

–w   Only create the **whatis** database. No manual reformatting is done.

–M   Update manual pages located in the specified **directory** (**/usr/share/man** by default).

–T   Use **tmac.an** in place of the standard manual page macros.

ENVIRONMENT

TROFF   The name of the formatter to use when the –t flag is given. If not set, 'troff' is used.

FILES

/usr/share/man	default manual directory location
/usr/share/man/man?/*.*	raw (nroff input) manual sections
/usr/share/man/cat?/*.*	preformatted **nroff**ed manual pages
/usr/share/man/fmt?/*.*	preformatted **troff**ed manual pages
/usr/share/man/whatis	**whatis** database location
/usr/ucblib/makewhatis	command script to make **whatis** database

SEE ALSO

man(1), nroff(1), troff(1), whatis(1)

DIAGNOSTICS

man?/xxx.? (.so'ed from man?/yyy.?): No such file or directory
    The file outside the parentheses is missing, and is referred to by the file inside them.

target of .so in man?/xxx.? must be relative to /usr/man
    catman only allows references to filenames that are relative to the directory /usr/share/man.

`opendir:man?: No such file or directory`
> A harmless warning message indicating that one of the directories **catman** normally looks for is missing.

`*.*: No such file or directory`
> A harmless warning message indicating **catman** came across an empty directory.

NAME

cb – C program beautifier

SYNOPSIS

cb [-s] [-j] [-l *leng*] [-V] [*file* . . .]

DESCRIPTION

The **cb** command reads syntactically correct C programs either from its arguments or from the standard input, and writes them on the standard output with
spacing and indentation that display the structure of the C code. By default, **cb**
preserves all user new-lines.

cb accepts the following options.

-s   Write the code in the style of Kernighan and Ritchie found in *The C
            Programming Language*.

-j   Put split lines back together.

-l *leng*   Split lines that are longer than *leng*.

-V   Print on standard error output the version of **cb** invoked.

NOTES

cb treats **asm** as a keyword.

The format of structure initializations is unchanged by **cb**.

Punctuation that is hidden in preprocessing directives causes indentation errors.

SEE ALSO

cc(1)

Kernighan, B. W., and Ritchie, D. M., *The C Programming Language*, Second Edition, Prentice-Hall, 1988

NAME

cc – C compiler

SYNOPSIS

cc [*options*] *file* . . .

DESCRIPTION

cc is the interface to the C compilation system. The compilation tools conceptually consist of a preprocessor, compiler, optimizer, basic block analyzer, assembler, and link editor. cc processes the supplied options and then executes the various tools with the proper arguments. cc accepts several types of files as arguments.

Files whose names end with .c are taken to be C source files and may be preprocessed, compiled, optimized, instrumented for profiling, assembled, and link edited. The compilation process may be stopped after the completion of any pass if the appropriate options are supplied. If the compilation process runs through the assembler, then an object file is produced whose name is that of the source with .o substituted for .c. However, the .o file is normally deleted if a single C file is compiled and then immediately link edited. In the same way, files whose names end in .s are taken to be assembly source files; they may be assembled and link edited. Files whose names end in .i are taken to be preprocessed C source files, and they may be compiled, optimized, instrumented for profiling, assembled, and link edited. Files whose names do not end in .c, .s, or .i are handed to the link editor, which produces a dynamically linked executable whose name by default is a.out.

Since cc usually creates files in the current directory during the compilation process, it is necessary to run cc in a directory in which a file can be created.

The following options are interpreted by cc:

–A *name*[(tokens)]
　　　　Associates *name* as a predicate with the specified *tokens* as if by a **#assert** preprocessing directive.

　　　　Preassertions:　　　system(unix)
　　　　　　　　　　　　　　cpu(i386)
　　　　　　　　　　　　　　machine(i386)

–A – Causes all predefined macros (other than those that begin with __) and predefined assertions to be forgotten.

–B *c*　　*c* can be either **dynamic** or **static**. **–B dynamic** causes the link editor to look for files named lib*x*.so and then for files named lib*x*.a when given the –l*x* option. **–B static** causes the link editor to look only for files named lib*x*.a. This option may be specified multiple times on the command line as a toggle. This option and its argument are passed to **ld**.

–C　　Cause the preprocessing phase to pass along all comments other than those on preprocessing directive lines.

–c　　Suppress the link editing phase of the compilation and do not remove any produced object files.

–D *name*[*=tokens*]

Associates *name* with the specified *tokens* as if by a **#define** preprocessing directive. If no *=tokens* is specified, the token **1** is supplied.

Predefinitions:　　**i386**
　　　　　　　　　　unix

–d *c*　*c* can be either **y** or **n**. **–dy** specifies dynamic linking, which is the default, in the link editor. **–dn** specifies static linking in the link editor. This option and its argument are passed to **ld**.

–E　　Only preprocess the named C files and send the result to the standard output. The output will contain preprocessing directives for use by the next pass of the compilation system.

–f　　This option is obsolete and will be ignored.

–G　　Used to direct the link editor to produce a shared object rather than a dynamically linked executable. This option is passed to **ld**. It cannot be used with the **–dn** option.

–g　　Cause the compiler to generate additional information needed for the use of **sdb**. Use of **sdb** on a program compiled with both the **–g** and **–O** options is not recommended unless the user understands the behavior of optimization.

–H　　Print, one per line, the path name of each file included during the current compilation on the standard error output.

–I *dir*　Alter the search for included files whose names do not begin with **/** to look in *dir* prior to the usual directories. The directories for multiple **–I** options are searched in the order specified.

–K [**PIC, minabi**]

–K PIC causes position-independent code (PIC) to be generated. **–K minabi** directs the compilation system to use a version of the C library that minimizes dynamic linking, without changing the application's ABI conformance (or non-conformance, as the case may be). Applications that use the Network Services Library or the X library may not use **–K minabi**.

–L *dir*　Add *dir* to the list of directories searched for libraries by **ld**. This option and its argument are passed to **ld**.

–l *name*

Search the library **lib***name***.so** or **lib***name***.a**. Its placement on the command line is significant as a library is searched at a point in time relative to the placement of other libraries and object files on the command line. This option and its argument are passed to **ld**.

–O　　Arrange for compilation phase optimization. This option has no effect on **.s** files.

–o *pathname*

Produce an output object file *pathname*, instead of the default **a.out**. This option and its argument are passed to **ld**.

-P   Only preprocess the named C files and leave the result in corresponding files suffixed **.i**. The output will not contain any preprocessing directives, unlike **-E**.

-p   Arrange for the compiler to produce code that counts the number of times each routine is called; also, if link editing takes place, profiled versions of **libc.a** and **libm.a** (with the **-lm** option) are linked if the **-dn** option is used. A **mon.out** file will then be produced at normal termination of execution of the object program. An execution profile can then be generated by use of **prof**.

-Q *c*   *c* can be either **y** or **n**. If *c* is **y**, identification information about each invoked compilation tool will be added to the output files (the default behavior). This can be useful for software administration. Giving **n** for *c* suppresses this information.

-q *c*   *c* can be either **l** or **p**. **-ql** causes the invocation of the basic block analyzer and arranges for the production of code that counts the number of times each source line is executed. A listing of these counts can be generated by use of **lprof**. **-qp** is a synonym for **-p**.

-S   Compile, optimize (if **-O** is present), and do not assemble or link edit the named C files. The assembler-language output is left in corresponding files suffixed **.s**.

-U *name*
        Causes any definition of *name* to be forgotten, as if by a **#undef** preprocessing directive. If the same *name* is specified for both **-D** and **-U**, *name* is not defined, regardless of the order of the options.

-V   Cause each invoked tool to print its version information on the standard error output.

-v   Cause the compiler to perform more and stricter semantic checks, and to enable certain **lint**-like checks on the named C files.

-W *tool*, arg_1[, arg_2 ...]
        Hand off the argument(s) arg_i each as a separate argument to *tool*. Each argument must be separated from the preceding by only a comma. (A comma can be part of an argument by escaping it by an immediately preceding backslash (\) character; the backslash is removed from the resulting argument.) *tool* can be one of the following:

          p   A synonym for **0**
          0   compiler
          2   optimizer
          b   basic block analyzer
          a   assembler
          l   link editor

        For example, **-Wa,-o,** *objfile* passes **-o** and *objfile* to the assembler, in that order; also **-Wl,-I,** *name* causes the linking phase to override the default name of the dynamic linker, **/usr/lib/libc.so.1**.

The order in which the argument(s) are passed to a tool with respect to the other specified command line options may change.

−X *c* Specify the degree of conformance to the ANSI C standard. *c* can be one of the following:

t (transition)
The compiled language includes all new features compatible with older (pre-ANSI) C (the default behavior). The compiler warns about all language constructs that have differing behavior between the new and old versions and uses the pre-ANSI C interpretation. This includes, for example, warning about the use of trigraphs the new escape sequence \a, and the changes to the integral promotion rules.

a (ANSI)
The compiled language includes all new features of ANSI C and uses the new interpretation of constructs with differing behavior. The compiler continues to warn about the integral promotion rule changes, but does not warn about trigraph replacements or new escape sequences.

c (conformance)
The compiled language and associated header files are ANSI C conforming, but include all conforming extensions of **−Xa**. Warnings will be produced about some of these. Also, only ANSI defined identifiers are visible in the standard header files.

The predefined macro __**STDC**__ has the value **0** for **−Xt** and **−Xa**, and **1** for **−Xc**. All warning messages about differing behavior can be eliminated in **−Xa** through appropriate coding; for example, use of casts can eliminate the integral promotion change warnings.

−Y *item*,*dir*
Specify a new directory *dir* for the location of *item*. *item* can consist of any of the characters representing tools listed under the **−W** option or the following characters representing directories containing special files:

F obsolete. Use **−YP** instead. For this release, **−YF** will be simulated using **−YP**. **−YF** will be removed in the next release.
I directory searched last for include files: *INCDIR* (see **−I**)
S directory containing the start-up object files: *LIBDIR*
L obsolete. Use **−YP** instead. For this release, **−YL** will be simulated using **−YP**. **−YL** will be removed in the next release.
U obsolete. Use **−YP** instead. For this release, **−YU** will be simulated using **−YP**. **−YU** will be removed in the next release.
P Change the default directories used for finding libraries. *dir* is a colon-separated path list.

If the location of a tool is being specified, then the new path name for the tool will be *dir*/*tool*. If more than one **−Y** option is applied to any one item, then the last occurrence holds.

cc recognizes -a, -B, -e, -h -m, -o, -r, -s, -t, -u, and -z and passes these options and their arguments to ld. cc also passes any unrecognized options to ld without any diagnostic.

When cc is put in a file *prefix*cc, the prefix will be recognized and used to prefix the names of each tool executed. For example, OLDcc will execute OLDacomp, OLDoptim, OLDbasicblk, OLDas, and OLDld, and will link the object file(s) with OLDcrt1.o. Therefore, be careful when moving cc around. The prefix applies to the compiler, optimizer, basic block analyzer, assembler, link editor, and the start-up routines.

FILES

file.c	C source file
file.i	preprocessed C source file
file.o	object file
file.s	assembly language file
a.out	link-edited output
LIBDIR/*crti.o	startup initialization code
LIBDIR/*crt1.o	startup routine
LIBDIR/*crtn.o	last startup routine
TMPDIR/*	temporary files
LIBDIR/acomp	preprocessor and compiler
LIBDIR/optim	optimizer
LIBDIR/basicblk	basic block analyzer
BINDIR/as	assembler
BINDIR/ld	link editor
LIBDIR/libc.so	shared standard C library
LIBDIR/libc.a	archive standard C library
INCDIR	usually /usr/include
LIBDIR	usually /usr/ccs/lib
BINDIR	usually /usr/ccs/bin
TMPDIR	usually /var/tmp but can be redefined by setting the environment variable TMPDIR (see tempnam in tmpnam(3S)).

SEE ALSO

as(1), ld(1), lint(1), lprof(1), prof(1), sdb(1), monitor(3C), tmpnam(3S)

The "C Compilation System" chapter in the *Programmer's Guide: ANSI C and Programming Support Tools*

Kernighan, B. W., and Ritchie, D. M., *The C Programming Language,* Second Edition, Prentice-Hall, 1988

American National Standard for Information Systems – Programming Language C, X3.159-1989

NOTES

Obsolescent but still recognized cc options include -f, -F, -YF, -YL, and -YU. The -ql and -O options do not work together; -O will be ignored.

NAME

cc – C compiler

SYNOPSIS

/usr/ucb/cc [*options*]

DESCRIPTION

/usr/ucb/cc is the C compiler for the BSD Compatibility Package. **/usr/ucb/cc** is identical to **/usr/bin/cc** (see **cc**(1)) except that BSD header files are used BSD libraries are linked *before* System V libraries.

/usr/ucb/cc accepts the same options as **/usr/bin/cc**, with the following exceptions:

–I *dir*   Search *dir* for included files whose names do not begin with a '/', prior to the usual directories. The directories fro multiple **–I** options are searched in the order specified. The preprocessor first searches for **#include** files in the directory containing *sourcefile*, and then in directories named with **–I** options (if any), then **/usr/ucbinclude**, and finally, in **/usr/include**.

–L *dir*   Add *dir* to the list of directories searched for libraries by **/usr/bin/cc**. This option is passed to **/usr/bin/ld**. Directories specified with this option are searched before **/usr/ucblib** and **/usr/lib**.

–Y LU, *dir*   Change the default directory used for finding libraries.

FILES

/usr/ucblib
/usr/lib/ld
/usr/ucblib/libucb.a
/usr/lib/libucb.a

NOTES

The **–Y LU**, *dir* option may have unexpected results, and should not be used. This option is not in the UNIX System V base.

SEE ALSO

ld(1)

as(1), ar(1), cc(1), ld(1), lorder(1), ranlib(1), strip(1), tsort(1), a.out(4) in the *Programmer's Reference Manual*

NAME

cd – change working directory

SYNOPSIS

cd [*directory*]

DESCRIPTION

If *directory* is not specified, the value of shell parameter $HOME is used as the new working directory. If *directory* specifies a complete path starting with /, ., or .., *directory* becomes the new working directory. If neither case applies, cd tries to find the designated directory relative to one of the paths specified by the $CDPATH shell variable. $CDPATH has the same syntax as, and similar semantics to, the $PATH shell variable. cd must have execute (search) permission in *directory*.

Because a new process is created to execute each command, cd would be ineffective if it were written as a normal command; therefore, it is recognized by and is internal to the shell.

SEE ALSO

pwd(1), sh(1)

chdir(2) in the *Programmer's Reference Manual*

NAME

cdc – change the delta comment of an SCCS delta

SYNOPSIS

cdc −r *SID* [−m[*mrlist*]] [−y[*comment*]] *file* . . .

DESCRIPTION

cdc changes the delta comment, for the SID (SCCS identification string) specified by the −r keyletter, of each named SCCS file.

The delta comment is the Modification Request (MR) and comment information normally specified via the −m and −y keyletters of the delta command.

If *file* is a directory, cdc behaves as though each file in the directory were specified as a named file, except that non-SCCS files (last component of the path name does not begin with s.) and unreadable files are silently ignored. If a name of − is given, the standard input is read (see the NOTES section) and each line of the standard input is taken to be the name of an SCCS file to be processed.

Arguments to cdc, which may appear in any order, consist of keyletter arguments and file names.

All the described keyletter arguments apply independently to each named file:

−r*SID*   Used to specify the *SCCS IDentification* (SID) string of a delta for which the delta comment is to be changed.

−m*mrlist*   If the SCCS file has the v flag set [see admin(1)] then a list of MR numbers to be added and/or deleted in the delta comment of the SID specified by the −r keyletter may be supplied. A null MR list has no effect.

mrlist entries are added to the list of MRs in the same manner as that of delta. In order to delete an MR, precede the MR number with the character ! (see the EXAMPLES section). If the MR to be deleted is currently in the list of MRs, it is removed and changed into a comment line. A list of all deleted MRs is placed in the comment section of the delta comment and preceded by a comment line stating that they were deleted.

If −m is not used and the standard input is a terminal, the prompt MRs? is issued on the standard output before the standard input is read; if the standard input is not a terminal, no prompt is issued. The MRs? prompt always precedes the comments? prompt (see −y keyletter).

mrlist entries in a list are separated by blanks and/or tab characters. An unescaped new-line character terminates the MR list.

Note that if the v flag has a value [see admin(1)], it is taken to be the name of a program (or shell procedure) that validates the correctness of the MR numbers. If a non-zero exit status is returned from the MR number validation program, cdc terminates and the delta comment remains unchanged.

-**y**[*comment*] Arbitrary text used to replace the *comment*(s) already existing for the delta specified by the -**r** keyletter. The previous comments are kept and preceded by a comment line stating that they were changed. A null *comment* has no effect.

If -**y** is not specified and the standard input is a terminal, the prompt **comments?** is issued on the standard output before the standard input is read; if the standard input is not a terminal, no prompt is issued. An unescaped new-line character terminates the *comment* text.

If you made the delta and have the appropriate file permissions, you can change its delta comment. If you own the file and directory you can modify the delta comment.

EXAMPLES

```
cdc -r1.6 -m"bl88-12345 !bl87-54321 bl89-00001" -ytrouble s.file
```

adds bl88-12345 and bl89-00001 to the MR list, removes bl87-54321 from the MR list, and adds the comment **trouble** to delta 1.6 of **s.file**.

Entering:

```
cdc -r1.6 s.file
MRs? !bl87-54321 bl88-12345 bl89-00001
comments? trouble
```

produces the same result.

FILES

x-file [see **delta**(1)]
z-file [see **delta**(1)]

SEE ALSO

admin(1), **delta**(1), **get**(1), **help**(1), **prs**(1), **sccsfile**(4)

DIAGNOSTICS

Use **help** for explanations.

NOTES

If SCCS file names are supplied to the **cdc** command via the standard input (- on the command line), then the -**m** and -**y** keyletters must also be used.

NAME

cflow – generate C flowgraph

SYNOPSIS

cflow [-r] [-ix] [-i_] [-d*num*] *files*

DESCRIPTION

The **cflow** command analyzes a collection of C, **yacc**, **lex**, assembler, and object files and builds a graph charting the external function references. Files suffixed with **.y**, **.1**, and **.c** are processed by **yacc**, **lex**, and the C compiler as appropriate. The results of the preprocessed files, and files suffixed with **.i**, are then run through the first pass of **lint**. Files suffixed with **.s** are assembled. Assembled files, and files suffixed with **.o**, have information extracted from their symbol tables. The results are collected and turned into a graph of external references that is written on the standard output.

Each line of output begins with a reference number, followed by a suitable number of tabs indicating the level, then the name of the global symbol followed by a colon and its definition. Normally only function names that do not begin with an underscore are listed (see the **-i** options below). For information extracted from C source, the definition consists of an abstract type declaration (e.g., **char** *), and, delimited by angle brackets, the name of the source file and the line number where the definition was found. Definitions extracted from object files indicate the file name and location counter under which the symbol appeared (e.g., *text*). Leading underscores in C-style external names are deleted. Once a definition of a name has been printed, subsequent references to that name contain only the reference number of the line where the definition may be found. For undefined references, only **< >** is printed.

As an example, suppose the following code is in **file.c**:

```
int   i;

main()
{
     f();
     g();
     f();
}

f()
{
     i = h();
}
```

The command

```
cflow -ix file.c
```

produces the output

```
1       main: int(), <file.c 4>
2               f: int(), <file.c 11>
3                   h: <>
4                       i: int, <file.c 1>
5               g: <>
```

When the nesting level becomes too deep, the output of **cflow** can be piped to the **pr** command, using the **-e** option, to compress the tab expansion to something less than every eight spaces.

In addition to the **-D**, **-I**, and **-U** options [which are interpreted just as they are by **cc**], the following options are interpreted by **cflow**:

-r   Reverse the "caller:callee" relationship producing an inverted listing showing the callers of each function. The listing is also sorted in lexicographical order by callee.

-ix   Include external and static data symbols. The default is to include only functions in the flowgraph.

-i_   Include names that begin with an underscore. The default is to exclude these functions (and data if **-ix** is used).

-d_num_   The _num_ decimal integer indicates the depth at which the flowgraph is cut off. By default this number is very large. Attempts to set the cutoff depth to a nonpositive integer will be ignored.

SEE ALSO
as(1), **cc**(1), **lex**(1), **lint**(1), **nm**(1), **yacc**(1)
pr(1) in the _User's Reference Manual_

DIAGNOSTICS
Complains about multiple definitions and only believes the first.

NOTES
Files produced by **lex** and **yacc** cause the reordering of line number declarations, which can confuse **cflow**. To get proper results, feed **cflow** the **yacc** or **lex** input.

NAME
>   checkfsys – check a file system

SYNOPSIS
>   checkfsys

DESCRIPTION
>   The **checkfsys** command allows you to check for and optionally repair a dam-
>   aged file system. The command invokes a visual interface (the check task avail-
>   able through the **sysadm** command). The initial prompt allows you to select the
>   device that contains the filesystem. Then you are asked to specify the type of
>   checking. The following choices are available:

>   **check only**
>   >   Check the file system. No repairs are attempted.

>   **interactive fix**
>   >   Repair the file system interactively. You are informed about each instance
>   >   of damage and asked if it should be repaired.

>   **automatic fix**
>   >   Repair the file system automatically. The program applies a standard
>   >   repair to each instance of damage.

>   The identical function is available under the **sysadm** menu:

>   >   **sysadm check**

NOTES
>   While automatic and interactive checks are generally successful, they can occa-
>   sionally lose a file or a file's name. Files with content but without names are put
>   in the *file-system*/**lost+found** directory.

>   If it is important not to lose data, check the file system first to see if it appears to
>   be damaged. If it does, use one of the repair options of the task.

DIAGNOSTICS
>   The **checkfsys** command exits with one of the following values:

>   0   Normal exit.

>   2   Invalid command syntax. A usage message is displayed.

>   7   The visual interface for this command is not available because it cannot
>   >   invoke **fmli**. (The FMLI package is not installed or is corrupted.)

SEE ALSO
>   fsck(1M), **makefsys**(1M), **mountfsys**(1M), **sysadm**(1M)

NAME
checknr – check nroff and troff input files; report possible errors

SYNOPSIS
/usr/ucb/checknr [-fs] [-a .*x1* .*y1* .*x2* .*y2* . . . .*xn* .*yn*]
[-c .*x1* .*x2* .*x3* . . . .*xn*] [*filename* . . .]

DESCRIPTION
The **checknr** command checks a list of **nroff** or **troff** input files for certain kinds of errors involving mismatched opening and closing delimiters and unknown commands. If no files are specified, **checknr** checks the standard input. Delimiters checked are:

Font changes using \f*x* . . . \fP.

Size changes using \s*x* . . . \s0.

Macros that come in open . . . close forms, for example, the **.TS** and **.TE** macros which must always come in pairs.

checknr knows about the **ms** and **me** macro packages.

checknr is intended to be used on documents that are prepared with **checknr** in mind. It expects a certain document writing style for \f and \s commands, in that each \f*x* must be terminated with \fP and each \s*x* must be terminated with \s0. While it will work to directly go into the next font or explicitly specify the original font or point size, and many existing documents actually do this, such a practice will produce complaints from **checknr**. Since it is probably better to use the \fP and \s0 forms anyway, you should think of this as a contribution to your document preparation style.

The following options are available:

-f   Ignore \f font changes.

-s   Ignore \s size changes.

-a .*x1* .*y1* . . .
Add pairs of macros to the list. The pairs of macros are assumed to be those (such as **.DS** and **.DE**) that should be checked for balance. The **-a** option must be followed by groups of six characters, each group defining a pair of macros. The six characters are a period, the first macro name, another period, and the second macro name. For example, to define a pair **.BS** and **.ES**, use **-a.BS.ES**

-c .*x1* . . .
Define commands which **checknr** would otherwise complain about as undefined.

SEE ALSO
eqn(1), nroff(1), troff(1), me(7), ms(7)

NOTES
There is no way to define a one-character macro name using the **-a** option.

NAME

chgrp – change the group ownership of a file

SYNOPSIS

chgrp [-R] [-h] *group file* . . .

DESCRIPTION

chgrp changes the group ID of the *files* given as arguments to *group*. The group may be either a decimal group ID or a group name found in the group ID file, /etc/group.

You must be the owner of the file, or be the super-user to use this command.

The operating system has a configuration option {_POSIX_CHOWN_RESTRICTED}, to restrict ownership changes. When this option is in effect, the owner of the file may change the group of the file only to a group to which the owner belongs. Only the super-user can arbitrarily change owner IDs whether this option is in effect or not.

chgrp has one option:

-R   Recursive. chgrp descends through the directory, and any subdirectories, setting the specified group ID as it proceeds. When symbolic links are encountered, they are traversed.

-h   If the file is a symbolic link, change the group of the symbolic link. Without this option, the group of the file referenced by the symbolic link is changed.

FILES

/etc/group

SEE ALSO

chmod(1), chown(1), id(1M)
chown(2) in the *Programmer's Reference Manual*.
group(4), passwd(4) in the *System Administrator's Reference Manual*.

NOTES

In a Remote File Sharing environment, you may not have the permissions that the output of the ls -l command leads you to believe. For more information see the *Network User's and Administrator's Guide*.

NAME

    chkey – change user encryption key

SYNOPSIS

    chkey

DESCRIPTION

    The **chkey** command prompts for a password and uses it to encrypt a new user encryption key. The encrypted key is stored in the **publickey**(4) database.

SEE ALSO

    keylogin(1), **keylogout**(1), **publickey**(4), **keyserv**(1M), **newkey**(1)

NAME
chmod – change file mode

SYNOPSIS
chmod [–R] *mode file* . . .
chmod [ugoa]{ + | – | = }[rwxlstugo] *file* . . .

DESCRIPTION
chmod changes or assigns the mode of a file. The mode of a file specifies its permissions and other attributes. The mode may be absolute or symbolic.

An absolute *mode* is specified using octal numbers:

    chmod *nnnn file* . . .

where *n* is a number from 0 to 7. An absolute mode is constructed from the OR
of any of the following modes:

4000	Set user ID on execution.
20#0	Set group ID on execution if # is **7**, **5**, **3**, or **1**.
	Enable mandatory locking if # is **6**, **4**, **2**, or **0**.
	This bit is ignored if the file is a directory; it may be set or cleared only using the symbolic mode.
1000	Turn on sticky bit [(see chmod(2)].
0400	Allow read by owner.
0200	Allow write by owner.
0100	Allow execute (search in directory) by owner.
0070	Allow read, write, and execute (search) by group.
0007	Allow read, write, and execute (search) by others.

Upon execution, the **setuid** and **setgid** modes affect interpreter scripts only if
the first line of those scripts is

    #! *pathname* [*arg*]

where *pathname* is the path of a command interpreter, such as **sh**. [See exec(2).]

A symbolic *mode* is specified in the following format:

    chmod [*who*] *operator* [*permission(s)*] *file* . . .

who is zero or more of the characters **u**, **g**, **o**, and **a** specifying whose permissions
are to be changed or assigned:

u	user's permissions
g	group's permissions
o	others' permissions
a	all permissions (user, group, and other)

If *who* is omitted, it defaults to **a**.

operator is one of +, –, or =, signifying how permissions are to be changed:

+	Add permissions.
–	Take away permissions.
=	Assign permissions absolutely.

Unlike other symbolic operations, = has an absolute effect in that it resets all other bits. Omitting *permission*(s) is useful only with = to take away all permissions.

permission(s) is any compatible combination of the following letters:

r	read permission
w	write permission
x	execute permission
s	user or group set-ID
t	sticky bit
l	mandatory locking
u, g, o	indicate that *permission* is to be taken from the current user, group or other mode respectively.

Permissions to a file may vary depending on your user identification number (UID) or group identification number (GID). Permissions are described in three sequences each having three characters:

User   Group   Other

rwx   rwx   rwx

This example (user, group, and others all have permission to read, write, and execute a given file) demonstrates two categories for granting permissions: the access class and the permissions themselves.

Multiple symbolic modes separated by commas may be given, though no spaces may intervene between these modes. Operations are performed in the order given. Multiple symbolic letters following a single operator cause the corresponding operations to be performed simultaneously.

The letter s is only meaningful with u or g, and t only works with u.

Mandatory file and record locking (l) refers to a file's ability to have its reading or writing permissions locked while a program is accessing that file. When locking is requested, the group ID of the user must be the same as the group ID of the file. It is not possible to permit group execution and enable a file to be locked on execution at the same time. In addition, it is not possible to turn on the set-group-ID bit and enable a file to be locked on execution at the same time. The following examples, therefore, are invalid and elicit error messages:

> chmod g+x,+l *file*
> chmod g+s,+l *file*

Only the owner of a file or directory (or the super-user) may change that file's or directory's mode. Only the super-user may set the sticky bit on a non-directory file. If you are not super-user, chmod will mask the sticky-bit but will not return an error. In order to turn on a file's set-group-ID bit, your own group ID must correspond to the file's and group execution must be set.

The −R option recursively descends through directory arguments, setting the mode for each file as described above.

EXAMPLES

Deny execute permission to everyone:

chmod **a-x** *file*

Allow read permission to everyone:

chmod **444** *file*

Make a file readable and writable by the group and others:

chmod **go+rw** *file*
chmod **066** *file*

Cause a file to be locked during access:

chmod **+l** *file*

Allow everyone to read, write, and execute the file and turn on the set group-ID.

chmod **=rwx,g+s** *file*
chmod **2777** *file*

Absolute changes don't work for the set-group-ID bit of a directory. You must use **g+s** or **g-s**.

SEE ALSO

ls(1).

chmod(2) in the *Programmer's Reference Manual*

NOTES

chmod permits you to produce useless modes so long as they are not illegal (for example, making a text file executable). **chmod** does not check the file type to see if mandatory locking is available.

NAME

chown – change file owner

SYNOPSIS

chown [-R] [-h] *owner file* ...

DESCRIPTION

chown changes the owner of the *files* to *owner*. The *owner* may be either a decimal user ID or a login name found in /etc/passwd file.

If chown is invoked by other than the super-user, the set-user-ID bit of the file mode, 04000, is cleared.

Only the owner of a file (or the super-user) may change the owner of that file.

Valid options to chown are:

-R   Recursive. chown descends through the directory, and any subdirectories, setting the ownership ID as it proceeds. When symbolic links are encountered, they are traversed.

-h   If the file is a symbolic link, change the owner of the symbolic link. Without this option, the owner of the file referenced by the symbolic link is changed.

The operating system has a configuration option {_POSIX_CHOWN_RESTRICTED}, to restrict ownership changes. When this option is in effect the owner of the file is prevented from changing the owner ID of the file. Only the super-user can arbitrarily change owner IDs whether this option is in effect or not.

FILES

/etc/passwd

SEE ALSO

chgrp(1), chmod(1)

chown(2) in the *Programmer's Reference Manual*

passwd(4) in the *System Administrator's Reference Manual*.

NOTES

In a Remote File Sharing environment, you may not have the permissions that the output of the ls -l command leads you to believe. For more information see the "Mapping Remote Users" section of the "RFS sysadm Interface" chapter of the *Network User's and Administrator's Guide*.

NAME

chown – change file owner

SYNOPSIS

/usr/ucb/chown [-fhR] *owner*[*.group*] *file . . .*

DESCRIPTION

chown changes the owner of the *files* to *owner*. The *owner* may be either a decimal user ID or a login name found in **/etc/passwd** file. The optional **.** *group* suffix may be used to change the group at the same time.

If chown is invoked by other than the super-user, the set-user-ID bit of the file mode, 04000, is cleared.

Only the super-user may change the owner of a file.

Valid options to chown are:

-f   Suppress error reporting

-h   If the file is a symbolic link, change the owner of the symbolic link. Without this option, the owner of the file referenced by the symbolic link is changed.

-R   Descend recursively through directories setting the ownership ID of all files in each directory entered.

FILES

/etc/group

/etc/passwd

NOTES

In a Remote File Sharing environment, you may not have the permissions that the output of the **ls** **-l** command leads you to believe. For more information see the "Mapping Remote Users" section of the Remote File Sharing chapter of the *System Administrator's Guide.*

SEE ALSO

chgrp(1), chmod(1) in the *User's Reference Manual*

chown(2) in the *Programmer's Reference Manual*

passwd(4) in the *System Administrator's Reference Manual*

NAME

chroot – change root directory for a command

SYNOPSIS

/usr/sbin/chroot *newroot command*

DESCRIPTION

chroot causes the given command to be executed relative to the new root. The meaning of any initial slashes (/) in the path names is changed for the command and any of its child processes to *newroot* . Furthermore, upon execution, the initial working directory is *newroot* .

Notice, however, that if you redirect the output of the command to a file:

      chroot   *newroot command* >**x**

will create the file **x** relative to the original root of the command, not the new one.

The new root path name is always relative to the current root: even if a **chroot** is currently in effect, the *newroot* argument is relative to the current root of the running process.

This command can be run only by the super-user.

SEE ALSO

cd(1) in the *User's Reference Manual*.
chroot(2) in the *Programmer's Reference Manual*.
Programmer's Guide: ANSI C and Programming Support Tools.

NOTES

One should exercise extreme caution when referencing device files in the new root file system.

When using **chroot**, do not exec a command that uses shared libraries. This will result in killing your process.

NAME

   chrtbl – generate character classification and conversion tables

SYNOPSIS

   chrtbl [*file*]

DESCRIPTION

   The **chrtbl** command creates two tables containing information on character
   classification, upper/lower-case conversion, character-set width, and numeric formatting. One table is an array of (257*2) + 7 bytes that is encoded so a table
   lookup can be used to determine the character classification of a character, convert a character [see **ctype**(3C)], and find the byte and screen width of a character in one of the supplementary code sets. The other table contains information
   about the format of non-monetary numeric quantities: the first byte specifies the
   decimal delimiter; the second byte specifies the thousands delimiter; and the
   remaining bytes comprise a null terminated string indicating the grouping (each
   element of the string is taken as an integer that indicates the number of digits
   that comprise the current group in a formatted non-monetary numeric quantity).

   chrtbl reads the user-defined character classification and conversion information
   from *file* and creates three output files in the current directory. To construct *file*,
   use the file supplied in **/usr/lib/locale/C/chrtbl_C** as a starting point. You
   may add entries, but do not change the original values supplied with the system.
   For example, for other locales you may wish to add eight-bit entries to the ASCII
   definitions provided in this file.

   One output file, **ctype.c** (a C-language source file), contains a (257*2)+7-byte
   array generated from processing the information from *file*. You should review
   the content of **ctype.c** to verify that the array is set up as you had planned. (In
   addition, an application program could use **ctype.c**.) The first 257 bytes of the
   array in **ctype.c** are used for character classification. The characters used for initializing these bytes of the array represent character classifications that are
   defined in **/usr/include/ctype.h**; for example, **_L** means a character is lower
   case and **_S| _B** means the character is both a spacing character and a blank. The
   second 257 bytes of the array are used for character conversion. These bytes of
   the array are initialized so that characters for which you do not provide conversion information will be converted to themselves. When you do provide conversion information, the first value of the pair is stored where the second one would
   be stored normally, and vice versa; for example, if you provide **<0x41 0x61>**,
   then **0x61** is stored where **0x41** would be stored normally, and **0x61** is stored
   where **0x41** would be stored normally. The last 7 bytes are used for character
   width information for up to three supplementary code sets.

   The second output file (a data file) contains the same information, but is structured for efficient use by the character classification and conversion routines (see
   ctype(3C)). The name of this output file is the value you assign to the keyword
   LC_CTYPE read in from *file*. Before this file can be used by the character
   classification and conversion routines, it must be installed in the
   /usr/lib/locale/*locale* directory with the name **LC_CTYPE** by someone who is
   super-user or a member of group **bin**. This file must be readable by user, group,
   and other; no other permissions should be set. To use the character classification

and conversion tables in this file, set the **LC_CTYPE** environment variable appropriately (see **environ**(5) or **setlocale**(3C)).

The third output file (a data file) is created only if numeric formatting information is specified in the input file. The name of this output file is the value you assign to the keyword **LC_NUMERIC** read in from *file*. Before this file can be used, it must be installed in the **/usr/lib/locale/***locale* directory with the name **LC_NUMERIC** by someone who is super-user or a member of group **bin**. This file must be readable by user, group, and other; no other permissions should be set. To use the numeric formatting information in this file, set the **LC_NUMERIC** environment variable appropriately (see **environ**(5) or **setlocale**(3C)).

The name of the locale where you install the files **LC_CTYPE** and **LC_NUMERIC** should correspond to the conventions defined in *file*. For example, if French conventions were defined, and the name for the French locale on your system is **french**, then you should install the files in **/usr/lib/locale/french**.

If no input file is given, or if the argument "–" is encountered, **chrtbl** reads from standard input.

The syntax of *file* allows the user to define the names of the data files created by **chrtbl**, the assignment of characters to character classifications, the relationship between upper and lower-case letters, byte and screen widths for up to three supplementary code sets, and three items of numeric formatting information: the decimal delimiter, the thousands delimiter and the grouping. The keywords recognized by **chrtbl** are:

LC_CTYPE	name of the data file created by **chrtbl** to contain character classification, conversion, and width information
isupper	character codes to be classified as upper-case letters
islower	character codes to be classified as lower-case letters
isdigit	character codes to be classified as numeric
isspace	character codes to be classified as spacing (delimiter) characters
ispunct	character codes to be classified as punctuation characters
iscntrl	character codes to be classified as control characters
isblank	character code for the blank (space) character
isxdigit	character codes to be classified as hexadecimal digits
ul	relationship between upper- and lower-case characters
cswidth	byte and screen width information (by default, each is one character wide)
LC_NUMERIC	name of the data file created by **chrtbl** to contain numeric formatting information
decimal_point	decimal delimiter
thousands_sep	thousands delimiter

grouping   string in which each element is taken as an integer that indicates the number of digits that comprise the current group in a
formatted non-monetary numeric quantity.

Any lines with the number sign (#) in the first column are treated as comments
and are ignored. Blank lines are also ignored.

Characters for **isupper**, **islower**, **isdigit**, **isspace**, **ispunct**, **iscntrl**,
isblank, **isxdigit**, and **ul** can be represented as a hexadecimal or octal constant
(for example, the letter **a** can be represented as **0x61** in hexadecimal or **0141** in
octal). Hexadecimal and octal constants may be separated by one or more space
and/or tab characters.

The dash character (-) may be used to indicate a range of consecutive numbers.
Zero or more space characters may be used for separating the dash character
from the numbers.

The backslash character (\) is used for line continuation. Only a carriage return
is permitted after the backslash character.

The relationship between upper- and lower-case letters (**ul**) is expressed as
ordered pairs of octal or hexadecimal constants: <*upper-case_character lower-
case_character*>. These two constants may be separated by one or more space
characters. Zero or more space characters may be used for separating the angle
brackets (< >) from the numbers.

The following is the format of an input specification for **cswidth**:

   n1:s1,n2:s2,n3:s3

where,
   n1   byte width for supplementary code set 1, required *s1*   screen
width for supplementary code set 1 *n2*   byte width for supplementary
code set 2 *s2*   screen width for supplementary code set 2 *n3*   byte
width for supplementary code set 3 *s3*   screen width for supplementary
code set 3

decimal_point and **thousands_sep** are specified by a single character that gives
the delimiter. **grouping** is specified by a quoted string in which each member
may be in octal or hex representation. For example, \3 or \x3 could be used to
set the value of a member of the string to 3.

EXAMPLE

The following is an example of an input file used to create the USA-ENGLISH code
set definition table in a file named **usa** and the non-monetary numeric formatting
information in a file name **num-usa**.

```
LC_CTYPE    usa
isupper     0x41 - 0x5a
islower     0x61 - 0x7a
isdigit     0x30 - 0x39
isspace     0x20 0x9 - 0xd
ispunct     0x21 - 0x2f 0x3a - 0x40        \
            0x5b - 0x60 0x7b - 0x7e
iscntrl     0x0 - 0x1f 0x7f
isblank     0x20
```

```
        isxdigit  0x30 - 0x39 0x61 - 0x66      \
                  0x41 - 0x46
        ul        <0x41 0x61> <0x42 0x62> <0x43 0x63>  \
                  <0x44 0x64> <0x45 0x65> <0x46 0x66>  \
                  <0x47 0x67> <0x48 0x68> <0x49 0x69>  \
                  <0x4a 0x6a> <0x4b 0x6b> <0x4c 0x6c>  \
                  <0x4d 0x6d> <0x4e 0x6e> <0x4f 0x6f>  \
                  <0x50 0x70> <0x51 0x71> <0x52 0x72>  \
                  <0x53 0x73> <0x54 0x74> <0x55 0x75>  \
                  <0x56 0x76> <0x57 0x77> <0x58 0x78>  \
                  <0x59 0x79> <0x5a 0x7a>
        cswidth            1:1,0:0,0:0
        LC_NUMERIC num_usa
        decimal_point          .
        thousands_sep          ,
        grouping               "\3"
```

FILES

/usr/lib/locale/*locale*/LC_CTYPE
> data files containing character classification, conversion, and character-set width information created by **chrtbl**

/usr/lib/locale/*locale*/LC_NUMERIC
> data files containing numeric formatting information created by **chrtbl**

/usr/include/ctype.h
> header file containing information used by character classification and conversion routines

/usr/lib/locale/C/chrtbl_C
> input file used to construct **LC_CTYPE** and **LC_NUMERIC** in the default locale.

SEE ALSO

environ(5)
ctype(3C), setlocale(3C) in the *Programmer's Reference Manual*

DIAGNOSTICS

The error messages produced by **chrtbl** are intended to be self-explanatory. They indicate errors in the command line or syntactic errors encountered within the input file.

NOTES

Changing the files in /usr/lib/locale/C will cause the system to behave unpredictably.

NAME

ckbinarsys – determine whether remote system can accept binary messages

SYNOPSIS

ckbinarsys [-S] -s *remote_system_name* -t *content_type*

DESCRIPTION

Because **rmail** can transport binary data, it may be important to determine whether a particular remote system (typically the next hop) can handle binary data via the chosen transport layer agent (uux, SMTP, and so on)

ckbinarsys consults the file **/etc/mail/binarsys** for information on a specific remote system. **ckbinarsys** returns its results via an appropriate exit code. An exit code of zero implies that it is OK to send a message with the indicated content type to the system specified. An exit code other than zero indicates that the remote system cannot properly handle messages with binary content.

The absence of the **binarsys** file will cause **ckbinarsys** to exit with a non-zero exit code.

Command-line arguments are:

-s *remote_system_name*
    Name of remote system to look up in **/etc/mail/binarsys**

-t *content_type*   Content type of message to be sent. When invoked by **rmail**, this will be one of two strings: **text** or **binary**, as determined by **mail** independent of any **Content-Type:** header lines that may be present within the message header. All other arguments are treated as equivalent to **binary**.

-S   Normally, **ckbinarsys** will print a message (if the binary mail is rejected) which would be suitable for **rmail** to return in the negative acknowledgement mail. When -S is specified, no message will be printed.

FILES

/etc/mail/binarsys
/usr/lib/mail/surrcmd/ckbinarsys

SEE ALSO

mailsurr(4), binarsys(4)
mail(1), uux(1) in the *User's Reference Manual*

NAME
　　　　ckbupscd – check file system backup schedule

SYNOPSIS
　　　　ckbupscd [–m]

DESCRIPTION
ckbupscd consults the file /etc/bupsched and prints the file system lists from lines with date and time specifications matching the current time. If the –m flag is present, an introductory message in the output is suppressed so that only the file system lists are printed. Entries in the bupsched file are printed under the control of cron.

The file bupsched should contain lines of four or more fields, separated by spaces or tabs. The first three fields (the schedule fields) specify a range of dates and times. The rest of the fields constitute a list of names of file systems to be printed if ckbupscd is run at some time within the range given by the schedule fields. The general format is:

time[,*time*] *day*[,*day*] *month*[,*month*] *fsyslist*

where:

time　　Specifies an hour of the day (0 through 23), matching any time within that hour, or an exact time of day (0:00 through 23:59).

day　　Specifies a day of the week (sun through sat) or day of the month (1 through 31).

month　Specifies the month in which the time and day fields are valid. Legal values are the month numbers (1 through 12).

fsyslist　The rest of the line is taken to be a file system list to print.

Multiple time, day, and month specifications may be separated by commas, in which case they are evaluated left to right.

An asterisk (*) always matches the current value for the field in which it appears.

A line beginning with a sharp sign (#) is interpreted as a comment and ignored.

The longest line allowed (including continuations) is 1024 characters.

EXAMPLES
The following are examples of lines which could appear in the /etc/bupsched file.

06:00-09:00　fri　1,2,3,4,5,6,7,8,9,10,11　/applic
　　　　Prints the file system name */applic* if ckbupscd is run between 6:00 A.M. and 9:00 A.M. any Friday during any month except December.

00:00-06:00,16:00-23:59　1,2,3,4,5,6,7　1,8　/
　　　　Prints a reminder to backup the root (/) file system if ckbupscd is run between the times of 4:00 P.M. and 6:00 A.M. during the first week of August or January.

FILES

/etc/bupsched   specification file containing times and file system to back up

SEE ALSO

cron(1M)
echo(1), sh(1), in the *User's Reference Manual*

NOTES

ckbupscd will report file systems due for backup if invoked any time in the
window. It does not know that backups may have just been done.

NAME

ckdate, errdate, helpdate, valdate – prompt for and validate a date

SYNOPSIS

ckdate [-Q] [-W *width*] [-f *format*] [-d *default*] [-h *help*] [-e *error*]
    [-p *prompt*] [-k *pid* [-s *signal*]]

errdate [-W *width*] [-e *error*] [-f *format*]

helpdate [-W *width*] [-h *help*] [-f *format*]

valdate [-f *format*] *input*

DESCRIPTION

ckdate prompts a user and validates the response. It defines, among other things, a prompt message whose response should be a date, text for help and error messages, and a default value (which is returned if the user responds with a RETURN). The user response must match the defined format for a date.

All messages are limited in length to 70 characters and are formatted automatically. Any white space used in the definition (including newline) is stripped. The -W option cancels the automatic formatting. When a tilde is placed at the beginning or end of a message definition, the default text is inserted at that point, allowing both custom text and the default text to be displayed.

If the prompt, help or error message is not defined, the default message (as defined under NOTES) is displayed.

Three visual tool modules are linked to the **ckdate** command. They are **errdate** (which formats and displays an error message), **helpdate** (which formats and displays a help message), and **valdate** (which validates a response). These modules should be used in conjunction with FMLI objects. In this instance, the FMLI object defines the prompt. When *format* is defined in the **errdate** and **helpdate** modules, the messages describe the expected format.

The options and arguments for this command are:

-Q   Do not allow quit as a valid response..

-W   Use *width* as the line length for prompt, help, and error messages.

-f   Verify input using *format*. Possible formats and their definitions are:
        %b = abbreviated month name
        %B = full month name
        %d = day of month (01 – 31)
        %D = date as %m/%d/%y (the default format)
        %e = day of month (1 – 31; single digits are preceded by a blank)
        %h = abbreviated month name (for example, jan, feb, mar)
        %m = month number (01 – 12)
        %y = year within century (for example, 91)
        %Y = year as *CCYY* (for example, 1991)

-d   The default value is *default*. The default is not validated and so does not have to meet any criteria.

-h   The help message is *help*.

-e   The error message is *error*.

-p   The prompt message is *prompt*.

-k   Send process ID *pid* a signal if the user chooses to abort.

-s   When quit is chosen, send *signal* to the process whose *pid* is specified by the -k option. If no signal is specified, use **SIGTERM**.

input   Input to be verified against format criteria.

EXIT CODES

0 = Successful execution
1 = EOF on input
2 = Usage error
3 = User termination (quit)
4 = Garbled format argument

NOTES

The default prompt for **ckdate** is:

    Enter the date [?,q]

The default error message is:

    ERROR - Please enter a date. Format is *format*.

The default help message is:

    Please enter a date. Format is *format*.

When the quit option is chosen (and allowed), **q** is returned along with the return code 3. The **valdate** module does not produce any output. It returns zero for success and non-zero for failure.

NAME

ckgid, errgid, helpgid, valgid – prompt for and validate a group ID

SYNOPSIS

ckgid [-Q] [-W *width*] [-m] [-d *default*] [-h *help*] [-e *error*] [-p *prompt*]
[-k *pid* [-s *signal*]]

errgid [-W *width*] [-e *error*]

helpgid [-W *width*] [-m] [-h *help*]

valgid *input*

DESCRIPTION

ckgid prompts a user and validates the response. It defines, among other things,
a prompt message whose response should be an existing group ID, text for help
and error messages, and a default value (which is returned if the user responds
with a RETURN).

All messages are limited in length to 70 characters and are formatted automatically. Any white space used in the definition (including newline) is stripped.
The -W option cancels the automatic formatting. When a tilde is placed at the
beginning or end of a message definition, the default text is inserted at that point,
allowing both custom text and the default text to be displayed.

If the prompt, help or error message is not defined, the default message (as
defined under NOTES) is displayed.

Three visual tool modules are linked to the **ckgid** command. They are **errgid**
(which formats and displays an error message), **helpgid** (which formats and
displays a help message), and **valgid** (which validates a response). These
modules should be used in conjunction with FML objects. In this instance, the
FML object defines the prompt.

The options and arguments for this command are:

-Q   Do not allow quit as a valid response.

-W   Use *width* as the line length for prompt, help, and error messages.

-m   Display a list of all groups when help is requested or when the user
       makes an error.

-d   The default value is *default*. The default is not validated and so does not
       have to meet any criteria.

-h   The help message is *help*.

-e   The error message is *error*.

-p   The prompt message is *prompt*.

-k   Send process ID *pid* a signal if the user chooses to abort.

-s   When quit is chosen, send *signal* to the process whose *pid* is specified by
       the -k option. If no signal is specified, use **SIGTERM**.

input Input to be verified against **/etc/group**

EXIT CODES
>0 = Successful execution
>1 = EOF on input
>2 = Usage error
>3 = User termination (quit)

NOTES
>The default prompt for **ckgid** is:
>>**Enter the name of an existing group [?,q]**
>
>The default error message is:
>>**ERROR - Please enter the name of an existing group.**
>>*(if the* **-m** *option of* **ckgid** *is used, a list of valid groups is displayed here)*
>
>The default help message is:
>>**Please enter an existing group name.**
>>*(if the* **-m** *option of* **ckgid** *is used, a list of valid groups is displayed here)*
>
>When the quit option is chosen (and allowed), **q** is returned along with the return code **3**. The **valgid** module does not produce any output. It returns zero for success and non-zero for failure.

NAME

ckint – display a prompt; verify and return an integer value

SYNOPSIS

ckint [-Q] [-W *width*] [-b *base*] [-d *default*] [-h *help*] [-e *error*]
[-p *prompt*] [-k *pid* [-s *signal*]]

errint [-W *width*] [-b *base*] [-e *error*]

helpint [-W *width*] [-b *base*] [-h *help*]

valint [-b *base*] *input*

DESCRIPTION

ckint prompts a user, then validates the response. It defines, among other things, a prompt message whose response should be an integer, text for help and error messages, and a default value (which is returned if the user responds with a RETURN).

All messages are limited in length to 70 characters and are formatted automatically. Any white space used in the definition (including newline) is stripped. The -W option cancels the automatic formatting. When a tilde is placed at the beginning or end of a message definition, the default text is inserted at that point, allowing both custom text and the default text to be displayed.

If the prompt, help or error message is not defined, the default message (as defined under NOTES) is displayed.

Three visual tool modules are linked to the ckint command. They are errint (which formats and displays an error message), helpint (which formats and displays a help message), and valint (which validates a response). These modules should be used in conjunction with FML objects. In this instance, the FML object defines the prompt. When *base* is defined in the errint and helpint modules, the messages includes the expected base of the input.

The options and arguments for this command are:

-Q　　Do not allow quit as a valid response.

-W　　Use *width* as the line length for prompt, help, and error messages.

-b　　The base for input is *base*. Must be 2 to 36, default is 10.

-d　　The default value is *default*. The default is not validated and so does not have to meet any criteria.

-h　　The help message is *help*.

-e　　The error message is *error*.

-p　　The prompt message is *prompt*.

-k　　Send process ID *pid* a signal if the user chooses to abort.

-s　　When quit is chosen, send *signal* to the process whose *pid* is specified by the -k option. If no signal is specified, use SIGTERM.

input　　Input to be verified against *base* criterion.

EXIT CODES

    0 = Successful execution
    1 = EOF on input
    2 = Usage error
    3 = User termination (quit)

NOTES

The default base 10 prompt for **ckint** is:

    `Enter an integer [?,q]`

The default base 10 error message is:

    `ERROR - Please enter an integer.`

The default base 10 help message is:

    `Please enter an integer.`

The messages are changed from "**integer**" to "**base** *base* **integer**" if the base is set to a number other than 10.

When the quit option is chosen (and allowed), **q** is returned along with the return code **3**. The **valint** module does not produce any output. It returns zero for success and non-zero for failure.

NAME

ckitem – build a menu; prompt for and return a menu item

SYNOPSIS

ckitem [-Q] [-W *width*] [-uno] [-f *file*] [-l *label*]
        [[-i *invis*] [-i *invis*] . . .] [-m *max*] [-d *default*] [-h *help*] [-e *error*]
        [-p *prompt*] [-k *pid* [-s *signal*]] [*choice1   choice2* . . .]

erritem [-W *width*] [-e *error*]   [*choice1   choice2* . . .]

helpitem [-W *width*] [-h *help*]   [*choice1   choice2* . . .]

DESCRIPTION

ckitem builds a menu and prompts the user to choose one item from a menu of items. It then verifies the response. Options for this command define, among other things, a prompt message whose response is a menu item, text for help and error messages, and a default value (which is returned if the user responds with a RETURN).

By default, the menu is formatted so that each item is prepended by a number and is printed in columns across the terminal. Column length is determined by the longest choice. Items are alphabetized.

All messages are limited in length to 70 characters and are formatted automatically. Any white space used in the definition (including newline) is stripped. The -W option cancels the automatic formatting. When a tilde is placed at the beginning or end of a message definition, the default text is inserted at that point, allowing both custom text and the default text to be displayed.

If the prompt, help or error message is not defined, the default message (as defined under NOTES) is displayed.

Two visual tool modules are linked to the ckitem command. They are erritem (which formats and displays an error message) and helpitem (which formats and displays a help message). These modules should be used in conjunction with FML objects. In this instance, the FML object defines the prompt. When *choice* is defined in these modules, the messages describe the available menu choice (or choices).

The options and arguments for this command are:

-Q   Do not allow quit as a valid response.

-W   Use *width* as the line length for prompt, help, and error messages.

-u   Display menu items as an unnumbered list.

-n   Do not display menu items in alphabetical order.

-o   Return only one menu token.

-f   *file* contains a list of menu items to be displayed. [The format of this file is: *token<tab>description*. Lines beginning with a pound sign ("#") are comments and are ignored.]

-l   Print *label* above the menu.

-i　　　*invis* specifies invisible menu choices (choices not to be printed in the menu). For example, "**all**" used as an invisible choice would mean it is a valid option but does not appear in the menu. Any number of invisible choices may be defined. Invisible choices should be made known to a user either in the prompt or in a help message.

-m　　The maximum number of menu choices allowed is *m*.

-d　　The default value is *default*. The default is not validated and so does not have to meet any criteria.

-h　　The help message is *help*.

-e　　The error message is *error*.

-p　　The prompt message is *prompt*.

-k　　Send process ID *pid* a signal if the user chooses to abort.

-s　　When quit is chosen, send *signal* to the process whose *pid* is specified by the -k option. If no signal is specified, use **SIGTERM**.

choice　Defines menu items. Items should be separated by white space or new-line.

EXIT CODES

0 = Successful execution
1 = EOF on input
2 = Usage error
3 = User termination (quit)
4 = No choices from which to choose

NOTES

The user may input the number of the menu item if choices are numbered or as much of the string required for a unique identification of the item. Long menus are paged with 10 items per page.

When menu entries are defined both in a file (by using the -f option) and also on the command line, they are usually combined alphabetically. However, if the -n option is used to suppress alphabetical ordering, then the entries defined in the file are shown first, followed by the options defined on the command line.

The default prompt for **ckitem** is:

　　　Enter selection [?,??,q]:

One question mark gives a help message and then redisplays the prompt. Two question marks gives a help message and then redisplays the menu label, the menu and the prompt.

The default error message is:

```
ERROR - Does not match an available menu selection.
Enter one of the following:
- the number of the menu item you wish to select
- the token associated withe the menu item,
- partial string which uniquely identifies the token
   for the menu item
- ?? to reprint the menu
```

The default help message is:

```
Enter one of the following:
- the number of the menu item you wish to select
- the token associated with the menu item,
- partial string which uniquely identifies the token
    for the menu item
- ?? to reprint the menu
```

When the quit option is chosen (and allowed), **q** is returned along with the return code 3.

NAME

　　ckkeywd – prompt for and validate a keyword

SYNOPSIS

　　ckkeywd [-Q] [-W *width*] [-d *default*] [-h *help*] [-e *error*] [-p *prompt*]
　　　　[-k *pid* [-s *signal*]] [*keyword* . . .]

DESCRIPTION

　　ckkeywd prompts a user and validates the response. It defines, among other
　　things, a prompt message whose response should be one of a list of keywords,
　　text for help and error messages, and a default value (which is returned if the
　　user responds with a RETURN). The answer returned from this command must
　　match one of the defined list of keywords.

　　All messages are limited in length to 70 characters and are formatted automati-
　　cally. Any white space used in the definition (including newline) is stripped.
　　The -W option cancels the automatic formatting. When a tilde is placed at the
　　beginning or end of a message definition, the default text is inserted at that point,
　　allowing both custom text and the default text to be displayed.

　　If the prompt, help or error message is not defined, the default message (as
　　defined under NOTES) is displayed.

　　-Q　　　　Do not allow quit as a valid response.

　　-W　　　　Use *width* as the line length for prompt, help, and error messages.

　　-d　　　　The default value is *default*. The default is not validated and so does
　　　　　　　not have to meet any criteria.

　　-h　　　　The help message is *help*.

　　-e　　　　The error message is *error*.

　　-p　　　　The prompt message is *prompt*.

　　-k　　　　Send process ID *pid* a signal if the user chooses to abort.

　　-s　　　　When quit is chosen, send *signal* to the process whose *pid* is specified
　　　　　　　by the -k option. If no signal is specified, use SIGTERM.

　　keyword　The keyword, or list of keywords, against which the answer is to be
　　　　　　　verified is *keyword*.

EXIT CODES

　　0 = Successful execution
　　1 = EOF on input
　　2 = Usage error
　　3 = User termination (quit)
　　4 = No keywords from which to choose

NOTES

　　The default prompt for ckkeywd is:

　　　　Enter appropriate value [*keyword*[, . . .],?,q]

The default error message is:

ERROR - Please enter one of the following keywords:
keyword[**,** . . .]

The default help message is:

Please enter one of the following keywords:
keyword[**,** . . .]

When the quit option is chosen (and allowed), **q** is returned along with the return code **3**.

NAME

    ckpath – display a prompt; verify and return a pathname

SYNOPSIS

    ckpath [**-Q**] [**-W** *width*] [**-a**| **1**] [*file_options*] [**-rtwx**] [**-d** *default*]
        [**-h** *help*] [**-e** *error*] [**-p** *prompt*] [**-k** *pid* [**-s** *signal*]]

    errpath [**-W** *width*] [**-a**| **1**] [*file_options*] [**-rtwx**] [**-e** *error*]

    helppath [**-W** *width*] [**-a**| **1**] [*file_options*] [**-rtwx**] [**-h** *help*]

    valpath [**-a**| **1**] [*file_options*] [**-rtwx**] *input*

DESCRIPTION

    ckpath prompts a user and validates the response. It defines, among other things, a prompt message whose response should be a pathname, text for help and error messages, and a default value (which is returned if the user responds with a RETURN).

    The pathname must obey the criteria specified by the first group of options. If no criteria are defined, the pathname must be for a normal file that does not yet exist. If neither **-a** (absolute) or **-1** (relative) is given, then either is assumed to be valid.

    All messages are limited in length to 70 characters and are formatted automatically. Any white space used in the definition (including newline) is stripped. The **-W** option cancels the automatic formatting. When a tilde is placed at the beginning or end of a message definition, the default text is inserted at that point, allowing both custom text and the default text to be displayed.

    If the prompt, help or error message is not defined, the default message (as defined under NOTES) is displayed.

    Three visual tool modules are linked to the **ckpath** command. They are **errpath** (which formats and displays an error message), **helppath** (which formats and displays a help message), and **valpath** (which validates a response). These modules should be used in conjunction with FACE objects. In this instance, the FACE object defines the prompt.

    The options and arguments for this command are:

    -Q   Do not allow quit as a valid response.

    -W   Use *width* as the line length for prompt, help, and error messages.

    -a   Pathname must be an absolute path.

    -1   Pathname must be a relative path.

    -r   Pathname must be readable.

    -t   Pathname must be creatable (touchable). Pathname is created if it does not already exist.

    -w   Pathname must be writable.

    -x   Pathname must be executable.

-d   The default value is *default*. The default is not validated and so does not have to meet any criteria.

-h   The help message is *help*.

-e   The error message is *error*.

-p   The prompt message is *prompt*.

-k   Send process ID *pid* a signal if the user chooses to abort.

-s   When quit is chosen, send *signal* to the process whose *pid* is specified by the **-k** option. If no signal is specified, use **SIGTERM**.

input   Input to be verified against validation options.

file_options are:

-b   Pathname must be a block special file.

-c   Pathname must be a character special file.

-f   Pathname must be a regular file.

-y   Pathname must be a directory.

-n   Pathname must not exist (must be new).

-o   Pathname must exist (must be old).

-z   Pathname must be a file with the size greater than 0 bytes.

The following *file_options* are mutually exclusive: **-bcfy, -no, -nz, -bz, -cz**.

EXIT CODES

0 = Successful execution
1 = EOF on input
2 = Usage error
3 = User termination (quit)
4 = Mutually exclusive options

NOTES

The text of the default messages for **ckpath** depends upon the criteria options that have been used. An example default prompt for **ckpath** (using the **-a** option) is:

```
Enter an absolute pathname [?,q]
```

An example default error message (using the **-a** option) is:

```
ERROR - Pathname must begin with a slash (/).
```

An example default help message is:

```
A pathname is a filename, optionally preceded by parent
directories. The pathname you enter:
- must contain 1 to NAME_MAX characters
- must not contain a spaces or special characters
```

NAME_MAX is a system variable is defined in **limits.h**.

When the quit option is chosen (and allowed), **q** is returned along with the return code **3**. The **valpath** module does not produce any output. It returns zero for success and non-zero for failure.

NAME
ckrange – prompt for and validate an integer

SYNOPSIS
ckrange [-Q] [-W *width*] [-l *lower*] [-u *upper*] [-b *base*] [-d *default*]
[-h *help*] [-e *error*] [-p *prompt*] [-k *pid* [-s *signal*]]

errange [-W *width*] [-l *lower*] [-u *upper*] [-e *error*] [-b *base*]

helprange [-W *width*] [-l *lower*] [-u *upper*] [-h *help*] [-b *base*]

valrange [-l *lower*] [-u *upper*] [-b *base*] *input*

DESCRIPTION
ckrange prompts a user and validates the response. It defines, among other things, a prompt message whose response should be an integer in the range specified, text for help and error messages, and a default value (which is returned if the user responds with a RETURN).

This command also defines a range for valid input. If either the lower or upper limit is left undefined, then the range is bounded on only one end.

All messages are limited in length to 70 characters and are formatted automatically. Any white space used in the definition (including newline) is stripped. The -W option cancels the automatic formatting. When a tilde is placed at the beginning or end of a message definition, the default text is inserted at that point, allowing both custom text and the default text to be displayed.

If the prompt, help or error message is not defined, the default message (as defined under NOTES) is displayed.

Three visual tool modules are linked to the **ckrange** command. They are **errange** (which formats and displays an error message), **helprange** (which formats and displays a help message), and **valrange** (which validates a response). These modules should be used in conjunction with FACE objects. In this instance, the FACE object defines the prompt.

The options and arguments for this command are:

-Q   Do not allow quit as a valid response.

-W   Use *width* as the line length for prompt, help, and error messages.

-l   The lower limit of the range is *lower*. Default is the machine's largest negative integer or long.

-u   The upper limit of the range is *upper*. Default is the machine's largest positive integer or long.

-b   The base for input is *base*. Must be 2 to 36, default is 10.

-d   The default value is *default*. The default is not validated and so does not have to meet any criteria. If *default* is non-numeric, **ckrange** returns 0 and not the alphabetic string.

-h   The help message is *help*.

-e   The error message is *error*.

-p   The prompt message is *prompt*.

-k   Send process ID *pid* a signal if the user chooses to abort.

-s   When quit is chosen, send *signal* to the process whose *pid* is specified by the **-k** option. If no signal is specified, use **SIGTERM**.

input   Input to be verified against upper and lower limits and base.

EXIT CODES

0 = Successful execution
1 = EOF on input
2 = Usage error
3 = User termination (quit)

NOTES

The default base 10 prompt for **ckrange** is:

Enter an integer between *lower* **and** *upper* [*lower–upper*,**q**,**?**]

The default base 10 error message is:

ERROR - Please enter an integer between *lower* **and** *upper*.

The default base 10 help message is:

Please enter an integer between *lower* **and** *upper*.

The messages are changed from "**integer**" to "**base** *base* **integer**" if the base is set to a number other than 10.

When the quit option is chosen (and allowed), **q** is returned along with the return code **3**. The **valrange** module does not produce any output. It returns zero for success and non-zero for failure.

NAME

ckstr – display a prompt; verify and return a string answer

SYNOPSIS

ckstr [**-Q**] [**-W** *width*] [[**-r** *regexp*] [**-r** *regexp*] ...] [**-l** *length*]
    [**-d** *default*] [**-h** *help*] [**-e** *error*] [**-p** *prompt*] [**-k** *pid* [**-s** *signal*]]

errstr [**-W** *width*] [**-e** *error*] [[**-r** *regexp*] [**-r** *regexp*] ...] [**-l** *length*]

helpstr [**-W** *width*] [**-h** *help*] [[**-r** *regexp*] [**-r** *regexp*] ...] [**-l** *length*]

valstr *input* [[**-r** *regexp*] [**-r** *regexp*] ...] [**-l** *length*]

DESCRIPTION

ckstr prompts a user and validates the response. It defines, among other things, a prompt message whose response should be a string, text for help and error messages, and a default value (which is returned if the user responds with a RETURN).

The answer returned from this command must match the defined regular expression and be no longer than the length specified. If no regular expression is given, valid input must be a string with a length less than or equal to the length defined with no internal, leading or trailing white space. If no length is defined, the length is not checked. Either a regular expression or a length must be given with the command.

All messages are limited in length to 70 characters and are formatted automatically. Any white space used in the definition (including newline) is stripped. The **-W** option cancels the automatic formatting. When a tilde is placed at the beginning or end of a message definition, the default text is inserted at that point, allowing both custom text and the default text to be displayed.

If the prompt, help or error message is not defined, the default message (as defined under NOTES) is displayed.

Three visual tool modules are linked to the **ckstr** command. They are **errstr** (which formats and displays an error message), **helpstr** (which formats and displays a help message), and **valstr** (which validates a response). These modules should be used in conjunction with FACE objects. In this instance, the FACE object defines the prompt.

The options and arguments for this command are:

-Q   Do not allow quit as a valid response.

-W   Use *width* as the line length for prompt, help, and error messages.

-r   Validate the input against regular expression *regexp*. May include white space. If multiple expressions are defined, the answer need match only one of them.

-l   The maximum length of the input is *length*.

-d   The default value is *default*. The default is not validated and so does not have to meet any criteria.

-h   The help message is *help*.

-e   The error message is *error*.

-p   The prompt message is *prompt*.

-k   Send process ID *pid* a signal if the user chooses to abort.

-s   When quit is chosen, send *signal* to the process whose *pid* is specified by the **-k** option. If no signal is specified, use **SIGTERM**.

input Input to be verified against format length and/or regular expression criteria.

EXIT CODES

0 = Successful execution
1 = EOF on input
2 = Usage error
3 = User termination (quit)

NOTES

The default prompt for **ckstr** is:

    Enter an appropriate value [?,q]

The default error message is dependent upon the type of validation involved. The user is told either that the length or the pattern matching failed.

The default help message is also dependent upon the type of validation involved. If a regular expression has been defined, the message is:

    Please enter a string which matches the following pattern:
    regexp

Other messages define the length requirement and the definition of a string.

When the quit option is chosen (and allowed), **q** is returned along with the return code **3**. The **valstr** module does not produce any output. It returns zero for success and non-zero for failure.

Unless a "**q**" for "quit" is disabled by the **-Q** option, a single "**q**" to the following

    ckstr -rq

is treated as a "quit" and not as a pattern match.

NAME

cktime – display a prompt; verify and return a time of day

SYNOPSIS

cktime [-Q] [-W *width*] [-f *format*] [-d *default*] [-h *help*] [-e *error*]
　　　[-p *prompt*] [-k *pid* [-s *signal*]]

errtime [-W *width*] [-e *error*] [-f *format*]

helptime [-W *width*] [-h *help*] [-f *format*]

valtime [-f *format*] *input*

DESCRIPTION

cktime prompts a user and validates the response. It defines, among other things, a prompt message whose response should be a time, text for help and error messages, and a default value (which is returned if the user responds with a RETURN). The user response must match the defined format for the time of day.

All messages are limited in length to 70 characters and are formatted automatically. Any white space used in the definition (including newline) is stripped. The -W option cancels the automatic formatting. When a tilde is placed at the beginning or end of a message definition, the default text is inserted at that point, allowing both custom text and the default text to be displayed.

If the prompt, help or error message is not defined, the default message (as defined under NOTES) is displayed.

Three visual tool modules are linked to the **cktime** command. They are **errtime** (which formats and displays an error message), **helptime** (which formats and displays a help message), and **valtime** (which validates a response). These modules should be used in conjunction with FMLI objects. In this instance, the FMLI object defines the prompt. When *format* is defined in the **errtime** and **helptime** modules, the messages describe the expected format.

The options and arguments for this command are:

-Q　　Do not allow quit as a valid response.

-W　　Use *width* as the line length for prompt, help, and error messages.

-f　　Verify the input against *format*. Possible formats and their definitions are:

　　　%H = hour (00 – 23)
　　　%I = hour (00 – 12)
　　　%M = minute (00 – 59)
　　　%p = ante meridian or post meridian
　　　%r = time as %I:%M:%S %p
　　　%R = time as %H:%M (the default format)
　　　%S = seconds (00 – 59)
　　　%T = time as %H:%M:%S

-d　　The default value is *default*. The default is not validated and so does not have to meet any criteria.

-h   The help message is *help*.

-e   The error message is *error*.

-p   The prompt message is *prompt*.

-k *pid* Send process ID *pid* a signal if the user chooses to abort.

-s *signal*
        When quit is chosen, send *signal* to the process whose *pid* is specified by the -k option. If no signal is specified, use **SIGTERM**.

input   Input to be verified against format criteria.

EXIT CODES

    0 = Successful execution
    1 = EOF on input
    2 = Usage error
    3 = User termination (quit)
    4 = Garbled format argument

NOTES

The default prompt for **cktime** is:

    Enter a time of day [?,q]

The default error message is:

    ERROR - Please enter the time of day. Format is *format*.

The default help message is:

    Please enter the time of day. Format is *format*.

When the quit option is chosen (and allowed), **q** is returned along with the return code **3**. The **valtime** module does not produce any output. It returns zero for success and non-zero for failure.

NAME

ckuid – prompt for and validate a user ID

SYNOPSIS

ckuid [-Q] [-W *width*] [-m] [-d *default*] [-h *help*] [-e *error*] [-p *prompt*]
[-k *pid* [-s *signal*]]

erruid [-W *width*] [-e *error*]

helpuid [-W *width*] [-m] [-h *help*]

valuid *input*

DESCRIPTION

ckuid prompts a user and validates the response. It defines, among other things, a prompt message whose response should be an existing user ID, text for help and error messages, and a default value (which is returned if the user responds with a RETURN).

All messages are limited in length to 70 characters and are formatted automatically. Any white space used in the definition (including newline) is stripped. The -W option cancels the automatic formatting. When a tilde is placed at the beginning or end of a message definition, the default text is inserted at that point, allowing both custom text and the default text to be displayed.

If the prompt, help or error message is not defined, the default message (as defined under NOTES) is displayed.

Three visual tool modules are linked to the **ckuid** command. They are **erruid** (which formats and displays an error message), **helpuid** (which formats and displays a help message), and **valuid** (which validates a response). These modules should be used in conjunction with FML objects. In this instance, the FML object defines the prompt.

The options and arguments for this command are:

-Q   Do not allow quit as a valid response.

-W   Use *width* as the line length for prompt, help, and error messages.

-m   Display a list of all logins when help is requested or when the user makes an error.

-d   The default value is *default*. The default is not validated and so does not have to meet any criteria.

-h   The help message is *help*.

-e   The error message is *error*.

-p   The prompt message is *prompt*.

-k   Send process ID *pid* a signal if the user chooses to abort.

-s   When quit is chosen, send *signal* to the process whose *pid* is specified by the -k option. If no signal is specified, use **SIGTERM**.

input   Input to be verified against **/etc/passwd**.

EXIT CODES

    0 = Successful execution

    1 = EOF on input

    2 = Usage error

    3 = User termination (quit)

NOTES

The default prompt for **ckuid** is:

    `Enter the login name of an existing user [?,q]`

The default error message is:

    `ERROR - Please enter the login name of an existing user.`

    (If the –m *option of* **ckuid** *is used, a list of valid users is also displayed.)*

The default help message is:

    `Please enter the login name of an existing user.`

    (If the –m *option of* **ckuid** *is used, a list of valid users is also displayed.)*

When the quit option is chosen (and allowed), **q** is returned along with the return code **3**. The **valuid** module does not produce any output. It returns zero for success and non-zero for failure.

NAME

ckyorn – prompt for and validate yes/no

SYNOPSIS

ckyorn [-Q] [-W *width*] [-d *default*] [-h *help*] [-e *error*] [-p *prompt*]
    [-k *pid* [-s *signal*]]

erryorn [-W *width*] [-e *error*]

helpyorn [-W *width*] [-h *help*]

valyorn *input*

DESCRIPTION

ckyorn prompts a user and validates the response. It defines, among other things, a prompt message for a yes or no answer, text for help and error messages, and a default value (which is returned if the user responds with a RETURN).

All messages are limited in length to 70 characters and are formatted automatically. Any white space used in the definition (including newline) is stripped. The -W option cancels the automatic formatting. For the -h and -e options, placing a tilde at the beginning or end of a message definition causes the default text to be inserted at that point. This allows both custom text and the default text to be displayed.

If the prompt, help or error message is not defined, the default message (as defined under NOTES) is displayed.

Three visual tool modules are linked to the ckyorn command. They are erryorn (which formats and displays an error message), helpyorn (which formats and displays a help message), and valyorn (which validates a response). These modules should be used in conjunction with FACE objects. In this instance, the FACE object defines the prompt.

The options and arguments for this command are:

-Q   Do not allow quit as a valid response.

-W   Use *width* as the line length for prompt, help, and error messages.

-d   The default value is *default*. The default is not validated and so does not have to meet any criteria.

-h   The help message is *help*.

-e   The error message is *error*.

-p   The prompt message is *prompt*.

-k   Send process ID *pid* a signal if the user chooses to abort.

-s   When quit is chosen, send *signal* to the process whose *pid* is specified by the -k option. If no signal is specified, use SIGTERM.

input   Input to be verified as y, yes, Y, Yes, YES or n, no, N, No, NO.

EXIT CODES
0 = Successful execution
1 = EOF on input
2 = Usage error
3 = User termination (quit)

NOTES

The default prompt for **ckyorn** is:

        Yes or No [y,n,?,q]

The default error message is:

        ERROR - Please enter yes or no.

The default help message is:

        Enter y or yes if your answer is yes;
        or no if your answer is no.

When the quit option is chosen (and allowed), **q** is returned along with the return code 3. The **valyorn** module does not produce any output. It returns zero for success and non-zero for failure.

NAME

    clear – clear the terminal screen

SYNOPSIS

    clear

DESCRIPTION

    clear clears your screen if this is possible. It looks in the environment for the terminal type and then in the **terminfo** database to figure out how to clear the screen.

SEE ALSO

    tput(1), terminfo(4)

NAME

cmp – compare two files

SYNOPSIS

cmp [-1] [-s] *file1 file2*

DESCRIPTION

The two files are compared. (If *file1* is –, the standard input is used.) Under default options, cmp makes no comment if the files are the same; if they differ, it announces the byte and line number at which the difference occurred. If one file is an initial subsequence of the other, that fact is noted.

Options:

-1   Print the byte number (decimal) and the differing bytes (octal) for each difference.

-s   Print nothing for differing files; return codes only.

SEE ALSO

comm(1), diff(1)

DIAGNOSTICS

Exit code 0 is returned for identical files, 1 for different files, and 2 for an inaccessible or missing argument.

NAME

cof2elf – COFF to ELF object file translation

SYNOPSIS

cof2elf [-iqV] [-Q{yn}] [-s *directory*] *files*

DESCRIPTION

cof2elf converts one or more COFF object *files* to ELF. This translation occurs in place, meaning the original file contents are modified. If an input file is an archive, each member will be translated as necessary, and the archive will be rebuilt with its members in the original order. cof2elf does not change input files that are not COFF.

Options have the following meanings.

-i   Normally, the files are modified only when full translation occurs. Unrecognized data, such as unknown relocation types, are treated as errors and prevent translation. Giving the –i flag ignores these partial translation conditions and modifies the file anyway.

-q   Normally, cof2elf prints a message for each file it examines, telling whether the file was translated, ignored, etc. The –q flag (for quiet) suppresses these messages.

-Q*arg* If *arg* is **y**, identification information about cof2elf will be added to the output files. This can be useful for software administration. Giving **n** for *arg* explicitly asks for no such information, which is the default behavior.

-s*directory* As mentioned above, cof2elf modifies the input files. This option saves a copy of the original files in the specified *directory*, which must exist. cof2elf does not save files it does not modify.

-V   This flag tells cof2elf to print a version message on standard error.

SEE ALSO

ld(1), elf(3E), a.out(4), ar(4)

NOTES

Some debugging information is discarded. Although this does not affect the behavior of a running program, it may affect the information available for symbolic debugging.

cof2elf translates only COFF relocatable files. It does not translate executable or static shared library files for two main reasons. First, the operating system supports executable files and static shared libraries, making translation unnecessary. Second, those files have specific address and alignment constraints determined by the file format. Matching the constraints with a different object file format is problematic.

When possible, programmers should recompile their source code to build new object files. cof2elf is provided for those times when source code is unavailable.

NAME

col – filter reverse line-feeds

SYNOPSIS

col [–b] [–f] [–x] [–p]

DESCRIPTION

col reads from the standard input and writes onto the standard output. It performs the line overlays implied by reverse line feeds (ASCII code ESC-**7**), and by forward and reverse half-line-feeds (ESC-**9** and ESC-**8**). col is particularly useful for filtering multicolumn output made with the .rt command of **nroff** and output resulting from use of the **tbl**(1) preprocessor.

If the **–b** option is given, col assumes that the output device in use is not capable of backspacing. In this case, if two or more characters are to appear in the same place, only the last one read will be output.

Although col accepts half-line motions in its input, it normally does not emit them on output. Instead, text that would appear between lines is moved to the next lower full-line boundary. This treatment can be suppressed by the **–f** (fine) option; in this case, the output from col may contain forward half-line-feeds (ESC-9), but will still never contain either kind of reverse line motion.

Unless the **–x** option is given, col will convert white space to tabs on output wherever possible to shorten printing time.

The ASCII control characters SO (\017) and SI (\016) are assumed by col to start and end text in an alternate character set. The character set to which each input character belongs is remembered, and on output SI and SO characters are generated as appropriate to ensure that each character is printed in the correct character set.

On input, the only control characters accepted are space, backspace, tab, return, new-line, SI, SO, VT (\013), and ESC followed by **7**, **8**, or **9**. The VT character is an alternate form of full reverse line-feed, included for compatibility with some earlier programs of this type. All other non-printing characters are ignored.

Normally, col will ignore any escape sequences unknown to it that are found in its input; the **–p** option may be used to cause col to output these sequences as regular characters, subject to overprinting from reverse line motions. The use of this option is highly discouraged unless the user is fully aware of the textual position of the escape sequences.

SEE ALSO

ascii(5)

nroff(1), tbl(1) in the *DOCUMENTER'S WORKBENCH Software Technical Discussion and Reference Manual* .

NOTES

The input format accepted by col matches the output produced by **nroff** with either the **–T37** or **–Tlp** options. Use **–T37** (and the **–f** option of col) if the ultimate disposition of the output of col will be a device that can interpret half-line motions, and **–Tlp** otherwise.

`col` cannot back up more than 128 lines or handle more than 800 characters per line.

Local vertical motions that would result in backing up over the first line of the document are ignored. As a result, the first line must not have any superscripts.

NAME

colltbl – create collation database

SYNOPSIS

colltbl [*file* | -]

DESCRIPTION

The colltbl command takes as input a specification file, *file*, that describes the collating sequence for a particular language and creates a database that can be read by strxfrm(3C) and strcoll(3C). strxfrm(3C) transforms its first argument and places the result in its second argument. The transformed string is such that it can be correctly ordered with other transformed strings by using strcmp(3C), strncmp(3C) or memcmp(3C). strcoll(3C) transforms its arguments and does a comparison.

If no input file is supplied, *stdin* is read.

The output file produced contains the database with collating sequence information in a form usable by system commands and routines. The name of this output file is the value you assign to the keyword codeset read in from *file*. Before this file can be used, it must be installed in the /usr/lib/locale/*locale* directory with the name LC_COLLATE by someone who is super-user or a member of group bin. *locale* corresponds to the language area whose collation sequence is described in *file*. This file must be readable by user, group, and other; no other permissions should be set. To use the collating sequence information in this file, set the LC_COLLATE environment variable appropriately (see environ(5) or setlocale(3C)).

The colltbl command can support languages whose collating sequence can be completely described by the following cases:

Ordering of single characters within the codeset. For example, in Swedish, V is sorted after U, before X and with W (V and W are considered identical as far as sorting is concerned).

Ordering of "double characters" in the collation sequence. For example, in Spanish, ch and ll are collated after c and l, respectively.

Ordering of a single character as if it consists of two characters. For example, in German, the "sharp s", β, is sorted as ss. This is a special instance of the next case below.

Substitution of one character string with another character string. In the example above, the string β is replaced with ss during sorting.

Ignoring certain characters in the codeset during collation. For example, if – were ignored during collation, then the strings re-locate and relo-cate would be equal.

Secondary ordering between characters. In the case where two characters are sorted together in the collation sequence, (i.e., they have the same "primary" ordering), there is sometimes a secondary ordering that is used if two strings are identical except for characters that have the same primary ordering. For example, in French, the letters e and è have the same primary ordering but e comes before è in the secondary ordering. Thus the word **lever** would be ordered before **lèver**, but **lèver** would be sorted before **levitate**. (Note that if **e** came before **è** in the primary ordering, then **lèver** would be sorted after **levitate**.)

The specification file consists of three types of statements:

1. **codeset**   *filename*

   filename is the name of the output file to be created by **colltbl**.

2. **order is**   *order_list*

   order_list is a list of symbols, separated by semicolons, that defines the collating sequence. The special symbol, **...**, specifies symbols that are lexically sequential in a short-hand form. For example,

          order is   **a;b;c;d;...;x;y;z**

   would specify the list of lower_case letters. Of course, this could be further compressed to just **a;...;z**.

   A symbol can be up to two bytes in length and can be represented in any one of the following ways:

   > the symbol itself (for example, **a** for the lower-case letter **a**),

   > in octal representation (for example, **\141** or **0141** for the letter **a**), or

   > in hexadecimal representation (for example, **\x61** or **0x61** for the letter **a**).

   Any combination of these may be used as well.

   The backslash character, **** , is used for continuation. No characters are permitted after the backslash character.

   Symbols enclosed in parenthesis are assigned the same primary ordering but different secondary ordering. Symbols enclosed in curly brackets are assigned only the same primary ordering. For example,

          order is   **a;b;c;ch;d;(e;è);f;...;z;**
                               {1;...;9};A;...;Z

   In the above example, **e** and **è** are assigned the same primary ordering and different secondary ordering, digits 1 through 9 are assigned the same primary ordering and no secondary ordering. Only primary ordering is assigned to the remaining symbols. Notice how double letters can be specified in the collating sequence (letter **ch** comes between **c** and **d**).

   If a character is not included in the **order is** statement it is excluded from the ordering and will be ignored during sorting.

3. **substitute** *string* **with** *repl*

   The **substitute** statement substitutes the string *string* with the string *repl*. This can be used, for example, to provide rules to sort the abbreviated month names numerically:

```
                    substitute "Jan" with "01"
                    substitute "Feb" with "02"
                           .
                           .
                           .
                    substitute "Dec" with "12"
```

A simpler use of the **substitute** statement that was mentioned above was to substitute a single character with two characters, as with the substitution of β with **ss** in German.

The **substitute** statement is optional. The **order is** and **codeset** statements must appear in the specification file.

Any lines in the specification file with a **#** in the first column are treated as comments and are ignored. Empty lines are also ignored.

EXAMPLE

The following example shows the collation specification required to support a hypothetical telephone book sorting sequence.

The sorting sequence is defined by the following rules:

a.   Upper and lower case letters must be sorted together, but upper case letters have precedence over lower case letters.

b.   All special characters and punctuation should be ignored.

c.   Digits must be sorted as their alphabetic counterparts (for example, **0** as **zero**, **1** as **one**).

d.   The **Ch**, **ch**, **CH** combinations must be collated between **C** and **D**.

e.   **V** and **W**, **v** and **w** must be collated together.

The input specification file to **colltbl** will contain:

```
        codeset     telephone

        order is    A;a;B;b;C;c;CH;Ch;ch;D;d;E;e;F;f;\
                    G;g;H;h;I;i;J;j;K;k;L;l;M;m;N;n;O;o;P;p;\
                    Q;q;R;r;S;s;T;t;U;u;{V;W};{v;w};X;x;Y;y;Z;z

        substitute "0" with "zero"
        substitute "1" with "one"
        substitute "2" with "two"
        substitute "3" with "three"
        substitute "4" with "four"
        substitute "5" with "five"
        substitute "6" with "six"
        substitute "7" with "seven"
        substitute "8" with "eight"
        substitute "9" with "nine"
```

FILES

/lib/locale/*locale*/LC_COLLATE
> LC_COLLATE database for *locale*

/usr/lib/locale/C/colltbl_C
> input file used to construct LC_COLLATE in the default locale.

SEE ALSO

memory(3C), setlocale(3C), strcoll(3C), string(3C), strxfrm(3C), environ(5) in the *Programmer's Reference Manual*

NAME

comb – combine SCCS deltas

SYNOPSIS

comb [-o] [-s] [-p*SID*] [-c*list*] *files*

DESCRIPTION

comb generates a shell procedure [see sh(1)] that, when run, reconstructs the given SCCS files. The reconstructed files are typically smaller than the original files. The arguments may be specified in any order, but all keyletter arguments apply to all named SCCS files. If a directory is named, comb behaves as though each file in the directory were specified as a named file, except that non-SCCS files (last component of the path name does not begin with s.) and unreadable files are silently ignored. If a name of – is given, the standard input is read; each line of the input is taken to be the name of an SCCS file to be processed; non-SCCS files and unreadable files are silently ignored. The generated shell procedure is written on the standard output.

The keyletter arguments are as follows. Each argument is explained as if only one named file is to be processed, but the effects of any keyletter argument apply independently to each named file.

-o　For each get -e, this argument causes the reconstructed file to be accessed at the release of the delta to be created, otherwise the reconstructed file would be accessed at the most recent ancestor. Use of the –o keyletter may decrease the size of the reconstructed SCCS file. It may also alter the shape of the delta tree of the original file.

-s　This argument causes comb to generate a shell procedure that, when run, produces a report that gives for each file: the file name, size (in blocks) after combining, original size (also in blocks), and percentage change computed by:

$$100 * (original - combined) / original$$

It is recommended that before any SCCS files are actually combined, one should use this option to determine exactly how much space is saved by the combining process.

-p*SID*　The SCCS identification string (SID) of the oldest delta to be preserved. All older deltas are discarded in the reconstructed file.

-c*list*　A *list* of deltas to be preserved. All other deltas are discarded. See get(1) for the syntax of a *list*.

If no keyletter arguments are specified, comb preserves only leaf deltas and the minimal number of ancestors needed to preserve the tree.

FILES

s.COMB　　　　the reconstructed SCCS file
comb?????　　temporary file

SEE ALSO

admin(1), delta(1), get(1), help(1), prs(1), sccsfile(4)

sh(1) in the *User's Reference Manual*

DIAGNOSTICS

Use **help**(1) for explanations.

NOTES

comb may rearrange the shape of the tree of deltas.

comb may not save any space; in fact, it is possible for the reconstructed file to be larger than the original.

NAME

comm – select or reject lines common to two sorted files

SYNOPSIS

comm [– [123]] *file1 file2*

DESCRIPTION

comm reads *file1* and *file2*, which should be ordered in ASCII collating sequence [see sort(1)], and produces a three-column output: lines only in *file1*; lines only in *file2*; and lines in both files. The file name – means the standard input.

Flags **1**, **2**, or **3** suppress printing of the corresponding column. Thus comm –12 prints only the lines common to the two files; comm –23 prints only lines in the first file but not in the second; comm –123 prints nothing.

SEE ALSO

cmp(1), diff(1), sort(1), uniq(1)

NAME

compress, uncompress, zcat – compress data for storage, uncompress and display compressed files

SYNOPSIS

compress [-dfFqcv] [-b *bits*] *file*

uncompress [-fqc] *file*

zcat *file*

DESCRIPTION

compress takes a file and compresses it to the smallest possible size, creates a compressed output file, and removes the original file unless the -c option is present. Compression is achieved by encoding common strings within the file. uncompress restores a previously compressed file to its uncompressed state and removes the compressed version. zcat uncompresses and displays a file on the standard output.

If no file is specified on the command line, input is taken from the standard input and the output is directed to the standard output. Output defaults to a file with the same filename as the input file with the suffix **.z** or it can be directed through the standard output. The output files have the same permissions and ownership as the corresponding input files or the user's standard permissions if output is directed through the standard output.

If no space is saved by compression, the output file is not written unless the -F flag is present on the command line.

OPTIONS

The following options are available from the command line:

-d   Decompresses a compressed file.

-c   Writes output on the standard output and does not remove original file.

-b *bits*   Specifies the maximum number of bits to use in encoding.

-f   Overwrites previous output file.

-F   Writes output file even if compression saves no space.

-q   Generates no output except error messages, if any.

-v   Prints the name of the file being compressed, the percentage of compression achieved. With uncompress, the name of of the uncompressed file is printed.

SEE ALSO

pack(1), ar(1), tar(1), cat(1)

NAME
>   comsat, in.comsat – biff server

SYNOPSIS
>   in.comsat

DESCRIPTION
>   comsat is the server process which listens for reports of incoming mail and notifies users who have requested to be told when mail arrives. It is invoked as needed by inetd(1M), and times out if inactive for a few minutes.
>
>   comsat listens on a datagram port associated with the **biff** service specification [see **services**(4)] for one line messages of the form
>
> >   *user@mailbox-offset*
>
>   If the *user* specified is logged in to the system and the associated terminal has the owner execute bit turned on (by a **biff y**), the *offset* is used as a seek offset into the appropriate mailbox file and the first 7 lines or 560 characters of the message are printed on the user's terminal. Lines which appear to be part of the message header other than the **From, To, Date**, or **Subject** lines are not printed when displaying the message.

FILES
>   /var/utmp　　　　　　who's logged on and on what terminals

SEE ALSO
>   services(4), inetd(1M)

NOTES
>   The message header filtering is prone to error.

NAME

    conflgs – change and display console flags

SYNOPSIS

    /etc/conflgs [-a 0| 1] [-c 0| 1] [-m 0| 1] [-r 0| 1] [-b baud] or
    /etc/conflgs [-c 0| 1] [-m 0| 1]

DESCRIPTION

    conflgs allows the remote console and console flags to be set and displayed. It can be used to enable or disable the remote console capability. conflgs allows console redirection (diagnostics and bootstrap input/output) to the second serial port to be enabled or disabled. Note that conflgs does not control what device is used as console — this is determined by whether or not the system is equipped with an integral console and by the COM2CONS tunable parameter. The console message flag and remote console message flag, which determine whether or not system error messages are directed to the console or remote console, can also be temporarily changed with conflgs.

    -a 0| 1 disable (0) or enable (1) diagnostics and bootstrap redirection to the second serial port. If enabled and the second serial port is used as the console, the baud rate specified with the -b option determines the baud rate used for the console. If the second serial port is used as the console but console redirection to the second serial port is disabled, the console baud rate is 9600.

    -r 0| 1 disable (0) or enable (1) the remote console feature. This controls console redirection to the first serial port and sets the remote console enable flag (RCEF). The baud rate specified with the -b option determines the baud rate used for the remote console.

    -c 0| 1 disable (0) or enable (1) sending system error messages to the console. This change only lasts until the system is rebooted. To permanently have system error messages directed to the console, change the CMF tunable parameter.

    -m 0| 1 disable (0) or enable (1) sending system error messages to the remote console. This change only lasts until the system is rebooted. The RCEF must be turned on before this flag for console messages to be seen on the remote console. On some systems, the RCEF is considered on and the remote console baud rate is fixed at 1200. To permanently have system error messages directed to the remote console, change the RCMF tunable parameter.

    If the -a and/or -r option is used, the -b baud option can be used to set the baud rate of the first or second serial port to baud. baud can be 1200 or 9600. If the -b option is not specified when enabling console redirection to the first or second serial port a default baud rate of 1200 is used. The baud rate specifies the baud rate to be used during diagnostics, bootstrap, and system initialization – until the multi-user state is reached. It does not take effect until the next system reboot or *init S*.

The **-a -r**, and **-b** options may or or may not be provided on all 386 machines.

The values of all the console flags are always displayed after the requested changes are made.

Note that the BIOS setup utility can also be used to change the whether or not console redirection to the first or second serial ports is enabled and their baud rates.

SEE ALSO

idtune(1M), init(1M)

NAME

convert – convert archive files to common formats

SYNOPSIS

convert [-x] *infile outfile*

DESCRIPTION

The **convert** command transforms input *infile1 to output outfile*. *infile* must be a UNIX System V Release 1.0 archive file and *outfile* will be the equivalent UNIX System V Release 2.0 archive file. All other types of input to the **convert** command will be passed unmodified from the input file to the output file (along with appropriate warning messages).

The **-x** option is required to convert a XENIX archive. (XENIX is a registered trademark of Microsoft Corporation.) Using this option will convert the general archive but leave archive members unmodified.

infile must be different from *outfile*.

FILES

TMPDIR/**conv**∗   temporary files

TMPDIR is usually **/usr/tmp** but can be redefined by setting the environment variable **TMPDIR** [see **tempnam**() in **tmpnam**(3S)].

SEE ALSO

ar(1), tmpnam(3S), a.out(4), ar(4)

NAME

cocreate, cosend, cocheck, coreceive, codestroy – communicate with a process

SYNOPSIS

cocreate [-r *rpath*] [-w *wpath*] [-i *id*] [-R *refname*] [-s *send_string*]
[-e *expect_string*] *command*

cosend [-n] *proc_id string*

cocheck *proc_id*

coreceive *proc_id*

codestroy [-R *refname*] *proc_id* [*string*]

DESCRIPTION

These co-processing functions provide a flexible means of interaction between FMLI and an independent process; especially, they enable FMLI to be responsive to asynchronous activity.

The **cocreate** function starts *command* as a co-process and initializes communications by setting up pipes between FMLI and the standard input and standard output of *command*. The argument *command* must be an executable and its arguments (if any). This means that *command* expects strings on its input (supplied by **cosend**) and sends information on its output that can be handled in various ways by FMLI. The following options can be used with **cocreate**.

-r *rpath*
If **-r** is specified, *rpath* is the pathname from which FMLI reads information. This option is usually used to set up communication with processes that naturally write to a certain path. If **-r** is not specified, **cocreate** will choose a unique path in **/var/tmp**.

-w *wpath*
If **-w** is specified, *wpath* is the pathname to which **cosend** writes information. This option is usually used so that one process can talk to many different FMLI processes through the same pipe. If **-w** is not specified, **cocreate** will choose a unique path in **/var/tmp**.

-i *id*
If **-i** is specified, *id* is an alternative name for the co-process initialized by this **cocreate**. If **-i** is not specified, *id* defaults to *command*. The argument *id* can later be used with the other co-processing functions rather than *command*. This option is typically used, since it facilitates the creation of two or more co-processes generated from the same *command*. (For example, **cocreate -i ID1 program args** and **cocreate -i ID2 program different_args**.)

-R *refname*
If **-R** is specified, *refname* is a local name for the co-process. Since the **cocreate** function can be issued more than once, a *refname* is useful when the same co-process is referenced a second or subsequent time. With the **-R** option, if the co-process already exists a new one will not be created: the same pipes will be shared. Then, *refname* can be used as an argument to the **-R** option to **codestroy** when you want to end a

particular connection to a co-process and leave other connections undisturbed. (The co-process is only killed after **codestroy** -R has been called as many times as **cocreate** -R was called.)

-**s** *send_string* The -**s** option specifies *send_string* as a string that will be appended to all output sent to the co-process using **cosend**. This option allows a co-process to know when input from FMLI has completed. The default *send_string* is a newline if -**s** is not specified.

-**e** *expect_string* The -**e** option specifies *expect_string* as a string that identifies the end of all output returned by the co-process. (Note: *expect_string* need only be the initial part of a line, and there must be a newline at the end of the co-process output). This option allows FMLI to know when output from the co-process has completed. The default *expect_string* is a newline if -**e** is not specified.

The **cosend** function sends *string* to the co-process identified by *proc_id* via the pipe set up by **cocreate** (optionally *wpath*), where *proc_id* can be either the *command* or *id* specified in **cocreate**. By default, **cosend** blocks, waiting for a response from the co-process. Also by default, FMLI does not send a *send_string* and does not expect an *expect_string* (except a newline). That is, it reads only one line of output from the co-process. If -**e** *expect_string* was not defined when the pipe was created, then the output of the co-process is any single string followed by a newline: any other lines of output remain on the pipe. If the -**e** option was specified when the pipe was created, **cosend** reads lines from the pipe until it reads a line starting with *expect_string*. All lines except the line starting with *expect_string* become the output of **cosend**. The following option can be used with **cosend**:

-**n**   If the -**n** option is specified, **cosend** will not wait for a response from the co-process. It simply returns, providing no output. If the -**n** option is not used, a co-process that does not answer will cause FMLI to permanently hang, waiting for input from the co-process.

The **cocheck** function determines if input is available from the process identified by *proc_id*, where *proc_id* can be either the *command* or *id* specified in **cocreate**. It returns a Boolean value, which makes **cocheck** useful in **if** statements and in other backquoted expressions in Boolean descriptors. **cocheck** receives no input from the co-process; it simply indicates if input is available from the co-process. You must use **coreceive** to actually accept the input. The **cocheck** function can be called from a **reread** descriptor to force a frame to update when new data is available. This is useful when the default value of a field in a form includes **coreceive**.

The **coreceive** function is used to read input from the co-process identified by *proc_id*, where *proc_id* can be either the *command* or *id* specified in **cocreate**. It should only be used when it has been determined, using **cocheck**, that input is actually available. If the -**e** option was used when the co-process was created, **coreceive** will continue to return lines of input until *expect_string* is read. At this point, **coreceive** will terminate. The output of **coreceive** is all the lines that were read excluding the line starting with *expect_string*. If the **-e** option was not used in the **cocreate**, each invocation of **coreceive** will return exactly one line from the co-process. If no input is available when **coreceive** is invoked, it will simply terminate without producing output.

The **codestroy** function terminates the read/write pipes to *proc-id*, where *proc_id* can be either the *command* or *id* specified in **cocreate**. It generates a SIGPIPE signal to the (child) co-process. This kills the co-process, unless the co-process ignores the SIGPIPE signal. If the co-process ignores the SIGPIPE, it will not die, even after the FMLI process terminates (the parent process id of the co-process will be 1).

The optional argument *string* is sent to the co-process before the co-process dies. If *string* is not supplied, a NULL string is passed, followed by the normal *send_string* (newline by default). That is, **codestroy** will call **cosend** *proc_id string*: this implies that **codestroy** will write any output generated by the co-process to *stdout*. For example, if an interactive co-process is written to expect a "quit" string when the communication is over, the **close** descriptor could be defined;

```
close=`codestroy ID 'quit' | message`
```

and any output generated by the co-process when the string **quit** is sent to it via **codestroy** (using **cosend**) would be redirected to the message line.

The **codestroy** function should usually be given the **-R** option, since you may have more than one process with the same name, and you do not want to kill the wrong one. **codestroy** keeps track of the number of *refnames* you have assigned to a process with **cocreate**, and when the last instance is killed, it kills the process (*id*) for you. **codestroy** is typically called as part of a **close** descriptor because **close** is evaluated when a frame is closed. This is important because the co-process will continue to run if **codestroy** is not issued.

When writing programs to use as co-processes, the following tips may be useful. If the co-process program is written in C language, be sure to flush output after writing to the pipe. (Currently, **awk**(1) and **sed**(1) cannot be used in a co-process program because they do not flush after lines of output.) Shell scripts are well-mannered, but slow. C language is recommended. If possible, use the default *send_string*, *rpath* and *wpath*. In most cases, *expect_string* will have to be specified. This, of course, depends on the co-process.

In the case where asynchronous communication from a co-process is desired, a co-process program should use **vsig** to force strings into the pipe and then signal FMLI that output from the co-process is available. This causes the **reread** descriptor of all frames to be evaluated immediately.

EXAMPLE

```
        .
        .
        .
    init=`cocreate -i BIGPROCESS initialize`
    close=`codestroy BIGPROCESS`
        .
        .
```

```
        .
        .
reread=`cocheck BIGPROCESS`
name=`cosend -n BIGPROCESS field1`
        .
        .
        .

        .
name="Receive field"
inactive=TRUE
value=`coreceive BIGPROCESS`
```

NOTES

Co-processes for trusted FMLI applications should use named pipes created by the application with the appropriate permissions; the default pipes created by FMLI are readable and writable by everyone. Handshaking can also be used to enhance security.

If **cosend** is used without the **-n** option, a co-process that does not answer will cause FMLI to permanently hang.

The use of non-alphabetic characters in input and output strings to a co-process should be avoided because they may not get transferred correctly.

SEE ALSO

vsig(1F)

awk(1), **cat**(1), **sed**(1), in the *UNIX System V Programmer's Reference Manual*

NAME

    copy – copy groups of files

SYNOPSIS

    copy [option]. . .source. . .dest

DESCRIPTION

The **copy** command copies the contents of directories to another directory. It is possible to copy whole file systems since directories are made when needed.

If files, directories, or special files do not exist at the destination, then they are created with the same modes and flags as the source. In addition, the super-user may set the user and group ID. The owner and mode are not changed if the destination file exists. Note that there may be more than one source directory. If so, the effect is the same as if the **copy** command had been issued for each source directory with the same destination directory for each copy.

All of the options must be given as separate arguments, and they may appear in any order even after the other arguments. The arguments are:

-a   Asks the user before attempting a copy. If the response does not begin with a "y", then a copy is not done. This option also sets the **ad** option.

-l   Uses links instead whenever they can be used. Otherwise a copy is done. Note that links are never done for special files or directories.

-n   Requires the destination file to be new. If not, then the **copy** command does not change the destination file. The -n flag is meaningless for directories. For special files an -n flag is assumed (that is, the destination of a special file must not exist).

-o   If set then every file copied has its owner and group set to those of source. If not set, then the file's owner is the user who invoked the program.

-m   If set, then every file copied has its modification time and access time set to that of the source. If not set, then the modification time is set to the time of the copy.

-r   If set, then every directory is recursively examined as it is encountered. If not set, then any directories that are found are ignored.

-ad   Asks the user whether an -r flag applies when a directory is discovered. If the answer does not begin with a "y", then the directory is ignored.

-v   If the verbose option is set, messages are printed that reveal what the program is doing.

source This may be a file, directory or special file. It must exist. If it is not a directory, then the results of the command are the same as for the **cp** command.

dest   The destination must be either a file or directory that is different from the source. If *source* and *destination* are anything but directories, then **copy** acts just like a **cp** command. If both are directories, then **copy** copies each file into the destination directory according to the flags that have been set.

NOTES

Special device files can be copied. When they are copied, any data associated with the specified device is not copied.

NAME

cp – copy files

SYNOPSIS

cp [-i] [-p] [-r] *file1* [*file2* . . .] *target*

DESCRIPTION

The **cp** command copies *filen* to *target*. *filen* and *target* may not have the same name. (Care must be taken when using **sh**(1) metacharacters.) If *target* is not a directory, only one file may be specified before it; if it is a directory, more than one file may be specified. If *target* does not exist, **cp** creates a file named *target*. If *target* exists and is not a directory, its contents are overwritten. If *target* is a directory, the file(s) are copied to that directory.

The following options are recognized:

-i   **cp** will prompt for confirmation whenever the copy would overwrite an existing *target*. A **y** answer means that the copy should proceed. Any other answer prevents **cp** from overwriting *target*.

-p   **cp** will duplicate not only the contents of *filen*, but also preserves the modification time and permission modes.

-r   If *filen* is a directory, **cp** will copy the directory and all its files, including any subdirectories and their files; *target* must be a directory.

If *filen* is a directory, *target* must be a directory in the same physical file system. *target* and *filen* do not have to share the same parent directory.

If *filen* is a file and *target* is a link to another file with links, the other links remain and *target* becomes a new file.

If *target* does not exist, **cp** creates a new file named *target* which has the same mode as *filen* except that the sticky bit is not set unless the user is a privileged user; the owner and group of *target* are those of the user.

If *target* is a file, its contents are overwritten, but the mode, owner, and group associated with it are not changed. The last modification time of *target* and the last access time of *filen* are set to the time the copy was made.

If *target* is a directory, then for each file named, a new file with the same mode is created in the target directory; the owner and the group are those of the user making the copy.

NOTES

A -- permits the user to mark the end of any command line options explicitly, thus allowing **cp** to recognize filename arguments that begin with a -. If a -- and a - both appear on the same command line, the second will be interpreted as a filename.

SEE ALSO

chmod(1), cpio(1), ln(1), mv(1), rm(1)

NAME

cpio – copy file archives in and out

SYNOPSIS

cpio **–i** [**bBcdfkmrsStuvV6KT**] [**–C** *bufsize*] [**–E** *file*] [**–H** *hdr*] [**–I** *file*
[**–M** *message*]] [**–R** *ID*]] [*pattern* . . .]

cpio **–o** [**aABcLvVKT**] [**–C** *bufsize*] [**–H** *hdr*] [**–O** *file* [**–M** *message*]]

cpio **–p** [**adlLmuvVKT**] [**–R** *ID*]] *directory*

DESCRIPTION

The **–i**, **–o**, and **–p** options select the action to be performed. The following list
describes each of the actions (which are mutually exclusive).

cpio **–i** (copy in) extracts files from the standard input, which is assumed to be
the product of a previous **cpio** **–o**. Only files with names that match *patterns* are
selected. *patterns* are regular expressions given in the filename-generating notation of **sh**(1). In *patterns*, meta-characters **?**, *, and **[** . . . **]** match the slash (**/**)
character, and backslash (****) is an escape character. A **!** meta-character means *not*.
(For example, the **!abc*** pattern would exclude all files that begin with **abc**.)
Multiple *patterns* may be specified and if no *patterns* are specified, the default for
patterns is * (that is, select all files). Each pattern must be enclosed in double
quotes; otherwise, the name of a file in the current directory might be used.
Extracted files are conditionally created and copied into the current directory tree
based on the options described below. The permissions of the files will be those
of the previous **cpio** **–o**. Owner and group permissions will be the same as the
current user unless the current user is super-user. If this is true, owner and
group permissions will be the same as those resulting from the previous **cpio** **–o**.

NOTE: If **cpio** **–i** tries to create a file that already exists and the existing file is
the same age or younger (newer), **cpio** will output a warning message and not
replace the file. (The **–u** option can be used to overwrite, unconditionally, the
existing file.) If file names are given as absolute pathnames to **cpio** **–o**, then
when the files are restored via **cpio** **–i**, they will be written to their original
directories regardless of the current directory. This behavior can be circumvented
by using the **–r** option.

cpio **–o** (copy out) reads the standard input to obtain a list of path names and
copies those files onto the standard output together with path name and status
information.

cpio **–p** (pass) reads the standard input to obtain a list of path names of files
that are conditionally created and copied into the destination *directory* tree based
on the options described below.

The meanings of the available options are

–a   Reset access times of input files after they have been copied. Access times
are not reset for linked files when **cpio** **–pla** is specified (mutually
exclusive with **–m**).

–A   Append files to an archive. The **–A** option requires the **–o** option. Valid
only with archives that are files, or that are on floppy diskettes or hard
disk partitions.

-b   Reverse the order of the bytes within each word. (Use only with the **-i** option.)

-B   Input/output is to be blocked 5,120 bytes to the record. The default buffer size is device dependent when this and the **-c** options are not used.

-c   Read or write header information in ASCII character form for portability. Always use this option (or the **-H** option) when the origin and the destination machines are different types (mutually exclusive with **-H** and **-6**). (The **-c** option implies expanded device numbers.)

-C *bufsize*
     Input/output is to be blocked *bufsize* bytes to the record, where *bufsize* is replaced by a positive integer. The default buffer size is device dependent when this and **-B** options are not used.

-d   Directories are to be created as needed.

-E *file* Specify an input file (*file*) that contains a list of filenames to be extracted from the archive (one filename per line).

-f   Copy in all files except those in *patterns*. (See the paragraph on **cpio -i** for a description of *patterns*.)

-H *hdr* Read or write header information in *hdr* format. Always use this option or the **-c** option when the origin and the destination machines are different types (mutually exclusive with **-c** and **-6**). Valid values for *hdr* are:

        crc or **CRC**   ASCII header with expanded device numbers and an additional per-file checksum

        ustar or **USTAR** IEEE/P1003 Data Interchange Standard header and format

        tar or **TAR**   **tar** header and format

        odc   ASCII header with small device numbers

-I *file* Read the contents of *file* as an input archive. If *file* is a character special device, and the current medium has been completely read, replace the medium and press RETURN to continue to the next medium. This option is used only with the **-i** option.

-k   Attempt to skip corrupted file headers and I/O errors that may be encountered. If you want to copy files from a medium that is corrupted or out of sequence, this option lets you read only those files with good headers. (For **cpio** archives that contain other **cpio** archives, if an error is encountered **cpio** may terminate prematurely. **cpio** will find the next good header, which may be one for a smaller archive, and terminate when the smaller archive's trailer is encountered.) Used only with the **-i** option.

-l   Whenever possible, link files rather than copying them. (Usable only with the **-p** option.)

-L   Follow symbolic links. The default is not to follow symbolic links.

-m   Retain previous file modification time. This option is ineffective on direc-
        tories that are being copied (mutually exclusive with -a).

-M *message*
        Define a *message* to use when switching media. When you use the -o or
        -I options and specify a character special device, you can use this option
        to define the message that is printed when you reach the end of the
        medium. One %d can be placed in *message* to print the sequence number
        of the next medium needed to continue.

-O *file* Direct the output of cpio to *file*. If *file* is a character special device and
        the current medium is full, replace the medium and press RETURN to con-
        tinue to the next medium. Use only with the -o option.

-r   Interactively rename files. If the user presses the RETURN key alone, the
        file is skipped. If the user types a "." the original pathname will be
        retained. (Not available with cpio -p.)

-R *ID* Reassign ownership and group information for each file to user *ID* (*ID*
        must be a valid user ID from /etc/passwd). This option is valid only for
        the super-user.

-s   Swap bytes within each half word.

-S   Swap halfwords within each word.

-t   Print a table of contents of the input. No files are created (mutually
        exclusive with -v).

-u   Copy unconditionally (normally, an older file will not replace a newer file
        with the same name).

-v   Verbose: causes a list of file names to be printed. When used with the -t
        option, the table of contents looks like the output of an ls -l command
        [see ls(1)].

-V   Special Verbose: print a dot for each file read or written. Useful to assure
        the user that cpio is working without printing out all file names.

-K   1K Blocks: force the blocking size to be a multiple of 1K.

-T   Truncate: truncate long file names to 14 characters.

-6   Process a UNIX System Sixth Edition archive format file. Use only with
        the -i option (mutually exclusive with -c and -H)).

NOTE: cpio assumes four-byte words.

If, when writing to a character device (-o) or reading from a character device
(-i), cpio reaches the end of a medium (such as the end of a diskette), and the
-O and -I options aren't used, cpio will print the following message:

        If you want to go on, type device/file name when ready.

To continue, you must replace the medium and type the character special device
name (/dev/rdsk/f0 for example) and press RETURN. You may want to continue by directing cpio to use a different device. For example, if you have two
floppy drives you may want to switch between them so cpio can proceed while

you are changing the floppies. (Simply pressing RETURN causes the **cpio** process to exit.)

EXAMPLES

The following examples show three uses of **cpio**.

When standard input is directed through a pipe to **cpio −o**, it groups the files so they can be directed (>) to a single file (**../newfile**). The −c option insures that the file will be portable to other machines (as would the −H option). Instead of **ls**(1), you could use **find**(1), **echo**(1), **cat**(1), and so on, to pipe a list of names to **cpio**. You could direct the output to a device instead of a file.

        ls | cpio −oc > ../newfile

cpio −i uses the output file of **cpio −o** (directed through a pipe with **cat** in the example below), extracts those files that match the patterns (**memo/a1, memo/b**∗), creates directories below the current directory as needed (−d option), and places the files in the appropriate directories. The −c option is used if the input file was created with a portable header. If no patterns were given, all files from **newfile** would be placed in the directory.

        cat newfile | cpio −icd "memo/a1" "memo/b∗"

cpio −p takes the file names piped to it and copies or links (−l option) those files to another directory (**newdir** in the example below). The −d option says to create directories as needed. The −m option says retain the modification time. (It is important to use the −**depth** option of **find**(1) to generate path names for **cpio**. This eliminates problems **cpio** could have trying to create files under read-only directories.) The destination directory, **newdir**, must exist.

        find . −depth −print | cpio −pdlmv newdir

Note that when you use **cpio** in conjunction with **find**, if you use the −**L** option with **cpio** then you must use the −**follow** option with **find** and vice versa. Otherwise there will be undesirable results.

SEE ALSO

ar(1), **cat**(1), **echo**(1), **find**(1), **ls**(1), **tar**(1)

archives(4) in the *System Administrator's Reference Manual*

NOTES

An archive created with the −c option on a System V Release 4 system cannot be read on System V Release 3.2 systems, or earlier. Use the −**H odc** option, which is equivalent to the header created by the −c option in earlier System V releases, if the **cpio** image will be read on a pre-System V Release 4 system.

System V Releases prior to Release 4 do not recognize symbolic links. The result of copying in a symbolic link on an older release will be a regular file that contains the pathname of the referenced file.

Path names are restricted to 256 characters for the binary (the default) and −**H odc** header formats. Otherwise, path names are restricted to 1024 characters.

Only the super-user can copy special files.

Blocks are reported in 512-byte quantities.

If a file has **000** permissions, contains more than 0 characters of data, and the user is not root, the file will not be saved or restored.

When attempting to redirect **stdin** or **stdout** from or to a character or block special device (for example, **/dev/diskette**), an error message "**Cannot read from device**" or "**Cannot write to device**," does not necessarily indicate that a true I/O error has occurred. More likely, the user does not have access to that device, and should request that the system administrator allocate that device for the user [see **admalloc**(1M)].

Prior to Release 4, the default buffer size was 512 bytes. Beginning with Release 4, the default buffer size is optimized for the device and using the **-C** option to specify a different block size may cause **cpio** to fail. Therefore, care must be taken when choosing the block size. For example, for floppy disks, *bufsize* must be a multiple of 512 (one floppy sector). To avoid wasting space on streaming tape drives, use the **-C** option with an appropriate block size.

NAME

crash – examine system images

SYNOPSIS

/usr/sbin/crash [–d *dumpfile*] [–n *namelist*] [–w *outputfile*]

DESCRIPTION

The **crash** command is used to examine the system memory image of a running or a crashed system by formatting and printing control structures, tables, and other information. Command line arguments to **crash** are *dumpfile*, *namelist*, and *outputfile*.

dumpfile is the file containing the system memory image. The default *dumpfile* is /dev/mem.

The text file *namelist* contains the symbol table information needed for symbolic access to the system memory image to be examined. The default *namelist* is /stand/unix. If a system image from another machine is to be examined, the corresponding text file must be copied from that machine.

When the **crash** command is invoked, a session is initiated. The output from a **crash** session is directed to *outputfile*. The default *outputfile* is the standard output.

Input during a **crash** session is of the form:

    function [*argument*. . .]

where *function* is one of the **crash** functions described in the "FUNCTIONS" subsection of this manual page, and *arguments* are qualifying data that indicate which items of the system image are to be printed.

The default for process-related items is the current process for a running system or the process that was running at the time of the crash for a crashed system. If the contents of a table are being dumped, the default is all active table entries.

The following function options are available to **crash** functions wherever they are semantically valid.

–e	Display every entry in a table.
–f	Display the full structure.
–p	Interpret all address arguments in the command line as physical addresses. If they are not physical addresses, results are inconsistent.
–s *process*	Specify a process slot other than the default.
–w *file*	Redirect the output of a function to *file*.

The functions **mode**, **defproc**, and **redirect** correspond to the function options –p, –s, and –w. The **mode** function may be used to set the address translation mode to physical or virtual for all subsequently entered functions; **defproc** sets the value of the process slot argument for subsequent functions; and **redirect** redirects all subsequent output.

Output from **crash** functions may be piped to another program in the following way:

> *function* [*argument . . .*] ! *shell_command*

For example,

> `mount ! grep rw`

writes all mount table entries with an **rw** flag to the standard output. The redirection option (**-w**) cannot be used with this feature.

Depending on the context of the function, numeric arguments are assumed to be in a specific radix. Counts are assumed to be decimal. Addresses are always hexadecimal. Table slot arguments larger than the size of the function will not be interpreted correctly. Use the *findslot* command to translate from an address to a table slot number. Default bases on all arguments may be overridden. The C conventions for designating the bases of numbers are recognized. A number that is usually interpreted as decimal is interpreted as hexadecimal if it is preceded by **0x** and as octal if it is preceded by **0**. Decimal override is designated by **0d**, and binary by **0b**.

Aliases for functions may be any uniquely identifiable initial substring of the function name. Traditional aliases of one letter, such as **p** for **proc**, remain valid.

Many functions accept different forms of entry for the same argument. Requests for table information will accept a table entry number or a range. A range of slot numbers may be specified in the form *a–b* where *a* and *b* are decimal numbers. An expression consists of two operands and an operator. An operand may be an address, a symbol, or a number; the operator may be +, –, *, /, &, or | . An operand that is a number should be preceded by a radix prefix if it is not a decimal number (**0** for octal, **0x** for hexadecimal, **0b** for binary). The expression must be enclosed in parentheses. Other functions accept any of these argument forms that are meaningful.

Two abbreviated arguments to **crash** functions are used throughout. Both accept data entered in several forms. They may be expanded into the following:

> *table_entry = address | slot | range*
>
> *start_addr = address | symbol | expression*

FUNCTIONS
? [**-w** *file*]
> List available functions.

! *command*
> Escape to the shell and execute *command*.

as [**-e**] [**-f**] [**-w** *file*] [*proc . . .*]
> Print information on process segments.

base [**-w** *file*] *number . . .*
> Print *number* in binary, octal, decimal, and hexadecimal. A number in a radix other than decimal should be preceded by a prefix that indicates its radix as follows: **0x**, hexadecimal; **0**, octal; and **0b**, binary.

buffer [-w *file*] [*-format*] *bufferslot*

buffer [-w *file*] [*-format*] [-p] *start_addr*
> Alias: **b**.
> Print the contents of a buffer in the designated format. The following format designations are recognized: -b, byte: -c, character; -d, decimal; -x, hexadecimal; -o, octal; and, -i, inode. If no format is given, the previous format is used. The default format at the beginning of a **crash** session is hexadecimal.

bufhdr [-f] [-w *file*] [[-p] *table_entry* . . .]
> Alias: **buf**.
> Print system buffer headers. The -f option produces different output depending on whether the buffer is local or remote (contains RFS data).

callout [-w *file*]
> Alias: **c**.
> Print the callout table.

class [-w *file*] [*table_entry* . . .]
> Print information about process scheduler classes.

dbfree [-w *file*] [*class* . . .]
> Print free streams data block headers. If a class is entered, only data block headers for the class specified is printed.

dblock [-e] [-w *file*] [-c *class* . . .]

dblock [-e] [-w *file*] [[-p] *table_entry* . . .]
> Print allocated streams data block headers. If the class option (-c) is used, only data block headers for the class specified is printed.

defproc [-w *file*] [-c]

defproc [-w *file*] [*slot*]
> Set the value of the default process slot argument. The default process slot argument may be set to the current slot number (-c) or the slot number may be specified. If no argument is entered, the value of the previously set slot number is printed. At the start of a **crash** session, the process slot is set to the current process.

dis [-w *file*] [-a] *start_addr* [*count*]

dis [-w *file*] [-a] -c [*count*]
> Disassemble *count* instructions starting at *start_addr*. The default count is 1. The absolute option (-a) specifies a non-symbolic disassembly. The -c option can be used in place of *start_addr* to continue disassembly at the address at which a previous disassembly ended.

dispq [-w *file*] [*table_entry* . . .]
> Print the dispatcher (scheduler) queues.

ds [-w *file*] *virtual_address* . . .
> Print the data symbol whose address is closest to, but not greater than, the address entered.

file [−e] [−w *file*] [[−p] *table_entry* . . .]
    Alias: **f**.
    Print the file table.

findaddr [−w *file*] *table slot*
    Print the address of *slot* in *table*. Only tables available to the **size** function are available to **findaddr**.

findslot [−w *file*] *virtual_address* . . .
    Print the table, entry slot number, and offset for the address entered. Only tables available to the **size** function are available to **findslot**.

fs [−w *file*] [[−p] *table_entry* . . .]
    Print the file system information table.

gdp [−e] [−f] [−w *file*] [[−p] *table_entry* . . .]
    Print the gift descriptor protocol table.

gdt [−e] [−w *file*] [*slot* [*count*]]
    table_entry . . .] Print the global descriptor table.

help [−w *file*] *function* . . .
    Print a description of the named function, including syntax and aliases.

idt [−e] [−w *file*] [*slot* [*count*]]
    Print the interrupt descriptor table.

inode [−e] [−f] [−w *file*] [[−p] *table_entry* . . .]
    Alias: **i**.
    Print the inode table, including file system switch information.

kfp [−w *file*] [*value* . . .]
    Print the kernel frame pointer (kfp) for the start of a kernel stack trace. If the value argument is supplied, the **p** is set to that value. If no argument is entered, the current value of the kfp is printed.

kmastat [−w *file*]
    Print kernel memory allocator statistics.

lck [−e] [−w *file*] [[−p] *table_entry* . . .]
    Alias: **l**.
    Print record locking information. If the −e option is used or table address arguments are given, the record lock list is printed. If no argument is entered, information on locks relative to inodes is printed.

ldt [−e] [−w *file*] [*process* [*slot* [*count*]]]
    Print the local descriptor table for the given process, for the current process if none is given.

linkblk [−e] [−w *file*] [[−p] *table_entry* . . .]
    Print the linkblk table.

map [−w *file*] *mapname* . . .
    Print the map structure of the given mapname.

mbfree [-w *file*]
> Print free streams message block headers.

mblock [-e] [-w *file*] [[-p] *table_entry* . . .]
> Print allocated streams message block headers.

mode [-w *file*] [*mode*]
> Set address translation of arguments to virtual (**v**) or physical (**p**) mode. If no mode argument is given, the current mode is printed. At the start of a **crash** session, the mode is virtual.

mount [-e] [-w *file*] [[-p] *table_entry* . . .]
> Alias: **m, vfs.**
> Print information about mounted file systems.

nm [-w *file*] *symbol* . . .
> Print value and type for the given symbol.

od [-p] [-w *file*] [-*format*] [-*mode*] [-s *process*] *start_addr* [*count*]
> Alias: **rd.**
> Print *count* values starting at *start_addr* in one of the following formats: character (-**c**), decimal (-**d**), hexadecimal (-**x**), octal (-**o**), ASCII (-**a**), or hexadecimal/character (-**h**), and one of the following modes: long (-**l**), short (-**t**), or byte (-**b**). The default mode for character and ASCII formats is byte; the default mode for decimal, hexadecimal, and octal formats is long. The format -**h** prints both hexadecimal and character representations of the addresses dumped; no mode needs to be specified. When format or mode is omitted, the previous value is used. At the start of a **crash** session, the format is hexadecimal and the mode is long. If no count is entered, 1 is assumed.

panic Print the latest system notices, warnings, and panic messages from the limited circular buffer kept in memory.

page [-e] [-w*file*] [[-p] *table_entry* . . .]
> Print information about pages.

pcb [-w *file*] [*process*]
> Print the process control block (TSS). If no arguments are given, the active TSS for the current process is printed.

prnode [-e] [-w *file*] [[-p] *table_entry* . . .]
> Print information about the private data of processes being traced.

proc [-e] [-f] [-w *file*] [[-p] *table_entry* . . . #*procid* . . .]

proc [-f] [-w *file*] [-r]
> Alias: **p.**
> Print the process table. Process table information may be specified in two ways. First, any mixture of table entries and process IDs may be entered. Each process ID must be preceded by a **#**. Alternatively, process table information for runnable processes may be specified with the runnable option (-**r**). The full option (-**f**) details most of the information in the process table as well as the region for that process.

ptbl [-e] [-w *file*] [-s*process*] [[-p] *addr* [*count*]]
　　　Print information on page descriptor tables.

pty [-f] [-e] [-w *file*] [-s] [-h] [-l]
　　　Print the pseudo ttys presently configured. The -l, -h and -h options
　　　give information about the STREAMS modules **ldterm, ptem** and **pckt**,
　　　respectively.

qrun [-w *file*]
　　　Print the list of scheduled streams queues.

queue [-e] [-w *file*] [[-p] *table_entry* . . .]
　　　Print streams queues.

quit　Alias: **q**.
　　　Terminate the **crash** session.

rcvd [-e] [-f] [-w *file*] [[-p] *table_entry* . . .]
　　　Print the receive descriptor table.

rduser [-e] [-f] [-w *file*] [[-p] *table_entry* . . .]
　　　Print the receive descriptor user table.

redirect [-w *file*] [-c]

redirect [-w *file*] [*newfile*]
　　　Used with a file name, redirects output of a **crash** session to *newfile*. If no
　　　argument is given, the file name to which output is being redirected is
　　　printed. Alternatively, the close option (-c) closes the previously set file
　　　and redirects output to the standard output.

resource [-e] [-w *file*] [[-p] *table_entry* . . .]
　　　Print the advertise table.

rtdptbl [-w *file*] [*table_entry* . . .]
　　　Print the real-time scheduler parameter table. See **rt_dptbl**(4).

rtproc [-w *file*]
　　　Print information about processes in the real-time scheduler class.

search [-p] [-w *file*] [-m *mask*] [-s *process*] *pattern start_addr length*
　　　Print the long words in memory that match *pattern*, beginning at the
　　　start_addr for *length* long words. The mask is ANDed (&) with each
　　　memory word and the result compared against the pattern. The mask
　　　defaults to **0xffffffff**.

size [-w *file*] [-x] [*structure_name* . . .]
　　　Print the size of the designated structure. The (-x) option prints the size
　　　in hexadecimal. If no argument is given, a list of the structure names for
　　　which sizes are available is printed.

sndd [-e] [-f] [-w *file*] [[-p] *table_entry* . . .]
　　　Print the send descriptor table.

snode [-e] [-f] [-w *file*] [[-p] *table_entry* . . .]
　　　Print information about open special files.

srmount [-e] [-w *file*] [[-p] *table_entry* . . .]
> Print the server mount table.

stack [-w *file*] [*process*]
> Alias: **s**.
> Dump the stack. If no arguments are entered, the kernel stack for the current process is printed. The interrupt stack and the stack for the current process are not available on a running system.

stat [-w *file*]
> Print system statistics.

stream [-e] [-f] [-w *file*] [[-p] *table_entry* . . .]
> Print the streams table.

strstat [-w *file*]
> Print streams statistics.

trace [-w *file*] [-r] [*process*]
> Alias: **t**.
> Print stack trace. The kfp value is used with the **-r** option; the **kfp** function prints or sets the kfp (kernel frame pointer) value.

ts [-w *file*] *virtual_address* . . .
> Print text symbol closest to the designated address.

tsdptbl [-w *file*] [*table_entry* . . .]
> Print the time-sharing scheduler parameter table. See **ts_dptbl**(4).

tsproc [-w *file*]
> Print information about processes in the time-sharing scheduler class.

tty [-e] [-f] [-l] [-w *file*] [-t *type* [[-p] *table_entry* . . .] | [-p] *start addr*]
> Valid types: **kd, asy, console, comports**.
> Print the tty table. If no arguments are given, the tty table for both tty types is printed. If the **-t** option is used, the table for the single tty type specified is printed. If no argument follows the type option, all entries in the table are printed. A single tty entry may be specified using *start_addr*. The **-l** option prints the line discipline information.

uinode [-e] [-f] [-w *file*] [[-p] *table_entry* . . .]
> Alias: **ui**.
> Print the ufs inode table.

user [-f] [-w *file*] [*process*]
> Alias: **u**.
> Print the ublock for the designated process.

var [-w *file*]
> Alias: **v**.
> Print the tunable system parameters.

vfs [-e] [-w *file*] [[-p] *table_entry* . . .]
> Alias: **mount, m**.
> Print information about mounted file systems.

vfssw [-w *file*] [[-p] *table_entry* . . .]
>   Print information about configured file system types.

vnode [-w *file*] [[-p] *vnode_addr* . . .]
>   Print information about vnodes.

vtop [-w *file*] [-s *process*] *start_addr* . . .
>   Print the physical address translation of the virtual address *start_addr*.

NAME

cron – clock daemon

SYNOPSIS

/usr/sbin/cron

DESCRIPTION

The **cron** command starts a process that executes commands at specified dates and times. Regularly scheduled commands can be specified according to instructions found in **crontab** files in the directory **/var/spool/cron/crontabs**. Users can submit their own **crontab** file via the **crontab** command. Commands which are to be executed only once may be submitted via the **at** command.

cron only examines **crontab** files and **at** command files during process initialization and when a file changes via the **crontab** or **at** commands. This reduces the overhead of checking for new or changed files at regularly scheduled intervals.

Since **cron** never exits, it should be executed only once. This is done routinely through **/sbin/rc2.d/S75cron** at system boot time. **/etc/cron.d/FIFO** is used as a lock file to prevent the execution of more than one **cron**.

To keep a log of all actions taken by **cron**, CRONLOG=YES (by default) must be specified in the **/etc/default/cron** file. If CRONLOG=NO is specified, no logging is done. Keeping the log is a user configurable option since **cron** usually creates huge log files.

FILES

/usr/sbin/cron.d	main cron directory
/etc/default/cron	used to maintain a log
/etc/cron.d/FIFO	used as a lock file
/var/cron/log	accounting information
/var/spool/cron	spool area

SEE ALSO

at(1), crontab(1), sh(1) in the *User's Reference Manual*

DIAGNOSTICS

A history of all actions taken by **cron** are recorded in **/var/cron/log**.

If cron fails it sends mail
check mail

NAME

crontab – user crontab file

SYNOPSIS

crontab [*file*]

crontab –e [-u *username*]

crontab –r [-u *username*]

crontab –l [-u *username*]

DESCRIPTION

crontab copies the specified file, or standard input if no file is specified, into a directory that holds all users' **crontab**s. The –e option edits a copy of the current user's **crontab** file, or creates an empty file to edit if **crontab** does not exist. When editing is complete, the file is installed as the user's **crontab** file. If -u *username* is given, the specified user's **crontab** file is edited, rather than the current user's **crontab** file; this may only be done by a privileged user. The -e option invokes the editor specified by the **VISUAL** environment variable, and if that is null, it looks at the **EDITOR** environment variable, and if that is null, it invokes ed [see ed(1)]. The –r option removes a user's **crontab** from the **crontab** directory. **crontab** –l will list the **crontab** file for the invoking user. Only a privileged user can use -u *username* following the –r or –l options to remove or list the **crontab** file of the specified user.

Note, the -u before the *username* only needs to be specified on Intel processor based computers. Others can specify *username* without the -u.

Users are permitted to use **crontab** if their names appear in the file /etc/cron.d/cron.allow. If that file does not exist, the file /etc/cron.d/cron.deny is checked to determine if the user should be denied access to **crontab**. If neither file exists, only root is allowed to submit a job. If **cron.allow** does not exist and **cron.deny** exists but is empty, global usage is permitted. The allow/deny files consist of one user name per line.

A crontab file consists of lines of six fields each. The fields are separated by spaces or tabs. The first five are integer patterns that specify the following:

minute (0– 59),
hour (0– 23),
day of the month (1– 31),
month of the year (1– 12),
day of the week (0– 6 with 0=Sunday).

Each of these patterns may be either an asterisk (meaning all legal values) or a list of elements separated by commas. An element is either a number or two numbers separated by a minus sign (meaning an inclusive range). Note that the specification of days may be made by two fields (day of the month and day of the week). If both are specified as a list of elements, both are adhered to. For example, 0 0 1,15 ∗ 1 would run a command on the first and fifteenth of each month, as well as on every Monday. To specify days by only one field, the other field should be set to ∗ (for example, 0 0 ∗ ∗ 1 would run a command only on Mondays).

The sixth field of a line in a crontab file is a string that is executed by the shell at the specified times. A percent character in this field (unless escaped by \) is translated to a new-line character. Only the first line (up to a % or end of line) of the command field is executed by the shell. The other lines are made available to the command as standard input.

Any line beginning with a # is a comment and will be ignored.

The shell is invoked from your $HOME directory with an arg0 of sh. Users who desire to have their .profile executed must explicitly do so in the crontab file. cron supplies a default environment for every shell, defining HOME, LOGNAME, SHELL(=/bin/sh), and PATH(=:/bin:/usr/bin:/usr/lbin).

If you do not redirect the standard output and standard error of your commands, any generated output or errors will be mailed to you.

FILES

/usr/sbin/cron.d	main cron directory
/var/spool/cron/crontabs	spool area
/var/cron/log	accounting information
/etc/cron.d/cron.allow	list of allowed users
/etc/cron.d/cron.deny	list of denied users

NOTES

If you inadvertently enter the **crontab** command with no argument(s), do not attempt to get out with a CTRL-D. This will cause all entries in your **crontab** file to be removed. Instead, exit with a DEL.

If a privileged user modifies another user's **crontab** file, resulting behavior may be unpredictable. Instead, the privileged user should first **su**(1M) to the other user's login before making any changes to the **crontab** file.

SEE ALSO

atq(1), atrm(1), ed(1), sh(1), su(1)

cron(1M) in the *System Administrator's Reference Manual*

NAME

crypt – encode/decode

SYNOPSIS

crypt [*password*]

crypt [-k]

DESCRIPTION

crypt reads from the standard input and writes on the standard output. The *password* is a key that selects a particular transformation. If no argument is given, **crypt** demands a key from the terminal and turns off printing while the key is being typed in. If the **-k** option is used, **crypt** will use the key assigned to the environment variable **CRYPTKEY**. **crypt** encrypts and decrypts with the same key:

```
crypt key <clear >cypher
crypt key <cypher | pr
```

Files encrypted by **crypt** are compatible with those treated by the editors **ed**(1), **edit**(1), **ex**(1), and **vi**(1) in encryption mode.

The security of encrypted files depends on three factors: the fundamental method must be hard to solve; direct search of the key space must be infeasible; "sneak paths" by which keys or clear text can become visible must be minimized.

crypt implements a one-rotor machine designed along the lines of the German Enigma, but with a 256-element rotor. Methods of attack on such machines are known, but not widely; moreover the amount of work required is likely to be large.

The transformation of a key into the internal settings of the machine is deliberately designed to be expensive, that is, to take a substantial fraction of a second to compute. However, if keys are restricted to (say) three lower-case letters, then encrypted files can be read by expending only a substantial fraction of five minutes of machine time.

If the key is an argument to the **crypt** command, it is potentially visible to users executing **ps**(1) or a derivative. The choice of keys and key security are the most vulnerable aspect of **crypt**.

FILES

/dev/tty   for typed key

SEE ALSO

ed(1), **edit**(1), **ex**(1), **makekey**(1), **nroff**(1), **pg**(1), **ps**(1), **stty**(1), **vi**(1)

NOTES

This command is provided with the Encryption Utilities, which is only available in the United States. If two or more files encrypted with the same key are concatenated and an attempt is made to decrypt the result, only the contents of the first of the original files will be decrypted correctly.

If output is piped to **nroff** and the encryption key is not given on the command line then do not pipe **crypt** through **pg**(1) or any other program that changes the **tty** settings. Doing so may cause **crypt** to leave terminal modes in a strange state [see **stty**(1)].

NAME

cscope – interactively examine a C program

SYNOPSIS

cscope [*options*] *files* . . .

DESCRIPTION

cscope is an interactive screen-oriented tool that allows the user to browse through C source files for specified elements of code.

By default, **cscope** examines the C (**.c** and **.h**), **lex** (**.1**), and **yacc** (**.y**) source files in the current directory. **cscope** may also be invoked for source files named on the command line. In either case, **cscope** searches the standard directories for **#include** files that it does not find in the current directory. **cscope** uses a symbol cross-reference, **cscope.out** by default, to locate functions, function calls, macros, variables, and preprocessor symbols in the files.

cscope builds the symbol cross-reference the first time it is used on the source files for the program being browsed. On a subsequent invocation, **cscope** rebuilds the cross-reference only if a source file has changed or the list of source files is different. When the cross-reference is rebuilt, the data for the unchanged files are copied from the old cross-reference, which makes rebuilding faster than the initial build.

The following options can appear in any combination:

–b	Build the cross-reference only.
–C	Ignore letter case when searching.
–c	Use only ASCII characters in the cross-reference file, that is, do not compress the data.
–d	Do not update the cross-reference.
–e	Suppress the **^e** command prompt between files.
–f *reffile*	Use *reffile* as the cross-reference file name instead of the default **cscope.out**.
–I *incdir*	Look in *incdir* (before looking in *INCDIR*, the standard place for header files, normally **/usr/include**) for any **#include** files whose names do not begin with **/** and that are not specified on the command line or in *namefile* below. (The **#include** files may be specified with either double quotes or angle brackets.) The *incdir* directory is searched in addition to the current directory (which is searched first) and the standard list (which is searched last). If more than one occurrence of **–I** appears, the directories are searched in the order they appear on the command line.
–i *namefile*	Browse through all source files whose names are listed in *namefile* (file names separated by spaces, tabs, or new-lines) instead of the default (**cscope.files**). If this option is specified, **cscope** ignores any files appearing on the command line.

–L	Do a single search with line-oriented output when used with the –*num pattern* option.
–l	Line-oriented interface (see "Line-Oriented Interface" below).
–*num pattern*	Go to input field *num* (counting from 0) and find *pattern*.
–P *path*	Prepend *path* to relative file names in a pre-built cross-reference file so you do not have to change to the directory where the cross-reference file was built. This option is only valid with the –d option.
–p *n*	Display the last *n* file path components instead of the default (1). Use 0 to not display the file name at all.
–s *dir*	Look in *dir* for additional source files. This option is ignored if source files are given on the command line.
–T	Use only the first eight characters to match against C symbols. A regular expression containing special characters other than a period (.) will not match any symbol if its minimum length is greater than eight characters.
–U	Do not check file time stamps (assume that no files have changed).
–u	Unconditionally build the cross-reference file (assume that all files have changed).
–V	Print on the first line of screen the version number of **cscope**.

The –I, –p, and –T options can also be in the **cscope.files** file.

Requesting the Initial Search

After the cross-reference is ready, **cscope** will display this menu:

```
Find this C symbol:
Find this function definition:
Find functions called by this function:
Find functions calling this function:
Find this text string:
Change this text string:
Find this egrep pattern:
Find this file:
Find files #including this file:
```

Press the **TAB** key repeatedly to move to the desired input field, type the text to search for, and then press the **RETURN** key.

Issuing Subsequent Requests

If the search is successful, any of these single-character commands can be used:

1-9	Edit the file referenced by the given line number.
SPACE	Display next set of matching lines.
+	Display next set of matching lines.

–	Display previous set of matching lines.
^e	Edit displayed files in order.
>	Append the displayed list of lines to a file.
|	Pipe all lines to a shell command.

At any time these single-character commands can also be used:

TAB	Move to next input field.
RETURN	Move to next input field.
^n	Move to next input field.
^p	Move to previous input field.
^y	Search with the last text typed.
^b	Move to previous input field and search pattern.
^f	Move to next input field and search pattern.
^c	Toggle ignore/use letter case when searching. (When ignoring letter case, search for **FILE** will match **File** and **file**.)
^r	Rebuild the cross-reference.
!	Start an interactive shell (type ^d to return to **cscope**).
^l	Redraw the screen.
?	Give help information about **cscope** commands.
^d	Exit **cscope**.

Note: If the first character of the text to be searched for matches one of the above commands, escape it by typing a \ (backslash) first.

Substituting New Text for Old Text

After the text to be changed has been typed, **cscope** will prompt for the new text, and then it will display the lines containing the old text. Select the lines to be changed with these single-character commands:

1-9	Mark or unmark the line to be changed.
*	Mark or unmark all displayed lines to be changed.
SPACE	Display next set of lines.
+	Display next set of lines.
–	Display previous set of lines.
a	Mark all lines to be changed.
^d	Change the marked lines and exit.
ESCAPE	Exit without changing the marked lines.
!	Start an interactive shell (type ^d to return to **cscope**).
^l	Redraw the screen.
?	Give help information about **cscope** commands.

Special Keys

If your terminal has arrow keys that work in **vi**(1), you can use them to move around the input fields. The up-arrow key is useful to move to the previous input field instead of using the **TAB** key repeatedly. If you have **CLEAR**, **NEXT**, or **PREV** keys they will act as the ^l, +, and – commands, respectively.

Line-Oriented Interface

The −l option lets you use **cscope** where a screen-oriented interface would not be useful, for example, from another screen-oriented program.

cscope will prompt with >> when it is ready for an input line starting with the field number (counting from 0) immediately followed by the search pattern, for example, **lmain** finds the definition of the **main** function.

If you just want a single search, instead of the **-l** option use the **-L** and *-num pattern* options, and you won't get the >> prompt.

For **-l**, cscope outputs the number of reference lines

> cscope: 2 lines

For each reference found, cscope outputs a line consisting of the file name, function name, line number, and line text, separated by spaces, for example,

> main.c main 161 main(argc, argv)

Note that the editor is not called to display a single reference, unlike the screen-oriented interface.

You can use the **r** command to rebuild the database.

cscope will quit when it detects end-of-file, or when the first character of an input line is **^d** or **q**.

ENVIRONMENT VARIABLES

EDITOR	Preferred editor, which defaults to **vi**(1).
INCLUDEDIRS	Colon-separated list of directories to search for **#include** files.
HOME	Home directory, which is automatically set at login.
SHELL	Preferred shell, which defaults to **sh**(1).
SOURCEDIRS	Colon-separated list of directories to search for additional source files.
TERM	Terminal type, which must be a screen terminal.
TERMINFO	Terminal information directory full path name. If your terminal is not in the standard **terminfo** directory, see **curses**(3X) and **terminfo**(4) for how to make your own terminal description.
TMPDIR	Temporary file directory, which defaults to **/var/tmp**.
VIEWER	Preferred file display program [such as **pg**], which overrides **EDITOR** (see above).
VPATH	A colon-separated list of directories, each of which has the same directory structure below it. If **VPATH** is set, cscope searches for source files in the directories specified; if it is not set, cscope searches only in the current directory.

FILES

cscope.files	Default files containing **-I**, **-p**, and **-T** options and the list of source files (overridden by the **-i** option).
cscope.out	Symbol cross-reference file, which is put in the home directory if it cannot be created in the current directory.
ncscope.out	Temporary file containing new cross-reference before it replaces the old cross-reference.
INCDIR	Standard directory for **#include** files (usually **/usr/include**).

SEE ALSO

The "**cscope**" chapter in the *Programmer's Guide: ANSI C and Programming Support Tools*

curses and **terminfo** in the *Programmer's Guide: Character User Interface (FMLI and ETI)*

NOTES

cscope recognizes function definitions of the form:

fname blank (*args*) *white arg_decs white* {

where:

fname	is the function name
blank	is zero or more spaces or tabs, not including newlines
args	is any string that does not contain a " or a newline
white	is zero or more spaces, tabs, or newlines
arg_decs	are zero or more argument declarations (*arg_decs* may include comments and white space)

It is not necessary for a function declaration to start at the beginning of a line. The return type may precede the function name; **cscope** will still recognize the declaration. Function definitions that deviate from this form will not be recognized by **cscope**.

The **Function** column of the search output for the menu option **Find functions called by this function:** input field will only display the first function called in the line, that is, for this function

```
e()
{
     return (f() + g());
}
```

the display would be

```
Functions called by this function: e

File Function Line
a.c  f      3 return(f() + g());
```

Occasionally, a function definition or call may not be recognized because of braces inside **#if** statements. Similarly, the use of a variable may be incorrectly recognized as a definition.

A **typedef** name preceding a preprocessor statement will be incorrectly recognized as a global definition, for example,

```
LDFILE *
#if AR16WR
```

Preprocessor statements can also prevent the recognition of a global definition, for example,

```
char flag
#ifdef ALLOCATE_STORAGE
        = -1
#endif
;
```

A function declaration inside a function is incorrectly recognized as a function call, for example,

```
f()
{
        void g();
}
```

is incorrectly recognized as a call to **g()**.

cscope recognizes C++ classes by looking for the class keyword, but doesn't recognize that a **struct** is also a class, so it doesn't recognize inline member function definitions in a structure. It also doesn't expect the class keyword in a **typedef**, so it incorrectly recognizes **X** as a definition in

```
typedef class X * Y;
```

It also doesn't recognize operator function definitions

```
Bool Feature::operator==(const Feature & other)
{
        ...
}
```

NAME

csh – shell command interpreter with a C-like syntax

SYNOPSIS

csh [**–bcefinstvVxX**] [*argument* . . .]

DESCRIPTION

csh, the C shell, is a command interpreter with a syntax reminiscent of the C language. It provides a number of convenient features for interactive use that are not available with the standard (Bourne) shell, including filename completion, command aliasing, history substitution, job control, and a number of built-in commands. As with the standard shell, the C shell provides variable, command and filename substitution.

Initialization and Termination

When first started, the C shell normally performs commands from the **.cshrc** file in your home directory, provided that it is readable and you either own it or your real group ID matches its group ID. If the shell is invoked with a name that starts with '–', as when started by **login**(1), the shell runs as a **login** shell. In this case, after executing commands from the **.cshrc** file, the shell executes commands from the **.login** file in your home directory; the same permission checks as those for **.cshrc** are applied to this file. Typically, the **.login** file contains commands to specify the terminal type and environment.

As a login shell terminates, it performs commands from the **.logout** file in your home directory; the same permission checks as those for **.cshrc** are applied to this file.

Interactive Operation

After startup processing is complete, an interactive C shell begins reading commands from the terminal, prompting with *hostname*% (or *hostname*# for the privileged user). The shell then repeatedly performs the following actions: a line of command input is read and broken into *words*. This sequence of words is placed on the history list and then parsed, as described under USAGE, below. Finally, the shell executes each command in the current line.

Noninteractive Operation

When running noninteractively, the shell does not prompt for input from the terminal. A noninteractive C shell can execute a command supplied as an *argument* on its command line, or interpret commands from a script.

The following options are available:

–b   Force a break from option processing. Subsequent command-line arguments are not interpreted as C shell options. This allows the passing of options to a script without confusion. The shell does not run a set-user-ID script unless this option is present.

–c   Read commands from the first filename *argument* (which must be present). Remaining arguments are placed in **argv**, the argument-list variable.

–e   Exit if a command terminates abnormally or yields a nonzero exit status.

−f	Fast start. Read neither the `.cshrc` file, nor the `.login` file (if a login shell) upon startup.
−i	Forced interactive. Prompt for command-line input, even if the standard input does not appear to be a terminal (character-special device).
−n	Parse (interpret), but do not execute commands. This option can be used to check C shell scripts for syntax errors.
−s	Take commands from the standard input.
−t	Read and execute a single command line. A '\' (backslash) can be used to escape each newline for continuation of the command line onto subsequent input lines.
−v	Verbose. Set the **verbose** predefined variable; command input is echoed after history substitution (but before other substitutions) and before execution.
−V	Set **verbose** before reading `.cshrc`.
−x	Echo. Set the **echo** variable; echo commands after all substitutions and just before execution.
−X	Set **echo** before reading `.cshrc`.

Except with the options −c, −i, −s or −t, the first nonoption *argument* is taken to be the name of a command or script. It is passed as argument zero, and subsequent arguments are added to the argument list for that command or script.

USAGE

Filename Completion

When enabled by setting the variable `filec`, an interactive C shell can complete a partially typed filename or user name. When an unambiguous partial filename is followed by an ESC character on the terminal input line, the shell fills in the remaining characters of a matching filename from the working directory.

If a partial filename is followed by the EOF character (usually typed as CTRL-d), the shell lists all filenames that match. It then prompts once again, supplying the incomplete command line typed in so far.

When the last (partial) word begins with a tilde (~), the shell attempts completion with a user name, rather than a file in the working directory.

The terminal bell signals errors or multiple matches; this can be inhibited by setting the variable **nobeep**. You can exclude files with certain suffixes by listing those suffixes in the variable **fignore**. If, however, the only possible completion includes a suffix in the list, it is not ignored. **fignore** does not affect the listing of filenames by the EOF character.

Lexical Structure

The shell splits input lines into words at space and tab characters, except as noted below. The characters &, |, ;, <, >, (, and) form separate words; if paired, the pairs form single words. These shell metacharacters can be made part of other words, and their special meaning can be suppressed by preceding them with a '\' (backslash). A newline preceded by a \ is equivalent to a space character.

In addition, a string enclosed in matched pairs of single-quotes (´), double-quotes ("), or backquotes (` ), forms a partial word; metacharacters in such a string, including any space or tab characters, do not form separate words. Within pairs of backquote ( `) or double-quote (") characters, a newline preceded by a '\' (backslash) gives a true newline character. Additional functions of each type of quote are described, below, under **Variable Substitution**, **Command Substitution**, and **Filename Substitution**.

When the shell's input is not a terminal, the character # introduces a comment that continues to the end of the input line. Its special meaning is suppressed when preceded by a \ or enclosed in matching quotes.

Command Line Parsing

A *simple command* is composed of a sequence of words. The first word (that is not part of an I/O redirection) specifies the command to be executed. A simple command, or a set of simple commands separated by | or |& characters, forms a *pipeline*. With |, the standard output of the preceding command is redirected to the standard input of the command that follows. With |&, both the standard error and the standard output are redirected through the pipeline.

Pipelines can be separated by semicolons (;), in which case they are executed sequentially. Pipelines that are separated by && or || form conditional sequences in which the execution of pipelines on the right depends upon the success or failure, respectively, of the pipeline on the left.

A pipeline or sequence can be enclosed within parentheses '( )' to form a simple command that can be a component in a pipeline or sequence.

A sequence of pipelines can be executed asynchronously, or in the background by appending an '&'; rather than waiting for the sequence to finish before issuing a prompt, the shell displays the job number (see **Job Control**, below) and associated process IDs, and prompts immediately.

History Substitution

History substitution allows you to use words from previous command lines in the command line you are typing. This simplifies spelling corrections and the repetition of complicated commands or arguments. Command lines are saved in the history list, the size of which is controlled by the **history** variable. The most recent command is retained in any case. A history substitution begins with a ! (although you can change this with the **histchars** variable) and may occur anywhere on the command line; history substitutions do not nest. The ! can be escaped with \ to suppress its special meaning.

Input lines containing history substitutions are echoed on the terminal after being expanded, but before any other substitutions take place or the command gets executed.

Event Designators

An event designator is a reference to a command-line entry in the history list.

!   Start a history substitution, except when followed by a space character, tab, newline, = or (.

!!	Refer to the previous command. By itself, this substitution repeats the previous command.
!*n*	Refer to command-line *n* .
!-*n*	Refer to the current command-line minus *n*.
!str	Refer to the most recent command starting with **str**.
!?*str*[?]	Refer to the most recent command containing **str**.
!{...}	Insulate a history reference from adjacent characters (if necessary).

Word Designators

A ':' (colon) separates the event specification from the word designator. It can be omitted if the word designator begins with a ^, $, *, – or %. If the word is to be selected from the previous command, the second ! character can be omitted from the event specification. For instance, !!:1 and !:1 both refer to the first word of the previous command, while !!$ and !$ both refer to the last word in the previous command. Word designators include:

#	The entire command line typed so far.
0	The first input word (command).
n	The *n*'th argument.
^	The first argument, that is, **1**.
$	The last argument.
%	The word matched by (the most recent) ?*s* search.
x-*y*	A range of words; –*y* abbreviates 0–*y*.
*	All the arguments, or a null value if there is just one word in the event.
x★	Abbreviates *x*–$.
x–	Like *x*★ but omitting word $.

Modifiers

After the optional word designator, you can add a sequence of one or more of the following modifiers, each preceded by a :.

h	Remove a trailing pathname component, leaving the head.
r	Remove a trailing suffix of the form '.*xxx*', leaving the basename.
e	Remove all but the suffix.
s/*l*/*r*[/]	Substitute *r* for *l*.
t	Remove all leading pathname components, leaving the tail.
&	Repeat the previous substitution.
g	Apply the change to the first occurrence of a match in each word, by prefixing the above (for example, **g&**).
p	Print the new command but do not execute it.
q	Quote the substituted words, escaping further substitutions.
x	Like **q**, but break into words at each space character, tab or newline.

Unless preceded by a **g**, the modification is applied only to the first string that matches *l*; an error results if no string matches.

The left-hand side of substitutions are not regular expressions, but character strings. Any character can be used as the delimiter in place of /. A backslash quotes the delimiter character. The character &, in the right hand side, is replaced by the text from the left-hand-side. The & can be quoted with a backslash. A null *l* uses the previous string either from a *l* or from a contextual scan string *s* from !?*s*. You can omit the rightmost delimiter if a newline immediately follows *r*; the rightmost ? in a context scan can similarly be omitted.

Without an event specification, a history reference refers either to the previous command, or to a previous history reference on the command line (if any).

Quick Substitution
  ^*l*^*r*[^]   This is equivalent to the history substitution: `!:s^l^r[^]`.

Aliases

The C shell maintains a list of aliases that you can create, display, and modify using the **alias** and **unalias** commands. The shell checks the first word in each command to see if it matches the name of an existing alias. If it does, the command is reprocessed with the alias definition replacing its name; the history substitution mechanism is made available as though that command were the previous input line. This allows history substitutions, escaped with a backslash in the definition, to be replaced with actual command-line arguments when the alias is used. If no history substitution is called for, the arguments remain unchanged.

Aliases can be nested. That is, an alias definition can contain the name of another alias. Nested aliases are expanded before any history substitutions is applied. This is useful in pipelines such as

    `alias  lm  ´ls  -l  \!*  |  more´`

which when called, pipes the output of **ls**(1V) through **more**(1).

Except for the first word, the name of the alias may not appear in its definition, nor in any alias referred to by its definition. Such loops are detected, and cause an error message.

I/O Redirection

The following metacharacters indicate that the subsequent word is the name of a file to which the command's standard input, standard output, or standard error is redirected; this word is variable, command, and filename expanded separately from the rest of the command.

   <   Redirect the standard input.

   << *word*   Read the standard input, up to a line that is identical with *word*, and place the resulting lines in a temporary file. Unless *word* is escaped or quoted, variable and command substitutions are performed on these lines. Then, invoke the pipeline with the temporary file as its standard input. *word* is not subjected to variable, filename, or command substitution, and each line is compared to it before any substitutions are performed by the shell.

>   >!   >&   >&!

Redirect the standard output to a file. If the file does not exist, it is created. If it does exist, it is overwritten; its previous contents are lost.

When set, the variable **noclobber** prevents destruction of existing files. It also prevents redirection to terminals and **/dev/null**, unless one of the **!** forms is used. The **&** forms redirect both standard output and the the standard error (diagnostic output) to the file.

>>   >>&   >>!   >>&!

Append the standard output. Like **>**, but places output at the end of the file rather than overwriting it. If **noclobber** is set, it is an error for the file not to exist, unless one of the **!** forms is used. The **&** forms append both the standard error and standard output to the file.

Variable Substitution

The C shell maintains a set of *variables*, each of which is composed of a *name* and a *value*. A variable name consists of up to 20 letters and digits, and starts with a letter (the underscore is considered a letter). A variable's value is a space-separated list of zero or more words.

To refer to a variable's value, precede its name with a '**$**'. Certain references (described below) can be used to select specific words from the value, or to display other information about the variable. Braces can be used to insulate the reference from other characters in an input-line word.

Variable substitution takes place after the input line is analyzed, aliases are resolved, and I/O redirections are applied. Exceptions to this are variable references in I/O redirections (substituted at the time the redirection is made), and backquoted strings (see Command Substitution).

Variable substitution can be suppressed by preceding the **$** with a ****, except within double-quotes where it always occurs. Variable substitution is suppressed inside of single-quotes. A **$** is escaped if followed by a space character, tab or newline.

Variables can be created, displayed, or destroyed using the **set** and **unset** commands. Some variables are maintained or used by the shell. For instance, the **argv** variable contains an image of the shell's argument list. Of the variables used by the shell, a number are toggles; the shell does not care what their value is, only whether they are set or not.

Numerical values can be operated on as numbers (as with the **@** built-in). With numeric operations, an empty value is considered to be zero; the second and subsequent words of multiword values are ignored. For instance, when the **verbose** variable is set to any value (including an empty value), command input is echoed on the terminal.

Command and filename substitution is subsequently applied to the words that result from the variable substitution, except when suppressed by double-quotes, when **noglob** is set (suppressing filename substitution), or when the reference is quoted with the **:q** modifier. Within double-quotes, a reference is expanded to form (a portion of) a quoted string; multiword values are expanded to a string with embedded space characters. When the **:q** modifier is applied to the reference, it is expanded to a list of space-separated words, each of which is quoted to prevent subsequent command or filename substitutions.

Except as noted below, it is an error to refer to a variable that is not set.

$*var*
${*var*}　　　　　These are replaced by words from the value of *var*, each separated by a space character. If *var* is an environment variable, its value is returned (but ':' modifiers and the other forms given below are not available).

$*var*[*index*]
${*var*[*index*]}　These select only the indicated words from the value of *var*. Variable substitution is applied to *index*, which may consist of (or result in) a either single number, two numbers separated by a '–', or an asterisk. Words are indexed starting from 1; a '*' selects all words. If the first number of a range is omitted (as with **$argv[-2]**), it defaults to 1. If the last number of a range is omitted (as with **$argv[1-]**), it defaults to **$#***var* (the word count). It is not an error for a range to be empty if the second argument is omitted (or within range).

$#*name*
${#*name*}　　　　These give the number of words in the variable.

$0　　　　　　　　This substitutes the name of the file from which command input is being read. An error occurs if the name is not known.

$*n*
${*n*}　　　　　　Equivalent to **$argv[***n***]**.

$*　　　　　　　　Equivalent to **$argv[*]**.

The modifiers **:e**, **:h**, **:q**, **:r**, **:t** and **:x** can be applied (see **History Substitution**), as can **:gh**, **:gt** and **:gr**. If **{ }** (braces) are used, then the modifiers must appear within the braces. The current implementation allows only one such modifier per expansion.

The following references may not be modified with **:** modifiers.

$?*var*
${?*var*}　Substitutes the string 1 if *var* is set or 0 if it is not set.

$?0　　　Substitutes 1 if the current input filename is known, or 0 if it is not.

$$　　　　Substitute the process number of the (parent) shell.

$<　　　　Substitutes a line from the standard input, with no further interpretation thereafter. It can be used to read from the keyboard in a C shell script.

Command and Filename Substitutions

Command and filename substitutions are applied selectively to the arguments of built-in commands. Portions of expressions that are not evaluated are not expanded. For non-built-in commands, filename expansion of the command name is done separately from that of the argument list; expansion occurs in a subshell, after I/O redirection is performed.

Command Substitution

A command enclosed by backquotes (` ... `) is performed by a subshell. Its standard output is broken into separate words at each space character, tab and newline; null words are discarded. This text replaces the backquoted string on the current command line. Within double-quotes, only newline characters force new words; space and tab characters are preserved. However, a final newline is ignored. It is therefore possible for a command substitution to yield a partial word.

Filename Substitution

Unquoted words containing any of the characters *, ?, [or {, or that begin with ~, are expanded (also known as *globbing*) to an alphabetically sorted list of filenames, as follows:

*	Match any (zero or more) characters.
?	Match any single character.
[...]	Match any single character in the enclosed list(s) or range(s). A list is a string of characters. A range is two characters separated by a minus-sign (–), and includes all the characters in between in the ASCII collating sequence [see **ascii**(7)].
{ *str*, *str*, ... }	Expand to each string (or filename-matching pattern) in the comma-separated list. Unlike the pattern-matching expressions above, the expansion of this construct is not sorted. For instance, {b,a} expands to 'b' 'a', (not 'a' 'b'). As special cases, the characters { and }, along with the string { }, are passed undisturbed.
~[*user*]	Your home directory, as indicated by the value of the variable **home**, or that of *user*, as indicated by the password entry for *user*.

Only the patterns *, ? and [...] imply pattern matching; an error results if no filename matches a pattern that contains them. The '.' (dot character), when it is the first character in a filename or pathname component, must be matched explicitly. The / (slash) must also be matched explicitly.

Expressions and Operators

A number of C shell built-in commands accept expressions, in which the operators are similar to those of C and have the same precedence. These expressions typically appear in the **@**, **exit**, **if**, **set** and **while** commands, and are often used to regulate the flow of control for executing commands. Components of an expression are separated by white space.

Null or missing values are considered 0. The result of all expressions are strings, which may represent decimal numbers.

The following C shell operators are grouped in order of precedence:

(...)	grouping
~	one's complement
!	logical negation
* / %	multiplication, division, remainder (These are right associative, which can lead to unexpected results. Group combinations explicitly with parentheses.)
+ −	addition, subtraction (also right associative)
<< >>	bitwise shift left, bitwise shift right
< > <= >=	less than, greater than, less than or equal to, greater than or equal to
== != =~ !~	equal to, not equal to, filename-substitution pattern match (described below), filename-substitution pattern mismatch
&	bitwise AND
^	bitwise XOR (exclusive or)
|	bitwise inclusive OR
&&	logical AND
| |	logical OR

The operators: ==, !=, =~, and !~ compare their arguments as strings; other operators use numbers. The operators =~ and !~ each check whether or not a string to the left matches a filename substitution pattern on the right. This reduces the need for **switch** statements when pattern-matching between strings is all that is required.

Also available are file inquiries:

−**r** *filename*	Return true, or 1 if the user has read access. Otherwise it returns false, or 0.
−**w** *filename*	True if the user has write access.
−**x** *filename*	True if the user has execute permission (or search permission on a directory).
−**e** *filename*	True if *file* exists.
−**o** *filename*	True if the user owns *file*.
−**z** *filename*	True if *file* is of zero length (empty).
−**f** *filename*	True if *file* is a plain file.
−**d** *filename*	True if *file* is a directory.

If *file* does not exist or is inaccessible, then all inquiries return false.

An inquiry as to the success of a command is also available:

{ *command* } If *command* runs successfully, the expression evaluates to true, 1. Otherwise it evaluates to false 0. (Note that, conversely, *command* itself typically returns 0 when it runs successfully, or some other value if it encounters a problem. If you want to get at the status directly, use the value of the **status** variable rather than this expression).

Control Flow

The shell contains a number of commands to regulate the flow of control in scripts, and within limits, from the terminal. These commands operate by forcing the shell either to reread input (to *loop*), or to skip input under certain conditions (to *branch*).

Each occurrence of a **foreach, switch, while, if**...**then** and **else** built-in must appear as the first word on its own input line.

If the shell's input is not seekable and a loop is being read, that input is buffered. The shell performs seeks within the internal buffer to accomplish the rereading implied by the loop. (To the extent that this allows, backward **goto** commands will succeed on nonseekable inputs.)

Command Execution

If the command is a C shell built-in, the shell executes it directly. Otherwise, the shell searches for a file by that name with execute access. If the command-name contains a **/**, the shell takes it as a pathname, and searches for it. If the command-name does not contain a **/**, the shell attempts to resolve it to a pathname, searching each directory in the **path** variable for the command. To speed the search, the shell uses its hash table (see the **rehash** built-in) to eliminate directories that have no applicable files. This hashing can be disabled with the **–c** or **–t**, options, or the **unhash** built-in.

As a special case, if there is no **/** in the name of the script and there is an alias for the word **shell**, the expansion of the **shell** alias is prepended (without modification), to the command line. The system attempts to execute the first word of this special (late-occurring) alias, which should be a full pathname. Remaining words of the alias's definition, along with the text of the input line, are treated as arguments.

When a pathname is found that has proper execute permissions, the shell forks a new process and passes it, along with its arguments to the kernel (using the **execve**(2) system call). The kernel then attempts to overlay the new process with the desired program. If the file is an executable binary (in **a.out**(4) format) the kernel succeeds, and begins executing the new process. If the file is a text file, and the first line begins with **#!**, the next word is taken to be the pathname of a shell (or command) to interpret that script. Subsequent words on the first line are taken as options for that shell. The kernel invokes (overlays) the indicated shell, using the name of the script as an argument.

If neither of the above conditions holds, the kernel cannot overlay the file (the **execve**(2) call fails); the C shell then attempts to execute the file by spawning a new shell, as follows:

- If the first character of the file is a **#**, a C shell is invoked.

- Otherwise, a standard (Bourne) shell is invoked.

Signal Handling

The shell normally ignores QUIT signals. Background jobs are immune to signals generated from the keyboard, including hangups (HUP). Other signals have the values that the C shell inherited from its environment. The shell's handling of interrupt and terminate signals within scripts can be controlled by the **onintr** built-in. Login shells catch the TERM signal; otherwise this signal is passed on to child processes. In no case are interrupts allowed when a login shell is reading the `.logout` file.

Job Control

The shell associates a numbered *job* with each command sequence, to keep track of those commands that are running in the background or have been stopped with TSTP signals (typically CTRL-z). When a command, or command sequence (semicolon separated list), is started in the background using the `&` metacharacter, the shell displays a line with the job number in brackets, and a list of associated process numbers:

       [1] 1234

To see the current list of jobs, use the `jobs` built-in command. The job most recently stopped (or put into the background if none are stopped) is referred to as the *current* job, and is indicated with a '+'. The previous job is indicated with a '–'; when the current job is terminated or moved to the foreground, this job takes its place (becomes the new current job).

To manipulate jobs, refer to the `bg`, `fg`, `kill`, `stop` and `%` built-ins.

A reference to a job begins with a '%'. By itself, the percent-sign refers to the current job.

`%` `%+` `%%`	The current job.
`%–`	The previous job.
`%j`	Refer to job *j* as in: '`kill –9 %j`'. *j* can be a job number, or a string that uniquely specifies the command-line by which it was started; '`fg %vi`' might bring a stopped **vi** job to the foreground, for instance.
`%?`*string*	Specify the job for which the command-line uniquely contains *string*.

A job running in the background stops when it attempts to read from the terminal. Background jobs can normally produce output, but this can be suppressed using the '`stty tostop`' command.

Status Reporting

While running interactively, the shell tracks the status of each job and reports whenever a finishes or becomes blocked. It normally displays a message to this effect as it issues a prompt, so as to avoid disturbing the appearance of your input. When set, the `notify` variable indicates that the shell is to report status changes immediately. By default, the `notify` command marks the current process; after starting a background job, type `notify` to mark it.

Built-In Commands

Built-in commands are executed within the C shell. If a built-in command occurs as any component of a pipeline except the last, it is executed in a subshell.

:	Null command. This command is interpreted, but performs no action.

alias [*name* [*def*]]
> Assign *def* to the alias *name*. *def* is a list of words that may contain escaped history-substitution metasyntax. *name* is not allowed to be **alias** or **unalias**. If *def* is omitted, the alias *name* is displayed along with its current definition. If both *name* and *def* are omitted, all aliases are displayed.

bg [*%job*] ...
> Run the current or specified jobs in the background.

break Resume execution after the **end** of the nearest enclosing **foreach** or **while** loop. The remaining commands on the current line are executed. This allows multilevel breaks to be written as a list of **break** commands, all on one line.

breaksw Break from a **switch**, resuming after the **endsw**.

case *label*:
> A label in a **switch** statement.

cd [*dir*]
chdir [*dir*]
> Change the shell's working directory to directory *dir*. If no argument is given, change to the home directory of the user. If *dir* is a relative pathname not found in the current directory, check for it in those directories listed in the **cdpath** variable. If *dir* is the name of a shell variable whose value starts with a /, change to the directory named by that value.

continue Continue execution of the nearest enclosing **while** or **foreach**.

default: Labels the default case in a **switch** statement. The default should come after all **case** labels. Any remaining commands on the command line are first executed.

dirs [-1]
> Print the directory stack, most recent to the left; the first directory shown is the current directory. With the **-1** argument, produce an unabbreviated printout; use of the ~ notation is suppressed.

echo [-n] *list*
> The words in *list* are written to the shell's standard output, separated by space characters. The output is terminated with a newline unless the **-n** option is used.

eval *argument* ...
> Reads the arguments as input to the shell, and executes the resulting command(s). This is usually used to execute commands generated as the result of command or variable substitution, since parsing occurs before these substitutions. See **tset**(1) for an example of how to use **eval**.

exec *command*
> Execute *command* in place of the current shell, which terminates.

exit [*(expr)*]
:   The shell exits, either with the value of the STATUS variable, or with the value of the specified by the expression **expr**.

fg % [*job*]
:   Bring the current or specified *job* into the foreground.

foreach *var (wordlist)*

   . . .

end
:   The variable *var* is successively set to each member of *wordlist*. The sequence of commands between this command and the matching **end** is executed for each new value of *var*. (Both **foreach** and **end** must appear alone on separate lines.)

    The built-in command **continue** may be used to continue the loop prematurely and the built-in command **break** to terminate it prematurely. When this command is read from the terminal, the loop is read up once prompting with **?** before any statements in the loop are executed.

glob *wordlist*
:   Perform filename expansion on *wordlist*. Like **echo**, but no \ escapes are recognized. Words are delimited by **NULL** characters in the output.

goto *label*
:   The specified *label* is filename and command expanded to yield a label. The shell rewinds its input as much as possible and searches for a line of the form *label*: possibly preceded by space or tab characters. Execution continues after the indicated line. It is an error to jump to a label that occurs between a **while** or **for** built-in, and its corresponding **end**.

hashstat
:   Print a statistics line indicating how effective the internal hash table has been at locating commands (and avoiding **exec**s). An **exec** is attempted for each component of the *path* where the hash function indicates a possible hit, and in each component that does not begin with a '/'.

history [**-hr**] [*n*]
:   Display the history list; if *n* is given, display only the *n* most recent events.

    -r   Reverse the order of printout to be most recent first rather than oldest first.

    -h   Display the history list without leading numbers. This is used to produce files suitable for sourcing using the **-h** option to *source*.

if *(expr) command*
:   If the specified expression evaluates to true, the single *command* with arguments is executed. Variable substitution on *command* happens early, at the same time it does for the rest of the *if* command. *command* must be a simple command, not a pipeline, a command list, or a parenthesized command list. Note: I/O redirection occurs even if **expr** is false, when *command* is *not* executed (this is a bug).

if (*expr*) **then**

...

else if (*expr2*) **then**

...

else

...

endif   If **expr**"" is true, commands up to the first **else** are executed. Otherwise, if *expr2* is true, the commands between the **else if** and the second **else** are executed. Otherwise, commands between the **else** and the **endif** are executed. Any number of **else if** pairs are allowed, but only one **else**. Only one **endif** is needed, but it is required. The words **else** and **endif** must be the first nonwhite characters on a line. The **if** must appear alone on its input line or after an **else**.)

jobs[**-1**]

List the active jobs under job control.

     -1   List process IDs, in addition to the normal information.

kill [*-sig*] [*pid*] [*%job*] ...

kill -1   Send the TERM (terminate) signal, by default, or the signal specified, to the specified process ID, the *job* indicated, or the current *job*. Signals are either given by number or by name. There is no default. Typing **kill** does not send a signal to the current job. If the signal being sent is TERM (terminate) or HUP (hangup), then the job or process is sent a CONT (continue) signal as well.

     -1   List the signal names that can be sent.

limit [**-h**] [*resource* [*max-use*]]

Limit the consumption by the current process or any process it spawns, each not to exceed *max-use* on the specified *resource*. If *max-use* is omitted, print the current limit; if *resource* is omitted, display all limits.

     -h   Use hard limits instead of the current limits. Hard limits impose a ceiling on the values of the current limits. Only the privileged user may raise the hard limits.

resource is one of:

cputime	Maximum CPU seconds per process.
filesize	Largest single file allowed.
datasize	Maximum data size (including stack) for the process.
stacksize	Maximum stack size for the process.
coredumpsize	Maximum size of a core dump (file).

max-use is a number, with an optional scaling factor, as follows:

nh	Hours (for **cputime**).
nk	n kilobytes. This is the default for all but **cputime**.
nm	n megabytes or minutes (for **cputime**).
mm:ss	Minutes and seconds (for **cputime**).

login [*username* | **-p**]

Terminate a login shell and invoke **login**(1). The **.logout** file is not processed. If *username* is omitted, **login** prompts for the name of a user.

-p   Preserve the current environment (variables).

logout   Terminate a login shell.

nice [**+***n* | **−***n*] [*command*]

Increment the process priority value for the shell or for *command* by n. The higher the priority value, the lower the priority of a process, and the slower it runs. When given, *command* is always run in a subshell, and the restrictions placed on commands in simple **if** commands apply. If *command* is omitted, **nice** increments the value for the current shell. If no increment is specified, **nice** sets the process priority value to 4. The range of process priority values is from −20 to 20. Values of n outside this range set the value to the lower, or to the higher boundary, respectively.

+*n*   Increment the process priority value by n.

−*n*   Decrement by n. This argument can be used only by the privileged user.

nohup [*command*]

Run *command* with HUPs ignored. With no arguments, ignore HUPs throughout the remainder of a script. When given, *command* is always run in a subshell, and the restrictions placed on commands in simple **if** commands apply. All processes detached with **&** are effectively **nohup**'d.

notify [**%***job*] . . .

Notify the user asynchronously when the status of the current, or of specified jobs, changes.

onintr [**−** | *label*]

Control the action of the shell on interrupts. With no arguments, **onintr** restores the default action of the shell on interrupts. (The shell terminates shell scripts and returns to the terminal command input level). With the **−** argument, the shell ignores all interrupts. With a *label* argument, the shell executes a **goto** *label* when an interrupt is received or a child process terminates because it was interrupted.

popd [**+***n*] Pop the directory stack, and **cd** to the new top directory. The elements of the directory stack are numbered from 0 starting at the top.

+*n*   Discard the n'th entry in the stack.

pushd [+*n* | *dir*]
> Push a directory onto the directory stack. With no arguments, exchange the top two elements.
>
> +*n*   Rotate the *n*'th entry to the top of the stack and **cd** to it.
>
> *dir*   Push the current working directory onto the stack and change to *dir*.

rehash   Recompute the internal hash table of the contents of directories listed in the *path* variable to account for new commands added.

repeat *count command*
> Repeat *command count* times. *command* is subject to the same restrictions as with the one-line **if** statement.

set [*var* [= *value*]]
set *var* [*n*] = *word*
> With no arguments, **set** displays the values of all shell variables. Multiword values are displayed as a parenthesized list. With the *var* argument alone, **set** assigns an empty (null) value to the variable *var*. With arguments of the form *var* = *value* **set** assigns *value* to *var*, where *value* is one of:
>
> > *word*   A single word (or quoted string).
> >
> > (*wordlist*)   A space-separated list of words enclosed in parentheses.
>
> Values are command and filename expanded before being assigned. The form **set** *var* [*n*] = *word* replaces the *n*'th word in a multiword value with *word*.

setenv [*VAR* [*word*]]
> With no arguments, **setenv** displays all environment variables. With the *VAR* argument sets the environment variable *VAR* to have an empty (null) value. (By convention, environment variables are normally given upper-case names.) With both *VAR* and *word* arguments **setenv** sets the environment variable **NAME** to the value *word*, which must be either a single word or a quoted string. The most commonly used environment variables, **USER**, **TERM**, and **PATH**, are automatically imported to and exported from the **csh** variables **user**, **term**, and **path**; there is no need to use **setenv** for these. In addition, the shell sets the **PWD** environment variable from the **csh** variable **cwd** whenever the latter changes.

shift [*variable*]
> The components of **argv**, or *variable*, if supplied, are shifted to the left, discarding the first component. It is an error for the variable not to be set, or to have a null value.

source [**-h**] *name*

Reads commands from *name*. **source** commands may be nested, but if they are nested too deeply the shell may run out of file descriptors. An error in a sourced file at any level terminates all nested **source** commands.

-h   Place commands from the the file *name* on the history list without executing them.

stop [*%job*] ...

Stop the current or specified background job.

suspend   Stop the shell in its tracks, much as if it had been sent a stop signal with **^Z**. This is most often used to stop shells started by **su**.

switch (*string*)
case *label*:
...
breaksw
...
default:
...
breaksw
endsw   Each *label* is successively matched, against the specified *string*, which is first command and filename expanded. The file metacharacters *****, **?** and **[...]** may be used in the case labels, which are variable expanded. If none of the labels match before a default label is found, execution begins after the default label. Each **case** statement and the **default** statement must appear at the beginning of a line. The command **breaksw** continues execution after the **endsw**. Otherwise control falls through subsequent **case** and **default** statements as with C. If no label matches and there is no default, execution continues after the **endsw**.

time [*command*]

With no argument, print a summary of time used by this C shell and its children. With an optional *command*, execute *command* and print a summary of the time it uses.

umask [*value*]

Display the file creation mask. With *value* set the file creation mask. *value* is given in octal, and is XORed with the permissions of 666 for files and 777 for directories to arrive at the permissions for new files. Common values include 002, giving complete access to the group, and read (and directory search) access to others, or 022, giving read (and directory search) but not write permission to the group and others.

unalias *pattern*

Discard aliases that match (filename substitution) *pattern*. All aliases are removed by **unalias ***.

unhash   Disable the internal hash table.

unlimit [**-h**] [*resource*]

Remove a limitation on *resource*. If no *resource* is specified, then all *resource* limitations are removed. See the description of the **limit** command for the list of *resource* names.

-h   Remove corresponding hard limits. Only the privileged user may do this.

unset *pattern*

Remove variables whose names match (filename substitution) *pattern*. All variables are removed by 'unset *'; this has noticeably distasteful side-effects.

unsetenv *variable*

Remove *variable* from the environment. Pattern matching, as with **unset** is not performed.

wait   Wait for background jobs to finish (or for an interrupt) before prompting.

while (*expr*)

...

end   While **expr** is true (evaluates to non-zero), repeat commands between the **while** and the matching **end** statement. **break** and **continue** may be used to terminate or continue the loop prematurely. The **while** and **end** must appear alone on their input lines. If the shell's input is a terminal, it prompts for commands with a question-mark until the **end** command is entered and then performs the commands in the loop.

% [*job*] [**&**]

Bring the current or indicated *job* to the foreground. With the ampersand, continue running *job* in the background.

@ [*var* =**expr**]

@ [*var* [*n*] =**expr**]

With no arguments, display the values for all shell variables. With arguments, the variable *var*, or the *n*'th word in the value of *var* , to the value that **expr** evaluates to. (If [*n*] is supplied, both *var* and its *n*'th component must already exist.)

If the expression contains the characters **>**, **<**, **&** or **|**, then at least this part of **expr** must be placed within parentheses.

The operators ***=**, **+=**, etc., are available as in C. The space separating the name from the assignment operator is optional. Spaces are, however, mandatory in separating components of **expr** that would otherwise be single words.

Special postfix operators, **++** and **--** increment or decrement *name*, respectively.

Environment Variables and Predefined Shell Variables

Unlike the standard shell, the C shell maintains a distinction between environment variables, which are automatically exported to processes it invokes, and shell variables, which are not. Both types of variables are treated similarly under variable substitution. The shell sets the variables **argv**, **cwd**, **home**, **path**, **prompt**, **shell**, and **status** upon initialization. The shell copies the environment variable **USER** into the shell variable **user**, **TERM** into **term**, and **HOME** into **home**, and copies each back into the respective environment variable whenever the shell variables are reset. **PATH** and **path** are similarly handled. You need only set **path** once in the **.cshrc** or **.login** file. The environment variable **PWD** is set from **cwd** whenever the latter changes. The following shell variables have predefined meanings:

argv	Argument list. Contains the list of command line arguments supplied to the current invocation of the shell. This variable determines the value of the positional parameters $1, $2, and so on.
cdpath	Contains a list of directories to be searched by the **cd**, **chdir**, and **popd** commands, if the directory argument each accepts is not a subdirectory of the current directory.
cwd	The full pathname of the current directory.
echo	Echo commands (after substitutions), just before execution.
fignore	A list of filename suffixes to ignore when attempting filename completion. Typically the single word '.o'.
filec	Enable filename completion, in which case the CTRL-d character CTRL-d) and the ESC character have special significance when typed in at the end of a terminal input line:

                    EOT   Print a list of all filenames that start with the preceding string.

                    ESC   Replace the preceding string with the longest unambiguous extension.

hardpaths	If set, pathnames in the directory stack are resolved to contain no symbolic-link components.
histchars	A two-character string. The first character replaces ! as the history-substitution character. The second replaces the carat (^) for quick substitutions.
history	The number of lines saved in the history list. A very large number may use up all of the C shell's memory. If not set, the C shell saves only the most recent command.
home	The user's home directory. The filename expansion of ~ refers to the value of this variable.
ignoreeof	If set, the shell ignores EOF from terminals. This protects against accidentally killing a C shell by typing a CTRL-d.
mail	A list of files where the C shell checks for mail. If the first word of the value is a number, it specifies a mail checking interval in seconds (default 5 minutes).

nobeep
Suppress the bell during command completion when asking the C shell to extend an ambiguous filename.

noclobber
Restrict output redirection so that existing files are not destroyed by accident. **>** redirections can only be made to new files. **>>** redirections can only be made to existing files.

noglob
Inhibit filename substitution. This is most useful in shell scripts once filenames (if any) are obtained and no further expansion is desired.

nonomatch
Returns the filename substitution pattern, rather than an error, if the pattern is not matched. Malformed patterns still result in errors.

notify
If set, the shell notifies you immediately as jobs are completed, rather than waiting until just before issuing a prompt.

path
The list of directories in which to search for commands. **path** is initialized from the environment variable **PATH**, which the C shell updates whenever **path** changes. A null word specifies the current directory. The default is typically: (. **/usr/ucb /usr/bin**). If **path** becomes unset only full pathnames will execute. An interactive C shell will normally hash the contents of the directories listed after reading .cshrc, and whenever **path** is reset. If new commands are added, use the **rehash** command to update the table.

prompt
The string an interactive C shell prompts with. Noninteractive shells leave the **prompt** variable unset. Aliases and other commands in the .cshrc file that are only useful interactively, can be placed after the following test: 'if ($?prompt == 0) exit', to reduce startup time for noninteractive shells. A **!** in the **prompt** string is replaced by the current event number. The default prompt is *hostname*% for mere mortals, or *hostname*# for the privileged user.

savehist
The number of lines from the history list that are saved in ~/.history when the user logs out. Large values for **savehist** slow down the C shell during startup.

shell
The file in which the C shell resides. This is used in forking shells to interpret files that have execute bits set, but that are not executable by the system.

status
The status returned by the most recent command. If that command terminated abnormally, 0200 is added to the status. Built-in commands that fail return exit status 1, all other built-in commands set status to 0.

time
Control automatic timing of commands. Can be supplied with one or two values. The first is the reporting threshold in CPU seconds. The second is a string of tags and text indicating which resources to report on. A tag is a percent sign (**%**) followed by a single *upper-case* letter (unrecognized tags print as text):

%D   Average amount of unshared data space used in
        Kilobytes.
%E   Elapsed (wallclock) time for the command.
%F   Page faults.
%I   Number of block input operations.
%K   Average amount of unshared stack space used in
        Kilobytes.
%M   Maximum real memory used during execution of
        the process.
%O   Number of block output operations.
%P   Total CPU time — U (user) plus S (system) — as a
        percentage of E (elapsed) time.
%S   Number of seconds of CPU time consumed by the
        kernel on behalf of the user's process.
%U   Number of seconds of CPU time devoted to the
        user's process.
%W   Number of swaps.
%X   Average amount of shared memory used in Kilo-
        bytes.

The default summary display outputs from the %U, %S, %E, %P, %X,
%D, %I, %O, %F and %W tags, in that order.

verbose   Display each command after history substitution takes place.

FILES

~/.cshrc   Read at beginning of execution by each shell.
~/.login   Read by login shells after .cshrc at login.
~/.logout   Read by login shells at logout.
~/.history   Saved history for use at next login.
/usr/bin/sh   Standard shell, for shell scripts not starting with a '#'.
/tmp/sh*   Temporary file for '<<'.
/etc/passwd   Source of home directories for '~name'.

SEE ALSO

login(1), sh(1)
access(2), exec(2), fork(2), pipe(2) in the *Programmer's Reference Manual*
a.out(4), environ(4), termio(4), ascii(5) in the *System Administrator's Reference Manual*

DIAGNOSTICS

You have stopped jobs.
        You attempted to exit the C shell with stopped jobs under job control. An
        immediate second attempt to exit will succeed, terminating the stopped
        jobs.

NOTES

Words can be no longer than 1024 characters. The system limits argument lists to
1,048,576 characters. However, the maximum number of arguments to a command for which filename expansion applies is 1706. Command substitutions may
expand to no more characters than are allowed in the argument list. To detect
looping, the shell restricts the number of **alias** substitutions on a single line to
20.

When a command is restarted from a stop, the shell prints the directory it started in if this is different from the current directory; this can be misleading (that is, wrong) as the job may have changed directories internally.

Shell built-in functions are not stoppable/restartable. Command sequences of the form *a* ; *b* ; *c* are also not handled gracefully when stopping is attempted. If you suspend *b*, the shell never executes *c*. This is especially noticeable if the expansion results from an alias. It can be avoided by placing the sequence in parentheses to force it into a subshell.

Control over terminal output after processes are started is primitive; use the Sun Window system if you need better output control.

Multiline shell procedures should be provided, as they are with the standard (Bourne) shell.

Commands within loops, prompted for by ?, are not placed in the *history* list.

Control structures should be parsed rather than being recognized as built-in commands. This would allow control commands to be placed anywhere, to be combined with |, and to be used with & and ; metasyntax.

It should be possible to use the : modifiers on the output of command substitutions. There are two problems with : modifier usage on variable substitutions: not all of the modifiers are available, and only one modifier per substitution is allowed.

The **g** (global) flag in history substitutions applies only to the first match in each word, rather than all matches in all words. The the standard text editors consistently do the latter when given the **g** flag in a substitution command.

Quoting conventions are confusing. Overriding the escape character to force variable substitutions within double quotes is counterintuitive and inconsistent with the Bourne shell.

Symbolic links can fool the shell. Setting the **hardpaths** variable alleviates this.

'**set path**' should remove duplicate pathnames from the pathname list. These often occur because a shell script or a **.cshrc** file does something like '**set path=(/usr/local /usr/hosts $path)**' to ensure that the named directories are in the pathname list.

The only way to direct the standard output and standard error separately is by invoking a subshell, as follows:

      example% (*command* > *outfile*) >& *errorfile*

Although robust enough for general use, adventures into the esoteric periphery of the C shell may reveal unexpected quirks.

NAME
csplit – context split

SYNOPSIS
csplit [–s] [–k] [–f *prefix*] *file arg1* [... *argn*]

DESCRIPTION
csplit reads *file* and separates it into *n*+1 sections, defined by the arguments *arg1* ... *argn*. By default the sections are placed in **xx**00 ... **xx***n* (*n* may not be greater than 99). These sections get the following pieces of *file*:

00:    From the start of *file* up to (but not including) the line referenced by *arg1*.

01:    From the line referenced by *arg1* up to the line referenced by *arg2*.
       :
       :

n: From the line referenced by *argn* to the end of *file*.

If the *file* argument is a –, then standard input is used.

The options to csplit are:

–s   csplit normally prints the character counts for each file created. If the –s option is present, csplit suppresses the printing of all character counts.

–k   csplit normally removes created files if an error occurs. If the –k option is present, csplit leaves previously created files intact.

–f *prefix*   If the –f option is used, the created files are named *prefix*00 . . . *prefixn*. **The default is xx00 ... xx***n*.

The arguments (*arg1* ... *argn*) to csplit can be a combination of the following:

/*rexp*/   A file is to be created for the section from the current line up to (but not including) the line containing the regular expression *rexp*. The current line becomes the line containing *rexp*. This argument may be followed by an optional + or – some number of lines (e.g., **/Page/–5**). See **ed**(1) for a description of how to specify a regular expression.

%*rexp*%   This argument is the same as /*rexp*/, except that no file is created for the section.

lnno   A file is to be created from the current line up to (but not including) *lnno*. The current line becomes *lnno*.

{*num*}   Repeat argument. This argument may follow any of the above arguments. If it follows a *rexp* type argument, that argument is applied *num* more times. If it follows *lnno*, the file will be split every *lnno* lines (*num* times) from that point.

Enclose all *rexp* type arguments that contain blanks or other characters meaningful to the shell in the appropriate quotes. Regular expressions may not contain embedded new-lines. csplit does not affect the original file; it is the user's responsibility to remove it if it is no longer wanted.

EXAMPLES

```
csplit -f cobol file '/procedure division/' /par5./ /par16./
```

This example creates four files, **cobol00...cobol03**. After editing the "split" files, they can be recombined as follows:

```
cat cobol0[0-3] > file
```

Note that this example overwrites the original file.

```
csplit -k file 100 {99}
```

This example splits the file at every 100 lines, up to 10,000 lines. The **-k** option causes the created files to be retained if there are less than 10,000 lines; however, an error message would still be printed.

```
csplit -k prog.c '%main(%´ '/^}/+1' {20}
```

If **prog.c** follows the normal C coding convention (the last line of a routine consists only of a } in the first character position), this example creates a file for each separate C routine (up to 21) in **prog.c**.

SEE ALSO

ed(1), **sh**(1).

DIAGNOSTICS

Self-explanatory except for:

arg - **out of range**

which means that the given argument did not reference a line between the current position and the end of the file.

NAME

ct – spawn login to a remote terminal

SYNOPSIS

ct [*options*] *telno* . . .

DESCRIPTION

ct dials the telephone number of a modem that is attached to a terminal and spawns a **login** process to that terminal. *Telno* is a telephone number, with equal signs for secondary dial tones and minus signs for delays at appropriate places. (The set of legal characters for *telno* is **0** through **9**, **-**, **=**, **∗∗**, and **#**. The maximum length of *telno* is 31 characters). If more than one telephone number is specified, ct tries each in succession until one answers; this is useful for specifying alternate dialing paths.

ct tries each line listed in the file **/etc/uucp/Devices** until it finds an available line with appropriate attributes, or runs out of entries. ct uses the following options:

-h	Normally, ct hangs up the current line so it can be used to answer the incoming call. The **-h** option prevents this action. The **-h** option also waits for the termination of the specified ct process before returning control to the user's terminal.
-s *speed*	The data rate may be set with the **-s** option. *speed* is expressed in baud rates. The default baud rate is 1200.
-v	If the **-v** (verbose) option is used, ct sends a running narrative to the standard error output stream.
-w *n*	If there are no free lines ct asks if it should wait for one, and if so, for how many minutes it should wait before it gives up. ct continues to try to open the dialers at one-minute intervals until the specified limit is exceeded. This dialogue may be overridden by specifying the **-w** *n* option where *n* is the maximum number of minutes that ct is to wait for a line.
-x*n*	This option is used for debugging; it produces a detailed output of the program execution on standard error. *n* is a single number between **0** and **9**. As *n* increases to **9**, more detailed debugging information is given.

After the user on the destination terminal logs out, there are two things that could occur, depending on what type of port monitor is monitoring the port. In the case of no port monitor, ct prompts: **Reconnect?** If the response begins with the letter **n**, the line is dropped; otherwise, **ttymon** is started again and the **login:** prompt is printed. In the second case, where a port monitor is monitoring the port, the port monitor reissues the **login:** prompt.

The user should log out properly before disconnecting.

FILES

/etc/uucp/Devices
/var/adm/ctlog

SEE ALSO

cu(1C), login(1), uucp(1C)

ttymon(1M) in the *System Administrator's Reference Manual*

NOTES

The ct program will not work with a DATAKIT Multiplex interface.

For a shared port, one used for both dial-in and dial-out, the ttymon program running on the line must have the −r and −b options specified [see ttymon(1M)].

NAME

ctags – create a tags file for use with **vi**

SYNOPSIS

ctags [**–aBFtuvwx**] [**–f** *tagsfile*] *filename* . . .

DESCRIPTION

ctags makes a tags file for **ex**(1) from the specified C, Pascal, FORTRAN, YACC, and LEX sources. A tags file gives the locations of specified objects (in this case functions and typedefs) in a group of files. Each line of the tags file contains the object name, the file in which it is defined, and an address specification for the object definition. Functions are searched with a pattern, typedefs with a line number. Specifiers are given in separate fields on the line, separated by SPACE or TAB characters. Using the tags file, **ex** can quickly find these objects definitions.

Normally **ctags** places the tag descriptions in a file called **tags**; this may be overridden with the **–f** option.

Files with names ending in **.c** or **.h** are assumed to be C source files and are searched for C routine and macro definitions. Files with names ending in **.y** are assumed to be YACC source files. Files with names ending in **.l** are assumed to be LEX files. Others are first examined to see if they contain any Pascal or FORTRAN routine definitions; if not, they are processed again looking for C definitions.

The tag **main** is treated specially in C programs. The tag formed is created by prepending **M** to *filename*, with a trailing **.c** removed, if any, and leading pathname components also removed. This makes use of **ctags** practical in directories with more than one program.

The following options are available:

–a   Append output to an existing **tags** file.

–B   Use backward searching patterns (?...?).

–F   Use forward searching patterns (/.../) (default).

–t   Create tags for typedefs.

–u   Update the specified files in tags, that is, all references to them are deleted, and the new values are appended to the file. Beware: this option is implemented in a way which is rather slow; it is usually faster to simply rebuild the **tags** file.

–v   Produce on the standard output an index listing the function name, file name, and page number (assuming 64 line pages). Since the output will be sorted into lexicographic order, it may be desired to run the output through **sort –f**.

–w   Suppress warning diagnostics.

–x   Produce a list of object names, the line number and file name on which each is defined, as well as the text of that line and prints this on the standard output. This is a simple index which can be printed out as an off-line readable function index.

FILES

    tags   output tags file

USAGE

The **−v** option is mainly used with **vgrind** which will be part of the optional BSD Compatibility Package.

SEE ALSO

ex(1), **vgrind**(1), **vi**(1)

NOTES

Recognition of **functions, subroutines** and **procedures** for FORTRAN and Pascal is done is a very simpleminded way. No attempt is made to deal with block structure; if you have two Pascal procedures in different blocks with the same name you lose.

The method of deciding whether to look for C or Pascal and FORTRAN functions is a hack.

ctags does not know about **#ifdefs**.

ctags should know about Pascal types. Relies on the input being well formed to detect typedefs. Use of **−tx** shows only the last line of typedefs.

NAME

ctrace – C program debugger

SYNOPSIS

ctrace [*options*] [*file*]

DESCRIPTION

The **ctrace** command allows the user to monitor the sequential execution of a C
program as each program statement executes. The effect is similar to executing a
shell procedure with the **–x** option. **ctrace** reads the C program in *file* (or from
standard input if the user does not specify *file*), inserts statements to print the text
of each executable statement and the values of all variables referenced or
modified, and writes the modified program to the standard output. The output
of **ctrace** must be placed into a temporary file because the **cc**(1) command does
not allow the use of a pipe. This file can then be compiled and executed.

As each statement in the program executes, it will be listed at the terminal, followed by the name and value of any variables referenced or modified in the
statement; these variable names and values will be followed by any output from
the statement. Loops in the trace output are detected and tracing is stopped until
the loop is exited or a different sequence of statements within the loop is executed. A warning message is printed after each 1000 loop cycles to help the user
detect infinite loops. The trace output goes to the standard output so the user
can put it into a file for examination with an editor or the **bfs**(1) or **tail**(1) commands.

The options commonly used are:

–f *functions*   Trace only these *functions.*
–v *functions*   Trace all but these *functions.*

The user may want to add to the default formats for printing variables. Long
and pointer variables are always printed as signed integers. Pointers to character
arrays are also printed as strings if appropriate. **char**, **short**, and **int** variables
are also printed as signed integers and, if appropriate, as characters. **double**
variables are printed as floating point numbers in scientific notation. The user
can request that variables be printed in additional formats, if appropriate, with
these options:

–o   Octal
–x   Hexadecimal
–u   Unsigned
–e   Floating point

These options are used only in special circumstances:

–l *n*   Check *n* consecutively executed statements for looping trace output,
instead of the default of 20. Use 0 to get all the trace output from loops.
–s   Suppress redundant trace output from simple assignment statements and
string copy function calls. This option can hide a bug caused by use of
the = operator in place of the == operator.
–t *n*   Trace *n* variables per statement instead of the default of 10 (the maximum
number is 20). The diagnostics section explains when to use this option.

-P　　Preprocess the input before tracing it. The user can also use the −D, −I,
　　　and −U cc(1) options.

−p *string*

　　　Change the trace print function from the default of **printf**. For example,
　　　fprintf(stderr, would send the trace to the standard error output.

−r *f*　Use file *f* in place of the **runtime.c** trace function package. This replace-
　　　ment lets the user change the entire print function, instead of just the
　　　name and leading arguments (see the −p option).

−V　　Prints version information on the standard error.

−Q*arg*　If *arg* is **y**, identification information about **ctrace** will be added to the
　　　output files. This can be useful for software administration. Giving **n** for
　　　arg explicitly asks for no such information, which is the default behavior.

EXAMPLE

If the file **lc.c** contains this C program:

```
 1 #include <stdio.h>
 2 main()  /* count lines in input */
 3 {
 4    int c, nl;
 5
 6    nl = 0;
 7    while ((c = getchar()) != EOF)
 8          if (c = '\n')
 9                ++nl;
10    printf("%d\n", nl);
11 }
```

these commands and test data are entered:

```
cc lc.c
a.out
1
(cntl-d)
```

the program will be compiled and executed. The output of the program will be
the number **2**, which is incorrect because there is only one line in the test data.
The error in this program is common, but subtle. If the user invokes **ctrace**
with these commands:

```
ctrace lc.c >temp.c
cc temp.c
a.out
```

the output will be:

```
 2 main()
 6    nl = 0;
      /* nl == 0 */
 7    while ((c = getchar()) != EOF)
```

The program is now waiting for input. If the user enters the same test data as before, the output will be:

```
        /* c == 49 or '1' */
   8        if (c = '\n')
        /* c == 10 or '\n' */
   9            ++nl;
            /* nl == 1 */
   7    while ((c = getchar()) != EOF)
        /* c == 10 or '\n' */
   8        if (c = '\n')
        /* c == 10 or '\n' */
   9            ++nl;
            /* nl == 2 */
   7    while ((c = getchar()) != EOF)
```

If an end-of-file character (cntl-d) is entered, the final output will be:

```
        /* c == -1 */
  10    printf("%d\n", nl);
        /* nl == 2 */2
        return
```

Note the information printed out at the end of the trace line for the **nl** variable following line 10. Also note the **return** comment added by **ctrace** at the end of the trace output. This shows the implicit return at the terminating brace in the function.

The trace output shows that variable **c** is assigned the value '**1**' in line 7, but in line 8 it has the value '**\n**'. Once user attention is drawn to this **if** statement, he or she will probably realize that the assignment operator (**=**) was used in place of the equality operator (**==**). This error can easily be missed during code reading.

EXECUTION-TIME TRACE CONTROL

The default operation for **ctrace** is to trace the entire program file, unless the **–f** or **–v** options are used to trace specific functions. The default operation does not give the user statement-by-statement control of the tracing, nor does it let the user turn the tracing off and on when executing the traced program.

The user can do both of these by adding **ctroff**() and **ctron**() function calls to the program to turn the tracing off and on, respectively, at execution time. Thus, complex criteria can be arbitrarily coded for trace control with **if** statements, and this code can even be conditionally included because **ctrace** defines the **CTRACE** preprocessor variable. For example:

```
#ifdef CTRACE
        if (c == '!' && i > 1000)
                ctron();
#endif
```

These functions can also be called from **sdb**(1) if they are compiled with the **–g** option. For example, to trace all but lines 7 to 10 in the main function, enter:

```
sdb a.out
main:7b ctroff()
main:11b ctron()
r
```

The trace can be turned off and on by setting static variable tr_ct_ to 0 and 1, respectively. This on/off option is useful if a user is using a debugger that can not call these functions directly.

FILES

/usr/ccs/lib/ctrace/runtime.c   run-time trace package

SEE ALSO

sdb(1), ctype(3C), fclose(3S), printf(3S), string(3C)
bfs(1), tail(1) in the *User's Reference Manual*

DIAGNOSTICS

This section contains diagnostic messages from both **ctrace** and **cc**(1), since the traced code often gets some cc warning messages. The user can get cc error messages in some rare cases, all of which can be avoided.

ctrace Diagnostics

warning: some variables are not traced in this statement

> Only 10 variables are traced in a statement to prevent the C compiler "out of tree space; simplify expression" error. Use the −t option to increase this number.

warning: statement too long to trace

> This statement is over 400 characters long. Make sure that tabs are used to indent the code, not spaces.

cannot handle preprocessor code, use −P option

> This is usually caused by #ifdef/#endif preprocessor statements in the middle of a C statement, or by a semicolon at the end of a #define preprocessor statement.

'if ... else if' sequence too long

> Split the sequence by removing an else from the middle.

possible syntax error, try −P option

> Use the −P option to preprocess the **ctrace** input, along with any appropriate −D, −I, and −U preprocessor options.

NOTES

Defining a function with the same name as a system function may cause a syntax error if the number of arguments is changed. Just use a different name.

ctrace assumes that **BADMAG** is a preprocessor macro, and that **EOF** and **NULL** are #defined constants. Declaring any of these to be variables, e.g., "int EOF;", will cause a syntax error.

Pointer values are always treated as pointers to character strings.

ctrace does not know about the components of aggregates like structures, unions, and arrays. It cannot choose a format to print all the components of an aggregate when an assignment is made to the entire aggregate. **ctrace** may choose to print the address of an aggregate or use the wrong format (e.g., `3.149050e-311` for a structure with two integer members) when printing the value of an aggregate.

The loop trace output elimination is done separately for each file of a multi-file program. Separate output elimination can result in functions called from a loop still being traced, or the elimination of trace output from one function in a file until another in the same file is called.

NAME

cu – call another UNIX system

SYNOPSIS

cu [options] [destination]

DESCRIPTION

cu calls up another UNIX system, a terminal, or possibly a non-UNIX system. It manages an interactive conversation with possible transfers of files. It is convenient to think of cu as operating in two phases. The first phase is the connection phase in which the connection is established. cu then enters the conversation phase. The –d option is the only one that applies to both phases.

–d   Causes diagnostic traces to be printed.

The cu command sets the input and output conversion mode to on or off, as appropriate, to avoid a character conversion on the local system when accessing the remote system.

On the remote system, the input and output conversion should be set manually, as cu cannot know whether input conversion is required or not. In most cases, remote systems can be used with input conversion on; however, when transferring files, this should be set to off before invoking the file transfer command in order to avoid unexpected conversion of the file contents.

Connection Phase

cu uses the same mechanism that **uucp** does to establish a connection. This means that it will use the **uucp** control files **/etc/uucp/Devices** and **/etc/uucp/Systems**. This gives cu the ability to choose from several different media to establish the connection. The possible media include telephone lines, direct connections, and local area networks (LANs). The **Devices** file contains a list of media that are available on your system. The **Systems** file contains information for connecting to remote systems, but it is not generally readable.

The *destination* parameter from the command line is used to tell cu what system you wish to connect to. The *destination* can be blank, a telephone number, a system name, or a LAN-specific address. A telephone number is a string consisting of the tone dial characters (the digits 0 through 9, *, and #) plus the special characters = and –. The equal sign designates a secondary dial tone and the minus sign creates a 4 second delay. A system name is the name of any computer that **uucp** can call; the **uuname** command prints a list of these names. The documentation for your LAN will show the form of the LAN-specific address.

If cu's default behavior is invoked (not using the –c or –l options), cu will use *destination* to determine which medium to use. If *destination* is a telephone number, cu will assume that you wish to use a telephone line and it will select an automatic call unit (ACU). If the *destination* is not a telephone number, then cu will assume that it is a system name. cu will follow the **uucp** calling mechanism and use the **Systems** and **Devices** files to obtain the best available connection. Since cu will choose a speed that is appropriate for the medium that it selects, you may not use the –s option when *destination* is a system name.

The −c and −1 options modify this default behavior. −c is most often used to select a LAN by specifying a Type field from the **Devices** file. Here, *destination* is assumed to be a system name. If the connection attempt to *system name* fails, a connection will be attempted using *destination* as a LAN-specific address. The −1 option is used to specify a device associated with a direct connection. If the connection is truly a direct connection to the remote machine, then there is no need to specify a *destination*. This is the only case where a blank *destination* is allowed. On the other hand, there may be cases in which the specified device connects to a dialer, so it is valid to specify a telephone number as a *destination*. The −c and −1 options should not be specified on the same command line.

cu accepts many options. The −c, −1, and −s options play a part in selecting the medium; the remaining options are used in configuring the line.

−s*speed*   Specifies the transmission speed (300, 1200, 2400, 4800, 9600). The default value is "Any" speed which will depend on the order of the lines in the **/etc/uucp/Devices** file. Most modems are either 300, 1200, or 2400 baud. Directly connected lines may be set to a speed higher than 2400 baud.

−c*type*   The first field in the **Devices** file is the "Type" field. The −c option forces cu to only use entries in the "Type" field that match the user specified *type*. The specified *type* is usually the name of a local area network.

−1*line*   Specifies a device name to use as the communication line. This can be used to override the search that would otherwise take place for the first available line having the right speed. When the −1 option is used without the −s option, the speed of a line is taken from the **Devices** file record in which *line* matches the second field (the Line field). When the −1 and −s options are both used together, cu will search the **Devices** file to check if the requested speed for the requested line is available. If so, the connection will be made at the requested speed, otherwise, an error message will be printed and the call will not be made. In the general case where a specified device is a directly connected asynchronous line (e.g., **/dev/term/**ab), a telephone number (*telno*) is not required. The specified device need not be in the **/dev** directory. If the specified device is associated with an auto dialer, a telephone number must be provided. If *destination* is used with this option, it must be a telephone number.

−b*n*   Forces *n* to be the number of bits processed on the line. *n* is either 7 or 8. This allows connection between systems with different character sizes. By default, the character size of the line is set to the same as the current local terminal.

−e   Set an EVEN data parity. This option designates that EVEN parity is to be generated for data sent to the remote system.

−h   Set communication mode to half-duplex. This option emulates the local **echo**(1) command in order to support calls to other computer systems that expect terminals to be set to half-duplex mode.

−n	Request user prompt for telephone number. For added security, this option will prompt the user to provide the telephone number to be dialed, rather than taking it from the command line.
−o	Set an ODD data parity. This option designates that ODD parity is to be generated for data sent to the remote system.
−t	Used to dial a terminal which has been set to auto answer. Appropriate mapping of carriage-return to carriage-return-line-feed pairs is set.

Conversation Phase

After making the connection, **cu** runs as two processes: the *transmit* process reads data from the standard input and, except for lines beginning with ~, passes it to the remote system; the *receive* process accepts data from the remote system and, except for lines beginning with ~, passes it to the standard output. Normally, an automatic DC3/DC1 protocol is used to control input from the remote so the buffer is not overrun. Lines beginning with ~ have special meanings.

The *transmit* process interprets the following user-initiated commands:

~.	terminate the conversation.
~!	escape to an interactive shell on the local system.
~!*cmd*...	run *cmd* on the local system (via **sh −c**).
~$*cmd*...	run *cmd* locally and send its output to the remote system.
~%cd	change the directory on the local system. Note: ~!**cd** will cause the command to be run by a sub-shell, probably not what was intended.
~%take *from* [*to*]	copy file *from* (on the remote system) to file *to* on the local system. If *to* is omitted, the *from* argument is used in both places.
~%put *from* [*to*]	copy file *from* (on local system) to file *to* on remote system. If *to* is omitted, the *from* argument is used in both places.
~~ *line*	send the line ~ *line* to the remote system.
~%break	transmit a BREAK to the remote system (which can also be specified as ~%b).
~%debug	toggles the −d debugging option on or off (which can also be specified as ~%d).
~t	prints the values of the termio structure variables for the user's terminal (useful for debugging).
~l	prints the values of the termio structure variables for the remote communication line (useful for debugging).
~%ifc	toggles between DC3/DC1 input control protocol and no input control. This is useful when the remote system does not respond properly to the DC3 and DC1 characters. (can also be specified as ~%nostop).

~%ofc   toggles the output flow control setting. When enabled, out-
                         going data flow may be controlled by the remote host (can
                         also be specified as ~%noostop).

~%divert   allow/disallow unsolicited diversions. That is, diversions
                         not specified by ~%take.

~%old   allow/disallow old style syntax for received diversions.

The *receive* process normally copies data from the remote system to the standard
output of the local system. It may also direct the output to local files.

The use of ~%put requires stty(1) and cat(1) on the remote side. It also requires
that the current control characters on the remote system be identical to the
current control characters on the local system. Backslashes are inserted at
appropriate places for these control characters.

The use of ~%take requires the existence of echo(1) and cat(1) on the remote system. Also, tabs mode [see stty(1)] should be set on the remote system if tabs
are to be copied without expansion to spaces.

When cu is used on system X to connect to system Y and subsequently used on
system Y to connect to system Z, commands on system Y can be executed by
using ~~. Executing a tilde command reminds the user of the local system uname.
For example, uname can be executed on Z, X, and Y as follows:

        uname
        Z
        ~[X]!uname
        X
        ~~[Y]!uname
        Y

In general, ~ causes the command to be executed on the original machine. ~~
causes the command to be executed on the next machine in the chain.

EXAMPLES

To dial a system whose telephone number is 9 1 201 555 1234 using 1200 baud
(where dialtone is expected after the 9):

        cu   -s1200   9=12015551234

If the speed is not specified, "Any" is the default value.

To log on a system that is on a Datakit VCS local area network, but which has
not been defined by your administrator [i.e., is not entered in the
/etc/uucp/Systems file(s)]:

        cu -c *DK address*

DK is the name of the Datakit local area network, and *address* is the Datakit
address which is of the form, /area/exchange/machine.

To log on a system connected by a direct line:

        cu   -l   /dev/term/XX

or

        cu -l term/XX

To dial a system with a specific line and speed:

        cu -s1200 -l term/XX

To dial a system using a specific line associated with an auto dialer:

        cu -l culXX 9=12015551234

To use a system name:

        cu *systemname*

FILES

        /etc/uucp/Sysfiles
        /etc/uucp/Systems
        /etc/uucp/Devices
        /var/spool/locks/*

SEE ALSO

cat(1), ct(1C), echo(1), stty(1), uucp(1C), uname(1), uuname(1)
System Administrator's Guide

DIAGNOSTICS

Exit code is zero for normal exit, otherwise, one.

NOTES

The cu command does not do any integrity checking on data it transfers. Data fields with special cu characters may not be transmitted properly. Depending on the interconnection hardware, it may be necessary to use a ~. to terminate the conversion, even if stty 0 has been used. Non-printing characters are not dependably transmitted using either the ~%put or ~%take commands. cu, between an IMBR1 and a PENRIL modem, will not return a login prompt immediately upon connection. A carriage return will return the prompt.

~%put and ~%take cannot be used over multiple links. Files must be moved one link at a time.

There is an artificial slowing of transmission by cu during the ~%put operation so that loss of data is unlikely. Files transferred using ~%take or ~%put must contain a trailing newline, otherwise, the operation will hang. Entering a CTRL-d command usually clears the hang condition.

NAME

custom - install specific portions of a UNIX package

SYNOPSIS

custom [-ir] [*package*]] [-m *device*] [-f [*file*]]

DESCRIPTION

custom allows the super-user to create a custom installation by selectively installing or deleting portions of the UNIX packages to or from the 386 operating system. It can be used interactively or it can be invoked from the command line with applicable command options.

Files are extracted or deleted in *packages*. A *package* is a collection of individual files that are grouped together in *sets*.

When in interactive mode, custom prompts you for volume 1 of the new product distribution and extracts the product information necessary to support it. The following menu provides support for adding or removing a package:

1. Install one or more packages
2. Remove one or more packages
3. List the files in a package
4. Install a single file
5. Select a new set to customize
6. Display current disk usage
7. Help

When you enter a menu option, you are prompted for further information. The following describes what actions are necessary for each menu option:

1. Install

   Prompts for one or more package names

   Calculates which installation volumes (distribution media) are needed and then prompts the user for the correct volume numbers. If multiple packages are specified, the names should be separated by spaces on the command line.

   This option, as well as "2" and "3," displays a list of available packages in the selected set. Each line describes the package name, whether the package is fully installed, not installed or partially installed, the size of the package (in 512 byte blocks), and a one line description of the package contents.

2. Remove

   Prompts for one or more package names.

   Deletes the correct files in the specified package. If multiple packages are specified, the names should be separated by spaces on the command line.

   Displays available packages (see option "1").

3. List files in a package

   Lists all files in the specified package

Prompts for one or more package names. Enter the name of the desired package(s).

Displays available packages (see option "1").

4. Install a single file

Retrieves the specified file from the distribution set

Filename should be a full pathname relative to the root directory "/".

5. Select a new set

Allows the user to work from a different set

6. Display current disk usage

Tells current disk usage.

7. Help

Prints a page of instructions to help you use *custom*.

-**s** A set identifier

-**i** Install the specified package(s)

-**r** Remove the specified package(s)

-**l** List the files in the specified package(s)

-**f** Install the specified file

The -**m** flag specifies the media device. The default is **/dev/install** (which is always the 0 device, as in **/dev/fd0**). This is very useful if the system has a 5.25-inch drive on **/dev/fd0** and a 3.5-inch floppy on **/dev/fd1** and it is necessary to install 3.5-inch media. For example:

```
custom -m /dev/rfd196ds9
```

This will override the default device and use the one supplied with the -**m** flag.

If any information is missing from the command line, **custom** prompts for the missing data.

NOTES

When installing some XENIX applications, error messages such as "**bad gid**" or "**bad uid**" may be printed. These messages occur because XENIX and UNIX assign UID and GID numbers differently. If necessary, the file and/or directory permissions can be altered with "**chmod**(1)" after installation.

FILES

/etc/perms/*

SEE ALSO

fixperm(1M) , df(1M), du(1M), install(1M)

NAME

    custom – install specific portions of certain UNIX or XENIX packages

SYNOPSIS

    custom [-s *set*] [-ilr] [*package*]] [-f [*file*]] [-m *device*]

DESCRIPTION

    custom allows the super-user to create a custom installation by selectively install-ling or deleting portions of UNIX or XENIX packages to or from the 386 operating system. It can be used interactively or it can be invoked from the command line with applicable command options.

    Files are extracted or deleted in *packages*. A *package* is a collection of individual files that are grouped together in *sets*.

    When in interactive mode, custom prompts you for volume 1 of the new product distribution and extracts the product information necessary to support it. The following menu provides support for adding or removing a package:

        1. Install one or more packages
        2. Remove one or more packages
        3. List available packages
        4. List the files in a package
        5. Install a single file
        6. Select a new set to customize
        7. Display current disk usage
        8. Help

    When you enter a menu option, you are prompted for further information. The following describes what actions are necessary for each menu option:

1. Install one or more packages

    Prompts for one or more package names. Enter the name of the desired package(s).

    Calculates which installation volumes (distribution media) are needed and then prompts the user for the correct volume numbers. If multiple pack-ages are specified, the names should be separated by spaces on the com-mand line.

    This option, as well as options 2 and 3, displays a list of available packages in the selected set. Each line describes the package name, whether the package is fully installed, not installed or partially installed, the size of the package (in 512 byte blocks), and a one line description of the package contents.

2. Remove one or more packages

    Prompts for one or more package names. Enter the name of the desired package(s).

    Deletes the correct files in the specified package. If multiple packages are specified, the names should be separated by spaces on the command line.

3. List available packages

   Prompts for one or more package names. Enter the name of the desired package(s).

   Displays available packages (see option 1).

4. List the files in a package

   Lists all files in the specified package.

   Prompts for one or more package names. Enter the name of the desired package(s).

5. Install a single file

   Retrieves the specified file from the distribution set.

   Filename should be a full pathname relative to the **root** directory (**/**).

6. Select a new set to customize

   Allows the user to work from a different set .

7. Display current disk usage

   Tells current disk usage.

8. Help

   Prints a page of instructions to help you use **custom.**

Options

-s   A set identifier

-i   Install the specified package(s)

-r   Remove the specified package(s)

-l   List the files in the specified package(s)

-f   Install the specified file

-m   Install from device (*device* must be **/dev/install** for floppy drive 0 or **/dev/install1** for floppy drive 1)

FILES

/etc/perms/*

SEE ALSO

df(1M), du(1M), fixperm(1M), install(1M)

NAME

cut – cut out selected fields of each line of a file

SYNOPSIS

cut –c*list* [*file* ...]

cut –f*list* [–d*char*] [–s] [*file* ...]

DESCRIPTION

Use **cut** to cut out columns from a table or fields from each line of a file; in data base parlance, it implements the projection of a relation. The fields as specified by *list* can be fixed length, i.e., character positions as on a punched card (–c option) or the length can vary from line to line and be marked with a field delimiter character like *tab* (–f option). **cut** can be used as a filter; if no files are given, the standard input is used. In addition, a file name of "–" explicitly refers to standard input.

The meanings of the options are:

list   A comma-separated list of integer field numbers (in increasing order), with optional – to indicate ranges [e.g., **1,4,7**; **1–3,8**; **–5,10** (short for **1–5,10**); or **3–** (short for third through last field)].

–c*list*   The *list* following –c (no space) specifies character positions (e.g., –c1–72 would pass the first 72 characters of each line).

–f*list*   The *list* following –f is a list of fields assumed to be separated in the file by a delimiter character (see –d); e.g., –f1,7 copies the first and seventh field only. Lines with no field delimiters will be passed through intact (useful for table subheadings), unless –s is specified.

–d*char*   The character following –d is the field delimiter (–f option only). Default is *tab*. Space or other characters with special meaning to the shell must be quoted.

–s   Suppresses lines with no delimiter characters in case of –f option. Unless specified, lines with no delimiters will be passed through untouched.

Either the –c or –f option must be specified.

Use **grep**(1) to make horizontal "cuts" (by context) through a file, or **paste**(1) to put files together column-wise (i.e., horizontally). To reorder columns in a table, use **cut** and **paste**.

EXAMPLES

cut –d: –f1,5 /etc/passwd   mapping of user IDs to names

name=`who am i | cut –f1 –d" "`   to set **name** to current login name.

DIAGNOSTICS

I "ERROR: line too long"
                A line can have no more than 1023 characters or fields, or there is no new-line character.

"ERROR: bad list for c / f option"
                Missing –c or –f option or incorrectly specified *list*. No error occurs if a line has fewer fields than the *list* calls for.

"ERROR: no fields"
> The *list* is empty.

"ERROR: no delimeter"
> Missing *char* on −d option.

"ERROR: cannot handle multiple adjacent backspaces"
> Adjacent backspaces cannot be processed correctly.

"WARNING: cannot open <filename>"
> Either *filename* cannot be read or does not exist. If multiple filenames are present, processing continues.

SEE ALSO

grep(1), paste(1)

NAME

cvtomflib - convert OMF (XENIX) libraries to ELF

SYNOPSIS

cvtomflib [-v] [-o *outfile*] *library* [*library*. . .]

DESCRIPTION

cvtomflib converts libraries of OMF objects to libraries of ELF objects. It is intended for use with application packages that provide only OMF libraries that could not otherwise be used with the Standard C Development Environment.

The options have the following meanings.

-v   Verbose output is produced for each converted object. Without this option, cvtomflib does its work silently.

-o   This option allows the user to specify a new name, *outfile*, for the converted library without changing the original. This option is only available when a single library is being converted.

NOTES

The original order of objects within the library is retained.

Each library is converted in the directory in which it's located. Without the -o option, the converted library will overwrite the original; therefore, you may want to copy the original library before conversion.

NAME
cxref – generate C program cross-reference

SYNOPSIS
cxref [*options*] *files*

DESCRIPTION
The **cxref** command analyzes a collection of C files and builds a cross-reference table. **cxref** uses a special version of **cc** to include **#define**'d information in its symbol table. It generates a list of all symbols (auto, static, and global) in each individual file, or, with the **-c** option, in combination. The table includes four fields: NAME, FILE, FUNCTION, and LINE. The line numbers appearing in the LINE field also show reference marks as appropriate. The reference marks include:

> assignment   =
> declaration   –
> definition   *

If no reference marks appear, you can assume a general reference.

OPTIONS
cxref interprets the **-D**, **-I**, **-U** options in the same manner that **cc** does. In addition, **cxref** interprets the following options:

-c   Combine the source files into a single report. Without the **-c** option, **cxref** generates a separate report for each file on the command line.

-d   Disables printing declarations, making the report easier to read.

-l   Does not print local variables. Prints only global and file scope statistics.

-o *file*   Direct output to *file*.

-s   Operates silently; does not print input file names.

-t   Format listing for 80-column width.

-w*num*   Width option that formats output no wider than *num* (decimal) columns. This option will default to 80 if *num* is not specified or is less than 51.

-C   Runs only the first pass of **cxref**, creating a **.cx** file that can later be passed to **cxref**. This is similar to the **-c** option of **cc** or **lint**.

-F   Prints the full path of the referenced file names.

-L*cols*   Modifies the number of columns in the LINE field. If you do not specify a number, **cxref** defaults to five columns.

-V   Prints version information on the standard error.

-W*name,file, function, line*
> Changes the default width of at least one field. The default widths are:

Field	Characters
NAME	15
FILE	13
FUNCTION	15
LINE	20 (4 per column)

FILES

TMPDIR/**tcx.** *   temporary files

TMPDIR/**cx.** *   temporary files

LIBDIR/**xref**   accessed by **cxref**

LIBDIR   usually **/usr/ccs/lib**

TMPDIR   usually **/var/tmp** but can be redefined by setting the environment variable **TMPDIR** [see **tempnam** in tmpnam(3S)].

EXAMPLE

a.c

```
1    main()
2    {
3           int i;
4           extern char c;
5
6           i=65;
7           c=(char)i;
8    }
```

Resulting cross-reference table:

NAME	FILE	FUNCTION	LINE		
c	a.c	---	4-	7=	
i	a.c	main	3*	6=	7
main	a.c	---	2*		
u3b2	predefined	---	0*		
unix	predefined	---	0*		

SEE ALSO

cc(1), lint(1)

DIAGNOSTICS

Error messages usually mean you cannot compile the files.

NAME

    `date` – print and set the date

SYNOPSIS

    `date` [`-u`] [`+` *format*]

    `date` [`-a` [`–`] *sss.fff*] [`-u`] [[*mmdd*] *HHMM* | *mmddHHMM* [*cc*] *yy*]

DESCRIPTION

    If no argument is given, or if the argument begins with `+`, the current date and time are printed. Otherwise, the current date is set (only by super-user).

    `-a` [`–`] *sss.fff*

            Slowly adjust the time by *sss.fff* seconds (*fff* represents fractions of a second). This adjustment can be positive or negative. The system's clock will be sped up or slowed down until it has drifted by the number of seconds specified.

    `-u`   Display (or set) the date in Greenwich Mean Time (GMT—universal time), bypassing the normal conversion to (or from) local time.

    mm   is the month number

    dd   is the day number in the month

    HH   is the hour number (24 hour system)

    MM   is the minute number

    cc   is the century minus one

    yy   is the last 2 digits of the year number

            The month, day, year, and century may be omitted; the current values are supplied as defaults. For example:

                `date 10080045`

            sets the date to Oct 8, 12:45 AM. The current year is the default because no year is supplied. The system operates in GMT. `date` takes care of the conversion to and from local standard and daylight time. Only the super-user may change the date. After successfully setting the date and time, `date` displays the new date according to the default format. The `date` command uses `TZ` to determine the correct time zone information [see `environ`(5)].

    `+` *format*   If the argument begins with `+`, the output of `date` is under the control of the user. Each Field Descriptor, described below, is preceded by `%` and is replaced in the output by its corresponding value. A single `%` is encoded by `%%`. All other characters are copied to the output without change. The string is always terminated with a new-line character. If the argument contains embedded blanks it must be quoted (see the EXAMPLE section).

    Specifications of native language translations of month and weekday names are supported. The month and weekday names used for a language are based on the locale specified by the environment variables `LC_TIME` and `LANG` (see `environ`(5)).

The month and weekday names used for a language are taken from a file whose format is specified in **strftime**(4). This file also defines country-specific date and time formats such as **%c**, which specifies the default date format. The following form is the default for **%c**:

> %a %b %e %T %Z %Y
> e.g., Fri Dec 23 10:10:42 EST 1988

Field Descriptors (must be preceded by a **%**):

a	abbreviated weekday name
A	full weekday name
b	abbreviated month name
B	full month name
c	country-specific date and time format
d	day of month – 01 to 31
D	date as **%m/%d/%y**
e	day of month – 1 to 31 (single digits are preceded by a blank)
h	abbreviated month name (alias for **%b**)
H	hour – 00 to 23
I	hour – 01 to 12
j	day of year – 001 to 366
m	month of year – 01 to 12
M	minute – 00 to 59
n	insert a new-line character
p	string containing ante-meridian or post-meridian indicator (by default, AM or PM)
r	time as **%I:%M:%S %p**
R	time as **%H:%M**
S	second – 00 to 61, allows for leap seconds
t	insert a tab character
T	time as **%H:%M:%S**
U	week number of year (Sunday as the first day of the week) – 00 to 53
w	day of week – Sunday = 0
W	week number of year (Monday as the first day of the week) – 00 to 53
x	Country-specific date format
X	Country-specific time format
y	year within century – 00 to 99
Y	year as *ccyy* (4 digits)
z	timezone name

EXAMPLE

The command

> date '+DATE: %m/%d/%y%nTIME: %H:%M:%S'

generates as output:

> DATE: 08/01/76
> TIME: 14:45:05

DIAGNOSTICS

`No permission` You are not the super-user and you try to change the date.
`bad conversion` The date set is syntactically incorrect.

NOTES

Should you need to change the date while the system is running multi-user, use the `datetime` command of `sysadm`(1M).

If you attempt to set the current date to one of the dates that the standard and alternate time zones change (for example, the date that daylight time is starting or ending), and you attempt to set the time to a time in the interval between the end of standard time and the beginning of the alternate time (or the end of the alternate time and the beginning of standard time), the results are unpredictable.

SEE ALSO

`sysadm`(1M), `strftime`(4), `environ`(5) in the *System Administrator's Reference Manual*

NAME

dbcmd – load command and macro files into a kernel executable file

SYNOPSIS

dbcmd *file macro*

DESCRIPTION

dbcmd loads the contents of the specified macros into the kernel executable *file*. The next time the kernel is rebooted with *file*, the loaded commands are part of the kernel debugger.

SEE ALSO

kdb(1M), dbsym(1M), kcrash(1M)

NAME
    dbsym – add symbols to kernel debugger

SYNOPSIS
    dbsym [**-v**] *file1 file2*

DESCRIPTION
    dbsym extracts the symbolic names and addresses from the kernel executable file,
    file1, and enters the data into *file2*. When the system is rebooted with *file2*, the
    symbolic information can now be used by the kernel debugger. Note that *file1*
    and *file2* can be the same.

    -v   The verbose option , **-v**, displays various symbol information.

SEE ALSO
    kdb(1M), **dbcmd**(1M), **kcrash**(1M)

NAME

dc – desk calculator

SYNOPSIS

dc [*file*]

DESCRIPTION

dc is an arbitrary precision arithmetic package. Ordinarily it operates on decimal integers, but one may specify an input base, output base, and a number of fractional digits to be maintained. [**bc** is a preprocessor for **dc** that provides infix notation and a C-like syntax that implements functions. **bc** also provides reasonable control structures for programs. See **bc**(1).] The overall structure of **dc** is a stacking (reverse Polish) calculator. If an argument is given, input is taken from that file until its end, then from the standard input. The following constructions are recognized:

number
> The value of the number is pushed on the stack. A number is an unbroken string of the digits 0–9. It may be preceded by an underscore (_) to input a negative number. Numbers may contain decimal points.

+ − / * % ^
> The top two values on the stack are added (+), subtracted (−), multiplied (*), divided (/), remaindered (%), or exponentiated (^). The two entries are popped off the stack; the result is pushed on the stack in their place. Any fractional part of an exponent is ignored.

sx
> The top of the stack is popped and stored into a register named x, where x may be any character. If the **s** is capitalized, x is treated as a stack and the value is pushed on it.

lx
> The value in register x is pushed on the stack. The register x is not altered. All registers start with zero value. If the **l** is capitalized, register x is treated as a stack and its top value is popped onto the main stack.

d
> The top value on the stack is duplicated.

p
> The top value on the stack is printed. The top value remains unchanged.

P
> Interprets the top of the stack as an ASCII string, removes it, and prints it.

f
> All values on the stack are printed.

q
> Exits the program. If executing a string, the recursion level is popped by two.

Q
> Exits the program. The top value on the stack is popped and the string execution level is popped by that value.

x
> Treats the top element of the stack as a character string and executes it as a string of **dc** commands.

X
> Replaces the number on the top of the stack with its scale factor.

[. . .]
> Puts the bracketed ASCII string onto the top of the stack.

$<x$ $>x$ $=x$

    The top two elements of the stack are popped and compared. Register x is evaluated if they obey the stated relation.

v   Replaces the top element on the stack by its square root. Any existing fractional part of the argument is taken into account, but otherwise the scale factor is ignored.

!   Interprets the rest of the line as a UNIX system command.

c   All values on the stack are popped.

i   The top value on the stack is popped and used as the number radix for further input.

I   Pushes the input base on the top of the stack.

o   The top value on the stack is popped and used as the number radix for further output.

O   Pushes the output base on the top of the stack.

k   The top of the stack is popped, and that value is used as a non-negative scale factor: the appropriate number of places are printed on output, and maintained during multiplication, division, and exponentiation. The interaction of scale factor, input base, and output base will be reasonable if all are changed together.

z   The stack level is pushed onto the stack.

Z   Replaces the number on the top of the stack with its length.

?   A line of input is taken from the input source (usually the terminal) and executed.

; :   are used by **bc**(1) for array operations.

EXAMPLE

    This example prints the first ten values of n!:

```
[la1+dsa*pla10>y]sy
0sa1
lyx
```

SEE ALSO

    bc(1)

DIAGNOSTICS

    `x is unimplemented`: x is an octal number.

    `stack empty`: not enough elements on the stack to do what was asked.

    `Out of space`: the free list is exhausted (too many digits).

    `Out of headers`: too many numbers being kept around.

    `Out of pushdown`: too many items on the stack.

    `Nesting Depth`: too many levels of nested execution.

NAME

dcopy (generic) – copy file systems for optimal access time

SYNOPSIS

dcopy [-F *FSType*] [-V] [*current_options*] [-o *specific_options*] *inputfs outputfs*

DESCRIPTION

dcopy copies file system *inputfs* to *outputfs*. *inputfs* is the device file for the existing file system; *outputfs* is the device file to hold the reorganized result. For the most effective optimization *inputfs* should be the raw device and *outputfs* should be the block device. Both *inputfs* and *outputfs* should be unmounted file systems.

current_options are options supported by the **s5**-specific module of **dcopy**. Other FSTypes do not necessarily support these options. *specific_options* indicate suboptions specified in a comma-separated list of suboptions and/or keyword-attribute pairs for interpretation by the *FSType*-specific module of the command.

The options are:

-F   Specify the *FSType* on which to operate. The *FSType* should either be specified here or be determinable from **/etc/vfstab** by matching the *inputfs* (device) with an entry in the table.

-V   Echo the complete command line, but do not execute the command. The command line is generated by using the options and arguments provided by the user and adding to them information derived from **/etc/vfstab**. This option should be used to verify and validate the command line.

-o   Specify FSType-specific options.

NOTE

This command may not be supported for all FSTypes.

FILES

/etc/vfstab   list of default parameters for each file system

SEE ALSO

vfstab(4)

Manual pages for the FSType-specific modules of **dcopy**

NAME
: dcopy (s5) – copy **s5** file systems for optimal access time

SYNOPSIS
: dcopy [-F s5] [*generic_options*] [-s*X*] [-a*n*] [-d] [-v] [-f*fsize*[:*isize*]] *inputfs outputfs*

DESCRIPTION

generic_options are options supported by the generic **dcopy** command.

With no options, **dcopy** copies files from *inputfs* compressing directories by removing vacant entries, and spacing consecutive blocks in a file by the optimal rotational gap.

The options are:

-F s5
: Specifies the **s5**-FSType. Need not be supplied if the information may be obtained from **/etc/vfstab** by matching the *inputfs* device with an entry in the file.

-s*X*
: Supply device information for creating an optimal organization of blocks in a file. *X* must be of the form *cylinder size:gap size.*

-a*n*
: Place the files not accessed in *n* days after the free blocks of the destination file system If no *n* is specified then no movement occurs.

-d
: Leave order of directory entries as is. The default is to move subdirectories to the beginning of directories.

-v
: Reports how many files were processed and how big the source and destination freelists are.

-f *fsize*[:*isize*]
: Specify the *outputfs* file system (*fsize*) and inode list (*isize*) sizes in logical blocks. If the suboption (or :*isize*) is not given, the values from *inputfs* are used.

dcopy catches interrupts and quits and reports on its progress. To terminate **dcopy**, send a quit signal followed by an interrupt or quit.

NOTES

fsck should be run on the new file system created by **dcopy** before it is mounted.

FILES

/etc/mnttab   list of file systems currently mounted

SEE ALSO

generic **dcopy**(1M), **fsck**(1M), **mkfs**(1M)

NAME

　　dd – convert and copy a file

SYNOPSIS

　　dd [option=value] ...

DESCRIPTION

　　dd copies the specified input file to the specified output with possible conversions. The standard input and output are used by default. The input and output block sizes may be specified to take advantage of raw physical I/O.

option	**values**
if=*file*	input file name; standard input is default
of=*file*	output file name; standard output is default
ibs=*n*	input block size *n* bytes (default 512)
obs=*n*	output block size *n* bytes (default 512)
bs=*n*	set both input and output block size, superseding *ibs* and *obs*; also, if no conversion is specified, preserve the input block size instead of packing short blocks into the output buffer (this is particularly efficient since no in-core copy need be done)
cbs=*n*	conversion buffer size (logical record length)
files=*n*	copy and concatenate *n* input files before terminating (makes sense only where input is a magnetic tape or similar device)
skip=*n*	skip *n* input blocks before starting copy (appropriate for magnetic tape, where *iseek* is undefined)
iseek=*n*	seek *n* blocks from beginning of input file before copying (appropriate for disk files, where *skip* can be incredibly slow)
oseek=*n*	seek *n* blocks from beginning of output file before copying
seek=*n*	identical to *oseek*, retained for backward compatibility
count=*n*	copy only *n* input blocks
conv=ascii	convert EBCDIC to ASCII
ebcdic	convert ASCII to EBCDIC
ibm	slightly different map of ASCII to EBCDIC
block	convert new-line terminated ASCII records to fixed length
unblock	convert fixed length ASCII records to new-line terminated records
lcase	map alphabetics to lower case
ucase	map alphabetics to upper case
swab	swap every pair of bytes
noerror	do not stop processing on an error (limit of 5 consecutive errors)
sync	pad every input block to *ibs*
. . . , . . .	several comma-separated conversions

　　Where sizes are specified, a number of bytes is expected. A number may end with **k**, **b**, or **w** to specify multiplication by 1024, 512, or 2, respectively; a pair of numbers may be separated by **x** to indicate multiplication.

cbs is used only if **ascii**, *unblock*, *ebcdic*, *ibm*, or *block* conversion is specified. In the first two cases, *cbs* characters are copied into the conversion buffer, any specified character mapping is done, trailing blanks are trimmed and a new-line is added before sending the line to the output. In the latter three cases, characters are read into the conversion buffer and blanks are added to make up an output record of size *cbs*. If *cbs* is unspecified or zero, the **ascii**, *ebcdic*, and *ibm* options convert the character set without changing the block structure of the input file; the *unblock* and *block* options become a simple file copy.

After completion, **dd** reports the number of whole and partial input and output blocks.

EXAMPLE

This command will read an EBCDIC tape blocked ten 80-byte EBCDIC card images per tape block into the ASCII file *x*:

    dd if=/dev/rmt/0h of=x ibs=800 obs=8k cbs=80 conv=ascii,lcase

Note the use of raw magnetic tape. **dd** is especially suited to I/O on the raw physical devices because it allows reading and writing in arbitrary block sizes.

SEE ALSO

cp(1)

NOTES

Do not use **dd** to copy files between filesystems having different block sizes.

Using a blocked device to copy a file will result in extra nulls being added to the file to pad the final block to the block boundary.

DIAGNOSTICS

f+p records in(out)   numbers of full and partial blocks read(written)

NAME

delsysadm – sysadm interface menu or task removal tool

SYNOPSIS

delsysadm *task* | [−r] *menu*

DESCRIPTION

The delsysadm command deletes a *task* or *menu* from the sysadm interface and modifies the interface directory structure on the target machine.

task | *menu*   The logical name and location of the menu or task within the interface menu hierarchy. Begin with the top menu **main** and proceed to where the menu or the task resides, separating each name with colons. See EXAMPLES.

If the −r option is used, this command will recursively remove all sub-menus and tasks for this menu. If the −r option is not used, the menu must be empty.

delsysadm should only be used to remove items added as "on-line" changes with the edsysadm command. Such an addition will have a package instance tag of ONLINE. If the task or menu (and its sub-menus and tasks) have any package instance tags other than ONLINE, you are asked whether to continue with the removal or to exit. Under these circumstances, you probably do not want to continue and you should rely on the package involved to take the necessary actions to delete this type of entry.

The command exits successfully or provides the error code within an error message.

EXAMPLES

To remove the nformat task, execute:

            delsysadm main:applications:ndevices:nformat.

DIAGNOSTICS

    0   Successful execution
    2   Invalid syntax
    3   Menu or task does not exist
    4   Menu not empty
    5   Unable to update interface menu structure

NOTES

Any menu that was originally a placeholder menu (one that only appears if sub-menus exist under it) will be returned to placeholder status when a deletion leaves it empty.

When the −r option is used, delsysadm checks for dependencies before removing any subentries. (A dependency exists if the menu being removed contains an entry placed there by an application package). If a dependency is found, the user is shown a list of packages that depend on the menu being deleted and asked whether or not to continue. If the answer is yes, the menu and all of its menus and tasks are removed (even those shown to have dependencies). If the answer is no, the menu is not deleted.

delsysadm should only be used to remove menu or task entries that have been added to the interface with edsysadm.

SEE ALSO

edsysadm(1M), sysadm(1M)

NAME

delta – make a delta (change) to an SCCS file

SYNOPSIS

delta [–r*SID*] [–s] [–n] [–g*list*] [–m[*mrlist*]] [–y[*comment*]] [–p] *files*

DESCRIPTION

delta is used to permanently introduce into the named SCCS file changes that were made to the file retrieved by **get –e** (called the g-file or generated file).

delta makes a delta to each named SCCS file. If a directory is named, **delta** behaves as though each file in the directory were specified as a named file, except that non-SCCS files (last component of the path name does not begin with **s.**) and unreadable files are silently ignored. If a name of – is given, the standard input is read (see the NOTES section); each line of the standard input is taken to be the name of an SCCS file to be processed.

delta may issue prompts on the standard output depending on certain keyletters specified and flags [see **admin**(1)] that may be present in the SCCS file (see –m and –y keyletters below).

Keyletter arguments apply independently to each named file.

–r*SID*   Uniquely identifies which delta is to be made to the SCCS file. The use of this keyletter is necessary only if two or more outstanding **get**s for editing (**get –e**) on the same SCCS file were done by the same person (login name). The SID value specified with the –r keyletter can be either the SID specified on the **get** command line or the SID to be made as reported by the **get** command [see **get**(1)]. A diagnostic results if the specified SID is ambiguous, or, if necessary and omitted on the command line.

–s   Suppresses the issue, on the standard output, of the created delta's SID, as well as the number of lines inserted, deleted and unchanged in the SCCS file.

–n   Specifies retention of the edited g-file (normally removed at completion of delta processing).

–g*list*   Specify a *list* [see **get**(1) for the definition of *list*] of deltas that are to be ignored when the file is accessed at the change level (SID) created by this delta.

–m[*mrlist*]   If the SCCS file has the **v** flag set [see **admin**(1)] then a Modification Request (MR) number must be supplied as the reason for creating the new delta. If –m is not used and the standard input is a terminal, the prompt **MRs?** is issued on the standard output before the standard input is read; if the standard input is not a terminal, no prompt is issued. The **MRs?** prompt always precedes the **comments?** prompt (see –y keyletter). MRs in a list are separated by blanks and/or tab characters. An unescaped new-line character terminates the MR list. Note that if the **v** flag has a value [see **admin**(1)], it is taken to be the name of a program (or shell procedure) that will validate the correctness of the MR numbers. If a non-zero exit status is returned from the MR number validation program, **delta** terminates. (It is assumed that the MR numbers were not all valid.)

−**y**[*comment*]   Arbitrary text used to describe the reason for making the delta. A null string is considered a valid *comment*. If −**y** is not specified and the standard input is a terminal, the prompt **comments?** is issued on the standard output before the standard input is read; if the standard input is not a terminal, no prompt is issued. An unescaped new-line character terminates the comment text.

−**p**   Causes **delta** to print (on the standard output) the SCCS file differences before and after the delta is applied in a **diff**(1) format.

FILES

g-file   Existed before the execution of **delta**; removed after completion of **delta**.

p-file   Existed before the execution of **delta**; may exist after completion of **delta**.

q-file   Created during the execution of **delta**; removed after completion of **delta**.

x-file   Created during the execution of **delta**; renamed to SCCS file after completion of **delta**.

z-file   Created during the execution of **delta**; removed during the execution of **delta**.

d-file   Created during the execution of **delta**; removed after completion of **delta**.

bdiff   Program to compute differences between the "gotten" file and the g-file.

SEE ALSO

admin(1), **cdc**(1), **get**(1), **help**(1), **prs**(1), **rmdel**(1), **sccsfile**(4)
bdiff(1) in the *User's Reference Manual*

DIAGNOSTICS

Use **help**(1) for explanations.

NOTES

A **get** of many SCCS files, followed by a **delta** of those files, should be avoided when the **get** generates a large amount of data. Instead, multiple **get**/**delta** sequences should be used.

If the standard input (−) is specified on the **delta** command line, the −**m** (if necessary) and −**y** keyletters must also be present. Omission of these keyletters causes an error.

Comments are limited to text strings of at most 1024 characters. Line lengths greater than 1000 characters cause undefined results.

NAME

deroff – remove **nroff/troff**, **tbl**, and **eqn** constructs

SYNOPSIS

deroff [**–m** *x*] [**–w**] [*file . . .*]

DESCRIPTION

deroff reads each of the *files* in sequence and removes all **troff**(1) requests,
macro calls, backslash constructs, **eqn**(1) constructs (between **.EQ** and **.EN** lines,
and between delimiters), and **tbl**(1) descriptions, perhaps replacing them with
white space (blanks and blank lines), and writes the remainder of the file on the
standard output. **deroff** follows chains of included files (**.so** and **.nx troff**
commands); if a file has already been included, a **.so** naming that file is ignored
and a **.nx** naming that file terminates execution. If no input file is given, **deroff**
reads the standard input.

The **–m** option may be followed by an **m**, **s**, or **l**. The **–mm** option causes the macros to be interpreted so that only running text (that is, no text from macro lines)
is output. The **–ml** option forces the **–mm** option and also causes deletion of lists
associated with the **mm** macros.

If the **–w** option is given, the output is a word list, one "word" per line, with all
other characters deleted. Otherwise, the output follows the original, with the
deletions mentioned above. In text, a "word" is any string that *contains* at least
two letters and is composed of letters, digits, ampersands (**&**), and apostrophes
(**'**); in a macro call, however, a "word" is a string that *begins* with at least two
letters and contains a total of at least three letters. Delimiters are any characters
other than letters, digits, apostrophes, and ampersands. Trailing apostrophes and
ampersands are removed from "words."

SEE ALSO

eqn(1), **nroff**(1), **tbl**(1), **troff**(1) in the *DOCUMENTER'S WORKBENCH
Software Technical Discussion and Reference Manual*

NOTES

deroff is not a complete **troff** interpreter, so it can be confused by subtle constructs. Most such errors result in too much rather than too little output.

The **–ml** option does not handle nested lists correctly.

troff(1), **nroff**(1), and **eqn**(1) are not part of this UNIX system release.

NAME

deroff – remove **nroff**, **troff**, **tbl** and **eqn** constructs

SYNOPSIS

`/usr/ucb/deroff` [`–w`] *filename* . . .

DESCRIPTION

The **deroff** command reads each file in sequence and removes all **nroff** and **troff** command lines, backslash constructions, macro definitions, **eqn** constructs (between **.EQ** and **.EN** lines or between delimiters), and table descriptions and writes the remainder on the standard output. **deroff** follows chains of included files (**.so** and **.nx** commands); if a file has already been included, a **.so** is ignored and a **.nx** terminates execution. If no input file is given, **deroff** reads from the standard input file.

OPTIONS

–w   Generate a word list, one word per line. A 'word' is a string of letters, digits, and apostrophes, beginning with a letter; apostrophes are removed. All other characters are ignored.

SEE ALSO

eqn(1), **nroff**(1), **tbl**(1), **troff**(1)

NOTES

deroff is not a complete **troff** interpreter, so it can be confused by subtle constructs. Most errors result in too much rather than too little output.

deroff does not work well with files that use **.so** to source in the standard macro package files.

NAME
     devattr – lists device attributes

SYNOPSIS
     devattr [-v] *device* [*attribute* [. . .]]

DESCRIPTION
     devattr displays the values for a device's attributes. The display can be
     presented in two formats. Used without the -v option, only the attribute values
     are shown. Used with the -v option, the attributes are shown in an
     attribute=value format. When no attributes are given on the command line, all
     attributes for the specified device are displayed in alphabetical order by attribute
     name. If attributes are given on the command line, only those are shown and
     they are displayed in command line order.

     The options and arguments for this command are:

     -v   Specifies verbose format. Attribute values are displayed in an
                     attribute=value format.
     device   Defines the device whose attributes should be displayed. Can be
                     the pathname of the device or the device alias.
     attribute   Defines which attribute, or attributes, should be shown. Default is
                     to show all attributes for a device. See the **putdev**(1M) manual
                     page for a complete listing and description of available attributes.

ERRORS
     The command will exit with one of the following values:

     0 = successful completion of the task.

     1 = command syntax incorrect, invalid option used, or internal error occurred.

     2 = device table could not be opened for reading.

     3 = requested device could not be found in the device table.

     4 = requested attribute not defined for specified device.

FILES
     /etc/device.tab

SEE ALSO
     putdev(1M).
     devattr(3X), listdev(3X) in the *Programmer's Reference Manual*

NAME

devfree – release devices from exclusive use

SYNOPSIS

devfree *key* [*device* [. . .]]

DESCRIPTION

devfree releases devices from exclusive use. Exclusive use is requested with the command **devreserv**.

When **devfree** is invoked with only the *key* argument, it releases all devices that have been reserved for that *key*. When called with *key* and *device* arguments, **devfree** releases the specified devices that have been reserved with that *key*.

The arguments for this command are:

key   Designates the unique key on which the device was reserved.

device   Defines device that this command will release from exclusive use. Can be the pathname of the device or the device alias.

ERRORS

The command will exit with one of the following values:

0 = successful completion of the task.

1 = command syntax incorrect, invalid option used, or internal error occurred.

2 = device table or device reservation table could not be opened for reading.

3 = reservation release could not be completely fulfilled because one or more of the devices was not reserved or was not reserved on the specified key.

FILES

/etc/device.tab
/etc/devlkfile

NOTES

The commands **devreserv** and **devfree** are used to manage the availability of devices on a system. These commands do not place any constraints on the access to the device. They serve only as a centralized bookkeeping point for those who wish to use them. Processes that do not use **devreserv** may concurrently use a device with a process that has reserved that device.

SEE ALSO

devfree(3X), **devreserv**(1), **devreserv**(3X), **reservdev**(3X)

NAME

devnm – device name

SYNOPSIS

/usr/sbin/devnm [*name* . . .]

DESCRIPTION

The **devnm** command identifies the special file associated with the mounted file system where the argument *name* resides. One or more *name*s can be specified.

This command is most commonly used by the **brc** command to construct a mount table entry for the **root** device.

EXAMPLE

The command:

    /usr/sbin/devnm /usr

produces:

    /dev/dsk/c1d0s2 /usr

if **/usr** is mounted on **/dev/dsk/c1d0s2**.

FILES

/dev/dsk/*
/etc/mnttab

SEE ALSO

brc(1M), mnttab(4)

NAME

devreserv – reserve devices for exclusive use

SYNOPSIS

devreserv [key [devicelist ...]]

DESCRIPTION

devreserv reserves devices for exclusive use. When the device is no longer required, use devfree to release it.

devreserv reserves at most one device per devicelist. Each list is searched in linear order until the first available device is found. If a device cannot be reserved from each list, the entire reservation fails.

When devreserv is invoked without arguments, it lists the devices that are currently reserved and the keys to which they are reserved. When devreserv is invoked with only the key argument, it lists the devices currently reserved to that key.

The arguments for this command are:

key   Designates a unique key on which the device will be reserved. The key must be a positive integer.

devicelist   Defines a list of devices that devreserv will search to find an available device. (The list must be formatted as a single argument to the shell.)

EXAMPLE

To reserve a floppy disk and a cartridge tape:

```
$ key=$$
$ echo "The current Process ID is equal to: $key"
The Current Process ID is equal to: 10658
$ devreserv $key diskette1,ctape1
```

To list all devices currently reserved:

```
$ devreserv
disk1         2423
diskette1     10658
ctape1        10658
```

To list all devices currently reserved to a particular key:

```
$ devreserv $key
diskette1
ctape1
```

ERRORS

The command will exit with one of the following values:

0 = successful completion of the task.

1 = command syntax incorrect, invalid option used, or internal error occurred.

2 = device table or device reservation table could not be opened for reading.

3 = device reservation request could not be fulfilled.

FILES

/etc/device.tab
/etc/devlkfile

NOTES

The commands **devreserv** and **devfree** are used to manage the availability of devices on a system. Their use is on a participatory basis and they do not place any constraints on the actual access to the device. They provide a centralized bookkeeping point for those who wish to use them. To summarize, devices which have been reserved cannot be used by processes which utilize the device reservation functions until the reservation has been canceled. However, processes that do not use device reservation may use a device that has been reserved since such a process would not have checked for its reservation status.

SEE ALSO

devfree(1M)

NAME

  df (generic), **dfspace** – report number of free disk blocks and files/free disk space

SYNOPSIS

  df [**-F** *FSType*] [**-befgiklntV**] [*current_options*] [**-o** *specific_options*]
    [*directory | special | resource. . .*]

  dfspace [**-F** *FSType*]

DESCRIPTION

  The **df** command prints the allocation portions of the generic superblock for mounted or unmounted file systems, directories or mounted resources. *directory* represents a valid directory name. If *directory* is specified, **df** reports on the device that contains the *directory*. *special* represents a special device (for example, **/dev/dsk/0s1**). *resource* is an RFS/NFS resource name. If arguments to **df** are pathnames, **df** produces a report on the file system containing the named file.

  The **df** command reports sizes in 512 byte blocks. It will report 2 blocks less free space, rather than 1 block, since the file uses one system block of 1-24 bytes.

  The directory **/etc/fscmd.d/TYPE** contains programs for each filesystem type; **df** invokes the appropriate binary. **/etc/fscmd.d** is linked to **/etc/fs**.

  current_options are options supported by the **s5**-specific module of **df**. Other FSTypes do not necessarily support these options. *specific_options* indicate suboptions specified in a comma-separated list of suboptions and/or keyword-attribute pairs for interpretation by the *FSType*-specific module of the command.

  The generic options are:

  -F   Specify the *FSType* on which to operate. This is only needed if the file system is unmounted. The *FSType* should be specified here or are determined from **/etc/vfstab** by matching the *mount_point*, *special*, or *resource* with an entry in the table.

  -b   Print only the number of kilobytes free.

  -e   Print only the number of files free.

  -f   Reports only an actual count of the blocks in the free list (free inodes arn not reported). With this option, **df** reports on raw devices.

  -g   Print the entire **statvfs** structure. Used only for mounted file systems. Cannot be used with *current_options* or with the **-o** option. This option will override the **-b**, **-e**, **-k̄**, **-n**, and **-t** options.

  -i   Display the total number of inodes, the number of free inodes, the number of used inodes, and the percentage of inodes in use.

  -k   Print allocation in kilobytes. This option should be invoked by itself because its output format is different from that of the other options.

  -l   Report on local file systems only. Used only for mounted file systems. Can not be used with *current_options* or with the **-o** option.

-n   Print only the *FSType* name. Invoked with no arguments this option prints a list of mounted file system types. Used only for mounted file systems. Can not be used with *current_options* or with the -o option.

-t   Causes total allocated block figures to be reported as well as number of free blocks.

-v   Echo the complete command line, but do not execute the command. The command line is generated by using the options and arguments provided by the user and adding to them information derived from **/etc/mnttab** or **/etc/vfstab**. This option should be used to verify and validate the command line.

-o   Specify FSType-specific options.

-v   Reports percent of blocks used as well as the number of blocks used and free. The -v option cannot be used with other options.

If no arguments or options are specified, the free space on all local and remotely mounted file systems is printed.

dfspace is a shell script that uses the **df** command. **dfspace** reports the available disk space for all mounted file systems with the exception of pseudo file systems such as **/proc**. **dfspace** reports the free disk space in mega bytes and also as a percentage of total disk space.

Without arguments, **dfspace** reports the free disk space on all file systems.

The option for **dfspace** is:

-F *FSType*   find free disk space on *FSType* file system.

NOTES

The -F option is intended for use with unmounted file systems.

This command may not be supported for all FSTypes.

If options -g or -n are used when there are remotely mounted resources, **df** will try to determine the remote resource's file system type. If it can be determined, **df** will print the file system type; otherwise, it will print **unknown**.

FILES

/dev/dsk/*

/etc/mnttab   list of filesystems currently mounted

/etc/vfstab   list of default parameters for each file system

SEE ALSO

mount(1M), mnttab(4), vfstab(4)

statvfs(2) in the *Programmer's Reference Manual*

Manual pages for the FSType-specific modules of **df** in the *System Administrator's Reference Manual*

NAME

df (s5) – report number of free disk blocks and i-nodes for **s5** file systems

SYNOPSIS

df [**-F s5**] [*generic_options*] [**-f**] [*directory... | special...*]

DESCRIPTION

generic_options are options supported by the generic **df** command.

The **df** command prints out the number of free blocks and free i-nodes in **s5** file systems or directories by examining the counts kept in the super-blocks. The *special* device name (e.g., **/dev/dsk/***, where the value of * is machine-dependent) or mount point *directory* name (e.g., **/usr**) must be specified. If *directory* is specified, the report presents information for the device that contains the directory.

The options are:

-F s5   Specifies the **s5**-FSType.

-f   An actual count of the blocks in the free list is made, rather than taking the figure from the super-block.

NOTE

The **-f** option can be used with the **-t**, **-b**, and **-e** options. The **-k** option overrides the **-f** option.

FILES

/dev/dsk/*

SEE ALSO

generic **df**(1M).

NAME

df (ufs) – report free disk space on **ufs** file systems

SYNOPSIS

df [**-F ufs**] [*generic_options*] [**-o i**] [*directory* | *special*]

DESCRIPTION

generic_options are options supported by the generic **df** command.

df displays the amount of disk space occupied by **ufs** file systems, the amount of used and available space, and how much of the file system's total capacity has been used.

Note that the amount of space reported as used and available is less than the amount of space in the file system; this is because the system reserves a fraction of the space in the file system to allow its file system allocation routines to work well. The amount reserved is typically about 10%; this may be adjusted using **tunefs**(1M). When all the space on the file system except for this reserve is in use, only the super-user can allocate new files and data blocks to existing files. When the file system is overallocated in this way, **df** may report that the file system is more than 100% utilized.

The options are:

-F ufs

    Specifies the **ufs**-FSType.

-o   Specify **ufs** file system specific options. The available option is:

    i   Report the number of used and free inodes. May not be used with *generic_options*.

NOTES

df calculates its results differently for mounted and unmounted file systems. For mounted systems the 10% reserved space mentioned above is included in the number of kilobytes used. For unmounted systems the 10% reservation is not included in the number of kilobytes used.

The **-b** and **-e** options override the **-t** option.

FILES

/etc/mnttab   list of file systems currently mounted

SEE ALSO

generic **df**(1M), **du**(1M), **quot**(1M), **tunefs**(1M), **mnttab**(4)

NAME

df – report free disk space on file systems

SYNOPSIS

df [-a] [-i] [-t *type*] [*filesystem* . . .] [*filename* . . .]

DESCRIPTION

df displays the amount of disk space occupied by currently mounted file systems, the amount of used and available space, and how much of the file system's total capacity has been used. Used without arguments, df reports on all mounted file systems, producing something like:

```
Filesystem  kbytes  used  avail  capacity  Mounted on
/dev/root    7445   4714  1986     70%     /
/dev/0s10    5148   3279  1868     64%     /stand
```

Note that **used+avail** is less than the amount of space in the file system (kbytes); this is because the system reserves a fraction of the space in the file system to allow its file system allocation routines to work well. The amount reserved is typically about 10%; this may be adjusted using **tunefs**(1M). When all the space on a file system except for this reserve is in use, only the super-user can allocate new files and data blocks to existing files. When a file system is overallocated in this way, df may report that the file system is more than 100% utilized.

If arguments to df are disk partitions (for example, **/dev/root** or *pathnames*, df produces a report on the file system containing the named file. Thus **df .** shows the amount of space on the file system containing the current directory.

Options

The options for df are as follows:

-a   Reports on all filesystems including the uninteresting ones which have zero total blocks. (For example, *automounter*)

-i   Report the number of used and free inodes.

-t *type*   Report on filesystems of a given *type* (for example, **nfs** or **4.2**).

FILES

/etc/mtab   List of filesystems currently mounted.

SEE ALSO

du(1M), quot(1M), and tunefs(1M) in the *System Administrator's Reference Manual*

NAME

dfmounts – display mounted resource information

SYNOPSIS

dfmounts [–**F** *fstype*] [–**h**] [–**o** *specific_options*] [*restriction* . . .]

DESCRIPTION

dfmounts shows the local resources shared through a distributed file system *fstype* along with a list of clients that have the resource mounted. If *restriction* is not specified, dfmounts displays remote resources mounted on the local system. *Specific_options* as well as the availability and semantics of *restriction* are specific to particular distributed file system types.

If dfmounts is entered without arguments, all remote resources currently mounted on the local system are displayed, regardless of file system type.

The output of dfmounts consists of an optional header line (suppressed with the –h flag) followed by a list of lines containing whitespace-separated fields. For each resource, the fields are:

         resource server pathname clients

where

resource	Specifies the resource name that must be given to the mount(1M) command.
server	Specifies the system from which the resource was mounted.
pathname	Specifies the pathname that must be given to the share(1M) command.
clients	Lists the systems, comma-separated, by which the resource was mounted. Clients are listed in the form *domain.*, *domain.system*, or *system*, depending on the file system type.

A field may be null. Each null field is indicated by a hyphen (–) unless the remainder of the fields on the line are also null. In this case, it may be omitted.

Fields with whitespace are enclosed in quotation marks (" ").

NOTES

dfmounts may not indicate the correct state if you mount a single resource on more than one directory.

FILES

/etc/dfs/fstypes

SEE ALSO

dfshares(1M), mount(1M), share(1M), unshare(1M)

NAME
dfmounts – display mounted NFS resource information

SYNOPSIS
dfmounts [–F nfs] [–h] [*server* . . .]

DESCRIPTION
dfmounts shows the local resources shared through Network File System, along with a list of clients that have mounted the resource. The –F flag may be omitted if NFS is the only file system type listed in the file /etc/dfs/fstypes.

The *server* option displays information about the resources mounted from each server, where *server* can be any system on the network. If no server is specified, then *server* is assumed to be the local system.

dfmounts without options displays all remote resources mounted on the local system, regardless of file system type.

The output of dfmounts consists of an optional header line (suppressed with the –h flag) followed by a list of lines containing whitespace-separated fields. For each resource, the fields are:

> *resource server pathname clients* . . .

where

resource	Specifies the resource name that must be given to the mount(1M) command.
server	Specifies the system from which the resource was mounted.
pathname	Specifies the pathname that must be given to the share(1M) command.
clients	A comma-separated list of systems that have mounted the resource.

FILES
/etc/dfs/fstypes

SEE ALSO
mount(1M), share(1M), unshare(1M).

NAME
>   dfmounts – display mounted RFS resource information

SYNOPSIS
>   dfmounts [-F rfs] [-h] [*resource_name* . . .]

DESCRIPTION
>   dfmounts shows the local resources shared through Remote File Sharing, along
>   with a list of clients that have mounted the resource. The -F flag may be omitted
>   if rfs is the first file system type listed in the file /etc/dfs/fstypes.
>
>   The output of *dfmounts* consists of an optional header line (suppressed with the
>   -h flag) followed by a list of lines containing whitespace-separated fields. For
>   each resource, the fields are:
>
>>   *resource server path clients* . . .
>
>   where
>
>>   *resource*   Specifies the resource name that must be given to the
>>   mount (1M) command.
>>
>>   *server*   Specifies the system from which the resource was mounted.
>>
>>   *path*   Specifies the full pathname that must be given to the
>>   share (1M) command.
>>
>>   *clients*   A comma-separated list of systems that have mounted the
>>   resource.
>
>   A field may be null. Each null field is indicated by a hyphen (–) unless the
>   remainder of the fields on the line are also null. In this case, it may be omitted.
>
>   Only a privileged user can execute this command.

FILES
>   /etc/dfs/fstypes

SEE ALSO
>   dfmounts(1M), share(1M), unshare(1M), fumount(1M), mount(1M)

NAME

dfshares – list available resources from remote or local systems

SYNOPSIS

dfshares [**-F** *fstype*] [**-h**] [**-o** *specific_options*] [*server* . . .]

DESCRIPTION

dfshares provides information about resources available to the host through a distributed file system of type *fstype*. *Specific_options* as well as the semantics of *server* are specific to particular distributed file systems.

If **dfshares** is entered without arguments, all resources currently shared on the local system are displayed, regardless of file system type.

The output of **dfshares** consists of an optional header line (suppressed with the **-h** flag) followed by a list of lines containing whitespace-separated fields. For each resource, the fields are:

> *resource server access transport description ...*

where

resource	Specifies the resource name that must be given to the **mount**(1M) command.
server	Specifies the name of the system that is making the resource available.
access	Specifies the access permissions granted to the client systems, either **ro** (for read-only) or **rw** (for read/write). If **dfshares** cannot determine access permissions, a hyphen (–) is displayed.
transport	Specifies the transport provider over which the *resource* is shared.
description	Describes the resource.

A field may be null. Each null field is indicated by a hyphen (–) unless the remainder of the fields on the line are also null. In this case, it may be omitted.

FILES

`/etc/dfs/fstypes`

SEE ALSO

dfmounts(1M), **mount**(1M), **share**(1M), **unshare**(1M)

NAME

dfshares – list available NFS resources from remote systems

SYNOPSIS

dfshares [-F nfs] [-h] [*server* . . .]

DESCRIPTION

dfshares provides information about resources available to the host through Network File System. The -F flag may be omitted if NFS is the first file system type listed in the file /etc/dfs/fstypes.

The query may be restricted to the output of resources available from one or more servers.

The *server* option displays information about the resources shared by each server, where *server* can be any system on the network. If no server is specified, then *server* is assumed to be the local system.

dfshares without arguments displays all resources shared on the local system, regardless of file system type.

The output of dfshares consists of an optional header line (suppressed with the -h flag) followed by a list of lines containing whitespace-separated fields. For each resource, the fields are:

   resource server access transport

where

resource	Specifies the resource name that must be given to the mount(1M) command.
server	Specifies the system that is making the resource available.
access	Specifies the access permissions granted to the client systems; however, dfshares cannot determine this information for an NFS resource and populates the field with a hyphen (-).
transport	Specifies the transport provider over which the *resource* is shared; however, dfshares cannot determine this information for an NFS resource and populates the field with a hyphen (-).

FILES

/etc/dfs/fstypes

SEE ALSO

share(1M), unshare(1M), mount(1M)

NAME
dfshares – list available RFS resources from remote systems

SYNOPSIS
dfshares [-F rfs] [-h] [*server* . . .]

DESCRIPTION
dfshares provides information about resources available to the host through Remote File Sharing. The -F flag may be omitted if rfs is the first file system type listed in the file /etc/dfs/fstypes.

The query may be restricted to the output of resources available from one or more servers. If no *server* is specified, all resources in the host's domain are displayed. A *server* may be given in the following form:

system	Specifies a system in the host's domain.
domain.	Specifies all systems in *domain*.
domain.system	Specifies *system* in *domain*.

The output of dfshares consists of an optional header line (suppressed with the -h flag) followed by a list of lines containing whitespace-separated fields. For each resource, the fields are:

resource server access transport description

where

resource	Specifies the resource name that must be given to the mount(1M) command.
server	Specifies the system that is making the resource available.
access	Specifies the access permissions granted to the client systems, either ro (for read-only) or rw (for read and write).
transport	Specifies the transport provider over which the *resource* is shared.
description	Describes the resource.

A field may be null. Each null field is indicated by a hyphen (–) unless the remainder of the fields on the line are also null. In this case, it may be omitted.

ERRORS
If your host machine cannot contact the domain name server, or the argument specified is syntactically incorrect, an error message is sent to standard error.

FILES
/etc/dfs/fstypes

SEE ALSO
share(1M), unshare(1M), mount(1M)

NAME

    `diff` – differential file comparator

SYNOPSIS

    `diff` [`–bitw`] [`–c`| `–e`| `–f` | `–h`| `–n`] *filename1 filename2*
    `diff` [`–bitw`] [`–C` *number*] *filename1 filename2*
    `diff` [`–bitw`] [`–D` *string*] *filename1 filename2*
    `diff` [`–bitw`] [`–c`| `–e`| `–f`| `–h`| `–n`] [`–l`] [`–r`] [`–s`] [`–S` *name*] *directory1*
    directory2

DESCRIPTION

    `diff` tells what lines must be changed in two files to bring them into agreement. If *filename1* (*filename2*) is –, the standard input is used. If *filename1* (*filename2*) is a directory, then a file in that directory with the name *filename2* (*filename1*) is used. The normal output contains lines of these forms:

        n1 **a** *n3,n4*
        n1,n2 **d** *n3*
        n1,n2 **c** *n3,n4*

These lines resemble **ed** commands to convert *filename1* into *filename2*. The numbers after the letters pertain to *filename2*. In fact, by exchanging **a** for **d** and reading backward one may ascertain equally how to convert *filename2* into *filename1*. As in **ed**, identical pairs, where *n1* = *n2* or *n3* = *n4*, are abbreviated as a single number.

Following each of these lines come all the lines that are affected in the first file flagged by <, then all the lines that are affected in the second file flagged by >.

  `–b`   Ignores trailing blanks (spaces and tabs) and treats other strings of blanks as equivalent.

  `–i`   Ignores the case of letters; for example, 'A' will compare equal to 'a'.

  `–t`   Expands TAB characters in output lines. Normal or –c output adds character(s) to the front of each line that may adversely affect the indentation of the original source lines and make the output lines difficult to interpret. This option will preserve the original source's indentation.

  `–w`   Ignores all blanks (SPACE and TAB characters) and treats all other strings of blanks as equivalent; for example, 'if (a == b)' will compare equal to 'if(a= =b)'.

The following options are mutually exclusive:

  `–c`   Produces a listing of differences with three lines of context. With this option output format is modified slightly: output begins with identification of the files involved and their creation dates, then each change is separated by a line with a dozen *'s. The lines removed from *filename1* are marked with '—'; those added to *filename2* are marked '+'. Lines that are changed from one file to the other are marked in both files with '!'.

−C *number*
> Produces a listing of differences identical to that produced by **−c** with *number* lines of context.

−e
> Produces a script of *a*, *c*, and *d* commands for the editor **ed**, which will recreate *filename2* from *filename1*. In connection with **−e**, the following shell program may help maintain multiple versions of a file. Only an ancestral file ($1) and a chain of version-to-version **ed** scripts ($2,$3,...) made by **diff** need be on hand. A "latest version" appears on the standard output.

> (shift; cat $*; echo '1,$p') | ed − $1

Except in rare circumstances, **diff** finds a smallest sufficient set of file differences.

−f
> Produces a similar script, not useful with **ed**, in the opposite order.

−h
> Does a fast, half-hearted job. It works only when changed stretches are short and well separated, but does work on files of unlimited length. Options **−e** and **−f** are unavailable with **−h**.

−n
> Produces a script similar to **−e**, but in the opposite order and with a count of changed lines on each insert or delete command.

−D *string*
> Creates a merged version of *filename1* and *filename2* with C preprocessor controls included so that a compilation of the result without defining *string* is equivalent to compiling *filename1*, while defining *string* will yield *filename2*.

The following options are used for comparing directories:

−l
> Produce output in long format. Before the **diff**, each text file is piped through **pr**(1) to paginate it. Other differences are remembered and summarized after all text file differences are reported.

−r
> Applies **diff** recursively to common subdirectories encountered.

−s
> Reports files that are the identical; these would not otherwise be mentioned.

−S *name*
> Starts a directory **diff** in the middle, beginning with the file *name*.

FILES
> /tmp/d?????
> /usr/lib/diffh for −h
> /usr/bin/pr

SEE ALSO
> **bdiff**(1), **cmp**(1), **comm**(1), **ed**(1), **pr**(1)

DIAGNOSTICS
> Exit status is 0 for no differences, 1 for some differences, 2 for trouble.

NOTES

Editing scripts produced under the **-e** or **-f** option are naive about creating lines consisting of a single period (.).

Missing newline at end of file X

indicates that the last line of file X did not have a new-line. If the lines are different, they will be flagged and output; although the output will seem to indicate they are the same.

NAME
diff3 – 3-way differential file comparison

SYNOPSIS
diff3 [**–exEX3**] *file1 file2 file3*

DESCRIPTION
diff3 compares three versions of a file, and publishes disagreeing ranges of text flagged with these codes:

====	all three files differ
====1	*file1* is different
====2	*file2* is different
====3	*file3* is different

The type of change suffered in converting a given range of a given file to some other is indicated in one of these ways:

f **:** *n1* **a**	Text is to be appended after line number *n1* in file *f*, where *f* = 1, 2, or 3.
f **:** *n1* **,** *n2* **c**	Text is to be changed in the range line *n1* to line *n2*. If *n1* = *n2*, the range may be abbreviated to *n1*.

The original contents of the range follows immediately after a **c** indication. When the contents of two files are identical, the contents of the lower-numbered file is suppressed.

–e Produce a script for the editor **ed**(1) that will incorporate into *file1* all changes between *file2* and *file3*, that is, the changes that normally would be flagged **====** and **====3**.

–x Produce a script to incorporate only changes flagged **====**.

–3 Produce a script to incorporate only changes flagged **====3**.

–E Produce a script that will incorporate all changes between *file2* and *file3*, but treat overlapping changes (that is, changes that would be flagged with **====** in the normal listing) differently. The overlapping lines from both files will be inserted by the edit script, bracketed by **<<<<<<** and **>>>>>>** lines.

–X Produce a script that will incorporate only changes flagged **====**, but treat these changes in the manner of the **–E** option.

The following command will apply the resulting script to *file1*.

    (cat script; echo '1,$p') | ed – *file1*

FILES
/tmp/d3∗
/usr/lib/diff3prog

SEE ALSO
diff(1)

NOTES

Text lines that consist of a single **.** will defeat **–e**.
Files longer than 64K bytes will not work.

NAME

diffmk – mark differences between versions of a **troff** input file

SYNOPSIS

/usr/ucb/diffmk *oldfile newfile markedfile*

DESCRIPTION

The **diffmk** command compares two versions of a file and creates a third version that includes "change mark" (.**mc**) commands for **nroff** and **troff**. *oldfile* and *newfile* are the old and new versions of the file. **diffmk** generates *markedfile*, which, contains the text from *newfile* with **troff**(1) "change mark" requests (.**mc**) inserted where *newfile* differs from *oldfile*. When *markedfile* is formatted, changed or inserted text is shown by a ⏐ at the right margin of each line. The position of deleted text is shown by a single *.

diffmk can also be used in conjunction with the proper **troff** requests to produce program listings with marked changes. In the following command line:

          diffmk old.c new.c marked.c ; nroff reqs marked.c ⏐ pr

the file **reqs** contains the following **troff** requests:

          .pl 1
          .ll 77
          .nf
          .eo
          .nh

which eliminate page breaks, adjust the line length, set no-fill mode, ignore escape characters, and turn off hyphenation, respectively.

If the characters ⏐ and * are inappropriate, you might run *markedfile* through **sed** to globally change them.

SEE ALSO

nroff(1), **troff**(1)

diff(1), **sed**(1) in the *User's Reference Manual*

NOTES

Aesthetic considerations may dictate manual adjustment of some output. File differences involving only formatting requests may produce undesirable output, that is, replacing .**sp** by .**sp 2** will produce a "change mark" on the preceding or following line of output.

NAME

> **dircmp** – directory comparison

SYNOPSIS

> **dircmp** [–d] [–s] [–w*n*] *dir1 dir2*

DESCRIPTION

> **dircmp** examines *dir1* and *dir2* and generates various tabulated information about the contents of the directories. Listings of files that are unique to each directory are generated for all the options. If no option is entered, a list is output indicating whether the file names common to both directories have the same contents.

> –d   Compare the contents of files with the same name in both directories and output a list telling what must be changed in the two files to bring them into agreement. The list format is described in **diff**(1).

> –s   Suppress messages about identical files.

> –w*n*   Change the width of the output line to *n* characters. The default width is 72.

SEE ALSO

> **cmp**(1), **diff**(1)

NAME

dis – object code disassembler

SYNOPSIS

dis [–o] [–V] [–L] [–s] [–d *sec*] [–D *sec*] [–F *function*] [–t *sec*] [–l *string*] *file* . . .

DESCRIPTION

The **dis** command produces an assembly language listing of *file*, which may be an object file or an archive of object files. The listing includes assembly statements and an octal or hexadecimal representation of the binary that produced those statements.

The following *options* are interpreted by the disassembler and may be specified in any order.

–d *sec*   Disassemble the named section as data, printing the offset of the data from the beginning of the section.

–D *sec*   Disassemble the named section as data, printing the actual address of the data.

–F *function*   Disassemble only the named function in each object file specified on the command line. The –F option may be specified multiple times on the command line.

–L   Lookup source labels for subsequent printing. This option works only if the file was compiled with additional debugging information (for example, the –g option of **cc**).

–l *string*   Disassemble the archive file specified by *string*. For example, one would issue the command **dis –l x –l z** to disassemble **libx.a** and **libz.a**, which are assumed to be in *LIBDIR*.

–o   Print numbers in octal. The default is hexadecimal.

–s   Perform symbolic disassembly where possible. Symbolic disassembly output will appear on the line following the instruction. Symbol names will be printed using C syntax.

–t *sec*   Disassemble the named section as text.

–V   Print, on standard error, the version number of the disassembler being executed.

If the –d, –D or –t options are specified, only those named sections from each user-supplied file name will be disassembled. Otherwise, all sections containing text will be disassembled.

On output, a number enclosed in brackets at the beginning of a line, such as [5], indicates that the break-pointable line number starts with the following instruction. These line numbers will be printed only if the file was compiled with additional debugging information [for example, the –g option of **cc**]. An expression such as <40> in the operand field or in the symbolic disassembly, following a relative displacement for control transfer instructions, is the computed address within the section to which control will be transferred. A function name will appear in the first column, followed by ( ) if the object file contains a symbol table.

FILES

LIBDIR   usually **/usr/ccs/lib**

SEE ALSO

as(1), cc(1), ld(1), a.out(4)

DIAGNOSTICS

The self-explanatory diagnostics indicate errors in the command line or problems encountered with the specified files.

NOTES

Since the **-da** option did not adhere to the command syntax rules, it has been replaced by **-D**.

At this time, symbolic disassembly does not take advantage of additional information available if the file is compiled with the **-g** option.

NAME
        diskadd – disk set up utility

SYNOPSIS
        diskadd [*disk_number*]

DESCRIPTION
        The initial system disk is set up during system installation. Additional disks
        must be set up using **diskadd**. **diskadd** is an interactive command which
        prompts the user for information about the setup of the disk.

        The optional argument *disk_number* is used to represent the SCSI disk device to be
        added to the system. If no argument or a 1 is supplied, **diskadd** will be executed
        for the second integral disk. The format of the *disk_number* argument is:

                c*xtydz*

                        x =   controller number, (0 - 2)
                        y =   Target controller SCSI ID, (0 - 6)
                        z =   Logical Unit ID number, (0 - 3).

        The tasks which are required for the setup of disks include the following steps.
        First the **fdisk**(1M) command is invoked to partition the disk. This step breaks
        up the disk into logical portions for the UNIX Operating system and for the DOS
        Operating system. The **disksetup**(1M) command is invoked next for surface
        analysis, creating/writing the **pdinfo**, VTOC and alternates info (for non-SCSI
        drives) to the disk, issuing the needed **mkfs** calls, and mounting filesystems. The
        surface analysis is done to catch any detectable defects and remap them. On
        SCSI disks, the formatting of the disk will remap any detectable defects, so the
        surface analysis is optional, but recommended. The creation of the VTOC divides
        the UNIX system partition into slices. Slices are created to contain a filesystem or
        act as a raw device (e.g., the **swap** or **dump** device). The execution of the
        mkfs(1M) command for the needed filesystems handles the creation of a specific
        type of filesystem on a slice. If automatic mounting was requested, directories
        are created in the root filesystem to hold the new filesystems, they are mounted,
        and **/etc/vfstab** is updated to remount them on subsequent bootups of the sys-
        tem.

        The device files will be present prior to running **diskadd**. The device files for an
        second integral disk **/dev/rdsk/1s*** and **/dev/dsk/1s***, are always present.

        If swap/paging space is added on the new drive, it must be made available for
        system use with the **swap**(1M) program.

NOTES
        Due to compatibility considerations, when you set-up a UFS filesystem greater
        than 128 MB, it will hold only 64k inodes. To create more than 64k inodes, either
        recreate the filesystem using **mkfs** or use the UFS filesystem debugger to allocate
        more inodes.

FILES
        /dev/dsk/1s?
        /dev/dsk/c?t?d?s?
        /dev/rdsk/1s*

    /dev/rdsk/c?t?d?s0
    /etc/vfstab

SEE ALSO

      fdisk(1M), mkdir(1M) mkfs(1M), swap(1M)

NAME

disksetup – disk set up utility

SYNOPSIS

/etc/disksetup -I -B [-d *defaults-file*] -b*boot-file raw-device* (Install primary disk)
/etc/disksetup -I [-d *defaults-file*] *raw-device* (Install additional disk)
/etc/disksetup -b *boot-file raw-device* (write boot code to the disk)

DESCRIPTION

-I   will cause the *raw-device* to be installed (surface analysis, creation/writing the pdinfo, VTOC, and alternates tables (for non-SCSI drives).

-B   is flag to designate that the raw-device will be the system boot device.

-d *defaults-file*
          is used to pass in a default layout for the raw-device. The information from the defaults file will be used to generate the default slices for the UNIX System partition. The layout of the file is explained in one of the following sections.

-b *boot-file*
          will cause the **disksetup** to write the boot code found the boot file into the boot slice of the UNIX System partition. The boot code can be in either **ELF** or **COFF** format. Only the required sections/segments will be loaded. The boot file provided with the system is **/etc/boot**.

raw-device
          the required raw-device argument is the character special device for the disk drive to be accessed. It should the slice 0 device to represent the entire device (for example, **/dev/rdsk/0s0** or **/dev/rdsk/c0t0d0s0**).

disksetup handles the low level activities required to install the primary drive or additional drives. The tasks which are required for the setup of disks include surface analysis, assisting a user create the layout of slices (either through a set of defaults or by querying them), writing the pdinfo, VTOC and alternates tables out to the drive, issuing need **mkfs** calls, creating mount points, mounting filesystems and updating the **/etc/vfstab** file. program.

In regards to **disksetup**'s method for assisting a user define the layout of slices, if no no defaults-file is provided, a user is queried first on which slices they wish to create, and then are queried on the sizes for those slices. (The user must ultimately confirm their choices and can repeat the above steps if they are unsatisfied with their choices.) If a defaults-file is provided, a default layout of slices will be created based on the defaults-file. If the user selects the default layout a VTOC representing the default layout is written to the drive. If the user does not select the default layout they will be allowed to specify the sizes for slices defined in the defaults-file.

The layout for the defaults-file is as follows:

```
slice #          slice name FStype              slice size
1         /           s5          35M
2         /dev/swap   -           2m
3         /usr        ufs         60W
4         /home       ufs         40W
10        /stand            bfs         5M
```

The slice number is the entry in VTOC where the slice will be located. Slice name is mount point if the slice is a filesystem or descriptive name if no file system will be created. *FStype* is the file system type for the slice where s5, **ufs** and **bfs** mean that type of **mkfs** is to be issued, an - means issue no **mkfs** for this slice. Slice size is an integer value followed by size specifier character. The M size specifier character means megabytes (MB), so 35M means 35 MB slice size. The m size specifier means times the size of memory, so assuming 4 MB of memory 2m means 8 MB slice size. The W size specifier character means weighted proportion. To calculate a weighted proportion of xW, x is divided by the sum of the W requests and then that value is multiplied with the remaining disk space (after M and m type requests were handled) to give the slice size. Assuming a 100 MB disk with 4 MB of memory, the above defaults file would yield:

```
slice 1 35M = 35 MB size
slice 2 2m = (2 * 4MB) = 8 MB size
slice 3 60W = (60/100 * 52 MB) = 31 MB size
slice 4 40W = (40/100 * 52 MB) = 21 MB size
slice 5 5M = 5 MB size
```

FILES

```
/dev/dsk/1s?
/dev/dsk/c?t?d?s?
/dev/rdsk/1s*
/dev/rdsk/c?t?d?s0
/etc/vfstab
```

SEE ALSO

fdisk(1M), mkdir(1M) mkfs(1M), mount(1M), swap(1M).

NAME

diskusg – generate disk accounting data by user ID

SYNOPSIS

/usr/lib/acct/diskusg [*options*] [*files*]

DESCRIPTION

diskusg generates intermediate disk accounting information from data in *files,* or the standard input if omitted. **diskusg** output lines on the standard output, one per user, in the following format: *uid login #blocks*

where

uid	the numerical user ID of the user.
login	the login name of the user; and
#blocks	the total number of disk blocks allocated to this user.

diskusg normally reads only the inodes of file systems for disk accounting. In this case, *files* are the special filenames of these devices.

diskusg recognizes the following options:

-s   the input data is already in **diskusg** output format. **diskusg** combines all lines for a single user into a single line.

-v   verbose. Print a list on standard error of all files that are charged to no one.

-i *fnmlist*   ignore the data on those file systems whose file system name is in *fnmlist*. *fnmlist* is a list of file system names separated by commas or enclosed within quotes. **diskusg** compares each name in this list with the file system name stored in the volume ID [see **labelit**(1M)].

-p *file*   use *file* as the name of the password file to generate login names. **/etc/passwd** is used by default.

-u *file*   write records to *file* of files that are charged to no one. Records consist of the special file name, the inode number, and the user ID.

The output of **diskusg** is normally the input to **acctdisk** [see **acct**(1M)] which generates total accounting records that can be merged with other accounting records. **diskusg** is normally run in **dodisk** [see **acctsh**(1M)].

EXAMPLES

The following will generate daily disk accounting information for **root** on **/dev/dsk/c1d0s0**:

    diskusg /dev/dsk/c1d0s0 | acctdisk > disktacct

FILES

/etc/passwd   used for user ID to login name conversions

SEE ALSO

acct(1M), **acctsh**(1M), **acct**(4)

NOTES

diskusg only works for S5 file systems. acctdusg (see acct(1M)) works for all file systems, but is slower than diskusg.

NAME

dispadmin – process scheduler administration

SYNOPSIS

dispadmin -l
dispadmin -c *class* -g [-r *res*]
dispadmin -c *class* -s *file*

DESCRIPTION

The **dispadmin** command displays or changes process scheduler parameters while the system is running.

The **-l** option lists the scheduler classes currently configured in the system.

The **-c** option specifies the class whose parameters are to be displayed or changed. Valid *class* values are **RT** for the real-time class and **TS** for the time-sharing class.

The **-g** option gets the parameters for the specified class and writes them to the standard output. Parameters for the real-time class are described on **rt_dptbl**(4). Parameters for the time-sharing class are described on **ts_dptbl**(4).

When using the **-g** option you may also use the **-r** option to specify a resolution to be used for outputting the time quantum values. If no resolution is specified, time quantum values are in milliseconds. If *res* is specified it must be a positive integer between 1 and 1000000000 inclusive, and the resolution used is the reciprocal of *res* in seconds. For example, a *res* value of 10 yields time quantum values expressed in tenths of a second; a *res* value of 1000000 yields time quantum values expressed in microseconds. If the time quantum cannot be expressed as an integer in the specified resolution, it is rounded up to the next integral multiple of the specified resolution.

The **-s** option sets scheduler parameters for the specified class using the values in *file*. These values overwrite the current values in memory—they become the parameters that control scheduling of processes in the specified class. The values in *file* must be in the format output by the **-g** option. Moreover, the values must describe a table that is the same size (has same number of priority levels) as the table being overwritten. Super-user privileges are required in order to use the **-s** option.

The **-g** and **-s** options are mutually exclusive: you may not retrieve the table at the same time you are overwriting it.

dispadmin does some limited sanity checking on the values supplied in *file* to verify that they are within their required bounds. The sanity checking, however, does not attempt to analyze the effect that the new values have on the performance of the system. Inappropriate values can have a dramatic negative effect on system performance. See the *System Administrator's Guide* for more information.

EXAMPLES

The following command retrieves the current scheduler parameters for the real-time class from kernel memory and writes them to the standard output. Time quantum values are in microseconds.

```
dispadmin -c RT -g -r 1000000
```

The following command overwrites the current scheduler parameters for the real-time class with the values specified in **rt.config**.

    dispadmin -c RT -s rt.config

The following command retrieves the current scheduler parameters for the time-sharing class from kernel memory and writes them to the standard output. Time quantum values are in nanoseconds.

    dispadmin -c TS -g -r 1000000000

The following command overwrites the current scheduler parameters for the time-sharing class with the values specified in **ts.config**.

    dispadmin -c TS -s ts.config

DIAGNOSTICS

dispadmin prints an appropriate diagnostic message if it fails to overwrite the current scheduler parameters due to lack of required permissions or a problem with the specified input file.

SEE ALSO

priocntl(1), priocntl(2), rt_dptbl(4), ts_dptbl(4)

NAME

dispgid – displays a list of all valid group names

SYNOPSIS

dispgid

DESCRIPTION

dispgid displays a list of all group names on the system (one group per line).

EXIT CODES

0 = Successful execution

1 = Cannot read the group file

NAME
    dispuid – displays a list of all valid user names

SYNOPSIS
    dispuid

DESCRIPTION
    dispuid displays a list of all user names on the system (one line per name).

EXIT CODES
    0 = Successful execution
    1 = Cannot read the password file

NAME
       dname – print Remote File Sharing domain and network names

SYNOPSIS
       dname [–D *domain*] [–N *netspeclist*] [–dna]

DESCRIPTION
       dname prints or defines a host's Remote File Sharing domain name or the
       network(s) used by Remote File Sharing as transport provider(s). When used
       with d, n, or a options, dname can be run by any user to print the domain name,
       transport provider name(s), or both. Only a user with root permission can use
       the –D *domain* option to set the domain name for the host or –N *netspeclist* to set
       the network specification used for Remote File Sharing. *netspeclist* is a comma-
       separated list of transport providers (*tp1,tp2,. . .*). The value of each transport
       provider is the network device name, relative to the */dev* directory. For example,
       the STARLAN NETWORK uses starlan.

       domain must consist of no more than 14 characters, consisting of any combination
       of letters (upper and lower case), digits, hyphens (–), and underscores (_).

       When dname is used to change a domain name, the host's password is removed.
       The administrator will be prompted for a new password the next time Remote
       File Sharing is started [rfstart(1M)].

       If dname is used with no options, it will default to dname –d.

NOTES
       You cannot use the –N or –D options while Remote File Sharing is running.

SEE ALSO
       rfstart(1M)

NAME

   domainname – get/set name of current secure RPC domain

SYNOPSIS

   domainname [*newname*]

DESCRIPTION

   The **domainname** command is used on secure RPC machines. With no argument, the name of the machine's secure RPC domain is written to standard output.

   The **domainname** command with an argument sets the name of the secure RPC domain to *newname*. *newname* may be up to 255 characters long.

   domainname is normally run by the RPC administrator on all machines to set the name of the secure RPC domain. To use secure RPC, machines must have secure RPC domain names.

NOTES

   Secure RPC domain names are not related to and should not be confused with RFS domains.

   The RPC package expects the *newname* argument to be a valid filename for the underlying file system in use on the networked machines using secure RPC. For example, machines based on the s5 file system should not have domain names longer than 14 characters in length or problems may occur when using secure RPC.

   The secure RPC domain name set by **domainname** will not be remembered across reboots. To give a machine a "permanent" name, set the **SRPC_DOMAIN** tunable in **/etc/master.d/name** to the secure RPC domain name.

SEE ALSO

   RPC Administration in the *Programmer's Guide: Networking Interfaces*

NAME

dos: **doscat, doscp, dosdir, dosformat, dosmkdir, dosls, dosrm, dosrmdir** – access and manipulate DOS files

SYNOPSIS

doscat [**-r** | **-m**] *file* . . .

doscp [**-r** | **-m**] *file1 file2*

doscp [**-r** | **-m**] *file* . . . *directory*

dosdir *directory*

dosformat [**-fqv**] *drive*

dosls *directory* . . .

dosmkdir *directory* . . .

dosrm *file* . . .

dosrmdir *directory* . . .

DESCRIPTION

The **dos** commands allow access to files and directories on a DOS hard disk partition or diskette. The DOS partition must be bootable, although not active.

Below is a description of the **dos** commands:

doscat   Copies one or more DOS files to the standard output. If **-r** is given, the files are copied without newline conversions. If **-m** is given, the files are copied with newline conversions.

doscp   Copies files from/to a DOS diskette or a DOS hard disk partition to/from a UNIX file system. **doscp** will rename a file while it is copying. For example, the command:

         doscp a:file1 file2

         copies the file named **file1** from the DOS disk to the UNIX file system and renames it file2.

         If *directory* is given, one or more *files* are copied to that directory. If **-r** is given, the files are copied without new line conversions. If **-m** is given, the files are copied with newline conversions.

dosdir   Lists DOS files in the standard DOS style directory format. (See the DOS **DIR** command.)

dosformat Creates a DOS 2.0 formatted diskette. It cannot be used to format a hard disk partition. The drive must be specified using the UNIX special file names. For example, if your system has two floppy drives, the first a 3.5" and the second a 5.25", then the following special file names would be used to format low and high density floppies:

DOS Format	UNIX special file name
1.4 MB	/dev/rdsk/f03ht
720 KB	/dev/rdsk/f03dt
1.2 MB	/dev/rdsk/f15ht
360 KB	/dev/rdsk/f15d9t

In the above special file names, **f0** refers to the first floppy drive, and **f1** refers to the second floppy drive.

The **-f** option suppresses the interactive feature. The **-q** (quiet) option is used to suppress information normally displayed during **dosformat**, but it does not suppress the interactive feature. The **-v** option prompts the user for a volume label after the diskette has been formatted. The maximum size of the volume label is 11 characters.

dosls　　Lists DOS directories and files in a UNIX system style format [see **ls**(1)].

dosrm　　Removes DOS files.

dosmkdir　　Creates DOS directories.

dosrmdir　　Deletes DOS directories.

The *file* and *directory* arguments for DOS files and directories have the form:

　　device:*name*

where *device* is a UNIX system path name for the special device file containing the DOS disk, and *name* is a path name to a file or directory on the DOS disk. The two components are separated by a colon (:). For example, the argument:

　　/dev/rdsk/f0t:/src/file.c

specifies the DOS file **file.asm** in the directory **/src** on diskette **/dev/rdsk/fd0t**. Note that slashes (and not backslashes) are used as file name separators for DOS path names. Arguments without a *device*: are assumed to be UNIX files.

For convenience, the user-configurable default file **/etc/default/msdos** can define DOS drive names to be used in place of the special device file path names. It may contain the following lines:

　　A=/dev/rdsk/f0t
　　C=/dev/rdsk/0s5
　　D=/dev/rdsk/1s5

The drive letter **A** may be used in place of special device file path name **/dev/rdsk/f0t** when referencing DOS files (see "Examples" below). The drive letter **C** or **D** refer to the DOS partition on the first or second hard disk.

The commands operate on the following types of disks:

　　DOS partitions on a hard disk
　　5-1/4 inch DOS
　　3-1/2 inch DOS
　　8, 9, 15, or 18 sectors per track

40 tracks per side
1 or 2 sides
DOS versions 1.0, 2.0, or 3.0

In the case of **doscp**, certain name conversions can be performed when copying a UNIX system file. File names with a base name longer than eight characters are truncated. Filename extensions (the part of the name following the separating period) longer than three characters are truncated. For example, the file 123456789.12345 becomes 12345678.123. A message informs the user that the name has been changed and the altered name is displayed. File names containing illegal DOS characters are stripped when writing to the DOS format. A message informs the user that characters have been removed and displays the name as written.

All DOS text files use a carriage-return/linefeed combination, CR-LF, to indicate a newline. UNIX system text files use a single newline LF character. When the **doscat** and **doscp** commands transfer DOS text files to UNIX system text files, they automatically strip the CR. When text files are transferred to DOS, the commands insert a CR before each LF character.

Under some circumstances, the automatic newline conversions do not occur. The -**m** option may be used to ensure the newline conversion. The -**r** option can be used to override the automatic conversion and force the command to perform a true byte copy regardless of file type.

EXAMPLES
```
doscat /dev/rdsk/f0t:tmp/output.1
doscat /tmp/f1 /tmp/f2/A:prog/output.1

dosdir /dev/rdsk/f0t:/prog
dosdir /D:/prog

doscp /mine/file.out/dev/rdsk/f0t:/mine/file.2
doscp /tmp/f1 /tmp/f2 D:

dosformat /dev/rdsk/f0d8dt

dosls /dev/rdsk:/src
dosls B:

dosmkdir /dev/fd0:/usr/docs

dosrm /dev/rdsk:/docs/memo.txt
dosrm /A:/docs/memo1.txt

dosrmdir /dev/rdsk:/usr/docs
```

FILES

`/etc/default/msdos`	Default information
`/dev/rdsk/f0t`	Floppy disk devices
`/dev/rdsk/0s5`	Hard disk devices

SEE ALSO

`directory`(3C) in the *Programmer's Reference Manual*

See your MS-DOS Documentation.

NOTES

It is not possible to refer to DOS directories with wild card specifications.

The programs mentioned above cooperate among themselves so no two programs will access the same DOS disk simultaneously. If a process attempts to access a device already in use, it displays the error message **Device Busy**, and exits with and exit code of 1.

The device argument to dosformat must be specific. For example, use **/dev/rdsk/f03ht** not **/dev/rdsk/f0t** or **a:**.

The DOS partition hard disk device names correspond as follows:

/dev/dsk/0s5	is equivalent to /dev/hd0d
/dev/rdsk/0s5	is equivalent to /dev/rhd0d
/dev/dsk/1s5	is equivalent to /dev/hd1d
/dev/rdsk/1s5	is equivalent to /dev/rhd1d

All of the DOS utilities leave temporary files in **/tmp**. These files are automatically removed when the system is rebooted. They can also be manually removed.

You must have DOS 3.3 or earlier. Extended DOS partitions are not supported.

NAME

download – host resident PostScript font downloader

SYNOPSIS

download [*options*] [*files*]

DESCRIPTION

download prepends host resident fonts to *files* and writes the results on the standard output. If no *files* are specified, or if – is one of the input *files*, the standard input is read. download assumes the input *files* make up a single PostScript job and that requested fonts can be included at the start of each input *file*. The following *options* are understood:

-f   Force a complete scan of each input *file*. In the absence of an explicit comment pointing download to the end of the file, the default scan stops immediately after the PostScript header comments.

-p *printer*   Before downloading, check the list of printer-resident fonts in /etc/lp/printers/*printer*/residentfonts.

-m *name*   Use *name* as the font map table. A *name* that begins with / is the full pathname of the map table and is used as is. Otherwise *name* is appended to the pathname of the host font directory.

-H *dir*   Use *dir* as the host font directory. The default is /usr/lib/lp/postscript.

Requested fonts are named in a comment (marked with %%DocumentFonts:) in the input *files*. Available fonts are the ones listed in the map table selected using the -m option.

The map table consists of fontname–filename pairs. The fontname is the full name of the PostScript font, exactly as it would appear in a %%DocumentFonts: comment. The filename is the pathname of the host resident font. A filename that begins with a / is used as is. Otherwise the pathname is relative to the host font directory. Comments are introduced by % (as in PostScript) and extend to the end of the line.

The only candidates for downloading are fonts listed in the map table that point download to readable files. A font is downloaded once, at most. Requests for unlisted fonts or inaccessible files are ignored. All requests are ignored if the map table can't be read.

EXAMPLES

The following map table could be used to control the downloading of the Bookman font family:

```
%
% The first string is the full PostScript font name.
% The second string is the file name - relative to the
% host font directory unless it begins with a /.
%
    Bookman-Light            bookman/light
    Bookman-LightItalic      bookman/lightitalic
    Bookman-Demi             bookman/demi
    Bookman-DemiItalic       bookman/demiitalic
```

Using the file **myprinter/map** (in the default host font directory) as the map table, you could download fonts by issuing the following command:

> **download −m** *myprinter/map file*

DIAGNOSTICS

An exit status of **0** is returned if *files* were successfully processed.

NOTES

The **download** program should be part of a more general program.

download does not look for **%%PageFonts:** comments and there is no way to force multiple downloads of a particular font.

We do not recommend the use of full pathnames in either map tables or the names of map tables.

SEE ALSO

dpost(1), **postdaisy**(1), **postdmd**(1), **postio**(1), **postmd**(1), **postprint**(1), **posttek**(1)

NAME

dpost – **troff** postprocessor for PostScript printers

SYNOPSIS

/usr/lib/lp/postscript/dpost [*options*] [*files*]

DESCRIPTION

dpost translates *files* created by **troff**(1) into PostScript and writes the results on the standard output. If no *files* are specified, or if – is one of the input *files*, the standard input is read. The following *options* are understood:

–c *num*   Print *num* copies of each page. By default only one copy is printed.

–e *num*   Sets the text encoding level to *num*. The recognized choices are 0, 1, and 2. The size of the output file and print time should decrease as *num* increases. Level 2 encoding will typically be about 20 percent faster than level 0, which is the default and produces output essentially identical to previous versions of **dpost**.

–m *num*   Magnify each logical page by the factor *num*. Pages are scaled uniformly about the origin, which is located near the upper left corner of each page. The default magnification is 1.0.

–n *num*   Print *num* logical pages on each piece of paper, where *num* can be any positive integer. By default, *num* is set to 1.

–o *list*   Print those pages for which numbers are given in the comma-separated *list*. The list contains single numbers *N* and ranges *N1–N2*. A missing *N1* means the lowest numbered page, a missing *N2* means the highest.

–p *mode*   Print *files* in either portrait or landscape *mode*. Only the first character of *mode* is significant. The default *mode* is portrait.

–w *num*   Set the line width used to implement *troff* graphics commands to *num* points, where a point is approximately 1/72 of an inch. By default, *num* is set to 0.3 points.

–x *num*   Translate the origin *num* inches along the positive x axis. The default coordinate system has the origin fixed near the upper left corner of the page, with positive x to the right and positive y down the page. Positive *num* moves everything right. The default offset is 0 inches.

–y *num*   Translate the origin *num* inches along the positive y axis. Positive *num* moves text up the page. The default offset is 0.

–F d*ir*   Use *dir* as the font directory. The default *dir* is **/usr/lib/font**, and *dpost* reads binary font files from directory **/usr/lib/font/devpost**.

–H *dir*   Use *dir* as the host resident font directory. Files in this directory should be complete PostScript font descriptions, and must be assigned a name that corresponds to the appropriate two-character **troff** font name. Each font file is copied to the

output file only when needed and at most once during each job.
There is no default directory.

−L *file*   Use *file* as the PostScript prologue which, by default, is
`/usr/lib/postscript/dpost.ps`.

−o   Disables PostScript picture inclusion. A recommended option
when **dpost** is run by a spooler in a networked environment.

−T *name*   Use font files for device *name* as the best description of available
PostScript fonts. By default, *name* is set to **post** and **dpost**
reads binary files from `/usr/lib/font/devpost`.

The *files* should be prepared by **troff**. The default font files in
`/usr/lib/font/devpost` produce the best and most efficient output. They
assume a resolution of 720 dpi, and can be used to format files by adding the
−Tpost option to the **troff** call. Older versions of the **eqn** and **pic** preproces-
sors need to know the resolution that **troff** will be using to format the *files*. If
those are the versions installed on your system, use the −r720 option with **eqn**
and −T720 with **pic**.

dpost makes no assumptions about resolutions. The first **x res** command sets
the resolution used to translate the input *files*, the `DESC.out` file, usually
`/usr/lib/font/devpost/DESC.out`, defines the resolution used in the binary
font files, and the PostScript prologue is responsible for setting up an appropriate
user coordinate system.

EXAMPLES

If the old versions of **eqn** and **pic** are installed on your system, you can obtain
the best possible looking output by issuing a command line such as the following:

       `pic -T720` *file* `| tbl | eqn -r720 | troff -mm -Tpost | dpost`

Otherwise,

       `pic` *file* `| tbl | eqn | troff -mm -Tpost | dpost`

should give the best results.

NOTES

Output files often do not conform to Adobe's file structuring conventions. Piping
the output of **dpost** through **postreverse** should produce a minimally conforming PostScript file.

Although **dpost** can handle files formatted for any device, emulation is expensive
and can easily double the print time and the size of the output file. No attempt
has been made to implement the character sets or fonts available on all devices
supported by **troff**. Missing characters will be replaced by white space, and
unrecognized fonts will usually default to one of the Times fonts (that is, R, I, B,
or BI).

An **x res** command must precede the first **x init** command, and all the input
files should have been prepared for the same output device.

Use of the −T option is not encouraged. Its only purpose is to enable the use of
other PostScript font and device description files, that perhaps use different resolutions, character sets, or fonts.

Although level 0 encoding is the only scheme that has been thoroughly tested, level 2 is fast and may be worth a try.

DIAGNOSTICS

An exit status of 0 is returned if *files* have been translated successfully, while 2 often indicates a syntax error in the input *files*.

FILES

```
/usr/lib/font/devpost/*.out
/usr/lib/font/devpost/charlib/*
/usr/lib/lp/postscript/dpost.ps
/usr/lib/lp/postscript/color.ps
/usr/lib/lp/postscript/draw.ps
/usr/lib/lp/postscript/forms.ps
/usr/lib/lp/postscript/ps.requests
/usr/lib/macros/pictures
/usr/lib/macros/color
```

SEE ALSO

download(1), postdaisy(1), postdmd(1), postio(1), postmd(1), postprint(1), postreverse(1), posttek(1), troff(1) devpost(5), troff(5)

NAME

    du – summarize disk usage

SYNOPSIS

    du [-sar] [*name* ...]

DESCRIPTION

    The du command reports the number of blocks contained in all files and (recursively) directories within each directory and file specified. The block count includes the indirect blocks of the file. If no *name*s are given, the current directory is used.

    The optional arguments are as follows:

    -s   causes only the grand total (for each of the specified *name*s) to be given.

    -a   causes an output line to be generated for each file.

    If neither -s or -a is specified, an output line is generated for each directory only.

    -r   will cause du to generate messages about directories that cannot be be read, files that cannot be opened, etc., rather than being silent (the default).

    A file with two or more links is only counted once.

NOTES

    If the -a option is not used, non-directories given as arguments are not listed.

    If there are links between files in different directories where the directories are on separate branches of the file system hierarchy, du will count the excess files more than once.

    Files with holes in them will get an incorrect block count.

SEE ALSO

    See the chapter on file system administration in the *System Administrator's Guide*.

NAME

　　　du – display the number of disk blocks used per directory or file

SYNOPSIS

　　　/usr/ucb/du [-a] [-s] [*filename* . . .]

DESCRIPTION

　　　du gives the number of kilobytes contained in all files and, recursively, directories within each specified directory or file *filename*. If *filename* is missing, '.' (the current directory) is used.

　　　A file which has multiple links to it is only counted once.

OPTIONS

　　　-a　　　Generate an entry for each file.

　　　-s　　　Only display the grand total for each of the specified *filenames*.

　　　Entries are generated only for each directory in the absence of options.

EXAMPLE

　　　Here is an example of using du in a directory. We used the pwd(1) command to identify the directory, then used du to show the usage of all the subdirectories in that directory. The grand total for the directory is the last entry in the display:

```
% pwd
/usr/ralph/misc
% du
5       ./jokes
33      ./squash
44      ./tech.papers/lpr.document
217     ./tech.papers/new.manager
401     ./tech.papers
144     ./memos
80      ./letters
388     ./window
93      ./messages
15      ./useful.news
1211    .
%
```

SEE ALSO

　　　df(1M), pwd(1) in the *User's Reference Manual*
　　　quot(1M) in the *System Administrator's Reference Manual*

NOTES

　　　Filename arguments that are not directory names are ignored, unless you use -a.

　　　If there are too many distinct linked files, du will count the excess files more than once.

NAME

dump – dump selected parts of an object file

SYNOPSIS

dump [*options*] *files*

DESCRIPTION

The **dump** command dumps selected parts of each of its object *file* arguments.

This command will accept both object files and archives of object files. It processes each file argument according to one or more of the following options:

-a   Dump the archive header of each member of an archive.

-C   Dump decoded C++ symbol table names.

-c   Dump the string table(s).

-D   Dump debugging information.

-f   Dump each file header.

-g   Dump the global symbols in the symbol table of an archive.

-h   Dump the section headers.

-L   Dump dynamic linking information and static shared library information, if available.

-l   Dump line number information.

-o   Dump each program execution header.

-r   Dump relocation information.

-s   Dump section contents in hexadecimal.

-T *index* or -T *index1*,*index2*
           Dump only the indexed symbol table entry defined by *index* or a range of entries defined by *index1*,*index2*.

-t   Dump symbol table entries.

-u   When reading a COFF object file, **dump** translates the file to ELF internally (this translation does not affect the file contents). This option controls how much translation occurs from COFF values to ELF. Normally (without –u), the COFF values are preserved as much as possible, showing the actual bytes in the file. If –u is used, **dump** updates the values and completes the internal translation, giving a consistent ELF view of the contents. Although the bytes displayed under this option might not match the file itself, they show how the file would look if it were converted to ELF. (See **cof2elf**(1) for more information.)

-V   Print version information.

The following modifiers are used in conjunction with the options listed above to modify their capabilities.

-d *number* or **-d** *number1*,*number2*

Dump the section number indicated by *number* or the range of sections starting at *number1* and ending at *number2*. This modifier can be used with **-h**, **-s**, and **-r**. When **-d** is used with **-h** or **-s**, the argument is treated as the number of a section or range of sections. When **-d** is used with **-r**, the argument is treated as the number of the section or range of sections to which the relocation applies. For example, to print out all relocation entries associated with the **.text** section, specify the number of the section as the argument to **-d**. If **.text** is section number 2 in the file, **dump** **-r** **-d** **2** will print all associated entries. To print out a specific relocation section use **dump** **-s** **-n** *name* for raw data output, or **dump** **-sv** **-n** *name* for interpreted output.

-n *name*

Dump information pertaining only to the named entity. This modifier can be used with **-h**, **-s**, **-r**, and **-t**. When **-n** is used with **-h** or **-s**, the argument will be treated as the name of a section. When **-n** is used with **-t** or **-r**, the argument will be treated as the name of a symbol. For example, **dump** **-t** **-n** **.text** will dump the symbol table entry associated with the symbol whose name is **.text**, where **dump** **-h** **-n** **.text** will dump the section header information for the **.text** section.

-p

Suppress printing of the headings.

-v

Dump information in symbolic representation rather than numeric. This modifier can be used with **-a** (date, user id, group id), **-f** (class, data, type, machine, version, flags), **-h** (type, flags), **-o** (type, flags), **-r** (name, type), **-s** (interpret section contents wherever possible), **-t** (type, bind), and **-L** (value). When **-v** is used with **-s**, all sections that can be interpreted, such as the string table or symbol table, will be interpreted. For example, **dump** **-sv** **-n** **.symtab** *files* will produce the same formatted output as **dump** **-tv** *files*, but **dump** **-s** **-n** **.symtab** *files* will print raw data in hexadecimal. Without additional modifiers, **dump** **-sv** *files* will dump all sections in the files interpreting all those that it can and dumping the rest (such as **.text** or **.data**) as raw data.

The **dump** command attempts to format the information it dumps in a meaningful way, printing certain information in character, hexadecimal, octal or decimal representation as appropriate.

SEE ALSO

a.out(4), ar(4)

NAME

    echo – echo arguments

SYNOPSIS

    echo [*arg*] . . .

    echo [–n] [*arg*]

DESCRIPTION

    echo writes its arguments separated by blanks and terminated by a new-line on the standard output.

    The **/usr/bin/sh** version understands the following C-like escape conventions; beware of conflicts with the shell's use of \ :

\ b	backspace
\ c	print line without new-line
\ f	form-feed
\ n	new-line
\ r	carriage return
\ t	tab
\v	vertical tab
\\	backslash
\ 0*n*	where *n* is the 8-bit character whose ASCII code is the 1-, 2- or 3-digit octal number representing that character.

    The following option is available to **/usr/bin/sh** users only if **/usr/ucb** precedes **/usr/bin** in the user's PATH. It is available to **/usr/csh** users, regardless of PATH:

        –n   Do not add the newline to the output.

    echo is useful for producing diagnostics in command files, for sending known data into a pipe, and for displaying the contents of environment variables.

SEE ALSO

    sh(1).

NOTES

    The –n option is a transition aid for BSD applications, and may not be supported in future releases.

    When representing an 8-bit character by using the escape convention \ 0*n*, the *n* must **always** be preceded by the digit zero (0).

    For example, typing: **echo** ´WARNING:\ 07´ will print the phrase WARNING: and sound the "bell" on your terminal. The use of single (or double) quotes (or two backslashes) is required to protect the "\" that precedes the "07".

    Following the \ 0, up to three digits are used in constructing the octal output character. If, following the \ 0*n*, you want to echo additional digits that are not part of the octal representation, you must use the full 3-digit *n*. For example, if you want to echo "ESC 7" you must use the three digits "033" rather than just the two digits "33" after the \ 0.

2 digits	Incorrect: produces:	`echo "\0337"	od -xc` `df0a` `337`	(hex) (ascii)
3 digits	Correct: produces:	`echo "\00337"	od -xc` `1b37 0a00` `033 7`	(hex) (ascii)

For the octal equivalents of each character, see ascii(5), in the *System Administrator's Reference Manual.*

NAME

echo – put string on virtual output

SYNOPSIS

echo [*string . . .*]

DESCRIPTION

The **echo** function directs each string it is passed to *stdout*. It is often used in conditional execution or for passing a string to another command.

EXAMPLES

Set the **done** descriptor to **help** if a test fails:

```
done=`if [ -s $F1 ];
    then echo close;
    else echo help;
    fi`
```

SEE ALSO

echo(1)

NAME

echo – echo arguments

SYNOPSIS

/usr/ucb/echo [arg] . . .

/usr/ucb/echo [**–n**] [arg]

DESCRIPTION

echo writes its arguments separated by blanks and terminated by a new-line on the standard output.

The **/usr/bin/sh** version understands the following C-like escape conventions; beware of conflicts with the shell's use of \:

\b	backspace
\c	print line without new-line
\f	form-feed
\n	new-line
\r	carriage return
\t	tab
\v	vertical tab
\\	backslash
\0n	where n is the 8-bit character whose ASCII code is the 1-, 2- or 3-digit octal number representing that character.

The following option is available to **/usr/bin/sh** users only if **/usr/ucb** precedes **/usr/bin** in the user's PATH. It is available to **/usr/csh** users, regardless of PATH:

–n　　Do not add the newline to the output.

echo is useful for producing diagnostics in command files and for sending known data into a pipe.

SEE ALSO

sh(1) in the *User's Reference Manual*

NOTES

The **–n** option is a transition aid for BSD applications, and may not be supported in future releases.

The When representing an 8-bit character by using the escape convention \0n, the n must **always** be preceded by the digit zero (0).

For example, typing: **echo** ´**WARNING:\07**´ will print the phrase **WARNING:** and sound the "bell" on your terminal. The use of single (or double) quotes (or two backslashes) is required to protect the "\" that precedes the "07".

For the octal equivalents of each character, see ascii(5), in the *System Administrator's Reference Manual*.

NAME

ed, red – text editor

SYNOPSIS

ed [-s] [-p *string*] [-x] [-c] [*file*]

red [-s] [-p *string*] [-x] [-c] [*file*]

DESCRIPTION

ed is the standard text editor. If the *file* argument is given, ed simulates an e command (see below) on the named file; that is to say, the file is read into ed's buffer so that it can be edited.

-s   Suppresses the printing of character counts by e, r, and w commands, of diagnostics from e and q commands, and of the ! prompt after a !*shell command*.

-p   Allows the user to specify a prompt string.

-x   Encryption option; when used, ed simulates an X command and prompts the user for a key. This key is used to encrypt and decrypt text using the algorithm of crypt(1). The X command makes an educated guess to determine whether text read in is encrypted or not. The temporary buffer file is encrypted also, using a transformed version of the key typed in for the -x option. See crypt(1). Also, see the NOTES section at the end of this manual page.

-c   Encryption option; the same as the -x option, except that ed simulates a C command. The C command is like the X command, except that all text read in is assumed to have been encrypted.

ed operates on a copy of the file it is editing; changes made to the copy have no effect on the file until a w (write) command is given. The copy of the text being edited resides in a temporary file called the *buffer*. There is only one buffer.

red is a restricted version of ed. It will only allow editing of files in the current directory. It prohibits executing shell commands via !*shell command*. Attempts to bypass these restrictions result in an error message (restricted shell).

Both ed and red support the fspec(4) formatting capability. After including a format specification as the first line of *file* and invoking ed with your terminal in stty -tabs or stty tab3 mode [see stty(1)], the specified tab stops will automatically be used when scanning *file*. For example, if the first line of a file contained:

        <:t5,10,15 s72:>

tab stops would be set at columns 5, 10, and 15, and a maximum line length of 72 would be imposed. NOTE: when you are entering text into the file, this format is not in effect; instead, because of being in stty -tabs or stty tab3 mode, tabs are expanded to every eighth column.

Commands to ed have a simple and regular structure: zero, one, or two *addresses* followed by a single-character *command*, possibly followed by parameters to that command. These addresses specify one or more lines in the buffer. Every command that requires addresses has default addresses, so that the addresses can very often be omitted.

In general, only one command may appear on a line. Certain commands allow the input of text. This text is placed in the appropriate place in the buffer. While **ed** is accepting text, it is said to be in input mode. In this mode, no commands are recognized; all input is merely collected. Leave input mode by typing a period (**.**) at the beginning of a line, followed immediately by a carriage return.

ed supports a limited form of regular expression notation; regular expressions are used in addresses to specify lines and in some commands (for example, **s**) to specify portions of a line that are to be substituted. A regular expression (RE) specifies a set of character strings. A member of this set of strings is said to be matched by the regular expression. The regular expressions allowed by **ed** are constructed as follows:

The following one-character regular expressions match a single character:

1.1   An ordinary character (not one of those discussed in 1.2 below) is a one-character regular expression that matches itself.

1.2   A backslash (\) followed by any special character is a one-character regular expression that matches the special character itself. The special characters are:

    a.   **.**, *****, **[**, and **** (period, asterisk, left square bracket, and backslash, respectively), which are always special, except when they appear within square brackets (**[ ]**; see 1.4 below).

    b.   **^** (caret or circumflex), which is special at the beginning of an entire regular expression (see 4.1 and 4.3 below), or when it immediately follows the left of a pair of square brackets (**[ ]**) (see 1.4 below).

    c.   **$** (dollar sign), which is special at the **end** of an entire regular expression (see 4.2 below).

    d.   The character used to bound (that is, delimit) an entire regular expression, which is special for that regular expression (for example, see how slash (**/**) is used in the **g** command, below.)

1.3   A period (**.**) is a one-character regular expression that matches any character except new-line.

1.4   A non-empty string of characters enclosed in square brackets (**[ ]**) is a one-character regular expression that matches any one character in that string. If, however, the first character of the string is a circumflex (**^**), the one-character regular expression matches any character except new-line and the remaining characters in the string. The **^** has this special meaning only if it occurs first in the string. The minus (**–**) may be used to indicate a range of consecutive characters; for example, **[0–9]** is equivalent to **[0123456789]**. The **–** loses this special meaning if it occurs first (after an initial **^**, if any) or last in the string. The right square bracket (**]**) does not terminate such a string when it is the first character within it (after an initial **^**, if any); for example, **[ ]a–f]** matches either a right square bracket (**]**) or one of the ASCII letters **a** through **f** inclusive. The four characters listed in 1.2.a above stand for themselves within such a string of characters.

The following rules may be used to construct regular expressions from one-character regular expressions:

2.1   A one-character regular expression is a regular expression that matches whatever the one-character regular expression matches.

2.2   A one-character regular expression followed by an asterisk ($*$) is a regular expression that matches *zero* or more occurrences of the one-character regular expression. If there is any choice, the longest leftmost string that permits a match is chosen.

2.3   A one-character regular expression followed by \{m\}, \{m,\}, or \{m,n\} is a regular expression that matches a range of occurrences of the one-character regular expression. The values of m and n must be non-negative integers less than 256; \{m\} matches exactly m occurrences; \{m,\} matches at least m occurrences; \{m,n\} matches any number of occurrences between m and n inclusive. Whenever a choice exists, the regular expression matches as many occurrences as possible.

2.4   The concatenation of regular expressions is a regular expression that matches the concatenation of the strings matched by each component of the regular expression.

2.5   A regular expression enclosed between the character sequences \(and \) is a regular expression that matches whatever the unadorned regular expression matches.

2.6   The expression \$n$ matches the same string of characters as was matched by an expression enclosed between \(and \) earlier in the same regular expression. Here n is a digit; the sub-expression specified is that beginning with the n-th occurrence of \(counting from the left. For example, the expression ^\(.*\)\1$ matches a line consisting of two repeated appearances of the same string.

A regular expression may be constrained to match words.

3.1   \< constrains a regular expression to match the beginning of a string or to follow a character that is not a digit, underscore, or letter. The first character matching the regular expression must be a digit, underscore, or letter.

3.2   \> constrains a regular expression to match the end of a string or to precede a character that is not a digit, underscore, or letter.

An entire regular expression may be constrained to match only an initial segment or final segment of a line (or both).

4.1   A circumflex (^) at the beginning of an entire regular expression constrains that regular expression to match an initial segment of a line.

4.2   A dollar sign ($) at the end of an entire regular expression constrains that regular expression to match a final segment of a line.

4.3   The construction ^*entire regular expression*$ constrains the entire regular expression to match the entire line.

The null regular expression (for example, //) is equivalent to the last regular expression encountered. See also the last paragraph before FILES below.

To understand addressing in **ed** it is necessary to know that at any time there is a *current line*. Generally speaking, the current line is the last line affected by a command; the exact effect on the current line is discussed under the description of each command. *Addresses* are constructed as follows:

1.   The character **.** addresses the current line.

2.   The character **$** addresses the last line of the buffer.

3.   A decimal number *n* addresses the *n*-th line of the buffer.

4.   '*x* addresses the line marked with the mark name character *x*, which must be an ASCII lower-case letter (**a–z**). Lines are marked with the **k** command described below.

5.   A regular expression enclosed by slashes (**/**) addresses the first line found by searching forward from the line following the current line toward the end of the buffer and stopping at the first line containing a string matching the regular expression. If necessary, the search wraps around to the beginning of the buffer and continues up to and including the current line, so that the entire buffer is searched. See also the last paragraph before FILES below.

6.   A regular expression enclosed in question marks (**?**) addresses the first line found by searching backward from the line preceding the current line toward the beginning of the buffer and stopping at the first line containing a string matching the regular expression. If necessary, the search wraps around to the end of the buffer and continues up to and including the current line. See also the last paragraph before FILES below.

7.   An address followed by a plus sign (**+**) or a minus sign (**–**) followed by a decimal number specifies that address plus (respectively minus) the indicated number of lines. A shorthand for .+5 is .5.

8.   If an address begins with **+** or **–**, the addition or subtraction is taken with respect to the current line; for example, **–5** is understood to mean **.–5**.

9.   If an address ends with **+** or **–**, then 1 is added to or subtracted from the address, respectively. As a consequence of this rule and of Rule 8, immediately above, the address **–** refers to the line preceding the current line. (To maintain compatibility with earlier versions of the editor, the character ^ in addresses is entirely equivalent to **–**.) Moreover, trailing **+** and **–** characters have a cumulative effect, so **––** refers to the current line less 2.

10.   For convenience, a comma (**,**) stands for the address pair **1**, **$**, while a semicolon (**;**) stands for the pair **.**, **$**.

Commands may require zero, one, or two addresses. Commands that require no addresses regard the presence of an address as an error. Commands that accept one or two addresses assume default addresses when an insufficient number of addresses is given; if more addresses are given than such a command requires, the last one(s) are used.

Typically, addresses are separated from each other by a comma (,). They may also be separated by a semicolon (;). In the latter case, the first address is calculated, the current line (.) is set to that value, and then the second address is calculated. This feature can be used to determine the starting line for forward and backward searches (see Rules 5 and 6, above). The second address of any two-address sequence must correspond to a line in the buffer that follows the line corresponding to the first address.

In the following list of **ed** commands, the parentheses shown prior to the command are not part of the address; rather they show the default address(es) for the command.

It is generally illegal for more than one command to appear on a line. However, any command (except **e**, **f**, **r**, or **w**) may be suffixed by **l**, **n**, or **p** in which case the current line is either listed, numbered or printed, respectively, as discussed below under the **l**, **n**, and **p** commands.

(.)a
<text>
.

> The **a**ppend command accepts zero or more lines of text and appends it after the addressed line in the buffer. The current line (.) is left at the last inserted line, or, if there were none, at the addressed line. Address 0 is legal for this command: it causes the "appended" text to be placed at the beginning of the buffer. The maximum number of characters that may be entered from a terminal is 256 per line (including the new-line character).

(.)c
<text>
.

> The **c**hange command deletes the addressed lines from the buffer, then accepts zero or more lines of text that replaces these lines in the buffer. The current line (.) is left at the last line input, or, if there were none, at the first line that was not deleted.

c

> Same as the **X** command, described later, except that **ed** assumes all text read in for the **e** and **r** commands is encrypted unless a null key is typed in.

(. , .)d

> The **d**elete command deletes the addressed lines from the buffer. The line after the last line deleted becomes the current line; if the lines deleted were originally at the end of the buffer, the new last line becomes the current line.

e *file*

> The **e**dit command deletes the entire contents of the buffer and then reads the contents of *file* into the buffer. The current line (.) is set to the last line of the buffer. If *file* is not given, the currently remembered file name, if any, is used (see the **f** command). The number of characters read in is printed; *file* is remembered for possible use as a default file name in subsequent **e**, **r**, and **w** commands. If *file* is replaced by !, the rest of the line is

taken to be a shell [sh(1)] command whose output is to be read in. Such a shell command is not remembered as the current file name. See also DIAGNOSTICS below.

E *file*

    The **E**dit command is like **e**, except that the editor does not check to see if any changes have been made to the buffer since the last **w** command.

f *file*

    If *file* is given, the **f** ile-name command changes the currently remembered file name to *file*; otherwise, it prints the currently remembered file name.

(**1** , **$**) **g** /*regular expression* / *command list*

    In the **g**lobal command, the first step is to mark every line that matches the given regular expression. Then, for every such line, the given *command list* is executed with the current line (**.**) initially set to that line. A single command or the first of a list of commands appears on the same line as the global command. All lines of a multi-line list except the last line must be ended with a \; **a**, **i**, and **c** commands and associated input are permitted. The **.** terminating input mode may be omitted if it would be the last line of the *command list*. An empty *command list* is equivalent to the **p** command. The **g**, **G**, **v**, and **V** commands are not permitted in the *command list*. See also the NOTES and the last paragraph before FILES below.

(**1** , **$**) **G** /*regular expression* /

    In the interactive **G**lobal command, the first step is to mark every line that matches the given regular expression. Then, for every such line, that line is printed, the current line (**.**) is changed to that line, and any one command (other than one of the **a**, **c**, **i**, **g**, **G**, **v**, and **V** commands) may be input and is executed. After the execution of that command, the next marked line is printed, and so on; a new-line acts as a null command; an **&** causes the re-execution of the most recent command executed within the current invocation of **G**. Note that the commands input as part of the execution of the **G** command may address and affect any lines in the buffer. The **G** command can be terminated by an interrupt signal (ASCII DEL or BREAK).

h

    The **h**elp command gives a short error message that explains the reason for the most recent **?** diagnostic.

H

    The **H**elp command causes **ed** to enter a mode in which error messages are printed for all subsequent **?** diagnostics. It will also explain the previous **?** if there was one. The **H** command alternately turns this mode on and off; it is initially off.

(.)**i**
<text>
.

> The **i**nsert command accepts zero or more lines of text and inserts it
> before the addressed line in the buffer. The current line (**.**) is left at the
> last inserted line, or, if there were none, at the addressed line. This com-
> mand differs from the **a** command only in the placement of the input text.
> Address 0 is not legal for this command. The maximum number of char-
> acters that may be entered from a terminal is 256 per line (including the
> new-line character).

(. , . +1)**j**

> The **j**oin command joins contiguous lines by removing the appropriate
> new-line characters. If exactly one address is given, this command does
> nothing.

(.)**k**x

> The **m**ark command marks the addressed line with name x, which must
> be an ASCII lower-case letter (**a**–**z**). The address 'x then addresses this
> line; the current line (**.**) is unchanged.

(. , .)**l**

> The **l**ist command prints the addressed lines in an unambiguous way: a
> few non-printing characters (for example, *tab, backspace*) are represented by
> visually mnemonic overstrikes. All other non-printing characters are
> printed in octal, and long lines are folded. An **l** command may be
> appended to any command other than **e**, **f**, **r**, or **w**.

(. , .)**m**a

> The **m**ove command repositions the addressed line(s) after the line
> addressed by a. Address **0** is legal for a and causes the addressed line(s)
> to be moved to the beginning of the file. It is an error if address a falls
> within the range of moved lines; the current line (**.**) is left at the last line
> moved.

(. , .)**n**

> The **n**umber command prints the addressed lines, preceding each line by
> its line number and a tab character; the current line (**.**) is left at the last
> line printed. The **n** command may be appended to any command other
> than **e**, **f**, **r**, or **w**.

(. , .)**p**

> The **p**rint command prints the addressed lines; the current line (**.**) is left at
> the last line printed. The **p** command may be appended to any command
> other than **e**, **f**, **r**, or **w**. For example, **dp** deletes the current line and
> prints the new current line.

P

> The editor will prompt with a ∗ for all subsequent commands. The **P**
> command alternately turns this mode on and off; it is initially off.

q

    The **q**uit command causes **ed** to exit. No automatic write of a file is done; however, see
DIAGNOSTICS , below.

Q

    The editor exits without checking if changes have been made in the buffer since the last **w** command.

($)**r** *file*

    The **r**ead command reads the contents of *file* into the buffer. If *file* is not given, the currently remembered file name, if any, is used (see the **e** and **f** commands). The currently remembered file name is not changed unless *file* is the very first file name mentioned since **ed** was invoked. Address 0 is legal for **r** and causes the file to be read in at the beginning of the buffer. If the read is successful, the number of characters read in is printed; the current line (**.**) is set to the last line read in. If *file* is replaced by **!**, the rest of the line is taken to be a shell [see **sh**(1)] command whose output is to be read in. For example, **$r !ls** appends current directory to the end of the file being edited. Such a shell command is not remembered as the current file name.

(**.** , **.**)**s**/*regular expression*/*replacement*/   or
(**.** , **.**)**s**/*regular expression*/*replacement*/**g**   or
(**.** , **.**)**s**/*regular expression*/*replacement*/*n*   *n* = 1-512

    The **s**ubstitute command searches each addressed line for an occurrence of the specified regular expression. In each line in which a match is found, all (non-overlapped) matched strings are replaced by the *replacement* if the global replacement indicator **g** appears after the command. If the global indicator does not appear, only the first occurrence of the matched string is replaced. If a number *n*, appears after the command, only the *n*-th occurrence of the matched string on each addressed line is replaced. It is an error if the substitution fails on all addressed lines. Any character other than space or new-line may be used instead of **/** to delimit the regular expression and the *replacement*; the current line (**.**) is left at the last line on which a substitution occurred. See also the last paragraph before FILES below.

    An ampersand (**&**) appearing in the *replacement* is replaced by the string matching the regular expression on the current line. The special meaning of **&** in this context may be suppressed by preceding it by ****. As a more general feature, the characters *****n***, where *n* is a digit, are replaced by the text matched by the *n*-th regular subexpression of the specified regular expression enclosed between **\(** and **\)**. When nested parenthesized subexpressions are present, *n* is determined by counting occurrences of **\(** starting from the left. When the character **%** is the only character in the *replacement*, the *replacement* used in the most recent substitute command is used as the *replacement* in the current substitute command. The **%** loses its special meaning when it is in a replacement string of more than one character or is preceded by a ****.

A line may be split by substituting a new-line character into it. The new-line in the *replacement* must be escaped by preceding it by \. Such substitution cannot be done as part of a **g** or **v** command list.

(. , .)t*a*

This command acts just like the **m** command, except that a *copy* of the addressed lines is placed after address **a** (which may be 0); the current line (.) is left at the last line copied.

u

The **undo** command nullifies the effect of the most recent command that modified anything in the buffer, namely the most recent **a, c, d, g, i, j, m, r, s, t, v, G,** or **V** command.

(1 , $)v/*regular expression***/***command list*

This command is the same as the global command **g**, except that the lines marked during the first step are those that do not match the regular expression.

(1 , $)V/*regular expression***/**

This command is the same as the interactive global command **G**, except that the lines that are marked during the first step are those that do not match the regular expression.

(1 , $)w *file*

The **write** command writes the addressed lines into *file*. If *file* does not exist, it is created with mode **666** (readable and writable by everyone), unless your file creation mask dictates otherwise; see the description of the **umask** special command on **sh**(1). The currently remembered file name is not changed unless *file* is the very first file name mentioned since **ed** was invoked. If no file name is given, the currently remembered file name, if any, is used (see the **e** and **f** commands); the current line (.) is unchanged. If the command is successful, the number of characters written is printed. If *file* is replaced by **!**, the rest of the line is taken to be a shell [see **sh**(1)] command whose standard input is the addressed lines. Such a shell command is not remembered as the current file name.

(1 , $)W *file*

This command is the same as the **write** command above, except that it appends the addressed lines to the end of *file* if it exists. If *file* does not exist, it is created as described above for the *w* command.

x

A key is prompted for, and it is used in subsequent **e, r,** and **w** commands to decrypt and encrypt text using the **crypt**(1) algorithm. An educated guess is made to determine whether text read in for the **e** and **r** commands is encrypted. A null key turns off encryption. Subsequent **e, r,** and **w** commands will use this key to encrypt or decrypt the text [see **crypt**(1)]. An explicitly empty key turns off encryption. Also, see the **−x** option of **ed.**

($) =
> The line number of the addressed line is typed; the current line (.) is unchanged by this command.

!*shell command*
> The remainder of the line after the ! is sent to the UNIX system shell [see **sh**(1)] to be interpreted as a command. Within the text of that command, the unescaped character % is replaced with the remembered file name; if a ! appears as the first character of the shell command, it is replaced with the text of the previous shell command. Thus, !! will repeat the last shell command. If any expansion is performed, the expanded line is echoed; the current line (.) is unchanged.

(.+1)<new-line>
> An address alone on a line causes the addressed line to be printed. A new-line alone is equivalent to .+1p; it is useful for stepping forward through the buffer.

If an interrupt signal (ASCII DEL or BREAK) is sent, **ed** prints a ? and returns to its command level.

Some size limitations: 512 characters in a line, 256 characters in a global command list, and 64 characters in the pathname of a file (counting slashes). The limit on the number of lines depends on the amount of user memory: each line takes 1 word.

When reading a file, **ed** discards ASCII NUL characters.

If a file is not terminated by a new-line character, **ed** adds one and puts out a message explaining what it did.

If the closing delimiter of a regular expression or of a replacement string (for example, /) would be the last character before a new-line, that delimiter may be omitted, in which case the addressed line is printed. The following pairs of commands are equivalent:

        s/s1/s2   s/s1/s2/p g/s1 g/s1/p ?s1   ?s1?

FILES

$TMPDIR	if this environmental variable is not null, its value is used in place of /var/tmp as the directory name for the temporary work file.
/var/tmp	if /var/tmp exists, it is used as the directory name for the temporary work file.
/tmp	if the environmental variable TMPDIR does not exist or is null, and if /var/tmp does not exist, then /tmp is used as the directory name for the temporary work file.
ed.hup	work is saved here if the terminal is hung up.

SEE ALSO

edit(1), ex(1), grep(1), sed(1), sh(1), stty(1), umask(1), vi(1)

fspec(4), regexp(5) in the *System Administrator's Reference Manual*

DIAGNOSTICS

?	for command errors.
?file	for an inaccessible file.
	(use the **help** and **Help** commands for detailed explanations).

If changes have been made in the buffer since the last **w** command that wrote the entire buffer, **ed** warns the user if an attempt is made to destroy **ed**'s buffer via the **e** or **q** commands. It prints **?** and allows one to continue editing. A second **e** or **q** command at this point will take effect. The **−s** command-line option inhibits this feature.

NOTES

The **−** option, although it continues to be supported, has been replaced in the documentation by the **−s** option that follows the Command Syntax Standard [see **intro**(1)].

The encryption options and commands are provided with the Security Administration Utilities package, which is available only in the United States.

A **!** command cannot be subject to a **g** or a **v** command.

The **!** command and the **!** escape from the **e**, **r**, and **w** commands cannot be used if the editor is invoked from a restricted shell [see **sh**(1)].

The sequence **\n** in a regular expression does not match a new-line character.

If the editor input is coming from a command file (for example, **ed** *file* < *ed_cmd_file*), the editor exits at the first failure.

NAME

edit – text editor (variant of ex for casual users)

SYNOPSIS

edit [-r] [-x] [-C] *name*...

DESCRIPTION

edit is a variant of the text editor **ex** recommended for new or casual users who wish to use a command-oriented editor. It operates precisely as **ex** with the following options automatically set:

novice	ON
report	ON
showmode	ON
magic	OFF

These options can be turned on or off via the **set** command in **ex**(1).

-r   Recover file after an editor or system crash.

-x   Encryption option; when used the file will be encrypted as it is being written and will require an encryption key to be read. **edit** makes an educated guess to determine if a file is encrypted or not. See **crypt**(1). Also, see the NOTES section at the end of this manual page.

-C   Encryption option; the same as -x except that **edit** assumes files are encrypted.

The following brief introduction should help you get started with **edit**. If you are using a CRT terminal you may want to learn about the display editor **vi**.

To edit the contents of an existing file you begin with the command **edit** *name* to the shell. **edit** makes a copy of the file that you can then edit, and tells you how many lines and characters are in the file. To create a new file, you also begin with the command **edit** with a filename: **edit** *name*; the editor will tell you it is a **[New File]**.

The **edit** command prompt is the colon (:), which you should see after starting the editor. If you are editing an existing file, then you will have some lines in **edit**'s buffer (its name for the copy of the file you are editing). When you start editing, **edit** makes the last line of the file the current line. Most commands to **edit** use the current line if you do not tell them which line to use. Thus if you say **print** (which can be abbreviated **p**) and type carriage return (as you should after all **edit** commands), the current line will be printed. If you **delete** (d) the current line, **edit** will print the new current line, which is usually the next line in the file. If you **delete** the last line, then the new last line becomes the current one.

If you start with an empty file or wish to add some new lines, then the **append** (a) command can be used. After you execute this command (typing a carriage return after the word **append**), **edit** will read lines from your terminal until you type a line consisting of just a dot (.); it places these lines after the current line. The last line you type then becomes the current line. The **insert** (i) command is like **append**, but places the lines you type before, rather than after, the current line.

edit numbers the lines in the buffer, with the first line having number 1. If you execute the command **1**, then **edit** will type the first line of the buffer. If you then execute the command **d**, **edit** will delete the first line, line 2 will become line 1, and **edit** will print the current line (the new line 1) so you can see where you are. In general, the current line will always be the last line affected by a command.

You can make a change to some text within the current line by using the **substitute (s)** command: **s**/*old*/*new*/ where *old* is the string of characters you want to replace and *new* is the string of characters you want to replace *old* with.

The **file (f)** command will tell you how many lines there are in the buffer you are editing and will say **[Modified]** if you have changed the buffer. After modifying a file, you can save the contents of the file by executing a **write (w)** command. You can leave the editor by issuing a **quit (q)** command. If you run **edit** on a file, but do not change it, it is not necessary (but does no harm) to **write** the file back. If you try to **quit** from **edit** after modifying the buffer without writing it out, you will receive the message **No write since last change (:quit! overrides)**, and **edit** will wait for another command. If you do not want to write the buffer out, issue the **quit** command followed by an exclamation point (**q!**). The buffer is then irretrievably discarded and you return to the shell.

By using the **d** and **a** commands and giving line numbers to see lines in the file, you can make any changes you want. You should learn at least a few more things, however, if you will use **edit** more than a few times.

The **change (c)** command changes the current line to a sequence of lines you supply (as in **append**, you type lines up to a line consisting of only a dot (.). You can tell **change** to change more than one line by giving the line numbers of the lines you want to change, i.e., **3,5c**. You can print lines this way too: **1,23p** prints the first 23 lines of the file.

The **undo (u)** command reverses the effect of the last command you executed that changed the buffer. Thus if you execute a **substitute** command that does not do what you want, type **u** and the old contents of the line will be restored. You can also **undo** an **undo** command. **edit** will give you a warning message when a command affects more than one line of the buffer. Note that commands such as **write** and **quit** cannot be undone.

To look at the next line in the buffer, type carriage return. To look at a number of lines, type ^D (while holding down the control key, press d) rather than carriage return. This will show you a half-screen of lines on a CRT or 12 lines on a hardcopy terminal. You can look at nearby text by executing the **z** command. The current line will appear in the middle of the text displayed, and the last line displayed will become the current line; you can get back to the line where you were before you executed the **z** command by typing ´´. The **z** command has other options: **z-** prints a screen of text (or 24 lines) ending where you are; **z+** prints the next screenful. If you want less than a screenful of lines, type **z.11** to display five lines before and five lines after the current line. (Typing **z.**n, when n is an odd number, displays a total of n lines, centered about the current line; when n is an even number, it displays $n-1$ lines, so that the lines displayed are centered around the current line.) You can give counts after other commands; for

example, you can delete 5 lines starting with the current line with the command
`d5` .

To find things in the file, you can use line numbers if you happen to know them; since the line numbers change when you insert and delete lines this is somewhat unreliable. You can search backwards and forwards in the file for strings by giving commands of the form /*text*/ to search forward for *text* or ?*text*? to search backward for *text* . If a search reaches the end of the file without finding *text*, it wraps around and continues to search back to the line where you are. A useful feature here is a search of the form /^*text*/ which searches for *text* at the beginning of a line. Similarly /*text*$/ searches for *text* at the end of a line. You can leave off the trailing / or ? in these commands.

The current line has the symbolic name dot (`.`); this is most useful in a range of lines as in `.,$p` which prints the current line plus the rest of the lines in the file. To move to the last line in the file, you can refer to it by its symbolic name $. Thus the command `$d` deletes the last line in the file, no matter what the current line is. Arithmetic with line references is also possible. Thus the line `$-5` is the fifth before the last and `.+20` is 20 lines after the current line.

You can find out the current line by typing `.=`. This is useful if you wish to move or copy a section of text within a file or between files. Find the first and last line numbers you wish to copy or move. To move lines 10 through 20, type `10,20d a` to delete these lines from the file and place them in a buffer named **a**. **edit** has 26 such buffers named **a** through **z**. To put the contents of buffer **a** after the current line, type **put a**. If you want to move or copy these lines to another file, execute an **edit** (**e**) command after copying the lines; following the **e** command with the name of the other file you wish to edit, i.e., **edit chapter2**. To copy lines without deleting them, use **yank** (**y**) in place of **d**. If the text you wish to move or copy is all within one file, it is not necessary to use named buffers. For example, to move lines 10 through 20 to the end of the file, type `10,20m $`.

SEE ALSO

    ed(1), **ex**(1), **vi**(1)

NOTES

    The encryption options are provided with the Security Administration Utilities package, which is available only in the United States.

NAME

edquota – edit user quotas

SYNOPSIS

edquota [−p *proto_user*] *username*...
edquota −t

DESCRIPTION

edquota is a quota editor. One or more users may be specified on the command line. For each user a temporary file is created with an ASCII representation of the current disk quotas for that user for each mounted ufs file system that has a quotas file, and an editor is then invoked on the file. A null entry is used if no quotas file exists for a file system. The quotas may then be modified, new quotas added, etc. Upon leaving the editor, edquota reads the temporary file and modifies the binary quota files to reflect the changes made.

The editor invoked is vi(1) unless the EDITOR environment variable specifies otherwise.

Only the super-user may edit quotas. In order for quotas to be established on a file system, the root directory of the file system must contain a file, owned by root, called quotas. See quotaon(1M) for details.

proto_user and username can be numeric, corresponding to the uid of a user. Unassigned uids may be specified; unassigned names may not. In this way, default quotas can be established for users who are later assigned a uid.

The options are:

−p   Duplicate the quotas of the *proto_user* specified for each *username* specified. This is the normal mechanism used to initialize quotas for groups of users.

−t   Edit the soft time limits for each file system. If the time limits are zero, the default time limits in /usr/include/sys/fs/ufs_quota.h are used. Time units of sec(onds), min(utes), hour(s), day(s), week(s), and month(s) are understood. Time limits are printed in the greatest possible time unit such that the value is greater than or equal to one.

FILES

quotas   quota file at the file system root
/etc/mnttab   table of mounted file systems

SEE ALSO

quota(1M), quotacheck(1M), quotaon(1M), repquota(1M), vi(1)

NAME

edsysadm – sysadm interface editing tool

SYNOPSIS

edsysadm

DESCRIPTION

edsysadm is an interactive tool that adds or changes either menu and task definitions in the sysadm interface. It can be used to make changes directly on-line on a specific machine or to create changes that will become part of a software package. The command creates the administration files necessary to achieve the requested changes in the interface and either places them in the appropriate place for on-line changes or saves them to be included in a software package.

edsysadm presents several screens, first prompting for which type of menu item you want to change, **menu** or **task**, and then for what type of action to take, **add** or **change**. When you select **add**, a blank menu or task definition (as described below) is provided for you to fill in. When you select **change**, a series of screens is presented to help identify the definition you wish to change. The final screen presented is the menu or task definition filled in with its current values, which you can then edit.

The menu definition prompts and their descriptions are:

Menu Name
: The name of the new menu (as it should appear in the lefthand column of the screen). This field has a maximum length of 16 alphanumeric characters.

Menu Description
: A description of the new menu (as it should appear in the righthand column of the screen). This field has a maximum length of 58 characters and can consist of any alphanumeric character except at sign (@), carat (^), tilde (˜), back grave (`), grave ('), and double quotes (").

Menu Location
: The location of the menu in the menu hierarchy, expressed as a menu pathname. The pathname should begin with the main menu followed by all other menus that must be traversed (in the order they are traversed) to access this menu. Each menu name must be separated by colons. For example, the menu location for a menu entry being added to the Applications menu is **main:applications**. Do not include the menu name in this location definition. The complete pathname to this menu entry will be the menu location plus the menu name defined at the first prompt.

    This is a scrollable field, showing a maximum of 50 alphanumeric characters at a time.

Menu Help File Name

Pathname to the item help file for this menu entry. If it resides in the directory from which you invoked **edsysadm**, you do not need to give a full pathname. If you name an item help file that does not exist, you are placed in an editor (as defined by **$EDITOR**) to create one. The new file is created in the current directory and named **Help**.

The task definition prompts and their descriptions are:

Task Name

The name of the new task (as it should appear in the lefthand column of the screen). This field has a maximum length of 16 alphanumeric characters.

Task Description

A description of the new task (as it should appear in the righthand column of the screen). This field has a maximum length of 58 characters and can consist of any alphanumeric character except at sign (@), carat (^), tilde (~), back grave ('), grave ('), and double quotes (").

Task Location

The location of the task in the menu hierarchy, expressed as a pathname. The pathname should begin with the main menu followed by all other menus that must be traversed (in the order they are traversed) to access this task. Each menu name must be separated by colons. For example, the task location for a task entry being added to the applications menu is **main:applications**. Do not include the task name in this location definition. The complete pathname to this task entry will be the task location as well as the task name defined at the first prompt.

This is a scrollable field, showing a maximum of 50 alphanumeric characters at a time.

Task Help File Name

Pathname to the item help file for this task entry. If it resides in the directory from which you invoked **edsysadm**, you do not need to give a full pathname. If you name an item help file that does not exist, you are placed in an editor (as defined by **$EDITOR**) to create one. The new file is created in the current directory and named **Help**.

Task Action

The FACE form name or executable that will be run when this task is selected. This is a scrollable field, showing a maximum of 58 alphanumeric characters at a time. This pathname can be relative to the current directory as well as absolute.

Task Files

Any FACE objects or other executables that support the task action listed above and might be called from within that action. *Do not include the help file name or the task action in this list*. Pathnames can be relative to the current directory as well as absolute. A dot (.) implies "all files in the current directory" and includes files in subdirectories.

This is a scrollable field, showing a maximum of 50 alphanumeric characters at a time.

Once the menu or task has been defined, screens for installing the menu or task or saving them for packaging are presented. The package creation or on-line installation is verified and you are informed upon completion.

NOTES

For package creation or modification, this command automatically creates a menu information file and a **prototype** file in the current directory (the directory from which the command is executed). The menu information file is used during package installation to modify menus in the menu structure. A **prototype** file is an installation file which gives a listing of package contents. The **prototype** file created by **edsysadm** lists the files defined under task action and gives them the special installation class of "admin". The contents of this **prototype** file must be incorporated in the package **prototype** file.

For on-line installation, **edsysadm** automatically creates a menu information file and adds or modifies the interface menu structure directly.

The item help file must follow the format shown in the *Application Programmer's Guide* in the "Customizing the Administration Interace" chapter or in the *System Administrator's Guide* in the "Customizing the **sysadm** Interface" appendix.

SEE ALSO

delsysadm(1M), pkgmk(1), prototype(4), sysadm(1M)

NAME

edvtoc – VTOC (Volume Table of Contents) editing utility

SYNOPSIS

edvtoc -f *vtoc-file raw-device*

DESCRIPTION

The **edvtoc** command allows you to edit the contents of the VTOC (Volume Table Of Contents). The required procedure for editing the VTOC includes three steps. First, run **prtvtoc** [see prtvtoc(1M)] using the **-f** option. Second, edit the file created by **prtvtoc** to reflect the needed changes to the VTOC. Third, run **edvtoc** using the edited file.

edvtoc provides four functions; reading/interpreting the *vtoc-file*, limited validity checking of the new VTOC, displaying the new VTOC, and writing the VTOC to the disk if the user requests it.

When editing the VTOC, the following entries are the valid slice tags and slice permission flags.

Slice Tags

#define	V_BOOT	0x01	/* Boot slice */
#define	V_ROOT	0x02	/* Root filesystem */
#define	V_SWAP	0x03	/* Swap filesystem */
#define	V_USR	0x04	/* Usr filesystem */
#define	V_BACKUP	0x05	/* full disk */
#define	V_ALTS	0x06	/* alternate sector space */
#define	V_OTHER	0x07	/* non-unix space */
#define	V_ALTTRK	0x08	/* alternate track space */
#define	V_STAND	0x09	/* Stand slice */
#define	V_VAR	0x0a	/* Var slice */
#define	V_HOME	0x0b	/* Home slice */
#define	V_DUMP	0x0c	/* dump slice */

Slice Permission Flags

#define	V_UNMNT	0x01	/* Unmountable partition */
#define	V_RONLY	0x10	/* Read only */
#define	V_VALID	0x200	/* Partition is valid to use */

The start and size value are in absolute sector numbers where the first sector on the drive is 0 (which is reserved for the partition table). Slices should start and end on a cylinder boundary if possible. The head, cylinder and sectors/track information provided by **prtvtoc -p** will assist in the calculations. Slices should not overlap (slice 0 is the exception, it describes the entire UNIX partition).

OPTIONS

–f *vtoc-file*   writes the current contents of the VTOC into the *vtoc-file* in a condensed format. The format of the file is slice number, slice tag value, slice flag value, slice start sector, slice size (in sectors). The purpose of this file is to be input for the **edvtoc** command.

raw-device   *raw-device* is the character special device for the disk drive to be accessed. It must be the slice 0 device to represent the entire device (for example, **/dev/rdsk/0s0** or **/dev/rdsk/c0t0d0s0**).

FILES

/dev/dsk/0s0
/dev/rdsk/1s0
/dev/rdsk/c?t?d?s0

SEE ALSO

prtvtoc(1M)

NAME

egrep – search a file for a pattern using full regular expressions

SYNOPSIS

egrep [*options*] *full_regular_expression* [*file* . . .]

DESCRIPTION

egrep (expression **grep**) searches files for a pattern of characters and prints all lines that contain that pattern. **egrep** uses full regular expressions (expressions that have string values that use the full set of alphanumeric and special characters) to match the patterns. It uses a fast deterministic algorithm that sometimes needs exponential space.

egrep accepts the same full regular expressions accepted by **ed**, with six exceptions:

```
\ (     \ <     \ {m
\ )     \ >     n\ }
```

(The regular expressions \ (and \ ) should not be confused with parentheses used for grouping.) In addition, **egrep** accepts the following expressions:

1. A full regular expression followed by **+** that matches one or more occurrences of the full regular expression.
2. A full regular expression followed by **?** that matches 0 or 1 occurrences of the full regular expression.
3. Full regular expressions separated by | or by a newline that match strings that are matched by any of the expressions.
4. A full regular expression that may be enclosed in parentheses ( ) for grouping.

Be careful using the characters **$**, *, [, ^, |, (,), and \ in *full_regular_expression*, because they are also meaningful to the shell. It is safest to enclose the entire *full_regular_expression* in single quotes ' . . . '.

The order of precedence of operators is [ ], then * ? +, then concatenation, then | and newline.

If no files are specified, **egrep** assumes standard input. Normally, each line found is copied to the standard output. The filename is printed before each line found if there is more than one input file.

Command line options are:

-b Precede each line by the block number on which it was found. This can be useful in locating block numbers by context (first block is 0).

-c Print only a count of the lines that contain the pattern.

-i Ignore uppercase/lowercase distinction during comparisons.

-h Suppress printing of filenames when searching multiple files.

-l Print the names of files with matching lines once, separated by newlines. Does not repeat the names of files when the pattern is found more than once.

-n   Precede each line by its line number in the file (first line is 1).

-v   Print all lines except those that contain the pattern.

-e *special_expression*

Search for a *special_expression* (*full_regular_expression* that begins with a −).

-f *file*

Take the list of *full_regular_expressions* from *file*.

SEE ALSO

ed(1), **fgrep**(1), **grep**(1), **sed**(1), **sh**(1)

DIAGNOSTICS

Exit status is 0 if any matches are found, 1 if none, 2 for syntax errors or inaccessible files (even if matches were found).

NOTES

Ideally there should be only one **grep** command, but there is not a single algorithm that spans a wide enough range of space-time tradeoffs. Lines are limited to **BUFSIZ** characters; longer lines are truncated. **BUFSIZ** is defined in **/usr/include/stdio.h**.

NAME

enable, disable – enable/disable LP printers

SYNOPSIS

enable *printers*

disable [*options*] *printers*

DESCRIPTION

The **enable** command activates the named *printers*, enabling them to print requests submitted by the **lp** command. If the printer is remote, the command will only enable the transfer of requests to the remote system; the **enable** command must be run again, on the remote system, to activate the printer. (Run **lpstat -p** to get the status of printers.)

The **disable** command deactivates the named *printers*, disabling them from printing requests submitted by **lp**. By default, any requests that are currently printing on the designated printers will be reprinted in their entirety either on the same printer or on another member of the same class of printers. If the printer is remote, this command will only stop the transmission of jobs to the remote system. The **disable** command must be run on the remote system to disable the printer. (Run **lpstat -p** to get the status of printers.) Options for use with **disable** are:

-c   Cancel any requests that are currently printing on any of the designated printers. This option cannot be used with the **-w** option. If the printer is remote, the **-c** option will be silently ignored.

-r *reason*   Assign a *reason* for the disabling of the printers. This *reason* applies to all *printers* specified. This *reason* is reported by **lpstat -p**. *reason* must be enclosed in quotes if it contains blanks. The default reason is **unknown reason** for existing printers, and **new printer** for printers just added to the system but not yet enabled.

-w   Wait until the request currently being printed is finished before disabling the specified printer. This option cannot be used with the **-c** option. If the printer is remote, the **-w** option will be silently ignored.

FILES

/var/spool/lp/*

SEE ALSO

lp(1), lpstat(1)

NAME

env – set environment for command execution

SYNOPSIS

env [-] [name=value] . . . [command args]

DESCRIPTION

env obtains the current *environment*, modifies it according to its arguments, then executes the command with the modified environment. Arguments of the form *name=value* are merged into the inherited environment before the command is executed. The – flag causes the inherited environment to be ignored completely, so that the command is executed with exactly the environment specified by the arguments.

If no command is specified, the resulting environment is printed, one name-value pair per line.

SEE ALSO

sh(1)

exec(2) in the *Programmer's Reference Manual*

profile(4), environ(5) in the *System Administrator's Reference Manual*

NAME

eqn, neqn, checkeq – typeset mathematics

SYNOPSIS

/usr/ucb/eqn [–d*xy*] [–f*n*] [–p*n*] [–s*n*] [*filename*] . . .

/usr/ucb/neqn [*filename*] . . .

/usr/ucb/checkeq [*filename*] . . .

DESCRIPTION

The **eqn** and **neqn** commands are language processors to assist in describing equations. **eqn** is a preprocessor for **troff**(1) and is intended for devices that can print **troff**'s output. **neqn** is a preprocessor for **nroff**(1) and is intended for use with terminals.

checkeq reports missing or unbalanced delimiters and **.EQ**/**.EN** pairs.

If no *filenames* are specified, **eqn** and **neqn** read from the standard input. A line beginning with **.EQ** marks the start of an equation; the end of an equation is marked by a line beginning with **.EN**. Neither of these lines is altered, so they may be defined in macro packages to get centering, numbering, etc. It is also possible to set two characters as ''delimiters''; subsequent text between delimiters is also treated as **eqn** input.

The following options are available for **eqn** and **neqn**:

–d*xy*　Set equation delimiters set to characters *x* and *y* with the command-line argument. The more common way to do this is with **delim***xy* between **.EQ** and **.EN**. The left and right delimiters may be identical. Delimiters are turned off by **delim off** appearing in the text. All text that is neither between delimiters nor between **.EQ** and **.EN** is passed through untouched.

–f*n*　　Change font to *n* globally in the document. The font can also be changed globally in the body of the document by using the **gfont** directive.

–p*n*　　Reduce subscripts and superscripts by *n* point sizes from the previous size. In the absence of the **–p** option, subscripts and superscripts are reduced by 3 point sizes from the previous size.

–s*n*　　Set equations in point size *n* globally in the document. The point size can also be changed globally in the body of the document by using the **gsize** directive.

–T*dev*　Prepare output for device *dev*. If no **–T** option is present, **eqn** looks at the environment variable **TYPESETTER** to see what the intended output device is. If no such variable is found in the environment, a system-dependent default device is assumed. Not available using **neqn**.

USAGE

eqn Language

Tokens within **eqn** are separated by braces, double quotes, tildes, circumflexes, SPACE, TAB, or NEWLINE characters. Braces { } are used for grouping; generally speaking, anywhere a single character like *x* could appear, a complicated construction enclosed in braces may be used instead. Tilde (~) represents a full SPACE in the output, circumflex (^) half as much.

Subscripts and superscripts are produced with the keywords **sub** and **sup**. Thus
'**x sub i**' makes x_i, '**a sub i sup 2**' produces a_i^2, and '**e sup {x sup 2 + y sup 2}**' gives $e^{x^2+y^2}$.

Fractions are made with **over**: '**a over b**' yields $\dfrac{a}{b}$.

sqrt makes square roots: '**1 over down 10 sqrt {ax sup 2 +bx+c}**' results in

$$\frac{1}{\sqrt{ax^2+bx+c}}.$$

Although **eqn** tries to get most things at the right place on the paper, occasionally you will need to tune the output to make it just right. In the previous example, a local motion, *down 10* was used to get more space between the square root and the line above it.

The keywords **from** and **to** introduce lower and upper limits on arbitrary things: $\lim\limits_{n\to\infty}\sum\limits_{0}^{n}x_i$ is made with '**lim from {n-> inf } sum from 0 to n x sub i**'.

Left and right brackets, braces, etc., of the right height are made with **left** and **right**: '**left [x sup 2 + y sup 2 over alpha right] ~=~1**' produces

$$\left[x^2+\frac{y^2}{\alpha}\right]\ =\ 1.$$

The **right** clause is optional. Legal characters after **left** and **right** are braces, brackets, bars, **c** and **f** for ceiling and floor, and **""** for nothing at all (useful for a right-side-only bracket).

Vertical piles of things are made with **pile**, **lpile**, **cpile**, and **rpile**: '**pile {a above b above c}**' produces $\begin{array}{c}a\\b\\c\end{array}$. There can be an arbitrary number of elements in a pile. **lpile** left-justifies, **pile** and **cpile** center, with different vertical spacing, and **rpile** right justifies.

Matrices are made with **matrix**: '**matrix { lcol { x sub i above y sub 2 } ccol { 1 above 2 } }**' produces $\begin{array}{cc}x_i & 1\\y_2 & 2\end{array}$. In addition, there is **rcol** for a right-justified column.

Diacritical marks are made with **dot**, **dotdot**, **hat**, **tilde**, **bar**, **vec**, **dyad**, and **under**: '**x dot = f(t) bar**' is $\dot{x}=\overline{f(t)}$, '**y dotdot bar ~=~ n under**' is $\ddot{y}=\underline{n}$, and '**x vec ~=~ y dyad**' is $\vec{x}=\overleftrightarrow{y}$.

Sizes and font can be changed with **size** *n* or **size** ±*n*, **roman**, *italic*, **bold**, and **font** *n*. Size and fonts can be changed globally in a document by **gsize** *n* and **gfont** *n*, or by the command-line arguments −s*n* and −f*n*.

Successive display arguments can be lined up. Place **mark** before the desired lineup point in the first equation; place **lineup** at the place that is to line up vertically in subsequent equations.

Shorthands may be defined or existing keywords redefined with **define**:

> **define** *thing* **%** *replacement* **%**

defines a new token called *thing* which will be replaced by *replacement* whenever it appears thereafter. The **%** may be any character that does not occur in *replacement*.

Keywords like **sum** ($\sum$), **int** ($\int$), **inf** (∞), and shorthands like **>=** ($\geq$), **->** ($\rightarrow$), and **!=** ($\neq$) are recognized. Greek letters are spelled out in the desired case, as in **alpha** or **GAMMA**. Mathematical words like sin, cos, and log are made Roman automatically. **troff**(1) four-character escapes like \(bu ($\bullet$) can be used anywhere. Strings enclosed in double quotes "..." are passed through untouched; this permits keywords to be entered as text, and can be used to communicate with **troff** when all else fails.

EXAMPLE

> **eqn** *filename* . . . | **troff**
>
> **neqn** *filename* . . . | **nroff**

SEE ALSO

> **tbl**(1), **troff**(1), **eqnchar**(5), **ms**(5)

NOTES

> To embolden digits, parens, etc., it is necessary to quote them, as in **bold "12.3"**.

NAME
     evgainit – Extended VGA keyboard/display driver initialization

SYNOPSIS
     evgainit *card-type*

DESCRIPTION
     evgainit is used to initialize the keyboard/display driver (see the **keyboard**(7) manual page) if extended VGA graphics modes are being used on certain video cards.

     The keyboard/display driver provides the interface to the video card. evgainit informs the keyboard/display driver which video card is installed and should be rerun each time the system is booted.

     In many cases the keyboard/display driver can determine which card is being used and therefore this command need not be run. For example, you don't need to run **evgainit** for the following cards:

     AT&T VDC 400, VDC 600, or VDC 750.

     Any card that doesn't have extended VGA capability (i.e. 800x600 pixels).

     Any card that is only VGA (640x480 pixels) or EGA (640x350 pixels).

     Any extended VGA cards (listed below) that will not be set to graphics modes with resolutions greater than 640x480 pixels.

     evgainit must be run, however, for the following cards before attempting to use resolutions greater than 640x480 pixels. The following list shows the *card-type* argument value that should be used for each video card:

card-type	Video Card(s)
vega	Video 7 800x600, Video 7 VEGA VGA Adaptor
stbga	STB VGA Extra/EM, Extra/EM-16
sigma/h	SIGMA VGA/H
pvga1a	Paradise PVGA1A
dell	Dell VGA
vram	Video 7 VRAM VGA
orvga	Orchid Designer VGA, Designer 800 VGA, ProDesigner VGA
orvgani	Orchid Designer, ProDesigner VGA (non-interlaced)
tvga	Tseng Labs
tvgani	Tseng Labs (non-interlaced)
gvga	Genoa Super VGA
pega	Paradise PEGA2
gega	Genoa EGA
fastwrite	Video 7 FastWrite VGA
won	ATI VGA Wonder

     The command can only be run with super user privileges.

EXAMPLES

For an STB Extra/EM-16 video card, **evgainit** should be invoked as:

    evgainit stb

This command could be run automatically from the **inittab** file (see the **inittab**(4) manual page) or could be run by super user after each system reboot.

SEE ALSO

keyboard(7), console(7), inittab(4).
"Video Interface" in the *Integrated Software Developer's Guide.*

NAME

ex – text editor

SYNOPSIS

ex [–**s**] [–**v**] [–**t** *tag*] [–**r** *file*] [–**L**] [–**R**] [–**x**] [–**C**] [–**c** *command*] *file* ...

DESCRIPTION

ex is the root of a family of editors: **ex** and **vi**. **ex** is a superset of **ed**, with the most notable extension being a display editing facility. Display based editing is the focus of **vi**.

If you have a CRT terminal, you may wish to use a display based editor; in this case see **vi**(1), which is a command which focuses on the display-editing portion of **ex**.

For ed Users

If you have used **ed** you will find that, in addition to having all of the **ed** commands available, **ex** has a number of additional features useful on CRT terminals. Intelligent terminals and high speed terminals are very pleasant to use with **vi**. Generally, the **ex** editor uses far more of the capabilities of terminals than **ed** does, and uses the terminal capability data base [see **terminfo**(4)] and the type of the terminal you are using from the environmental variable TERM to determine how to drive your terminal efficiently. The editor makes use of features such as insert and delete character and line in its **visual** command (which can be abbreviated **vi**) and which is the central mode of editing when using the **vi** command.

ex contains a number of features for easily viewing the text of the file. The **z** command gives easy access to windows of text. Typing **^D** (control-d) causes the editor to scroll a half-window of text and is more useful for quickly stepping through a file than just typing return. Of course, the screen-oriented **visual** mode gives constant access to editing context.

ex gives you help when you make mistakes. The **undo** (**u**) command allows you to reverse any single change which goes astray. **ex** gives you a lot of feedback, normally printing changed lines, and indicates when more than a few lines are affected by a command so that it is easy to detect when a command has affected more lines than it should have.

The editor also normally prevents overwriting existing files, unless you edited them, so that you do not accidentally overwrite a file other than the one you are editing. If the system (or editor) crashes, or you accidentally hang up the telephone, you can use the editor **recover** command (or –**r** *file* option) to retrieve your work. This will get you back to within a few lines of where you left off.

ex has several features for dealing with more than one file at a time. You can give it a list of files on the command line and use the **next** (**n**) command to deal with each in turn. The **next** command can also be given a list of file names, or a pattern as used by the shell to specify a new set of files to be dealt with. In general, file names in the editor may be formed with full shell metasyntax. The metacharacter '%' is also available in forming file names and is replaced by the name of the current file.

The editor has a group of buffers whose names are the ASCII lower-case letters (**a-z**). You can place text in these named buffers where it is available to be inserted elsewhere in the file. The contents of these buffers remain available when you begin editing a new file using the **edit** (**e**) command.

There is a command **&** in **ex** which repeats the last **substitute** command. In addition, there is a confirmed substitute command. You give a range of substitutions to be done and the editor interactively asks whether each substitution is desired.

It is possible to ignore the case of letters in searches and substitutions. **ex** also allows regular expressions which match words to be constructed. This is convenient, for example, in searching for the word "edit" if your document also contains the word "editor."

ex has a set of options which you can set to tailor it to your liking. One option which is very useful is the **autoindent** option that allows the editor to supply leading white space to align text automatically. You can then use **^D** as a backtab and space or tab to move forward to align new code easily.

Miscellaneous useful features include an intelligent **join** (**j**) command that supplies white space between joined lines automatically, commands **<** and **>** which shift groups of lines, and the ability to filter portions of the buffer through commands such as **sort**.

Invocation Options

The following invocation options are interpreted by **ex** (previously documented options are discussed in the **NOTES** section at the end of this manual page):

-s   Suppress all interactive-user feedback. This is useful in processing editor scripts.

-v   Invoke **vi**.

-t *tag*   Edit the file containing the *tag* and position the editor at its definition.

-r *file*   Edit *file* after an editor or system crash. (Recovers the version of *file* that was in the buffer when the crash occurred.)

-L   List the names of all files saved as the result of an editor or system crash.

-R   **Readonly** mode; the **readonly** flag is set, preventing accidental overwriting of the file.

-x   Encryption option; when used, **ex** simulates an **X** command and prompts the user for a key. This key is used to encrypt and decrypt text using the algorithm of the **crypt** command. The **X** command makes an educated guess to determine whether text read in is encrypted or not. The temporary buffer file is encrypted also, using a transformed version of the key typed in for the **-x** option. See **crypt**(1). Also, see the **NOTES** section at the end of this manual page.

−C	Encryption option; the same as the **−x** option, except that **ex** simulates a C command. The C command is like the **X** command, except that all text read in is assumed to have been encrypted.
−c *command*	Begin editing by executing the specified editor *command* (usually a search or positioning command).

The *file* argument indicates one or more files to be edited.

ex States

Command	Normal and initial state. Input prompted for by **:**. Your line kill character cancels a partial command.
Insert	Entered by **a**, **i**, or **c**. Arbitrary text may be entered. Insert state normally is terminated by a line having only "**.**" on it, or, abnormally, with an interrupt.
Visual	Entered by typing **vi**; terminated by typing **Q** or **^** (control-\).

ex Command Names and Abbreviations

abbrev	**ab**	map		set	**se**
append	**a**	mark	**ma**	shell	**sh**
args	**ar**	move	**m**	source	**so**
change	**c**	next	**n**	substitute	**s**
copy	**co**	number	**nu**	unabbrev	**unab**
delete	**d**	preserve	**pre**	undo	**u**
edit	**e**	print	**p**	unmap	**unm**
file	**f**	put	**pu**	version	**ve**
global	**g**	quit	**q**	visual	**vi**
insert	**i**	read	**r**	write	**w**
join	**j**	recover	**rec**	xit	**x**
list	**l**	rewind	**rew**	yank	**ya**

ex Commands

forced encryption	**C**	heuristic encryption	**X**
resubst	**&**	print next	**CR**
rshift	**>**	lshift	**<**
scroll	**^D**	window	**z**
shell escape	**!**		

ex Command Addresses

n	line *n*	*/pat*	next with *pat*
.	current	*?pat*	previous with *pat*
$	last	*x−n*	*n* before *x*
+	next	*x,y*	*x* through *y*
−	previous	*´x*	marked with *x*
+*n*	*n* forward	*´ ´*	previous context
%	1,$		

Initializing options

EXINIT	place **set**'s here in environment variable
$HOME/.exrc	editor initialization file
./.exrc	editor initialization file
set *x*	enable option *x*
set no*x*	disable option *x*
set *x***=val**	give value *val* to option *x*
set	show changed options
set all	show all options
set *x***?**	show value of option *x*

Most useful options and their abbreviations

autoindent	**ai**	supply indent
autowrite	**aw**	write before changing files
directory		pathname of directory for temporary work files
exrc	**ex**	allow **vi/ex** to read the **.exrc** in the current directory. This option is set in the **EXINIT** shell variable or in the **.exrc** file in the **$HOME** directory.
ignorecase	**ic**	ignore case of letters in scanning
list		print **^I** for tab, $ at end
magic		treat **.** **[** ***** special in patterns
modelines		first five lines and last five lines executed as **vi/ex** commands if they are of the form **ex:***command***:** or **vi:***command***:**
number	**nu**	number lines
paragraphs	**para**	macro names that start paragraphs
redraw		simulate smart terminal
report		informs you if the number of lines modified by the last command is greater than the value of the **report** variable
scroll		command mode lines
sections	**sect**	macro names that start sections
shiftwidth	**sw**	for < >, and input **^D**
showmatch	**sm**	to) and } as typed
showmode	**smd**	show insert mode in **vi**
slowopen	**slow**	stop updates during insert
term		specifies to **vi** the type of terminal being used (the default is the value of the environmental variable **TERM**)
window		visual mode lines
wrapmargin	**wm**	automatic line splitting
wrapscan	**ws**	search around end (or beginning) of buffer

Scanning pattern formation

^	beginning of line
$	end of line
.	any character
\\<	beginning of word
\\>	end of word
[str]	any character in *str*
[^str]	any character not in *str*
[x–y]	any character between *x* and *y*
*	any number of preceding characters

AUTHOR

vi and **ex** are based on software developed by The University of California, Berkeley California, Computer Science Division, Department of Electrical Engineering and Computer Science.

FILES

/usr/lib/exstrings	error messages
/usr/lib/exrecover	recover command
/usr/lib/expreserve	preserve command
/usr/share/lib/terminfo/*	describes capabilities of terminals
$HOME/.exrc	editor startup file
./.exrc	editor startup file
/tmp/Ex*nnnnn*	editor temporary
/tmp/Rx*nnnnn*	named buffer temporary
/var/preserve/login	preservation directory
	(where **login** is the user's login)

NOTES

Several options, although they continue to be supported, have been replaced in the documentation by options that follow the Command Syntax Standard [see **intro**(1)]. The – option has been replaced by **-s**, a **-r** option that is not followed with an option-argument has been replaced by **-L**, and +*command* has been replaced by **-c** *command*.

The encryption options and commands are provided with the Security Administration Utilities package, which is available only in the United States.

The **z** command prints the number of logical rather than physical lines. More than a screen full of output may result if long lines are present.

File input/output errors do not print a name if the command line **-s** option is used.

There is no easy way to do a single scan ignoring case.

The editor does not warn if text is placed in named buffers and not used before exiting the editor.

Null characters are discarded in input files and cannot appear in resultant files.

SEE ALSO

    crypt(1), **ed**(1), **edit**(1), **grep**(1), **sed**(1), **sort**(1), **vi**(1)
    curses(3X), in the *Programmer's Reference Manual*
    term(4), **terminfo**(4) in the *System Administrator's Reference Manual*
    User's Guide
    Editing Guide
    curses/terminfo chapter of the *Programmer's Guide*

NAME

expr – evaluate arguments as an expression

SYNOPSIS

expr *arguments*

DESCRIPTION

The *arguments* are taken as an expression. After evaluation, the result is written on the standard output. Terms of the expression must be separated by blanks. Characters special to the shell must be escaped. Note that **0** is returned to indicate a zero value, rather than the null string. Strings containing blanks or other special characters should be quoted. Integer-valued arguments may be preceded by a unary minus sign. Internally, integers are treated as 32-bit, 2s complement numbers. The length of the expression is limited to 512 characters.

The operators and keywords are listed below. Characters that need to be escaped in the shell [see **sh**(1)] are preceded by \. The list is in order of increasing precedence, with equal precedence operators grouped within **{ }** symbols.

expr **|** *expr*
> returns the first *expr* if it is neither null nor **0**, otherwise returns the second *expr*.

expr **&** *expr*
> returns the first *expr* if neither *expr* is null or **0**, otherwise returns **0**.

expr { **=, \>, \>=, \<, \<=, != }** *expr*
> returns the result of an integer comparison if both arguments are integers, otherwise returns the result of a lexical comparison.

expr { **+, –** } *expr*
> addition or subtraction of integer-valued arguments.

expr { *****, /****, % } *expr*
> multiplication, division, or remainder of the integer-valued arguments.

expr **:** *expr*
> The matching operator **:** compares the first argument with the second argument, which must be a regular expression. Regular expression syntax is the same as that of **ed**(1), except that all patterns are "anchored" (i.e., begin with **^**) and, therefore, **^** is not a special character, in that context. Normally, the matching operator returns the number of bytes matched (**0** on failure). Alternatively, the **(** . . . **)** pattern symbols can be used to return a portion of the first argument.

match *expr expr*
> Compare the first argument with the second argument which must be a regular expression. Regular expression syntax is the same as that of **ed**(1), except that all patterns are anchored (for example, begin with **^**) and, therefore, **^** is not a special character, in that context. Normally, the number of characters matched (0 on failure) is returned. Alternatively, the **(** . . . **)** pattern symbols can be used to return a portion of the first argument.

length *string*
> Return the length of *string*.

substr *string index count*
> Return the portion of *string* composed of at most *count* characters start-
> ing at the character position of *string* as expressed by *index* (where the
> first character of *string* is index 1, not 0).

index *string character_sequence*
> Return the index of the first character in *string* that is also in
> *character_sequence* or 0 to indicate no match.

EXAMPLES
Add 1 to the shell variable **a**:

> a=` expr $a + 1`

The following example emulates **basename**(1)—it returns the last segment of the
path name **$a**. For **$a** equal to either **/usr/abc/file** or just **file**, the example
returns **file**. (Watch out for **/** alone as an argument: **expr** takes it as the division operator; see the NOTES below.)

> expr $a : ´.*/\(.*\)´ \| $a

Here is a better version of the previous example. The addition of the **//** characters eliminates any ambiguity about the division operator and simplifies the
whole expression.

> expr //$a : ´.*/\(.*\)´

Return the number of characters in **$VAR**:

> expr $VAR : ´.*´

SEE ALSO
ed(1), **sh**(1)

DIAGNOSTICS
As a side effect of expression evaluation, **expr** returns the following exit values:
> 0 if the expression is neither null nor **0**
> 1 if the expression *is* null or **0**
> 2 for invalid expressions.

syntax error	for operator/operand errors
non-numeric argument	if arithmetic is attempted on such a string

NOTES
After argument processing by the shell, **expr** cannot tell the difference between
an operator and an operand except by the value. If **$a** is an **=**, the command:

> expr $a = ´=´

looks like:

> expr = = =

as the arguments are passed to **expr** (and they are all taken as the **=** operator).
The following works:

> expr X$a = X=

NAME

exstr – extract strings from source files

SYNOPSIS

exstr *file* . . .

exstr **-e** *file* . . .

exstr **-r** [**-d**] *file* . . .

DESCRIPTION

The **exstr** utility is used to extract strings from C language source files and replace them by calls to the message retrieval function [see **gettxt**(3C)]. This utility will extract all character strings surrounded by double quotes, not just strings used as arguments to the **printf** command or the **printf** routine. In the first form, **exstr** finds all strings in the source files and writes them on the standard output. Each string is preceded by the source file name and a colon. The meanings of the options are:

-e   Extract a list of strings from the named C language source files, with positional information. This list is produced on standard output in the following format:

> *file:line:position:msgfile:msgnum:string*
>
> | | |
> |---|---|
> | *file* | the name of a C language source file |
> | *line* | line number in the file |
> | *position* | character position in the line |
> | *msgfile* | null |
> | *msgnum* | null |
> | *string* | the extracted text string |

Normally you would redirect this output into a file. Then you would edit this file to add the values you want to use for *msgfile* and *msgnum*:

> | | |
> |---|---|
> | *msgfile* | the file that contains the text strings that will replace *string*. A file with this name must be created and installed in the appropriate place by the **mkmsgs**(1) utility. |
> | *msgnum* | the sequence number of the string in *msgfile*. |

The next step is to use **exstr** **-r** to replace *string*s in *file*.

-r   Replace strings in a C language source file with function calls to the message retrieval function **gettxt**.

-d   This option is used together with the **-r** option. If the message retrieval fails when **gettxt** is invoked at run time, then the extracted string is printed.

You would use the capability provided by **exstr** on an application program that needs to run in an international environment and have messages print in more than one language. **exstr** replaces text strings with function calls that point at strings in a message database. The database used depends on the runtime value of the **LC_MESSAGES** environment variable [see **environ**(5)].

The first step is to use **exstr -e** to extract a list of strings and save it in a file. Next, examine this list and determine which strings can be translated and subsequently retrieved by the message retrieval function. Then, modify this file by deleting lines that can't be translated and, for lines that can be translated, by adding the message file names and the message numbers as the fourth (*msgfile*) and fifth (*msgnum*) entries on a line. The message files named must have been created by **mkmsgs**(1) and exist in **/usr/lib/locale/**locale**/LC_MESSAGES**. The directory *locale* corresponds to the language in which the text strings are written [see **setlocale**(3C)]. The message numbers used must correspond to the sequence numbers of strings in the message files.

Now use this modified file as input to **exstr -r** to produce a new version of the original C language source file in which the strings have been replaced by calls to the message retrieval function **gettxt**. The *msgfile* and *msgnum* fields are used to construct the first argument to **gettxt**. The second argument to **gettxt** is printed if the message retrieval fails at run time. This argument is the null string, unless the **-d** option is used.

This utility cannot replace strings in all instances. For example, a static initialized character string cannot be replaced by a function call, or a string could be in the form of an escape sequence that cannot be translated. In order not to break existing code, the files created by invoking **exstr -e** must be examined and lines containing strings not replaceable by function calls must be deleted. In some cases the code may require modifications so that strings can be extracted and replaced by calls to the message retrieval function.

EXAMPLES

The following examples show uses of **exstr**.

Assume that the file **foo.c** contains two strings:

```
main()
{
        printf("This is an example\n");
        printf("Hello world!\n");
}
```

The **exstr** utility, invoked with the argument **foo.c**, extracts strings from the named file and prints them on the standard output.

exstr foo.c produces the following output:

```
foo.c:This is an example\n
foo.c:Hello world!\n
```

exstr -e foo.c > foo.stringsout produces the following output in the file **foo.stringsout**:

```
foo.c:3:8:::This is an example\n
foo.c:4:8:::Hello world!\n
```

You must edit **foo.stringsout** to add the values you want to use for the *msgfile* and *msgnum* fields before these strings can be replaced by calls to the retrieval function. If **UX** is the name of the message file, and the numbers **1** and **2** represent the sequence number of the strings in the file, here is what **foo.stringsout** looks like after you add this information:

```
foo.c:3:8:UX:1:This is an example\n
foo.c:4:8:UX:2:Hello world!\n
```

The **exstr** utility can now be invoked with the **-r** option to replace the strings in the source file by calls to the message retrieval function **gettxt**.

exstr -r foo.c <foo.stringsout >intlfoo.c produces the following output:

```
extern char *gettxt();
main()
{
        printf(gettxt("UX:1", ""));
        printf(gettxt("UX:2", ""));
}
```

exstr -rd foo.c <foo.stringsout >intlfoo.c uses the extracted strings as a second argument to **gettxt**.

```
extern char *gettxt();
main()
{
        printf(gettxt("UX:1", "This is an example\n"));
        printf(gettxt("UX:2", "Hello world!\n"));
}
```

FILES

/usr/lib/locale/*locale*/LC_MESSAGES/*   files created by mkmsgs(1)

SEE ALSO

gettxt(1), mkmsgs(1), printf(1), srchtxt(1), gettxt(3C), printf(3S), setlocale(3C), environ(5)

DIAGNOSTICS

The error messages produced by **exstr** are intended to be self-explanatory. They indicate errors in the command line or format errors encountered within the input file.

NAME

face – executable for the Framed Access Command Environment Interface

SYNOPSIS

face [–i *init_file*] [–c *command_file*] [–a *alias_file*] [*file* . . .]

DESCRIPTION

file is the full pathname of the file describing the object to be opened initially, and must follow the naming convention **Menu.**xxx for a menu, **Form.**xxx for a form, and **Text.**xxx for a text file, where xxx is any string that conforms to the UNIX system file naming conventions. The FMLI descriptor **lifetime** will be ignored for all frames opened by argument to **face**. These frames have a lifetime of **immortal** by default. If *file* is not specified on the command line, the FACE Menu will be opened along with those objects specified by the **LOGINWIN** environment variables. These variables are found in the user's **.environ** file.

FILES

$HOME/pref/.environ

SEE ALSO

env(4)

DIAGNOSTICS

The **face** command will exit with a non-zero exit code if the user is not properly set up as a FACE user.

NAME

factor – obtain the prime factors of a number

SYNOPSIS

factor [*integer*]

DESCRIPTION

When you use **factor** without an argument, it waits for you to give it an integer. After you give it a positive integer less than or equal to 10^{14}, it factors the integer, prints its prime factors the proper number of times, and then waits for another integer. **factor** exits if it encounters a zero or any non-numeric character.

If you invoke **factor** with an argument, it factors the integer as described above, and then it exits.

The maximum time to factor an integer is proportional to $\sqrt{n}$. **factor** will take this time when n is prime or the square of a prime.

DIAGNOSTICS

factor prints the error message, Ouch, for input out of range or for garbage input.

NAME

fastboot, fasthalt – reboot/halt the system without checking the disks

SYNOPSIS

/usr/ucb/fastboot [*boot-options*]

/usr/ucb/fasthalt [*halt-options*]

DESCRIPTION

fastboot and fasthalt are shell scripts that invoke reboot and halt with the proper arguments.

These commands are provided for compatibility only.

FILES

/etc/rc

SEE ALSO

halt(1M), reboot(1M)

fsck(1M), init(1M), rc0(1M), rc2(1M), rc6(1M) in the *System Administrator's Reference Manual*

NAME
    fdetach – detach a name from a STREAMS-based file descriptor

SYNOPSIS
    fdetach path

DESCRIPTION
    The fdetach command detaches a STREAMS-based file descriptor from a name in
    the file system. *path* is the path name of the object in the file system name space,
    which was previously attached [see fattach(3C)]. The user must be the owner
    of the file or a user with the appropriate privileges. All subsequent operations on
    path will operate on the file system node and not on the STREAMS file. The per-
    missions and status of the node are restored to the state the node was in before
    the STREAMS file was attached to it.

SEE ALSO
    fattach(3C), fdetach(3C), streamio(7)
    Programmer's Guide: STREAMS

NAME

fdisk – create or modify hard disk partition table

SYNOPSIS

fdisk [*argument*]

DESCRIPTION

This command is used to create and modify the partition table that is put in the first sector of the hard disk. This table is used by DOS and by the first-stage bootstrap to identify parts of the disk reserved for different operating systems, and to identify the partition containing the second-stage bootstrap (the active partition). The optional argument can be used to specify the raw device associated with the hard disk; the default value is /dev/rdsk/0s0 for integral disks. For SCSI disks, there is no default value. However if the default on your system is set to 0s0, then it is linked to /dev/rdsk/c0t0d0s0. If the default is set to 1s0, then it is linked to /dev/rdsk/c0t1d0s0.

The program displays the partition table as it exists on the disk, and then presents a menu allowing the user to modify the table. The menu, questions, warnings, and error messages are intended to be self-explanatory.

If there is no partition table on the disk, the user is given the option of creating a default partitioning or specifying the initial table values. The default partitioning allows 10% of the disk for MS-DOS and 90% for the UNIX System, and makes the UNIX System partition active. In either case, when the initial table is created, fdisk also writes out the first-stage bootstrap code [see hd(7)] along with the partition table. After the initial table is created, only the table is changed; the bootstrap is not modified.

Menu Options

The following are the menu options given by the fdisk program:

Create a partition

> This option allows the user to create a new partition. The maximum number of partitions is 4. The program will ask for the type of the partition (MS-DOS, UNIX System, or other). It will then ask for the size of the partition as a percentage of the disk. The user may also enter the letter c at this point, in which case the program will ask for the starting cylinder number and size of the partition in cylinders. If a c is not entered, the program will determine the starting cylinder number where the partition will fit. In either case, if the partition would overlap an existing partition, or will not fit, a message is displayed and the program returns to the original menu.

Change Active (Boot from) partition

> This option allows the user to specify the partition where the first-stage bootstrap will look for the second-stage bootstrap, otherwise known as the active partition.

Delete a partition

> This option allows the user to delete a previously created partition. Note that this will destroy all data in that partition.

Exit   This option writes the new version of the table created during this session with **fdisk** out to the hard disk, and exits the program.

Cancel This option exits without modifying the partition table.

DIAGNOSTICS

Most messages will be self-explanatory. The following may appear immediately after starting the program:

fdisk: cannot open <device>
> This indicates that the device name argument is not valid.

fdisk: unable to get device parameters for device <device>
> This indicates a problem with the configuration of the hard disk, or an error in the hard disk driver.

fdisk: error reading partition table
> This indicates that some error occurred when trying initially to read the hard disk. This could be a problem with the hard disk controller or driver, or with the configuration of the hard disk.

This message may appear after selecting the **Exit** option from the menu.

fdisk: error writing boot record
> This indicates that some error occurred when trying to write the new partition table out to the hard disk. This could be a problem with the hard disk controller, the disk itself, the driver, or the configuration of the hard disk.

FILES

/dev/rdsk/0s0 for integral disks
/dev/rdsk/c?t?d?s0 for SCSI disks

SEE ALSO

mkpart(1M), disk(7), hd(7)

NOTES

Compatible with MS-DOS Versions 3.2, 3.3, and 4.0. Partitions set up using the MS-DOS 4.0 **fdisk** command that are greater than 32 MB will appear in the UNIX System display as "other". Partitions created with MS-DOS that are less than 32 MB will appear correctly as DOS partitions.

The DOS 4.01 **fdisk** program assumes it can store diagnostic information in cylinder 1020 on the hard disk. If a UNIX System partition is created that uses cylinder 1020, DOS 4.01 **fdisk** will be unable to create a DOS partition. Therefore, the user must either create the UNIX System partition at the front of the disk so that cylinder 1020 is not used, or create the DOS partition using the UNIX System **fdisk** (not DOS **fdisk**) and never delete it.

When setting up a DOS 4.01 partition on the hard disk to co-reside with a UNIX partition that has already been set up, do not allow **fdisk** to create the largest possible partition and make it active (as the **fdisk** prompt requests). Instead, the user should manually set it up to line up against the UNIX partition. Note that this applies to when the user boots DOS 4.01 from floppy disk (not from within UNIX) and runs **fdisk**.

NAME

fdp – create, or restore from, a full file system archive

SYNOPSIS

fdp −B [−dovAENS] [−c *count*] *bkjobid odpname odpdev odplab descript*

fdp −RC [−dovAENS] [−c *count*] *odpname odpdev redpname redev rsjobid descript*

DESCRIPTION

The **fdp** command is invoked as a child process by other shell commands. The command name, **fdp**, is read either from the *bkhist.tab* file or the **bkreg -m** command and option. The -B, -R, and -C options are passed to **fdp** by the shell commands **backup**, and **restore**. The other options are passed from the **bkhist.tab** file or the **bkreg -p** command and option. The arguments are sent to **fdp** from various locations in the backup service.

fdp −B is invoked as a child process by the **backdaemon** command to perform a backup of the data partition *odpdev* (the originating data partition). All blocks in the data partition are archived. The resulting backup is created in the format described on **dd**(1). The backup is recorded in the backup history log, /etc/bkup/bkhist.tab.

fdp −RC is invoked as a child process by the **rsoper** command to restore the entire data partition from an archive created by **fdp −B**. The data partition archive is assumed to be in the format described on **dd**(1). *dd(1)* format.

The arguments to **fdp** are defined as follows:

bkjobid   the job id assigned by *backup*. The method uses the *bkjobid* when it creates history log entries.

odpname   the name of the data partition that is to be backed up. Unused by **fdp**, but supplied by **backup** for command-line compatibility with other archiving methods.

odpdev   the name of the block special device on which the data partition resides.

odplab   the volume name on the file system [see **labelit**(1M)]. Unused by **fdp**, but supplied by **backup** for command-line compatibility with other archiving methods.

descript   is a description for a destination device in the form:

        dgroup:dname:dchar:dlabels

dgroup specifies a device group [see **devgroup.tab**(4)].
dname specifies a particular device name [see **device.tab**(4)].
dchars specifies characteristics associated with the device. If specified, *dchar* overrides the defaults for the specified device and group. [See **device.tab**(4) for a further description of device characteristics].
dlabels specifies the volume names for the media to be used for reading or writing the archive.

rsjobid   the job id assigned by **restore**.

redev   if non-null, the partition to be restored to instead of *ofsdev*.

redpname   unused, but provided for consistency with other methods.

Options

Some options are only significant during **fdp** **−B** invocations; they are accepted but ignored during **fdp** **−R** invocations because the command is invoked and options are specified automatically by **restore**. These options are flagged with an asterisk (*).

c*count*   Archives or restores only the first *count* (512 byte) blocks of data in the data partition.

d*   Inhibits recording the archive in the backup history log.

o   Permits the user to override media insertion requests [see **getvol**(1M) and the description of the **−o** option].

v*   Validates the archive as it is written. A checksum is computed as the archive is being written; as each medium is completed, it is re-read and the checksum recomputed to verify that each block is readable and correct. If either check fails, the medium is considered unreadable. If **−A** has been specified, the archiving operation fails; otherwise, the operator is prompted to replace the failed medium.

A   Establishes automated mode, (that is, does not prompt the user to insert or remove media).

E*   Reports an estimate of media usage for the archive; then performs the backup.

N*   Reports an estimate of media usage for the archive; does not perform the backup.

S   Displays a period (.) for every 100 (512 byte) blocks read-from or written-to the archive on the destination device.

User Interactions

The connection between an archiving method and **backup** is more complex than a simple fork/exec or pipe. The **backup** command is responsible for all interactions with the user, either directly, or through the **bkoper** command. Therefore, **fdp** neither reads from standard-input nor writes to standard-output or standard-error. A method library must be used [see **libbrmeth**(3)] to communicate reports (estimates, filenames, periods, status, and so on) to **backup**.

DIAGNOSTICS

The exit codes for **fdp** are the following:

0   successful completion of the task

1   one or more parameters to **fdp** are invalid.

2   an error has occurred which caused **fdp** to fail to complete all portions of its task.

FILES

`/etc/bkup/bkexcept.tab`	lists the files that are to be excluded from an incremental file system backup.
`/etc/bkup/bkhist.tab`	lists the labels of all volumes that have been used for backup operations.
`/etc/bkup/rsstatus.tab`	tracks the status of all restore requests from users.
`/etc/bkup/bklog`	logs errors generated by the backup methods and the **backup** command
`/etc/bkup/rslog`	logs errors generated by the restore methods and the **restore** command
`$TMP/filelist$$`	temporarily stores a table of contents for a backup archive.

SEE ALSO

backup(1M), device.tab(4), fdp(1), ffile(1), fimage(1), getvol(1M), incfile(1), labelit(1M), libbrmeth(3), prtvtoc(1M), rsoper(1M)

NAME

ff (generic) – list file names and statistics for a file system

SYNOPSIS

ff [–F *FSType*] [–v] [*current_options*] [–o *specific_options*] *special* . . .

DESCRIPTION

ff reads the files and directories of the *special* file. I-node data is saved for files which match the selection criteria which is either the *inode* number and/or *inode* age. Output consists of the path name and other file information. Output fields are positional. The output is produced in i-node order. The default line produced by ff is:

> *path-name   i-number*

current_options are options supported by the s5-specific module of ff. Other FSTypes do not necessarily support these options. *specific_options* indicate suboptions specified in a comma-separated list of suboptions and/or keyword-attribute pairs for interpretation by the *FSType*-specific module of the command.

The options are:

–F   Specify the *FSType* on which to operate. The *FSType* should either be specified here or be determinable from /etc/vfstab by matching the *special* with an entry in the table.

–v   Echo the complete command line, but do not execute the command. The command line is generated by using the options and arguments provided by the user and adding to them information derived from /etc/vfstab. This option should be used to verify and validate the command line.

–o   Specify FSType-specific options.

NOTE

This command may not be supported for all FSTypes.

FILES

/etc/vfstab   list of default parameters for each file system

SEE ALSO

ncheck(1M), vfstab(4)
find(1) in the *User's Reference Manual*
Manual pages for the FSType-specific modules of ff

NAME

ff (s5) – display i-list information

SYNOPSIS

ff [**-F s5**] [*generic_options*] [**-I**] [**-l**] [**-p***prefix*] [**-s**] [**-u**] [**-a***n*] [**-m***n*] [**-c***n*] [**-n***file*] [**-i***i-node-list*] *special*. . .

DESCRIPTION

generic_options are options supported by the generic **ff** command.

ff reads the i-list and directories of the *special* file, assuming it is an **s5** file system. I-node data is saved for files which match the selection criteria. Output consists of the pathname for each saved i-node, plus other file information requested using the print *options* below. Output fields are positional. The output is produced in i-node order; fields are separated by tabs. The default line produced by **ff** is:

> *pathname i-number*

The pathname is preceded by a **.** (dot) unless the **-p** option is specified.

The maximum information the command will provide is:

> *pathname i-number size uid*

The argument *n* in the *option* descriptions that follow is used as a decimal integer (optionally signed), where **+** *n* means more than *n*, **–** *n* means less than *n*, and *n* means exactly *n*. A day is defined as a 24 hour period.

The options are:

-F s5	Specifies the **s5**-FSType.
-I	Do not print the i-node number after each pathname.
-l	Generate a supplementary list of all pathnames for multiply-linked files.
-p*prefix*	The specified *prefix* will be added to each generated pathname. The default is **.** (dot).
-s	Print the file size, in bytes, after each pathname.
-u	Print the owner's login name after each pathname.
-a*n*	Select if the i-node has been accessed in *n* days.
-m*n*	Select if the i-node has been modified in *n* days.
-c*n*	Select if the i-node has been changed in *n* days.
-n*file*	Select if the i-node has been modified more recently than the argument *file*.
-i*i-node-list*	Generate names for only those i-nodes specified in *i-node-list*. *i-node-list* is a list of numbers separated by commas and without spaces.

NOTE

If the −1 option is not specified, only a single pathname out of all possible ones is generated for a multiply-linked i-node. If −1 is specified, all possible names for every linked file on the file system are included in the output. If -1 and -i are both specified, then only the names for linked files matching an i-node listed in the i-node list are displayed.

SEE ALSO

generic **ff**(1M), **ncheck**(1M).
find(1) in the *User's Reference Manual*

NAME

ff (ufs) – list file names and statistics for a **ufs** file system

SYNOPSIS

ff [-F ufs] [*generic_options*] [-I] [-l] [-p*prefix*] [-s] [-u] [-a*n*] [-m*n*]
[-c*n*] [-n*file*] [-i*i-node-list*] [-o a,m,s] *special*...

DESCRIPTION

generic_options are options supported by the generic **ff** command.

ff reads the i-list and directories of the *special* file, assuming it is a file system. Inode data is saved for files which match the selection criteria. Output consists of the pathname for each saved inode, plus other file information requested using the options below. Output fields are positional. The output is produced in inode order; fields are separated by TAB characters. The default line produced by **ff** is:

     pathname i-number

The options are:

  -F ufs   Specifies the **ufs**-FSType.

  -I   Do not print the i-node number after each pathname.

  -l   Generate a supplementary list of all pathnames for multiply-linked files.

  -p*prefix*   The specified *prefix* will be added to each generated pathname. The default is **.** (dot).

  -s   Print the file size, in bytes, after each pathname.

  -u   Print the owner's login name after each pathname.

  -a*n*   Select if the i-node has been accessed in *n* days.

  -m*n*   Select if the i-node has been modified in *n* days.

  -c*n*   Select if the i-node has been changed in *n* days.

  -n*file*   Select if the i-node has been modified more recently than the argument *file*.

  -i*i-node-list* Generate names for only those i-nodes specified in *i-node-list*. *i-node-list* is a list of numbers separated by commas and without spaces.

  -o   Specify **ufs** file system specific options. The options available are:

         a   Print the '.' and '..' directory entries.

         m   Print mode information.

         s   Print only special files and files with set-user-ID mode.

NOTE

If the **-l** option is not specified, only a single pathname out of all possible ones is generated for a multiply-linked inode. If **-l** is specified, all possible names for every linked file on the file system are included in the output. However, no selection criteria apply to the names generated.

SEE ALSO

find(1), generic ff(1M), ncheck(1M)

NAME
　　ffile – create, or restore from, a full file system archive

SYNOPSIS
　　ffile **-B** [*-dlmortvAENSV*] *bkjobid ofsname ofsdev ofslab descript*

　　ffile **-RC** [*-dlmortvAENSV*] *ofsname ofsdev refsname redev rsjobid descript*

　　ffile **-RF** [*-dlmortvAENSV*] *ofsname ofsdev descript rsjobid:uid:date:type:name*
　　[:[*rename*]:[*inode*]] . . .

DESCRIPTION
　　The **ffile** command is invoked as a child process by other shell commands. The
　　command name, **ffile**, is read either from the **bkhist.tab** file or the **bkreg -m**
　　command and option. The **-B**, **-R**, **-F**, and **-C** options are passed to **ffile** by
　　the shell commands **backup**, **restore**, and **urestore**. The other options are
　　passed from the **bkhist.tab** or the **bkreg -p** command and option. The argu-
　　ments are sent to **ffile** from various locations in the backup service.

　　ffile -B is invoked as a child process by **bkdaemon** to perform a full backup of
　　the file system *ofsname* (the originating file system). All files in *ofsname* are
　　archived. The resulting backup is created in the format described on **cpio**(4).
　　The　　backup　　is　　recorded　　in　　the　　backup　　history　　log,
　　/usr/oam/bkrs/tables/bkhist.tab.

　　ffile -RC and **RF** are invoked as child processes by **rsoper** to extract files from
　　an full file system archive created by **ffile -B**. The file system archive is
　　assumed to be in the format described on **cpio**(4).

　　If the **-RC** option is selected, the entire file system is restored.

　　If the **-RF** option is specified, only selected objects from the archive are restored.
　　Each 7-tuple, composed of *rsjobid:uid:date:type:name:rename:inode*, specifies an
　　object to be restored from the file system archive. The 7-tuple objects come to
　　ffile from **rsstatus.tab**.

　　The arguments to **ffile** are defined as follows:

　　bkjobid　　the job id assigned by **backup**. The method uses the *bkjobid* when it
　　　　　　　　creates history log and table-of-contents entries.

　　ofsname　　the name of the file system that is to be backed up.

　　ofsdev　　the name of the block special device on which the file system resides.

　　ofslab　　the volume name on the file system [see **labelit**(1M)].

　　descript　　is a description for a destination device in the form:

　　　　　　　　dgroup:dname:dchar:dlabels

　　　　　　dgroup specifies a device group [see **devgroup.tab**(4)].
　　　　　　dname specifies a particular device name [see **device.tab**(4)].
　　　　　　dchars specifies characteristics associated with the device. If specified,
　　　　　　dchar overrides the defaults for the specified device and group. [See
　　　　　　device.tab(4) for a further description of device characteristics.]
　　　　　　dlabels specifies the volume names for the media to be used for read-
　　　　　　ing or writing the archive.

refsname   if non-null, the name of the file system to be restored to instead of *ofsname*. At least one of *refsname* and *redev* must be null.

redev   if non-null, the partition to be restored to instead of *ofsdev*. At least one of *refsname* and *redev* must be null.

rsjobid   the restore jobid assigned by **restore** or **urestore**.

uid   the real uid of the user who requested the object to be restored. It must match the uid of the owner of the object at the time the archive was made, or it must be the superuser uid.

date   the newest "last modification time" that is acceptable for a restorable object. The object is restored from the archive immediately older than this date. *date* is a hexadecimal representation of the date and time provided by the **time** system call [see **time**(2)].

type   either **F** or **D**, indicating that the object is a file or a directory, respectively.

name   the name the object had in the file system archive.

rename   the name that the object should be restored to (it may differ from the name the object had in the file system archive). If omitted, the object is restored to *name*.

inode   the inode number of the object as it was stored in the file system archive. *[inode]* is not used by **ffile -R**, and is provided only for command-line compatibility with other restoration methods.

Options

Some options are only significant during **ffile -B** invocations; they are accepted but ignored during **ffile -R** invocations because the command is invoked and options are specified automatically by **restore**. These options are flagged with an asterisk (*).

d*   Inhibits recording of the archive in the backup history log.

l*   Creates a long form of the backup history log that includes a table-of-contents for the archive. This includes the data used to generate a listing of each file in the archive (like that produced by the **ls -l** command).

m*   Mounts the originating file system read-only before starting the backup and remounts it with its original permissions after completing the backup. Cannot be used with **root** or **/usr** file systems.

o   Permits the user to override media insertion requests [see **getvol**(1M) and the description of the **-o** option].

r*   Includes remotely mounted resources in the archive.

t*   Creates a table of contents for the backup on additional media instead of in the backup history log.

v*   Validates the archive as it is written. A checksum is computed as the archive is being written; as each medium is completed, it is re-read and the checksum recomputed to verify that each block is readable and correct. If either check fails, the medium is considered unreadable. If **-A** has been specified, the archiving operation fails; otherwise, the operator is prompted to replace the failed medium.

A   Establishes automated mode, (i.e., does not prompt the user to insert or remove media).

E*   Reports an estimate of media usage for the archive; then performs the backup.

N*   Reports an estimate of media usage for the archive; does not perform the backup.

S   Displays a period (.) for every 100 (512 byte) blocks read-from or written-to the archive on the destination device.

V   Displays the name of each file written-to or extracted-from the archive on the destination device.

User Interactions

The connection between an archiving method and **backup** is more complex than a simple fork/exec or pipe. The **backup** command is responsible for all interactions with the user, either directly, or through **bkoper**. Therefore, **ffile** neither reads from standard-input nor writes to standard-output or standard-error. A method library must be used [see **libbrmeth**(3)] to communicate reports (estimates, filenames, periods, status, etc.) to **backup**.

DIAGNOSTICS

The exit codes for **ffile** are the following:

0   successful completion of the task
1   one or more parameters to **ffile** are invalid.
2   an error has occurred which caused **ffile** to fail to complete all portions of its task.

FILES

/usr/oam/bkrs/tables/bkexcept.tab
      lists the files that are to be excluded from an incremental file system backup.

/usr/oam/bkrs/tables/bkhist.tab
      lists the labels of all volumes that have been used for backup operations.

/usr/oam/bkrs/tables/rsstatus.tab
      tracks the status ofall restore requests from users.

/usr/oam/bkrs/logs/bklog logs errors generated by the backup methods and the **backup** command

/usr/oam/bkrs/logs/rslog logs errors generated by the restore methods and the **restore** command

$TMP/filelist$$ temporarily stores a table of contents for a backup archive.

SEE ALSO

backup(1M), bkoper(1M) cpio(1), cpio(4), device.tab(4), fdp(1), ffile(1), fimage(1), getvol(1M), incfile(1), labelit(1M), libbrmeth(3), ls(1), restore(1M), rsoper(1M), time(2), urestore(1)

NAME

fgrep – search a file for a character string

SYNOPSIS

fgrep [options] string [file . . .]

DESCRIPTION

fgrep (fixed string grep) searches files for a character string and prints all lines that contain that string. fgrep is different from grep and egrep because it searches for a string instead of searching for a pattern that matches an expression. It uses a fast and compact algorithm.

The characters $, *, [, ^, |, (,), and \ are interpreted literally by fgrep, that is, fgrep does not recognize full regular expressions as does egrep. Because these characters have special meaning to the shell, it is safest to enclose the entire *string* in single quotes ' . . . '.

If no files are specified, fgrep assumes standard input. Normally, each line found is copied to the standard output. The filename is printed before each line found if there is more than one input file.

Command line options are:

- **-b** Precede each line by the block number on which it was found. This can be useful in locating block numbers by context (first block is 0).
- **-c** Print only a count of the lines that contain the pattern.
- **-h** Suppress printing of filenames when searching multiple files.
- **-i** Ignore uppercase/lowercase distinction during comparisons.
- **-l** Print the names of files with matching lines once, separated by newlines. Does not repeat the names of files when the pattern is found more than once.
- **-n** Precede each line by its line number in the file (first line is 1).
- **-v** Print all lines except those that contain the pattern.
- **-x** Print only lines matched entirely.
- **-e** *special_string*
   Search for a *special_string* (*string* begins with a -).
- **-f** *file*
   Take the list of *strings* from *file*.

SEE ALSO

ed(1), egrep(1), grep(1), sed(1), sh(1

DIAGNOSTICS

Exit status is 0 if any matches are found, 1 if none, 2 for syntax errors or inaccessible files (even if matches were found).

NOTES

Ideally there should be only one grep command, but there is not a single algorithm that spans a wide enough range of space-time tradeoffs. Lines are limited to BUFSIZ characters; longer lines are truncated. BUFSIZ is defined in /usr/include/stdio.h.

NAME

file – determine file type

SYNOPSIS

file [–h] [–m *mfile*] [–f *ffile*] *arg* ...
file [–h] [–m *mfile*] –f *ffile*
file –c [–m *mfile*]

DESCRIPTION

file performs a series of tests on each file supplied by *arg* and, optionally, on each file supplied in *ffile* in an attempt to classify it. If *arg* appears to be a text file, file examines the first 512 bytes and tries to guess its programming language. If *arg* is an executable a.out, file prints the version stamp, provided it is greater than 0. If *arg* is a symbolic link, by default the link is followed and file tests the file that the symbolic link references.

–c   Check the magic file for format errors. For reasons of efficiency, this validation is normally not carried out.

–f *ffile*   *ffile* contains the names of the files to be examined.

–h   Do not follow symbolic links.

–m *mfile*   Use *mfile* as an alternate magic file, instead of /etc/magic.

file uses /etc/magic to identify files that have a magic number. A magic number is a numeric or string constant that indicates the file type. Commentary at the beginning of /etc/magic explains its format.

FILES

/etc/magic

SEE ALSO

filehdr(4) in the *System Administrator's Reference Manual*

DIAGNOSTICS

If the –h option is specified and *arg* is a symbolic link, file prints the error message:

symbolic link to *arg*

NAME

fimage – create, restore an image archive of a filesystem

SYNOPSIS

fimage **-B** [**-dlmotuvAENS**] *bkjobid ofsname ofsdev ofslab descript*

fimage **-RC** [**-dlmotuvAENS**] *ofsname ofsdev refsname redev rsjobid descript*

fimage **-RF** [**-dlmotuvAENS**] *ofsname ofsdev descript rsjobid:uid:date:type:name*
        [:[*rename*]:[*inode*]] . . .

DESCRIPTION

The **fimage** command is invoked as a child process by other shell commands. The command name, **fimage**, is read either from the **bkhist.tab** file or the **bkreg -m** command and option. The **-B**, **-R**, **-F**, and **-C** options are passed to **fimage** by the shell commands **backup**, **restore**, and **urestore** described below. The other options are passed from the **bkhist.tab** file or the **bkreg -p** command and option. The arguments are sent to **fimage** from various locations in the backup service. **fimage** neither reads from standard-input nor writes to standard-output or standard-error.

fimage -B is invoked as a child process by **bkdaemon** to perform an image backup of the filesystem *ofsname* (the originating filesystem). All files in *ofsname* are archived. The resulting backup is created in the format described on **volcopy**(1M). The backup is recorded in the backup history log, **/etc/bkup/bkhist.tab**.

fimage -RC and **-RF** are invoked as child processes by the **rsoper** command to extract files from an image archive created by **fimage -B**. The filesystem archive is assumed to be in the format described on **volcopy** format.

If the **-RC** option is selected, the entire filesystem is restored.

If the **-RF** option is specified, only selected objects from the archive are restored. Each 7-tuple, composed of *rsjobid:uid:date:type:name:rename:inode*, specifies an object to be restored from the filesystem archive. The 7-tuple objects come to **fimage** from the **rsstatus.tab** file.

The arguments to **fimage** are defined as follows:

bkjobid   the job id assigned by **backup**. The method uses the *bkjobid* when it creates history log and table-of-contents entries.

ofsname   the name of the file system that is to be backed up.

ofsdev   the name of the block special device on which the file system resides.

ofslab   the volume name on the file system [see **labelit**(1M)].

descript   is a description for a destination device in the form:
           dgroup:dname:dchar:dlabels
     dgroup specifies a device group [see **devgroup.tab**(4)].
     dname specifies a particular device name [see **device.tab**(4)].
     dchars specifies characteristics associated with the device. If specified, *dchar* overrides the defaults for the specified device and group. [See **device.tab**(4) for a further description of device characteristics.] *dlabels* specifies the volume names for the media to be used for reading or writing the archive.

refsname   if non-null, the name of the file system to be restored to instead of *ofsname*. At least one of *refsname* and *redev* must be null.

redev   if non-null, the partition to be restored to instead of *ofsdev*. At least one of *refsname* and *redev* must be null.

rsjobid   the restore jobid assigned by **restore** or **urestore**.

uid   the real uid of the user who requested the object to be restored. It must match the uid of the owner of the object at the time the archive was made, or it must be the superuser uid.

date   the newest "last modification time" that is acceptable for a restorable object. The object is restored from the archive immediately older than this date. *date* is a hexadecimal representation of the date and time provided by the **time** system call [see **time**(2)].

type   either **F** or **D**, indicating that the object is a file or a directory, respectively.

name   the name the object had in the file system archive.

rename   the name that the object should be restored to (it may differ from the name the object had in the file system archive). If omitted, the object is restored to *name*.

inode   the inode number of the object as it was stored in the file system archive. *[inode]* is not used by **ffile -R**, and is provided only for command-line compatibility with other restoration methods.

Options

Some options are only significant during **fimage -B** invocations; they are accepted but ignored during **fimage -R** invocations because the command is invoked and options are specified automatically by **restore**. These options are flagged with an asterisk (*).

d*   Inhibits recording the archive in the backup history log.

l*   Creates a long form of the backup history log that includes a table-of-contents for the archive. This includes the data used to generate a listing of each file in the archive (like that produced by the **ls -l** command).

m*   Mounts the originating filesystem read-only before starting the backup and remounts it with its original permissions after completing the backup. Cannot be used with **root** or **/usr** filesystems.

o   Permits the user to override media insertion requests [see **getvol**(1M) and the description of the **-o** option].

t*   Creates a table of contents for the backup on additional media instead of in the backup history log.

u*   Unmounts the originating filesystem before the backup is begun. After the backup is complete, remounts the filesystem under its original permission. This option cannot be used with a **root** or **usr** filesystem. The **-u** option overrides the **-m** option.

v*   Validates the archive as it is written. A checksum is computed as the archive is being written; as each medium is completed, it is re-read and the checksum recomputed to verify that each block is readable and correct. If either check fails, the medium is considered unreadable. If **−A** has been specified, the archiving operation fails; otherwise, the operator is prompted to replace the failed medium.

A   Do not prompt the user for removable media operations (automated operation).

E*   Reports an estimate of media usage for the archive; then performs the backup.

N*   Reports an estimate of media usage for the archive; does not perform the backup.

S   Displays a period (.) for every 100 (512 byte) blocks read-from or written-to the archive on the destination device.

User Interactions

The connection between an archiving method and **backup** is more complex than a simple fork/exec or pipe. The **backup** command is responsible for all interactions with the user, either directly, or through **bkoper**. Therefore, **ffile** neither reads from standard-input nor writes to standard-output or standard-error. A method library must be used [see **libbrmeth**(3)] to communicate reports (estimates, filenames, periods, status, etc.) to **backup**.

DIAGNOSTICS

The exit codes for **ffile** are the following:

0   successful completion of the task
1   one or more parameters to **ffile** are invalid.
2   an error has occurred which caused **ffile** to fail to complete all portions of its task.

FILES

`/etc/bkup/bkhist.tab`	lists the labels of all volumes that have been used for backup operations.
`/etc/bkup/rsstatus.tab`	tracks the status of all restore requests from users.
`/etc/bkup/bklog`	logs errors generated by the backup methods and the **backup** command
`/etc/bkup/rslog`	logs errors generated by the restore methods and the **restore** command
`$TMP/filelist$$`	temporarily stores a table of contents for a backup archive.

SEE ALSO

backup(1M), bkoper(1M) **device.tab**(4), **fdp**(1), **ffile**(1), fimage(1), getvol(1M), **incfile**(1), **labelit**(1M), **libbrmeth**(3), **ls**(1), restore(1M), rsoper(1M), **time**(2), **urestore**(1), **volcopy**(1M)

NAME

find – find files

SYNOPSIS

find *path-name-list expression*

DESCRIPTION

find recursively descends the directory hierarchy for each path name in the *path-name-list* (that is, one or more path names) seeking files that match a boolean *expression* written in the primaries given below. In the descriptions, the argument n is used as a decimal integer where $+n$ means more than n, $-n$ means less than n and n means exactly n. Valid expressions are:

-name *pattern*   True if *pattern* matches the current file name. Normal shell file name generation characters [see **sh**(1)] may be used. A backslash (\ ) is used as an escape character within the pattern. The pattern should be escaped or quoted when **find** is invoked from the shell.

-perm [-]*onum*   True if the file permission flags exactly match the octal number *onum* (see **chmod**(1)). If *onum* is prefixed by a minus sign (-), only the bits that are set in *onum* are compared with the file permission flags, and the expression evaluates true if they match.

-size *n*[c]   True if the file is *n* blocks long (512 bytes per block). If *n* is followed by a **c**, the size is in characters.

-atime *n*   True if the file was accessed *n* days ago. The access time of directories in *path-name-list* is changed by **find** itself.

-mtime *n*   True if the file's data was modified *n* days ago.

-ctime *n*   True if the file's status was changed *n* days ago.

-exec *cmd*   True if the executed *cmd* returns a zero value as exit status. The end of *cmd* must be punctuated by an escaped semicolon. A command argument {} is replaced by the current path name.

-ok *cmd*   Like **-exec** except that the generated command line is printed with a question mark first, and is executed only if the user responds by typing **y**.

-print   Always true; causes the current path name to be printed.

-newer *file*   True if the current file has been modified more recently than the argument *file*.

-depth   Always true; causes descent of the directory hierarchy to be done so that all entries in a directory are acted on before the directory itself. This can be useful when **find** is used with **cpio**(1) to transfer files that are contained in directories without write permission.

-mount   Always true; restricts the search to the file system containing the directory specified.

-local	True if the file physically resides on the local system.
(*expression*)	True if the parenthesized expression is true (parentheses are special to the shell and must be escaped).
-type *c*	True if the type of the file is *c*, where *c* is **b**, **c**, **d**, **l**, **p**, or **f** for block special file, character special file, directory, symbolic link, fifo (named pipe), or plain file, respectively.
-follow	Always true; causes symbolic links to be followed. When following symbolic links, **find** keeps track of the directories visited so that it can detect infinite loops; for example, such a loop would occur if a symbolic link pointed to an ancestor. This expression should not be used with the **-type l** expression.
-links *n*	True if the file has *n* links.
-user *uname*	True if the file belongs to the user *uname*. If *uname* is numeric and does not appear as a login name in the **/etc/passwd** file, it is taken as a user ID.
-nouser	True if the file belongs to a user not in the **/etc/passwd** file.
-group *gname*	True if the file belongs to the group *gname*. If *gname* is numeric and does not appear in the **/etc/group** file, it is taken as a group ID.
-nogroup	True if the file belongs to a group not in the **/etc/group** file.
-fstype *type*	True if the filesystem to which the file belongs is of type *type*.
-inum *n*	True if the file has inode number *n*.
-prune	Always yields true. Do not examine any directories or files in the directory structure below the *pattern* just matched. See the examples, below.

The primaries may be combined using the following operators (in order of decreasing precedence):

1. The negation of a primary (**!** is the unary *not* operator).

2. Concatenation of primaries (the *and* operation is implied by the juxtaposition of two primaries).

3. Alternation of primaries (**-o** is the *or* operator).

Note that when you use **find** in conjunction with **cpio**, if you use the **-L** option with **cpio** then you must use the **-follow** expression with **find** and vice versa. Otherwise there will be undesirable results.

EXAMPLES

Remove all files in your home directory named **a.out** or **.o** that have not been accessed for a week:

```
find $HOME \( -name a.out -o -name '*.o' \) -atime +7 -exec rm {} \;
```

Recursively print all file names in the current directory and below, but skipping SCCS directories:

```
find . -name SCCS -prune -o -print
```

Recursively print all file names in the current directory and below, skipping the contents of SCCS directories, but printing out the SCCS directory name:

```
find . -print -name SCCS -prune
```

FILES

/etc/passwd, /etc/group

SEE ALSO

chmod(1), sh(1), test(1)
stat(2), and umask(2) in the *Programmer's Reference Manual*
fs(4) in the *System Administrator's Reference Manual*

NOTE

When using **find** to determine files modified within a range of time, one must use the **?time** argument BEFORE the **-print** argument otherwise **find** will give all files.

The following option is obsolete and will not be supported in future releases.

-cpio *device*   Always true; write the current file on *device* in cpio(1) format (5120-byte records).

NAME
finger – display information about local and remote users

SYNOPSIS
finger [–bfhilmpqsw] *username*. . .

finger [–l] *username@hostname*. . . (TC/IP)

DESCRIPTION
By default, the **finger** command displays information about each , logged-in user, including login name, full name, terminal name (prepended with a '*' if write-permission is denied), idle time, login time, and location if known.

Idle time is minutes if it is a single integer, hours and minutes if a ':' is present, or days and hours if a **d** is present.

When one or more *username* arguments are given, more detailed information is given for each *username* specified, whether they are logged in or not. *username* must be that of a local user, and may be a first or last name, or an account name. When **finger** is used to find users on a remote device, the user and the name of the remote device are specified in the form *username@hostname*. Information is presented in a multi-line format, and includes, in addition to the information mentioned above:

> the user's home directory and login shell

> time the user logged in if currently logged in, or the time the user last logged in if not, as well as the terminal or host from which the user logged in and, if a terminal.

> last time the user received mail, and the last time the user read their mail

> any plan contained in the file **.plan** in the user's home directory

> and any project on which the user is working described in the file **.project** (also in the user's home directory)

The following options are available:

–b   Suppress printing the user's home directory and shell in a long format printout.

–f   Suppress printing the header that is normally printed in a non-long format printout.

–h   Suppress printing of the **.project** file in a long format printout.

–i   Force "idle" output format, which is similar to short format except that only the login name, terminal, login time, and idle time are printed.

–l   Force long output format.

–m   Match arguments only on user name (not first or last name).

–p   Suppress printing of the **.plan** file in a long format printout.

–q   Force quick output format, which is similar to short format except that only the login name, terminal, and login time are printed.

-s   Force short output format.

-w   Suppress printing the full name in a short format printout.

Within the TCP/IP network, the -1 option can be used remotely.

FILES

/var/adm/utmp	who is logged in
/etc/passwd	for users' names
/var/adm/lastlog	last login times
~/.plan	plans
~/.project	projects

SEE ALSO

passwd(1), who(1), whois(1)

NOTES

Only the first line of the ~/.project file is printed.

NAME

`fingerd, in.fingerd` – remote user information server

SYNOPSIS

`in.fingerd`

DESCRIPTION

`fingerd` implements the server side of the Name/Finger protocol, specified in RFC 742. The Name/Finger protocol provides a remote interface to programs which display information on system status and individual users. The protocol imposes little structure on the format of the exchange between client and server. The client provides a single command line to the finger server which returns a printable reply.

`fingerd` waits for connections on TCP port 79. Once connected it reads a single command line terminated by a <RETURN-LINE-FEED> which is passed to `finger`(1). `fingerd` closes its connections as soon as the output is finished.

If the line is null (only a RETURN-LINEFEED is sent) then `finger` returns a default report that lists all users logged into the system at that moment.

If a user name is specified (for instance, **eric**<RETURN-LINE-FEED>) then the response lists more extended information for only that particular user, whether logged in or not. Allowable names in the command line include both login names and user names. If a name is ambiguous, all possible derivations are returned.

FILES

`/var/utmp`	who is logged in
`/etc/passwd`	for users' names
`/var/adm/lastlog`	last login times
`$HOME/.plan`	plans
`$HOME/.project`	projects

SEE ALSO

`finger`(1)

Harrenstien, Ken, *NAME/FINGER*, RFC 742, Network Information Center, SRI International, Menlo Park, Calif., December 1977

NOTES

Connecting directly to the server from a TIP or an equally narrow-minded TELNET-protocol user program can result in meaningless attempts at option negotiation being sent to the server, which will foul up the command line interpretation. `fingerd` should be taught to filter out IAC's and perhaps even respond negatively (IAC *will not*) to all option commands received.

NAME

fixperm – correct or initialize XENIX file permissions and ownership

SYNOPSIS

fixperm [**-acDfgilnSsvw** [**-d** *package*] [**-u** *package*]] *specfile*

DESCRIPTION

For each line in the specification file *specfile*, **fixperm** makes the listed pathname conform to a specification. **fixperm** is typically used by the super-user to configure a XENIX system upon installation. It has been provided for use with any existing XENIX packages that you may have that you wish to install on the UNIX system. Nonsuper-users can only use **fixperm** with the **-D** , **-f** , **-l** , or **-n** options.

The following options are available:

Option	Description
-a	All files in the perm file must exist. This means that files marked as optional (type letter is in capital letters) must be present.
-c	Creates empty files and missing directories.
-D	Lists directories only on standard output. Does not modify target files.
-d *package*	Processes input lines beginning with given package specifier string (see above). For instance, -dBASE processes only items specified as belonging to the Basic utilities set. The default action is to process all lines.
-f	Lists files only on standard output. Does not modify target files.
-g	Lists all devices on the standard output. Target files are not modified (analogous to **-l**, **-f**, and **-D**).
-i	Checks to see if the selected packages are installed. Return values are

> 0:   `package completely installed`
> 4:   `package not installed`
> 5:   `package partially installed`

	If the equivalent package was installed as a UNIX package, **-i** will not detect it.
-l	Lists files and directories on standard output. Does not modify target files.
-n	Reports errors only. Does not modify target files.
-S	Issues a complaint if files are not in x.out format.
-s	Modifies special device files in addition to the rest of the permlist.
-u *package*	Causes similar action to **-d** option but processes items that are not part of the given package.

-v   *(verbose)*   Issues a complaint if executable files are 1) word-swapped, 2) not fixed-stack, 3) not separate I and D, or 4) not stripped.

-w   Lists location (volume number) of the specified files or directories.

Specification File Format

Each nonblank line in the specification file consists of either a comment or an item specification. A comment is any text from a pound sign "#" up to the end of the line. There is one item specification per line. User and group id numbers must be specified at the top of the specification file for each user and group mentioned in the file.

An item specification consists of a package specifier, a permission specification, owner and group specifications, the number of links on the file, the filename, and an optional volume number.

The package specifier is an arbitrary string that is the name of a package within a distribution set. A package is a set of files.

A permission specification follows the package specifier. The permission specification consists of a file type, followed by a numeric permission specification. The item specification is one of the following characters:

Character	Description
x	executable
a	archive
e	empty file (create if -c option given)
b	block device
c	character device
d	directory
f	text file
p	named pipe

If the item specification is given as an uppercase letter, the file associated with it is optional, and **fixperm** will not return an error message if it does not exist.

The numeric permission conforms to the scheme described in **chmod** (1). The owner and group permissions are in the third column separated by a slash, such as "bin/bin". The fourth column indicates the number of links. If there are links to the file, the next line contains the linked filename with no other information. The fifth column is a pathname. The pathname must be relative (not preceded by a slash "/"). The sixth column is only used for special files, major and minor device numbers, or volume numbers.

EXAMPLES

The following two lines make a distribution and invoke **tar**(1) to archive only the files in **my_package** on **/dev/sample** :

```
/etc/fixperm -f /etc/perm/my_package> list
tar cfF /dev/sample list
```

This command line reports package errors:

```
/etc/fixperm -nd my_package
```

NOTES

fixperm is usually only run by a shell script at installation.

fixperm should only be run from the directory to which the target files are relative.

SEE ALSO

custom(1)

NAME

  fixperm – correct or initialize file permissions and ownership

SYNOPSIS

  fixperm [-cDjilnSsvw [-d *package*] [-u *package*]] *specfile*

DESCRIPTION

  For each line in the specification file *specfile*, fixperm makes the listed pathname conform to a specification. fixperm is typically used to configure a XENIX system upon installation. Nonsuper-users can only use fixperm with the -D, -f, -l, or -n options. Only super-users can use the -c, -d, -i, -n, -S, -u, -v, and -w options.

  The following options are available:

  -c   Creates empty files and missing directories.

  -D   Lists directories only on standard output. Does not modify target files.

  -d *package*   Processes input lines beginning with given package specifier string (see above). For instance, -dBASE processes only items specified as belonging to the Basic utilities set. The default action is to process all lines.

  -f   Lists files only on standard output. Does not modify target files.

  -i   Checks only if the selected packages are installed. Return values are:

                    0: package completely installed
                    4: package not installed
                    5: package partially installed

  -l   Lists files and directories on standard output. Does not modify target files.

  -n   Reports errors only. Does not modify target files.

  -S   Issues a complaint if files are not in x.out format.

  -s   Modifies special device files in addition to the rest of the perm-list.

  -u *package*   Causes similar action to -d option, but processes items that are not part of the given package.

  -v   Issues a complaint if executable files are:

                    1) word-swapped
                    2) not fixed-stack
                    3) not separate I and D
                    4) not stripped

  -w   Lists location (volume number) of the specified files or directories.

Specification File Format

Each nonblank line in the specification file consists of either a comment or an item specification. A comment is any text from a pound sign "#" up to the end of the line. There is one item specification per line. User and group id numbers must be specified at the top of the specification file for each user and group mentioned in the file.

An item specification consists of a package specifier, a permission specification, owner and group specifications, the number of links on the file, the filename, and an optional volume number.

The package specifier is an arbitrary string that is the name of a package within a distribution set. A package is a set of files.

A permission specification follows the package specifier. The permission specification consists of a file type, followed by a numeric permission specification. The item specification is one of the following characters:

x   executable
a   archive
e   empty file (create if -c option given)
b   block device
c   character device
d   directory
f   text file
p   named pipe

If the item specification is given as an uppercase letter, the file associated with it is optional, and **fixperm** will not return an error message if it does not exist.

The numeric permission conforms to the scheme described in **chmod**. The owner and group permissions are in the third column separated by slash, such as "**bin/bin**". The fourth column indicates the number of links. If there are links to the file, the next line contains the linked filename with no other information. The fifth column is a pathname. The pathname must be relative (not preceded by a slash "/"). The sixth column is only used for special files, major and minor device numbers, or volume numbers.

EXAMPLES

The following two lines make a distribution and invoke **tar** to archive only the files in **base.perms** on **/dev/sample**:

```
/etc/fixperm -f/etc/base.perms>list
tar cfF /dev/sample list
```

This command line reports **BASE** package errors:

```
/etc/fixperm -nd BASE
```

NOTES

fixperm is usually only run by a shell script at installation.

NAME

fixshlib – alters executables to call SCO UNIX System V/386 Release 3.2-compatible libnsl

SYNOPSIS

fixshlib *filename*

DESCRIPTION

SCO applications installed with the custom command [see custom(1M) in the *System Administrator's Reference Manual*] will automatically have references to **libnsl** changed to reference an SCO UNIX System V/386 Release 3.2-compatible **libnsl** (**shlib/libNSL_s**). However, you may need to run **fixshlib** on any SCO UNIX System V/386 Release 3.2 application that is not installed using the **custom** command. The **fixshlib** command will alter the executable to use the SCO UNIX System V/386 Release 3.2-compatible **libnsl**.

When executing the command, *filename* is the pathname of the executable to be modified.

DIAGNOSTICS

If **filename** is not a COFF format **a.out** executable, you will see the following error message:

```
unknown file type - possibly bad magic: Error 0
```

SEE ALSO

custom(1M) in the *System Administrator's Reference Manual*

NOTES

Using the **fixshlib** command on a COFF executable built or intended to run on non-SCO UNIX system implementations could cause the executable to fail. If your executable fails because of this, there is no way to restore the executable. The associated application should be re-installed.

NAME

fmlcut – cut out selected fields of each line of a file

SYNOPSIS

fmlcut –c*list* [*file* . . .]

fmlcut –f*list* [–d *char*] [–s] [*file* . . .]

DESCRIPTION

The **fmlcut** function cuts out columns from a table or fields from each line in *file*; in database parlance, it implements the projection of a relation. **fmlcut** can be used as a filter; if *file* is not specified or is -, the standard input is read. *list* specifies the fields to be selected. Fields can be fixed length (character positions) or variable length (separated by a field delimiter character), depending on whether -c or -f is specified.

Note that either the –c or the –f option must be specified.

The meanings of the options are:

list   A comma-separated list of integer field numbers (in increasing order), with optional – to indicate ranges For example: **1,4,7**; **1-3,8**; **–5,10** (short for **1-5,10**); or **3-** (short for third through last field).

–c*list*   If -c is specified, *list* specifies character positions (for example, –c1-72 would pass the first 72 characters of each line). Note that no space intervenes between -c and *list*.

–f*list*   If -f is specified, *list* is a list of fields assumed to be separated in the file by the default delimiter character, **TAB**, or by *char* if the -d option is specified. For example, –f1,7 copies the first and seventh field only. Lines with no delimiter characters are passed through intact (useful for table subheadings), unless -s is specified. Note that no space intervenes between -f and *list*. The following options can be used if you have specified -f.

  –d*char*   If –d is specified, *char* is the field delimiter. Space or other characters with special meaning to FMLI must be quoted. Note that no space intervenes between -d and *char*. The default field delimiter is **TAB**.

  –s   Suppresses lines with no delimiter characters. If -s is not specified, lines with no delimiters will be passed through untouched.

EXAMPLES

fmlcut –d: –f1,5 /etc/passwd   gets login IDs and names

`who am i | fmlcut –f1 –d" "`   gets the current login name

DIAGNOSTICS

fmlcut returns the following exit values:

0   when the selected field is successfully cut out

2   on syntax errors

The following error messages may be displayed on the FMLI message line:

ERROR: `line too long`
A line has more than 1023 characters or fields, or there is no new-line character.

ERROR: `bad list for c / f option`
Missing −c or −f option or incorrectly specified *list*. No error occurs if a line has fewer fields than the *list* calls for.

ERROR: `no fields`
The *list* is empty.

ERROR: `no delimiter`
Missing *char* on −d option.

NOTES

`fmlcut` cannot correctly process lines longer than 1023 characters, or lines with no newline character.

SEE ALSO

`fmlgrep`(1F)

NAME

  fmlexpr – evaluate arguments as an expression

SYNOPSIS

  fmlexpr *arguments*

DESCRIPTION

The **fmlexpr** function evaluates its arguments as an expression. After evaluation, the result is written on the standard output. Terms of the expression must be separated by blanks. Characters special to FMLI must be escaped. Note that **0** is returned to indicate a zero value, rather than the null string. Strings containing blanks or other special characters should be quoted. Integer-valued arguments may be preceded by a unary minus sign. Internally, integers are treated as 32-bit, 2s complement numbers.

The operators and keywords are listed below. Characters that need to be escaped are preceded by \. The list is in order of increasing precedence, with equal precedence operators grouped within **{ }** symbols.

expr \ | *expr*

  returns the first *expr* if it is neither null nor **0**, otherwise returns the second *expr*.

expr \& *expr*

  returns the first *expr* if neither *expr* is null or **0**, otherwise returns **0**.

expr { **=, \>, \>=, \<, \<=, != }** *expr*

  returns the result of an integer comparison if both arguments are integers, otherwise returns the result of a lexical comparison.

expr { **+, −** } *expr*

  addition or subtraction of integer-valued arguments.

expr { ***, /, %** } *expr*

  multiplication, division, or remainder of the integer-valued arguments.

expr **:** *expr*

  The matching operator **:** compares the first argument with the second argument which must be a regular expression. Regular expression syntax is the same as that of **ed**(1), except that all patterns are "anchored" (that is, begin with **^**) and, therefore, **^** is not a special character, in that context. Normally, the matching operator returns the number of bytes matched (**0** on failure). Alternatively, the **\(. . . \)** pattern symbols can be used to return a portion of the first argument.

EXAMPLES

  1.   Add 1 to the variable **a**:

          'fmlexpr $a + 1 | set -l a'

  2.   For $a equal to either "**/usr/abc/***file*" or just "*file*":

          fmlexpr $a : .*/\(.*\) \| $a

returns the last segment of a path name (for example, *file*). Watch out for / alone as an argument: **fmlexpr** will take it as the division operator (see NOTES below).

3.   A better representation of example 2.

         fmlexpr //$a : .*/\(.*\)

The addition of the // characters eliminates any ambiguity about the division operator (because it makes it impossible for the left-hand expression to be interpreted as the division operator), and simplifies the whole expression.

4.   Return the number of characters in $VAR.

         fmlexpr $VAR : .*

DIAGNOSTICS

As a side effect of expression evaluation, **fmlexpr** returns the following exit values:

0   if the expression is neither null nor 0 (that is, TRUE)
1   if the expression is null or 0 (that is, FALSE)
2   for invalid expressions (that is, FALSE).

syntax error   for operator/operand errors
non-numeric argument   if arithmetic is attempted on such a string

In the case of syntax errors and non-numeric arguments, an error message will be printed at the current cursor position. Use **refresh** to redraw the screen.

NOTES

After argument processing by FMLI, **fmlexpr** cannot tell the difference between an operator and an operand except by the value. If $a is an =, the command:

         fmlexpr $a = =

looks like:

         fmlexpr = = =

as the arguments are passed to **fmlexpr** (and they will all be taken as the = operator). The following works, and returns TRUE:

         fmlexpr X$a = X=

SEE ALSO

ed(1), **expr**(1), **set**(1F), **sh**(1)

NAME

fmlgrep – search a file for a pattern

SYNOPSIS

fmlgrep [*options*] *limited_regular_expression* [*file* . . .]

DESCRIPTION

fmlgrep searches *file* for a pattern and prints all lines that contain that pattern. The **fmlgrep** function uses limited regular expressions (expressions that have string values that use a subset of the possible alphanumeric and special characters) like those used with **ed**(1) to match the patterns. It uses a compact non-deterministic algorithm.

Be careful when using FMLI special characters (for example, **$**, **`**, **´**, **"**) in *limited_regular_expression*. It is safest to enclose the entire *limited_regular_expression* in single quotes ´ . . . ´ .

If *file* is not specified, **fmlgrep** assumes standard input. Normally, each line matched is copied to standard output. The file name is printed before each line matched if there is more than one input file.

Command line options are:

-b   Precede each line by the block number on which it was found. This can be useful in locating block numbers by context (first block is 0).

-c   Print only a count of the lines that contain the pattern.

-i   Ignore upper/lower case distinction during comparisons.

-l   Print only the names of files with matching lines, separated by new-lines. Does not repeat the names of files when the pattern is found more than once.

-n   Precede each line by its line number in the file (first line is 1).

-s   Suppress error messages about nonexistent or unreadable files.

-v   Print all lines except those that contain the pattern.

DIAGNOSTICS

fmlgrep returns the following exit values:

0 if the pattern is found (that is, TRUE)
1 if the pattern is not found (that is, FALSE)
2 if an invalid expression was used or *file* is inaccessible

NOTES

Lines are limited to BUFSIZ characters; longer lines are truncated. BUFSIZ is defined in **/usr/include/stdio.h**.

If there is a line with embedded nulls, **fmlgrep** will only match up to the first null; if it matches, it will print the entire line.

SEE ALSO

fmlcut(1F)

ed(1), **egrep**(1), **fgrep**(1), **grep**(1) in the *UNIX System V Programmer's Reference Manual*

NAME

fmli – invoke FMLI

SYNOPSIS

fmli [-a *alias_file*] [-c *command_file*] [-i *initialization_file*] *file* ...

DESCRIPTION

The fmli command invokes the Form and Menu Language Interpreter and opens the frame(s) specified by the *file* argument. The *file* argument is the pathname of the initial frame definition file(s), and must follow the naming convention **Menu.***xxx*, **Form.***xxx* or **Text.***xxx* for a menu, form or text frame respectively, where *xxx* is any string that conforms to UNIX system file naming conventions. The FMLI descriptor **lifetime** will be ignored for all frames opened by argument to fmli. These frames have a lifetime of **immortal** by default.

The available options are as follows:

-a   If -a is specified, *alias_file* is the name of a file which contains lines of the form *alias=pathname*. Thereafter, *$alias* can be used in definition files to simplify references to objects or devices with lengthy pathnames, or to define a search path (similar to **$PATH** in the UNIX system shell).

-c   If -c is specified, *command_file* is the name of a file in which default FMLI commands can be disabled, and new application-specific commands can be defined. The contents of *command_file* are reflected in the FMLI Command Menu.

-i   If -i is specified, *initialization_file* is the name of a file in which the following characteristics of the application as a whole can be specified:

  A transient introductory frame displaying product information

  A banner, its position, and other elements of the banner line

  Color attributes for all elements of the screen

  Screen Labeled Keys (SLKs) and their layout on the screen.

Environment Variables

LOADPFK

When this variable is set to **yes**, **true**, or the null string, it directs FMLI to download alternative keystroke sequences into the function keys of terminals (such as the AT&T 5620 and 630) that do not have fixed, preset values for them. See the appendix titled "Keyboard and Mouse Support" of the *Programmer's Guide: Character User Interface (FMLI and ETI)* for more information on automatic function key downloading.

COLUMNS

Can be used to override the width of the logical screen defined for the terminal set in **TERM**. For terminals with a 132-column mode, for example, invoking FMLI with the line

  COLUMNS=132 fmli *frame-file*

will allow this wider screen width to be used.

LINES
Can be used to override the length of the logical screen defined for the terminal set in **TERM**.

EXAMPLES
To invoke **fmli**:

```
fmli Menu.start
```

where **Menu.start** is an example of *file* named according to the file name conventions for menu definition files explained above.

To invoke **fmli** and name an initialization file:

```
fmli -i init.myapp Menu.start
```

where **init.myapp** is an example of *initialization_file*.

DIAGNOSTICS
If *file* is not supplied to the **fmli** command, **fmli** returns the message:

```
Initial object must be specified.
```

If *file* does not exist or is not readable, **fmli** returns an error message and exits. The example command line above returns the following message and exits:

```
Can't open object "Menu.start"
```

If *file* exists, but does not start with one of the three correct object names (**Menu.**, **Form.**, or **Text.**) or if it is named correctly but does not contain the proper data, **fmli** starts to build the screen by putting out the screen labels for function keys, after which it flashes the message:

```
I do not recognize that kind of object
```

and then exits.

FILES
/usr/bin/fmli

SEE ALSO
vsig(1F)

NAME

fmt – simple text formatters

SYNOPSIS

fmt [**-cs**] [**-w** *width*] [*file* ...]

DESCRIPTION

fmt is a simple text formatter that fills and joins lines to produce output lines of (up to) the number of characters specified in the **-w** *width* option. The default *width* is 72. **fmt** concatenates the *inputfiles* listed as arguments. If none are given, **fmt** formats text from the standard input.

Blank lines are preserved in the output, as is the spacing between words. **fmt** does not fill lines beginning with a "**.**" (dot), for compatibility with **nroff**(1). Nor does it fill lines starting with "**From:**".

Indentation is preserved in the output, and input lines with differing indentation are not joined (unless **-c** is used).

fmt can also be used as an in-line text filter for **vi**(1); the **vi** command:

    ! } fmt

reformats the text between the cursor location and the end of the paragraph.

OPTIONS

-c   Crown margin mode. Preserve the indentation of the first two lines within a paragraph, and align the left margin of each subsequent line with that of the second line. This is useful for tagged paragraphs.

-s   Split lines only. Do not join short lines to form longer ones. This prevents sample lines of code, and other such formatted text, from being unduly combined.

-w *width*   Fill output lines to up to *width* columns.

SEE ALSO

nroff(1), **vi**(1)

NOTES

The **-w** *width* option is acceptable for BSD compatibility, but it may go away in future releases.

NAME

fmtmsg – display a message on **stderr** or system console

SYNOPSIS

fmtmsg [**-c** *class*] [**-u** *subclass*] [**-l** *label*] [**-s** *severity*] [**-t** *tag*] [**-a** *action*] *text*

DESCRIPTION

Based on a message's classification component, **fmtmsg** either writes a formatted message to **stderr** or writes a formatted message to the console.

A formatted message consists of up to five standard components as defined below. The classification and subclass components are not displayed as part of the standard message, but rather define the source of the message and direct the display of the formatted message. The valid options are:

-c *class*   Describes the source of the message. Valid keywords are:

        hard   The source of the condition is hardware.
        soft   The source of the condition is software.
        firm   The source of the condition is firmware.

-u *subclass*   A list of keywords (separated by commas) that further defines the message and directs the display of the message. Valid keywords are:

        appl   The condition originated in an application. This keyword should not be used in combination with either **util** or **opsys**.
        util   The condition originated in a utility. This keyword should not be used in combination with either **appl** or **opsys**.
        opsys   The message originated in the kernel. This keyword should not be used in combination with either **appl** or **util**.
        recov   The application will recover from the condition. This keyword should not be used in combination with **nrecov**.
        nrecov   The application will not recover from the condition. This keyword should not be used in combination with **recov**.
        print   Print the message to the standard error stream **stderr**.
        console   Write the message to the system console. **print**, **console**, or both may be used.

-l *label*   Identifies the source of the message.

-s *severity*   Indicates the seriousness of the error. The keywords and definitions of the standard levels of *severity* are:

        halt   The application has encountered a severe fault and is halting.

	`error`	The application has detected a fault.
	`warn`	The application has detected a condition that is out of the ordinary and might be a problem.
	`info`	The application is providing information about a condition that is not in error.

-t *tag*   The string containing an identifier for the message.

-a *action*   A text string describing the first step in the error recovery process. This string must be written so that the entire *action* argument is interpreted as a single argument. **fmtmsg** precedes each action string with the **TO FIX:** prefix.

text   A text string describing the condition. Must be written so that the entire *text* argument is interpreted as a single argument.

The environment variables **MSGVERB** and **SEV_LEVEL** control the behavior of **fmtmsg**. **MSGVERB** is set by the administrator in the **/etc/profile** for the system. Users can override the value of **MSGVERB** set by the system by resetting **MSGVERB** in their own **.profile** files or by changing the value in their current shell session. **SEV_LEVEL** can be used in shell scripts.

MSGVERB tells **fmtmsg** which message components to select when writing messages to **stderr**. The value of **MSGVERB** is a colon separated list of optional keywords. **MSGVERB** can be set as follows:

     MSGVERB=[*keyword*[**:***keyword*[**:**. . .]]]
     export MSGVERB

Valid *keywords* are: **label**, **severity**, **text**, **action**, and **tag**. If **MSGVERB** contains a keyword for a component and the component's value is not the component's null value, **fmtmsg** includes that component in the message when writing the message to **stderr**. If **MSGVERB** does not include a keyword for a message component, that component is not included in the display of the message. The keywords may appear in any order. If **MSGVERB** is not defined, if its value is the null string, if its value is not of the correct format, or if it contains keywords other than the valid ones listed above, **fmtmsg** selects all components.

MSGVERB affects only which message components are selected for display. All message components are included in console messages.

SEV_LEVEL defines severity levels and associates print strings with them for use by **fmtmsg**. The standard severity levels shown below cannot be modified. Additional severity levels can be defined, redefined, and removed.

     0   (no severity is used)
     1   HALT
     2   ERROR
     3   WARNING
     4   INFO

SEV_LEVEL is set as follows:

SEV_LEVEL=[*description*[**:***description*[**:**. . .]]]
export SEV_LEVEL

description is a comma-separated list containing three fields:

description=*severity_keyword***,** *level***,** *printstring*

severity_keyword is a character string used as the keyword with the **−s** *severity* option to **fmtmsg**.

level is a character string that evaluates to a positive integer (other than **0, 1, 2, 3,** or **4,** which are reserved for the standard severity levels). If the keyword *severity_keyword* is used, *level* is the severity value passed on to **fmtmsg**(3C).

printstring is the character string used by **fmtmsg** in the standard message format whenever the severity value *level* is used.

If **SEV_LEVEL** is not defined, or if its value is null, no severity levels other than the defaults are available. If a *description* in the colon separated list is not a comma separated list containing three fields, or if the second field of a comma separated list does not evaluate to a positive integer, that *description* in the colon separated list is ignored.

DIAGNOSTICS

The exit codes for **fmtmsg** are the following:

0   All the requested functions were executed successfully.

1   The command contains a syntax error, an invalid option, or an invalid argument to an option.

2   The function executed with partial success, however the message was not displayed on **stderr**.

4   The function executed with partial success, however the message was not displayed on the system console.

32   No requested functions were executed successfully.

EXAMPLES

Example 1: The following example of **fmtmsg** produces a complete message in the standard message format and displays it to the standard error stream:

```
fmtmsg −c soft −u recov,print,appl −l UX:cat −s error −t
UX:cat:001 −a "refer to manual" "invalid syntax"
```

produces:

```
UX:cat: ERROR: invalid syntax
TO FIX: refer to manual    UX:cat:001
```

Example 2: When the environment variable **MSGVERB** is set as follows:

```
MSGVERB=severity:text:action
```

and Example 1 is used, **fmtmsg** produces:

```
ERROR: invalid syntax
TO FIX: refer to manual
```

Example 3: When the environment variable **SEV_LEVEL** is set as follows:

```
SEV_LEVEL=note,5,NOTE
```

the following **fmtmsg** command:

```
fmtmsg  -c  soft  -u  print  -l  UX:cat  -s  note  -a  "refer  to
manual"  "invalid syntax"
```

produces:

```
UX:cat: NOTE: invalid syntax
TO FIX: refer to manual
```

and displays the message on **stderr**.

SEE ALSO

　　addseverity(3C), **fmtmsg**(3C) in the *Programmer's Reference Manual*

NAME

    `fold` – fold long lines

SYNOPSIS

    `fold` [**–w** *width* | *–width*] [*filename* . . .]

DESCRIPTION

    Fold the contents of the specified *filename*s, or the standard input if no files are specified, breaking the lines to have maximum width *width*. The default for *width* is 80. *width* should be a multiple of 8 if tabs are present, or the tabs should be expanded.

SEE ALSO

    `pr`(1)

NOTES

    Folding may not work correctly if underlining is present.

    The **-w** *width* option is provided as a transition tool only. It will be removed in future releases.

NAME
format – format floppy disk tracks

SYNOPSIS
/bin/format [–vVE] [–f *first*] [–l *last*] [–i *interleave*] *device* [t]

DESCRIPTION
The **format** command formats floppy disks. Unless otherwise specified, formatting starts at track 0 and continues until an error is returned at the end of a partition.

The **–f** and **–l** options specify the first and last track to be formatted. The default interleave of 2 may be modified by using the **–i** option. *device* must specify a raw (character) floppy device. The **t** indicates the entire disk. Absence of this letter indicates that the first track of the diskette cannot be accessed.

–v   verbose.

–V   verify. After tracks are formatted, a random sector is chosen and a write of test data is done into it. The sector is then read back and a comparison is made.

–E   exhaustive verify. Every sector is verified by write/read/compare.

FILES
/dev/rdsk/∗ raw device for partition to be formatted

SEE ALSO
mkpart(1M), fd(7)

NAME

    fromsmtp – receive RFC822 mail from SMTP

SYNOPSIS

    fromsmtp [**−d**] [**−h** *host*] [**−s** *sender*] *to* . . .

DESCRIPTION

    fromsmtp reads an RFC822 message from its standard input, does some conversion of the message to make it acceptable to UNIX System mail, and pipes the result to **rmail**. The *to* arguments are passed as arguments to **rmail**. **fromsmtp** is normally invoked by **smtpd** to deliver incoming mail messages.

    The **−d** option may be used for debugging **fromsmtp**. It will cause the command line for **rmail** to be echoed to standard output, as well as the results of the message (after conversion). The message will not be given to **rmail** when this option is used.

    The **−h** *host* option may be used to prepend a host or network name to the front of the sender path in the **From** line at the beginning of the message. This is useful if you need to identify which of several possible networks a message was received from (for possible use in replying).

    The **−s** *sender* option is used to give a default sender name, in case **fromsmtp** cannot determine the name of the sender from the message it reads. If this option is not used, the default sender name **unknown** will be used.

FILES

    /usr/bin/rmail   where converted mail is piped to

SEE ALSO

    rmail(1M), **smtpd**(1M)

    RFC822 – Standard for the Format of ARPA Internet Text Messages

NAME
fsba – file system block analyzer

SYNOPSIS
/usr/sbin/fsba [–b *target_block_size*] *file-system1* [*file-system2* . . .]

DESCRIPTION
The fsba command determines the disk space required to store the data from an existing file system in a new file system with the specified logical block size. Each *file-system* listed on the command line refers to an existing file system and should be specified by device name (for example, /dev/rdsk/*, where the value of * is machine dependent).

The *target_block_size* specifies the logical block size in bytes of the new file system. Valid target block sizes are 512, 1024, and 2048. Default target block size is 1024. A block size of 2048 is supported only if the 2K file system package is installed.

The fsba command prints information about how many 512-byte disk sectors are allocated to store the data in the old (existing) file system and how many would be required to store the same data in a new file system with the specified logical block size. It also prints the number of allocated and free i-nodes for the existing file system.

If the number of free sectors listed for the new file system is negative, the data will not fit in the new file system unless the new file system is larger than the existing file system. The new file system must be made at least as large as the number of sectors listed by fsba as allocated for the new file system. The maximum size of the new file system is limited by the size of the disk partition used for the new file system.

Note that it is possible to specify a *target_block_size* that is smaller than the logical block size of the existing file system. In this case the new file system would require fewer sectors to store the data.

SEE ALSO
mkfs(1M), prtvtoc(1M)

NAME

fsck (generic) – check and repair file systems

SYNOPSIS

fsck [-F *FSType*] [-V] [-m] [*special* . . .]

fsck [-F *FSType*] [-V] [*current_options*] [-o *specific_options*] [*special* . . .]

DESCRIPTION

fsck audits and interactively repairs inconsistent conditions for file systems. If the file system is inconsistent the user is prompted for concurrence before each correction is attempted. It should be noted that some corrective actions will result in some loss of data. The amount and severity of data loss may be determined from the diagnostic output. The default action for each correction is to wait for the user to respond **yes** or **no**. If the user does not have write permission fsck defaults to a **no** action.

The file system should be unmounted when fsck is used. If this is not possible, care should be taken that the system is quiescent and that it is rebooted immediately afterwards if the file system is a critical one, for example **root**.

current_options are options supported by the **s5**-specific module of fsck. Other *FSTypes* do not necessarily support these options. *specific_options* indicate suboptions specified in a comma-separated list of suboptions and/or keyword-attribute pairs for interpretation by the *FSType*-specific module of the command.

special represents a block or character special device (e.g., **/dev/rdsk/***, where the value of * is machine dependent). It is preferable that a character special device be used. fsck will not work on a block device if it is mounted. If *special* is not supplied, fsck looks through **/etc/vfstab** and executes fsck for all character specials in the **fsckdev** field of **/etc/vfstab** for which there is a numeric entry in the **fsckpass** field.

The options are:

-F   Specify the *FSType* on which to operate. The *FSType* should either be specified here or be determinable from **/etc/vfstab** by matching the *special* with an entry in the table.

-V   Echo the complete command line, but do not execute the command. The command line is generated by using the options and arguments provided by the user and adding to them information derived from **/etc/vfstab**. This option should be used to verify and validate the command line.

-m   Check but don't repair. This option checks that the file system is suitable for mounting.

-o   Specify *FSType*-specific options.

NOTE

This command may not be supported for all *FSTypes*.

FILES

    `/etc/vfstab`   list of default parameters for each file system

SEE ALSO

    `checkfsys`(1M), `mkfs`(1M), `vfstab`(4)

    Manual pages for the *FSType*-specific modules of **fsck**

NAME

fsck (bfs) - check and repair **bfs** file systems

SYNOPSIS

fsck [-F bfs] [*generic_options*] [*special* . . .]

fsck [-F bfs] [*generic_optionsi*] [-y | -n] [*special* . . .]

DESCRIPTION

generic_options are options supported by the generic **fsck** command.

fsck checks to see if compaction was in process but was not completed, perhaps as a result of a system crash. If it was, **fsck** completes the compaction of the file [see **fs_bfs**(4)].

The options are:

-y   Assume a yes response to all questions asked by **fsck**.

-n   Assume a no response to all questions asked by **fsck**.

SEE ALSO

checkfsys(1M), generic **fsck**(1M), **mkfs**(1M), **fs_bfs**(4)

See the chapter on file systems in the *System Administrator's Guide*

NAME

fsck (s5) – check and repair s5 file systems

SYNOPSIS

fsck [–F s5] [*generic_options*] [*special. . .*]

fsck [–F s5] [*generic_options*] [–y] [–n] [–p] [–sX] [–SX] [–t*file*] [–1] [–q] [–D] [–f] [*special...*]

DESCRIPTION

generic_options are options supported by the generic **fsck** command.

The options are:

–F s5   Specifies the s5-FSType.

–y   Assume a **yes** response to all questions asked by **fsck**.

–n   Assume a **no** response to all questions asked by **fsck**; do not open the file system for writing.

–p   Correct inconsistencies that can be fixed automatically, that is, inconsistencies that are deemed harmless and can be fixed without confirmation by the administrator. Examples of such inconsistencies are unreferenced i-nodes, incorrect counts in the superblocks, and missing blocks in the free list.

–sX Ignore the actual free list and (unconditionally) reconstruct a new one by rewriting the super-block of the file system. The file system should be unmounted while this is done; if this is not possible, care should be taken that the system is quiescent and that it is rebooted immediately afterwards. This precaution is necessary so that the old, bad, in-core copy of the superblock will not continue to be used, or written on the file system.

             The **–s**X suboption allows for creating an optimal free-list organization.

             If X is not given, the values used when the file system was created are used. The format of X is *cylinder size:gap size*.

–sX Conditionally reconstruct the free list. This suboption is like **–s**X above except that the free list is rebuilt only if there were no discrepancies discovered in the file system. Using **s** will force a **no** response to all questions asked by **fsck**. This suboption is useful for forcing free list reorganization on uncontaminated file systems.

–t_file_   If **fsck** cannot obtain enough memory to keep its tables, it uses a scratch file. If the **t** option is specified, the *file* named is used as the scratch file, if needed. Without the **t** option, **fsck** will prompt the user for the name of the scratch file. The file chosen should not be on the file system being checked, and if it is not a special file or did not already exist, it is removed when **fsck** completes.

–1   Identify damaged files by their logical names.

-q   Quiet **fsck**. Unreferenced **fifos** will silently be removed. If **fsck** requires it, counts in the superblock will be automatically fixed and the free list salvaged.

-D   Directories are checked for bad blocks. Useful after system crashes.

-f   Fast check. Check block and sizes and check the free list. The free list will be reconstructed if it is necessary.

Inconsistencies checked are as follows:

1. Blocks claimed by more than one i-node or the free list.
2. Blocks claimed by an i-node or the free list outside the range of the file system.
3. Incorrect link counts.
4. Size checks:
    Incorrect number of blocks.
    Directory size not 16-byte aligned.
5. Bad i-node format.
6. Blocks not accounted for anywhere.
7. Directory checks:
    File pointing to unallocated i-node.
    I-node number out of range.
8. Super Block checks:
    More than 65536 i-nodes.
    More blocks for i-nodes than there are in the file system.
9. Bad free block list format.
10. Total free block and/or free i-node count incorrect.

Orphaned files and directories (allocated but unreferenced) are, with the user's concurrence, reconnected by placing them in the **lost+found** directory, if the files are nonempty. The user will be notified if the file or directory is empty or not. Empty files or directories are removed, as long as the **n** suboption is not specified. **fsck** will force the reconnection of nonempty directories. The name assigned is the i-node number.

NOTE

Checking the raw device is almost always faster.

I-node numbers for **.** and **. .** in each directory are not checked for validity.

SEE ALSO

checkfsys(1M), **crash**(1M), generic **fsck**(1M), **mkfs**(1M), **ncheck**(1M), **fs**(4)

NAME

fsck (ufs) – file system consistency check and interactive repair

SYNOPSIS

fsck [**-F ufs**] [*generic_options*] [*special ...*]

fsck [**-F ufs**] [*generic_options*] [(**-y**|**-Y**)|(**-n**|**-N**)] [**-o p,b=#,w**] [*special ....*]

DESCRIPTION

generic_options are options supported by the generic **fsck** command. *current_options* are options supported by the **s5**-specific module of the **fsck** command.

fsck audits and interactively repairs inconsistent conditions on file systems. In this case, it asks for confirmation before attempting any corrections. Inconsistencies other than those mentioned above can often result in some loss of data. The amount and severity of data lost can be determined from the diagnostic output.

fsck corrects innocuous inconsistencies such as: unreferenced inodes, too-large link counts in inodes, missing blocks in the free list, blocks appearing in the free list and also in files, or incorrect counts in the super block, automatically. It displays a message for each inconsistency corrected that identifies the nature of, and file system on which, the correction is to take place. After successfully correcting a file system, **fsck** prints the number of files on that file system, the number of used and free blocks, and the percentage of fragmentation.

The default action for each correction is to wait for the operator to respond either **yes** or **no**. If the operator does not have write permission on the file system, **fsck** will default to a **-n** (no corrections) action.

Inconsistencies checked are as follows:

Blocks claimed by more than one inode or the free list.

Blocks claimed by an inode or the free list outside the range of the file system.

Incorrect link counts.

Incorrect directory sizes.

Bad inode format.

Blocks not accounted for anywhere.

Directory checks, file pointing to unallocated inode, inode number out of range, absence of '.' and '..' as the first two entries in each directory.

Super Block checks: more blocks for inodes than there are in the file system.

Bad free block list format.

Total free block and/or free inode count incorrect.

Orphaned files and directories (allocated but unreferenced) are, with the operator's concurrence, reconnected by placing them in the **lost+found** directory. The name assigned is the inode number. If the **lost+found** directory does not exist, it is created. If there is insufficient space its size is increased.

A file system may be specified by giving the name of the block or character special device on which it resides, or by giving the name of its mount point.

The options are:

−F ufs   Specifies the **ufs**-FSType.

−y | −Y   Assume a yes response to all questions asked by **fsck**.

−n | −N   Assume a no response to all questions asked by **fsck**; do not open
              the file system for writing.

−o   Specify **ufs** file system specific suboptions. These suboptions can be
              any combination of the following:

    p   Check the filesystem non-interactively. Exit if there is a prob-
              lem requiring intervention.

    b=#   Use the block specified as the super block for the file system.
              Block 32 is always an alternate super block.

NOTES

Checking the character special device is almost always faster.

SEE ALSO

checkfsys(1M), **crash**(1M), generic **fsck**(1M), **mkfs**(1M), **ufs**(4)

NAME

fsdb (generic) – file system debugger

SYNOPSIS

fsdb [**-F** *FSType*] [**-V**] [*current_options*] [**-o** *specific_options*] *special*

DESCRIPTION

fsdb is a file system debugger which allows for the manual repair of a file system after a crash. *special* is a special device used to indicate the file system to be debugged. **fsdb** is intended for experienced users only. *FSType* is the file system type to be debugged. Since different *FSTypes* have different structures and hence different debugging capabilities the manual pages for the *FSType*-specific **fsdb** should be consulted for a more detailed description of the debugging capabilities.

current_options are options supported by the **s5**-specific module of **fsdb**. Other *FSTypes* do not necessarily support these options. *specific_options* indicate suboptions specified in a comma-separated list of suboptions and/or keyword-attribute pairs for interpretation by the *FSType*-specific module of the command.

The options are:

-F   Specify the *FSType* on which to operate. The *FSType* should either be specified here or be determinable from **/etc/vfstab** by matching the *special* with an entry in the table.

-V   Echo the complete command line, but do not execute the command. The command line is generated by using the options and arguments provided by the user and adding to them information derived from **/etc/vfstab**. This option should be used to verify and validate the command line.

-o   Specify *FSType*-specific options.

NOTE

This command may not be supported for all *FSTypes*.

FILES

/etc/vfstab   list of default parameters for each file system

SEE ALSO

mkfs(1M), **vfstab**(4).
Manual pages for the *FSType*-specific modules of **fsdb**

NAME

  fsdb (s5) – **s5** file system debugger

SYNOPSIS

  fsdb [–**F** **s5**] [*generic_options*] [–**z** *i-number*] *special* [–]

DESCRIPTION

  generic_options are options supported by the generic **fsdb** command.

  fsdb can be used to patch up a damaged **s5** file system after a crash. *special* is a special device used to indicate the file system to be debugged. It has conversions to translate block and i-numbers into their corresponding disk addresses. Also included are mnemonic offsets to access different parts of an i-node. These greatly simplify the process of correcting control block entries or descending the file system tree.

  fsdb contains several error-checking routines to verify i-node and block addresses. These can be disabled if necessary by invoking **fsdb** with the optional – argument or by the use of the **O** symbol. (**fsdb** reads the i-size and f-size entries from the superblock of the file system as the basis for these checks.)

  The options are:

  –**F s5**   Specifies the **s5**-FSType.

  –**z** *i-number*   Clear the i-node identified by *i-number*. Non-interactive.

  Numbers are considered decimal by default. Octal numbers must be prefixed with a zero. During any assignment operation, numbers are checked for a possible truncation error due to a size mismatch between source and destination.

  fsdb reads a block at a time and will therefore work with raw as well as block I/O. A buffer management routine is used to retain commonly used blocks of data in order to reduce the number of read system calls. All assignment operations result in an immediate write-through of the corresponding block.

  The symbols recognized by **fsdb** are:

#	absolute address
i	convert from i-number to i-node address
b	convert to block address
d	directory slot offset
+ , –	address arithmetic
q	quit
> , <	save, restore an address
=	numerical assignment
=+	incremental assignment
=–	decremental assignment
="	character string assignment
O	error checking flip flop
p	general print facilities
f	file print facility
B	byte mode

W	word mode
D	double word mode
!	escape to shell

The print facilities generate a formatted output in various styles. The current address is normalized to an appropriate boundary before printing begins. It advances with the printing and is left at the address of the last item printed. The output can be terminated at any time by typing the delete character. If a number follows the **p** symbol, that many entries are printed. A check is made to detect block boundary overflows since logically sequential blocks are generally not physically sequential. If a count of zero is used, all entries to the end of the current block are printed. The print options available are:

i	print as i-nodes
d	print as directories
o	print as octal words
e	print as decimal words
c	print as characters
b	print as octal bytes

The **f** symbol is used to print data blocks associated with the current i-node. If followed by a number, that block of the file is printed. (Blocks are numbered from zero.) The desired print option letter follows the block number, if present, or the **f** symbol. This print facility works for small as well as large files. It checks for special devices and that the block pointers used to find the data are not zero.

Dots, tabs, and spaces may be used as function delimiters but are not necessary. A line with just a new-line character will increment the current address by the size of the data type last printed. That is, the address is set to the next byte, word, double word, directory entry or i-node, allowing the user to step through a region of a file system. Information is printed in a format appropriate to the data type. Bytes, words and double words are displayed with the octal address followed by the value in octal and decimal. A **.B** or **.D** is appended to the address for byte and double word values, respectively. Directories are printed as a directory slot offset followed by the decimal i-number and the character representation of the entry name. I-nodes are printed with labeled fields describing each element.

The following mnemonics are used for i-node examination and refer to the current working i-node:

md	mode
ln	link count
uid	user ID number
gid	group ID number
sz	file size
a #	data block numbers (0 – 12)
at	access time
mt	modification time
maj	major device number

             `min`   minor device number

EXAMPLES

`386i`	prints i-number 386 in an i-node format. This now becomes the current working i-node.
`ln=4`	changes the link count for the working i-node to 4.
`ln=+1`	increments the link count by 1.
`fc`	prints, in ASCII, block zero of the file associated with the working i-node.
`2i.fd`	prints the first 32 directory entries for the root i-node of this file system.
`d5i.fc`	changes the current i-node to that associated with the 5th directory entry (numbered from zero) found from the above command. The first logical block of the file is then printed in ASCII.
`512B.p0o`	prints the superblock of this file system in octal.
`2i.a0b.d7=3`	changes the i-number for the seventh directory slot in the root directory to 3. This example also shows how several operations can be combined on one command line.
`d7.nm="`*name*`"`	changes the name field in the directory slot to the given string. Quotes are optional when used with **nm** if the first character is alphabetic.
`a2b.p0d`	prints the third block of the current i-node as directory entries.

SEE ALSO

fsck(1M), generic **fsdb**(1M), **dir**(4), **fs**(4)

NAME
    fsdb (ufs) – **ufs** file system debugger

SYNOPSIS
    fsdb [**−F ufs**] [*generic_options*] [**-z** *i-number*] *special*

DESCRIPTION
    generic_options are options supported by the generic **fsdb** command.

    The options are:

    −F ufs
        Specifies the **ufs**-FSType.

    -z *i-number*
        Clear the i-node identified by *i-number*. Non-interactive.

SEE ALSO
    fsck(1M), generic **fsdb**(1M), **dir**(4), ufs **fs**(4)

NAME
> fsirand – install random inode generation numbers

SYNOPSIS
> /usr/ucb/fsirand [-p] *special*

DESCRIPTION
> **fsirand** installs random inode generation numbers on all the inodes on device *special*, and also installs a filesystem ID in the superblock. This helps increase the security of filesystems exported by NFS.
>
> **fsirand** must be used only on an unmounted filesystem that has been checked with **fsck**(1M). The only exception is that it can be used on the root filesystem in single-user mode, if the system is immediately re-booted afterwords.
>
> The **-p** option prints out the generation numbers for all the inodes, but does not change the generation numbers.

SEE ALSO
> **fsck**(1M) in the *System Administrator's Reference Manual*

NAME

fstyp (generic) – determine file system type

SYNOPSIS

fstyp [–v] *special*

DESCRIPTION

fstyp allows the user to determine the file system type of unmounted file systems using heuristic programs.

An **fstyp** module for each file system type to be checked is executed; each of these modules applies some appropriate heuristic to determine whether the supplied *special* file is of the type for which it checks. If it is, the program prints on standard output the usual file-system identifier for that type and exits with a return code of 0; if none of the modules succeed, the error message **unknown_fstyp (no matches)** is returned and the exit status is 1. If more than one module succeeds the error message **unknown_fstyp (multiple matches)** is returned and the exit status is 2.

The options are:

–v   Produce verbose output. This is usually information about the file systems superblock and varies across different *FSTypes*.

NOTES

The use of heuristics implies that the result of **fstyp** is not guaranteed to be accurate.

NAME

ftp – file transfer program

SYNOPSIS

ftp [**–dgintv**] [*hostname*]

DESCRIPTION

The **ftp** command is the user interface to the ARPANET standard File Transfer Protocol (FTP). **ftp** transfers files to and from a remote network site.

The client host with which **ftp** is to communicate may be specified on the command line. If this is done, **ftp** immediately attempts to establish a connection to an FTP server on that host; otherwise, **ftp** enters its command interpreter and awaits instructions from the user. When **ftp** is awaiting commands from the user, it displays the prompt **ftp>**.

The following options may be specified at the command line, or to the command interpreter:

–d   Enable debugging.

–g   Disable filename globbing.

–i   Turn off interactive prompting during multiple file transfers.

–n   Do not attempt auto-login upon initial connection. If auto-login is not disabled, **ftp** checks the **.netrc** file in the user's home directory for an entry describing an account on the remote machine. If no entry exists, **ftp** will prompt for the login name of the account on the remote machine (the default is the login name on the local machine), and, if necessary, for a password and an account with which to log in.

–t   Enable packet tracing (unimplemented).

–v   Show all responses from the remote server, as well as report on data transfer statistics. This is turned on by default if **ftp** is running interactively with its input coming from the user's terminal.

The following commands can be specified to the command interpreter:

! [*command*]
      Run *command* as a shell command on the local machine. If no *command* is given, invoke an interactive shell.

$ *macro-name* [*args*]
      Execute the macro *macro-name* that was defined with the **macdef** command. Arguments are passed to the macro unglobbed.

account [*passwd*]
      Supply a supplemental password required by a remote system for access to resources once a login has been successfully completed. If no argument is included, the user will be prompted for an account password in a non-echoing input mode.

append *local-file* [*remote-file*]

Append a local file to a file on the remote machine. If *remote-file* is not specified, the local file name is used, subject to alteration by any **ntrans** or **nmap** settings. File transfer uses the current settings for representation type, file structure, and transfer mode.

ascii Set the representation type to network ASCII. This is the default type.

bell Sound a bell after each file transfer command is completed.

binary

Set the representation type to image.

bye Terminate the FTP session with the remote server and exit **ftp**. An EOF will also terminate the session and exit.

case Toggle remote computer file name case mapping during **mget** commands. When **case** is on (default is off), remote computer file names with all letters in upper case are written in the local directory with the letters mapped to lower case.

cd *remote-directory*

Change the working directory on the remote machine to *remote-directory*.

cdup Change the remote machine working directory to the parent of the current remote machine working directory.

close Terminate the FTP session with the remote server, and return to the command interpreter. Any defined macros are erased.

cr Toggle RETURN stripping during network ASCII type file retrieval. Records are denoted by a RETURN/LINEFEED sequence during network ASCII type file transfer. When **cr** is on (the default), RETURN characters are stripped from this sequence to conform with the UNIX system single LINEFEED record delimiter. Records on non-UNIX-system remote hosts may contain single LINEFEED characters; when an network ASCII type transfer is made, these LINEFEED characters may be distinguished from a record delimiter only when **cr** is off.

delete *remote-file*

Delete the file *remote-file* on the remote machine.

debug

Toggle debugging mode. When debugging is on, **ftp** prints each command sent to the remote machine, preceded by the string **-->**.

dir [*remote-directory*] [*local-file*]

Print a listing of the directory contents in the directory, *remote-directory*, and, optionally, placing the output in *local-file*. If no directory is specified, the current working directory on the remote machine is used. If no local file is specified, or *local-file* is **-**, output is sent to the terminal.

disconnect

A synonym for **close**.

form [*format-name*]
Set the carriage control format subtype of the representation type to *format-name*. The only valid *format-name* is **non-print**, which corresponds to the default non-print subtype.

get *remote-file* [*local-file*]
Retrieve the *remote-file* and store it on the local machine. If the local file name is not specified, it is given the same name it has on the remote machine, subject to alteration by the current **case**, **ntrans**, and **nmap** settings. The current settings for representation type, file structure, and transfer mode are used while transferring the file.

glob Toggle filename expansion, or globbing, for **mdelete**, **mget** and **mput**. If globbing is turned off, filenames are taken literally.

Globbing for **mput** is done as in **sh**(1). For **mdelete** and **mget**, each remote file name is expanded separately on the remote machine, and the lists are not merged.

Expansion of a directory name is likely to be radically different from expansion of the name of an ordinary file: the exact result depends on the remote operating system and FTP server, and can be previewed by doing **mls** *remote-files* –.

mget and **mput** are not meant to transfer entire directory subtrees of files. You can do this by transferring a **tar**(1) archive of the subtree (using a representation type of image as set by the **binary** command).

hash Toggle hash-sign (#) printing for each data block transferred. The size of a data block is 8192 bytes.

help [*command*]
Print an informative message about the meaning of *command*. If no argument is given, **ftp** prints a list of the known commands.

lcd [*directory*]
Change the working directory on the local machine. If no *directory* is specified, the user's home directory is used.

ls [*remote-directory*] [*local-file*]
Print an abbreviated listing of the contents of a directory on the remote machine. If *remote-directory* is left unspecified, the current working directory is used. If no local file is specified, or if *local-file* is –, the output is sent to the terminal.

macdef *macro-name*
Define a macro. Subsequent lines are stored as the macro *macro-name*; a null line (consecutive NEWLINE characters in a file or RETURN characters from the terminal) terminates macro input mode. There is a limit of 16 macros and 4096 total characters in all defined macros. Macros remain defined until a **close** command is executed.

The macro processor interprets $ and \ as special characters. A $ followed by a number (or numbers) is replaced by the corresponding argument on the macro invocation command line. A $ followed by an **i** signals that macro processor that the executing macro is to be looped. On the first pass $i is replaced by the first argument on the macro invocation command line, on the second pass it is replaced by the second argument, and so on. A \ followed by any character is replaced by that character. Use the \ to prevent special treatment of the $.

mdelete [*remote-files*]
Delete the *remote-files* on the remote machine.

mdir *remote-files local-file*
Like **dir**, except multiple remote files may be specified. If interactive prompting is on, **ftp** will prompt the user to verify that the last argument is indeed the target local file for receiving **mdir** output.

mget *remote-files*
Expand the *remote-files* on the remote machine and do a **get** for each file name thus produced. See **glob** for details on the filename expansion. Resulting file names will then be processed according to **case**, **ntrans**, and **nmap** settings. Files are transferred into the local working directory, which can be changed with **lcd** *directory*; new local directories can be created with **!** **mkdir** *directory*.

mkdir *directory-name*
Make a directory on the remote machine.

mls *remote-files local-file*
Like **ls**(1), except multiple remote files may be specified. If interactive prompting is on, **ftp** will prompt the user to verify that the last argument is indeed the target local file for receiving **mls** output.

mode [*mode-name*]
Set the transfer mode to *mode-name*. The only valid *mode-name* is **stream**, which corresponds to the default stream mode. This implementation only supports **stream**, and requires that it be specified.

mput *local-files*
Expand wild cards in the list of local files given as arguments and do a **put** for each file in the resulting list. See **glob** for details of filename expansion. Resulting file names will then be processed according to **ntrans** and **nmap** settings.

nmap [*inpattern outpattern*]
Set or unset the filename mapping mechanism. If no arguments are specified, the filename mapping mechanism is unset. If arguments are specified, remote filenames are mapped during **mput** commands and **put** commands issued without a specified remote target filename. If arguments are specified, local filenames are mapped during **mget** commands and **get** commands issued without a specified local target filename.

This command is useful when connecting to a non-UNIX-system remote host with different file naming conventions or practices. The mapping follows the pattern set by *inpattern* and *outpattern*. *inpattern* is a template for incoming filenames (which may have already been processed according to the **ntrans** and **case** settings). Variable templating is accomplished by including the sequences $1, $2, ..., $9 in *inpattern*. Use \ to prevent this special treatment of the $ character. All other characters are treated literally, and are used to determine the **nmap** *inpattern* variable values.

For example, given *inpattern* **$1.$2** and the remote file name **mydata.data**, **$1** would have the value **mydata**, and **$2** would have the value **data**.

The *outpattern* determines the resulting mapped filename. The sequences **$1**, **$2**, ..., **$9** are replaced by any value resulting from the *inpattern* template. The sequence **$0** is replaced by the original filename. Additionally, the sequence [*seq1* , *seq2*] is replaced by *seq1* if *seq1* is not a null string; otherwise it is replaced by *seq2*.

For example, the command **nmap $1.$2.$3 [$1,$2].[$2,file]** would yield the output filename **myfile.data** for input filenames **myfile.data** and **myfile.data.old**, **myfile.file** for the input filename **myfile**, and **myfile.myfile** for the input filename **myfile**. SPACE characters may be included in *outpattern*, as in the example **nmap $1 | sed "s/ *$//" >** **$1**. Use the \ character to prevent special treatment of the **$**, **[**, **]**, and **,** characters.

ntrans [*inchars* [*outchars*]]

Set or unset the filename character translation mechanism. If no arguments are specified, the filename character translation mechanism is unset. If arguments are specified, characters in remote filenames are translated during **mput** commands and **put** commands issued without a specified remote target filename, and characters in local filenames are translated during **mget** commands and **get** commands issued without a specified local target filename.

This command is useful when connecting to a non-UNIX-system remote host with different file naming conventions or practices. Characters in a filename matching a character in *inchars* are replaced with the corresponding character in *outchars*. If the character's position in *inchars* is longer than the length of *outchars*, the character is deleted from the file name.

open *host* [*port*]

Establish a connection to the specified *host* FTP server. An optional port number may be supplied, in which case, **ftp** will attempt to contact an FTP server at that port. If the *auto-login* option is on (default setting), **ftp** will also attempt to automatically log the user in to the FTP server.

prompt

Toggle interactive prompting. Interactive prompting occurs during multiple file transfers to allow the user to selectively retrieve or store files. By default, prompting is turned on. If prompting is turned off, any **mget** or **mput** will transfer all files, and any **mdelete** will delete all files.

proxy *ftp-command*

Execute an FTP command on a secondary control connection. This command allows simultaneous connection to two remote FTP servers for transferring files between the two servers. The first **proxy** command should be an **open**, to establish the secondary control connection. Enter the command **proxy ?** to see other FTP commands executable on the secondary connection.

The following commands behave differently when prefaced by **proxy**: **open** will not define new macros during the auto-login process, **close** will not erase existing macro definitions, **get** and **mget** transfer files from the host on the primary control connection to the host on the secondary control connection, and **put**, **mputd**, and **append** transfer files from the host on the secondary control connection to the host on the primary control connection.

Third party file transfers depend upon support of the **PASV** command by the server on the secondary control connection.

put *local-file* [*remote-file*]
Store a local file on the remote machine. If *remote-file* is left unspecified, the local file name is used after processing according to any **ntrans** or **nmap** settings in naming the remote file. File transfer uses the current settings for representation type, file structure, and transfer mode.

pwd Print the name of the current working directory on the remote machine.

quit A synonym for **bye**.

quote *arg1 arg2 ...*
Send the arguments specified, verbatim, to the remote FTP server. A single FTP reply code is expected in return. (The **remotehelp** command displays a list of valid arguments.)

quote should be used only by experienced users who are familiar with the FTP protocol.

recv *remote-file* [*local-file*]
A synonym for **get**.

remotehelp [*command-name*]
Request help from the remote FTP server. If a *command-name* is specified it is supplied to the server as well.

rename *from to*
Rename the file *from* on the remote machine to have the name *to*.

reset Clear reply queue. This command re-synchronizes command/reply sequencing with the remote FTP server. Resynchronization may be necessary following a violation of the FTP protocol by the remote server.

rmdir *directory-name*
Delete a directory on the remote machine.

runique
Toggle storing of files on the local system with unique filenames. If a file already exists with a name equal to the target local filename for a **get** or **mget** command, a **.1** is appended to the name. If the resulting name matches another existing file, a **.2** is appended to the original name. If this process continues up to **.99**, an error message is printed, and the transfer does not take place. The generated unique filename will be

reported. **runique** will not affect local files generated from a shell command. The default value is off.

send *local-file* [*remote-file*]
    A synonym for **put**.

sendport
    Toggle the use of **PORT** commands. By default, **ftp** will attempt to use a **PORT** command when establishing a connection for each data transfer. The use of **PORT** commands can prevent delays when performing multiple file transfers. If the **PORT** command fails, **ftp** will use the default data port. When the use of **PORT** commands is disabled, no attempt will be made to use **PORT** commands for each data transfer. This is useful when connected to certain FTP implementations that ignore **PORT** commands but incorrectly indicate they have been accepted.

status
    Show the current status of **ftp**.

struct [*struct-name*]
    Set the file structure to *struct-name*. The only valid *struct-name* is **file**, which corresponds to the default file structure. The implementation only supports **file**, and requires that it be specified.

sunique
    Toggle storing of files on remote machine under unique file names. The remote FTP server must support the **STOU** command for successful completion. The remote server will report the unique name. Default value is off.

tenex Set the representation type to that needed to talk to TENEX machines.

trace Toggle packet tracing (unimplemented).

type [*type-name*]
    Set the representation type to *type-name*. The valid *type-name*s are **ascii** for network ASCII, **binary** or **image** for image, and **tenex** for local byte size with a byte size of 8 (used to talk to TENEX machines). If no type is specified, the current type is printed. The default type is network ASCII.

user *user-name* [*password*] [*account*]
    Identify yourself to the remote FTP server. If the password is not specified and the server requires it, **ftp** will prompt the user for it (after disabling local echo). If an account field is not specified, and the FTP server requires it, the user will be prompted for it. If an account field is specified, an account command will be relayed to the remote server after the login sequence is completed if the remote server did not require it for logging in. Unless **ftp** is invoked with auto-login disabled, this process is done automatically on initial connection to the FTP server.

verbose
    Toggle verbose mode. In verbose mode, all responses from the FTP server are displayed to the user. In addition, if verbose mode is on, when a file transfer completes, statistics regarding the efficiency of the transfer are

reported. By default, verbose mode is on if **ftp**'s commands are coming from a terminal, and off otherwise.

? [*command*]
> A synonym for **help**.

Command arguments which have embedded spaces may be quoted with quote (") marks.

If any command argument which is not indicated as being optional is not specified, **ftp** will prompt for that argument.

ABORTING A FILE TRANSFER

To abort a file transfer, use the terminal interrupt key. Sending transfers will be immediately halted. Receiving transfers will be halted by sending an FTP protocol **ABOR** command to the remote server, and discarding any further data received. The speed at which this is accomplished depends upon the remote server's support for **ABOR** processing. If the remote server does not support the **ABOR** command, an **ftp>** prompt will not appear until the remote server has completed sending the requested file.

The terminal interrupt key sequence will be ignored when **ftp** has completed any local processing and is awaiting a reply from the remote server. A long delay in this mode may result from the **ABOR** processing described above, or from unexpected behavior by the remote server, including violations of the ftp protocol. If the delay results from unexpected remote server behavior, the local **ftp** program must be killed by hand.

FILE NAMING CONVENTIONS

Local files specified as arguments to **ftp** commands are processed according to the following rules.

1)   If the file name – is specified, the standard input (for reading) or standard output (for writing) is used.

2)   If the first character of the file name is |, the remainder of the argument is interpreted as a shell command. **ftp** then forks a shell, using **popen**(3S) with the argument supplied, and reads (writes) from the standard output (standard input) of that shell. If the shell command includes SPACE characters, the argument must be quoted; for example "**| ls -lt**". A particularly useful example of this mechanism is: "**dir | more**".

3)   Failing the above checks, if globbing is enabled, local file names are expanded according to the rules used in the **sh**(1); see the **glob** command. If the **ftp** command expects a single local file (for example, **put**), only the first filename generated by the globbing operation is used.

4)   For **mget** commands and **get** commands with unspecified local file names, the local filename is the remote filename, which may be altered by a **case**, **ntrans**, or **nmap** setting. The resulting filename may then be altered if **runique** is on.

5)   For **mput** commands and **put** commands with unspecified remote file names, the remote filename is the local filename, which may be altered by a **ntrans** or **nmap** setting. The resulting filename may then be altered by the remote server if **sunique** is on.

FILE TRANSFER PARAMETERS

The FTP specification specifies many parameters which may affect a file transfer.

The representation type may be one of network ASCII, EBCDIC, image, or local byte size with a specified byte size (for PDP-10's and PDP-20's mostly). The network ASCII and EBCDIC types have a further subtype which specifies whether vertical format control (NEWLINE characters, form feeds, etc.) are to be passed through (non-print), provided in TELNET format (TELNET format controls), or provided in ASA (FORTRAN) (carriage control (ASA)) format. **ftp** supports the network ASCII (subtype non-print only) and image types, plus local byte size with a byte size of 8 for communicating with TENEX machines.

The file structure may be one of **file** (no record structure), **record**, or **page**. **ftp** supports only the default value, which is **file**.

The transfer mode may be one of **stream**, **block**, or **compressed**. **ftp** supports only the default value, which is **stream**.

SEE ALSO

ls(1), **rcp**(1), **tar**(1), **sh**(1), **ftpd**(1M), **popen**(3S), **netrc**(4)

NOTES

Correct execution of many commands depends upon proper behavior by the remote server.

An error in the treatment of carriage returns in the 4.2 BSD code handling transfers with a representation type of network ASCII has been corrected. This correction may result in incorrect transfers of binary files to and from 4.2 BSD servers using a representation type of network ASCII. Avoid this problem by using the image type.

NAME

    `ftpd` – file transfer protocol server

SYNOPSIS

    `in.ftpd` [`-dl`] [`-t`*timeout*]

DESCRIPTION

    `ftpd` is the Internet File Transfer Protocol (FTP) server process. The server is invoked by the Internet daemon `inetd`(1M) each time a connection to the FTP service [see `services`(4)] is made, with the connection available as descriptor 0.

    Inactive connections are timed out after 90 seconds.

    The following options are available:

    `-d`   Write Debugging information into the system log.

    `-l`   Write each FTP session into the system log.

    `-t`*timeout*

        Set the inactivity timeout period to *timeout*, in seconds. The FTP server will timeout an inactive session after 15 minutes.

Requests

    The FTP server currently supports the following FTP requests; case is not distinguished.

Request	Description
ABOR	abort previous command
ACCT	specify account (ignored)
ALLO	allocate storage (vacuously)
APPE	append to a file
CDUP	change to parent of current working directory
CWD	change working directory
DELE	delete a file
HELP	give help information
LIST	give list files in a directory (`ls -lg`)
MKD	make a directory
MODE	specify data transfer *mode*
NLST	give name list of files in directory (`ls`)
NOOP	do nothing
PASS	specify password
PASV	prepare for server-to-server transfer
PORT	specify data connection port
PWD	print the current working directory

QUIT	terminate session
RETR	retrieve a file
RMD	remove a directory
RNFR	specify rename-from file name
RNTO	specify rename-to file name
STOR	store a file
STOU	store a file with a unique name
STRU	specify data transfer *structure*
TYPE	specify data transfer *type*
USER	specify user name
XCUP	change to parent of current working directory
XCWD	change working directory
XMKD	make a directory
XPWD	print the current working directory
XRMD	remove a directory

The remaining FTP requests specified in RFC 959 are recognized, but not implemented.

The FTP server will abort an active file transfer only when the **ABOR** command is preceded by a Telnet Interrupt Process (IP) signal and a Telnet Synch signal in the command Telnet stream, as described in RFC 959.

ftpd interprets file names according to the globbing conventions used by **sh**(1). This allows users to utilize the metacharacters: * ? [ ] { } ~

ftpd authenticates users according to four rules.

1)   The user name must be in the password data base, **/etc/passwd**, and not have a null password. In this case a password must be provided by the client before any file operations may be performed.

2)   If the user name appears in the file **/etc/ftpusers**, **ftp** access is denied.

3)   **ftp** access is denied unless the user's shell (from **/etc/passwd**) is listed in the file **/etc/shells**, or the user's shell is one of the following:

```
/bin/sh
/bin/ksh
/bin/csh
/usr/bin/sh
/usr/bin/ksh
/usr/bin/csh
```

4)   If the user name is anonymous or ftp, an anonymous FTP account must be present in the password file (user ftp). In this case the user is allowed to log in by specifying any password (by convention this is given as the client host's name).

In the last case, **ftpd** takes special measures to restrict the client's access privileges. The server performs a **chroot**(2) command to the home directory of the ftp user. In order that system security is not breached, it is recommended that the ftp subtree be constructed with care; the following rules are recommended.

home_directory
        Make the home directory owned by **ftp** and unwritable by anyone.

home_directory/**usr/bin**
        Make this directory owned by the super-user and unwritable by anyone. The program **ls**(1) must be present to support the list commands. This program should have mode 111.

home_directory/**etc**
        Make this directory owned by the super-user and unwritable by anyone. Copies of the files **passwd**(4), **group**(4), and **netconfig** must be present for the **ls** command to work properly. These files should be mode 444.

home_directory/**pub**
        Make this directory mode 777 and owned by **ftp**. Users should then place files which are to be accessible via the anonymous account in this directory.

home_directory/**dev**
        Make this directory owned by the super-user and unwritable by anyone. Change directories to this directory and do the following:

```
FTP="'grep ^ftp: /etc/passwd | cut -d: -f6'"
MAJORMINOR="'ls -l /dev/tcp | nawk '{ gsub(/,/, ""); print $5, $6}''
mknod $FTP/dev/tcp c $MAJORMINOR
chmod 666 $FTP/dev/tcp
```

SEE ALSO

   ftp(1), getsockopt(3N), passwd(4), services(4)

   Postel, Jon, and Joyce Reynolds, *File Transfer Protocol (FTP)*, RFC 959, Network Information Center, SRI International, Menlo Park, Calif., October 1985

NOTES

   The anonymous account is inherently dangerous and should be avoided when possible.

   The server must run as the super-user to create sockets with privileged port numbers. It maintains an effective user ID of the logged in user, changing to user ID 0 only when binding addresses to sockets. The possible security holes have been extensively scrutinized, but are possibly incomplete.

`/etc/ftpusers` contains a list of users who cannot access the system; the format of the file is one username per line.

NAME

　　fumount – forced unmount of advertised resources

SYNOPSIS

　　fumount [-w *sec*] *resource* [[-w *sec*] *resource*]. . .

DESCRIPTION

　　fumount unadvertises each *resource* and disconnects remote access to the *resource*. The **-w** *sec* causes a delay of *sec* seconds prior to the disconnect from the *resource* specified immediately after the **-w**.

　　When the forced unmount occurs, an administrative shell script is started on each remote computer that has the resource mounted (**/usr/bin/rfuadmin**). If a grace period of several seconds is specified with **-w**, **rfuadmin** is started with the **fuwarn** option. When the actual forced unmount is ready to occur, **rfuadmin** is started with the **fumount** option. See the **rfuadmin**(1M) manual page for information on the action taken in response to the forced unmount.

　　This command is restricted to the super-user.

ERRORS

　　If *resource* (1) does not physically reside on the local machine, (2) is an invalid resource name, (3) is not currently advertised and is not remotely mounted, or (4) the command is not run with super-user privileges, an error message will be sent to standard error.

SEE ALSO

　　adv(1M), **mount**(1M), **rfuadmin**(1M), **rfudaemon**(1M), **rmount**(1M), **unadv**(1M)

NAME

    fusage – disk access profiler

SYNOPSIS

    fusage [[*mount_point*] | [*advertised_resource*] | [*block_special_device*] [. . .]]

DESCRIPTION

    When used with no options, **fusage** reports block I/O transfers, in kilobytes, to and from all locally mounted file systems and advertised Remote File Sharing resources on a per client basis. The count data are cumulative since the time of the mount. When used with an option, **fusage** reports on the named file system, advertised resource, or block special device.

    The report includes one section for each file system and advertised resource and has one entry for each machine that has the directory remotely mounted, ordered by decreasing usage. Sections are ordered by device name; advertised resources that are not complete file systems will immediately follow the sections for the file systems they are in.

SEE ALSO

    adv(1M), **mount**(1M), **df**(1M), **crash**(1M)

NAME

fuser – identify processes using a file or file structure

SYNOPSIS

/usr/sbin/fuser [–[c|f]ku] *files* | *resources* [[–] [–[c|f]ku]
files | *resources*] . . .

DESCRIPTION

fuser outputs the process IDs of the processes that are using the *files* or remote
resources specified as arguments. Each process ID is followed by one of these
letter codes, which identify how the process is using the file:

c   as its current directory.

r   as its root directory, which was set up by the **chroot**(1M) command.

o   as an open file.

t   as its text file.

a   as its trace file located in the **/proc** directory.

For block special devices with mounted file systems, processes using any file on
that device are listed. For remote resource names, processes using any file associated with that remote resource (Remote File Sharing) are reported. For all other
types of files (text files, executables, directories, devices, etc.) only the processes
using that file are reported.

The following options may be used with **fuser**:

–c   may be used with files that are mount points for file systems. With that
        option the report is for use of the mount point and any files within that
        mounted file system.

–f   when this is used, the report is only for the named file, not for files within
        a mounted file system.

–u   the user login name, in parentheses, also follows the process ID.

–k   the SIGKILL signal is sent to each process. Since this option spawns kills
        for each process, the kill messages may not show up immediately [see
        kill(2)].

If more than one group of files are specified, the options may be respecified for
each additional group of files. A lone dash cancels the options currently in force.

The process IDs are printed as a single line on the standard output, separated by
spaces and terminated with a single new line. All other output is written on
standard error.

Any user with permission to read **/dev/kmem** and **/dev/mem** can use **fuser**.
Only the super-user can terminate another user's process

EXAMPLES

fuser –ku /dev/dsk/1s?

      if typed by a user with appropriate privileges, terminates all processes
      that are preventing disk drive one from being unmounted, listing the pro-
      cess ID and login name of each as it is killed.

```
fuser -u /etc/passwd
```
lists process IDs and login names of processes that have the password file open.

```
fuser -ku /dev/dsk/1s? -u /etc/passwd
```
executes both of the above examples in a single command line.

```
fuser -cu /home
```
if the **/dev/dsk/c1d0s9** device is mounted on /home, lists process ID's and login names of processes that are using **/dev/dsk/c1d0s9**.

FILES

/stand/unix	for system namelist
/dev/kmem	for system image
/dev/mem	also for system image

NOTE

If an RFS resource from a pre System V Release 4 server is mounted, **fuser** can only report on use of the whole file system, not on individual files within it.

Because **fuser** works with a snapshot of the system image, it may miss processes that begin using a file while **fuser** is running. Also, processes reported as using a file may have stopped using it while **fuser** was running. These factors should discourage the use of the **-k** option.

fuser does not report all possible usages of a file (for example, a mapped file).

SEE ALSO

mount(1M), **chroot**(1M)
ps(1) in the *User's Reference Manual*
kill(2), **signal**(2), **proc(4)** in the *Programmer's Reference Manual*

NAME
fwtmp, wtmpfix – manipulate connect accounting records

SYNOPSIS
/usr/lib/acct/fwtmp [-ic]
/usr/lib/acct/wtmpfix [files]

DESCRIPTION
fwtmp reads from the standard input and writes to the standard output, converting binary records of the type found in /var/adm/wtmp to formatted ASCII
records. The ASCII version is useful when it is necessary to edit bad records.

The argument −ic is used to denote that input is in ASCII form, and output is to
be written in binary form.

wtmpfix examines the standard input or named files in utmp.h format, corrects
the time/date stamps to make the entries consistent, and writes to the standard
output. A − can be used in place of files to indicate the standard input. If
time/date corrections are not performed, acctcon will fault when it encounters
certain date-change records.

Each time the date is set, a pair of date change records are written to
/var/adm/wtmp. The first record is the old date denoted by the string "old
time" placed in the line field and the flag OLD_TIME placed in the type field of
the utmp structure. The second record specifies the new date and is denoted by
the string new time placed in the line field and the flag NEW_TIME placed in the
type field. wtmpfix uses these records to synchronize all time stamps in the file.

In addition to correcting time/date stamps, wtmpfix will check the validity of the
name field to ensure that it consists solely of alphanumeric characters or spaces.
If it encounters a name that is considered invalid, it will change the login name to
INVALID and write a diagnostic to the standard error. In this way, wtmpfix
reduces the chance that acctcon will fail when processing connect accounting
records.

FILES
/var/adm/wtmp
/usr/include/utmp.h

SEE ALSO
acct(1M),   acctcms(1M),   acctcon(1M),   acctmerg(1M),   acctprc(1M),
acctsh(1M), runacct(1M), acct(4), utmp(4)
acctcom(1), ed(1) in the User's Reference Manual
acct(2) in the Programmer's Reference Manual

NAME

    gcore – get core images of running processes

SYNOPSIS

    gcore [–o *filename*] *process-id* . . .

DESCRIPTION

    gcore creates a core image of each specified process. Such an image may be used with debuggers such as **sdb**. The name of the core image file for the process whose process ID is *process-id* will be **core.***process-id*.

    The –o option substitutes *filename* in place of **core** as the first part of the name of the core image files.

FILES

    core.*process-id*   core images

SEE ALSO

    kill(1), **csh**(1)
    sdb(1), **ptrace**(2) in the *Programmer's Reference Manual*

NAME

gencat – generate a formatted message catalogue

SYNOPSIS

gencat [-m] [-f *format*] *catfile msgfile* ...

DESCRIPTION

The **gencat** utility merges the message text source file(s) msgfile into a formatted message database *catfile*. The database *catfile* will be created if it does not already exist. If *catfile* does exist its messages will be included in the new *catfile*. If set and message numbers collide, the new message-text defined in *msgfile* will replace the old message text currently contained in *catfile*. The message text source file (or set of files) input to **gencat** can contain either set and message numbers or simply message numbers, in which case the set **NL_SETD** [see **nl_types**(5)] is assumed.

The **-f** option allows different format message catalogues to be generated. Arguments that can be used with this option are:

SVR4   Produces the System V Release 4 format catalogue. (This is the default if **-f** or **-m** are not specified.)

m   This is equivalent to the **-m** option.

XENIX Produces message catalogues suitable for use with SCO UNIX/XENIX applications.

If the **-m** or **-f** options are not used, the format of an existing message catalogue will be retained. The **-f** option can be used to change the format of a catalogue.

The format of a message text source file is defined as follows. Note that the fields of a message text source line are separated by a single ASCII space or tab character. Any other ASCII spaces or tabs are considered as being part of the subsequent field.

$set   n comment

Where *n* specifies the set identifier of the following messages until the next **$set**, **$delset** or end-of-file appears. *n* must be a number in the range (1–{**NL_SETMAX**}). Set identifiers within a single source file need not be contiguous. Any string following the set identifier is treated as a comment. If no **$set** directive is specified in a message text source file, all messages will be located in the default message set **NL_SETD**.

$delset   n comment

Deletes message set *n* from an existing message catalogue. Any string following the set number is treated as a comment.

(Note: if *n* is not a valid set it is ignored.)

$ comment

A line beginning with a dollar symbol $ followed by an ASCII space or tab character is treated as a comment.

m message-text

The *m* denotes the message identifier, which is a number in the range (1–{**NL_MSGMAX**}). The message-text is stored in the message catalogue with the set identifier specified by the last **$set** directive, and with message identifier *m*. If the message-text is empty, and an ASCII space or tab field separator is present, an empty string is stored in the message catalogue. If a message source line has a message number, but neither a field separator nor message-text , the existing message with that number (if any) is deleted from the catalogue. Message identifiers need not be contiguous. The length of message-text must be in the range (0–{**NL_TEXTMAX**}).

$quote c
This line specifies an optional quote character *c*, which can be used to surround message-text so that trailing spaces or null (empty) messages are visible in a message source line. By default, or if an empty **$quote** directive is supplied, no quoting of message-text will be recognized.

Empty lines in a message text source file are ignored.

Text strings can contain the special characters and escape sequences defined in the following table:

Description	Symbol	Sequence
newline	NL(LF)	\n
horizontal tab	HT	\t
vertical tab	VT	\v
backspace	BS	\b
carriage return	CR	\r
form feed	FF	\f
backslash	\	\\
bit pattern	ddd	\ddd

The escape sequence **\ddd** consists of backslash followed by 1, 2 or 3 octal digits, which are taken to specify the value of the desired character. If the character following a backslash is not one of those specified, the backslash is ignored.

Backslash followed by an ASCII newline character is also used to continue a string on the following line. Thus, the following two lines describe a single message string:

```
1 This line continues \
to the next line
```

which is equivalent to:

```
1 This line continues to the next line
```

NOTES
This version of gencat is built upon the **mkmsgs** utility. The gencat database comprises of two files *catfile***.m** *which is an* **mkmsgs** format catalogue and the file *catfile* which contains the information required to translate an set and message number into a simple message number which can be used in a call to **gettxt**.

Using **gettxt** constrains the catalogues to be located in a subdirectory under **/usr/lib/locale**. This restriction is lifted by placing only a symbolic link to the catalogue in the directory **/usr/lib/locale/Xopen/LC_MESSAGES** when the catalogue is opened. It is this link that **gettxt** uses when attempting to access the catalogue. The link is removed when the catalogue is closed but occasionally as applications exit abnormally without closing catalogues redundant symbolic links will be left in the directory.

For compatibility with previous version of **gencat** released in a number of specialized internationalization products, the **-m** option is supplied. This option will cause gencat to build a single file *catfile* which is compatible with the format catalogues produced by the earlier versions. The retrieval routines detect the type of catalogue they are using and will act appropriately.

SEE ALSO

mkmsgs(1)

catopen(3C), catgets(3C), catclose(3C), gettxt(3C), nl_types(5) in the *Programmer's Reference Manual*.

NAME

gencc – create a front-end to the cc command

SYNOPSIS

gencc

DESCRIPTION

The **gencc** command is an interactive command designed to aid in the creation of a front-end to the **cc** command. Since hard-coded pathnames have been eliminated from the C Compilation System (CCS), it is possible to move pieces of the CCS to new locations without recompilation. The new locations of moved pieces can be specified through the –Y option to the **cc** command. However, it is inconvenient to supply the proper –Y options with every invocation of the **cc** command. Further, if a system administrator moves pieces of the CCS, such movement should be invisible to users.

The front-end to the **cc** command that **gencc** generates is a one-line shell script that calls the **cc** command with the proper –Y options specified. The front-end to the **cc** command will also pass all user-supplied options to the **cc** command.

gencc prompts for the location of each tool and directory that can be respecified by a –Y option to the **cc** command. If no location is specified, it assumes that that piece of the CCS has not been relocated. After all the locations have been prompted for, **gencc** will create the front-end to the **cc** command.

gencc creates the front-end to the **cc** command in the current working directory and gives the file the same name as the **cc** command. Thus, **gencc** can not be run in the same directory containing the actual **cc** command. Further, if a system administrator has redistributed the CCS, the actual **cc** command should be placed in a location that is not typically in a user's path (e.g., **/usr/lib**). Such placement will prevent users from accidentally invoking the **cc** command without using the front-end.

NOTES

gencc does not produce any warnings if a tool or directory does not exist at the specified location. Also, **gencc** does not actually move any files to new locations. The **gencc** command is obsolete.

FILES

./cc   front-end to cc

SEE ALSO

cc(1)

NAME

get – get a version of an SCCS file

SYNOPSIS

get [−a*seq-no.*] [−c*cutoff*] [−i*list*] [−r*SID*] [−w*string*] [−x*list*] [−l[p]] [−b] [−e] [−g]
[−k] [−m] [−n] [−p] [−s] [−t] *file*. . .

DESCRIPTION

get generates an ASCII text file from each named SCCS file according to the
specifications given by its keyletter arguments, which begin with −. The arguments may be specified in any order, but all keyletter arguments apply to all
named SCCS files. If a directory is named, get behaves as though each file in the
directory were specified as a named file, except that non-SCCS files (last component of the path name does not begin with s.) and unreadable files are
silently ignored. If a name of − is given, the standard input is read; each line of
the standard input is taken to be the name of an SCCS file to be processed.

The generated text is normally written into a file called the g-file whose name is
derived from the SCCS file name by simply removing the leading "s." (see also
the FILES section below).

Each of the keyletter arguments is explained below as though only one SCCS file
is to be processed, but the effects of any keyletter argument apply independently
to each named file.

    −r*SID*   The SCCS identification string (SID) of the version (delta) of an
                 SCCS file to be retrieved. Table 1 below shows, for the most use-
                 ful cases, what version of an SCCS file is retrieved (as well as the
                 SID of the version to be eventually created by delta(1) if the −e
                 keyletter is also used), as a function of the SID specified.

    −c*cutoff*   Cutoff date-time, in the form:

                 YY[*MM*[*DD*[*HH*[*MM*[*SS*]]]]]

                 No changes (deltas) to the SCCS file that were created after the
                 specified *cutoff* date-time are included in the generated ASCII text
                 file. Units omitted from the date-time default to their maximum
                 possible values; that is, −c7502 is equivalent to −c750228235959.
                 Any number of non-numeric characters may separate the two-
                 digit pieces of the *cutoff* date-time. This feature allows one to
                 specify a *cutoff* date in the form:

                 −c"77/2/2 9:22:25".

    −i*list*   A *list* of deltas to be included (forced to be applied) in the crea-
                 tion of the generated file. The *list* has the following syntax:

                 <list> ::= <range> | <list> , <range>
                 <range> ::= SID | SID − SID

                 SID, the SCCS Identification of a delta, may be in any form shown
                 in the "SID Specified" column of Table 1.

−**x**_list_   A _list_ of deltas to be excluded in the creation of the generated file. See the −**i** keyletter for the _list_ format.

−**e**   Indicates that the **get** is for the purpose of editing or making a change (delta) to the SCCS file via a subsequent use of **delta**(1). The −**e** keyletter used in a **get** for a particular version (SID) of the SCCS file prevents further **get**s for editing on the same SID until **delta** is executed or the **j** (joint edit) flag is set in the SCCS file [see **admin**(1)]. Concurrent use of **get** −**e** for different SIDs is always allowed.

     If the g-file generated by **get** with an −**e** keyletter is accidentally ruined in the process of editing it, it may be regenerated by re-executing the **get** command with the −**k** keyletter in place of the −**e** keyletter.

     SCCS file protection specified via the ceiling, floor, and authorized user list stored in the SCCS file [see **admin**(1)] are enforced when the −**e** keyletter is used.

−**b**   Used with the −**e** keyletter to indicate that the new delta should have an SID in a new branch as shown in Table 1. This keyletter is ignored if the **b** flag is not present in the file [see **admin**(1)] or if the retrieved **delta** is not a leaf **delta**. (A leaf **delta** is one that has no successors on the SCCS file tree.) A branch **delta** may always be created from a non-leaf **delta**. Partial SIDs are interpreted as shown in the "SID Retrieved" column of Table 1.

−**k**   Suppresses replacement of identification keywords (see below) in the retrieved text by their value. The −**k** keyletter is implied by the −**e** keyletter.

−**l**[**p**]   Causes a delta summary to be written into an l-file. If −**lp** is used, then an l-file is not created; the delta summary is written on the standard output instead. See IDENTIFICATION KEYWORDS for detailed information on the l-file.

−**p**   Causes the text retrieved from the SCCS file to be written on the standard output. No g-file is created. All output that normally goes to the standard output goes to file descriptor 2 instead, unless the −**s** keyletter is used, in which case it disappears.

−**s**   Suppresses all output normally written on the standard output. However, fatal error messages (which always go to file descriptor 2) remain unaffected.

−**m**   Causes each text line retrieved from the SCCS file to be preceded by the SID of the delta that inserted the text line in the SCCS file. The format is: SID, followed by a horizontal tab, followed by the text line.

−**n**   Causes each generated text line to be preceded with the %M% identification keyword value (see below). The format is: %M% value, followed by a horizontal tab, followed by the text line. When both the −**m** and −**n** keyletters are used, the format is: %M%

value, followed by a horizontal tab, followed by the **-m** keyletter generated format.

-g   Suppresses the actual retrieval of text from the SCCS file. It is primarily used to generate an l-file, or to verify the existence of a particular SID.

-t   Used to access the most recently created delta in a given release (for example, **-r1**), or release and level (for example, **-r1.2**).

-w *string*   Substitute *string* for all occurrences of %W% when getting the file. Substitution occurs prior to keyword expansion.

-a*seq-no.*   The delta sequence number of the SCCS file delta (version) to be retrieved. This keyletter is used by the **comb** command; it is not a generally useful keyletter. If both the **-r** and **-a** keyletters are specified, only the **-a** keyletter is used. Care should be taken when using the **-a** keyletter in conjunction with the **-e** keyletter, as the SID of the delta to be created may not be what one expects. The **-r** keyletter can be used with the **-a** and **-e** keyletters to control the naming of the SID of the delta to be created.

For each file processed, **get** responds (on the standard output) with the SID being accessed and with the number of lines retrieved from the SCCS file.

If the **-e** keyletter is used, the SID of the delta to be made appears after the SID accessed and before the number of lines generated. If there is more than one named file or if a directory or standard input is named, each file name is printed (preceded by a new-line) before it is processed. If the **-i** keyletter is used, included deltas are listed following the notation "**Included**"; if the **-x** keyletter is used, excluded deltas are listed following the notation "**Excluded**".

TABLE 1. Determination of SCCS Identification String

SID* Specified	−b Keyletter Used†	Other Conditions	SID Retrieved	SID of Delta to be Created
none‡	no	R defaults to mR	mR.mL	mR.(mL+1)
none‡	yes	R defaults to mR	mR.mL	mR.mL.(mB+1).1
R	no	R > mR	mR.mL	R.1***
R	no	R = mR	mR.mL	mR.(mL+1)
R	yes	R > mR	mR.mL	mR.mL.(mB+1).1
R	yes	R = mR	mR.mL	mR.mL.(mB+1).1
R	−	R < mR and R does *not* exist	hR.mL**	hR.mL.(mB+1).1
R	−	Trunk succ.# in release > R and R exists	R.mL	R.mL.(mB+1).1
R.L	no	No trunk succ.	R.L	R.(L+1)
R.L	yes	No trunk succ.	R.L	R.L.(mB+1).1
R.L	−	Trunk succ. in release ≥ R	R.L	R.L.(mB+1).1
R.L.B	no	No branch succ.	R.L.B.mS	R.L.B.(mS+1)
R.L.B	yes	No branch succ.	R.L.B.mS	R.L.(mB+1).1
R.L.B.S	no	No branch succ.	R.L.B.S	R.L.B.(S+1)
R.L.B.S	yes	No branch succ.	R.L.B.S	R.L.(mB+1).1
R.L.B.S	−	Branch succ.	R.L.B.S	R.L.(mB+1).1

* "R", "L", "B", and "S" are the "release", "level", "branch", and "sequence" components of the SID, respectively; "m" means "maximum". Thus, for example, "R.mL" means "the maximum level number within release R"; "R.L.(mB+1).1" means "the first sequence number on the new branch (that is, maximum branch number plus one) of level L within release R". Note that if the SID specified is of the form "R.L", "R.L.B", or "R.L.B.S", each of the specified components must exist.

** "hR" is the highest existing release that is lower than the specified, nonexistent, release R.

*** This is used to force creation of the first delta in a new release.

Successor.

† The −b keyletter is effective only if the b flag [see **admin**(1)] is present in the file. An entry of − means "irrelevant".

‡ This case applies if the d (default SID) flag is not present in the file. If the d flag is present in the file, then the SID obtained from the d flag is interpreted as if it had been specified on the command line. Thus, one of the other cases in this table applies.

IDENTIFICATION KEYWORDS

Identifying information is inserted into the text retrieved from the SCCS file by replacing identification keywords with their value wherever they occur. The following keywords may be used in the text stored in an SCCS file:

Keyword   Value

%M%   Module name: either the value of the **m** flag in the file [see **admin**(1)], or if absent, the name of the SCCS file with the leading **s.** removed.

%I%   SCCS identification (SID) (**%R%.%L%.%B%.%S%**) of the retrieved text.

%R%   Release.

%L%   Level.

%B%   Branch.

%S%   Sequence.

%D%   Current date (*YY/MM/DD*).

%H%   Current date (*MM/DD/YY*).

%T%   Current time (*HH:MM:SS*).

%E%   Date newest applied delta was created (*YY/MM/DD*).

%G%   Date newest applied delta was created (*MM/DD/YY*).

%U%   Time newest applied delta was created (*HH:MM:SS*).

%Y%   Module type: value of the **t** flag in the SCCS file [see **admin**(1)].

%F%   SCCS file name.

%P%   Fully qualified SCCS file name.

%Q%   The value of the **q** flag in the file [see **admin**(1)].

%C%   Current line number. This keyword is intended for identifying messages output by the program such as "this should not have happened" type errors. It is not intended to be used on every line to provide sequence numbers.

%Z%   The four-character string **@(#)** recognizable by the **what** command.

%W%   A shorthand notation for constructing **what** strings for UNIX System program files. %W% = %Z%%M%<tab>%I%

%A%   Another shorthand notation for constructing **what** strings for non-UNIX System program files: %A% = %Z%%Y% %M% %I%%Z%

Several auxiliary files may be created by **get**. These files are known generically as the g-file, l-file, p-file, and z-file. The letter before the hyphen is called the tag. An auxiliary file name is formed from the SCCS file name: the last component of all SCCS file names must be of the form **s.***module-name*, the auxiliary files are named by replacing the leading **s** with the tag. The g-file is an exception to this scheme: the g-file is named by removing the **s.** prefix. For example, **s.xyz.c**, the auxiliary file names would be **xyz.c**, **l.xyz.c**, **p.xyz.c**, and **z.xyz.c**, respectively.

The g-file, which contains the generated text, is created in the current directory (unless the **-p** keyletter is used). A g-file is created in all cases, whether or not any lines of text were generated by the **get**. It is owned by the real user. If the **-k** keyletter is used or implied, its mode is 644; otherwise its mode is 444. Only the real user need have write permission in the current directory.

The l-file contains a table showing which deltas were applied in generating the retrieved text. The l-file is created in the current directory if the **-l** keyletter is used; its mode is 444 and it is owned by the real user. Only the real user need have write permission in the current directory.

Lines in the l-file have the following format:

    a.   A blank character if the delta was applied; ∗ otherwise.

    b.   A blank character if the delta was applied or was not applied and ignored; ∗ if the delta was not applied and was not ignored.

    c.   A code indicating a "special" reason why the delta was or was not applied: "**I**" (included), "**X**" (excluded), or "**C**" (cut off by a **–c** keyletter).

    d.   Blank.

    e.   SCCS identification (SID).

    f.   Tab character.

    g.   Date and time (in the form *YY/MM/DD HH:MM:SS*) of creation.

    h.   Blank.

    i.   Login name of person who created **delta**.

The comments and MR data follow on subsequent lines, indented one horizontal tab character. A blank line terminates each entry.

The p-file is used to pass information resulting from a **get** with an **–e** keyletter along to **delta**. Its contents are also used to prevent a subsequent execution of **get** with an **–e** keyletter for the same SID until **delta** is executed or the joint edit flag, **j**, [see **admin**(1)] is set in the SCCS file. The p-file is created in the directory containing the SCCS file and the effective user must have write permission in that directory. Its mode is 644 and it is owned by the effective user. The format of the p-file is: the gotten SID, followed by a blank, followed by the SID that the new delta will have when it is made, followed by a blank, followed by the login name of the real user, followed by a blank, followed by the date-time the **get** was executed, followed by a blank and the **–i** keyletter argument if it was present, followed by a blank and the **–x** keyletter argument if it was present, followed by a new-line. There can be an arbitrary number of lines in the p-file at any time; no two lines can have the same new delta SID.

The z-file serves as a lock-out mechanism against simultaneous updates. Its contents are the binary (2 bytes) process ID of the command (that is, **get**) that created it. The z-file is created in the directory containing the SCCS file for the duration of **get**. The same protection restrictions as those for the p-file apply for the z-file. The z-file is created with mode 444.

FILES

g-file	Created by the execution of **get**.
p-file	[see **delta**(1)]
q-file	[see **delta**(1)]
z-file	[see **delta**(1)]
bdiff	Program to compute differences between the "gotten" file and the g-file.

SEE ALSO

    admin(1), **delta**(1), **help**(1), **prs**(1), **what**(1)

    bdiff(1) in the *User's Reference Manual*

DIAGNOSTICS

Use **help**(1) for explanations.

NOTES

If the effective user has write permission (either explicitly or implicitly) in the directory containing the SCCS files, but the real user does not, then only one file may be named when the **-e** keyletter is used.

NAME

getdev – lists devices based on criteria

SYNOPSIS

getdev [-ae] [criteria [...]] [device [...]]

DESCRIPTION

getdev generates a list of devices that match certain criteria. The criteria includes a list of attributes (given in expressions) and a list of devices. If no criteria is given, all devices are included in the list.

Devices must satisfy at least one of the criteria in the list unless the −a option is used. Then, only those devices which match all of the criteria in a list will be included.

Devices which are defined on the command line and which match the criteria are included in the generated list. However, if the −e flag is used, the list becomes a set of devices to be *excluded* from the list.

Criteria Expression Types

There are four possible expression types which the criteria specified in the *criteria* argument may follow:

attribute=*value*   Selects all devices whose attribute *attribute* is defined and is equal to *value*.

attribute!=*value*   Selects all devices whose attribute *attribute* is defined and does not equal *value*.

attribute:*   Selects all devices which have the attribute *attribute* defined.

attribute!:*   Selects all devices which do not have the attribute *attribute* defined.

See the **putdev**(1M) manual page for a complete listing and description of available attributes.

Options and Arguments

The options and arguments for this command are:

−a   Specifies that a device must match all criteria to be included in the list generated by this command. The flag has no effect if no criteria are defined.

−e   Specifies that the list of devices which follows on the command line should be *excluded* from the list generated by this command. (Without the −e the named devices are *included* in the generated list.) The flag has no effect if no devices are defined.

criteria   Defines criteria that a device must match to be included in the generated list. Should be given in expressions.

device   Defines devices which should be included in the generated list. Can be the pathname of the device or the device alias.

ERRORS

The command will exit with one of the following values:

0 =   Successful completion of the task.

1 =   Command syntax incorrect, invalid option used, or internal error occurred.

2 =   Device table could not be opened for reading.

FILES

/etc/device.tab

SEE ALSO

devattr(1), getdgrp(1), putdev(1), putdgrp(1), getdev(3X).

NAME

getdgrp – lists device groups which contain devices that match criteria

SYNOPSIS

getdgrp [–ael] [criteria [...]] [dgroup [...]]

DESCRIPTION

getdgrp generates a list of device groups that contain devices matching the given criteria. The criteria is given in the form of expressions.

criteria can be one expression or a list of expressions which a device must meet for its group to be included in the list generated by getdgrp. If no criteria is given, all device groups are included in the list.

Devices must satisfy at least one of the criteria in the list. However, the –a flag can be used to define that a "logical and" operation should be performed. Then, only those groups containing devices which match all of the criteria in a list will be included.

dgroup defines a set of device groups to be included in the list. Device groups that are defined and which contain devices matching the criteria are included. However, if the –e flag is used, this list defines a set of device groups to be excluded. When the –e option is used and criteria is also defined, the generated list will include device groups containing devices which match the criteria and are not in the command line list.

Criteria Expression Types

There are four possible expressions types:

attribute=value   Selects all device groups with a member whose attribute attribute is defined and is equal to value.

attribute!=value   Selects all device groups with a member whose attribute attribute is defined and does not equal value.

attribute:*   Selects all device groups with a member which has the attribute attribute defined.

attribute!:*   Selects all device groups with a member which does not have the attribute attribute defined.

See the putdev(1M) manual page for a complete listing and description of available attributes.

Options and Arguments

The options and arguments for this command are:

–a   Specifies that a device must match all criteria before a device group to which it belongs can be included in the list generated by this command. The flag has no effect if no criteria are defined.

–e   Specifies that the list of device groups on the command line should be excluded from the list generated by this command. (Without the –e the named device groups are the only ones which can be included in the generated list.) The flag has no effect if no device groups are defined.

-l   Specifies that all device groups (subject to the **-e** option and
                      the *dgroup* list) should be listed even if they contain no valid
                      device members. This option has no affect if *criteria* is
                      specified on the command line.

criteria   Defines criteria that a device must match before a device
                      group to which it belongs can be included in the generated
                      list.

dgroup   Defines device groups which should be included in or
                      excluded from the generated list.

ERRORS

The command will exit with one of the following values:

0 =   successful completion of the task.

1 =   command syntax incorrect, invalid option used, or internal error occurred.

2 =   device table or device group table could not be opened for reading.

FILES

/etc/device.tab
/etc/dgroup.tab

SEE ALSO

devattr(1), getdev(1), putdev(1), putdgrp(1), getdgrp(3X)

NAME

getfrm – returns the current frameID number

SYNOPSIS

getfrm

DESCRIPTION

getfrm returns the current frameID number. The frameID number is a number assigned to the frame by FMLI and displayed flush left in the frame's title bar. If a frame is closed its frameID number may be reused when a new frame is opened. getfrm takes no arguments.

EXAMPLES

If a menu whose frameID is 3 defines an item to have this **action** descriptor:

    action=open text stdtext `getfrm`

the text frame defined in the definition file **stdtext** would be passed the argument 3 when it is opened.

NOTES

It is not a good idea to use **getfrm** in a backquoted expression coded on a line by itself. Stand-alone backquoted expressions are evaluated before any descriptors are parsed, thus the frame is not yet fully current, and may not have been assigned a frameID number.

NAME

getitems – return a list of currently marked menu items

SYNOPSIS

getitems [*delimiter_string*]

DESCRIPTION

The **getitems** function returns the value of **lininfo** if defined, else it returns the value of the **name** descriptor, for all currently marked menu items. Each value in the list is delimited by *delimiter_string*. The default value of *delimiter_string* is newline.

EXAMPLE

The **done** descriptor in the following menu definition file executes **getitems** when the user presses ENTER (note that the menu is multiselect):

```
Menu="Example"
multiselect=TRUE
done=`getitems ":" | message`

name="Item 1"
action=`message "You selected item 1"`

name="Item 2"
lininfo="This is item 2"
action=`message "You selected item 2"`

name="Item 3"
action=`message "You selected item 3"`
```

If a user marked all three items in this menu, pressing ENTER would cause the following string to be displayed on the message line:

```
Item 1:This is item 2:Item 3
```

Note that because **lininfo** is defined for the second menu item, its value is displayed instead of the value of the **name** descriptor.

NAME

getopt – parse command options

SYNOPSIS

set -- ` getopt *optstring* $* `

DESCRIPTION

The **getopts** command supercedes **getopt**. For more information, see the NOTES below.

getopt is used to break up options in command lines for easy parsing by shell procedures and to check for legal options. *optstring* is a string of recognized option letters; see **getopt**(3C). If a letter is followed by a colon, the option is expected to have an argument which may or may not be separated from it by white space. The special option -- is used to delimit the end of the options. If it is used explicitly, **getopt** recognizes it; otherwise, **getopt** generates it; in either case, **getopt** places it at the end of the options. The positional parameters ($1 $2 ...) of the shell are reset so that each option is preceded by a - and is in its own positional parameter; each option argument is also parsed into its own positional parameter.

EXAMPLE

The following code fragment shows how one might process the arguments for a command that can take the options **a** or **b**, as well as the option **o**, which requires an argument:

```
set -- ` getopt abo: $* `
if [ $? != 0 ]
then
        echo $USAGE
        exit 2
fi
for i in $*
do
        case $i in
        -a | -b)        FLAG=$i; shift;;
        -o)             OARG=$2; shift 2;;
        --)             shift; break;;
        esac
done
```

This code accepts any of the following as equivalent:

```
cmd -aoarg file file
cmd -a -o arg file file
cmd -oarg -a file file
cmd -a -oarg -- file file
```

SEE ALSO

getopts(1), sh(1)

getopt(3C) in the *Programmer's Reference Manual*

DIAGNOSTICS

     `getopt` prints an error message on the standard error when it encounters an option letter not included in *optstring*.

NOTES

     `getopt` will not be supported in the next major release. For this release a conversion tool has been provided, **getoptcvt**. For more information about **getopts** and **getoptcvt**, see `getopts`(1).

     Reset `optind` to 1 when rescanning the options.

     `getopt` does not support the part of Rule 8 of the command syntax standard [see `intro`(1)] that permits groups of option-arguments following an option to be separated by white space and quoted. For example,

         `cmd -a -b -o "xxx z yy" file`

     is not handled correctly. To correct this deficiency, use the **getopts** command in place of **getopt**.

     If an option that takes an option-argument is followed by a value that is the same as one of the options listed in *optstring* (referring to the earlier EXAMPLE section, but using the following command line: `cmd -o -a file`), `getopt` always treats **-a** as an option-argument to **-o**; it never recognizes **-a** as an option. For this case, the **for** loop in the example shifts past the *file* argument.

NAME

getopts, getoptcvt – parse command options

SYNOPSIS

getopts *optstring name* [*arg . . .*]

/usr/lib/getoptcvt [–b] *file*

DESCRIPTION

getopts is used by shell procedures to parse positional parameters and to check for valid options. It supports all applicable rules of the command syntax standard (see Rules 3-10, intro(1)). It should be used in place of the getopt command. (See the NOTES section below.)

optstring must contain the option letters the command using getopts will recognize; if a letter is followed by a colon, the option is expected to have an argument, or group of arguments, which must be separated from it by white space.

Each time it is invoked, getopts places the next option in the shell variable *name* and the index of the next argument to be processed in the shell variable OPTIND. Whenever the shell or a shell procedure is invoked, OPTIND is initialized to 1. (OPTIND is not initialized to 1 when a shell function is called.)

When an option requires an option-argument, getopts places it in the shell variable OPTARG.

If an illegal option is encountered, ? will be placed in *name*.

When the end of options is encountered, getopts exits with a non-zero exit status. The special option –– may be used to delimit the end of the options.

By default, getopts parses the positional parameters. If extra arguments (*arg . . .*) are given on the getopts command line, getopts parses them instead.

/usr/lib/getoptcvt reads the shell script in *file*, converts it to use getopts instead of getopt, and writes the results on the standard output.

–b   Make the converted script portable to earlier releases of the UNIX system. /usr/lib/getoptcvt modifies the shell script in *file* so that when the resulting shell script is executed, it determines at run time whether to invoke getopts or getopt.

So all new commands will adhere to the command syntax standard described in intro(1), they should use getopts or getopt to parse positional parameters and check for options that are valid for that command (see the NOTES section below).

EXAMPLE

The following fragment of a shell program shows how one might process the arguments for a command that can take the options a or b, as well as the option o, which requires an option-argument:

```
while getopts abo: c
do
        case $c in
        a | b)          FLAG=$c;;
        o)              OARG=$OPTARG;;
        \?)             echo $USAGE
                        exit 2;;
```

```
            esac
      done
      shift ` expr $OPTIND - 1`
```

This code accepts any of the following as equivalent:

```
      cmd -a -b -o "xxx z yy" file
      cmd -a -b -o "xxx z yy" -- file
      cmd -ab -o xxx,z,yy file
      cmd -ab -o "xxx z yy" file
      cmd -o xxx,z,yy -b -a file
```

SEE ALSO

intro(1), **sh**(1)

getopt(3C) in the *Programmer's Reference Manual*

NOTES

Although the following command syntax rule [see **intro**(1)] relaxations are permitted under the current implementation, they should not be used because they may not be supported in future releases of the system. As in the EXAMPLE section above, **a** and **b** are options, and the option **o** requires an option-argument. The following example violates Rule 5: options with option-arguments must not be grouped with other options:

```
      cmd -aboxxx file
```

The following example violates Rule 6: there must be white space after an option that takes an option-argument:

```
      cmd -ab -oxxx file
```

Changing the value of the shell variable OPTIND or parsing different sets of arguments may lead to unexpected results.

DIAGNOSTICS

getopts prints an error message on the standard error when it encounters an option letter not included in *optstring*.

NAME

`gettable` – get DoD Internet format host table from a host

SYNOPSIS

`gettable` *host*

DESCRIPTION

`gettable` is a simple program used to obtain the DoD Internet host table from a hostname server. The indicated *host* is queried for the table. The table, if retrieved, is placed in the file **hosts.txt**.

`gettable` operates by opening a TCP connection to the port indicated in the service specification for hostname. A request is then made for all names and the resultant information is placed in the output file.

`gettable` is best used in conjunction with the **htable**(1M) program which converts the DoD Internet host table format to that used by the network library lookup routines.

SEE ALSO

`htable`(1M)

Harrenstien, Ken, Mary Stahl, and Elizabeth Feinler, *HOSTNAME Server*, RFC 953, Network Information Center, SRI International, Menlo Park, Calif., October 1985

NOTES

Should allow requests for only part of the database.

NAME

gettxt – retrieve a text string from a message data base

SYNOPSIS

gettxt *msgfile*:*msgnum* [*dflt_msg*]

DESCRIPTION

gettxt retrieves a text string from a message file in the directory **/usr/lib/locale/***locale***/LC_MESSAGES**. The directory name *locale* corresponds to the language in which the text strings are written; see **setlocale**(3C).

msgfile   Name of the file from which to retrieve *msgnum*. The name can be up to 14 characters in length, but may not contain either \0 (null) or the characters / (slash) or : (colon).

msgnum   Sequence number of the string to retrieve from *msgfile*. The strings in *msgfile* are numbered sequentially from 1 to *n*, where *n* is the number of strings in the file.

dflt_msg   Default string to be displayed if **gettxt** fails to retrieve *msgnum* from *msgfile*. Nongraphic characters must be represented as alphabetic escape sequences.

The text string to be retrieved is in the file *msgfile*, created by the **mkmsgs**(1) utility and installed under the directory **/usr/lib/locale/***locale***/LC_MESSAGES**. You control which directory is searched by setting the environment variable **LC_MESSAGES**. If **LC_MESSAGES** is not set, the environment variable **LANG** will be used. If **LANG** is not set, the files containing the strings are under the directory **/usr/lib/locale/C/LC_MESSAGES**.

If **gettxt** fails to retrieve a message in the requested language, it will try to retrieve the same message from **/usr/lib/locale/C/LC_MESSAGES/***msgfile*. If this also fails, and if *dflt_msg* is present and non-empty, then it will display the value of *dflt_msg*; if *dflt_msg* is not present or is empty, then it will display the string **Message not found!!\n**.

EXAMPLE

If the environment variables **LANG** or **LC_MESSAGES** have not been set to other than their default values,

     gettxt UX:10 "hello world\n"

will try to retrieve the 10th message from **/usr/lib/locale/C/LC_MESSAGES/UX**. If the retrieval fails, the message "hello world," followed by a new-line, will be displayed.

FILES

/usr/lib/locale/C/LC_MESSAGES/∗   default message files created by **mkmsgs**(1)

/usr/lib/locale/*locale***/LC_MESSAGES/**∗   message files for different languages created by **mkmsgs**(1)

SEE ALSO

exstr(1), **mkmsgs**(1), **srchtxt**(1)
gettxt(3C), **setlocale**(3C) in the *Programmer's Reference Manual*

NAME

getty – set terminal type, modes, speed, and line discipline

SYNOPSIS

getty [–h] [–t *timeout*] *line* [*speed* [*type* [*linedisc*]]]

getty –c *file*

DESCRIPTION

getty is included for compatibility with previous releases for the few applications that still call getty directly. getty can only be executed by the superuser, that is, by a process with the user ID **root**. Initially getty prints the login prompt, waits for the user's login name, and then invokes the **login** command. getty attempts to adapt the system to the terminal speed by using the options and arguments specified on the command line.

line   The name of a TTY line in **/dev** to which getty is to attach itself. getty uses this string as the name of a file in the **/dev** directory to open for reading and writing.

–h   If the –h flag is not set, a hangup will be forced by setting the speed to zero before setting the speed to the default or specified speed.

–t *timeout*
specifies that getty should exit if the open on the line succeeds and no one types anything in *timeout* seconds.

speed   The *speed* argument is a label to a speed and TTY definition in the file **/etc/ttydefs**. This definition tells getty at what speed to run initially, what the initial TTY settings are, and what speed to try next, should the user indicate, by pressing the BREAK key, that the speed is inappropriate. The default *speed* is 1200 baud.

type and *linedisc*
These options are obsolete and will be ignored.

–c *file*   The –c option is no longer supported. Instead use **sttydefs –l** to list the contents of the **/etc/ttydefs** file and perform a validity check on the file.

When given no optional arguments, getty specifies the following: The *speed* of the interface is set to 1200 baud, either parity is allowed, new-line characters are converted to carriage return-line feed, and tab expansion is performed on the standard output. getty types the login prompt before reading the user's name a character at a time. If a null character (or framing error) is received, it is assumed to be the result of the user pressing the BREAK key. This will cause getty to attempt the next *speed* in the series. The series that getty tries is determined by what it finds in **/etc/ttydefs**.

NOTES

Administrators and developers are encouraged to use **ttymon**(1M) as support for getty may be dropped in the future.

FILES

`/etc/ttydefs`

SEE ALSO

`sttydefs`(1M), `tty`(7), `ttymon`(1M)
`ct`(1C), `login`(1) in the *User's Reference Manual*
`ioctl`(2) in the *Programmer's Reference Manual*

NAME

getvol – verifies device accessibility

SYNOPSIS

getvol **-n** [**-1** *label*] *device*

getvol [**-f**| **-F**] [**-wo**] [**-1** *label*| **-x** *label*] *device*

DESCRIPTION

getvol verifies that the specified device is accessible and that a volume of the appropriate medium has been inserted. The command is interactive and displays instructional prompts, describes errors, and shows required label information.

Options and arguments for this command are:

-n   Runs the command in non-interactive mode. The volume is assumed to be inserted upon command invocation.

-1   Specifies that the label *label* must exist on the inserted volume (can be overriden by the –o option).

-f   Formats the volume after insertion, using the format command defined for this device in the device table.

-F   Formats the volume after insertion and places a file system on the device. Also uses the format command defined for this device in the device table.

-w   Allows administrator to write a new label on the device. User is prompted to supply the label text. This option is ineffective if the **-n** option is enabled.

-o   Allows the administrator to override a label check.

-x   Specifies that the label *label* must exist on the device. This option should be used in place of the **-1** option when the label can only be verified by visual means. Use of the option causes a message to be displayed asking the administrator to visually verify that the label is indeed *label*.

device   Names the device which should be verified for accessibility.

ERRORS

The command will exit with one of the following values:

0 =   successful completion of the task.

1 =   command syntax incorrect, invalid option used, or internal error occurred.

3 =   device table could not be opened for reading.

NOTES

This command uses the device table to determine the characteristics of the device when performing the volume label checking.

FILES

/etc/device.tab

SEE ALSO

getvol(3X)

NAME

grep – search a file for a pattern

SYNOPSIS

grep [*options*] *limited_regular_expression* [*file* . . .]

DESCRIPTION

grep searches files for a pattern and prints all lines that contain that pattern. grep uses limited regular expressions (expressions that have string values that use a subset of the possible alphanumeric and special characters) like those used with ed(1) to match the patterns. It uses a compact non-deterministic algorithm.

Be careful using the characters $, *, [, ^, |, (,), and \ in the *limited_regular_expression* because they are also meaningful to the shell. It is safest to enclose the entire *limited_regular_expression* in single quotes ′ . . . ′.

If no files are specified, grep assumes standard input. Normally, each line found is copied to standard output. The filename is printed before each line found if there is more than one input file.

Command line options are:

-b　　Precede each line by the block number on which it was found. This can be useful in locating block numbers by context (first block is 0).

-c　　Print only a count of the lines that contain the pattern.

-e *special_expression*
　　　Search for a *special_expression* (*full_regular_expression* that begins with a –).

-f *file*
　　　Take the list of *full_regular_expressions* from *file*.

-i　　Ignore uppercase/lowercase distinction during comparisons.

-h　　Prevents the name of the file containing the matching line from being appended to that line. Used when searching multiple files.

-l　　Print the names of files with matching lines once, separated by newlines. Does not repeat the names of files when the pattern is found more than once.

-n　　Precede each line by its line number in the file (first line is 1).

-s　　Suppress error messages about nonexistent or unreadable files

-v　　Print all lines except those that contain the pattern.

SEE ALSO

ed(1), egrep(1), fgrep(1), sed(1), sh(1)

DIAGNOSTICS

Exit status is 0 if any matches are found, 1 if none, 2 for syntax errors or inaccessible files (even if matches were found).

NOTES

Lines are limited to BUFSIZ characters; longer lines are truncated. BUFSIZ is defined in /usr/include/stdio.h.

If there is a line with embedded nulls, grep will only match up to the first null; if it matches, it will print the entire line.

NAME

groupadd – add (create) a new group definition on the system

SYNOPSIS

groupadd [-g *gid* [-o]] *group*

DESCRIPTION

The **groupadd** command creates a new group definition on the system by adding the appropriate entry to the **/etc/group** file.

The following options are available:

-g *gid*   The group ID for the new group. This group ID must be a non-negative decimal integer below MAXUID as defined in the **<param.h>** header file. By default, a unique group ID is allocated in the valid range. Group IDs from 0-99 are reserved.

-o   This option allows the *gid* to be duplicated (non-unique).

group   A string of printable characters that specifies the name of the new group. It may not include a colon (:) or newline (\\n).

FILES

/etc/group

SEE ALSO

groupdel(1M), groupmod(1M), logins(1M), useradd(1M), userdel(1M), usermod(1M), users(1)

DIAGNOSTICS

The **groupadd** command exits with one of the following values:

0   Success.

2   Invalid command syntax; a usage message for the **groupadd** command is displayed.

3   An invalid argument was provided to an option.

4   *gid* is not unique (when the **-o** option is not used).

9   *group* is not unique.

10   Cannot update the **/etc/group** file.

NAME

groupdel – delete a group definition from the system

SYNOPSIS

groupdel *group*

DESCRIPTION

The **groupdel** command deletes a group definition from the system. It deletes the appropriate entry from the **/etc/group** file.

The following options are available:

group   A string of printable characters that specifies the group to be deleted.

FILES

/etc/group

SEE ALSO

groupadd(1M), groupmod(1M), logins(1M), useradd(1M), userdel(1M), usermod(1M), users(1)

DIAGNOSTICS

The **groupdel** command exits with one of the following values:

0   Success.

2   Invalid command syntax. A usage message for the **groupdel** command is displayed.

6   **group** does not exist.

10   Cannot update the **/etc/group** file.

NAME

groupmod – modify a group definition on the system

SYNOPSIS

groupmod -g *gid* [-o] *group*
groupmod -n *name group*

DESCRIPTION

The **groupmod** command modifies the definition of the specified group by modifying the appropriate entry in the **/etc/group** file.

The following options are available:

-g *gid*   Changes the value of the group id to *gid*. *gid* must be a non-negative decimal integer below **MAXUID** as defined in <**param.h**>.

-o   This option allows the *gid* to be duplicated (non-unique).

-n *name*
         A string of printable characters that specifies a new name for the group. It may not include a colon (:) or newline (\n).

group   The current name of the group to be modified.

FILES

/etc/group

SEE ALSO

groupadd(1M),   groupdel(1M),   logins(1M),   useradd(1M),   userdel(1M),
usermod(1M).

DIAGNOSTICS

The **groupmod** command exits with one of the following values:

0   Success.

2   Invalid command syntax. A usage message for the **groupmod** command is displayed.

3   An invalid argument was provided to an option.

4   *gid* is not unique (when the **-o** option is not used).

6   *group* does not exist.

9   *name* already exists as a group name.

10   Cannot update the **/etc/group** file.

NAME

    groups – print group membership of user

SYNOPSIS

    groups [*user*]

DESCRIPTION

    The command **groups** prints on standard output the groups to which you or the optionally specified user belong. Each user belongs to a group specified in **/etc/passwd** and possibly to other groups as specified in **/etc/group**.

SEE ALSO

    setgroups(2), group(4), passwd(4)

FILES

    /etc/passwd
    /etc/group

NAME

    groups – display a user's group memberships

SYNOPSIS

    /usr/ucb/groups [*user* . . .]

DESCRIPTION

    With no arguments, **groups** displays the groups to which you belong; else it displays the groups to which the **user** belongs. Each user belongs to a group specified in the password file **/etc/passwd** and possibly to other groups as specified in the file **/etc/group**. If you do not own a file but belong to the group which it is owned by then you are granted group access to the file.

FILES

    /etc/passwd
    /etc/group

SEE ALSO

    getgroups(2) in the *Programmer's Reference Manual*

NOTES

    This command is obsolescent.

NAME

grpck – check group database entries

SYNOPSIS

/usr/ucb/grpck [*filename*]

DESCRIPTION

grpck checks that a file in group(4) does not contain any errors; it checks the /etc/group file by default.

This command differs from /usr/sbin/grpck in its ability to correctly parse YP entries in /etc/passwd.

FILES

/etc/group

SEE ALSO

group(4), passwd(4) in the *System Administrator's Reference Manual*

DIAGNOSTICS

Too many/few fields
> An entry in the group file does not have the proper number of fields.

No group name
> The group name field of an entry is empty.

Bad character(s) in group name
> The group name in an entry contains characters other than lower-case letters and digits.

Invalid GID
> The group ID field in an entry is not numeric or is greater than 65535.

Null login name
> A login name in the list of login names in an entry is null.

Login name not found in password file
> A login name in the list of login names in an entry is not in the password file.

NAME
halt – stop the processor

SYNOPSIS
/usr/ucb/halt [-nqy]

DESCRIPTION
halt writes out any information pending to the disks and then stops the processor.

halt normally logs the system shutdown to the system log daemon, syslogd(1M), and places a shutdown record in the login accounting file /var/adm/wtmp. These actions are inhibited if the –n or –q options are present.

The following options are available:

-n   Prevent the *sync* before stopping.

-q   Quick halt. No graceful shutdown is attempted.

-y   Halt the system, even from a dialup terminal.

FILES
/var/adm/wtmp   login accounting file

SEE ALSO
reboot(1M), syslogd(1M)
shutdown(1M), init(1M) in the *System Administrator's Reference Manual*

NOTES
This command is equivalent to init 0.

NAME

　　hd – display files in hexadecimal format

SYNOPSIS

　　hd [-*format* [-**s** *offset*] [-**n** *count*] [*file*]

DESCRIPTION

The **hd** command displays the contents of files in hexadecimal octal, decimal and character formats. Control over the specification of ranges of characters is also available. The default behavior is with the following flags set: "-**abx** -**A**". This says that addresses (file offsets) and bytes are printed in hexadecimal and that characters are also printed. If no *file* argument is given, the standard input is read.

Options include:

-**s** *offset*　　Specify the beginning offset in the file where printing is to begin. If no 'file' argument is given, or if a seek fails because the input is a pipe, 'offset' bytes are read from the input and discarded. Otherwise, a seek error will terminate processing of the current file.

　　　　　　The *offset* may be given in decimal, hexadecimal (preceded by '**0x**'), or octal (preceded by a '**0**'). It is optionally followed by one of the following multipliers: **w, l, b,** or **k**; for words (2 bytes), long words (4 bytes), blocks (512 bytes), or **K** bytes (1024 bytes). Note that this is the once case where "**b**" does not stand for bytes. Since specifying a hexadecimal offset in blocks would result in an ambiguous trailing '**b**', any offset and multiplier may be separated by an asterisk (*).

-**n** *count*　　Specify the number of bytes to process. The *count* is in the same format as *offset*, above.

Format Flags

Format flags may specify addresses, characters, bytes, words (2 bytes), or longs (4 bytes) to be printed in hexadecimal, decimal, or octal. Two special formats may also be indicated: test or **ASCII**. Format and base specifiers amy be freely combined and repeated as desired in order to specify different bases (hexadecimal, decimal or octal) for different output formats (addresses, characters, etc.). All format flags appearing in a single argument are applied as appropriate to all other flags in that argument.

acbwlA　　Output format specifiers for address, characters, bytes, words, longs and ASCII, respectively. Only one base specifier will be used for addresses; the address will appear on the first line of output that begins each new offset in the input.

　　　　　　The character format prints printable characters unchanged, special C escapes as defined in the language, and remaining values in the specified base.

　　　　　　The ASCII format prints all printable characters unchanged, and all others as a period (.). This format appears to the right of the first of other specified output formats. A base specifier has no meaning with the ASCII format. If no other output format (other than addresses) is given, **bx** is assumed. If no base specifier is given, all of **xdo** are used.

xdo   Output base specifiers for hexadecimal, decimal and octal. If no
           format specifier is given, all of **acbwl** are used.

t   Print a test file, each line preceded by the address in the file. Nor-
           mally, lines should be terminated by a **\n** character; but long lines will
           be broken up. Control characters in the range 0x00 to 0x1f are rpinted
           as '**^@**' to '**^_**'. Bytes with the high bit set are preceded by a tilde (˜)
           and printed as if the high bit were not set. The special characters (ˆ,˜,\)
           are preceded by a backslash (\) to escape their special meaning. As
           special cases, two values are represented numerically as '\177' and
           '\377'. This flag will override all output format specifiers except
           addresses.

NAME

    head – display first few lines of files

SYNOPSIS

    head [*–n*] [*file . . .*]

DESCRIPTION

    head copies the first *n* lines of each *file* to the standard output. If no *file* is given, **head** copies lines from the standard input. The default value of *n* is 10 lines.

    When more than one file is specified, the start of each file will look like:

        `==>`*file*`<==`

    Thus, a common way to display a set of short files, identifying each one, is:

        head *–9999 file1 file2 . . .*

SEE ALSO

    cat(1), **more**(1), **pg**(1), **tail**(1)

NAME

help – ask for help with message numbers or SCCS commands

SYNOPSIS

help [*args*]

DESCRIPTION

help finds information to explain a message from a command or explain the use of a SCCS command. Zero or more arguments may be supplied. If no arguments are given, help will prompt for one.

The arguments may be either information within the parentheses following a message or SCCS command names.

The response of the program will be the explanatory information related to the argument, if there is any.

When all else fails, try "help stuck".

FILES

LIBDIR/**help**	directory containing files of message text.
LIBDIR/**help/helploc**	file containing locations of help files not in *LIBDIR*/**help**.
LIBDIR	usually **/usr/ccs/lib**

NAME

   hostid – print the numeric identifier of the current host

SYNOPSIS

   /usr/ucb/hostid

DESCRIPTION

   The **hostid** command prints the identifier of the current host in hexadecimal. This numeric value is likely to differ when **hostid** is run on a different machine.

SEE ALSO

   gethostid(2)
   sysinfo(2) in the *Programmer's Reference Manual*

NAME

hostname – set or print name of current host system

SYNOPSIS

/usr/ucb/hostname [*name-of-host*]

DESCRIPTION

The **hostname** command prints the name of the current host, as given before the **login** prompt. The super-user can set the hostname by giving an argument.

SEE ALSO

uname(1) in the *User's Reference Manual*

NAME
htable – convert DoD Internet format host table

SYNOPSIS
htable *filename*

DESCRIPTION
htable converts a host table in the format specified by RFC 952 to the format used by the network library routines. Three files are created as a result of running htable: hosts, networks, and gateways. The hosts file is used by the gethostent(3N) routines in mapping host names to addresses. The networks file is used by the getnetent(3N) routines in mapping network names to numbers. The gateways file is used by the routing daemon in identifying passive Internet gateways; see routed(1M) for an explanation.

If any of the files localhosts, localnetworks, or localgateways are present in the current directory, the file's contents are prepended to the output file without interpretation. This allows sites to maintain local aliases and entries which are not normally present in the master database.

htable is best used in conjunction with the gettable(1M) program which retrieves the DoD Internet host table from a host.

FILES
localhosts
localnetworks
localgateways

SEE ALSO
gethostent(3N), getnetent(3N), gettable(1M), routed(1M)

Harrenstien, Ken, Mary Stahl, and Elizabeth Feinler, *DoD Internet Host Table Specification*, RFC 952, Network Information Center, SRI International, Menlo Park, Calif., October 1985

NOTES
Does not properly calculate the gateways file.

NAME

iconv – code set conversion utility

SYNOPSIS

iconv -f *fromcode* -t *tocode* [*file*]

DESCRIPTION

iconv converts the characters or sequences of characters in *file* from one code set to another and writes the results to standard output. Should no conversion exist for a particular character then it is converted to the underscore '_' in the target codeset.

The required arguments *fromcode* and *tocode* identify the input and output code sets, respectively. If no *file* argument is specified on the command line, iconv reads the standard input.

iconv will always convert to or from the ISO 8859-1 Latin alphabet No.1, from or to an ISO 646 ASCII variant codeset for a particular language. The ISO 8859-1 codeset will support the majority of 8 bit codesets. The conversions attempted by iconv accommodate the most commonly used languages.

The following table lists the supported conversions.

Code Set Conversions Supported				
Code	Symbol	Target Code	Symbol	comment
ISO 646	646	ISO 8859-1	8859	US Ascii
ISO 646de	646de	ISO 8859-1	8859	German
ISO 646da	646da	ISO 8859-1	8859	Danish
ISO 646en	646en	ISO 8859-1	8859	English Ascii
ISO 646es	646es	ISO 8859-1	8859	Spanish
ISO 646fr	646fr	ISO 8859-1	8859	French
ISO 646it	646it	ISO 8859-1	8859	Italian
ISO 646sv	646sv	ISO 8859-1	8859	Swedish
ISO 8859-1	8859	ISO 646	646	7 bit Ascii
ISO 8859-1	8859	ISO 646de	646de	German
ISO 8859-1	8859	ISO 646da	646da	Danish
ISO 8859-1	8859	ISO 646en	646en	English Ascii
ISO 8859-1	8859	ISO 646es	646es	Spanish
ISO 8859-1	8859	ISO 646fr	646fr	French
ISO 8859-1	8859	ISO 646it	646it	Italian
ISO 8859-1	8859	ISO 646sv	646sv	Swedish

The conversions are performed according to the tables found on the iconv(5) manual page.

EXAMPLES

The following converts the contents of file **mail1** from code set **8859** to **646fr** and stores the results in file **mail.local**.

```
iconv -f 8859 -t 646fr mail1 > mail.local
```

FILES

`/usr/lib/iconv/iconv_data`	lists the conversions supported
`/usr/lib/iconv/*`	conversion tables

SEE ALSO

iconv(5) in the *System Administrator's Reference Manual*

DIAGNOSTICS

iconv returns 0 upon successful completion, 1 otherwise.

NAME

id – print the user name and ID, and group name and ID

SYNOPSIS

id [-a]

DESCRIPTION

id displays the calling process's ID and name. It also displays the group ID and name. If the real effective IDs do not match, both are printed.

The -a option reports all the groups to which the invoking process belongs. ID, and your username. If your real and effective IDs do not match, both are printed.

The -a option reports all the groups to which the invoking user belongs.

SEE ALSO

getuid(2) in the *Programmer's Reference Manual*

NAME

idbuild – build new UNIX System kernel

SYNOPSIS

/etc/conf/bin/idbuild

DESCRIPTION

This script builds a new UNIX System kernel using the current system configuration in etc/conf/. Kernel reconfigurations are usually done after a device driver is installed, or system tunable parameters are modified. The script uses the shell variable ROOT from the user's environment as its starting path. Except for the special case of kernel development in a non-root source tree, the shell variable ROOT should always be set to null or to "/". idbuild exits with a return code of zero on success and non-zero on failure.

Building a new UNIX System image consists of generating new system configuration files, then link-editing the kernel and device driver object modules in the etc/conf/pack.d object tree. This is done by idbuild by calling the following commands:

etc/conf/bin/idconfig   To build kernel configuration files.

etc/conf/bin/idmkunix   To process the configuration files and link-edit a new UNIX System image.

The system configuration files are built by processing the Master and System files representing device driver and tunable parameter specifications. For the i386 UNIX System the files etc/conf/cf.d/mdevice, and etc/conf/cf.d/mtune represent the Master information. The files etc/conf/cf.d/stune, and the files specified in etc/conf/sdevice.d/* represent the System information. The kernel also has file system type information defined in the files specified by etc/conf/sfsys.d/* and etc/conf/mfsys.d/* .

Once a new UNIX System kernel has been configured, a lock file is set in etc/.new_unix which causes the new kernel to replace /unix on the next system shutdown (i.e., on the next entry to the *init 0* state). Upon the next system boot, the new kernel will be executed.

ERROR MESSAGES

Since idbuild calls other system commands to accomplish system reconfiguration and link editing, it will report all errors encountered by those commands, then clean up intermediate files created in the process. In general, the exit value 1 indicates an error was encountered by idbuild .

The errors encountered fall into the following categories:

Master file error messages.
System file error messages.
Tunable file error messages.
Compiler and Link-editor error messages.

All error messages are designed to be self-explanatory.

SEE ALSO

idinstall(1m), idtune(1m).

mdevice(4), mfsys(4), mtune(4), sdevice(4), sfsys(4), stune(4) in the *Programmer's Reference Manual.*

NAME

idcheck – returns selected information

SYNOPSIS

`/etc/conf/bin/idcheck`

DESCRIPTION

This command returns selected information about the system configuration. It is useful in add-on device Driver Software Package (DSP) installation scripts to determine if a particular device driver has already been installed, or to verify that a particular interrupt vector, I/O address or other selectable parameter is in fact available for use. The various forms are:

> **idcheck –p** *device-name* [**-i dir**] [**-r**]
>
> **idcheck–v** *vector* [**-i dir**] [**-r**]
>
> **idcheck–d** *dma-channel* [**-i dir**] [**-r**]
>
> **idcheck–a –1** *lower_address* **–u** *upper_address* [**-i dir**] [**-r**]
>
> **idcheck –c –1** *lower_address* **–u** *upper_address* [**-i dir**] [**-r**]

This command scans the System and Master modules and returns:

> 100 if an error occurs.
>
> 0 if no conflict exists.
>
> a positive number greater than 0 and less than 100 if a conflict exists.

The command line options are:

-r Report device name of any conflicting device on stdout.

-p *device-name* This option checks for the existence of four different components of the DSP. The exit code is the addition of the return codes from the four checks.

Add 1 to the exit code if the DSP directory under **/etc/conf/pack.d** exists.

Add 2 to the exit code if the Master module has been installed.

Add 4 to the exit code if the System module has been installed.

Add 8 to the exit code if the Kernel was built with the System module.

Add 16 to the exit code if a Driver.o is part of the DSP (vs. a **stubs.c** file).

-v *vector* Returns 'type' field of device that is using the vector specified (that is, another DSP is already using the vector).

-d *dma-channel* Returns 1 if the dma channel specified is being used.

-a This option checks whether the IOA region bounded by "*lower*" and "*upper*" conflict with another DSP ("*lower*" and "*upper*" are specified with the **-1** and **-u** options). The exit code is the addition of two different return codes.

Add 1 to the exit code if the IOA region overlaps with another device.

Add 2 to the exit code if the IOA region overlaps with another device and that device has the 'O' option specified in the *type* field of the Master module. The 'O' option permits a driver to overlap the IOA region of another driver.

−c   Returns 1 if the CMA region bounded by *"lower"* and *"upper"* conflict with another DSP (*"lower"* and *"upper"* are specified with the −1 and −u options).

−l *address*   Lower bound of address range specified in hex. The leading 0x is unnecessary.

−u *address*   Upper bound of address range specified in hex. The leading 0x is unnecessary.

−i *dir*   Specifies the directory in which the ID files **sdevice** and **mdevice** reside. The default directory is **/etc/conf/cf.d** .

ERROR MESSAGES

There are no error messages or checks for valid arguments to options. **idcheck** interprets these arguments using the rules of **scanf**(3) and queries the **sdevice** and **mdevice** files. For example, if a letter is used in the place of a digit, **scanf** (3) will translate the letter to 0. **idcheck** will then use this value in its query.

SEE ALSO

idinstall(1M)
mdevice(4), sdevice(4) in the *Programmer's Reference Manual*

NAME

idconfig – produce a new kernel configuration

SYNOPSIS

/etc/conf/bin/idconfig

DESCRIPTION

The **idconfig** command takes as its input a collection of files specifying the configuration of the next UNIX System to be built. A collection of output files for use by **idmkunix** is produced.

The input files expected by **idconfig** are as follows:

mdevice	– Master device specifications
sdevice	– System device specifications
mtune	– Master parameter specifications
stune	– System parameter specifications
mfsys	– File system type master data
sfsys	– File system type system data
sassign	– Device Assignment File

The output files produced by **idconfig** are as follows:

conf.c	– Kernel data structures and function definitions
config.h	– Kernel parameter and device definitions
vector.c	– Interrupt vector definitions
direct	– Listing of all driver components included in the build
fsconf.c	– File system type configuration data

The command line options are as follows:

-o *directory*   Output files will be created in the directory specified rather than /etc/conf/cf.d.

-i *directory*   Input files that normally reside in /etc/conf/cf.d can be found in the directory specified.

-r *directory*   The directory specified will be used as the ID "root" directory rather than /etc/conf.

-d *file*   Use *file* name rather than **sdevice** for input.

-t *file*   Use *file* name rather than **stune** for input.

-T *file*   Use *file* name rather than **mtune** for input.

-a *file*   Use *file* name rather than **sassign** for input.

-c *file*   Redirect **conf.c** output to *file* name.

-h *file*   Redirect **config.h** output to *file* name.

-v *file*   Redirect **vector.c** output to *file* name.

-p *file*   Redirect **direct** output to *file* name.

-D, -m, -s   These options are no longer supported.

-#   Print debugging information.

This version of UNIX supports multiple major numbers for drivers. **idconfig** generates additional constants (via defines) in the **config.h** file so that they can be used by the driver (as they will get referenced in the **space.c** file to generate appropriate data structures. The information provided by these constants is how many major numbers were assigned to the device and what are their values. The names of the constants are as follows:

    PRFX_CMAJOR_X

    PRFX_BMAJOR_X

where **PRFX** stands for device prefix. In case of a SCSI device, it would be a SCSI device. The **X** stands for the list subscript, starting with subscript 0.

In addition, the configuration file **conf.c** that initializes **bdevsw[]** and **cdevsw[]** tables will also add entries for each of the major numbers and, as such, the same driver entry points will be repeated for each one of the entries.

ERROR MESSAGES

An exit value of zero indicates success. If an error **i** was encountered, **idconfig** will exit with a non-zero value and report an error message. All error messages are designed to be self-explanatory.

SEE ALSO

dmkunix(1M), **idbuild**(1M), **idinstall**(1M), **mdevice**(4), **mtune**(4), **sdevice**(4), **stune**(4)

NAME

idinstall – add, delete, update, or get device driver configuration data

SYNOPSIS

/etc/conf/bin/idinstall –[adug] [–e] –[msoptnirhcl] *dev_name*

DESCRIPTION

The **idinstall** command is called by a Driver Software Package (DSP) Install script or Remove script to Add (**–a**), Delete (**–d**), Update (**–u**), or Get (**–g**) device driver configuration data. **idinstall** expects to find driver component files in the current directory. When components are installed or updated, they are moved or appended to files in the **/etc/conf** directory and then deleted from the current directory unless the **–k** flag is used. The options for the command are as follows:

Action Specifiers:

     –a   Add the DSP components

     –d   Remove the DSP components

     –u   Update the DSP components

     –g   Get the DSP components (print to std out, except Master)

Component Specifiers: (*)

     –m   Master component

     –s   System component

     –o   Driver.o component

     –p   Space.c component

     –t   Stubs.c component

     –n   Node (special file) component

     –i   Inittab component

     –r   Device Initialization (rc) component

     –h   Device shutdown (sd) component

     –c   Mfsys component: file system type config (Master) data

     –l   Sfsys component: file system type local (System) data

         (*) If no component is specified, the default is all except for the **–g** option where a single component must be specified explicitly.

Miscellaneous:

     –e   Disable free disk space check

     –k   Keep files (do not remove from current directory) on add or update.

In the simplest case of installing a new DSP, the command syntax used by the DSP's Install script should be **idinstall –a** *dev_name*. In this case the command will require and install a Driver.o, Master and System entry, and optionally install the Space.c, Stubs.c, Node, Init, Rc, Shutdown, Mfsys, and Sfsys components if those modules are present in the current directory.

The Driver.o, Space.c, and Stubs.c files are moved to a directory in **/etc/conf/pack.d**. The *dev_name* is passed as an argument, which is used as the directory name. The remaining components are stored in the corresponding directories under **/etc/conf** in a file whose name is *dev_name*. For example, the Node file would be moved to **/etc/conf/node.d/dev_name**.

The **idinstall -m** usage provides an interface to the **idmaster** command which will add, delete, and update **mdevice** file entries using a Master file from the local directory. An interface is provided here so that driver writers have a consistent interface to install any DSP component.

As stated above, driver writers will generally use only the **idinstall -a** *dev_name* form of the command. Other options of **idinstall** are provided to allow an Update DSP (that is, one that replaces an existing device driver component) to be installed, and to support installation of multiple controller boards of the same type.

If the call to **idinstall** uses the **-u** (update) option, it will:

overlay the files of the old DSP with the files of the new DSP.

invoke the **idmaster** command with the 'update' option if a Master module is part of the new DSP.

idinstall also does a verification that enough free disk space is available to start the reconfiguration process. This is done by calling the **idspace** command. **idinstall** will fail if insufficient space exists, and exit with a non-zero return code. The **-e** option bypasses this check.

This version of UNIX Supports Multiple Major numbers per device. For the case of a DSP package where **idinstall** is invoked by the installation software in the DSP, the range specification will be used. The range "3.6" will mean four major numbers are being requested. The *ID* Software will then look for the first four available (consecutive) major numbers.

If a driver supports both block and character I/O both block and character majors are assigned by **idinstall**. These major numbers do not have to be the same. For SCSI developers who require them to be the same, a new field 'v' has to be added to the third field of the master file.

idinstall makes a record of the last device installed in a file (**/etc/.last_dev_add**), and saves all removed files from the last delete operation in a directory (**/etc/.last_dev_del**). These files are recovered by **/etc/conf/bin/idmkenv** whenever it is determined that a system reconfiguration was aborted due to a power failure or unexpected system reboot.

ERROR MESSAGES

An exit value of zero indicates success. If an error was encountered, **idinstall** will exit with a non-zero value, and report an error message. All error messages are designed to be self-explanatory. Typical error message that can be generated by **idinstall** are as follows:

```
Device package already exists.
Cannot make the driver package directory.
Cannot remove driver package directory.
Local directory does not contain a Driver object (Driver.o) file.
Local directory does not contain a Master file.
Local directory does not contain a System file.
Cannot remove driver entry.
```

SEE ALSO

idspace(1M), idcheck(1M)

mdevice(4), sdevice(4) in the *Programmer's Reference Manual*

NAME

idload – Remote File Sharing user and group mapping

SYNOPSIS

idload [-n] [-g g_rules] [-u u_rules] [directory]
idload -k

DESCRIPTION

idload is used on Remote File Sharing server machines to build translation tables for user and group ids. It takes your /etc/passwd and /etc/group files and produces translation tables for user and group ids from remote machines, according to the rules set down in the u_rules and g_rules files. If you are mapping by user and group name, you will need copies of remote /etc/passwd and /etc/group files. If no rules files are specified, remote user and group ids are mapped to MAXUID+1 (this is an id number that is one higher than the highest number you could assign on your system.)

By default, the remote password and group files are assumed to reside in /etc/rfs/auth.info/domain/nodename/[passwd| group]. The directory argument indicates that some directory structure other than /etc/rfs/auth.info contains the domain/nodename passwd and group files. (nodename is the name of the computer the files are from and domain is the domain that computer is a member of.)

You must run idload to put the mapping into place. Global mapping will take effect immediately for machines that have one of your resources currently mounted. Mapping for other specific machines will take effect when each machine mounts one of your resources.

-n   This is used to do a trial run of the id mapping. No translation table will be produced, however, a display of the mapping is output to the terminal (stdout).

-k   This is used to print the idmapping that is currently in use. (Specific mapping for remote machines will not be shown until that machine mounts one of your resources.)

-u u_rules The u_rules file contains the rules for user id translation. The default rules file is /etc/rfs/auth.info/uid.rules.

-g g_rules The g_rules file contains the rules for group id translation. The default rules file is /etc/rfs/auth.info/gid.rules.

This command is restricted to the super-user.

Rules

The rules files have two types of sections (both optional): global and host. There can be only one global section, though there can be one host section for each computer you want to map.

The global section describes the default conditions for translation for any machines that are not explicitly referenced in a host section. If the global section is missing, the default action is to map all remote user and group ids from undefined computers to **MAXUID+1**. The syntax of the first line of the **global** section is:

> **global**

A **host** section is used for each machine or group of machines that you want to map differently from the global definitions. The syntax of the first line of each **host** section is:

> **host** *name* . . .

where *name* is replaced by the full name of a computer (*domain.nodename*).

The format of a rules file is described below. (All lines are optional, but must appear in the order shown.)

```
global
default local | transparent
exclude remote_id-remote_id | remote_id
map remote_id:local

host domain.nodename [domain.nodename. . .]
default local | transparent
exclude remote_id-remote_id | remote_id | remote_name
map remote:local | remote | all
```

Each of these instruction types is described below.

The line

> **default** *local* | **transparent**

defines the mode of mapping for remote users that are not specifically mapped in instructions in other lines. **transparent** means that each remote user and group id will have the same numeric value locally unless it appears in the **exclude** instruction. *local* can be replaced by a local user name or id to map all users into a particular local name or id number. If the default line is omitted, all users that are not specifically mapped are mapped into a "special guest" login id.

The line

> **exclude** *remote_id-remote_id* | *remote_id* | *remote_name*

defines remote ids that will be excluded from the **default** mapping. The **exclude** instruction must precede any **map** instructions in a block. You can use a range of id numbers, a single id number, or a single name. (*remote_name* cannot be used in a **global** block.)

The line

> **map** *remote:local* | *remote* | **all**

defines the local ids and names that remote ids and names will be mapped into. *remote* is either a remote id number or remote name; *local* is either a local id number or local name. Placing a colon between a *remote* and a *local* will give the value on the left the permissions of the value on the right. A single *remote* name or id will assign the user or group permissions of the same local name or id. **all** is a predefined alias for the set of all user and group ids found in the local

/etc/passwd and /etc/group files. (You cannot map by remote name in global blocks.)

Note: idload will always output warning messages for map all, since password files always contain multiple administrative user names with the same id number. The first mapping attempt on the id number will succeed, each subsequent attempts will produce a warning.

Remote File Sharing doesn't need to be running to use idload.

EXIT STATUS

On successful completion, idload will produce one or more translation tables and return a successful exit status. If idload fails, the command will return an exit status of zero and not produce a translation table.

ERRORS

If (1) either rules file cannot be found or opened, (2) there are syntax errors in the rules file, (3) there are semantic errors in the rules file, (4) host password or group information could not be found, or (5) the command is not run with super-user privileges, an error message will be sent to standard error. Partial failures will cause a warning message to appear, though the process will continue.

FILES

/etc/passwd
/etc/group
/etc/rfs/auth.info/*domain*/*nodename*/[user| group]
/etc/rfs/auth.info/uid.rules
/etc/rfs/auth.info/gid.rules

SEE ALSO

mount(1M)
"Remote File Sharing" chapter of the *System Administrator's Guide* for detailed information on ID mapping

NAME

    idmkinit – reads files containing specifications

SYNOPSIS

    `/etc/conf/bin/idmkinit`

DESCRIPTION

    This command reads the files containing specifications of `/etc/inittab` entries from `/etc/conf/init.d` and constructs a new `inittab` file in `/etc/conf/cf.d` . It returns 0 on success and a positive number on error.

    The files in `/etc/conf/init.d` are copies of the Init modules in device Driver Software Packages (DSP). There is at most one Init file per DSP. Each file contains one line for each `inittab` entry to be installed. There may be multiple lines (that is, multiple `inittab` entries) per file. An `inittab` entry has the form (the *id* field is often called the *tag*):

        id:rstate:action:process

    The Init module entry must have one of the following forms:

        action:process

        rstate:action:process

        id:rstate:action:process

    When **idmkinit** encounters an entry of the first type, a valid *id* field will be generated, and an *rstate* field of 2 (indicating run on init state 2) will be generated. When an entry of the second type is encountered only the *id* field is prepended. An entry of the third type is incorporated into the new `inittab` unchanged.

    Since add-on `inittab` entries specify init state 2 for their *rstate* field most often, an entry of the first type should almost always be used. An entry of the second type may be specified if you need to specify other than state 2. DSP's should avoid specifying the *id* field as in the third entry, since other add-on applications or DSPs may have already used the *id* value you have chosen. The `/etc/init` program will encounter serious errors if one or more `inittab` entries contain the same *id* field.

    idmkinit determines which of the three forms above is being used for the entry by requiring each entry to have a valid action keyword. Valid action values are as follows:

        `off`
        `respawn`
        `ondemand`
        `once`
        `wait`
        `boot`
        `bootwait`
        `powerfail`
        `powerwait`
        `initdefault`
        `sysinit`

The **idmkinit** command is called automatically upon entering init State 2 on the next system reboot after a kernel reconfiguration to establish the correct **/etc/inittab** for the running **/unix** kernel. **idmkinit** can be called as a user level command to test modification of **inittab** before a DSP is actually built. It is also useful in installation scripts that do not reconfigure the kernel, but need to create **inittab** entries. In this case, the **inittab** generated by **idmkinit** must be copied to **/etc/inittab** , and a **telinit q** command must be run to make the new entry take affect.

The command line options are:

-o *directory*   **inittab** will be created in the directory specified rather than **/etc/conf/cf.d** .

-i *directory*   The ID file **init.base**, which normally resides in **/etc/conf/cf.d**, can be found in the directory specified.

-e *directory*   The Init modules that are usually in **/etc/conf/init.d** can be found in the directory specified.

-#   Print debugging information.

ERROR MESSAGES

An exit value of zero indicates success. If an error was encountered, **idmkinit** will exit with a non-zero value and report an error message. All error messages are designed to be self-explanatory.

SEE ALSO

idbuild(1), **idinstall**(1M), **idmknod**(1M), **init**(1M)

inittab(4) in the *Programmer's Reference Manual*

NAME

idmknod – removes nodes and reads specifications of nodes

SYNOPSIS

idmknod [*options*]

DESCRIPTION

This command performs the following functions:

Removes the nodes for non-required devices (those that do not have an **r** in field 3 of the the device's **mdevice** entry) from **/dev**. Ordinary files will not be removed. If the **/dev** directory contains subdirectories, those subdirectories will be traversed and nodes found for non-required devices will be removed as well. If empty subdirectories result due to the removal of nodes, the subdirectories are then removed.

Reads the specifications of nodes given in the files contained in **/etc/conf/node.d** and installs these nodes in **/dev**. If the node specification defines a path containing subdirectories, the subdirectories will be made automatically.

Returns 0 on success and a positive number on error.

The **idmknod** command is run automatically upon entering init state 2 on the next system reboot after a kernel reconfiguration to establish the correct representation of device nodes in the **/dev** directory for the running **/unix** kernel. **idmknod** can be called as a user level command to test modification of the **/dev** directory before a Driver Software Package (DSP) is actually built. It is also useful in installation scripts that do not reconfigure the kernel, but need to create **/dev** entries.

The files in **/etc/conf/node.d** are copies of the I. Node modules installed by device DSPs. There is at most one file per DSP. Each file contains one line for each node that is to be installed. The format of each line is:

Name of device entry (field 1) in the **mdevice** file.
(The **mdevice** entry will be the line installed by the DSP from its *Master* module.) This field must be from 1 to 8 characters in length. The first character must be a letter. The others may be letters, digits, or underscores.

Name of node to be inserted in **/dev**.
The first character must be a letter. The others may be letters, digits, or underscores. This field can be a path relative to **/dev** , and **idmknod** will create subdirectories as needed.

The character **b** or **c**.
A **b** indicates that the node is a 'block' type device and **c** indicates 'character' type device.

For devices having multiple major numbers, the following scheme is used to specify which device nodes belong to which major. The third field is expanded to specify a major number offset as follows:

"[b/c]: maj_off", where [b/c] refers to either block or character major and maj_off refers to an offset number within the major number range in the mdevice file. For example, a specification "C:2" refers to a character major offset 2, which for a major range of "15-18" would translate to character major 17.

Minor device number.
If this field is a non-numeric, it is assumed to be a request for a streams clone device node, and idmknod will set the minor number to the value of the major number of the device specified [see mknod(2) in the *Programmer's Reference Manual* for information on minor device number values].

User id.
The integer value in this field describes the ownership of the node to be made.

Group id.
The integer value in this field describes the group ownership of the node to be created.

Permission.
The value expected must be in octal form, in the manner in which permissions are described to the chmod(1) command (i.e. 0777).

Some example node file entries are as follows:

asy tty00 c 1   makes /dev/tty00 for device asy using minor device 1.

qt rmt/c0s0 c 4   makes /dev/rmt/c0s0 for device qt using minor device 4.

clone net/nau/clone c nau
                makes /dev/net/nau/clone for device clone. The minor device number is set to the major device number of device nau.

scsi tty1 C:0 5   makes tty1 for device scsi using minor device 1 major_number offset 0.

The command line options are:

−o *directory*   Nodes will be installed in the directory specified rather than /dev.

−i *directory*   The file mdevice which normally resides in /etc/conf/cf.d , can be found in the directory specified.

−e *directory*   The *Node* modules that normally reside in /etc/conf/node.d can be found in the directory specified.

−s   Suppress removing nodes (just add new nodes).

ERROR MESSAGES
An exit value of zero indicates success. If an error was encountered due to a syntax or format error in a *node* entry, an advisory message will be printed to *stdout* and the command will continue. If a serious error is encountered (that is, a required file cannot be found), idmknod will exit with a non-zero value and report an error message. All error messages are designed to be self-explanatory.

SEE ALSO
idinstall(1M), idmkinit(1M)
mdevice(4), mknod(2), sdevice(4) in the *Programmer's Reference Manual*

NAME

idmkunix – build new UNIX System kernel

SYNOPSIS

/etc/conf/bin/idmkunix

DESCRIPTION

The idmkunix command creates a bootable UNIX Operating System kernel in the directory /etc/conf/cf.d . The component kernel "core" files and device driver object files contained in subdirectories of /etc/conf/pack.d are used as input along with device and parameter definition files produced by idconfig. In brief, the required input files are as follows:

/etc/conf/cf.d/conf.c	– Kernel data structures and function definitions
/etc/conf/cf.d/config.h	– Kernel parameter and device definitions
/etc/conf/cf.d/vector.c	– Interrupt vector definitions
/etc/conf/cf.d/direct	– Listing of all driver components included in the build
/etc/conf/cf.d/fsconf.c	– File system type configuration data
/etc/conf/cf.d/vuifile	– Memory management definitions for the kernel
/etc/conf/pack.d/*/Driver.o	– Component kernel object files
/etc/conf/pack.d/*/space.c	– Component kernel space allocation files
/etc/conf/pack.d/*/stubs.c	– Component kernel stubs files

The command line options are as follows:

-o *directory*   The file *unix* be created in the directory specified rather than /etc/conf/cf.d.

-i *directory*   Input files that normally reside in /etc/conf/cf.d can be found in the directory specified.

-r *directory*   The directory specified will be used as the ID "root" directory rather than /etc/conf .

-c, cc, -l, ld   These options are no longer supported.

-#   Print debugging information.

ERROR MESSAGES

An exit value of zero indicates success. If an error was encountered, idmkunix will exit with a non-zero value and report an error message. All error messages are designed to be self-explanatory.

SEE ALSO

idbuild(1M), idconfig(1M), idinstall(1M), mdevice(4), mtune(4), sdevice(4), stune(4)

NAME

idspace – investigates free space

SYNOPSIS

/etc/conf/bin/idspace [-i *inodes*] [-r *blocks*] [-u *blocks*]
   [-t *blocks*]

DESCRIPTION

This command investigates free space in /, /usr, and /tmp file systems to determine whether sufficient disk blocks and inodes exist in each of potentially 3 file
systems. The default tests that idspace performs are as follows:

> Verify that the **root** file system (/) has 400 blocks more than the size of
> the current /unix. This verifies that a device driver being added to the
> current /unix can be built and placed in the **root** directory. A check is
> also made to insure that 100 inodes exist in the **root** directory.

> Determine whether a /usr file system exists. If it does exist, a test is
> made that 400 free blocks and 100 inodes are available in that file system.
> If the file system does not exist, idspace does not complain since files
> created in /usr by the reconfiguration process will be created in the **root**
> file system and space requirements are covered by the test in (1.) above.

> Determine whether a /tmp file system exists. If it does exist, a test is
> made that 400 free blocks and 100 inodes are available in that file system.
> If the file system does not exist, idspace does not complain since files
> created in /tmp by the reconfiguration process will be created in the **root**
> file system and space requirements are covered by the test in (1.) above.

The command line options are:

-i *inodes*   This option overrides the default test for 100 inode in all of the
idspace checks.

-r *blocks*   This option overrides the default test for /unix size + 400 blocks
when checking the **root** (/) file system. When the -r option is used,
the /usr and /tmp file systems are not tested unless explicitly
specified.

-u *blocks*   This option overrides the default test for 400 blocks when checking
the /usr file system. When the -u option is used, the **root** (/) and
/tmp file systems are not tested unless explicitly specified. If /usr is
not a separate file system, an error is reported.

-t *blocks*   This option overrides the default test for 400 blocks when checking
the /tmp file system. When the -t option is used, the **root** (/) and
/usr file systems are not tested unless explicitly specified. If /tmp is
not a separate file system, an error is reported.

ERROR MESSAGES

An exit value of zero indicates success. If insufficient space exists in a file system or an error was encountered due to a syntax or format error, **idspace** will report a message. All error messages are designed to be self-explanatory. The specific exit values are as follows:

0   success.

1   command syntax error, or needed file does not exist.

2   file system has insufficient space or inodes.

3   requested file system does not exist (−u and −t options only).

SEE ALSO

idbuild(1M), idinstall(1M)

NAME
idtune – attempts to set value of a tunable parameter

SYNOPSIS
/etc/conf/bin/idtune [-f | -m] *name value*

DESCRIPTION
This script attempts to set the value of a tunable parameter. The tunable parameter to be changed is indicated by *name*. The desired value for the tunable parameter is *value*.

If there is already a value for this parameter (in the **stune** file), the user will normally be asked to confirm the change with the following message:

> **Tunable Parameter** *name* **is currently set to** *old_value*.
> **Is it OK to change it to** *value*? **(y/n)**

If the user answers y, the change will be made. Otherwise, the tunable parameter will not be changed, and the following message will be displayed:

> *name* left at *old_value*.

However, if the **-f** (force) option is used, the change will always be made and no messages will ever be given.

If the **-m** (minimum) option is used and there is an existing value which is greater than the desired value, no change will be made and no message will be given.

If system tunable parameters are being modified as part of a device driver or application add-on package, it may not be desirable to prompt the user with the above question. The add-on package Install script may chose to override the existing value using the **-f** or **-m** options. However, care must be taken not to invalidate a tunable parameter modified earlier by the user or another add-on package.

In order for the change in parameter to become effective, the UNIX System kernel must be rebuilt and the system rebooted.

DIAGNOSTICS
The exit status will ne non-zero if errors are encountered.

SEE ALSO
idbuild(1).

mtune(4), stune(4) in the *Programmer's Reference Manual*.

NAME

ifconfig – configure network interface parameters

SYNOPSIS

ifconfig *interface* [*address_family*] [*address* [*dest_address*]] [*parameters*]
[**netmask** *mask*] [**broadcast** *address*] [**metric** *n*]

ifconfig *interface* [*protocol_family*]

DESCRIPTION

ifconfig is used to assign an address to a network interface and/or to configure network interface parameters. ifconfig must be used at boot time to define the network address of each interface present on a machine; it may also be used at a later time to redefine an interface's address or other operating parameters. Used without options, ifconfig displays the current configuration for a network interface. If a protocol family is specified, ifconfig will report only the details specific to that protocol family. Only the super-user may modify the configuration of a network interface.

The *interface* parameter is a string of the form name unit, for example **emd1**.

Since an interface may receive transmissions in differing protocols, each of which may require separate naming schemes, the parameters and addresses are interpreted according to the rules of some address family, specified by the *address_family* parameter. The address families currently supported are **ether** and **inet**. If no address family is specified, **inet** is assumed.

For the DARPA Internet family (**inet**), the address is either a host name present in the host name data base [see **hosts**(4)], or a DARPA Internet address expressed in the Internet standard dot notation. Typically, an Internet address specified in dot notation will consist of your system's network number and the machine's unique host number. A typical Internet address is **192.9.200.44**, where **192.9.200** is the network number and **44** is the machine's host number.

For the **ether** address family, the address is an Ethernet address represented as *x*:*x*:*x*:*x*:*x*:*x* where *x* is a hexadecimal number between 0 and ff. Only the super-user may use the **ether** address family.

If the *dest_address* parameter is supplied in addition to the *address* parameter, it specifies the address of the correspondent on the other end of a point to point link.

OPTIONS

The following *parameters* may be set with ifconfig:

up   Mark an interface up. This may be used to enable an interface after an ifconfig down. It happens automatically when setting the first address on an interface. If the interface was reset when previously marked down, the hardware will be re-initialized.

down   Mark an interface down. When an interface is marked down, the system will not attempt to transmit messages through that interface. If possible, the interface will be reset to disable reception as well. This action does not automatically disable routes using the interface.

trailers   (inet only) Enable the use of a trailer link level encapsulation when sending. If a network interface supports trailer encapsulation, the system will, when possible, encapsulate outgoing messages in a manner which minimizes the number of memory to memory copy operations performed by the receiver. This feature is machine-dependent, and therefore not recommended. On networks that support the Address Resolution Protocol [see **arp**(7)]; currently, only 10 Mb/s Ethernet), this flag indicates that the system should request that other systems use trailer encapsulation when sending to this host. Similarly, trailer encapsulations will be used when sending to other hosts that have made such requests.

-trailers   Disable the use of a trailer link level encapsulation.

arp   Enable the use of the Address Resolution Protocol in mapping between network level addresses and link level addresses (default). This is currently implemented for mapping between DARPA Internet addresses and 10Mb/s Ethernet addresses.

-arp   Disable the use of the Address Resolution Protocol.

metric *n*   Set the routing metric of the interface to *n*, default 0. The routing metric is used by the routing protocol [**routed**(1M)]. Higher metrics have the effect of making a route less favorable; metrics are counted as additional hops to the destination network or host.

netmask *mask*
            (inet only) Specify how much of the address to reserve for subdividing networks into sub-networks. The mask includes the network part of the local address and the subnet part, which is taken from the host field of the address. The mask can be specified as a single hexadecimal number with a leading 0x, with a dot-notation Internet address, or with a pseudo-network name listed in the network table **networks**(4). The mask contains 1's for the bit positions in the 32-bit address which are to be used for the network and subnet parts, and 0's for the host part. The mask should contain at least the standard network portion, and the subnet field should be contiguous with the network portion.

broadcast *address*
            (inet only) Specify the address to use to represent broadcasts to the network. The default broadcast address is the address with a host part of all 1's.

EXAMPLES

If your workstation is not attached to an Ethernet, the **emd1** interface should be marked down as follows:

```
ifconfig emd1 down
```

FILES

    /dev/nit
    /etc/netmasks

SEE ALSO

    netstat(1M), netmasks(4)

DIAGNOSTICS

Messages indicating the specified interface does not exist, the requested address is unknown, or the user is not privileged and tried to alter an interface's configuration.

NAME
>   incfile – create, restore an incremental filesystem archive

SYNOPSIS
>   incfile -B [-dilmortvxAENSV] *bkjobid ofsname ofsdev ofslab descript*
>
>   incfile -T *bkjobid tocfname descript*
>
>   incfile -RC [-dilmortvxAENSV] *ofsname ofsdev refsname redev rsjobid descript*
>
>   incfile -RF [-dilmortvxAENSV] *ofsname ofsdev descript rsjobid:uid:date:type:name*
>   [:[rename]:[inode]] ...

DESCRIPTION
>   incfile is invoked as a child process by other shell commands. The command
>   name, incfile, is read either from the bkhist.tab file or the bkreg -m com-
>   mand and option. The -B, -T, -R, -F, and -C options are passed to incfile
>   by the shell commands backup, restore, and *urestore(1)* described below. The
>   minus options are passed from the bkhist.tab file or the bkreg -p command
>   and option. The arguments are sent to incfile from various locations in the
>   backup service.
>
>   incfile -B is invoked as a child process by the bkdaemon command to perform
>   an incremental backup of the filesystem *ofsname* (the originating filesystem). All
>   files in *ofsname* that have been modified or have had an inode change since the
>   last full backup are archived. The resulting backup is created in cpio file format.
>   The backup is recorded in the backup history log, /etc/bkup/bkhist.tab.

> *bkjobid*   the job id assigned by backup. The method uses the *bkjobid* when it
>   creates history log and table-of-contents entries.
>
> *ofsname*   the name of the filesystem that is to be backed up.
>
> *ofsdev*   the name of the UNIX block special device on which the filesystem
>   resides.
>
> *ofslab*   the volume name on the filesystem [see labelit(1M)].
>
> *descript*   is a description for a destination device in the form:
>
>>   *dgroup:dname:dchar:dlabels*
>
>   *dgroup* specifies a device group [see devgroup.tab(4)].
>   *dname* specifies a particular device name [see device.tab(4)].
>   *dchars* specifies characteristics associated with the device. If specified,
>   *dchar* overrides the defaults for the specified device and group. [See
>   device.tab(4) for a further description of device characteristics].
>   *dlabels* specifies the volume names for the media to be used for read-
>   ing or writing the archive.

>   incfile -T is invoked as a child process by the backup to archive a table-of-
>   contents on the volumes described by *descript*.

> *tocfname*   the name of the file containing the table-of-contents.

>   incfile -RC and incfile -RF are invoked as child processes by the rsoper
>   command to extract files from an incremental filesystem archive created by
>   incfile -B. The filesystem archive is assumed to be in cpio format.

If the **-RC** option is selected, all files recorded in the archive are restored.

refsname   if non-null, the name of the filesystem to be restored to instead of *ofsname*.

redev   if non-null, the partition to be restored to instead of *ofsdev*.

At least one of *refsname* and *redev* must be null.

If the **-RF** option is specified, only selected objects from the archive are restored. Each 7-tuple, composed of *rsjobid:uid:date:type:name:rename:inode*, specifies an object to be restored from the filesystem archive. The 7-tuple objects come to **incfile** from the **rsstatus.tab** file.

rsjobid   the restore jobid assigned by **restore** or **urestore**.

uid   the real uid of the user who requested the object to be restored. It must match the uid of the owner of the object at the time the archive was made, or it must be the superuser uid.

date   the newest "last modification time" that is acceptable for a restorable object. The object is restored from the archive immediately older than this date. *date* is a hexadecimal representation of the date and time provided by the **time** system call.

type   either **F** or **D**, indicating that the object is a file or a directory, respectively.

name   the name the object had in the filesystem archive.

rename   the name that the object should be restored to (it may differ from the name the object had in the filesystem archive). If omitted, the object is restored to *name*.

inode   the inode number of the object as it was stored in the filesystem archive. *[inode]* is not used by **incfile -R**, and is provided only for command-line compatibility with other restoral methods.

Options

Some options are only significant during **incfile -B** invocations; they are accepted but ignored during **incfile -R** invocations because the command is invoked and options are specified automatically by **restore**. These options are flagged with an asterisk (*).

d*   Inhibits the recording of the archive in the backup history log.

i*   Excludes from the backup those files that have only had an inode change.

l*   Creates a long form of the backup history log that includes a table of contents for the archive. This includes the data used to generate a listing of each file in the archive like that produced by the **ls -l** command.

m*   Mounts the originating filesystem read-only before starting the backup and remounts it with its original permissions after completing the backup. Cannot be used with **root** or **/usr** filesystems.

o	Permits the user to override media insertion requests [see the **getvol**(1M), **-o** option].
r*	Includes remotely mounted resources in the archive.
t*	Creates a table of contents for the backup on additional media instead of in the backup history log.
v*	Validates the archive as it is written. A checksum is computed as the archive is being written; as each medium is completed, it is re-read and the checksum is recomputed to verify that each block is readable and correct. If either check fails, the medium is considered unreadable. If **−A** has been specified, the archiving operation fails; otherwise, the operator is prompted to replace the failed medium.
x*	Ignores the exception list; backs up all changed or modified files.
A	Establishes automated mode, (i.e., does not prompt the user to insert or remove media).
E*	Reports an estimate of media usage for the archive, then performs the backup.
N*	Reports an estimate of media usage for the archive, but does not perform the backup.
S	Displays a period (.) for every 100 (512 byte) blocks read-from or written-to the archive on the destination device.
V	Displays the name of each file written-to or extracted-from the archive on the destination device.

User Interactions

The connection between an archiving method and the **backup** command is more complex than a simple **fork/exec** or **pipe**. The **backup** command is responsible for all interactions with the user, either directly, or through the **bkoper** command. Therefore, **incfile** neither reads from standard-input nor writes to standard-output or standard-error. A method library must be used [see **libbrmeth**(3)] to communicate reports (estimates, filenames, periods, status, etc.) to the **backup** command.

DIAGNOSTICS

The exit codes for **incfile** are the following:

0 = successful completion of the task
1 = one or more parameters to **incfile** are invalid.
2 = an error has occurred which caused **incfile** to fail to complete all portions of its task.

FILES

/etc/bkup/bkexcept.tab	lists the files that are to be excluded from an incremental filesystem backup.
/etc/bkup/bkhist.tab	lists the labels of all volumes that have been used for backup operations.

`/etc/bkup/rsstatus.tab`	tracks the status of all restore requests from users.
`/etc/bkup/bklog`	lists errors generated by the backup methods and the **backup** command.
`/etc/bkup/rslog`	logs errors generated by the restore methods and the **restore** command.
$TMP/filelist$$	temporarily stores a table of contents for a backup archive.

SEE ALSO

backup(1M), bkoper(1M) cpio(1), cpio(4), device.tab(4), fdp(1), ff(1M), ffile(1), fimage(1), getvol(1M), incfile(1), labelit(1M), libbrmeth(3), ls(1), restore(1M), rsoper(1M), time(2)

NAME

indicator – display application specific alarms and/or the ''working'' indicator

SYNOPSIS

indicator [-b [*n*]] [-c *column*] [-1 *length*] [-o] [-w] [*string* ...]

DESCRIPTION

The **indicator** function displays application specific alarms or the ''working'' indicator, or both, on the FMLI banner line. By default, **indicator** ???? The argument *string* is a string to be displayed on the banner line, and should always be the last argument given. Note that *string* is not automatically cleared from the banner line.

The following options are available:

-b *n*   The -b option rings the terminal bell *n* times, where *n* is an integer from 1 to 10. The default value is 1. If the terminal has no bell, the screen is flashed instead, if possible.

-c *column*   The -c option defines the column of the banner line at which to start the indicator string. The argument *column* must be an integer from 0 to DISPLAYW-1. If the -c option is not used, *column* defaults to 0.

-1 *length*   The -1 option defines the maximum length of the string displayed. If *string* is longer than *length* characters, it will be truncated. The argument *length* must be an integer from 1 to DISPLAYW. If the -1 option is not used, *length* defaults to DISPLAYW. NOTE: if *string* doesn't fit it will be truncated.

-o   The -o option causes **indicator** to duplicate its output to *stdout*.

-w   The -w option turns on the working indicator.

EXAMPLES

When the value entered in a form field is invalid, the following use of **indicator** will ring the bell three times and display the word WRONG starting at column 1 of the banner line.

```
invalidmsg=`indicator -b 3 -c 1 "WRONG"`
```

To clear the indicator after telling the user the entry is wrong:

```
invalidmsg=`indicator -b 9 -c 1 "WRONG"; sleep(3);
        indicator -c 1 "      "`
```

In this example the value of **invalidmsg** (in this case the default value **Input is not valid**), still appears on the FMLI message line.

NAME

indxbib – create an inverted index to a bibliographic database

SYNOPSIS

/usr/ucb/indxbib *database-file* . . .

DESCRIPTION

indxbib makes an inverted index to the named *database-file* (which must reside within the current directory), typically for use by lookbib and refer. A *database* contains bibliographic references (or other kinds of information) separated by blank lines.

A bibliographic reference is a set of lines, constituting fields of bibliographic information. Each field starts on a line beginning with a '%', followed by a key-letter, then a blank, and finally the contents of the field, which may continue until the next line starting with '%' (see addbib).

indxbib is a shell script that calls two programs: mkey and inv. mkey truncates words to 6 characters, and maps upper case to lower case. It also discards words shorter than 3 characters, words among the 100 most common English words, and numbers (dates) < 1900 or > 2000. These parameters can be changed.

indxbib creates an entry file (with a .ia suffix), a posting file (.ib), and a tag file (.ic), in the working directory.

FILES

```
/usr/ucblib/reftools/mkey
/usr/ucblib/reftools/inv
*.ia            entry file
*.ib            posting file
*.ic            tag file
*.ig            reference file
```

SEE ALSO

addbib(1), lookbib(1), refer(1), roffbib(1), sortbib(1)

NOTES

All dates should probably be indexed, since many disciplines refer to literature written in the 1800s or earlier.

indxbib does not recognize pathnames.

NAME

inetd – Internet services daemon

SYNOPSIS

inetd [–d] [–s] [*configuration-file*]

DESCRIPTION

inetd, the Internet services daemon, is normally run at boot time by the Service Access Facility (SAF). When started, inetd reads its configuration information from *configuration-file*, the default being /etc/inetd.conf. See inetd.conf(4) for more information on the format of this file. It listens for connections on the Internet addresses of the services that its configuration file specifies. When a connection is found, it invokes the server daemon specified by that configuration file for the service requested. Once a server process exits, inetd continues to listen on the socket.

The –s option allows you to run inetd "stand-alone," outside the Service Access Facility (SAF).

Rather than having several daemon processes with sparsely distributed requests each running concurrently, inetd reduces the load on the system by invoking Internet servers only as they are needed.

inetd itself provides a number of simple TCP-based services. These include echo, discard, chargen (character generator), daytime (human readable time), and time (machine readable time, in the form of the number of seconds since midnight, January 1, 1900). For details of these services, consult the appropriate RFC, as listed below, from the Network Information Center.

inetd rereads its configuration file whenever it receives a hangup signal, SIGHUP. New services can be activated, and existing services deleted or modified in between whenever the file is reread.

SEE ALSO

comsat(1M), ftpd(1M), rexecd(1M), rlogind(1M), rshd(1M), telnetd(1M), tftpd(1M), inetd.conf(4)

Postel, Jon, "Echo Protocol," RFC 862, Network Information Center, SRI International, Menlo Park, Calif., May 1983

Postel, Jon, "Discard Protocol," RFC 863, Network Information Center, SRI International, Menlo Park, Calif., May 1983

Postel, Jon, "Character Generater Protocol," RFC 864, Network Information Center, SRI International, Menlo Park, Calif., May 1983

Postel, Jon, "Daytime Protocol," RFC 867, Network Information Center, SRI International, Menlo Park, Calif., May 1983

Postel, Jon, and Ken Harrenstien, "Time Protocol," RFC 868, Network Information Center, SRI International, Menlo Park, Calif., May 1983

NAME

infocmp – compare or print out *terminfo* descriptions

SYNOPSIS

infocmp [-d] [-c] [-n] [-I] [-L] [-C] [-r] [-u] [-s d| i| l| c] [-v] [-V]
[-1] [-w *width*] [-A *directory*] [-B *directory*] [*termname* . . .]

DESCRIPTION

infocmp can be used to compare a binary **terminfo** entry with other terminfo entries, rewrite a **terminfo** description to take advantage of the **use=** terminfo field, or print out a **terminfo** description from the binary file (**term**) in a variety of formats. In all cases, the boolean fields will be printed first, followed by the numeric fields, followed by the string fields.

Default Options

If no options are specified and zero or one *termnames* are specified, the **-I** option will be assumed. If more than one *termname* is specified, the **-d** option will be assumed.

Comparison Options [–d] [–c] [–n]

infocmp compares the **terminfo** description of the first terminal *termname* with each of the descriptions given by the entries for the other terminal's *termnames*. If a capability is defined for only one of the terminals, the value returned will depend on the type of the capability: **F** for boolean variables, **-1** for integer variables, and **NULL** for string variables.

-d   produces a list of each capability that is different between two entries. This option is useful to show the difference between two entries, created by different people, for the same or similar terminals.

-c   produces a list of each capability that is common between two entries. Capabilities that are not set are ignored. This option can be used as a quick check to see if the **-u** option is worth using.

-n   produces a list of each capability that is in neither entry. If no *termnames* are given, the environment variable **TERM** will be used for both of the *termnames*. This can be used as a quick check to see if anything was left out of a description.

Source Listing Options [–I] [–L] [–C] [–r]

The **-I**, **-L**, and **-C** options will produce a source listing for each terminal named.

-I   use the **terminfo** names
-L   use the long C variable name listed in <**term.h**>
-C   use the **termcap** names
-r   when using **-C**, put out all capabilities in **termcap** form

If no *termnames* are given, the environment variable **TERM** will be used for the terminal name.

The source produced by the **-C** option may be used directly as a **termcap** entry, but not all of the parameterized strings may be changed to the **termcap** format. infocmp will attempt to convert most of the parameterized information, but anything not converted will be plainly marked in the output and commented out. These should be edited by hand.

All padding information for strings will be collected together and placed at the beginning of the string where **termcap** expects it. Mandatory padding (padding information with a trailing '/') will become optional.

All **termcap** variables no longer supported by **terminfo**, but which are derivable from other **terminfo** variables, will be output. Not all **terminfo** capabilities will be translated; only those variables which were part of **termcap** will normally be output. Specifying the **-r** option will take off this restriction, allowing all capabilities to be output in *termcap* form.

Note that because padding is collected to the beginning of the capability, not all capabilities are output. Mandatory padding is not supported. Because **termcap** strings are not as flexible, it is not always possible to convert a **terminfo** string capability into an equivalent **termcap** format. A subsequent conversion of the **termcap** file back into **terminfo** format will not necessarily reproduce the original **terminfo** source.

Some common **terminfo** parameter sequences, their **termcap** equivalents, and some terminal types which commonly have such sequences, are:

terminfo	termcap	Representative Terminals
%p1%c	%.	adm
%p1%d	%d	hp, ANSI standard, vt100
%p1%'x'%+%c	%+x	concept
%i	%i	ANSI standard, vt100
%p1%?%'x'%>%t%p1%'y'%+%;	%>xy	concept
%p2 is printed before %p1	%r	hp

Use= Option [-u]

    -u   produces a **terminfo** source description of the first terminal *termname* which is relative to the sum of the descriptions given by the entries for the other terminals *termnames*. It does this by analyzing the differences between the first *termname* and the other *termnames* and producing a description with **use=** fields for the other terminals. In this manner, it is possible to retrofit generic terminfo entries into a terminal's description. Or, if two similar terminals exist, but were coded at different times or by different people so that each description is a full description, using **infocmp** will show what can be done to change one description to be relative to the other.

A capability will get printed with an at-sign (@) if it no longer exists in the first *termname*, but one of the other *termname* entries contains a value for it. A capability's value gets printed if the value in the first *termname* is not found in any of the other *termname* entries, or if the first of the other *termname* entries that has this capability gives a different value for the capability than that in the first *termname*.

The order of the other *termname* entries is significant. Since the terminfo compiler **tic** does a left-to-right scan of the capabilities, specifying two **use=** entries that contain differing entries for the same capabilities will produce different results depending on the order that the entries are given in. **infocmp** will flag any such inconsistencies between the other *termname* entries as they are found.

Alternatively, specifying a capability *after* a **use=** entry that contains that capability will cause the second specification to be ignored. Using **infocmp** to recreate a description can be a useful check to make sure that everything was specified correctly in the original source description.

Another error that does not cause incorrect compiled files, but will slow down the compilation time, is specifying extra **use=** fields that are superfluous. **infocmp** will flag any other *termname* **use=** fields that were not needed.

Other Options [–s d| i| l| c] [–v] [–V] [–1] [–w *width***]**

    -s   sorts the fields within each type according to the argument below:

           d   leave fields in the order that they are stored in the *terminfo* database.

           i   sort by *terminfo* name.

           l   sort by the long C variable name.

           c   sort by the *termcap* name.

           If the **-s** option is not given, the fields printed out will be sorted alphabetically by the **terminfo** name within each type, except in the case of the **–C** or the **–L** options, which cause the sorting to be done by the **termcap** name or the long C variable name, respectively.

    -v   prints out tracing information on standard error as the program runs.

    -V   prints out the version of the program in use on standard error and exit.

    -1   causes the fields to be printed out one to a line. Otherwise, the fields will be printed several to a line to a maximum width of 60 characters.

    -w   changes the output to *width* characters.

Changing Databases [–A *directory***] [–B** *directory***]**

The location of the compiled **terminfo** database is taken from the environment variable **TERMINFO** . If the variable is not defined, or the terminal is not found in that location, the system **terminfo** database, usually in /usr/share/lib/terminfo, will be used. The options **–A** and **–B** may be used to override this location. The **–A** option will set **TERMINFO** for the first *termname* and the **–B** option will set **TERMINFO** for the other *termnames*. With this, it is possible to compare descriptions for a terminal with the same name located in two different databases. This is useful for comparing descriptions for the same terminal created by different people.

FILES

    /usr/share/lib/terminfo/?/*   Compiled terminal description database.

SEE ALSO

    curses(3X), **captoinfo**(1M), **terminfo**(4), **tic**(1M)

NAME

init, `telinit` – process control initialization

SYNOPSIS

`/sbin/init` [`0123456SsQqabc`]

`/sbin/telinit` [`0123456SsQqabc`]

DESCRIPTION

init

init is a general process spawner. Its primary role is to create processes from information stored in the file **/etc/inittab** [see **inittab**(4)].

At any given time, the system is in one of eight possible run levels. A run level is a software configuration of the system under which only a selected group of processes exist. The processes spawned by init for each of these run levels is defined in **/etc/inittab**. init can be in one of eight run levels, **0–6** and **S** or **s** (run levels **S** and **s** are identical). The run level changes when a privileged user runs **/sbin/init**. This user-spawned init sends appropriate signals to the original init spawned by the operating system when the system was booted, telling it which run level to change to.

The following are the arguments to init.

0   shut the machine down so it is safe to remove the power. Have the machine remove power if it can.

1   put the system in system administrator mode. All file systems are mounted. Only a small set of essential kernel processes are left running. This mode is for administrative tasks such as installing optional utility packages. All files are accessible and no users are logged in on the system.

2   put the system in multi-user mode. All multi-user environment terminal processes and daemons are spawned. This state is commonly referred to as the multi-user state.

3   start the remote file sharing processes and daemons. Mount and advertise remote resources. Run level **3** extends multi-user mode and is known as the remote-file-sharing state.

4   is available to be defined as an alternative multi-user environment configuration. It is not necessary for system operation and is usually not used.

5   Stop the UNIX system and go to the firmware monitor.

6   Stop the UNIX system and reboot to the state defined by the **init-default** entry in **/etc/inittab**.

a,b,c   process only those **/etc/inittab** entries having the **a**, **b**, or **c** run level set. These are pseudo-states, which may be defined to run certain commands, but which do not cause the current run level to change.

Q,q   re-examine /etc/inittab.

S,s   enter single-user mode. When this occurs, the terminal which exe-
        cuted this command becomes the system console. This is the only run
        level that doesn't require the existence of a properly formatted
        /etc/inittab file. If this file does not exist, then by default the only
        legal run level that init can enter is the single-user mode. When the
        system comes up to S or s, file systems for users' files are not
        mounted and only essential kernel processes are running. When the
        system comes down to S or s, all mounted file systems remain
        mounted, and all processes started by init that should only be run-
        ning in multi-user mode are killed. In addition, any process that has a
        utmp entry will be killed. This last condition insures that all port
        monitors started by the SAC are killed and all services started by these
        port monitors, including ttymon login services, are killed. Other
        processes not started directly by init will remain running. For exam-
        ple, cron remains running.

When a UNIX system is booted, init is invoked and the following occurs. First,
init looks in /etc/inittab for the initdefault entry [see inittab(4)]. If
there is one, init will usually use the run level specified in that entry as the initial run level to enter. If there is no initdefault entry in /etc/inittab, init
requests that the user enter a run level from the virtual system console. If an S or
s is entered, init goes to the single-user state. In the single-user state the virtual
console terminal is assigned to the user's terminal and is opened for reading and
writing. The command /sbin/su is invoked and a message is generated on the
physical console saying where the virtual console has been relocated. Use either
init or telinit, to signal init to change the run level of the system. Note that
if the shell is terminated (via an end-of-file), init will only re-initialize to the
single-user state if the /etc/inittab file does not exist.

If a 0 through 6 is entered, init enters the corresponding run level. Run levels
0, 5, and 6 are reserved states for shutting the system down. Run levels 2, 3, and
4 are available as multi-user operating states.

If this is the first time since power up that init has entered a run level other
than single-user state, init first scans /etc/inittab for boot and bootwait
entries [see inittab(4)]. These entries are performed before any other processing
of /etc/inittab takes place, providing that the run level entered matches that of
the entry. In this way any special initialization of the operating system, such as
mounting file systems, can take place before users are allowed onto the system.
init then scans /etc/inittab and executes all other entries that are to be processed for that run level.

To spawn each process in /etc/inittab, init reads each entry and for each
entry that should be respawned, it forks a child process. After it has spawned all
of the processes specified by /etc/inittab, init waits for one of its descendant
processes to die, a powerfail signal, or a signal from another init or telinit
process to change the system's run level. When one of these conditions occurs,
init re-examines /etc/inittab. New entries can be added to /etc/inittab at
any time; however, init still waits for one of the above three conditions to occur

before re-examining `/etc/inittab`. To get around this, `init Q` or `init q` command wakes `init` to re-examine `/etc/inittab` immediately.

When `init` comes up at boot time and whenever the system changes from the single-user state to another run state, `init` sets the `ioctl`(2) states of the virtual console to those modes saved in the file `/etc/ioctl.syscon`. This file is written by `init` whenever the single-user state is entered.

When a run level change request is made `init` sends the warning signal (SIGTERM) to all processes that are undefined in the target run level. `init` waits five seconds before forcibly terminating these processes via the kill signal (SIGKILL).

When `init` receives a signal telling it that a process it spawned has died, it records the fact and the reason it died in `/var/adm/utmp` and `/var/adm/wtmp` if it exists [see `who`(1)]. A history of the processes spawned is kept in `/var/adm/wtmp`.

If `init` receives a **powerfail** signal (SIGPWR) it scans `/etc/inittab` for special entries of the type **powerfail** and **powerwait**. These entries are invoked (if the run levels permit) before any further processing takes place. In this way `init` can perform various cleanup and recording functions during the powerdown of the operating system.

telinit

`telinit`, which is linked to `/sbin/init`, is used to direct the actions of `init`. It takes a one-character argument and signals `init` to take the appropriate action.

FILES

```
/etc/inittab
/var/adm/utmp
/var/adm/wtmp
/etc/ioctl.syscon
/dev/console
```

SEE ALSO

`ttymon`(1M), `shutdown`(1M), `inittab`(4), `utmp`(4), `utmpx`(4), `termio`(7)
`login`(1), `sh`(1), `stty`(1), `who`(1) in the *User's Reference Manual*
`kill`(2) in the *Programmer's Reference Manual*

DIAGNOSTICS

If `init` finds that it is respawning an entry from `/etc/inittab` more than ten times in two minutes, it will assume that there is an error in the command string in the entry, and generate an error message on the system console. It will then refuse to respawn this entry until either five minutes has elapsed or it receives a signal from a user-spawned `init` or `telinit`. This prevents `init` from eating up system resources when someone makes a typographical error in the `inittab` file or a program is removed that is referenced in `/etc/inittab`.

When attempting to boot the system, failure of `init` to prompt for a new run level may be because the virtual system console is linked to a device other than the physical system console.

NOTES

init and telinit can be run only by a privileged user.

The S or s state must not be used indiscriminately in the /etc/inittab file. A good rule to follow when modifying this file is to avoid adding this state to any line other than the initdefault.

If a default state is not specified in the initdefault entry in /etc/inittab, state 6 is entered. Consequently, the system will loop, that is, it will go to firmware and reboot continuously.

If the utmp file cannot be created when booting the system, the system will boot to state "s" regardless of the state specified in the *initdefault* entry in /etc/inittab. This can happen if the /var filesystem is not accessible.

In the event of a file table overflow condition, init uses the file descriptor associated with /etc/inittab that was retained from the last time it accessed the file. This prevents init from going into single user mode when it cannot obtain a file descriptor to open /etc/inittab.

NAME

install – install commands

SYNOPSIS

/usr/sbin/install [–c *dira*] [–f *dirb*] [–i] [–n *dirc*] [–m *mode*] [–u *user*] [–g *group*] [–o] [–s] *file* [*dirx* . . .]

DESCRIPTION

The install command is most commonly used in "makefiles" [see make(1)] to install a *file* (updated target file) in a specific place within a file system. Each *file* is installed by copying it into the appropriate directory, thereby retaining the mode and owner of the original command. The program prints messages telling the user exactly what files it is replacing or creating and where they are going.

If no options or directories (*dirx* . . .) are given, install will search a set of default directories (/bin, /usr/bin, /etc, /lib, and /usr/lib, in that order) for a file with the same name as *file*. When the first occurrence is found, install issues a message saying that it is overwriting that file with *file*, and proceeds to do so. If the file is not found, the program states this and exits without further action.

If one or more directories (*dirx* ...) are specified after *file*, those directories will be searched before the directories specified in the default list.

The meanings of the options are:

–c *dira*   Installs a new command (*file*) in the directory specified by *dira*, only if it is not found. If it is found, install issues a message saying that the file already exists, and exits without overwriting it. May be used alone or with the –s option.

–f *dirb*   Forces *file* to be installed in given directory, whether or not one already exists. If the file being installed does not already exist, the mode and owner of the new file will be set to 755 and bin, respectively. If the file already exists, the mode and owner will be that of the already existing file. May be used alone or with the –o or –s options.

–i   Ignores default directory list, searching only through the given directories (*dirx* ...). May be used alone or with any other options except –c and –f.

–n *dirc*   If *file* is not found in any of the searched directories, it is put in the directory specified in *dirc*. The mode and owner of the new file will be set to 755 and bin, respectively. May be used alone or with any other options except –c and –f.

–m *mode*   The mode of the new file is set to *mode*.

–u *user*   The owner of the new file is set to *user*.

–g *group*   The group id of the new file is set to *group*. Only available to the superuser.

    −o   If *file* is found, this option saves the "found" file by copying it to OLD*file* in the directory in which it was found. This option is useful when installing a frequently used file such as **/bin/sh** or **/lib/saf/ttymon**, where the existing file cannot be removed. May be used alone or with any other options except **−c**.

    −s   Suppresses printing of messages other than error messages. May be used alone or with any other options.

SEE ALSO
    make(1)

NAME
install – install files

SYNOPSIS
/usr/ucb/install [−cs] [−g *group*] [−m *mode*] [−o *owner*] *file1 file2*

/usr/ucb/install [−cs] [−g *group*] [−m *mode*] [−o *owner*] *file* . . . *directory*

/usr/ucb/install −d [−g *group*] [−m *mode*] [−o *owner*] *directory*

DESCRIPTION
Install is used within makefiles to copy new versions of files into a destination directory and to create the destination directory itself.

The first two forms are similar to the **cp**(1) command with the addition that executable files can be stripped during the copy and the owner, group, and mode of the installed file(s) can be given.

The third form can be used to create a destination directory with the required owner, group and permissions.

Note: **install** uses no special privileges to copy files from one place to another. The implications of this are:

> You must have permission to read the files to be installed.

> You must have permission to copy into the destination file or directory.

> You must have permission to change the modes on the final copy of the file if you want to use the −m option to change modes.

> You must be superuser if you want to specify the ownership of the installed file with −o. If you are not the super-user, or if −o is not in effect, the installed file will be owned by you, regardless of who owns the original.

OPTIONS
−g *group*   Set the group ownership of the installed file or directory. (staff by default)

−m *mode*   Set the mode for the installed file or directory. (0755 by default)

−o *owner*   If run as root, set the ownership of the installed file to the user-ID of *owner*.

−c   Copy files. In fact **install** *always* copies files, but the −c option is retained for backwards compatibility with old shell scripts that might otherwise break.

−s   Strip executable files as they are copied.

−d   Create a directory. Missing parent directories are created as required as in **mkdir −p**. If the directory already exists, the owner, group and mode will be set to the values given on the command line.

SEE ALSO
chown(1)

chgrp(1), chmod(1), cp(1), mkdir(1), strip(1) in the *User's Reference Manual*
install(1M) in the *System Administrator's Reference Manual*

NAME

`installf` – add a file to the software installation database

SYNOPSIS

`installf` [`-c` *class*] *pkginst pathname* [*ftype* [[*major minor*]
[*mode owner group*]]

`installf` [`-c` *class*] *pkginst* –

`installf` `-f` [`-c` *class*] *pkginst*

DESCRIPTION

`installf` is a tool available for use from within custom procedure scripts such as **preinstall, postinstall, preremove**, and **postremove**. `installf` informs the system that a pathname not listed in the **pkgmap** file is being created or modified. It should be invoked before any file modifications have occurred.

When the second synopsis is used, the pathname descriptions will be read from standard input. These descriptions are the same as would be given in the first synopsis but the information is given in the form of a list. (The descriptions should be in the form: *pathname* [*ftype* [[*major minor*] [*mode owner group*]]].)

After all files have been appropriately created and/or modified, `installf` should be invoked with the `-f` synopsis to indicate that installation is final. Links will be created at this time and, if attribute information for a pathname was not specified during the original invocation of `installf` or was not already stored on the system, the current attribute values for the pathname will be stored. Otherwise, `installf` verifies that attribute values match those given on the command line, making corrections as necessary. In all cases, the current content information is calculated and stored appropriately.

`-c` *class*   Class to which installed objects should be associated. Default class is **none**.

pkginst   A short string used to designate a package. It is composed of one or two parts: *pkg* (an abbreviation for the package name) or, if more than one instance of that package exists, *pkg* plus *inst* (an instance identifier). (The term "package instance" is used loosely: it refers to all instantiations of *pkginst*, even those that do not include instance identifiers.)

The package name abbreviation (*pkg*) is the mandatory part of *pkginst*. To create such an abbreviation, assign it with the **PKG** parameter. For example, to assign the abbreviation **sds** to the Software Distribution Service package, enter **PKG=sds**.

The second part (*inst*), which is required only if you have more than one instance of the package in question, is a suffix that identifies the instance. This suffix is either a number (preceded by a period) or any short mnemonic string you choose. If you don't assign your own instance identifier when one is required, the system assigns a numeric one by default. For example, if you have three instances of the Software Distribution Service package and you don't create your own mnemonic identifiers (such as **old** and **beta**), the system adds the suffixes **.2** and **.3** to the second and third packages, automatically.

To indicate all instances of a package, specify **inst.***. (When using this format, enclose the command line in single quotes to prevent the shell from interpreting the * character.) Use the token **all** to refer to all packages available on the source medium.

pathname Pathname that is being created or modified.

ftype A one-character field that indicates the file type. Possible file types include:

    f   a standard executable or data file

    e   a file to be edited upon installation or removal

    v   volatile file (one whose contents are expected to change)

    d   directory

    x   an exclusive directory

    l   linked file

    p   named pipe

    c   character special device

    b   block special device

    s   symbolic link

major The major device number. The field is only specified for block or character special devices.

minor The minor device number. The field is only specified for block or character special devices.

mode The octal mode of the file (for example, 0664). A question mark (**?**) indicates that the mode will be left unchanged, implying that the file already exists on the target machine. This field is not used for linked or symbolically linked files.

owner The owner of the file (for example, **bin** or **root**). The field is limited to 14 characters in length. A question mark (**?**) indicates that the owner will be left unchanged, implying that the file already exists on the target machine. This field is not used for linked or symbolically linked files.

group The group to which the file belongs (for example, **bin** or **sys**). The field is limited to 14 characters in length. A question mark (**?**) indicates that the group will be left unchanged, implying that the file already exists on the target machine. This field is not used for linked or symbolically linked files.

−f Indicates that installation is complete. This option is used with the final invocation of **installf** (for all files of a given class).

NOTES

When *ftype* is specified, all applicable fields, as shown below, must be defined:

ftype	*Required Fields*
p x d f v or e	mode owner group
c or b	major minor mode owner group

The **installf** command will create directories, named pipes and special devices on the original invocation. Links are created when **installf** is invoked with the −**f** option to indicate installation is complete.

Links should be specified as *path1=path2*. *path1* indicates the destination and *path2* indicates the source file.

For symbolically linked files, *path2* can be a relative pathname, such as **./** or **../**. For example, if you enter a line such as

    s /foo/bar/etc/mount=../usr/sbin/mount

path2 (**/foo/bar/etc/mount**) will be a symbolic link to **../usr/sbin/mount**.

Files installed with **installf** will be placed in the class *none*, unless a class is defined with the command. Subsequently, they will be removed when the associated package is deleted. If this file should not be deleted at the same time as the package, be certain to assign it to a class which is ignored at removal time. If special action is required for the file before removal, a class must be defined with the command and an appropriate class action script delivered with the package.

When classes are used, **installf** must be used as follows:

    installf -c class1 . . .
    installf -f -c class1 . . .
    installf -c class2 . . .
    installf -f -c class2 . . .

EXAMPLE

The following example shows the use of **installf** invoked from an optional preinstall or postinstall script:

```
#create /dev/xt directory
#(needs to be done before drvinstall)
installf $PKGINST /dev/xt d 755 root sys || exit 2
majno='/usr/sbin/drvinstall -m /etc/master.d/xt \
     -d $BASEDIR/data/xt.o -v1.0' || exit 2
i=00
while [ $i -lt $limit ]
do
     for j in 0 1 2 3 4 5 6 7
     do
             echo /dev/xt$i$j c $majno 'expr $i * 8 + $j' \
                  644 root sys |
             echo /dev/xt$i$j=/dev/xt/$i$j
     done
     i='expr $i + 1'
     [ $i -le 9 ] && i="0$i" #add leading zero
done | installf $PKGINST - || exit 2

# finalized installation, create links
installf -f $PKGINST || exit 2
```

SEE ALSO
compver(4), copyright(4), depend(4), pkgadd(1M), pkgask(1M), pkgchk(1M), pkginfo(1), pkginfo(4), pkgmap(4), pkgmk(1), pkgparam(1), pkgproto(1), pkgtrans(1), pkgrm(1M), removef(1M) space(4)

NAME

ipcrm – remove a message queue, semaphore set, or shared memory ID

SYNOPSIS

ipcrm [*options*]

DESCRIPTION

ipcrm removes one or more messages, semaphores, or shared memory identifiers. The identifiers are specified by the following *options*:

-q *msqid*   Remove the message queue identifier *msqid* from the system and destroy the message queue and data structure associated with it.

-m *shmid*   Remove the shared memory identifier *shmid* from the system. The shared memory segment and data structure associated with it are destroyed after the last detach.

-s *semid*   Remove the semaphore identifier *semid* from the system and destroy the set of semaphores and data structure associated with it.

-Q *msgkey*   Remove the message queue identifier, created with key *msgkey*, from the system and destroy the message queue and data structure associated with it.

-M *shmkey*   Removes the shared memory identifier, created with key *shmkey*, from the system. The shared memory segment and data structure associated with it are destroyed after the last detach.

-S *semkey*   Remove the semaphore identifier, created with key *semkey*, from the system and destroy the set of semaphores and data structure associated with it.

The details of the removes are described in msgctl(2), shmctl(2), and semctl(2). Use the ipcs command to find the identifiers and keys.

SEE ALSO

ipcs(1)

msgctl(2), msgget(2), msgop(2), semctl(2), semget(2), semop(2), shmctl(2), shmget(2), shmop(2) in the *Programmer's Reference Manual*

NAME

ipcs – report inter-process communication facilities status

SYNOPSIS

ipcs [*options*]

DESCRIPTION

ipcs prints information about active inter-process communication facilities. Without *options*, information is printed in short format for message queues, shared memory, and semaphores that are currently active in the system. Otherwise, the information that is displayed is controlled by the following *options*:

-q   Print information about active message queues.

-m   Print information about active shared memory segments.

-s   Print information about active semaphores.

If −q, −m, or −s are specified, information about only those indicated is printed. If none of these three are specified, information about all three is printed subject to these options:

-b   Print information on biggest allowable size: maximum number of bytes in messages on queue for message queues, size of segments for shared memory, and number of semaphores in each set for semaphores. See below for meaning of columns in a listing.

-c   Print creator's login name and group name. See below.

-o   Print information on outstanding usage: number of messages on queue and total number of bytes in messages on queue for message queues and number of processes attached to shared memory segments.

-p   Print process number information: process ID of last process to send a message, process ID of last process to receive a message on message queues, process ID of creating process, and process ID of last process to attach or detach on shared memory segments. See below.

-t   Print time information: time of the last control operation that changed the access permissions for all facilities, time of last **msgsnd** and last **msgrcv** on message queues, time of last **shmat** and last **shmdt** on shared memory, time of last **semop** on semaphores. See below.

-a   Use all print options. (This is a shorthand notation for −b, −c, −o, −p, and −t.)

−C *corefile*
       Use the file *corefile* in place of /dev/kmem.

−N *namelist*
       Use the file *namelist* in place of /stand/unix.

-X   Print information about XENIX interprocess communication, in addition to the standard interprocess communication status. The XENIX process information describes a second set of semaphores and shared memory.

Note that the **-p** option does not print process number information for XENIX shared memory, and the **-t** option does not print time information about XENIX semaphores and shared memory.

The column headings and the meaning of the columns in an **ipcs** listing are given below; the letters in parentheses indicate the options that cause the corresponding heading to appear; "all" means that the heading always appears. Note that these options only determine what information is provided for each facility; they do not determine which facilities are listed.

T   (all)   Type of the facility:

          q   message queue
          m   shared memory segment
          s   semaphore

ID   (all)   The identifier for the facility entry.

KEY   (all)   The key used as an argument to **msgget**, **semget**, or **shmget** to create the facility entry. (Note:The key of a shared memory segment is changed to **IPC_PRIVATE** when the segment has been removed until all processes attached to the segment detach it.).TP **MODE**   (all) The facility access modes and flags: The mode consists of 11 characters that are interpreted as follows. The first two characters are:

          R   A process is waiting on a *msgrcv*.
          S   A process is waiting on a *msgsnd*.
          D   The associated shared memory segment has been removed. It will disappear when the last process attached to the segment detaches it.
          C   The associated shared memory segment is to be cleared when the first attach is executed.
          –   The corresponding special flag is not set.

The next nine characters are interpreted as three sets of three bits each. The first set refers to the owner's permissions; the next to permissions of others in the user-group of the facility entry; and the last to all others. Within each set, the first character indicates permission to read, the second character indicates permission to write or alter the facility entry, and the last character is currently unused.

The permissions are indicated as follows:

          r   Read permission is granted.
          w   Write permission is granted.
          a   Alter permission is granted.
          –   The indicated permission is not granted.

OWNER (all)   The login name of the owner of the facility entry.

GROUP (all)   The group name of the group of the owner of the facility entry.

CREATOR   (a,c)   The login name of the creator of the facility entry.

CGROUP   (a,c)   The group name of the group of the creator of the facility entry.

CBYTES   (a,o)   The number of bytes in messages currently outstanding on the associated message queue.

QNUM   (a,o)   The number of messages currently outstanding on the associated message queue.

QBYTES   (a,b)   The maximum number of bytes allowed in messages outstanding on the associated message queue.

LSPID   (a,p)   The process ID of the last process to send a message to the associated queue.

LRPID   (a,p)   The process ID of the last process to receive a message from the associated queue.

STIME   (a,t)   The time the last message was sent to the associated queue.

RTIME   (a,t)   The time the last message was received from the associated queue.

CTIME   (a,t)   The time when the associated entry was created or changed.

NATTCH   (a,o)   The number of processes attached to the associated shared memory segment.

SEGSZ   (a,b)   The size of the associated shared memory segment.

CPID   (a,p)   The process ID of the creator of the shared memory entry.

LPID   (a,p)   The process ID of the last process to attach or detach the shared memory segment.

ATIME   (a,t)   The time the last attach was completed to the associated shared memory segment.

DTIME   (a,t)   The time the last detach was completed on the associated shared memory segment.

NSEMS   (a,b)   The number of semaphores in the set associated with the semaphore entry.

OTIME   (a,t)   The time the last semaphore operation was completed on the set associated with the semaphore entry.

FILES

```
/stand/unix     system namelist
/dev/kmem       memory
/etc/passwd     user names
/etc/group      group names
```

NOTES

If the user specifies either the –C or –N flag, the real and effective *UID/GID* is set to the real *UID/GID* of the user invoking **ipcs**.

Things can change while **ipcs** is running; the information it gives is guaranteed to be accurate only when it was retrieved.

SEE ALSO

msgop(2), **semop**(2), **shmop**(2) in the *Programmer's Reference Manual*

NAME

ismpx – return windowing terminal state

SYNOPSIS

ismpx [-s]

DESCRIPTION

The **ismpx** command reports whether its standard input is connected to a multiplexed **xt** channel; that is, whether it's running under **layers** or not. It is useful for shell scripts that download programs to a windowing terminal.

ismpx prints **yes** and returns **0** if invoked under **layers**, and prints **no** and returns **1** otherwise.

-s   Do not print anything; just return the proper exit status.

SEE ALSO

layers(1), jwin(1), xt(7)

EXAMPLE

```
if ismpx -s
then
        jwin
fi
```

NAME

join – relational database operator

SYNOPSIS

join [*options*] *file1 file2*

DESCRIPTION

join forms, on the standard output, a join of the two relations specified by the lines of *file1* and *file2*. If *file1* is −, the standard input is used.

file1 and *file2* must be sorted in increasing ASCII collating sequence on the fields on which they are to be joined, normally the first in each line [see sort(1)].

There is one line in the output for each pair of lines in *file1* and *file2* that have identical join fields. The output line normally consists of the common field, then the rest of the line from *file1*, then the rest of the line from *file2*.

The default input field separators are blank, tab, or new-line. In this case, multiple separators count as one field separator, and leading separators are ignored. The default output field separator is a blank.

Some of the options below use the argument *n*. This argument should be a **1** or a **2** referring to either *file1* or *file2*, respectively. The following options are recognized:

−a*n*   In addition to the normal output, produce a line for each unpairable line in file *n*, where *n* is 1 or 2.

−e *s*   Replace empty output fields with string *s*.

−j*n m*   Join on the *m*th field of file *n*. If *n* is missing, use the *m*th field in each file. Fields are numbered starting with **1**.

−o *list*   Each output line includes the fields specified in *list*, each element of which has the form *n.m*, where *n* is a file number and *m* is a field number. The common field is not printed unless specifically requested.

−t*c*   Use character *c* as a separator (tab character). Every appearance of *c* in a line is significant. The character *c* is used as the field separator for both input and output.

EXAMPLE

The following command line will join the password file and the group file, matching on the numeric group ID, and outputting the login name, the group name and the login directory. It is assumed that the files have been sorted in ASCII collating sequence on the group ID fields.

        join −j1 4 −j2 3 −o 1.1 2.1 1.6 −t: /etc/passwd /etc/group

SEE ALSO

awk(1), comm(1), sort(1), uniq(1).

NOTES

With default field separation, the collating sequence is that of **sort** −b; with −t, the sequence is that of a plain sort.

The conventions of the **join**, **sort**, **comm**, **uniq**, and **awk** commands are wildly incongruous.

Filenames that are numeric may cause conflict when the **-o** option is used just before listing filenames.

NAME

jterm – reset layer of windowing terminal

SYNOPSIS

jterm

DESCRIPTION

The **jterm** command is used to reset a layer of a windowing terminal after downloading a terminal program that changes the terminal attributes of the layer. It is functional only under **layers**. In practice, it is most commonly used to restart the default terminal emulator after using an alternate one provided with a terminal-specific application package. For example, on the AT&T 630 MTG terminal, after executing the **xproof** command in a layer, issuing the **jterm** command will restart the default terminal emulator in that layer.

EXIT STATUS

Returns **0** upon successful completion, **1** otherwise.

NOTES

The layer that is reset is the one attached to standard error — that is, the window you are in when you type the **jterm** command.

SEE ALSO

layers(1)

NAME

jwin – print size of layer

SYNOPSIS

jwin

DESCRIPTION

jwin is functional only under **layers**(1) and is used to determine the size of the window associated with the current process. It prints the width and the height of the window in bytes (number of characters across and number of lines, respectively). For bit-mapped terminals only, it also prints the width and height of the window in bits.

EXIT STATUS

Returns **0** on successful completion, **1** otherwise.

DIAGNOSTICS

If **layers**(1) has not been invoked, an error message is printed:

```
jwin: not mpx
```

NOTE

The window whose size is printed is the one attached to standard input; that is, the window you are in when you type the **jwin** command.

SEE ALSO

layers(1)

EXAMPLE

```
jwin
bytes:  86 25
bits:   780 406
```

NAME

kcrash – examine system images

SYNOPSIS

kcrash [-w] [-k] *dumpfile* [*namelist*]

DESCRIPTION

The kcrash program is similar to the crash(1M) program in that it examines system crash dumps. Command line arguments to kcrash are *dumpfile* and *namelist*.

dumpfile is the file containing the system memory image. The default *dumpfile* is /dev/mem.

The text file *namelist* contains the symbol table information needed for symbolic access to the system memory image to be examined. The default *namelist* is /stand/unix.

Unlike crash, the kcrash command interface is based on the kernel debugger [see kdb(1M)]. All commands accepted by the kernel debugger can be used identically in kcrash, with the following exceptions:

I/O commands (such as in, out, and so forth) do not work.

Execution commands (such as go, tr, and so forth) do not work.

Multiprocessor commands (such as gos, ss, cpu, and so forth) do not work.

Instruction and memory breakpoint commands do not work.

Commands that modify memory (actually modify the crash dump file) work only if the -w flag is present in the command line.

If the -k flag is present, *dumpfile* can be /dev/mem, allowing kcrash to be used on the running system. In addition, the following commands work only in kcrash (not in the kernel debugger):

< *file* << *file*	Read and execute commands from the given file. Note that these commands are like dbcmd(1M) used with the kernel debugger.
! shell-command *!! shell-command*	Execute the given shell command.
q qq quit	Quit kcrash.

FILES

/crash/crash.*	crash dumps
/crash/macros/*	macros that are useful for kernel debugging
/unix	default *namelist*

SEE ALSO

crash(1M), kdb(1M), dbcmd(1M), and dbsym(1M)

NAME

kdb – kernel debugger

SYNOPSIS

kdb

DESCRIPTION

KDB is a kernel debugger that works like a Reverse Polish Notation (RPN) calculator. KDB can set breakpoints, display kernel stack traces and various kernel
structures, and modify the contents of memory, I/O, and registers. The debugger
supports basic arithmetic operations, conditional execution, variables, and macros.
KDB does conversions from a kernel symbol name to its virtual address, from a
virtual address to the value at that address, and from a virtual address to the
name of the nearest kernel symbol. You have a choice of different numeric bases,
address spaces, and operand sizes.

This is an advanced tool, only for those who are thoroughly familiar with the
UNIX kernel. Because UNIX systems differ, you could possibly damage your system by following some of the examples in this discussion.

You can invoke the debugger by using the **kdb** command or the
sysi86(SI86TODEMON) system call on all systems, <CTRL-Alt-d> (from the console only) on an AT bus system, or the interrupt character (from the console only)
on a Multibus system. In addition, KDB is entered automatically under various
conditions, such as panics and breakpoint traps. Any time the **kdb>>** prompt
appears, you are in the debugger. I/O is done via the console (kd), or a serial
terminal.

To exit the debugger, type <CTRL-d> or q.

When you exit and re-enter the debugger, its state is preserved, including the
contents of the value stack.

USING KDB AS A CALCULATOR

KDB operates as an RPN calculator, similar to **dc**(1). This calculator has a 32-
level value stack for storing results and intermediate values. Commands and
values you enter operate on the value stack, which is an internal data structure in
KDB. It has no connection with the kernel stack or any other stack in the system.

To use KDB, at the **kdb>>** prompt type one or more items (values or commands)
on a line. Separate items with spaces or tabs. Press <Enter> to end a line and
send its contents to KDB for processing. Each item is processed separately, from
left to right.

The values can be:

Numbers   Use positive or negative integers. Numbers must begin
                         with a digit, or a minus sign for negative numbers. Begin
                         octal numbers with "0o" and hex numbers with "0x". Oth-
                         erwise, numbers are assumed to be in the default base —
                         the default is hex, unless you change it. (See "Resetting
                         the Numeric Base" for instructions.)

Character constants   You can have KDB convert characters to a number by entering one to four characters inside single quotes. C-style escapes are supported in character constants.

Strings   Use C-style strings, enclosed in double quotes.

Kernel symbol names   When you type a kernel symbol name, its address is pushed onto the value stack.

When you enter a number or a string, it is pushed onto the value stack, becoming the new TOS (Top Of Stack). Values remain on the value stack until they are popped off as a result of a command.

In the descriptions below, [TOS] means the value on the top of the stack and [TOS-1] means the value just below it (pushed previously).

Stack Operations

KDB provides these commands for examining or changing the value stack:

stk	print all values on the stack
p	print [TOS]
dup	push [TOS]
pop	pop 1 value
clrstk	pop all values

stk   For example, starting with an empty value stack, this input:

    5 "xyzzy" 7 stk

displays the entire stack:

    5
    "xyzzy"
    7

p   At this point, the input:

    p

displays the top value on the stack, which is:

    7

The next example uses the **p** command to display the address of a kernel symbol. The input:

    lbolt p

produces an address something like this:

    D01821BC

dup   This command is useful when you want to use a value twice in a calculation. For example:

    5 3 * dup 2 + * p

would produce the output:

    FF

which is the value of (((5 * 3) + 2) * (5 * 3)).

`pop`   This command removes the top value from the value stack. For example, if this is the stack:

> 5
> **"xyzzy"**
> 7

the input:

> **pop stk**

removes the top value from the stack and displays the resulting stack:

> 5
> **"xyzzy"**

`clrstk` This command clears the value stack. Remember that the contents of the stack are saved when you exit and re-enter KDB.

Arithmetic Operations

You can perform arithmetic operations on the top values on the stack:

+	compute [TOS-1] + [TOS]; pop 2; push result
-	compute [TOS-1] - [TOS]; pop 2; push result
*	compute [TOS-1] * [TOS]; pop 2; push result
/	compute [TOS-1] / [TOS]; pop 2; push result
%	compute [TOS-1] % [TOS]; pop 2; push result
>>	compute [TOS-1] >> [TOS]; pop 2; push result
<<	compute [TOS-1] << [TOS]; pop 2; push result
<	compute [TOS-1] < [TOS]; pop 2; push result
>	compute [TOS-1] > [TOS]; pop 2; push result
==	compute [TOS-1] == [TOS]; pop 2; push result
!=	compute [TOS-1] != [TOS]; pop 2; push result
&	compute [TOS-1] & [TOS]; pop 2; push result
|	compute [TOS-1] | [TOS]; pop 2; push result
^	compute [TOS-1] ^ [TOS]; pop 2; push result
&&	compute [TOS-1] && [TOS]; pop 2; push result
||	compute [TOS-1] || [TOS]; pop 2; push result
!	replace [TOS] with ![TOS]
++	replace [TOS] with [TOS] + 1
--	replace [TOS] with [TOS] - 1

For example, this input (subtracting 5 from 7):

> **7 5 - p**

would produce this output:

> 2

The power of KDB's calculator feature lies in its ability to evaluate expressions like this:

> **callout 16 +**

This pushes the address of the callout table on the stack and adds 16 to it. If the size of a callout table entry is 16 bytes, the result of the calculation is the address of the second entry in the callout table. (Use the **size** command of **crash**(1M) to find the sizes of common system tables.)

WARNING: Make sure the divide operator (slash character) is both preceded and followed by spaces. If any other character appears next to the slash, it indicates a suffix instead of division.

READING AND WRITING TO MEMORY

These commands still operate like an RPN calculator, but they perform specific debugging operations instead of calculations. To examine and set the contents of memory (and I/O) use the commands:

r	replace [TOS] with the value at virtual address [TOS]
w	write [TOS-1] into virtual address [TOS]; pop 2
dump	show [TOS] bytes starting at virtual address [TOS-1]; pop 2

r For example, you can find the *value* of the (long) kernel variable, **lbolt**, by typing:

    lbolt r p

This puts the virtual address of **lbolt** on the stack, replaces it with the value found at that address, and prints the result.

w To change the value of **lbolt** to 2000, type:

    2000 lbolt w

This writes 2000 at **lbolt's** virtual address.

You could increment **lbolt** by typing:

    lbolt r ++ lbolt w

This puts the virtual address of **lbolt** on the stack, replaces it with the value found at that address, adds 1 to the value, and writes the result at **lbolt's** virtual address.

dump This command displays a range of memory, both in hex and ASCII. For example, if you typed:

    putbuf 10 dump

which shows 10 bytes, starting at the virtual address of **putbuf**, you would see something like:

    6572206C 6D206C61 726F6D65 .... D0108C60 l real memor....

In each line, the block of four values on the left shows the values of 16 bytes, displayed as four 4-byte longwords in hex. The dots represent values outside of the requested range. (**dump** may also display question marks here; that means the address is invalid). The next column is the address of the first of the 16 bytes. The last column is the same 16 bytes displayed in ASCII. Dots here represent values outside the requested range or unprintable characters.

Suffixes

Suffixes can be appended to many KDB commands. They always begin with the slash character (/).

WARNING: Don't leave spaces before or after the slash character. When the slash is preceded and followed by a space, it indicates division instead of a suffix.

Operand-size suffixes

The **r**, **w** and **dump** commands can also work with units of bytes and words, as well as the default longs. To do this, append one of these suffixes to the command:

/b   byte
/w   word (2 bytes)
/l   long (4 bytes)—this is the default.

For example, to display the value of a short (2-byte) variable at address 0xD0008120, type:

    0xD0008120 r/w p

Entering the **dump** command with **/b** displays 16 1-byte values per line, with **/w** displays eight 2-byte values per line, and with **/l** (or nothing) displays four 4-byte values per line.

Address-space suffixes

The **r**, **w** and **dump** commands, by default, work with kernel virtual addresses. You can change to physical addresses, I/O addresses, or user process virtual addresses by appending one of these suffixes to the command:

/k   kernel virtual — the default
/p   physical
/io   I/O port
/u#   user process number # virtual (# is a process
        slot number in hex)

/p   For example, to dump 40 (hex) bytes in longword format from physical address 2000, type:

            2000 40 dump/p

        The default address is kernel virtual, so the **/p** suffix is required for the physical address. Note that an operand-size suffix is not required, because long is the default.

/io   For example, to read from port 300 (in bytes) and display the result, type:

            300 r/io/b p

/u#   For example, to dump 20 longwords from process 16's u area at an offset of 1000, type:

            1000 u + 20 dump/u16

Suffix formats.
Address-space suffixes can be combined with operand-size suffixes; only the first slash is required. For example, to do the read from I/O port 300 shown above, any of these command lines is acceptable:

```
300 r/io/b
300 r/b/io
300 r/iob
300 r/bio
```

Suffixes can also be attached directly to an address as shorthand for "read and print." Thus, `2000 r/p p` can be shortened to `2000/p`.

Since the default address-space is kernel virtual, the common operation of "read and print from kernel virtual" can be even further shortened. Type `lbolt/` to read and print the value of the (long) kernel variable, `lbolt`.

DISPLAYING AND WRITING TO REGISTERS

You can examine the CPU's general registers (and a couple of pseudo-registers) with these commands:

%eax	push the contents of 32-bit register eax
%ebx	push the contents of 32-bit register ebx
%ecx	push the contents of 32-bit register ecx
%edx	push the contents of 32-bit register edx
%esi	push the contents of 32-bit register esi
%edi	push the contents of 32-bit register edi
%ebp	push the contents of 32-bit register ebp
%esp	push the contents of 32-bit register esp
%eip	push the contents of 32-bit register eip
%efl	push the contents of 32-bit register efl
%cs	push the contents of 16-bit register cs
%ds	push the contents of 16-bit register ds
%es	push the contents of 16-bit register es
%fs	push the contents of 16-bit register fs
%gs	push the contents of 16-bit register gs
%err	push the error number
%trap	push the trap number
%ax	push the contents of 16-bit register ax
%bx	push the contents of 16-bit register bx
%cx	push the contents of 16-bit register cx
%dx	push the contents of 16-bit register dx
%si	push the contents of 16-bit register si
%di	push the contents of 16-bit register di
%bp	push the contents of 16-bit register bp
%sp	push the contents of 16-bit register sp
%ip	push the contents of 16-bit register ip
%fl	push the contents of 16-bit register fl
%al	push the contents of 8-bit register al
%ah	push the contents of 8-bit register ah
%bl	push the contents of 8-bit register bl

%bh	push the contents of 8-bit register **bh**
%cl	push the contents of 8-bit register **cl**
%ch	push the contents of 8-bit register **ch**
%dl	push the contents of 8-bit register **dl**
%dh	push the contents of 8-bit register **dh**

You can modify the values of general-purpose registers with these commands:

w%eax	write [TOS] into 32-bit register **eax**; pop 1
w%ebx	write [TOS] into 32-bit register **ebx**; pop 1
w%ecx	write [TOS] into 32-bit register **ecx**; pop 1
w%edx	write [TOS] into 32-bit register **edx**; pop 1
w%esi	write [TOS] into 32-bit register **esi**; pop 1
w%edi	write [TOS] into 32-bit register **edi**; pop 1
w%ebp	write [TOS] into 32-bit register **ebp**; pop 1
w%esp	write [TOS] into 32-bit register **esp**; pop 1
w%eip	write [TOS] into 32-bit register **eip**; pop 1
w%efl	write [TOS] into 32-bit register **efl**; pop 1
w%cs	write [TOS] into 16-bit register **cs**; pop 1
w%ds	write [TOS] into 16-bit register **ds**; pop 1
w%es	write [TOS] into 16-bit register **es**; pop 1
w%fs	write [TOS] into 16-bit register **fs**; pop 1
w%gs	write [TOS] into 16-bit register **gs**; pop 1
w%err	write [TOS] into the error number pseudo-register; pop 1
w%trap	write [TOS] into the trap number pseudo-register; pop 1
w%ax	write [TOS] into 16-bit register **ax**; pop 1
w%bx	write [TOS] into 16-bit register **bx**; pop 1
w%cx	write [TOS] into 16-bit register **cx**; pop 1
w%dx	write [TOS] into 16-bit register **dx**; pop 1
w%si	write [TOS] into 16-bit register **si**; pop 1
w%di	write [TOS] into 16-bit register **di**; pop 1
w%bp	write [TOS] into 16-bit register **bp**; pop 1
w%sp	write [TOS] into 16-bit register **sp**; pop 1
w%ip	write [TOS] into 16-bit register **ip**; pop 1
w%fl	write [TOS] into 16-bit register **fl**; pop 1
w%al	write [TOS] into 8-bit register **al**; pop 1
w%ah	write [TOS] into 8-bit register **ah**; pop 1
w%bl	write [TOS] into 8-bit register **bl**; pop 1
w%bh	write [TOS] into 8-bit register **bh**; pop 1
w%cl	write [TOS] into 8-bit register **cl**; pop 1
w%ch	write [TOS] into 8-bit register **ch**; pop 1
w%dl	write [TOS] into 8-bit register **dl**; pop 1
w%dh	write [TOS] into 8-bit register **dh**; pop 1

Register Sets

The commands listed above can also be used to access specific register sets. Multiple sets of general registers may have been saved on the kernel stack (one for each interrupt, trap, and so on). For more information see "Printing Kernel Stack Traces."

Register sets are numbered from 0 to 19, with 0 being the current (most recent) set. By default, the general-register commands use register set 0, but you can override this with a *register-set suffix:*

> /rs#   register set number #

Note that by combining suffixes, you can access any register of any process. For example, you can get the **eax** register from process 5's register set 1 by typing:

> %eax/u5rs1

to push the contents of that register (**%eax**) in register set 1 (/**rs1**) of user process 5 (/**u5**).

CPU Control Registers

In addition to the general registers, you can examine the values of CPU control registers with these commands:

> cr0   push the contents of register **cr0**
> cr2   push the contents of register **cr2**
> cr3   push the contents of register **cr3**

CREATING DEBUGGER VARIABLES

KDB allows you to create named variables that are stored in the debugger and hold debugger values (numbers or strings). Two KDB commands apply to variables:

> = *variable*   store [TOS] in [variable]; pop 1
> **vars**   show values of debugger variables

= *variable*   This command assigns a value to a debugger variable. For example:

> 5 = abc

creates the variable **abc** if it does not exist, and sets the variable equal to 5. Now whenever you use the variable name, its value is pushed onto the stack. For example:

> abc abc + 2 - p

(5 + 5 - 2) will yield **8**.

Note that variable names share the same namespace as debugger macros and kernel global symbols.

vars   To look at all the existing variables, use the **vars** command. Variables are shown in the following format:

> *name = value*

The vars command also lists macros, in this format:

> *name :: value*

SETTING BREAKPOINTS

Set and modify breakpoints with these commands:

> B   set breakpoint #[TOS] at address [TOS-1]; pop 2
> -or-   set breakpoint #[TOS] at address [TOS-2] with command string

	[TOS-1]; pop 3
b	set first free breakpoint address [TOS]; pop 1
-or-	set first free breakpoint at address [TOS-1] with command string [TOS]; pop 2
brkoff	disable breakpoint #[TOS]; pop 1
brkon	re-enable breakpoint #[TOS]; pop 1
brksoff	disable all breakpoints
brkson	re-enable all (disabled) breakpoints
trace	set breakpoint #[TOS] trace count to [TOS-1]; pop 2
clrbrk	clear breakpoint #[TOS]; pop 1
clrbrks	clear all breakpoints
curbrk	push the current breakpoint number, or -1 if not entered from a breakpoint
?brk	show current breakpoint settings

You can have up to 20 breakpoints, numbered 0 through 19, set at one time.

B and b The **B** command lets you set specific breakpoints, while the **b** command automatically picks the first un-set breakpoint.

This example sets breakpoint 3 at a specific address:

`0xD0125098 3 B`

Normally, you'll just set a breakpoint at a certain address. For example:

`read b`

This sets an instruction breakpoint at the beginning of the kernel **read** routine, using the next available breakpoint number. When the specified address is executed (after exiting from the debugger), you enter the debugger again, with a message indicating which breakpoint was triggered.

Debugger command strings can be added to the breakpoint commands. Enter a quoted string of commands after the address:

`read "stack" b`

which is used as a series of debugger commands that are executed when the breakpoint is triggered. If there are several items in the string, separate them with spaces:

`ie6unitdata_req "300 r/bio p" b`

After these commands are executed, you are prompted for debugger commands, as usual, unless the **q** (**quit**) command is executed in the command string.

You can append breakpoint-type suffixes to the breakpoint commands (**B** and **b**). By default, breakpoints are "instruction" breakpoints, which trigger when the specified address is executed. The suffixes cause breakpoints to trigger on data accesses instead. The breakpoint-type suffixes are:

/a	data access breakpoint
/m	data modify breakpoint
/i	instruction execution breakpoint—this is the default

With access and modify breakpoints, you can also use operand-size suffixes to control the size of the address range that will trigger the breakpoint. The default is /l (4 bytes); you can also use /w (word) and /b (byte). (See the earlier discussion of suffixes under "Reading and Writing to Memory" for more information.)

brkoff and brkon

These commands let you temporarily disable and re-enable a breakpoint, instead of clearing it with clrbrk and then re-entering it later. This is especially handy for breakpoints with command strings.

trace

This command sets a trace count for a breakpoint. This causes the debugger to just print a message and decrement the count when the breakpoint is triggered, instead of entering the debugger, until the count reaches zero. Commands attached to the breakpoint are not executed.

?brk

Use this command to determine the current breakpoint settings. Each set breakpoint is displayed, with (1) the breakpoint number, the address (both (2) in hex and (3) symbolic), (4) the current state, and (5) the type:

```
0: 0xD003907C(read) ON /i
1      2            3  4  5
```

The possible states are:

ON	set and enabled
DISABLED	set, but currently disabled
OFF	un-set (these breakpoints are not displayed by ?brk)

The possible types (in this example /i) are the same as the breakpoint-type suffixes described earlier.

If a breakpoint has a non-zero trace count, that is displayed after the breakpoint state. If a breakpoint has a command string, it is displayed at the end of the line. For example, with a count of 5 and a stack command, the above breakpoint would display as:

```
0: 0xD003907C(read) ON  0x5 /i "stack"
```

SINGLE-STEPPING THROUGH INSTRUCTIONS

You can use these commands for single-stepping:

s	single step 1 instruction
ss	single step [TOS] instructions; pop 1
S	single step 1 instruction (passing calls)
SS	single step [TOS] instructions (passing calls); pop 1

s and ss single-step all instructions. S and SS single-step all instructions except call instructions. They don't step down into the called routine, but instead skip ahead to the return from the call, treating the whole subroutine sequence as a single instruction.

EXAMINING KERNEL DATA STRUCTURES

KDB provides commands for looking at certain kernel structures:

ps	show process information
sleeping	show list of sleeping processes
pinode	print s5 inode at address [TOS]; pop 1
puinode	print ufs inode at address [TOS]; pop 1
pprnode	print /proc inode at address [TOS]; pop 1
psnode	print snode at address [TOS]; pop 1
pvfs	print vfs struct at address [TOS]; pop 1
pvnode	print vnode at address [TOS]; pop 1

The **sleeping** command shows sleeping processes with their process table slot numbers and the channels on which they are waiting. This information can be used with the **call** and **pstack** commands.

The **ps** command shows information about each active process in the system. This information includes process IDs, flags, states, and command names. The current process is marked with an asterisk (*****) after its state code.

PRINTING KERNEL STACK TRACES

KDB provides the following commands to look at kernel stack traces:

stack	kernel stack trace for the current process
pstack	kernel stack trace for process [TOS]; pop 1
stackargs	set max # arguments in stack trace to [TOS]; pop 1
stackdump	show contents of kernel stack in hex

Note that the argument to **pstack** can be specified either as a process table slot number, the address of the process structure, or **-1** for the current process. (**-1 pstack** is equivalent to the **stack** command.)

The output of **stack** and **pstack** have the same format. A typical stack trace (for the current process, entered via <CTRL-Alt-d>) looks like this:

```
DEBUGGER ENTERED FROM USER REQUEST
  kdcksysrq(D101FD40 D00DE624 81)..........ebp:E0000D30  ret:D008F592
*kdintr+0x186(1 0).......................ebp:E0000D74  ret:D0011A3A
INTERRUPT 0x1 from 158:D001218A (ebp:E0000D84)
    eax:      8 ebx:       0 ecx:FFFFFFFF edx:       8 efl: 246 ds:160
    esi:D00EDDD0 edi:D106BC00 esp:E0000DC8 ebp:E0000DE0 regset:0 es:160
  idle(0 D00EDDD0 D106BC00)...............(ebp:E0000DC4) ret:D006F11F
  pswtch(D002464C 0 D00F9090).............ebp:E0000DE0  ret:D00122ED
  swtch(0 D00F9090 D101A160)..............(ebp:E0000DE4) ret:D002464C
  sleep(D0038B0C 14 D00BCA3C).............ebp:E0000DFC  ret:D0038D6F
  fsflush(0 E0000002 E0000002)............ebp:E0000E38  ret:D001E24B
  main+0x5FB().............................ebp:E0000E70
```

The stack trace shows a history of which routine called which other routine, up until the point the debugger was entered (or in the case of a non-current process, until the process was context-switched out).

The most-recently-entered routine is shown on the first line. In the example, the debugger was entered from **kdcksysrq**, which, in turn, was called by **kdintr**; **idle** was called from **pswtch**, and so on. The stack trace ends at the point the kernel was entered from user mode. In the case of a system process (as shown here) where there is no user mode, the stack trace ends at the call from **main**.

Routine Trace Format

The trace for each routine has four parts: (1) its address, (2) the arguments passed to it, (3) the value of its **ebp** register, and (4) its return address. For example:

```
fsflush(0 E0000002 E0000002)............ebp:E0000E38  ret:D001E24B
   1    ----------2---------            ------3-----   ------4-----
```

Address.

> The address that was called usually appears in symbolic form. A routine name may also include:

An offset (a plus sign (+) and a hex number): ***kdintr+0x186**
> The offset may mean that the actual address called was somewhere past the start of the indicated routine. This will most likely happen if a subroutine was declared "static." Since the debugger only has access to global symbols, it finds the nearest preceding global symbol.
>
> The offset may also mean that the exact address called cannot be determined. The address displayed in this case is the return address into this routine from the routine it called. This will most likely happen if this routine was called indirectly via a function pointer.

An asterisk (*): ***kdintr+0x186**
> This means the routine was called indirectly. There is insufficient information in the stack format to be 100% sure of the correctness of indirect call traces.

A tilde (~)
> This is used where there is some uncertainty in the stack trace that did not arise from indirect calls.

Whenever you see an asterisk or a tilde in a stack trace, there is a small chance that some part of the stack trace from that point on is incorrect.

Arguments.

> The arguments passed to the routine appear as a list of hex numbers, enclosed in parentheses. Since the actual number of arguments passed cannot be determined, KDB assumes that each routine has no more than a certain maximum number of arguments. The default is three, but you can change it with the **stackargs** command. If a routine actually has:

Fewer arguments than displayed:
> Only the first ones are real. In rare cases when the debugger can deduce that a routine could not have been called with the maximum number of arguments (because there isn't enough room on the stack), it displays

only the maximum possible number of arguments. In the above stack
trace, the call to **kdintr** is shown with only two arguments (1 0).

More arguments than displayed:
Increase the number with **stackargs** and then display the stack trace
again, or dump out a portion of the stack directly in order to see all the
arguments (continue to the next section for details).

ebp register.
The value of the **ebp** register inside the routine is shown as a hex number
following **ebp:**. This value can be used as a "frame pointer" to access
arguments and local variables for the routine. The following diagram
illustrates the stack layout.

```
                         |          . . .            |
                         +---------------------------+
    [EBP] + 0xC  | argument 2                |
                         +---------------------------+
    [EBP] + 8    | argument 1                |
                         +---------------------------+
    [EBP] + 4    | return address            |
                         +---------------------------+
    [EBP]  --->  | saved EBP from caller     |
                         +---------------------------+
    [EBP] - 4    | local or saved register   |
                         +---------------------------+
    [EBP] - 8    | local or saved register   |
                         +---------------------------+
                         |          . . .            |
```

For example, if you want to see all the arguments to a routine that takes five
arguments, find its **ebp** value from the stack trace — say **0xE0000E0C** — and
enter these commands:

    0xE0000E0C 8 + 5 4 * dump

or, more succinctly:

    0xE0000E14 14 dump

Any **ebp** value in parentheses is a computed value (see the **ebp** values for **idle**
and **switch** in the example). In these cases, due to code optimization or partial
execution, the **ebp** value has not been set up for one or more routines. KDB computes the value **ebp** ought to have had and displays it in parentheses.

Return address.
This is the address this routine returns to in its caller. It is shown as a
hex number following **ret:**.

Trap Frames
In addition to lines for each routine, stack traces will often include "trap frames"
created when an event causes suspension of current processing, saving all register
values on the stack. Typical events are interrupts, hardware exceptions, and

system calls. Trap frames are three lines each, starting with an upper-case, non-indented keyword (like INTERRUPT in the example). The next two lines contain the values of the registers at the time the event occurred. The first line of a trap frame is in one of these formats:

```
INTERRUPT 0x1 from 158:D001218A (ebp:E0000D84)
TRAP 0x1(err 0x0)from 158:D001218A (ebp:E0000D94,ss:esp:1F:80468E8)
SYSTEM CALL from 158:D001218A (ebp: E0000D94, ss:esp: 1F:80468E8)
SIGNAL RETURN from 158:D001218A (ebp: E0000D94, ss:esp: 1F:80468E8)
```

These represent interrupts, hardware exception traps, system calls, and returns from old-style signal handlers, respectively. The number after **INTERRUPT** is the interrupt vector number (IRQ). The number after **TRAP** is the hardware exception number; the most common are **0x1** for breakpoint traps and **0xE** for page faults.

The colon-separated numbers after the word **from** are the segment and offset (**cs** and **eip**) at the time the event occurred. The values in parentheses show the **ebp** value for the beginning of the trap frame, and the user stack pointer segment and offset at the time the event occurred. The user stack information is only displayed if the trap frame is for an entry into the kernel from user mode.

RESETTING THE NUMERIC BASE

If you don't start numbers with "0o" (for octal) or "0x" (for hex), KDB assumes they are in the default numeric base. Initially, the defaults for both input and output are set to 16 (hex), but you can use these commands to change them:

ibase	set default input base to [TOS]; pop 1
ibinary	set default input base to 2
ioctal	set default input base to 8
idecimal	set default input base to 10
ihex	set default input base to 16
obase	set output base to [TOS]; pop 1
ooctal	set output base to 8
odecimal	set output base to 10
ohex	set output base to 16

CONVERTING ADDRESS SPACES

Use these commands to convert a virtual address to a physical address:

kvtop	convert kernel virtual address [TOS] to physical
uvtop	convert user proc #[TOS] address [TOS-1] to physical; pop 1

DOING CONDITIONAL EXECUTION

KDB provides two commands for conditional execution:

then	if [TOS] = 0, skip to **endif**; pop 1
endif	end scope of **then** command

In other words, a sequence like:

```
<condition> then <commands> endif
```

executes **<commands>** if and only if the **<condition>** is true (non-zero).

These are mostly useful for macros and breakpoint command strings. For example, imagine you wish to set a breakpoint for when the function **inb** is called with **2E** as its first argument. Use the following command:

```
inb "%esp 4 + r 2E != then q" b
```

This says to set a breakpoint at **inb**, but enter the debugger only if the contents of **(%esp+4)** are equal to **2E**. This works because **esp** points to the return address on the stack, and the longword after that is the first argument. For the second argument, you would add 8 instead of 4 (see the "Printing Kernel Stack Traces" section for details of the stack layout).

If you do a **?brk** command, the display for that breakpoint includes the string of debugger commands:

```
0: 0xD003907C(inb) ON  /i "%esp 4 + r 2E != then q"
```

CALLING A KERNEL FUNCTION

Use this command to call an arbitrary kernel function:

> **call**   call the function at address [TOS-1] with [TOS] arguments, given by [TOS-([TOS]+1)], ... [TOS-2]; pop [TOS]+2

To call **psignal**() with two arguments, the current process and **9**, type:

```
curproc r 9 psignal 2 call
```

curproc r gives the value of the current process, the first argument, and **9** is the second argument. **psignal** is converted into the address at which that function can be called, and **2** specifies the number of arguments to pass to **psignal**().

DOING A SYSTEM DUMP

This command causes a system dump and forces a reboot:

> **sysdump**   cause a system dump

All of memory and the current state is dumped to the dump partition on the disk, so you can use **crash**(1M) to do a postmortem.

MISCELLANEOUS COMMANDS

Some miscellaneous KDB commands are:

> **findsym**   print kernel symbol with address closest to [TOS]; pop 1
> **dis**   disassemble [TOS] instructions starting at address [TOS-1]; pop 2
> **nonverbose** turn verbose mode off
> **verbose**   turn verbose mode on
> **newdebug** switch to another debugger on next debugger entry
> **help**   print a help message
> **?**   print a help message (same as **help**)
> **cmds**   print a list of all debugger commands

WRITING MACROS

KDB provides the ability to assign a string of commands to a single new command name, called a macro. When a debugging task involves repeating the same set of commands many times (possibly doing other things in between), it is easier to define a macro and use it in place of the whole set of commands.

These commands are used for macros:

```
:: macro    define [macro] as command string [TOS];  pop 1
P           print [TOS] in raw form;  pop 1
PP          print [TOS] values in raw form,
            from [TOS-[TOS]], ... [TOS-1]; pop [TOS]+1
vars        show values of debugger macros and variables
```

: : macro   Use this command to define macros. For example:

```
"curproc r 16 - p" :: newaddr
```

Note that macro names share the same namespace as debugger variables and kernel global symbols.

P and PP   These commands are provided to aid in writing macros. **P** and **PP** print values in raw form, without the embellishments provided by the **p** command, such as quotes around strings and automatic newlines after each value. This allows complete control over formatting. For example, the input:

```
"The value of curproc is " curproc r ".\n" 3 PP
```

might produce the output:

```
The value of curproc is 0xD1011E80.
```

To put something like this into a macro means putting strings inside strings, so you'll have to escape the inner quotes:

```
"\"The value of curproc is \" curproc r \".\n\" 3 PP" ::
pcurproc
```

vars   Use this command to show the macro definitions. Macros are shown in this format:

name **::** *value*

Note that the **vars** command also shows the values of variables, in this format:

name **=** *value*

EXECUTING DEBUGGER COMMANDS AT BOOT TIME

KDB allows you to specify an arbitrary command sequence to be executed at boot time, when the system is coming up (specifically, from **main()** at the time of the **io_start** routines). You can do this by writing the commands into the file **$ROOT/etc/conf/cf.d/kdb.rc**, then rebuilding the kernel with **idbuild**.

Instead of rebuilding the kernel with **idbuild**, you can modify the KDB information in an already-built kernel by typing the command:

```
unixsyms -i /etc/conf/cf.d/kdb.rc /unix
```

At boot time, after the (possibly blank) string is executed, the system enters KDB at the **kdb>>** prompt, unless a **q** command was executed as part of the string — just like conditional breakpoints. (A non-existent or zero-length **kdb.rc** file acts as a single **q** command, so KDB is not entered.)

USING A SERIAL TERMINAL

KDB can be used from a serial terminal as well as the console. This is particularly useful if you are trying to debug a scenario that involves graphics or multiple virtual terminals on the console.

Before you attempt to use the debugger from a serial terminal, make sure there is a **getty** or **ttymon** running on it. It may be either logged in or waiting at the login prompt. This ensures that the baud rate and other parameters are properly set.

You can switch from the console to a terminal, and vice-versa, with the **newterm** command. This immediately switches you to the new terminal. The debugger continues to use this terminal until you give it the **newterm** command again, even if you exit and re-enter KDB.

The **newterm** command does not take an argument. On a 386, the serial terminal is assumed to be **tty00**, the terminal on the com1 port. You can change the device used by editing the **/etc/conf/pack.d/kdb-util/space.c** file, rebuilding the kernel and rebooting. If the terminal is attached to the com2 port, set the device to **tty01** by changing all occurrences of **asyputchar** and **asygetchar** to **asyputchar2** and **asygetchar2**, respectively, and changing the minor number of the device from 0 to 1. The first lines of 386-specific code should look like this:

```
#ifdef AT386
int asyputchar2(), asygetchar2();
static struct conssw asysw = {
     asyputchar2,    1,    asygetchar2
};
#endif
```

To use terminals on both com1 and com2 ports, you can set up **newterm** to cycle from the console to **tty00** to **tty01** and back to the console. Edit all the 386-specific code in the **space.c** file to look like this:

```
#ifdef AT386
int asyputchar(), asygetchar();
int asyputchar2(), asygetchar2();
static struct conssw asysw = {
     asyputchar,    0,    asygetchar
};
static struct conssw asysw2 = {
     asyputchar2,    1,    asygetchar2
};
#endif
         .
         .
         .

#ifdef AT386
     &asysw,
     &asysw2,
#endif
```

Once you exit from KDB, you can invoke it again from either the console or a serial terminal. Use the **kdb** command to invoke the debugger from a terminal; <CTRL-Alt-d> only works from the console. Regardless of where you invoke KDB, its I/O appears where you directed it during the last KDB session.

ENTERING THE DEBUGGER FROM A DRIVER

If you are debugging a device driver or another part of the kernel, you can directly invoke the kernel debugger by including this code in your driver:

```
#include <sys/xdebug.h>

(*cdebugger) (DR_OTHER, NO_FRAME);
```

DR_OTHER tells the debugger that the reason for entering is "other." See **sys/xdebug.h** for a list of other reason codes.

Note that this mechanism cannot be used for debugging early kernel startup code or driver **init** routines, since the debugger cannot be used until its **init** routine (**kdb_init**) has been called.

DISABLING THE <CTRL-Alt-d> SEQUENCE

As a security feature, KDB can only be called from the console via <CTRL-Alt-d> if the **kdb_security** flag was set to 0 when the kernel was built. To disable the <CTRL-Alt-d> key sequence, reset the **kdb_security** flag by using **/etc/conf/bin/idtune** to change the KDBSECURITY tunable to 1. Note that the flag setting does not affect the **kdb** command.

COMMAND SUMMARY

+	compute [TOS-1] + [TOS]; pop 2; push result
-	compute [TOS-1] - [TOS]; pop 2; push result
*	compute [TOS-1] * [TOS]; pop 2; push result
/	compute [TOS-1] / [TOS]; pop 2; push result
%	compute [TOS-1] % [TOS]; pop 2; push result
>>	compute [TOS-1] >> [TOS]; pop 2; push result
<<	compute [TOS-1] << [TOS]; pop 2; push result
<	compute [TOS-1] < [TOS]; pop 2; push result
>	compute [TOS-1] > [TOS]; pop 2; push result
==	compute [TOS-1] == [TOS]; pop 2; push result
!=	compute [TOS-1] != [TOS]; pop 2; push result
&	compute [TOS-1] & [TOS]; pop 2; push result
|	compute [TOS-1] | [TOS]; pop 2; push result
^	compute [TOS-1] ^ [TOS]; pop 2; push result
&&	compute [TOS-1] && [TOS]; pop 2; push result
||	compute [TOS-1] || [TOS]; pop 2; push result
!	replace [TOS] with ![TOS]
++	replace [TOS] with [TOS] + 1
--	replace [TOS] with [TOS] - 1
%eax	push the contents of 32-bit register **eax**
%ebx	push the contents of 32-bit register **ebx**
%ecx	push the contents of 32-bit register **ecx**

%edx	push the contents of 32-bit register **edx**
%esi	push the contents of 32-bit register **esi**
%edi	push the contents of 32-bit register **edi**
%ebp	push the contents of 32-bit register **ebp**
%esp	push the contents of 32-bit register **esp**
%eip	push the contents of 32-bit register **eip**
%efl	push the contents of 32-bit register **efl**
%cs	push the contents of 16-bit register **cs**
%ds	push the contents of 16-bit register **ds**
%es	push the contents of 16-bit register **es**
%fs	push the contents of 16-bit register **fs**
%gs	push the contents of 16-bit register **gs**
%err	push the error number
%trap	push the trap number
%ax	push the contents of 16-bit register **ax**
%bx	push the contents of 16-bit register **bx**
%cx	push the contents of 16-bit register **cx**
%dx	push the contents of 16-bit register **dx**
%si	push the contents of 16-bit register **si**
%di	push the contents of 16-bit register **di**
%bp	push the contents of 16-bit register **bp**
%sp	push the contents of 16-bit register **sp**
%ip	push the contents of 16-bit register **ip**
%fl	push the contents of 16-bit register **fl**
%al	push the contents of 8-bit register **al**
%ah	push the contents of 8-bit register **ah**
%bl	push the contents of 8-bit register **bl**
%bh	push the contents of 8-bit register **bh**
%cl	push the contents of 8-bit register **cl**
%ch	push the contents of 8-bit register **ch**
%dl	push the contents of 8-bit register **dl**
%dh	push the contents of 8-bit register **dh**
= variable	store [TOS] in [variable]; pop 1
:: macro	define [macro] as command string [TOS]; pop 1
?	print a help message (same as **help**)
?brk	show current breakpoint settings
B	set breakpoint #[TOS] at address [TOS-1]; pop 2 -or- set brkpoint #[TOS] at address [TOS-2] w/command string [TOS-1]; pop 3
b	set 1st free breakpoint address [TOS]; pop 1 -or- set 1st free brkpoint at address [TOS-1] w/command string [TOS]; pop 2
brkoff	disable breakpoint #[TOS]; pop 1
brkon	re-enable breakpoint #[TOS]; pop 1
brksoff	disable all breakpoints
brkson	re-enable all (disabled) breakpoints
call	call the function at address [TOS-1] with [TOS] arguments, given by [TOS-([TOS]+1)], ... [TOS-2]; pop [TOS]+2

clrbrk	clear breakpoint #[TOS]; pop 1
clrbrks	clear all breakpoints
clrstk	pop all values
cmds	print a list of all debugger commands
cr0	push the contents of register cr0
cr2	push the contents of register cr2
cr3	push the contents of register cr3
curbrk	push the current breakpoint number, or -1 if not entered from a breakpoint
dis	disassemble [TOS] instructions starting at address [TOS-1]; pop 2
dump	show [TOS] bytes starting at virtual address [TOS-1]; pop 2
dup	push [TOS]
endif	end scope of **then** command
findsym	print kernel symbol with address closest to [TOS]; pop 1
help	print a help message
ibase	set default input base to [TOS]; pop 1
ibinary	set default input base to 2
ioctal	set default input base to 8
idecimal	set default input base to 10
ihex	set default input base to 16
kvtop	convert kernel virtual addr [TOS] to physical
newterm	alternate debugger I/O between console and tty00
newdebug	switch to another debugger on next debugger entry
nonverbose	turn verbose mode off
obase	set output base to [TOS]; pop 1
odecimal	set output base to 10
ohex	set output base to 16
ooctal	set output base to 8
P	print [TOS] in raw form; pop 1
p	print [TOS]
PP	print [TOS] values in raw form, from [TOS-[TOS]], ... [TOS-1]; pop [TOS]+1
pinode	print s5 inode at address [TOS]; pop 1
pop	pop 1 value
pprnode	print /proc inode at address [TOS]; pop 1
psnode	print snode at address [TOS]; pop 1
ps	show process information
pstack	kernel stack trace for process [TOS]; pop 1
pvfs	print vfs struct at address [TOS]; pop 1
pvnode	print vnode at address [TOS]; pop 1
puinode	print ufs inode at address [TOS]; pop 1
q	quit—exit from the debugger
r	replace [TOS] with the value at virtual address [TOS]
S	single step 1 instruction (passing calls)
s	single step 1 instruction
sleeping	show list of sleeping processes

ss	single step [TOS] instructions (passing calls); pop 1
ss	single step [TOS] instructions; pop 1
stack	kernel stack trace for the current process
stackargs	set max # arguments in stack trace to [TOS]; pop 1
stackdump	show contents of kernel stack in hex
stk	print all values on the stack
sysdump	cause a system dump
then	if [TOS] = 0, skip to **endif**; pop 1
trace	set breakpoint #[TOS] trace count to [TOS-1]; pop 2
uvtop	convert user process #[TOS] address [TOS-1] to physical; pop 1
vars	show values of debugger variables
verbose	turn verbose mode on
w	write [TOS-1] into virtual address [TOS]; pop 2
w%eax	write [TOS] into 32-bit register **eax**; pop 1
w%ebx	write [TOS] into 32-bit register **ebx**; pop 1
w%ecx	write [TOS] into 32-bit register **ecx**; pop 1
w%edx	write [TOS] into 32-bit register **edx**; pop 1
w%esi	write [TOS] into 32-bit register **esi**; pop 1
w%edi	write [TOS] into 32-bit register **edi**; pop 1
w%ebp	write [TOS] into 32-bit register **ebp**; pop 1
w%esp	write [TOS] into 32-bit register **esp**; pop 1
w%eip	write [TOS] into 32-bit register **eip**; pop 1
w%efl	write [TOS] into 32-bit register **efl**; pop 1
w%cs	write [TOS] into 16-bit register **cs**; pop 1
w%ds	write [TOS] into 16-bit register **ds**; pop 1
w%es	write [TOS] into 16-bit register **es**; pop 1
w%fs	write [TOS] into 16-bit register **fs**; pop 1
w%gs	write [TOS] into 16-bit register **gs**; pop 1
w%err	write [TOS] into the error number pseudo-register; pop 1
w%trap	write [TOS] into the trap number pseudo-register; pop 1
w%ax	write [TOS] into 16-bit register **ax**; pop 1
w%bx	write [TOS] into 16-bit register **bx**; pop 1
w%cx	write [TOS] into 16-bit register **cx**; pop 1
w%dx	write [TOS] into 16-bit register **dx**; pop 1
w%si	write [TOS] into 16-bit register **si**; pop 1
w%di	write [TOS] into 16-bit register **di**; pop 1
w%bp	write [TOS] into 16-bit register **bp**; pop 1
w%sp	write [TOS] into 16-bit register **sp**; pop 1
w%ip	write [TOS] into 16-bit register **ip**; pop 1
w%fl	write [TOS] into 16-bit register **fl**; pop 1
w%al	write [TOS] into 8-bit register **al**; pop 1
w%ah	write [TOS] into 8-bit register **ah**; pop 1
w%bl	write [TOS] into 8-bit register **bl**; pop 1
w%bh	write [TOS] into 8-bit register **bh**; pop 1
w%cl	write [TOS] into 8-bit register **cl**; pop 1
w%ch	write [TOS] into 8-bit register **ch**; pop 1

    w%dl   write [TOS] into 8-bit register dl; pop 1
    w%dh   write [TOS] into 8-bit register dh; pop 1

Command Suffixes
    Operand size
    /b   byte
    /w   word (2 bytes)
    /l   long (4 bytes)—this is the default
    Address space
    /k   kernel virtual—this is the default
    /p   physical
    /io   I/O port
    /u#   user process number # virtual
    Register set
    /rs#   register set number #
    Breakpoint type
    /a   data access breakpoint
    /m   data modify breakpoint
    /i   instruction execution breakpoint—this is the default

Old Commands
    These commands from previous versions are supported as aliases to new com-
    mands:

    Old   New
    Command   Equivalent
    r1   r/b
    r2   r/w
    r4   r/l
    w1   w/b
    w2   w/w
    w4   w/l
    rp1   r/b/p
    rp2   r/w/p
    rp4   r/l/p
    wp1   w/b/p
    wp2   w/w/p
    wp4   w/l/p
    rio1   r/b/io
    rio2   r/w/io
    rio4   r/l/io
    wio1   w/b/io
    wio2   w/w/io
    wio4   w/l/io
    .trap   %trap
    trc0   0 trace
    trc1   1 trace
    trc2   2 trace

`trc3`	3 trace
`db?`	?brk

These old commands are supported:

`.i`	push breakpoint type: instruction
`.a`	push breakpoint type: access byte
`.m`	push breakpoint type: modify byte
`.aw`	push breakpoint type: access word
`.mw`	push breakpoint type: modify word
`.al`	push breakpoint type: access long
`.ml`	push breakpoint type: modify long
`.clr`	push breakpoint type: clear breakpoint
`brk0`	set breakpoint 0 to type [TOS] at address [TOS-1]; pop 2
`brk1`	set breakpoint 1 to type [TOS] at address [TOS-1]; pop 2
`brk2`	set breakpoint 2 to type [TOS] at address [TOS-1]; pop 2
`brk3`	set breakpoint 3 to type [TOS] at address [TOS-1]; pop 2

SEE ALSO

`crash`(1M)

`dc`(1) in the *User's Reference Manual*
The discussion of the UNIX kernel in the *System Administrator's Guide*

NAME

kdb – multiprocessor kernel debugger

SYNOPSIS

kdb

DESCRIPTION

The multiprocessor kernel debugger is a simple debugger that resides in the kernel and allows the programmer to examine and modify memory, disassemble instructions, download and execute programs, set breakpoints, and single-step instructions, on all the online processors.

You can configure the kernel debugger as part of the kernel load file (/unix). The UNIX System V Release 4 *System Administrator's Guide* contains information about rebuilding the kernel. After loading the debugger, type CTRL-ALT-D to enter it.

Multiprocessor Support

The multiprocessor kernel debugger allows each processor independently to be either in the debugger or running at any time. Processors in the debugger are in one of two modes: *master mode* or *slave mode*. At most, one processor is in master mode at any time, although master mode may be transferred among the processors with a debugger command described below. When any processor enters the debugger from a state in which all processors are running, that processor becomes the master and forces all the other processors to become slaves, thereby suspending execution over the entire multiprocessor system. All the commands described below execute on the current master processor unless otherwise noted. Slave processors do nothing until instructed by the master as a result of a debugger command.

The console device is physically attached to only one processor in the multiprocessor system; that processor is termed the *console processor*. All debugger I/O is routed through the console processor, no matter which processor is master. Because the debugger allows independent control over processors, it is possible to "detach" the console processor from the master processor. This results in the loss of interaction between the debugger and the user (for example, by resuming execution on the console processor by using the **gos** command when it is in slave mode). The debugger prints a warning about this condition when it detects it. There are two methods for the console processor to resume performing console I/O to the debugger. The console processor can voluntarily enter the debugger (by hitting a breakpoint or otherwise trapping into the debugger). Or, failing that, the user can type the debugger keystroke, control-alt-D, on the console. Either of these will force the console processor back into slave mode and back into performing console I/O on behalf of the current master processor.

Commands

All debugger commands are brief mnemonics (usually two characters) followed by zero or more arguments. In the following descriptions, optional arguments are enclosed in square brackets. Arguments are separated by spaces or commas, and each argument must be one of the following:

A number in the current input radix (default hexadecimal), or in a different radix as specified by a prefix: 0x for hexadecimal, 0t for decimal, 0o for octal, or 0b for binary.

A percent sign followed by a register name, meaning the contents of that register, such as %eax, %esp, %eflags. Only 32-bit registers are allowed; 8- or 16-bit registers are invalid.

A percent sign followed by b and an instruction breakpoint number, meaning the address referred to by that breakpoint, such as %bx .

A dollar sign ($), meaning the address of the last memory location that was displayed.

The name of a kernel symbol. This works only if the kernel debugger has been loaded with the symbol table by using the **dbsym**(1M) command. A sharp (#) prefix to a name forces the interpretation as a symbol, and not a hexadecimal number. (Without this, the name "add," for example, would always be interpreted as 0x**ADD**.)

The name of a user-defined debugger variable.

Any of the above combined by using the usual arithmetic operators (+ – * / & | ^), the relational operators as used in the C programming language (== != <> <= >=), or the C language pointer-dereference operator (*). Two special operators perform instruction arithmetic: A @– B backs up B instructions from address A; A @+ B advances B instructions from address A; where A and B are expressions. All operators have equal precedence. Use parentheses to force a particular order of evaluation. Division by zero yields zero.

A string surrounded by single-quotes (') or double-quotes ("). The C escape for the newline character (\n) may be used in the string.

A percent sign followed by s and an expression, meaning the null-terminated character string starting at that memory address.

A percent sign followed by p and an expression, meaning the physical memory address corresponding to that virtual address.

A percent sign followed by v and an expression, to test that virtual address' validity. If the virtual address is valid, this operation evaluates to 1, otherwise to 0.

Any numeric expression preceded by ~, meaning the ones-complement of the number.

Input Commands

The multiprocessor debugger prompts with Κ*n*> , where *n* is the processor identification number (*cpuid*) of the current master processor, in hexadecimal. This prompt indicates that the debugger is ready to accept any of the commands described below. Input characters can be erased with BACKSPACE or DEL. An entire input line can be erased with control-U or control-X. In addition, the debugger supports flow control (CTRL-S, CTRL-Q) and keyboard interrupt (CTRL-C).

Before each time the debugger issues a prompt, it checks the state of each processor and notifies the user of those processors that have entered slave mode since the last check. In this way, the user is kept informed of the activities on all the processors.

After a breakpoint or debug trap, the debugger prints a status line describing the trap, immediately followed by the K prompt, and is again ready to accept commands. In the case of a trace trap, the debugger automatically supplies the expected command, **tr**. If you want to enter a different command, erase the **tr** and retype a new command.

During any of the display, modify, examine, or write commands, you can enter one of the following:

RETURN	Move to the next item.
+*n*	Move to the *n*th next item.
-	Move to the previous item.
-*n*	Move to the *n*th previous item.
=*addr*	Move to the item at address *addr*. Only valid when operating on memory, not on registers.
n	Change the value of the item to *n*. Only valid for modify or write commands, not display or examine. The **mi** command allows you to enter multiple numbers separated by spaces, to change more than one byte.
.	(Or any character other than + - = or a hex number.) Exits the command and returns to the debugger prompt.

If an attempt is made to access an invalid virtual address, the command and all levels of invoked macros will be aborted and the debugger will prompt for the next command.

Display Commands

These commands allow you to examine memory only. This prevents accidental modification of system memory when in the debugger.

dl *addr* [*count*]

> Display memory as long integers (4 byte hex integers), 32 bytes at a time. If a *count* is given, memory is displayed 32 * *count* bytes at a time.

dw *addr* [*count*]

> Display memory as words (2 byte hex integers), 32 bytes at a time.

db *addr* [*count*]

> Display memory as bytes (1 byte hex integers), 32 bytes at a time.

di [*addr*]   Display memory as disassembled instructions. The default *addr* is the contents of %eip.

dr [*addr*]   Display the CPU general registers stored at *addr*. The default *addr* is the automatically-determined register save area (see the rg command).

dR   Display the CPU "special" registers (debug, control, and table base registers).

dy *addr* [*count*]

> Similar to dl, but displays the long integers in symbolic form, if possible.

se *start end pattern* [*mask*]

> Search for the given pattern in the range of addresses starting at *start*, up to (but not including) *end*. The search is performed on long integers. If a *mask* is given, only those bits corresponding to 1 bits in the mask are significant in the search.

Examine Commands

el *addr*   Examine memory as longs, one at a time.

ew *addr*   Examine memory as words, one at a time.

eb *addr*   Examine memory as bytes, one at a time.

ei [*addr*] Examine memory as disassembled instructions. (Same as di.)

er   Examine CPU general registers, one at a time.

eR   Examine the CPU special registers, one at a time.

Modify Commands

ml *addr* Examine and optionally modify memory, as long integers.

mw *addr* Examine and optionally modify memory, as words.

mb *addr* Examine and optionally modify memory, as bytes.

mi [*addr*] Examine memory as instructions and optionally modify (as bytes).

mr Examine and optionally modify the CPU registers.

mR Examine and optionally modify the CPU special registers.

Write Commands

wl *addr* Write memory as long integers, without examining.

ww *addr* Write memory as words, without examining.

wb *addr* Write memory as bytes, without examining.

I/O Commands

in *addr*
ib *addr* Read a byte from the specified I/O port.

iw *addr* Read a word (2 bytes) from the specified I/O port.

il *addr* Read a long word (4 bytes) from the specified I/O port.

ou *addr value*
ob *addr value*
 Output a byte (*value*) to the specified I/O port.

ow *addr value*
 Output a word (*value*) to the specified I/O port.

ol *addr value*
 Output a long word (*value*) to the specified I/O port.

Execute Commands

go [*addr*] Resume execution on all processors. If an *addr* is given, the master processor resumes execution at *addr*.

gor [*addr*]
 Resume real-mode execution on the master processor, and normal execution on all other processors. If an *addr* is given, the master processor resumes execution at *addr*.

gos [*cpuid*]
 Resume execution on only the processors whose *cpuid*'s are listed. If no *cpuid*'s are given, it resumes execution on only the current master processor.

tr [*addr*] Trace: single step one instruction on the master processor. If an *addr* is given, the master processor resumes execution at *addr*.

trs [*cpuid*]
Trace (single step) on the slave processor identified by *cpuid*, or on the master processor if *cpuid* is omitted.

to [*addr*]   Trace over: single step over "call" instructions on the master processor. If an *addr* is given, the master processor resumes execution at *addr*.

tos [*cpuid*]
Trace (single step) over "call" instructions on the slave processor identified by *cpuid*, or on the master processor if *cpuid* is omitted.

stop [*cpuid*]
Suspend execution on the running processors whose *cpuid*'s are listed, and force them into slave mode. If no *cpuid*'s are given, it suspends every currently running processor.

call *addr* [**args**]
Call a function with the specified arguments and show the return value.

Multiprocessor Commands

These commands, together with the Execute Commands above, which start and stop processors, comprise the complete multiprocessor command set.

cpu *cpuid*   Switch master mode from the current master processor to the slave processor identified by *cpuid*. The current master processor becomes a slave, and the designated slave becomes the new master.

ss [*cpuid*]   Show the multiprocessor debugger status of the processor identified by *cpuid*, or of all processors if *cpuid* is omitted.

Instruction Breakpoint Commands

An instruction breakpoint invokes the debugger just prior to the execution of a specified instruction. There are a total of 16 instruction breakpoints available. Instruction breakpoints affect all processors; that is, every processor that hits an instruction breakpoint will enter the debugger. Chip breakpoints (see below) affect only the processor on which the breakpoint was set.

br [*addr*]
Set an instruction breakpoint. The default address is the contents of **%eip**.

bc [*addr*]
Clear (remove) an instruction breakpoint.

bC   Clear (remove) all instruction breakpoints.

bx [*addr*]
Set a temporary (one-shot) instruction breakpoint.

bo [*addr*]
> Turn an instruction breakpoint on or off. If a breakpoint is turned off, it acts as though it were cleared, but the breakpoint remains in the breakpoint table.

bp   Display instruction breakpoints.

Chip Breakpoint Commands

A chip breakpoint invokes the debugger when a specified memory location is referenced. There are a total of four chip breakpoints available. Chip breakpoints affect only the processor on which the breakpoint was set. Instruction breakpoints (see above) affect all processors.

ur *num type* [*addr*]
> Sets a chip breakpoint. *Num* must be 0 to 3, *addr* is the breakpoint address, and *type* gives the type of memory access that will trigger the breakpoint. Valid types are:
>
> | | |
> |---|---|
> | 0 | Execute |
> | 10 | Byte write |
> | 11 | Byte read/write |
> | 20 | Word write |
> | 21 | Word read/write |
> | 40 | Long write |
> | 41 | Long read/write |
>
> Note that the first digit specifies the breakpoint length and the second specifies the access type (write-only or read/write). The breakpoint is global unless the type is ORed with 100, which makes it local; or with 200, which makes it global and local. For example, 140 specifies a local long write-only breakpoint.

uc *num*   Clear a chip breakpoint.

uC   Clear all chip breakpoints.

ux *num type* [*addr*]
> Like **ur**, but set a temporary (one-shot) breakpoint.

up   Print all chip breakpoints.

Miscellaneous Commands

bt [*addr*]   Display a stack backtrace, using *addr* as a frame pointer. The default address is the contents of **%ebp**. This works only with C language routines in protected mode.

c3 [*addr*]   Use the specified physical address as the base of the page directory for translating linear-to-physical addresses. This address is obtained from the special register **CR3** if no **c3** command is given. To restore the base to that original value, use an *addr* of zero. If *addr* is missing, display the current page directory base.

ds *addr*   Print the value of the address as an offset from the nearest symbol.

fill *start end value*
> Fill memory from address *start* up to (but not including) address *end* with the byte *value*.

he or **help** or **?** or **??**
> List the debugger commands.

ma *addr*

map *addr*   Display the page directory and page table entries used to map the given linear address to a physical address. This behaves the same whether paging is on or off.

more [*lines*]
> Set the number of display lines to *lines*. If *lines* is greater than zero, it enables output paging. When *lines* or more contiguous lines of information are printed without asking the user for input, the message "**--press space for more--**" is displayed and output is temporarily suspended until the user presses the space bar. This prevents the debugger from printing too many lines of output at once on video terminals. If *lines* is zero, it disables output paging. Output paging is disabled by default. If *lines* is missing, it reports whether output paging is enabled or disabled.

pause   Pause until the user types something.

pf *"string"* [**args**. . .]

pg [*n*]   If *n* is 0, turn paging off. If *n* is 1, turn paging on. If *n* is missing, report whether paging is on or off. If paging is off, the debugger interprets all addresses as linear (virtual) addresses. (Breakpoints are always linear addresses.)

pr *addr* [*radix*]
> Print the value of the address given as an argument in the specified radix, or in the current input radix if *radix* is missing. This is most useful if *addr* is an expression (see the earlier discussion of arguments).

printf *"string"* [**args**. . .]
> Print the string. Percent signs in the string are treated as in **printf**(3S): **%d**, **%u**, **%x**, **%o**, **%b**, **%s**, **%c** are supported. In addition, **%y** prints its argument in symbolic form, if possible, and **%I** prints its argument in disassembled instruction form.

printbits *"bit-desc" word*
Display the bits that are set (the 1 bits) in *word* symbolically according to *bit-desc*, which is a colon-separated list of names associated with the corresponding bit positions, starting with bit 0 (the least significant bit). For example, **printbits ''X:Y:Z:FOO:BAR''** 0x9D prints **X Z FOO BAR**.

radix [*n*] Set the input radix to *n*. If *n* is omitted, display the current input radix. The default radix is hexadecimal.

read var Read an expression from the user and set the named debugger variable to the expression's value.

real [*n*] If *n* is 0, turn real-mode off. If *n* is 1, turn real-mode on. If *n* is missing, report whether real-mode is on or off. If real-mode is off, the debugger traces in protected mode. If real-mode is on, the debugger traces in real mode.

rg [*addr*] Change the pointer to the "register save area," from which all references to CPU registers retrieve registers. Normally, the register save area is set up automatically, but you can use a different set of registers when you use **rg** to change the pointer. To restore the pointer to its original value, use an *addr* of zero. If *addr* is missing, it displays the current register save area pointer.

set var value
Set the variable named by var to have the given value. If the variable var has not previously been defined, it becomes defined; if it was previously defined, its old value is lost.

sp [*addr*] *Addr* must be the address of a kernel **proc** structure. The debugger uses the context of that process to translate linear-to-physical addresses. Use of the **sp** command overrides the CR3 register: after an **sp** command, **c3** commands have no effect.

sy [*n*] [*max*]
If *n* is 0, turn symbolic display off. If *n* is 1, turn symbolic display on. If *n* is missing, report whether symbolic display is on or off. If *max* is given, it specifies the maximum offset for printing symbols. For example, if *max* is 1000, a symbol may be displayed in the form *name+NNN*, where *NNN* is 1 through 1000, but if *NNN* would be greater than 1000, the non-symbolic display format is used.

ve Print the version number of the debugger.

or **##** or **no**
No-op. Input lines beginning with **#** are treated as comments and ignored. **pr** *addr* [*radix*] Prints the value of the address given as an argument in the specified radix, or in the current input radix if *radix* is missing. This is most useful if *addr* is an expression (see the earlier discussion of arguments).

Macro Commands

define ''*name''* [*arg-desc*] [*maxsize*]

Defines a macro, with the given name and the specified argument description string. The optional *maxsize* argument specifies the maximum size (in bytes) of the macro; the default size is 4096 bytes. The macro can be invoked after its definition by simply typing its name like any other command. The *arg-desc* string describes to the debugger what arguments the macro expects. Each lower-case letter specifies the type of the corresponding argument, as follows:

> **a** or **i** address or integer, the result of an arbitrary expression
> **s** string
> **?** means the following arguments are optional
> * means any number of arguments or any type
> . means don't parse more arguments
> , is ignored.

For example, the argument description for the **se** command is "**aai?i**", and for **pf** it is "**s***". If *arg-desc* is missing, the macro will be defined as requiring no arguments. Any debugger commands can be entered as the body of the macro, although interactive commands, such as **di** are not recommended (see the **interact** command). The expression $*n*, where *n* is a digit from 1 to 9, is replaced on invocation with the *n*th argument to the macro. The expression **$#** evaluates to the number of arguments to the macro. Entry of the macro body is terminated by a period (.) anywhere in the macro body. Include a period in the macro body by preceding the character with a backslash (\).

args *n*

Set the number of macro arguments to *n*.

delm "*name*"

Erase (deletes) the named macro.

do "*name*" [**args**. . .]

Repeatedly call the named macro with any **args** specified, until an **exit** command is executed. This is the only explicit form of iteration the debugger provides. The **args** are passed to the named macro — and, if **setarg** is not used within the macro, — **args** is passed to every subsequent iteration of the named macro.

em ''*name''*
echo [*n*]

If *n* is 1, macros are echoed when they are invoked. If *n* is 0 (the default), macros are not echoed. If *n* is missing, the status of the echo flag is printed. If the **ec** command is given within a macro body, it is in effect for that macro only.

exit   Stop iterating a repeated macro call (see **do**). Note that **exit** does not terminate the execution of the current macro; it merely prevents further iterations.

interact *n*
        If *n* is 1, interactive commands (such as **di**, **bt**, and **dr**) when invoked during macro execution will read input from the user. If *n* is 0 (the default), interactive commands inside macros will read input from the macro body. The **interact** command affects only the currently-executing macro and has no effect outside a macro body.

lm [*"name"*]
        List the named macro. If the macro name is omitted, list all macros.

nx   Repeat the call to the previously invoked macro. The arguments used are those used on the previous call, possibly modified by any intervening **sa** commands.

onbreak [*"name"*]
        Set the on-break macro to the macro named by *name*. If *name* is omitted, disable the on-break macro feature. The on-break macro, if one is specified, is executed on every entrance to the debugger resulting from any trap or breakpoint. This feature is very handy for implementing conditional breakpoints.

sa *n value*
setarg *n value*
        Sets the *n*th macro argument to the given value. The value of *n* should be between 1 and 9. Useful within a macro to set up the arguments for the next call through an **nx** command.

Predefined Macros

buf *addr*   Print selected fields of a **struct buf** at the given address.

buf+ *addr*   Run **buf** *addr* and set up the debugger to display the next adjacent buffer.

buf- *addr*   Run **buf** *addr* and set up the debugger to display the previous adjacent buffer.

bufv *addr*   Run **buf** *addr* and set up the kernel debugger to display the buffer at **addr->av_forw** each time a carriage return is entered.

dscr *addr*   Print any 286/i386/i486 descriptor in its appropriate format.

dscr+ *addr*   Run **dscr** *addr* and set up the debugger to display the next adjacent descriptor.

xintrq *addr*
        Print all the inter-CPU interrupt queues.

xintrq+ *addr*
        Run **xintrq** *addr* and set up the kernel debugger to print the next adjacent inter-CPU interrupt queue.

inode *addr*   Print selected fields of a **struct inode** (in the same manner as **sys/inode.h**).

inode+ *addr*
>   Run **inode** *addr* and set the debugger up to print the next adjacent inode address.

mutex *addr*   Print selected fields of a **struct mutex**.

curlock   Print the master processor's **curlock** stack. (**curlock_aux** is a sub-macro used by **curlock**.)

percpu *addr*
>   Print selected fields of a **struct percpu**.

percpup+ *addr*
>   Run **percpu** *addr* and set the debugger up to display the next adjacent cpu address.

cpuinfo *cpuid*
>   Print selected fields of a **struct cpuinfo** for the given CPU.

proc *addr*   Print selected fields of a **struct proc**.

proc+ *addr*   Run **proc** *addr* and set up the debugger to display the next adjacent processor address.

ps   Simulate **/bin/ps -1**. (**ps_loop** and **psl** are submacros used by **ps**.)

pid *pid*   Find a process with the given *pid* (remember, the default debugger radix is hex, not decimal) and run **proc** on it. (**pid_search** is a sub-macro used by **pid**. **pidof** and **pgrpof** are submacros used by **proc**.)

btproc *addr*
>   Set the KDB process context to *addr* and run the backtrace **bt** command.

strstat   Prints selected STREAMS statistics. (**strstat_aux** is a submacro used by **strstat**.)

strmsg *addr*
>   Print selected fields of a **struct msgb**. (**strmsg_aux** and **strmsg_type** are submacros used by **strmsg**.)

strqueue *addr*
>   Print selected fields of a **struct queue**. (**strqueue_aux** is a sub-macro used by **strqueue**.)

strqueue_band *addr*
>   Print selected fields of a **struct qband**. (**strfollow** is a submacro used by **stream**.)

stream *addr*
>   Print selected fields of a **struct stdata** and substructures.

streams   Print all **streams** except **muxs**.

streams_muxs
>   Print all **streams**. (**streams_aux** is a submacro used by **streams** and **streams_muxs**.)

queues   Print all **streams** queues.

queues_flag
                Print all **streams** queues with none of the flags set. (**queues_aux**
                and **queues_loop** are submacros used by **queues** and **queues_flag**.)

stream_find *addr*
                Find and print a **stream** associated with the given **queue**.
                (**stream_find1** and **stream_find2** are submacros used by
                stream_find.)

flags *addr*   Print flags (in the same manner as **%eflags**) set in **dword** at *addr*.

tss *addr*   Print selected fields of a **struct tss386**.

tss+ *addr*   Run **tss** *addr* and set the debugger up to run **tss** on the next adja-
                cent address.

tty *addr*   Print selected fields of a **struct tty**.

tty+ *addr*   Run **tty** *addr* and set the debugger up to run **tty** on the next adja-
                cent address.

user *addr*   Print selected fields of a **struct user**.

vnode *addr*   Print selected fields of a **struct vnode**.

vnode+ *addr*
                Run **vnode** *addr* and set up the debugger to run **vnode** on the next
                adjacent address.

Conditional Commands

IF *expr*
EL
FI   If the expression evaluates to zero, all commands up to the matching
                EL or **FI** are skipped. If the expression is non-zero, execution
                proceeds normally to the matching **FI**, unless a matching **EL** is found,
                in which case, commands between the **EL** and the **FI** are skipped.
                During any of this "skipping," the prompt changes from *Kn>* to *-Kn>*
                to indicate that the commands are being read but not executed.

if *expr*
elseif *expr*
else
fi   Same as IF-EL-FI but with the **elseif** construct which allows chain-
                ing of conditional statements.

ifdef "*name*"
                Like **if**, but the condition is "true" if a macro named *name* exists.

ifsdef "*name*"
                Like **if**, but the condition is "true" if a symbol named *name* exists.

SEE ALSO
dbcmd(1M), dbsym(1M), and kcrash(1M)

NOTES

If you try to **go** at the exact address where a breakpoint is set, the breakpoint does not trigger.

The disassembler works only with protected mode (32 bit) instructions. It does not know how to disassemble 16 bit instructions.

FILES

`/etc/conf/macros.d`   Directory containing macro files.

NAME

keylogin – decrypt and store secret key

SYNOPSIS

keylogin

DESCRIPTION

The **keylogin** command prompts for a password, and uses it to decrypt the user's secret key stored in the **publickey**(4) database. Once decrypted, the user's key is stored by the local key server process, **keyserv**(1M), to be used by any secure network service, such as NFS.

SEE ALSO

chkey(1), keylogout(1), publickey(4), keyserv(1M), newkey(1)

NAME

> keyserv – server for storing public and private keys

SYNOPSIS

> keyserv [–n]

DESCRIPTION

> keyserv is a daemon that is used for storing the private encryption keys of each user logged into the system. These encryption keys are used for accessing secure network services such as secure NFS.

> Normally, root's key is read from the file **/etc/.rootkey** when the daemon is started. This is useful during power-fail reboots when no one is around to type a password.

> When the **–n** option is used, root's key is not read from **/etc/.rootkey**. Instead, **keyserv** prompts the user for the password to decrypt root's key stored in the **publickey**(4) database and then stores the decrypted key in **/etc/.rootkey** for future use. This option is useful if the **/etc/.rootkey** file ever gets out of date or corrupted.

> To start **keyserv** manually, you must be **root** with the appropriate privileges.

FILES

> /etc/.rootkey

SEE ALSO

> publickey(4)

NAME

kill – terminate a process by default

SYNOPSIS

```
kill [-signal] pid...
kill -signal -pgid...
kill -l
```

DESCRIPTION

kill sends a signal to the specified processes. The value of **signal** may be numeric or symbolic [see **signal**(5)]. The symbolic signal name is the name as it appears in **/usr/include/sys/signal.h**, with the **SIG** prefix stripped off. Signal 15 (**SIGTERM**) is sent by default; this will normally kill processes that do not catch or ignore the signal.

pid and *pgid* are unsigned numeric strings that identify which process(es) should receive the signal. If *pid* is used, the process with process ID *pid* is selected. If *pgid* is used, all processes with process group ID *pgid* are selected.

The process number of each asynchronous process started with **&** is reported by the shell (unless more than one process is started in a pipeline, in which case the number of the last process in the pipeline is reported). Process numbers can also be found by using **ps**(1).

When invoked with the **-1** option, kill will print a list of symbolic signal names. The details of the kill are described in **kill**(2). For example, if process number 0 is specified, all processes in the process group are signaled.

The signaled process must belong to the current user unless the user is the super-user.

SEE ALSO

ps(1), **sh**(1)
kill(2), **signal**(2), **signal**(5) in the *Programmer's Reference Manual*

NAME

    `killall` – kill all active processes

SYNOPSIS

    `/usr/sbin/killall` [*signal*]

DESCRIPTION

    `killall` is used by `/usr/sbin/shutdown` to kill all active processes not directly related to the shutdown procedure.

    `killall` terminates all processes with open files so that the mounted file systems will be unbusied and can be unmounted.

    `killall` sends *signal* [see `kill`(1)] to all processes not belonging to the above group of exclusions. If no *signal* is specified, a default of 15 (`SIGTERM`) is used.

FILES

    `/usr/sbin/shutdown`

SEE ALSO

    `fuser`(1M), `shutdown`(1M), `signal`(5)

    `kill`(1), `ps`(1) in the *User's Reference Manual*

    `signal`(2) in the *Programmer's Reference Manual*

NOTES

    The `killall` command can be run only by a privileged user.

NAME

ksh, **rksh** – KornShell, a standard/restricted command and programming language

SYNOPSIS

ksh [±**aefhikmnprstuvx**] [±**o** *option*] ... [–**c** *string*] [*arg* ...]
rksh [±**aefhikmnprstuvx**] [±**o** *option*] ... [–**c** *string*] [*arg* ...]

DESCRIPTION

ksh is a command and programming language that executes commands read from a terminal or a file. **rksh** is a restricted version of the command interpreter **ksh**; it is used to set up login names and execution environments whose capabilities are more controlled than those of the standard shell. See *Invocation* below for the meaning of arguments to the shell.

Definitions.

A *metacharacter* is one of the following characters:

     ;   &   (   ) | <   >   new-line   space   tab

A *blank* is a **tab** or a **space**. An *identifier* is a sequence of letters, digits, or underscores starting with a letter or underscore. Identifiers are used as names for *functions* and *variables*. A *word* is a sequence of *characters* separated by one or more non-quoted *metacharacters*.

A *command* is a sequence of characters in the syntax of the shell language. The shell reads each command and carries out the desired action either directly or by invoking separate utilities. A special command is a command that is carried out by the shell without creating a separate process. Except for documented side effects, most special commands can be implemented as separate utilities.

Commands.

A *simple-command* is a sequence of *blank* separated words which may be preceded by a variable assignment list (see *Environment* below). The first word specifies the name of the command to be executed. Except as specified below, the remaining words are passed as arguments to the invoked command. The command name is passed as argument 0 [see **exec**(2)]. The *value* of a simple-command is its exit status if it terminates normally, or (octal) 200+*status* if it terminates abnormally [see **signal**(2) for a list of status values].

A *pipeline* is a sequence of one or more *commands* separated by |. The standard output of each command but the last is connected by a **pipe**(2) to the standard input of the next command. Each command is run as a separate process; the shell waits for the last command to terminate. The exit status of a pipeline is the exit status of the last command.

A *list* is a sequence of one or more pipelines separated by ;, &, &&, or ||, and optionally terminated by ;, &, or |&. Of these five symbols, ;, &, and |& have equal precedence, which is lower than that of && and ||. The symbols && and || also have equal precedence. A semicolon (;) causes sequential execution of the preceding pipeline; an ampersand (&) causes asynchronous execution of the preceding pipeline (that is, the shell does *not* wait for that pipeline to finish). The symbol |& causes asynchronous execution of the preceding command or pipeline with a two-way pipe established to the parent shell. The standard input and output of the spawned command can be written to and read from by the parent

Shell using the **-p** option of the special commands **read** and **print** described later. The symbol **&&** (**|** **|**) causes the *list* following it to be executed only if the preceding pipeline returns a zero (non-zero) value. An arbitrary number of new-lines may appear in a *list,* instead of a semicolon, to delimit a command.

A *command* is either a simple-command or one of the following. Unless otherwise stated, the value returned by a command is that of the last simple-command executed in the command.

for *identifier* [**in** *word* ...] **;do** *list* **;done**
> Each time a **for** command is executed, *identifier* is set to the next *word* taken from the **in** *word* list. If **in** *word* ... is omitted, then the **for** command executes the **do** *list* once for each positional parameter that is set (see *Parameter Substitution* below). Execution ends when there are no more words in the list.

select *identifier* [**in** *word* ...] **;do** *list* **;done**
> A **select** command prints on standard error (file descriptor 2), the set of *word*s, each preceded by a number. If **in** *word* ... is omitted, then the positional parameters are used instead (see *Parameter Substitution* below). The **PS3** prompt is printed and a line is read from the standard input. If this line consists of the number of one of the listed *word*s, then the value of the parameter *identifier* is set to the *word* corresponding to this number. If this line is empty the selection list is printed again. Otherwise the value of the parameter *identifier* is set to **null**. The contents of the line read from standard input is saved in the variable **REPLY.** The *list* is executed for each selection until a **break** or *end-of-file* is encountered.

case *word* **in** [[**(**]*pattern* [**|** *pattern*] ... **)** *list* **;;**] ... **esac**
> A **case** command executes the *list* associated with the first *pattern* that matches *word*. The form of the patterns is the same as that used for file-name generation (see *File Name Generation* below).

if *list* **;then** *list* [**elif** *list* **;then** *list*] ... [**;else** *list*] **;fi**
> The *list* following **if** is executed and, if it returns a zero exit status, the *list* following the first **then** is executed. Otherwise, the *list* following **elif** is executed and, if its value is zero, the *list* following the next **then** is executed. Failing that, the **else** *list* is executed. If no **else** *list* or **then** *list* is executed, then the **if** command returns a zero exit status.

while *list* **;do** *list* **;done**
until *list* **;do** *list* **;done**
> A **while** command repeatedly executes the **while** *list* and, if the exit status of the last command in the list is zero, executes the **do** *list;* otherwise the loop terminates. If no commands in the **do** *list* are executed, then the **while** command returns a zero exit status; **until** may be used in place of **while** to negate the loop termination test.

(*list* **)**
> Execute *list* in a separate environment. Note, that if two adjacent open parentheses are needed for nesting, a space must be inserted to avoid arithmetic evaluation as described below.

{ *list* ; }
>   *list* is simply executed. The { must be followed by a space. Note that
>   unlike the metacharacters (and), { and } are *reserved words* and must be
>   typed at the beginning of a line or after a ; in order to be recognized.

[[*expression*]]
>   Evaluates *expression* and returns a zero exit status when *expression* is true.
>   See *Conditional Expressions* below, for a description of *expression*.

function *identifier* { *list* ; }
identifier () { *list* ; }
>   Define a function which is referenced by *identifier*. The body of the func-
>   tion is the *list* of commands between { and }. (see *Functions* below). The
>   { must be followed by a space.

time *pipeline*
>   The *pipeline* is executed and the elapsed time as well as the user and sys-
>   tem time are printed on standard error.

The following reserved words are only recognized as the first word of a command and when not quoted:

```
if      then    else    elif    fi      case    esac    for     while
until   do      done    {   }   function  select  time   [[  ]]
```

Comments.

A word beginning with # causes that word and all the following characters up to
a new-line to be ignored.

Aliasing.

The first word of each command is replaced by the text of an **alias** if an **alias**
for this word has been defined. An alias name consists of any number of characters excluding meta-characters, quoting characters, file expansion characters,
parameter and command substitution characters and =. The replacement string
can contain any valid Shell script including the metacharacters listed above. The
first word of each command in the replaced text, other than any that are in the
process of being replaced, will be tested for aliases. If the last character of the
alias value is a *blank* then the word following the alias will also be checked for
alias substitution. Aliases can be used to redefine special builtin commands but
cannot be used to redefine the reserved words listed above. Aliases can be
created, listed, and exported with the **alias** command and can be removed with
the **unalias** command. Exported aliases remain in effect for scripts invoked by
name, but must be reinitialized for separate invocations of the Shell (see *Invocation* below).

Aliasing is performed when scripts are read, not while they are executed. Therefore, for an alias to take effect the **alias** definition command has to be executed
before the command which references the alias is read.

Aliases are frequently used as a short hand for full path names. An option to the
aliasing facility allows the value of the alias to be automatically set to the full
pathname of the corresponding command. These aliases are called *tracked* aliases.
The value of a *tracked* alias is defined the first time the corresponding command is
looked up and becomes undefined each time the **PATH** variable is reset. These
aliases remain *tracked* so that the next subsequent reference will redefine the

value. Several tracked aliases are compiled into the shell. The **-h** option of the **set** command makes each referenced command name into a tracked alias.

The following *exported aliases* are compiled into the shell but can be unset or redefined:

```
autoload='typeset -fu'
false='let 0'
functions='typeset -f'
hash='alias -t'
history='fc -l'
integer='typeset -i'
nohup='nohup '
r='fc -e -'
true=':'
type='whence -v'
```

Tilde Substitution.

After alias substitution is performed, each word is checked to see if it begins with an unquoted ~. If it does, then the word up to a **/** is checked to see if it matches a user name in the **/etc/passwd** file. If a match is found, the ~ and the matched login name is replaced by the login directory of the matched user. This is called a *tilde* substitution. If no match is found, the original text is left unchanged. A ~ by itself, or in front of a **/**, is replaced by **$HOME**. A ~ followed by a **+** or **-** is replaced by **$PWD** and **$OLDPWD** respectively.

In addition, *tilde* substitution is attempted when the value of a *variable assignment* begins with a ~.

Command Substitution.

The standard output from a command enclosed in parentheses preceded by a dollar sign (**$( )**) or a pair of grave accents (**' '**) may be used as part or all of a word; trailing new-lines are removed. In the second (archaic) form, the string between the quotes is processed for special quoting characters before the command is executed (see *Quoting* below). The command substitution **$(cat file)** can be replaced by the equivalent but faster **$(<file)**. Command substitution of most special commands that do not perform input/output redirection are carried out without creating a separate process.

An arithmetic expression enclosed in double parentheses and preceded by a dollar sign [**$(())**] is replaced by the value of the arithmetic expression within the double parentheses.

Parameter Substitution.

A *parameter* is an *identifier*, one or more digits, or any of the characters *, @, #, ?, -, $, and !. A *variable* (a parameter denoted by an identifier) has a *value* and zero or more *attributes*. *Variables* can be assigned **values** and *attributes* by using the **typeset** special command. The attributes supported by the Shell are described later with the **typeset** special command. Exported parameters pass values and attributes to the environment.

The shell supports a one-dimensional array facility. An element of an array variable is referenced by a *subscript*. A *subscript* is denoted by a [, followed by an *arithmetic expression* (see *Arithmetic Evaluation* below) followed by a]. To assign values to an array, use **set** **-A** *name* *value* ... . The value of all subscripts must be in the range of 0 through 1023. Arrays need not be declared. Any reference to a variable with a valid subscript is legal and an array will be created if necessary. Referencing an array without a subscript is equivalent to referencing the element zero.

The *value* of a *variable* may also be assigned by writing:

> *name=value* [*name=value*] ...

If the integer attribute, **-i**, is set for *name* the *value* is subject to arithmetic evaluation as described below.

Positional parameters, parameters denoted by a number, may be assigned values with the **set** special command. Parameter **$0** is set from argument zero when the shell is invoked.

The character **$** is used to introduce substitutable *parameters*.

${*parameter*}
> The shell reads all the characters from **${** to the matching **}** as part of the same word even if it contains braces or metacharacters. The value, if any, of the parameter is substituted. The braces are required when *parameter* is followed by a letter, digit, or underscore that is not to be interpreted as part of its name or when a variable is subscripted. If *parameter* is one or more digits then it is a positional parameter. A positional parameter of more than one digit must be enclosed in braces. If *parameter* is ∗ or @, then all the positional parameters, starting with **$1**, are substituted (separated by a field separator character). If an array *identifier* with subscript ∗ or @ is used, then the value for each of the elements is substituted (separated by a field separator character).

${#*parameter*}
> If *parameter* is ∗ or @, the number of positional parameters is substituted. Otherwise, the length of the value of the *parameter* is substituted.

${#*identifier*[∗]}
> The number of elements in the array *identifier* is substituted.

${*parameter*:-*word*}
> If *parameter* is set and is non-null then substitute its value; otherwise substitute *word*.

${*parameter*:=*word*}
> If *parameter* is not set or is null then set it to *word*; the value of the parameter is then substituted. Positional parameters may not be assigned to in this way.

${*parameter*:?*word*}
> If *parameter* is set and is non-null then substitute its value; otherwise, print *word* and exit from the shell. If *word* is omitted then a standard message is printed.

${*parameter*:+*word*}
> If *parameter* is set and is non-null then substitute *word*; otherwise substitute nothing.

${*parameter*#*pattern*}
${*parameter*##*pattern*}

> If the Shell *pattern* matches the beginning of the value of *parameter*, then the value of this substitution is the value of the *parameter* with the matched portion deleted; otherwise the value of this *parameter* is substituted. In the first form the smallest matching pattern is deleted and in the second form the largest matching pattern is deleted.

${*parameter*%*pattern*}
${*parameter*%%*pattern*}

> If the Shell *pattern* matches the end of the value of *parameter*, then the value of this substitution is the value of the *parameter* with the matched part deleted; otherwise substitute the value of *parameter*. In the first form the smallest matching pattern is deleted and in the second form the largest matching pattern is deleted.

In the above, *word* is not evaluated unless it is to be used as the substituted string, so that, in the following example, **pwd** is executed only if **d** is not set or is null:

```
echo ${d:-$(pwd)}
```

If the colon (**:**) is omitted from the above expressions, then the shell only checks whether *parameter* is set or not.

The following parameters are automatically set by the shell:

#	The number of positional parameters in decimal.
-	Flags supplied to the shell on invocation or by the **set** command.
?	The decimal value returned by the last executed command.
$	The process number of this shell.
_	Initially, the value _ is an absolute pathname of the shell or script being executed as passed in the *environment*. Subsequently it is assigned the last argument of the previous command. This parameter is not set for commands which are asynchronous. This parameter is also used to hold the name of the matching **MAIL** file when checking for mail.
!	The process number of the last background command invoked.
ERRNO	The value of *errno* as set by the most recently failed system call. This value is system dependent and is intended for debugging purposes.
LINENO	The line number of the current line within the script or function being executed.
OLDPWD	The previous working directory set by the **cd** command.
OPTARG	The value of the last option argument processed by the **getopts** special command.
OPTIND	The index of the last option argument processed by the **getopts** special command.

PPID	The process number of the parent of the shell.
PWD	The present working directory set by the **cd** command.
RANDOM	Each time this variable is referenced, a random integer, uniformly distributed between 0 and 32767, is generated. The sequence of random numbers can be initialized by assigning a numeric value to **RANDOM**.
REPLY	This variable is set by the **select** statement and by the **read** special command when no arguments are supplied.
SECONDS	Each time this variable is referenced, the number of seconds since shell invocation is returned. If this variable is assigned a value, then the value returned upon reference will be the value that was assigned plus the number of seconds since the assignment.

The following variables are used by the shell:

CDPATH	The search path for the **cd** command.
COLUMNS	If this variable is set, the value is used to define the width of the edit window for the shell edit modes and for printing **select** lists.
EDITOR	If the value of this variable ends in **vi** and the **VISUAL** variable is not set, then the corresponding option (see *Special Command* **set** below) will be turned on.
ENV	If this variable is set, then parameter substitution is performed on the value to generate the pathname of the script that will be executed when the *shell* is invoked (see *Invocation* below). This file is typically used for *alias* and *function* definitions.
FCEDIT	The default editor name for the **fc** command.
FPATH	The search path for function definitions. This path is searched when a function with the **–u** attribute is referenced and when a command is not found. If an executable file is found, then it is read and executed in the current environment.
IFS	Internal field separators, normally **space**, **tab**, and **new-line** that is used to separate command words which result from command or parameter substitution and for separating words with the special command **read**. The first character of the **IFS** variable is used to separate arguments for the "$*" substitution (see *Quoting* below).
HISTFILE	If this variable is set when the shell is invoked, then the value is the pathname of the file that will be used to store the command history (see *Command re-entry* below).
HISTSIZE	If this variable is set when the shell is invoked, then the number of previously entered commands that are accessible by this shell will be greater than or equal to this number. The default is 128.
HOME	The default argument (home directory) for the **cd** command.
LINES	If this variable is set, the value is used to determine the column length for printing **select** lists. Select lists will print vertically until about two-thirds of **LINES** lines are filled.

MAIL   If this variable is set to the name of a mail file *and* the **MAIL-PATH** variable is not set, then the shell informs the user of arrival of mail in the specified file.

MAILCHECK   This variable specifies how often (in seconds) the shell will check for changes in the modification time of any of the files specified by the **MAILPATH** or **MAIL** variables. The default value is 600 seconds. When the time has elapsed the shell will check before issuing the next prompt.

MAILPATH   A colon (**:**) separated list of file names. If this variable is set then the shell informs the user of any modifications to the specified files that have occurred within the last **MAILCHECK** seconds. Each file name can be followed by a **?** and a message that will be printed. The message will undergo parameter substitution with the variable, **$_** defined as the name of the file that has changed. The default message is *you have mail in $_*.

PATH   The search path for commands (see *Execution* below). The user may not change **PATH** if executing under **rksh** (except in *.profile*).

PS1   The value of this variable is expanded for parameter substitution to define the primary prompt string which by default is "**$** ". The character **!** in the primary prompt string is replaced by the *command* number (see *Command Re-entry* below).

PS2   Secondary prompt string, by default "**>** ".

PS3   Selection prompt string used within a **select** loop, by default "**#?** ".

PS4   The value of this variable is expanded for parameter substitution and precedes each line of an execution trace. If omitted, the execution trace prompt is "**+** ".

SHELL   The pathname of the *shell* is kept in the environment. At invocation, if the basename of this variable matches the pattern ***r*sh**, then the shell becomes restricted.

TMOUT   If set to a value greater than zero, the shell will terminate if a command is not entered within the prescribed number of seconds after issuing the **PS1** prompt. (Note that the shell can be compiled with a maximum bound for this value which cannot be exceeded.)

VISUAL   If the value of this variable ends in **vi** then the corresponding option (see *Special Command* **set** below) will be turned on.

The shell gives default values to **PATH**, **PS1**, **PS2**, **MAILCHECK**, **TMOUT** and **IFS**. **HOME**, **MAIL** and **SHELL** are set by **login**(1).

Blank Interpretation.

After parameter and command substitution, the results of substitutions are scanned for the field separator characters (those found in **IFS**) and split into distinct arguments where such characters are found. Explicit null arguments (**""** or **' '**) are retained. Implicit null arguments (those resulting from *parameters* that have no values) are removed.

File Name Generation.

Following substitution, each command *word* is scanned for the characters *, ?, and [unless the −**f** option has been **set**. If one of these characters appears then the word is regarded as a *pattern*. The word is replaced with lexicographically sorted file names that match the pattern. If no file name is found that matches the pattern, then the word is left unchanged. When a *pattern* is used for file name generation, the character **.** at the start of a file name or immediately following a **/**, as well as the character **/** itself, must be matched explicitly. In other instances of pattern matching the **/** and **.** are not treated specially.

    *   Matches any string, including the null string.
    ?   Matches any single character.
    [...] Matches any one of the enclosed characters. A pair of characters separated by − matches any character lexically between the pair, inclusive. If the first character following the opening "[" is a "!" then any character not enclosed is matched. A − can be included in the character set by putting it as the first or last character.

A *pattern-list* is a list of one or more patterns separated from each other with a |. Composite patterns can be formed with one or more of the following:

    ? (*pattern-list*)
        Optionally matches any one of the given patterns.
    * (*pattern-list*)
        Matches zero or more occurrences of the given patterns.
    + (*pattern-list*)
        Matches one or more occurrences of the given patterns.
    @ (*pattern-list*)
        Matches exactly one of the given patterns.
    ! (*pattern-list*)
        Matches anything, except one of the given patterns.

Quoting.

Each of the *metacharacters* listed above (see *Definitions* above) has a special meaning to the shell and causes termination of a word unless quoted. A character may be *quoted* (that is, made to stand for itself) by preceding it with a \. The pair **\new-line** is removed. All characters enclosed between a pair of single quote marks (′ ′), are quoted. A single quote cannot appear within single quotes. Inside double quote marks ("**"**), parameter and command substitution occurs and \ quotes the characters \, ′, ", and **$**. The meaning of **$*** and **$@** is identical when not quoted or when used as a variable assignment value or as a file name. However, when used as a command argument, "**$***" is equivalent to "**$1***d***$2***d*...", where *d* is the first character of the **IFS** variable, whereas "**$@**" is equivalent to "**$1**"*d*"**$2**"*d*. . . Inside grave quote marks (′ ′) \ quotes the characters \, ′, and **$**. If the grave quotes occur within double quotes then \ also quotes the character ".

The special meaning of reserved words or aliases can be removed by quoting any character of the reserved word. The recognition of function names or special command names listed below cannot be altered by quoting them.

Arithmetic Evaluation.

An ability to perform integer arithmetic is provided with the special command **let**. Evaluations are performed using *long* arithmetic. Constants are of the form [*base*#]*n* where *base* is a decimal number between two and thirty-six representing the arithmetic base and *n* is a number in that base. If *base*# is omitted then base 10 is used.

An arithmetic expression uses the same syntax, precedence, and associativity of expression of the C language. All the integral operators, other than **++**, **− −**, **?:**, and **,** are supported. Variables can be referenced by name within an arithmetic expression without using the parameter substitution syntax. When a variable is referenced, its value is evaluated as an arithmetic expression.

An internal integer representation of a *variable* can be specified with the **−i** option of the **typeset** special command. Arithmetic evaluation is performed on the value of each assignment to a variable with the **−i** attribute. If you do not specify an arithmetic base, the first assignment to the variable determines the arithmetic base. This base is used when parameter substitution occurs.

Since many of the arithmetic operators require quoting, an alternative form of the **let** command is provided. For any command which begins with a **((**, all the characters until a matching **))** are treated as a quoted expression. More precisely, **((**. . .**))** is equivalent to **let "**. . .**"**.

Prompting.

When used interactively, the shell prompts with the parameter expanded value of **PS1** before reading a command. If at any time a new-line is typed and further input is needed to complete a command, then the secondary prompt (that is, the value of **PS2**) is issued.

Conditional Expressions.

A *conditional expression* is used with the **[[** compound command to test attributes of files and to compare strings. Word splitting and file name generation are not performed on the words between **[[** and **]]**. Each expression can be constructed from one or more of the following unary or binary expressions:

−a *file*	True, if *file* exists.
−b *file*	True, if *file* exists and is a block special file.
−c *file*	True, if *file* exists and is a character special file.
−d *file*	True, if *file* exists and is a directory.
−f *file*	True, if *file* exists and is an ordinary file.
−g *file*	True, if *file* exists and is has its **setgid** bit set.
−k *file*	True, if *file* exists and is has its sticky bit set.
−n *string*	True, if length of *string* is non-zero.
−o *option*	True, if option named *option* is on.
−p *file*	True, if *file* exists and is a fifo special file or a pipe.
−r *file*	True, if *file* exists and is readable by current process.
−s *file*	True, if *file* exists and has size greater than zero.
−t *fildes*	True, if file descriptor number *fildes* is open and associated with a terminal device.

−u *file*	True, if *file* exists and is has its setuid bit set.
−w *file*	True, if *file* exists and is writable by current process.
−x *file*	True, if *file* exists and is executable by current process. If *file* exists and is a directory, then the current process has permission to search in the directory.
−z *string*	True, if length of *string* is zero.
−L *file*	True, if *file* exists and is a symbolic link.
−O *file*	True, if *file* exists and is owned by the effective user id of this process.
−G *file*	True, if *file* exists and its group matches the effective group id of this process.
−S *file*	True, if *file* exists and is a socket.
file1 −nt *file2*	True, if *file1* exists and is newer than *file2*.
file1 −ot *file2*	True, if *file1* exists and is older than *file2*.
file1 −ef *file2*	True, if *file1* and *file2* exist and refer to the same file.
string = *pattern*	True, if *string* matches *pattern*.
string != *pattern*	True, if *string* does not match *pattern*.
string1 < *string2*	True, if *string1* comes before *string2* based on ASCII value of their characters.
string1 > *string2*	True, if *string1* comes after *string2* based on ASCII value of their characters.
exp1 −eq *exp2*	True, if *exp1* is equal to *exp2*.
exp1 −ne *exp2*	True, if *exp1* is not equal to *exp2*.
exp1 −lt *exp2*	True, if *exp1* is less than *exp2*.
exp1 −gt *exp2*	True, if *exp1* is greater than *exp2*.
exp1 −le *exp2*	True, if *exp1* is less than or equal to *exp2*.
exp1 −ge *exp2*	True, if *exp1* is greater than or equal to *exp2*.

In each of the above expressions, if *file* is of the form **/dev/fd/***n*, where *n* is an integer, then the test applied to the open file whose descriptor number is *n*.

A compound expression can be constructed from these primitives by using any of the following, listed in decreasing order of precedence.
(*expression*)
> True, if *expression* is true. Used to group expressions.

! *expression*
> True if *expression* is false.

expression1 && *expression2*
> True, if *expression1* and *expression2* are both true.

expression1 || *expression2*
> True, if either *expression1* or *expression2* is true.

Input/Output.

Before a command is executed, its input and output may be redirected using a special notation interpreted by the shell. The following may appear anywhere in a simple-command or may precede or follow a *command* and are *not* passed on to the invoked command. Command and parameter substitution occurs before *word* or *digit* is used except as noted below. File name generation occurs only if the pattern matches a single file and blank interpretation is not performed.

<*word*	Use file *word* as standard input (file descriptor 0).
>*word*	Use file *word* as standard output (file descriptor 1). If the file does not exist then it is created. If the file exists, is a regular file, and the **noclobber** option is on, this causes an error; otherwise, it is truncated to zero length.
>|*word*	Sames as >, except that it overrides the **noclobber** option.
>>*word*	Use file *word* as standard output. If the file exists then output is appended to it (by first seeking to the end-of-file); otherwise, the file is created.
<>*word*	Open file *word* for reading and writing as standard input.
<<[–]*word*	The shell input is read up to a line that is the same as *word*, or to an end-of-file. No parameter substitution, command substitution or file name generation is performed on *word*. The resulting document, called a *here-document*, becomes the standard input. If any character of *word* is quoted, then no interpretation is placed upon the characters of the document; otherwise, parameter and command substitution occurs, **\new-line** is ignored, and \ must be used to quote the characters \, **$**, ′, and the first character of *word*. If – is appended to <<, then all leading tabs are stripped from *word* and from the document.
<&*digit*	The standard input is duplicated from file descriptor *digit* [see **dup**(2)]. Similarly for the standard output using >& *digit*.
<&–	The standard input is closed. Similarly for the standard output using >&–.
<&p	The input from the co-process is moved to standard input.
>&p	The output to the co-process is moved to standard output.

If one of the above is preceded by a digit, then the file descriptor number referred to is that specified by the digit (instead of the default 0 or 1). For example:

> ... 2>&1

means file descriptor 2 is to be opened for writing as a duplicate of file descriptor 1.

The order in which redirections are specified is significant. The shell evaluates each redirection in terms of the (*file descriptor*, *file*) association at the time of evaluation. For example:

> ... 1>*fname* 2>&1

first associates file descriptor 1 with file *fname*. It then associates file descriptor 2 with the file associated with file descriptor 1 (that is, *fname*). If the order of redirections were reversed, file descriptor 2 would be associated with the terminal (assuming file descriptor 1 had been) and then file descriptor 1 would be associated with file *fname*.

If a command is followed by **&** and job control is not active, then the default standard input for the command is the empty file **/dev/null**. Otherwise, the environment for the execution of a command contains the file descriptors of the invoking shell as modified by input/output specifications.

Environment.

The *environment* [see **environ**(5)] is a list of name-value pairs that is passed to an executed program in the same way as a normal argument list. The names must be *identifiers* and the values are character strings. The shell interacts with the environment in several ways. On invocation, the shell scans the environment and creates a variable for each name found, giving it the corresponding value and marking it *export* . Executed commands inherit the environment. If the user modifies the values of these variables or creates new ones, using the **export** or **typeset -x** commands they become part of the environment. The environment seen by any executed command is thus composed of any name-value pairs originally inherited by the shell, whose values may be modified by the current shell, plus any additions which must be noted in **export** or **typeset -x** commands.

The environment for any *simple-command* or function may be augmented by prefixing it with one or more variable assignments. A variable assignment argument is a word of the form *identifier=value*. Thus:

> **TERM=450** *cmd args*   and
> (**export TERM; TERM=450;** *cmd args*)

are equivalent (as far as the above execution of *cmd* is concerned except for commands listed with one or two daggers, †, in the Special Commands section).

If the **-k** flag is set, *all* variable assignment arguments are placed in the environment, even if they occur after the command name. The following first prints **a=b c** and then **c:**

> echo a=b c
> set -k
> echo a=b c

This feature is intended for use with scripts written for early versions of the shell and its use in new scripts is strongly discouraged. It is likely to disappear someday.

Functions.

The **function** reserved word, described in the *Commands* section above, is used to define shell functions. Shell functions are read in and stored internally. Alias names are resolved when the function is read. Functions are executed like commands with the arguments passed as positional parameters (see *Execution* below).

Functions execute in the same process as the caller and share all files and present working directory with the caller. Traps caught by the caller are reset to their default action inside the function. A trap condition that is not caught or ignored by the function causes the function to terminate and the condition to be passed on to the caller. A trap on **EXIT** set inside a function is executed after the function completes in the environment of the caller. Ordinarily, variables are shared between the calling program and the function. However, the **typeset** special command used within a function defines local variables whose scope includes the current function and all functions it calls.

The special command **return** is used to return from function calls. Errors within functions return control to the caller.

Function identifiers can be listed with the **−f** or **+f** option of the **typeset** special command. The text of functions may also be listed with **−f**. Function can be undefined with the **−f** option of the **unset** special command.

Ordinarily, functions are unset when the shell executes a shell script. The **−xf** option of the **typeset** command allows a function to be exported to scripts that are executed without a separate invocation of the shell. Functions that need to be defined across separate invocations of the shell should be specified in the **ENV** file with the **−xf** option of **typeset**.

Jobs.

If the **monitor** option of the **set** command is turned on, an interactive shell associates a *job* with each pipeline. It keeps a table of current jobs, printed by the **jobs** command, and assigns them small integer numbers. When a job is started asynchronously with **&**, the shell prints a line which looks like:

        [1] 1234

indicating that the job which was started asynchronously was job number 1 and had one (top-level) process, whose process id was 1234.

If you are running a job and wish to do something else you may hit the key **^z** (CTRL-z) which sends a STOP signal to the current job. The shell will then normally indicate that the job has been 'Stopped', and print another prompt. You can then manipulate the state of this job, putting it in the background with the **bg** command, or run some other commands and then eventually bring the job back into the foreground with the foreground command **fg**. A **^z** takes effect immediately and is like an interrupt in that pending output and unread input are discarded when it is typed.

A job being run in the background will stop if it tries to read from the terminal. Background jobs are normally allowed to produce output, but this can be disabled by giving the command "stty tostop". If you set this tty option, then background jobs will stop when they try to produce output like they do when they try to read input.

There are several ways to refer to jobs in the shell. A job can be referred to by the process id of any process of the job or by one of the following:

%*number*	The job with the given number.
%*string*	Any job whose command line begins with *string*.
%?*string*	Any job whose command line contains *string*.
%%	Current job.
%+	Equivalent to %%.
%−	Previous job.

This shell learns immediately whenever a process changes state. It normally informs you whenever a job becomes blocked so that no further progress is possible, but only just before it prints a prompt. This is done so that it does not otherwise disturb your work.

When the monitor mode is on, each background job that completes triggers any trap set for **CHLD**.

When you try to leave the shell while jobs are running or stopped, you will be warned that 'You have stopped(running) jobs.' You may use the **jobs** command to see what they are. If you do this or immediately try to exit again, the shell will not warn you a second time, and the stopped jobs will be terminated.

Signals.

When a command is run in the background (that it, when it is followed by **&**) and the job **monitor** option is active, the command does not receive **INTERRUPT** or **QUIT** signals. When a command is run in the background (that it, when it is followed by **&**) and the job **monitor** option is not active, the command receives **INTERRUPT** or **QUIT** signals but ignores them. Otherwise, signals have the values inherited by the shell from its parent (but see also the **trap** command below).

Execution.

Each time a command is executed, the above substitutions are carried out. If the command name matches one of the *Special Commands* listed below, it is executed within the current shell process. Next, the command name is checked to see if it matches one of the user defined functions. If it does, the positional parameters are saved and then reset to the arguments of the *function* call. When the *function* completes or issues a **return**, the positional parameter list is restored and any trap set on **EXIT** within the function is executed. The value of a *function* is the value of the last command executed. A function is also executed in the current shell process. If a command name is not a *special command* or a user defined *function*, a process is created and an attempt is made to execute the command via **exec**(2).

The shell variable **PATH** defines the search path for the directory containing the command. Alternative directory names are separated by a colon (**:**). The default path is **/usr/bin:** (specifying **/usr/bin** and the current directory in that order). The current directory can be specified by two or more adjacent colons, or by a colon at the beginning or end of the path list. If the command name contains a **/** then the search path is not used. Otherwise, each directory in the path is searched for an executable file. If the file has execute permission but is not a directory or an **a.out** file, it is assumed to be a file containing shell commands. A sub-shell is spawned to read it. All non-exported aliases, functions, and variables, are removed in this case. A parenthesized command is executed in a sub-shell without removing non-exported quantities.

Command Re-entry.

The text of the last **HISTSIZE** (default 128) commands entered from a terminal device is saved in a *history* file. The file **$HOME/.sh_history** is used if the file denoted by the **HISTFILE** variable is not set or is not writable. A shell can access the commands of all *interactive* shells which use the same named **HISTFILE**. The special command **fc** is used to list or edit a portion of this file. The portion of the file to be edited or listed can be selected by number or by giving the first character or characters of the command. A single command or range of commands can be specified. If you do not specify an editor program as an argument to **fc** then the value of the variable **FCEDIT** is used. If **FCEDIT** is not defined then **/usr/bin/ed** is used. The edited command(s) is printed and re-executed upon leaving the editor. The editor name – is used to skip the editing phase and to re-execute the command. In this case a substitution variable of the form *old=new* can be used to modify the command before execution. For example, if **r** is aliased to ‘**fc −e −**’ then typing ‘**r bad=good c**’ will re-execute the most recent command which starts with the letter **c**, replacing the first occurrence of the string **bad** with the string **good**.

In-line Editing Options

Normally, each command line entered from a terminal device is simply typed followed by a new-line (‘RETURN’ or ‘LINE FEED’). If the **vi** option is active, the user can edit the command line. To be in this edit mode **set** the **vi** option. An editing option is automatically selected each time the **VISUAL** or **EDITOR** variable is assigned a value ending in either of these option names.

The editing features require that the user’s terminal accept ‘RETURN’ as carriage return without line feed and that a space (‘ ’) must overwrite the current character on the screen. ADM terminal users should set the "space - advance" switch to ‘space’. Hewlett-Packard series 2621 terminal users should set the straps to ‘bcGHxZ etX’.

The editing mode implements a concept where the user is looking through a window at the current line. The window width is the value of **COLUMNS** if it is defined, otherwise 80. If the line is longer than the window width minus two, a mark is displayed at the end of the window to notify the user. As the cursor moves and reaches the window boundaries the window will be centered about the cursor. The mark is a **>** (**<**, *****) if the line extends on the right (left, both) side(s) of the window.

The search commands in each edit mode provide access to the history file. Only strings are matched, not patterns, although a leading **^** in the string restricts the match to begin at the first character in the line.

vi Editing Mode

There are two typing modes. Initially, when you enter a command you are in the *input* mode. To edit, the user enters *control* mode by typing ESC (**\033**) and moves the cursor to the point needing correction and then inserts or deletes characters or words as needed. Most control commands accept an optional repeat *count* prior to the command.

When in **vi** mode on most systems, canonical processing is initially enabled and the command will be echoed again if the speed is 1200 baud or greater and it contains any control characters or less than one second has elapsed since the prompt was printed. The ESC character terminates canonical processing for the remainder of the command and the user can then modify the command line. This scheme has the advantages of canonical processing with the type-ahead echoing of raw mode.

If the option **viraw** is also set, the terminal will always have canonical processing disabled.

Input Edit Commands

By default the editor is in input mode.

erase	(User defined erase character as defined by the stty command, usually ^H or #.) Delete previous character.
^W	Delete the previous blank separated word.
^D	Terminate the shell.
^V	Escape next character. Editing characters, the user's erase or kill characters may be entered in a command line or in a search string if preceded by a ^V. The ^V removes the next character's editing features (if any).
\	Escape the next *erase* or **kill** character.

Motion Edit Commands

These commands will move the cursor.

[*count*]l	Cursor forward (right) one character.
[*count*]w	Cursor forward one alpha-numeric word.
[*count*]W	Cursor to the beginning of the next word that follows a blank.
[*count*]e	Cursor to end of word.
[*count*]E	Cursor to end of the current blank delimited word.
[*count*]h	Cursor backward (left) one character.
[*count*]b	Cursor backward one word.
[*count*]B	Cursor to preceding blank separated word.
[*count*]|	Cursor to column *count*.
[*count*]f*c*	Find the next character *c* in the current line.
[*count*]F*c*	Find the previous character *c* in the current line.
[*count*]t*c*	Equivalent to **f** followed by **h**.
[*count*]T*c*	Equivalent to **F** followed by **l**.
[*count*];	Repeats *count* times, the last single character find command, **f**, **F**, **t**, or **T**.
[*count*],	Reverses the last single character find command *count* times.
0	Cursor to start of line.
^	Cursor to first non-blank character in line.
$	Cursor to end of line.

Search Edit Commands

These commands access your command history.

[*count*]k	Fetch previous command. Each time **k** is entered the previous command back in time is accessed.
[*count*]–	Equivalent to **k**.

[*count*]ȷ   Fetch next command. Each time ȷ is entered the next com-
            mand forward in time is accessed.

[*count*]+   Equivalent to ȷ.

[*count*]G   The command number *count* is fetched. The default is the least
            recent history command.

/*string*   Search backward through history for a previous command con-
            taining *string*. *String* is terminated by a RETURN or
            NEW LINE. If string is preceded by a ^, the matched line
            must begin with *string*. If *string* is null the previous string will
            be used.

?*string*   Same as / except that search will be in the forward direction.

n   Search for next match of the last pattern to / or ? commands.

N   Search for next match of the last pattern to / or ?, but in
            reverse direction. Search history for the *string* entered by the
            previous / command.

Text Modification Edit Commands

These commands will modify the line.

a   Enter input mode and enter text after the current character.

A   Append text to the end of the line. Equivalent to $a.

[*count*]c*motion*

c[*count*]*motion*
            Delete current character through the character that *motion*
            would move the cursor to and enter input mode. If *motion* is c,
            the entire line will be deleted and input mode entered.

C   Delete the current character through the end of line and enter
            input mode. Equivalent to c$.

S   Equivalent to cc.

D   Delete the current character through the end of line.
            Equivalent to d$.

[*count*]d*motion*

d[*count*]*motion*
            Delete current character through the character that *motion*
            would move to. If *motion* is d, the entire line will be deleted.

i   Enter input mode and insert text before the current character.

I   Insert text before the beginning of the line. Equivalent to 0i.

[*count*]P   Place the previous text modification before the cursor.

[*count*]p   Place the previous text modification after the cursor.

R   Enter input mode and replace characters on the screen with
            characters you type overlay fashion.

[*count*]**r***c*	Replace the *count* character(s) starting at the current cursor position with *c*, and advance the cursor.
[*count*]**x**	Delete current character.
[*count*]**X**	Delete preceding character.
[*count*]**.**	Repeat the previous text modification command.
[*count*]**~**	Invert the case of the *count* character(s) starting at the current cursor position and advance the cursor.
[*count*]**_**	Causes the *count* word of the previous command to be appended and input mode entered. The last word is used if *count* is omitted.
*	Causes an ***** to be appended to the current word and file name generation attempted. If no match is found, it rings the bell. Otherwise, the word is replaced by the matching pattern and input mode is entered.
****	Filename completion. Replaces the current word with the longest common prefix of all filenames matching the current word with an asterisk appended. If the match is unique, a **/** is appended if the file is a directory and a space is appended if the file is not a directory.

Other Edit Commands

Miscellaneous commands.

[*count*]**y***motion*

y[*count*]*motion*
> Yank current character through character that *motion* would move the cursor to and puts them into the delete buffer. The text and cursor are unchanged.

Y	Yanks from current position to end of line. Equivalent to **y$**.
u	Undo the last text modifying command.
U	Undo all the text modifying commands performed on the line.
[*count*]**v**	Returns the command **fc -e ${VISUAL:-${EDITOR:-vi}}** *count* in the input buffer. If *count* is omitted, then the current line is used.
^L	Line feed and print current line. Has effect only in control mode.
^J	(New line) Execute the current line, regardless of mode.
^M	(Return) Execute the current line, regardless of mode.
#	Sends the line after inserting a **#** in front of the line. Useful for causing the current line to be inserted in the history without being executed.

=   List the file names that match the current word if an asterisk
          were appended it.

@*letter* Your alias list is searched for an alias by the name _*letter* and if
          an alias of this name is defined, its value will be inserted on
          the input queue for processing.

Special Commands.

The following simple-commands are executed in the shell process. Input/Output
redirection is permitted. Unless otherwise indicated, the output is written on file
descriptor 1 and the exit status, when there is no syntax error, is zero. Commands that are preceded by one or two † are treated specially in the following
ways:

1.   Variable assignment lists preceding the command remain in effect when
     the command completes.
2.   I/O redirections are processed after variable assignments.
3.   Errors cause a script that contains them to abort.
4.   Words, following a command preceded by †† that are in the format of a
     variable assignment, are expanded with the same rules as a variable
     assignment. This means that tilde substitution is performed after the =
     sign and word splitting and file name generation are not performed.

† **:** [*arg* ...]
     The command only expands parameters.

† **.** *file* [*arg* ...]
     Read the complete *file* then execute the commands. The commands are
     executed in the current Shell environment. The search path specified by
     PATH is used to find the directory containing *file*. If any arguments *arg* are
     given, they become the positional parameters. Otherwise the positional
     parameters are unchanged. The exit status is the exit status of the last
     command executed.

†† **alias** [**-tx**] [*name*[=*value*]] ...
     Alias with no arguments prints the list of aliases in the form *name=value*
     on standard output. An *alias* is defined for each name whose *value* is
     given. A trailing space in *value* causes the next word to be checked for
     alias substitution. The **-t** flag is used to set and list tracked aliases. The
     value of a tracked alias is the full pathname corresponding to the given
     name. The value becomes undefined when the value of **PATH** is reset but
     the aliases remain tracked. Without the **-t** flag, for each *name* in the argu-
     ment list for which no *value* is given, the name and value of the alias is
     printed. The **-x** flag is used to set or print exported aliases. An exported
     alias is defined for scripts invoked by name. The exit status is non-zero if
     a *name* is given, but no value, for which no alias has been defined.

bg [*job*...]
     This command is only on systems that support job control. Puts each
     specified *job* into the background. The current job is put in the back-
     ground if *job* is not specified. See *Jobs* for a description of the format of
     job.

† break [*n*]
>   Exit from the enclosing **for, while, until** or **select** loop, if any. If *n* is specified then break *n* levels.

† continue [*n*]
>   Resume the next iteration of the enclosing **for, while, until** or **select** loop. If *n* is specified then resume at the *n*-th enclosing loop.

cd [*arg*]
cd *old new*
>   This command can be in either of two forms. In the first form it changes the current directory to *arg*. If *arg* is – the directory is changed to the previous directory. The shell variable **HOME** is the default *arg*. The variable **PWD** is set to the current directory. The shell variable **CDPATH** defines the search path for the directory containing *arg*. Alternative directory names are separated by a colon (:). The default path is **<null>** (specifying the current directory). Note that the current directory is specified by a null path name, which can appear immediately after the equal sign or between the colon delimiters anywhere else in the path list. If *arg* begins with a / then the search path is not used. Otherwise, each directory in the path is searched for *arg*.

The second form of **cd** substitutes the string *new* for the string *old* in the current directory name, **PWD** and tries to change to this new directory.

The **cd** command may not be executed by **rksh**.

echo [*arg* ...]
>   See **echo**(1) for usage and description.

† eval [*arg* ...]
>   The arguments are read as input to the shell and the resulting command(s) executed.

† exec [*arg* ...]
>   If *arg* is given, the command specified by the arguments is executed in place of this shell without creating a new process. Input/output arguments may appear and affect the current process. If no arguments are given the effect of this command is to modify file descriptors as prescribed by the input/output redirection list. In this case, any file descriptor numbers greater than 2 that are opened with this mechanism are closed when invoking another program.

† exit [*n*]
>   Causes the shell to exit with the exit status specified by *n*. If *n* is omitted then the exit status is that of the last command executed. An end-of-file will also cause the shell to exit except for a shell which has the *ignoreeof* option (see **set** below) turned on.

†† export [*name*[=*value*]] ...
>   The given *name*s are marked for automatic export to the *environment* of subsequently-executed commands.

fc [−e *ename*] [−nlr] [*first* [*last*]]
fc −e − [*old=new*] [*command*]
> In the first form, a range of commands from *first* to *last* is selected from the last **HISTSIZE** commands that were typed at the terminal. The arguments *first* and *last* may be specified as a number or as a string. A string is used to locate the most recent command starting with the given string. A negative number is used as an offset to the current command number. If the flag −l, is selected, the commands are listed on standard output. Otherwise, the editor program *ename* is invoked on a file containing these keyboard commands. If *ename* is not supplied, then the value of the variable **FCEDIT** (default /usr/bin/ed) is used as the editor. When editing is complete, the edited command(s) is executed. If *last* is not specified then it will be set to *first*. If *first* is not specified the default is the previous command for editing and −16 for listing. The flag −r reverses the order of the commands and the flag −n suppresses command numbers when listing. In the second form the *command* is re-executed after the substitution *old=new* is performed.

fg [*job...*]
> This command is only on systems that support job control. Each *job* specified is brought to the foreground. Otherwise, the current job is brought into the foreground. See *Jobs* for a description of the format of *job*.

getopts *optstring name* [*arg ...*]
> Checks *arg* for legal options. If *arg* is omitted, the positional parameters are used. An option argument begins with a + or a −. An option not beginning with + or − or the argument −− ends the options. *optstring* contains the letters that **getopts** recognizes. If a letter is followed by a :, that option is expected to have an argument. The options can be separated from the argument by blanks.
>
> **getopts** places the next option letter it finds inside variable *name* each time it is invoked with a + prepended when *arg* begins with a +. The index of the next *arg* is stored in **OPTIND**. The option argument, if any, gets stored in **OPTARG**.
>
> A leading : in *optstring* causes **getopts** to store the letter of an invalid option in **OPTARG**, and to set *name* to ? for an unknown option and to : when a required option is missing. Otherwise, **getopts** prints an error message. The exit status is non-zero when there are no more options.

jobs [−lnp] [*job ...*]
> Lists information about each given job; or all active jobs if *job* is omitted. The −l flag lists process ids in addition to the normal information. The −n flag only displays jobs that have stopped or exited since last notified. The −p flag causes only the process group to be listed. See *Jobs* for a description of the format of *job*.

kill [-*sig*] *job* ...
kill -l

>Sends either the TERM (terminate) signal or the specified signal to the specified jobs or processes. Signals are either given by number or by names (as given in **/usr/include/signal.h**, stripped of the prefix "SIG"). If the signal being sent is TERM (terminate) or HUP (hangup), then the job or process will be sent a CONT (continue) signal if it is stopped. The argument *job* can the process id of a process that is not a member of one of the active jobs. See *Jobs* for a description of the format of *job*. In the second form, **kill -l**, the signal numbers and names are listed.

let *arg* ...

>Each *arg* is a separate *arithmetic expression* to be evaluated. See *Arithmetic Evaluation* above, for a description of arithmetic expression evaluation.

>The exit status is 0 if the value of the last expression is non-zero, and 1 otherwise.

† newgrp [*arg* ...]

>Equivalent to **exec /usr/bin/newgrp** *arg* ....

print [**-Rnprsu**[*n*]] [*arg* ...]

>The shell output mechanism. With no flags or with flag - or -- the arguments are printed on standard output as described by **echo**(1). In raw mode, **-R** or **-r**, the escape conventions of **echo** are ignored. The **-R** option will print all subsequent arguments and options other than **-n**. The **-p** option causes the arguments to be written onto the pipe of the process spawned with |**&** instead of standard output. The **-s** option causes the arguments to be written onto the history file instead of standard output. The **-u** flag can be used to specify a one digit file descriptor unit number **n** on which the output will be placed. The default is 1. If the flag **-n** is used, no **new-line** is added to the output.

pwd   Equivalent to **print -r - $PWD**

read [**-prsu**[*n*]] [*name?prompt*] [*name* ...]

>The shell input mechanism. One line is read and is broken up into fields using the characters in **IFS** as separators. In raw mode, **-r,** a \ at the end of a line does not signify line continuation. The first field is assigned to the first *name*, the second field to the second *name*, and so on, with left-over fields assigned to the last *name*. The **-p** option causes the input line to be taken from the input pipe of a process spawned by the shell using |**&**. If the **-s** flag is present, the input will be saved as a command in the history file. The flag **-u** can be used to specify a one digit file descriptor unit to read from. The file descriptor can be opened with the **exec** special command. The default value of *n* is 0. If *name* is omitted then **REPLY** is used as the default *name*. The exit status is 0 unless an end-of-file is encountered. An end-of-file with the **-p** option causes cleanup for this process so that another can be spawned. If the first argument contains a

?, the remainder of this word is used as a *prompt* on standard error when the shell is interactive. The exit status is 0 unless an end-of-file is encountered.

†† **readonly** [*name*[=*value*]] ...

The given *names* are marked readonly and these names cannot be changed by subsequent assignment.

† **return** [*n*]

Causes a shell *function* to return to the invoking script with the return status specified by *n*. If *n* is omitted then the return status is that of the last command executed. If **return** is invoked while not in a *function* or a **.** script, then it is the same as an **exit**.

set [±**aefhkmnpstuvx**] [±**o** *option*] ... [±**A** *name*] [*arg* ...]

The flags for this command have meaning as follows:

-A   Array assignment. Unset the variable *name* and assign values sequentially from the list *arg*. If **+A** is used, the variable *name* is not unset first.

-a   All subsequent variables that are defined are automatically exported.

-e   If a command has a non-zero exit status, execute the **ERR** trap, if set, and exit. This mode is disabled while reading profiles.

-f   Disables file name generation.

-h   Each command becomes a tracked alias when first encountered.

-k   All variable assignment arguments are placed in the environment for a command, not just those that precede the command name.

-m   Background jobs will run in a separate process group and a line will print upon completion. The exit status of background jobs is reported in a completion message. On systems with job control, this flag is turned on automatically for interactive shells.

-n   Read commands and check them for syntax errors, but do not execute them. Ignored for interactive shells.

-o   The following argument can be one of the following option names:

allexport	Same as **-a**.
errexit	Same as **-e**.
bgnice	All background jobs are run at a lower priority. This is the default mode.
ignoreeof	The shell will not exit on end-of-file. The command **exit** must be used.
keyword	Same as **-k**.
markdirs	All directory names resulting from file name generation have a trailing **/** appended.
monitor	Same as **-m**.
noclobber	Prevents redirection **>** from truncating existing files. Require **>|** to truncate a file when turned on.
noexec	Same as **-n**.
noglob	Same as **-f**.

nolog	Do not save function definitions in history file.
nounset	Same as **-u**.
privileged	Same as **-p**.
verbose	Same as **-v**.
trackall	Same as **-h**.
vi	Puts you in insert mode of a **vi** style in-line editor until you hit escape character **033**. This puts you in move mode. A return sends the line.
viraw	Each character is processed as it is typed in **vi** mode.
xtrace	Same as **-x**.

If no option name is supplied then the current option settings are printed.

-p　　Disables processing of the **$HOME/.profile** file and uses the file **/etc/suid_profile** instead of the **ENV** file. This mode is on whenever the effective uid (gid) is not equal to the real uid (gid). Turning this off causes the effective uid and gid to be set to the real uid and gid.

-s　　Sort the positional parameters lexicographically.

-t　　Exit after reading and executing one command.

-u　　Treat unset parameters as an error when substituting.

-v　　Print shell input lines as they are read.

-x　　Print commands and their arguments as they are executed.

-　　Turns off **-x** and **-v** flags and stops examining arguments for flags.

- -　　Do not change any of the flags; useful in setting **$1** to a value beginning with **-**. If no arguments follow this flag then the positional parameters are unset.

Using **+** rather than **-** causes these flags to be turned off. These flags can also be used upon invocation of the shell. The current set of flags may be found in **$-**. Unless **-A** is specified, the remaining arguments are positional parameters and are assigned, in order, to **$1 $2** .... If no arguments are given then the names and values of all variables are printed on the standard output.

† **shift** [*n*]

The positional parameters from **$*n*+1** ... are renamed **$1** ... , default *n* is 1. The parameter *n* can be any arithmetic expression that evaluates to a non-negative number less than or equal to **$#**.

† **times**　Print the accumulated user and system times for the shell and for processes run from the shell.

† **trap** [*arg*] [*sig*] ...

arg is a command to be read and executed when the shell receives signal(s) *sig*. (Note that *arg* is scanned once when the trap is set and once when the trap is taken.) Each *sig* can be given as a number or as the name of the signal. Trap commands are executed in order of signal number. Any attempt to set a trap on a signal that was ignored on entry to the current shell is ineffective. If *arg* is omitted or is **-**, then all trap(s) *sig* are reset to their original values. If *arg* is the null string then this signal is ignored by the shell and by the commands it invokes. If *sig* is **ERR** then *arg* will be executed whenever a command has a non-zero exit status. *sig* is **DEBUG** then *arg* will be executed after each command. If *sig* is **0** or **EXIT** and the **trap** statement is executed inside the body of a function, then the command *arg* is executed after the function completes. If *sig* is **0** or **EXIT** for a **trap** set outside any function then the command *arg* is executed on exit from the shell. The **trap** command with no arguments prints a list of commands associated with each signal number.

†† **typeset** [±**HLRZfilrtux**[*n*]] [*name*[=*value*]] ...

Sets attributes and values for shell variables. When invoked inside a function, a new instance of the variable *name* is created. The parameter value and type are restored when the function completes. The following list of attributes may be specified:

-H   This flag provides UNIX to host-name file mapping on non-UNIX machines.

-L   Left justify and remove leading blanks from *value*. If *n* is non-zero it defines the width of the field, otherwise it is determined by the width of the value of first assignment. When the variable is assigned to, it is filled on the right with blanks or truncated, if necessary, to fit into the field. Leading zeros are removed if the **-Z** flag is also set. The **-R** flag is turned off.

-R   Right justify and fill with leading blanks. If *n* is non-zero it defines the width of the field, otherwise it is determined by the width of the value of first assignment. The field is left filled with blanks or truncated from the end if the variable is reassigned. The **L** flag is turned off.

-Z   Right justify and fill with leading zeros if the first non-blank character is a digit and the **-L** flag has not been set. If *n* is non-zero it defines the width of the field, otherwise it is determined by the width of the value of first assignment.

-f   The names refer to function names rather than variable names. No assignments can be made and the only other valid flags are **-t**, **-u** and **-x**. The flag **-t** turns on execution tracing for this function. The flag **-u** causes this function to be marked undefined. The **FPATH** variable will be searched to find the function definition when the function is referenced. The flag **-x** allows the function definition to remain in effect across shell procedures invoked by name.

-i   Variable is an integer. This makes arithmetic faster. If *n* is non-zero it defines the output arithmetic base, otherwise the first assignment determines the output base.

-l   All upper-case characters converted to lower-case. The upper-case flag, **-u** is turned off.

-r   The given *names* are marked readonly and these names cannot be changed by subsequent assignment.

-t   Tags the variables. Tags are user definable and have no spe-
            cial meaning to the shell.

-u   All lower-case characters are converted to upper-case charac-
            ters. The lower-case flag, -l is turned off.

-x   The given *names* are marked for automatic export to the
            environment of subsequently-executed commands.

Using + rather than - causes these flags to be turned off. If no *name*
arguments are given but flags are specified, a list of *names* (and optionally the **values**) of the *variables* which have these flags set is printed.
(Using + rather than - keeps the values from being printed.) If no
names and flags are given, the *names* and *attributes* of all *variables* are
printed.

ulimit [-[HS][a | cdfnstv]]

ulimit [-[HS][c | d | f | n | s | t | v]] *limit*
            ulimit prints or sets hard or soft resource limits. These limits are
            described in **getrlimit**(2).

            If *limit* is not present, **ulimit** prints the specified limits. Any number
            of limits may be printed at one time. The -a option prints all limits.

            If *limit* is present, **ulimit** sets the specified limit to *limit*. The string
            unlimited requests the largest valid limit. Limits may be set for only
            one resource at a time. Any user may set a soft limit to any value
            below the hard limit. Any user may lower a hard limit. Only a
            super-user may raise a hard limit; see **su**(1).

            The -H option specifies a hard limit. The -S option specifies a soft
            limit. If neither option is specified, **ulimit** will set both limits and
            print the soft limit.

            The following options specify the resource whose limits are to be
            printed or set. If no option is specified, the file size limit is printed or
            set.

            -c   maximum core file size (in 512-byte blocks)

            -d   maximum size of data segment or heap (in kbytes)

            -f   maximum file size (in 512-byte blocks)

            -n   maximum file descriptor plus 1

            -s   maximum size of stack segment (in kbytes)

            -t   maximum CPU time (in seconds)

            -v   maximum size of virtual memory (in kbytes)

            If no option is given, -f is assumed.

umask [*mask*]
            The user file-creation mask is set to *mask* [see **umask**(2)]. *mask* can
            either be an octal number or a symbolic value as described in **chmod**(1).
            If a symbolic value is given, the new umask value is the complement of
            the result of applying *mask* to the complement of the previous umask
            value. If *mask* is omitted, the current value of the mask is printed.

unalias *name ...*
> The variables given by the list of *name*s are removed from the *alias* list.

unset [**-f**] *name ...*
> The variables given by the list of *name*s are unassigned, for example, their values and attributes are erased. Read-only variables cannot be unset. If the flag, **-f**, is set, then the names refer to *function* names. Unsetting **ERRNO**, **LINENO**, **MAILCHECK**, **OPTARG**, **OPTIND**, **RANDOM**, **SECONDS**, **TMOUT**, and _ causes removes their special meaning even if they are subsequently assigned to.

† **wait** [*job*]
> Wait for the specified *job* and report its termination status. If *job* is not given then all currently active child processes are waited for. The exit status from this command is that of the process waited for. See *Jobs* for a description of the format of *job*.

whence [**-pv**] *name ...*
> For each *name*, indicate how it would be interpreted if used as a command name.
>
> **-v**   produces a more verbose report.
>
> **-p**   does a path search for *name* even if name is an alias, a function, or a reserved word.

Invocation.

If the shell is invoked by **exec**(2), and the first character of argument zero ($0) is -, then the shell is assumed to be a **login** shell and commands are read from **/etc/profile** and then from either **.profile** in the current directory or **$HOME/.profile**, if either file exists. Next, commands are read from the file named by performing parameter substitution on the value of the environment variable **ENV** if the file exists. If the **-s** flag is not present and *arg* is, then a path search is performed on the first *arg* to determine the name of the script to execute. The script *arg* must have read permission and any **setuid** and **setgid** settings will be ignored. Commands are then read as described below; the following flags are interpreted by the shell when it is invoked:

-c *string*   If the **-c** flag is present then commands are read from *string*.

-s   If the **-s** flag is present or if no arguments remain then commands are read from the standard input. Shell output, except for the output of the *Special commands* listed above, is written to file descriptor 2.

-i   If the **-i** flag is present or if the shell input and output are attached to a terminal (as told by **ioctl**(2)) then this shell is *interactive*. In this case TERM is ignored (so that **kill 0** does not kill an interactive shell) and INTR is caught and ignored (so that **wait** is interruptible). In all cases, **QUIT** is ignored by the shell.

-r   If the **-r** flag is present the shell is a restricted shell.

The remaining flags and arguments are described under the **set** command above.

rksh Only.

rksh is used to set up login names and execution environments whose capabilities are more controlled than those of the standard shell. The actions of **rksh** are identical to those of **sh**, except that the following are disallowed:

changing directory [see **cd**(1)],
setting the value of **SHELL**, **ENV**, or **PATH,**
specifying path or command names containing **/,**
redirecting output (**>, >|** , **<>** , and **>>**).

The restrictions above are enforced after **.profile** and the **ENV** files are interpreted.

When a command to be executed is found to be a shell procedure, **rksh** invokes **ksh** to execute it. Thus, it is possible to provide to the end-user shell procedures that have access to the full power of the standard shell, while imposing a limited menu of commands; this scheme assumes that the end-user does not have write and execute permissions in the same directory.

The net effect of these rules is that the writer of the **.profile** has complete control over user actions, by performing guaranteed setup actions and leaving the user in an appropriate directory (probably not the login directory).

The system administrator often sets up a directory of commands (that is, **/usr/rbin**) that can be safely invoked by **rksh**.

EXIT STATUS

Errors detected by the shell, such as syntax errors, cause the shell to return a non-zero exit status. Otherwise, the shell returns the exit status of the last command executed (see also the **exit** command above). If the shell is being used non-interactively then execution of the shell file is abandoned. Run time errors detected by the shell are reported by printing the command or function name and the error condition. If the line number that the error occurred on is greater than one, then the line number is also printed in square brackets (**[]**) after the command or function name.

FILES

```
/etc/passwd
/etc/profile
/etc/suid_profile
$HOME/.profile
/tmp/sh*
/dev/null
```

SEE ALSO

cat(1), **cd**(1), **chmod**(1), **cut**(1), **echo**(1), **env**(1), **paste**(1), **stty**(1), **test**(1), **umask**(1), and **vi**(1)
dup(2), **exec**(2), **fork**(2), **ioctl**(2), **lseek**(2), **pipe**(2), **signal**(2), **umask**(2), **ulimit**(2), **wait**(2), and **rand**(3C) in the *Programmer's Reference Manual*
newgrp(1M), **a.out**(4), **profile**(4), and **environ**(4) in the *System Administrator's Reference Manual*

Morris I. Bolsky and David G. Korn, *The KornShell Command and Programming Language*, Prentice Hall, 1989.

NOTES

If a command which is a *tracked alias* is executed, and then a command with the same name is installed in a directory in the search path before the directory where the original command was found, the shell will continue to **exec** the original command. Use the **-t** option of the **alias** command to correct this situation.

Some very old shell scripts contain a ^ as a synonym for the pipe character. |.

Using the `fc` built-in command within a compound command will cause the whole command to disappear from the history file.

The built-in command . *file* reads the whole file before any commands are executed. Therefore, **alias** and **unalias** commands in the file will not apply to any functions defined in the file.

Traps are not processed while a job is waiting for a foreground process. Thus, a trap on `CHLD` won't be executed until the foreground job terminates.

NAME

labelit (generic) – provide labels for file systems

SYNOPSIS

labelit [-**F** *FSType*] [-**V**] [*current_options*] [-**o** *specific_options*] *special* [*operands*]

DESCRIPTION

labelit can be used to provide labels for unmounted disk file systems or file systems being copied to tape.

The *special* name should be the disk partition (for example, /**dev/rdsk/***, where the value of * is machine specific), or the cartridge tape (for example, /**dev/rmt/***). The device may not be on a remote machine. *operands* are *FSType*-specific and the manual page of the *FSType*-specific labelit command should be consulted for a detailed description.

current_options are options supported by the **s5**-specific module of labelit. Other *FSTypes* do not necessarily support these options. *specific_options* indicate suboptions specified in a comma-separated list of suboptions and/or keyword-attribute pairs for interpretation by the *FSType*-specific module of the command.

The options are:

-**F**   specify the *FSType* on which to operate. The *FSType* should either be specified here or be determinable from /**etc/vfstab** by matching *special* with an entry in the table.

-**V**   echo complete command line. This option is used to verify and validate the command line. Additional information obtained via a /**etc/vfstab** lookup is included in the output. The command is not executed.

-**o**   Specify *FSType*-specific options.

NOTE

This command may not be supported for all FSTypes.

FILES

/**etc/vfstab**   list of default parameters for each file system

SEE ALSO

makefsys(1M), vfstab(4)
Manual pages for the FSType-specific modules of labelit

NAME

labelit (s5) – provide labels for **s5** file systems

SYNOPSIS

labelit [–**F s5**] [*generic_options*] [–**n**] *special* [*fsname volume*]

DESCRIPTION

generic_options are options supported by the generic labelit command.

labelit can be used to provide labels for unmounted **s5** disk file systems or **s5** file systems being copied to tape.

With the optional arguments omitted, labelit prints current label values.

The *special* name should be the disk partition (e.g., **/dev/rdsk/***), or the cartridge tape (for example, **/dev/rmt/***, where the value of * is machine dependent.) The device may not be on a remote machine.

The *fsname* argument represents the mounted name (e.g., **root, usr,** etc.) of the file system.

Volume may be used to equate an internal name to a volume name applied externally to the hard disk, diskette or tape.

For file systems on disk, *fsname* and *volume* are recorded in the superblock.

The options are:

–**F s5**   Specifies the **s5**-FSType. Used to ensure that an **s5** file system is labelled.

–**n**   Provides for initial tape labeling only. (This destroys the previous contents of the tape.)

SEE ALSO

generic **labelit**(1M), **makefsys**(1M), s5_specific **mount**(1M), **fs**(4).

NAME

      labelit (ufs) – provide labels for **ufs** file systems

SYNOPSIS

      labelit [**–F ufs**] [*generic_options*] *special* [*fsname volume*]

DESCRIPTION

      generic_options are options supported by the generic **labelit** command.

      labelit can be used to provide labels for unmounted disk file systems or file systems being copied to tape.

      If neither *fsname* nor *volume* is specified, **labelit** prints the current values.

      The *special* name should be the physical disk section (for example, **/dev/rdsk/***, where * is machine specific), or the cartridge tape (for example, **/dev/rmt/***). The device may not be on a remote machine.

      The *fsname* argument represents the mounted name (for example, **root**, **usr**, etc.) of the file system.

      Volume may be used to equate an internal name to a volume name applied externally to the disk pack, diskette, or tape.

      The option is:

      –F ufs   Specifies the **ufs**-FSType.

SEE ALSO

      generic **labelit**(1M), **makefsys**(1M), **ufs**(4)

NAME
last – indicate last user or terminal logins

SYNOPSIS
last [−n *number* | −*number*] [−f *filename*] [*name* | *tty*] ...

DESCRIPTION
The **last** command looks in the **/var/adm/wtmp**, file which records all logins and logouts, for information about a user, a terminal or any group of users and terminals. Arguments specify names of users or terminals of interest. Names of terminals may be given fully or abbreviated. For example **last 10** is the same as **last term/10**. If multiple arguments are given, the information which applies to any of the arguments is printed. For example **last root console** lists all of root's sessions as well as all sessions on the console terminal. **last** displays the sessions of the specified users and terminals, most recent first, indicating the times at which the session began, the duration of the session, and the terminal which the session took place on. If the session is still continuing or was cut short by a reboot, **last** so indicates.

The pseudo-user **reboot** logs in at reboots of the system, thus

　　　　last reboot

will give an indication of mean time between reboot.

last with no arguments displays a record of all logins and logouts, in reverse order.

If **last** is interrupted, it indicates how far the search has progressed in **/var/adm/wtmp**. If interrupted with a quit signal (generated by a CTRL-\) **last** indicates how far the search has progressed so far, and the search continues.

The following options are available:

−n *number* | −*number*　　Limit the number of entries displayed to that specified by *number*. These options are identical; the −*number* option is provided as a transition tool only and will be removed in future releases.

−f *filename*　　Use *filename* as the name of the accounting file instead of **/var/adm/wtmp**.

FILES
/var/adm/wtmp　　accounting file

SEE ALSO
utmp(4) in the *System Administrator's Reference Manual*

NAME

lastcomm – show the last commands executed, in reverse order

SYNOPSIS

/usr/ucb/lastcomm [*command-name*] . . . [*user-name*] . . . [*terminal-name*] . . .

DESCRIPTION

The lastcomm command gives information on previously executed commands. lastcomm with no arguments displays information about all the commands recorded during the current accounting file's lifetime. If called with arguments, lastcomm only displays accounting entries with a matching *command-name*, *user-name*, or *terminal-name*.

EXAMPLE

The command:

        lastcomm a.out root term/01

would produce a listing of all the executions of commands named **a.out**, by user **root** while using the terminal **term/01**. and

        lastcomm root

would produce a listing of all the commands executed by user **root**.

For each process entry, lastcomm displays the following items of information:

the command name under which the process was called

one or more flags indicating special information about the process. The flags have the following meanings:

> **F**   The process performed a **fork** but not an **exec**.

> **S**   The process ran as a set-user-id program.

the name of the user who ran the process

the terminal which the user was logged in on at the time (if applicable)

the amount of CPU time used by the process (in seconds)

the date and time the process exited

FILES

/var/adm/pacct   accounting file

SEE ALSO

sigvec(3)

last(1) in the *User's Reference Manual*
acct(4), core(4) in the *System Administrator's Reference Manual*

NAME

layers – layer multiplexor for windowing terminals

SYNOPSIS

layers [–s] [–t] [–D [–m *max-pkt*] [–d] [–p] [–h *modlist*] [–f *file*] [*layersys-prgm*]

DESCRIPTION

layers manages asynchronous windows [see **layers**(5)] on a windowing terminal. Upon invocation, **layers** finds an unused **xt**(7) channel group and associates it with the terminal line on its standard output. It then waits for commands from the terminal.

Command-line options:

–s   Report protocol statistics on standard error at the end of the session after you exit from **layers**. The statistics may be printed during a session by invoking the program **xts**(1M).

–t   Turn on **xt**(7) driver packet tracing, and produces a trace dump on standard error at the end of the session after you exit from **layers**. The trace dump may be printed during a session by invoking the program **xtt**(1M).

–D   Send debugging messages to standard error.

–m *max-pkt*

Set maximum size for the data part of regular **xt** packets sent from the host to the terminal. Valid values are 32 to 252. This option also implies that regular rather than network **xt** protocol should be used. See **xtproto**(5).

–d   If a firmware patch has been downloaded, print out the sizes of the text, data, and bss portions of the firmware patch on standard error.

–p   If a firmware patch has been downloaded, print the down-loading protocol statistics and a trace on standard error.

–h *modlist*

Push a list of STREAMS modules separated by a comma on a layer.

–f *file*   Start **layers** with an initial configuration specified by *file*. Each line of the file represents a layer to be created, and has the following format:

origin_x origin_y corner_x corner_y command_list

The coordinates specify the size and position of the layer on the screen in the terminal's coordinate system. If all four are **0**, the user must define the layer interactively. *command_list*, a list of one or more commands, must be provided. It is executed in the new layer using the user's shell (by executing: **$SHELL -i -c "***command_list***"**). This means that the last command should invoke a shell, such as **/usr/bin/sh**. (If the last command is not a shell, then, when the last command has completed, the layer will not be functional.)

layersys-prgm

A file containing a firmware patch that the **layers** command downloads to the terminal before layers are created and *command_list* is executed.

Each layer is in most ways functionally identical to a separate terminal. Characters typed on the keyboard are sent to the standard input of the UNIX system process attached to the current layer (called the host process), and characters written on the standard output by the host process appear in that layer. When a layer is created, a separate shell is established and bound to the layer. If the environment variable **SHELL** is set, the user gets that shell: otherwise, **/usr/bin/sh** is used. In order to enable communications with other users via **write**(1), **layers** invokes the command **relogin**(1M) when the first layer is created. **relogin**(1M) will reassign that layer as the user's logged-in terminal. An alternative layer can be designated by using **relogin**(1M) directly. **layers** will restore the original assignment on termination.

Layers are created, deleted, reshaped, and otherwise manipulated in a terminal-dependent manner. For instance, the AT&T 630 MTG terminal provides a mouse-activated pop-up menu of layer operations. The method of ending a **layers** session is also defined by the terminal.

If a user wishes to take advantage of a terminal-specific application software package, the environment variable **DMD** should be set to the path name of the directory where the package was installed. Otherwise **DMD** should not be set.

EXAMPLES

A typical startup command is:

```
layers -f startup
```

where **startup** contains

```
8 8 700 200 date ; pwd ; exec $SHELL
8 300 780 850 exec $SHELL
```

The command

```
layers -h FILTER,LDTERM
```

pushes the STREAMS modules **FILTER** and **LDTERM** on each layer that is opened.

FILES

```
/dev/xt/??[0-7]
/usr/lib/layersys/lsys.8;7;3
$DMD/lib/layersys/lsys.8;?;?
```

SEE ALSO

ismpx(1), **jterm**(1), **jwin**(1), **sh**(1), **write**(1)
relogin(1M), **wtinit**(1M), **xts**(1M), **xtt**(1M), **jagent**(5), **layers**(5), **xtproto**(5), and **xt**(7)
libwindows(3X) in the *Programmer's Reference Manual*

NOTES

The **xt**(7) driver supports an alternate data transmission scheme known as ENCODING MODE. This mode makes **layers** operation possible even over data links which intercept control characters or do not transmit 8-bit characters. ENCODING MODE is selected either by setting a setup option on your windowing terminal or by setting the environment variable **DMDLOAD** to the value **hex** before running **layers**:   `DMDLOAD=hex; export DMDLOAD`

If, after executing **layers** **-f** *file*, the terminal does not respond in one or more of the layers, often the last command in the *command_list* for that layer did not invoke a shell.

To access this version of **layers**, make sure **/usr/bin** appears before any other directory, such as **$DMD/bin**, you have in your path that contains a layers program. [For information about defining the shell environmental variable **PATH** in your **.profile**, see **profile**(4).] Otherwise, if there is a terminal-dependent version of **layers**, you may get it instead of the correct one.

layers sends all debugging and error messages to standard error. Therefore, when invoking **layers** with the **–D, –d**, or **–p** option, it is necessary to redirect standard error to a file. For example,

```
layers -D 2>layers.msgs
```

If **layers** encounters an error condition and standard error is not redirected, the last error encountered will be printed when the **layers** commands exits.

When using **layers** the minimum acceptable baud rate is 1200. Behavior of **layers** is unpredictable when using baud rate below 1200.

When using V7/BSD/Xenix applications (for example, the **jim** editor) **layers** should be invoked as

```
layers -h ldterm,ttcompat
```

This pushes the **ttcompat** module on each window and converts the BSD interface into the **termio**(7) interface.

NAME

    ld – link editor for object files

SYNOPSIS

    ld [*options*] *files* . . .

DESCRIPTION

    The ld command combines relocatable object files, performs relocation, and resolves external symbols. ld operates in two modes, static or dynamic, as governed by the −d option. In static mode, −dn, relocatable object files given as arguments are combined to produce an executable object file; if the −r option is specified, relocatable object files are combined to produce one relocatable object file. In dynamic mode, −dy, the default, relocatable object files given as arguments are combined to produce an executable object file that will be linked at execution with any shared object files given as arguments; if the −G option is specified, relocatable object files are combined to produce a shared object. In all cases, the output of ld is left in a.out by default.

    If any argument is a library, it is searched exactly once at the point it is encountered in the argument list. The library may be either a relocatable archive or a shared object. For an archive library, only those routines defining an unresolved external reference are loaded. The archive library symbol table [see ar(4)] is searched sequentially with as many passes as are necessary to resolve external references that can be satisfied by library members. Thus, the ordering of members in the library is functionally unimportant, unless there exist multiple library members defining the same external symbol. A shared object consists of a single entity all of whose references must be resolved within the executable being built or within other shared objects with which it is linked.

    The following options are recognized by ld:

    −a   In static mode only, produce an executable object file; give errors for undefined references. This is the default behavior for static mode. −a may not be used with the −r option.

    −b   In dynamic mode only, when creating an executable, do not do special processing for relocations that reference symbols in shared objects. Without the −b option, the link editor will create special position-independent relocations for references to functions defined in shared objects and will arrange for data objects defined in shared objects to be copied into the memory image of the executable by the dynamic linker at run time. With the −b option, the output code may be more efficient, but it will be less sharable.

    −d[y| n]   When −dy, the default, is specified, ld uses dynamic linking; when −dn is specified, ld uses static linking.

    −e *epsym* Set the entry point address for the output file to be that of the symbol *epsym*.

    −h *name* In dynamic mode only, when building a shared object, record *name* in the object's dynamic section. *name* will be recorded in executables that are linked with this object rather than the object's UNIX System file name. Accordingly, *name* will be used by the dynamic linker as the name of the shared object to search for at run time.

−l*x*   Search a library lib*x*.so or lib*x*.a, the conventional names for shared object and archive libraries, respectively. In dynamic mode, unless the −Bstatic option is in effect, ld searches each directory specified in the library search path for a file lib*x*.so or lib*x*.a. The directory search stops at the first directory containing either. ld chooses the file ending in .so if −l*x* expands to two files whose names are of the form lib*x*.so and lib*x*.a. If no lib*x*.so is found, then ld accepts lib*x*.a. In static mode, or when the −Bstatic option is in effect, ld selects only the file ending in .a. A library is searched when its name is encountered, so the placement of −l is significant.

−m   Produce a memory map or listing of the input/output sections on the standard output.

−o *outfile*   Produce an output object file named *outfile*. The name of the default object file is a.out.

−r   Combine relocatable object files to produce one relocatable object file. ld will not complain about unresolved references. This option cannot be used in dynamic mode or with −a.

−s   Strip symbolic information from the output file. The debug and line sections and their associated relocation entries will be removed. Except for relocatable files or shared objects, the symbol table and string table sections will also be removed from the output object file.

−t   Turn off the warning about multiply defined symbols that are not the same size.

−u *symname*   Enter *symname* as an undefined symbol in the symbol table. This is useful for loading entirely from an archive library, since initially the symbol table is empty and an unresolved reference is needed to force the loading of the first routine. The placement of this option on the command line is significant; it must be placed before the library that will define the symbol.

−z defs   Force a fatal error if any undefined symbols remain at the end of the link. This is the default when building an executable. It is also useful when building a shared object to assure that the object is self-contained, that is, that all its symbolic references are resolved internally.

−z nodefs   Allow undefined symbols. This is the default when building a shared object. It may be used when building an executable in dynamic mode and linking with a shared object that has unresolved references in routines not used by that executable. This option should be used with caution.

−z text   In dynamic mode only, force a fatal error if any relocations against non-writable, allocatable sections remain.

-B [dynamic| static]

> Options governing library inclusion. **-Bdynamic** is valid in dynamic mode only. These options may be specified any number of times on the command line as toggles: if the **-Bstatic** option is given, no shared objects will be accepted until **-Bdynamic** is seen. See also the **-l** option.

-Bsymbolic

> In dynamic mode only, when building a shared object, bind references to global symbols to their definitions within the object, if definitions are available. Normally, references to global symbols within shared objects are not bound until run time, even if definitions are available, so that definitions of the same symbol in an executable or other shared objects can override the object's own definition. **ld** will issue warnings for undefined symbols unless **-z defs** overrides.

-G

> In dynamic mode only, produce a shared object. Undefined symbols are allowed.

-I *name*

> When building an executable, use *name* as the path name of the interpreter to be written into the program header. The default in static mode is no interpreter; in dynamic mode, the default is the name of the dynamic linker, **/usr/lib/libc.so.1**. Either case may be overridden by **-I**. **exec** will load this interpreter when it loads the **a.out** and will pass control to the interpreter rather than to the **a.out** directly.

-L *path*

> Add *path* to the library search directories. **ld** searches for libraries first in any directories specified with **-L** options, then in the standard directories. This option is effective only if it precedes the **-l** option on the command line.

-M *mapfile*

> In *static* mode only, read *mapfile* as a text file of directives to **ld**. Because these directives change the shape of the output file created by **ld**, use of this option is strongly discouraged.

-Q[y| n]

> Under **-Qy**, an **ident** string is added to the **.comment** section of the output file to identify the version of the link editor used to create the file. This will result in multiple **ld idents** when there have been multiple linking steps, such as when using **ld -r**. This is identical with the default action of the **cc** command. **-Qn** suppresses version.

-V

> Output a message giving information about the version of **ld** being used.

-YP, *dirlist*

> Change the default directories used for finding libraries. *dirlist* is a colon-separated path list.

The environment variable **LD_LIBRARY_PATH** may be used to specify library search directories. In the most general case, it will contain two directory lists separated by a semicolon:

> *dirlist1* **;** *dirlist2*

If **ld** is called with any number of occurrences of **-L**, as in

    ld . . . **-L***path1* . . . **-L***pathn* . . .

then the search path ordering is

    dirlist1 path1 . . . pathn dirlist2 LIBPATH

LD_LIBRARY_PATH is also used to specify library search directories to the dynamic linker at run time. That is, if **LD_LIBRARY_PATH** exists in the environment, the dynamic linker will search the directories named in it, before its default directory, for shared objects to be linked with the program at execution.

The environment variable **LD_RUN_PATH**, containing a directory list, may also be used to specify library search directories to the dynamic linker. If present and not null, it is passed to the dynamic linker by **ld** via data stored in the output object file.

FILES

lib*x*.**so**	libraries
lib*x*.a	libraries
a.out	output file
LIBPATH	usually **/usr/ccs/lib:/usr/lib**

SEE ALSO

as(1), **cc**(1), **exec**(2), **exit**(2), **end**(3C), **a.out**(4), **ar**(4)

The "C Compilation System" chapter and the "Mapfile Option" appendix in the *Programmer's Guide: ANSI C and Programming Support Tools*

NOTES

Through its options, the link editor gives users great flexibility; however, those who use the **-M** *mapfile* option must assume some added responsibilities. Use of this feature is strongly discouraged.

NAME

ld – link editor, dynamic link editor

SYNOPSIS

/usr/ucb/ld [*options*]

DESCRIPTION

/usr/ucb/ld is the link editor for the BSD Compatibility Package. /usr/ucb/ld
is identical to /usr/bin/ld [see ld(1)] except that BSD libraries and routines are
included *before* System V libraries and routines.

/usr/ucb/ld accepts the same options as /usr/bin/ld, with the following
exceptions:

−L *dir* Add *dir* to the list of directories searched for libraries by /usr/bin/ld.
Directories specified with this option are searched before /usr/ucblib
and /usr/lib.

−Y LU, *dir*
Change the default directory used for finding libraries. Warning: this
option may have unexpected results, and should not be used.

FILES

/usr/ucblib
/usr/lib
/usr/ucblib/libx.a
/usr/lib/libx.a

SEE ALSO

ar(1), as(1), cc(1), ld(1), lorder(1), strip(1), tsort(1) in the *Programmer's Reference Manual*

NAME

ldd – list dynamic dependencies

SYNOPSIS

ldd [−d | −r] *file*

DESCRIPTION

The **ldd** command lists the path names of all shared objects that would be loaded as a result of executing *file*. If *file* is a valid executable but does not require any shared objects, **ldd** will succeed, producing no output.

ldd may also be used to check the compatibility of *file* with the shared objects it uses. It does this by optionally printing warnings for any unresolved symbol references that would occur if *file* were executed. Two options govern this mode of **ldd**:

−d   Causes **ldd** to check all references to data objects.

−r   Causes **ldd** to check references to both data objects and functions.

Only one of the above options may be given during any single invocation of **ldd**.

SEE ALSO

cc(1), ld(1)

The "C Compilation System" chapter in the *Programmer's Guide: ANSI C and Programming Support Tools*

DIAGNOSTICS

ldd prints its record of shared object path names to **stdout**. The optional list of symbol resolution problems are printed to **stderr**. If *file* is not an executable file or cannot be opened for reading, a non-zero exit status is returned.

NOTES

ldd doesn't list shared objects explicitly attached via **dlopen**(3X).

ldd uses the same algorithm as the dynamic linker to locate shared objects.

NAME

ldsysdump – load system dump from floppy diskettes

SYNOPSIS

/usr/sbin/ldsysdump *destination_file*

DESCRIPTION

The ldsysdump command loads the memory image files from the floppy diskettes used to take a system dump and recombines them into a single file on the hard disk suitable for use by the **crash** command. The *destination_file* is the name of the hard disk file into which the data from the diskettes will be loaded.

When invoked, ldsysdump begins an interactive procedure that prompts the user to insert the diskettes to be loaded. The user has the option of quitting the session at any time. This allows only the portion of the system image needed to be dumped.

EXAMPLES

This example loads the three floppies produced via the **sysdump** command on a machine equipped with 2 MB of memory.

```
$ldsysdump /var/tmp/cdump

Insert first sysdump floppy.
Enter 'c' to continue, 'q' to quit: c

Loading sysdump
.............................................................
.......................................

Insert next sysdump floppy.
Enter 'c' to continue, 'q' to quit: c

Loading more sysdump
.............................................................
.......................................

Insert next sysdump floppy.
Enter 'c' to continue, 'q' to quit: c

Loading more sysdump
.............................................................
.......................................

3 Sysdump files coalesced, 4096 (512 byte) blocks
$
```

SEE ALSO

crash(1M), sysdump(8)
ulimit(2) in the *Programmer's Reference Manual*

DIAGNOSTICS

If a floppy diskette is inserted out of sequence a message is printed. The user is allowed to insert a new one and continue the session.

NOTES

The file size limit must be set large enough to hold the dump.

NAME

lex – generate programs for simple lexical tasks

SYNOPSIS

lex [-ctvn –V –Q[y|n]] [*file*]

DESCRIPTION

The **lex** command generates programs to be used in simple lexical analysis of text.

The input *files* (standard input default) contain strings and expressions to be searched for and C text to be executed when these strings are found.

lex generates a file named **lex.yy.c**. When **lex.yy.c** is compiled and linked with the lex library, it copies the input to the output except when a string specified in the file is found. When a specified string is found, then the corresponding program text is executed. The actual string matched is left in **yytext**, an external character array. Matching is done in order of the patterns in the *file*. The patterns may contain square brackets to indicate character classes, as in **[abx-z]** to indicate **a**, **b**, **x**, **y**, and **z**; and the operators *, +, and ? mean, respectively, any non-negative number of, any positive number of, and either zero or one occurrence of, the previous character or character class. Thus, **[a–zA–Z]+** matches a string of letters. The character **.** is the class of all ASCII characters except new-line. Parentheses for grouping and vertical bar for alternation are also supported. The notation $r\{d,e\}$ in a rule indicates between d and e instances of regular expression r. It has higher precedence than | , but lower than *, ?, +, and concatenation. The character ^ at the beginning of an expression permits a successful match only immediately after a new-line, and the character $ at the end of an expression requires a trailing new-line. The character / in an expression indicates trailing context; only the part of the expression up to the slash is returned in **yytext**, but the remainder of the expression must follow in the input stream. An operator character may be used as an ordinary symbol if it is within " symbols or preceded by \.

Three macros are expected: **input()** to read a character; **unput(**c**)** to replace a character read; and **output(**c**)** to place an output character. They are defined in terms of the standard streams, but you can override them. The program generated is named **yylex()**, and the lex library contains a **main()** that calls it. The macros **input** and **output** read from and write to **stdin** and **stdout**, respectively.

The function **yymore** accumulates additional characters into the same **yytext**. The function **yyless(**n**)** pushes back **yyleng** $-n$ characters into the input stream. (**yyleng** is an external **int** variable giving the length in bytes of **yytext**.) The function **yywrap** is called whenever the scanner reaches end of file and indicates whether normal wrapup should continue. The action **REJECT** on the right side of the rule causes the match to be rejected and the next suitable match executed. The action **ECHO** on the right side of the rule is equivalent to **printf("%s"**, **yytext**).

Any line beginning with a blank is assumed to contain only C text and is copied; if it precedes %%, it is copied into the external definition area of the **lex.yy.c** file. All rules should follow a %%, as in **yacc**. Lines preceding %% that begin with a non-blank character define the string on the left to be the remainder of the line; it can be called out later by surrounding it with {}. In this section, C code (and preprocessor statements) can also be included between %{ and %}. Note that curly brackets do not imply parentheses; only string substitution is done.

The external names generated by **lex** all begin with the prefix **yy** or **YY**.

The flags must appear before any files.

-c   Indicates C actions and is the default.

-t   Causes the **lex.yy.c** program to be written instead to standard output.

-v   Provides a two-line summary of statistics.

-n   Will not print out the –**v** summary.

-V   Print out version information on standard error.

-Q[y|n] Print out version information to output file **lex.yy.c** by using –**Qy**. The –**Qn** option does not print out version information and is the default.

Multiple files are treated as a single file. If no files are specified, standard input is used.

Certain default table sizes are too small for some users. The table sizes for the resulting finite state machine can be set in the definitions section:

%p n number of positions is n (default 2500)

%n n number of states is n (500)

%e n number of parse tree nodes is n (1000)

%a n number of transitions is n (2000)

%k n number of packed character classes is n (2500)

%o n size of output array is n (3000)

The use of one or more of the above automatically implies the –**v** option, unless the –**n** option is used.

EXAMPLE

```
D       [0-9]
%{
void
skipcommnts(void)
{
        for(;;)
        {
                while(input()!='*')
                        ;
                if(input()=='/')
                        return;
                else
```

```
                                unput(yytext[yyleng-1]);
                    }
          }
          %}
          %%
          if      printf("IF statement\n");
          [a-z]+  printf("tag, value %s\n",yytext);
          0{D}+   printf("octal number %s\n",yytext);
          {D}+    printf("decimal number %s\n",yytext);
          "++"    printf("unary op\n");
          "+"     printf("binary op\n");
          "\n"    ;/*no action */
          "/*"      skipcommnts();
          %%
```

SEE ALSO

yacc(1)

The "**lex**" chapter in the *Programmer's Guide: ANSI C and Programming Support Tools*

NAME

line – read one line

SYNOPSIS

line

DESCRIPTION

line copies one line (up to a new-line) from the standard input and writes it on the standard output. It returns an exit code of 1 on EOF and always prints at least a new-line. It is often used within shell files to read from the user's terminal.

SEE ALSO

sh(1)

read(2) in the *Programmer's Reference Manual*

NAME

link, unlink – link and unlink files and directories

SYNOPSIS

/usr/sbin/link *file1 file2*
/usr/sbin/unlink *file*

DESCRIPTION

The **link** command is used to create a file name that points to another file. Linked files and directories can be removed by the **unlink** command; however, it is strongly recommended that the **rm** and **rmdir** commands be used instead of the **unlink** command.

The only difference between **ln** and **link** and **unlink** is that the latter do exactly what they are told to do, abandoning all error checking. This is because they directly invoke the **link** and **unlink** system calls.

SEE ALSO

rm(1) in the *User's Reference Manual*
link(2), **unlink**(2) in the *Programmer's Reference Manual*

NOTES

These commands can be run only by the super-user.

NAME

lint – a C program checker

SYNOPSIS

lint [*options*] *files*

DESCRIPTION

lint detects features of C program files which are likely to be bugs, non-portable, or wasteful. It also checks type usage more strictly than the compiler. lint issues error and warning messages. Among the things it detects are unreachable statements, loops not entered at the top, automatic variables declared and not used, and logical expressions whose value is constant. lint checks for functions that return values in some places and not in others, functions called with varying numbers or types of arguments, and functions whose values are not used or whose values are used but none returned.

Arguments whose names end with .c are taken to be C source files. Arguments whose names end with .ln are taken to be the result of an earlier invocation of lint with either the −c or the −o option used. The .ln files are analogous to .o (object) files that are produced by the cc(1) command when given a .c file as input. Files with other suffixes are warned about and ignored.

lint takes all the .c, .ln, and llib-l*x*.ln (specified by −l*x*) files and processes them in their command line order. By default, lint appends the standard C lint library (llib-lc.ln) to the end of the list of files. When the −c option is used, the .ln and the llib-l*x*.ln files are ignored. When the −c option is not used, the second pass of lint checks the .ln and the llib-l*x*.ln list of files for mutual compatibility.

Any number of lint options may be used, in any order, intermixed with file-name arguments. The following options are used to suppress certain kinds of complaints:

-a   Suppress complaints about assignments of long values to variables that are not long.

-b   Suppress complaints about **break** statements that cannot be reached.

-h   Do not apply heuristic tests that attempt to intuit bugs, improve style, and reduce waste.

-m   Suppress complaints about external symbols that could be declared static.

-u   Suppress complaints about functions and external variables used and not defined, or defined and not used. (This option is suitable for running lint on a subset of files of a larger program).

-v   Suppress complaints about unused arguments in functions.

-x   Do not report variables referred to by external declarations but never used.

The following arguments alter **lint**'s behavior:

-I*dir*   Search for included header files in the directory *dir* before searching the current directory and/or the standard place.

-l*x*   Include the lint library **llib-l***x***.ln**. For example, you can include a lint version of the math library **llib-lm.ln** by inserting **-lm** on the command line. This argument does not suppress the default use of **llib-lc.ln**. These lint libraries must be in the assumed directory. This option can be used to reference local lint libraries and is useful in the development of multi-file projects.

-L*dir*   Search for lint libraries in *dir* before searching the standard place.

-n   Do not check compatibility against the standard C lint library.

-p   Attempt to check portability to other dialects of C. Along with stricter checking, this option causes all non-external names to be truncated to eight characters and all external names to be truncated to six characters and one case.

-s   Produce one-line diagnostics only. **lint** occasionally buffers messages to produce a compound report.

-k   Alter the behavior of /∗LINTED [*message*]∗/ directives. Normally, **lint** will suppress warning messages for the code following these directives. Instead of suppressing the messages, **lint** prints an additional message containing the comment inside the directive.

-y   Specify that the file being linted will be treated as if the /∗LINTLIBRARY∗/ directive had been used. A lint library is normally created by using the /∗LINTLIBRARY∗/ directive.

-F   Print pathnames of files. **lint** normally prints the filename without the path.

-c   Cause **lint** to produce a **.ln** file for every **.c** file on the command line. These **.ln** files are the product of **lint**'s first pass only, and are not checked for inter-function compatibility.

-o*x*   Cause **lint** to create a lint library with the name **llib-l***x***.ln**. The **-c** option nullifies any use of the **-o** option. The lint library produced is the input that is given to **lint**'s second pass. The **-o** option simply causes this file to be saved in the named lint library. To produce a **llib-l***x***.ln** without extraneous messages, use of the **-x** option is suggested. The **-v** option is useful if the source file(s) for the lint library are just external interfaces.

Some of the above settings are also available through the use of "lint comments" (see below).

-V   Write to standard error the product name and release.

-w*file* Write a **.ln** file to *file*, for use by **cflow**(1).

−R*file*   Write a `.ln` file to *file*, for use by **cxref**(1).

lint recognizes many **cc**(1) command line options, including **−D**, **−U**, **−g**, **−O**, **−Xt**, **−Xa**, and **−Xc**, although **−g** and **−O** are ignored. Unrecognized options are warned about and ignored. The predefined macro **lint** is defined to allow certain questionable code to be altered or removed for **lint**. Thus, the symbol **lint** should be thought of as a reserved word for all code that is planned to be checked by **lint**.

Certain conventional comments in the C source will change the behavior of **lint**:

/∗ARGSUSED*n*∗/
> makes **lint** check only the first *n* arguments for usage; a missing *n* is taken to be 0 (this option acts like the **−v** option for the next function).

/∗CONSTCOND∗/ or /∗CONSTANTCOND∗/ or /∗CONSTANTCONDITION∗/
> suppresses complaints about constant operands for the next expression.

/∗EMPTY∗/
> suppresses complaints about a null statement consequent on an if statement. This directive should be placed after the test expression, and before the semicolon. This directive is supplied to support empty if statements when a valid else statement follows. It suppresses messages on an empty **else** consequent.

/∗FALLTHRU∗/ or /∗FALLTHROUGH∗/
> suppresses complaints about fall through to a **case** or **default** labeled statement. This directive should be placed immediately preceding the label.

/∗LINTLIBRARY∗/
> at the beginning of a file shuts off complaints about unused functions and function arguments in this file. This is equivalent to using the **−v** and **−x** options.

/∗LINTED [*message*]∗/
> suppresses any intra-file warning except those dealing with unused variables or functions. This directive should be placed on the line immediately preceding where the lint warning occurred. The **−k** option alters the way in which **lint** handles this directive. Instead of suppressing messages, **lint** will print an additional message, if any, contained in the comment. This directive is useful in conjunction with the **−s** option for post-lint filtering.

/∗NOTREACHED∗/
> at appropriate points stops comments about unreachable code. [This comment is typically placed just after calls to functions like **exit**(2)].

/∗PRINTFLIKE*n*∗/
> makes **lint** check the first *(n-1)* arguments as usual. The *nth* argument is interpreted as a **printf** format string that is used to check the remaining arguments.

/*PROTOLIB*n**/
> causes **lint** to treat function declaration prototypes as function definitions if *n* is non-zero. This directive can only be used in conjunction with the
> /* LINTLIBRARY */ directive. If *n* is zero, function prototypes will be treated normally.

/*SCANFLIKE*n**/
> makes **lint** check the first *(n-1)* arguments as usual. The *nth* argument is interpreted as a **scanf** format string that is used to check the remaining arguments.

/*VARARGS*n**/
> suppresses the usual checking for variable numbers of arguments in the following function declaration. The data types of the first *n* arguments are checked; a missing *n* is taken to be 0. The use of the ellipsis terminator (. . .) in the definition is suggested in new or updated code.

lint produces its first output on a per-source-file basis. Complaints regarding included files are collected and printed after all source files have been processed, if **-s** is not specified. Finally, if the **-c** option is not used, information gathered from all input files is collected and checked for consistency. At this point, if it is not clear whether a complaint stems from a given source file or from one of its included files, the source filename will be printed followed by a question mark.

The behavior of the **-c** and the **-o** options allows for incremental use of **lint** on a set of C source files. Generally, one invokes **lint** once for each source file with the **-c** option. Each of these invocations produces a **.ln** file that corresponds to the **.c** file, and prints all messages that are about just that source file. After all the source files have been separately run through **lint**, it is invoked once more (without the **-c** option), listing all the **.ln** files with the needed **-l***x* options. This will print all the inter-file inconsistencies. This scheme works well with **make**; it allows **make** to be used to **lint** only the source files that have been modified since the last time the set of source files were **lint**ed.

FILES

LIBDIR	the directory where the lint libraries specified by the **-l***x* option must exist
LIBDIR/**lint[12]**	first and second passes
LIBDIR/**llib-lc.ln**	declarations for C Library functions (binary format; source is in *LIBDIR*/**llib-lc**)
LIBPATH/**llib-lm.ln**	declarations for Math Library functions (binary format; source is in *LIBDIR*/llib-lm)
TMPDIR/***lint***	temporaries
TMPDIR	usually **/var/tmp** but can be redefined by setting the environment variable **TMPDIR** [see **tempnam** in **tmpnam**(3S)].

LIBDIR	usually `/ccs/lib`
LIBPATH	usually `/usr/ccs/lib:/usr/lib`

SEE ALSO

cc(1), make(1)

See the "lint" chapter in the *C Programmer's Guide: ANSI C and Programming Support Tools.*

NAME

listdgrp – lists members of a device group

SYNOPSIS

listdgrp *dgroup*

DESCRIPTION

listdgrp displays the members of the device group specified by the *dgroup*.

ERRORS

This command will exit with one of the following values:

0 = successful completion of the task.

1 = command syntax incorrect, invalid option used, or internal error occurred.

2 = device group table could not be opened for reading.

3 = device group *dgroup* could not be found in the device group table.

EXAMPLE

To list the devices that belong to group **partitions**:

```
$ listdgrp partitions
root
swap
usr
```

FILES

/etc/dgroup.tab

SEE ALSO

putdgrp(1)

NAME

listen – network listener daemon

SYNOPSIS

/usr/lib/saf/listen [**−m** *devstem*] *net_spec*

DESCRIPTION

The **listen** process "listens" to a network for service requests, accepts requests when they arrive, and invokes servers in response to those service requests. The network listener process may be used with any connection-oriented network (more precisely, with any connection-oriented transport provider) that conforms to the Transport Interface (TLI) specification.

The listener internally generates a pathname for the minor device for each connection; it is this pathname that is used in the **utmp** entry for a service, if one is created. By default, this pathname is the concatenation of the prefix **/dev/***netspec* with the decimal representation of the minor device number. When the **−m** *devstem* option is specified, the listener will use *devstem* as the prefix for the pathname. In either case, the representation of the minor device number will be at least two digits (for example, 05 or 27), but will be longer when necessary to accommodate minor device numbers larger than 99.

SERVER INVOCATION

When a connection indication is received, the listener creates a new transport endpoint and accepts the connection on that endpoint. Before giving the file descriptor for this new connection to the server, any designated STREAMS modules are pushed and the configuration script is executed, if one exists. This file descriptor is appropriate for use with either TLI (see especially **t_sync(3N)**) or the sockets interface library.

By default, a new instance of the server is invoked for each connection. When the server is invoked, file descriptor 0 refers to the transport endpoint, and is open for reading and writing. File descriptors 1 and 2 are copies of file descriptor 0; no other file descriptors are open. The service is invoked with the user and group IDs of the user name under which the service was registered with the listener, and with the current directory set to the HOME directory of that user.

Alternatively, a service may be registered so that the listener will pass connections to a standing server process through a FIFO or a named STREAM, instead of invoking the server anew for each connection. In this case, the connection is passed in the form of a file descriptor that refers to the new transport endpoint. Before the file descriptor is sent to the server, the listener interprets any configuration script registered for that service using **doconfig**(3N), although **doconfig** is invoked with both the NORUN and NOASSIGN flags. The server receives the file descriptor for the connection in a **strrecvfd** structure via an I_RECVFD **ioctl**(2).

For more details about the listener and its administration, see **nlsadmin**(1M).

FILES

/etc/saf/*pmtag*/*

SEE ALSO
nlsadmin(1M), pmadm(1M), sac(1M), sacadm(1M),
doconfig(3N), nlsgetcall, nlsprovider(3N),
streamio(7)
Network Programmer's Guide

NOTES
When passing a connection to a standing server, the user and group IDs contained in the **strrecvfd** structure will be those for the listener (that is, they will both be 0); the user name under which the service was registered with the listener is not reflected in these IDs.

When operating multiple instances of the listener on a single transport provider, there is a potential race condition in the binding of addresses during initialization of the listeners if any of their services have dynamically assigned addresses. This condition would appear as an inability of the listener to bind a static-address service to its otherwise valid address, and would result from a dynamic-address service having been bound to that address by a different instance of the listener.

NAME
> listusers – list user login information

SYNOPSIS
> listusers [–g *groups*] [–l *logins*]

DESCRIPTION
> Executed without any options, this command displays a list of all user logins, sorted by login, and the account field value associated with each login in /etc/passwd.
>
> –g   Lists all user logins belonging to **group**, sorted by login. Multiple groups can be specified as a comma-separated list.
>
> –l   Lists the user login or logins specified by **logins**, sorted by login. Multiple logins can be specified as a comma-separated list.

NOTES
> A user login is one that has a UID of 100 or greater.
>
> The –l and –g options can be combined. User logins will be listed only once, even if they belong to more than one of the selected groups.

NAME

ln – link files

SYNOPSIS

ln [**-s**] [**-f**] [**-n**] *file1* [*file2* . . .] *target*

DESCRIPTION

The **ln** command links *filen* to *target* by creating a directory entry that refers to *target*. By using **ln** with one or more file names, the user may create one or more links to *target*.

The **ln** command may be used to create both hard links and symbolic links; by default it creates hard links. A hard link to a file is indistinguishable from the original directory entry. Any changes to a file are effective independent of the name used to reference the file. Hard links may not span file systems and may not refer to directories.

Without the **-s** option, **ln** is used to create hard links. *filen* is linked to *target*. If *target* is a directory, another file named *filen* is created in *target* and linked to the original *filen*. If *target* is a file, its contents are overwritten.

If **ln** determines that the mode of *target* forbids writing, it will print the mode [see **chmod**(2)], ask for a response, and read the standard input for one line. If the line begins with **y**, the link occurs, if permissible; otherwise, the command exits.

There are three options to **ln**. If multiple options are specified, the one with the highest priority is used and the remainder are ignored. The options, in descending order of priority, are:

-s   **ln** will create a symbolic link. A symbolic link contains the name of the file to which it is linked. Symbolic links may span file systems and may refer to directories. If the linkname exists, then do not overwrite the contents of the file. A symbolic link's permissions are always set to read, write, and execute permission for owner, group, and world (**777**).

-f   **ln** will link files without questioning the user, even if the mode of *target* forbids writing. Note that this is the default if the standard input is not a terminal.

-n   If the linkname is an existing file, do not overwrite the contents of the file. The **-f** option overrides this option.

If the **-s** option is used with two arguments, *target* may be an existing directory or a non-existent file. If *target* already exists and is not a directory, an error is returned. *filen* may be any path name and need not exist. If it exists, it may be a file or directory and may reside on a different file system from *target*. If *target* is an existing directory, a file is created in directory *target* whose name is *filen* or the last component of *filen*. This file is a symbolic link that references *filen*. If *target* does not exist, a file with name *target* is created and it is a symbolic link that references *filen*.

If the **-s** option is used with more than two arguments, *target* must be an existing directory or an error will be returned. For each *filen*, a file is created in *target* whose name is *filen* or its last component; each new *filen* is a symbolic link to the original *filen*. The *files* and *target* may reside on different file systems.

SEE ALSO

chmod(1), cp(1), mv(1), rm(1), **link**(2), readlink(2), **stat**(2), **symlink**(2)

NOTES

Doing operations that involve ".." (such as "**cd ..**") in a directory that is symbolically linked will reference the original directory not the target.

The **-s** option does not use the current working directory. In the command

         ln -s *path target*

path is taken literally without being evaluated against the current working directory.

NAME

ln – make hard or symbolic links to files

SYNOPSIS

/usr/ucb/ln [**-fs**] *filename* [*linkname*]
/usr/ucb/ln [**-fs**] *pathname* . . . *directory*

DESCRIPTION

/usr/ucb/ln creates an additional directory entry, called a link, to a file or directory. Any number of links can be assigned to a file. The number of links does
not affect other file attributes such as size, protections, data, and so on.

filename is the name of the original file or directory. *linkname* is the new name to
associate with the file or filename. If *linkname* is omitted, the last component of
filename is used as the name of the link.

If the last argument is the name of a directory, symbolic links are made in that
directory for each *pathname* argument; /usr/ucb/ln uses the last component of
each *pathname* as the name of each link in the named *directory*.

A hard link (the default) is a standard directory entry just like the one made
when the file was created. Hard links can only be made to existing files. Hard
links cannot be made across file systems (disk partitions, mounted file systems).
To remove a file, all hard links to it must be removed, including the name by
which it was first created; removing the last hard link releases the inode associated with the file.

A symbolic link, made with the **-s** option, is a special directory entry that points
to another named file. Symbolic links can span file systems and point to directories. In fact, you can create a symbolic link that points to a file that is currently
absent from the file system; removing the file that it points to does not affect or
alter the symbolic link itself.

A symbolic link to a directory behaves differently than you might expect in certain cases. While an ls(1V) on such a link displays the files in the pointed-to
directory, an 'ls -l' displays information about the link itself:

```
example% /usr/ucb/ln -s dir link
example% ls link
file1 file2 file3 file4
example% ls -l link
lrwxrwxrwx  1 user              7 Jan 11 23:27 link -> dir
```

When you **cd**(1) to a directory through a symbolic link, you wind up in the
pointed-to location within the file system. This means that the parent of the new
working directory is not the parent of the symbolic link, but rather, the parent of
the pointed-to directory. For instance, in the following case the final working
directory is /usr and not /home/user/linktest.

```
example% pwd
/home/user/linktest
example% /usr/ucb/ln -s /var/tmp symlink
example% cd symlink
example% cd ..
example% pwd
/usr
```

C shell user's can avoid any resulting navigation problems by using the pushd and popd built-in commands instead of cd.

OPTIONS

-f   Force a hard link to a directory — this option is only available to the super-user.

-s   Create a symbolic link or links.

EXAMPLE

The commands below illustrate the effects of the different forms of the /usr/ucb/ln command:

```
example% /usr/ucb/ln file link
example% ls -F file link
file    link
example% /usr/ucb/ln -s file symlink
example% ls -F file symlink
file    symlink@
example% ls -li file link symlink
 10606 -rw-r--r--  2 user        0 Jan 12 00:06 file
 10606 -rw-r--r--  2 user        0 Jan 12 00:06 link
 10607 lrwxrwxrwx  1 user        4 Jan 12 00:06 symlink -> file
example% /usr/ucb/ln -s nonesuch devoid
example% ls -F devoid
devoid@
example% cat devoid
devoid: No such file or directory
example% /usr/ucb/ln -s /proto/bin/* /tmp/bin
example% ls -F /proto/bin /tmp/bin
/proto/bin:
x*      y*      z*

/tmp/bin:
x@      y@      z@
```

SEE ALSO

cp(1), ls(1), mv(1), rm(1) in the *User's Reference Manual*

link(2), readlink(2), stat(2), symlink(2) in the *Programmer's Reference Manual*

NOTES

When the last argument is a directory, simple basenames should not be used for *pathname* arguments. If a basename is used, the resulting symbolic link points to itself:

```
example% /usr/ucb/ln -s file /tmp
example% ls -l /tmp/file
lrwxrwxrwx  1 user            4 Jan 12 00:16 /tmp/file -> file
example% cat /tmp/file
/tmp/file: Too many levels of symbolic links
```

To avoid this problem, use full pathnames, or prepend a reference to the PWD variable to files in the working directory:

```
example% rm /tmp/file
example% /usr/ucb/ln -s $PWD/file /tmp
lrwxrwxrwx  1 user
     4 Jan 12 00:16 /tmp/file -> /home/user/subdir/file
```

NAME

    `lockd` – network lock daemon

SYNOPSIS

    `/usr/lib/nfs/lockd` [`-t` *timeout*] [`-g` *graceperiod*]

DESCRIPTION

    `lockd` processes lock requests that are either sent locally by the kernel or remotely by another lock daemon. `lockd` forwards lock requests for remote data to the server site's lock daemon through RPC/XDR. `lockd` then requests the status monitor daemon, `statd`(1M), for monitor service. The reply to the lock request will not be sent to the kernel until the status daemon and the server site's lock daemon have replied.

    If either the status monitor or server site's lock daemon is unavailable, the reply to a lock request for remote data is delayed until all daemons become available.

    When a server recovers, it waits for a grace period for all client-site lock daemons to submit reclaim requests. Client-site lock daemons, on the other hand, are notified by the status monitor daemon of the server recovery and promptly resubmit previously granted lock requests. If a lock daemon fails to secure a previously granted lock at the server site, the it sends SIGLOST to a process.

OPTIONS

    `-t` *timeout*   Use *timeout* **seconds** as the interval instead of the default value (15 seconds) to retransmit lock request to the remote server.

    `-g` *graceperiod*   Use *graceperiod* **seconds** as the grace period duration instead of the default value (45 seconds).

SEE ALSO

    `statd`(1M), `fcntl`(2), `signal`(2), `lockf`(3C)

NAME

logger – add entries to the system log

SYNOPSIS

/usr/ucb/logger [-t *tag*] [-p *priority*] [-i] [-f *filename*] [*message*] . . .

DESCRIPTION

logger provides a method for adding one-line entries to the system log file from the command line. One or more *message* arguments can be given on the command line, in which case each is logged immediately. Otherwise, a *filename* can be specified, in which case each line in the file is logged. If neither is specified, logger reads and logs messages on a line-by-line basis from the standard input.

The following options are available:

-t *tag*   Mark each line added to the log with the specified *tag*.

-p *priority* Enter the message with the specified *priority*. The message priority can be specified numerically, or as a *facility.level* pair. For example, '-p local3.info' assigns the message priority to the **info** level in the **local3** facility. The default priority is **user.notice**.

-i   Log the process ID of the logger process with each line.

-f *filename* Use the contents of *filename* as the message to log.

message   If this is unspecified, either the file indicated with **-f** or the standard input is added to the log.

EXAMPLE

logger System rebooted

will log the message 'System rebooted' to the facility at priority **notice** to be treated by **syslogd** as other messages to the facility **notice** are.

logger -p local0.notice -t HOSTIDM -f /dev/idmc

will read from the file **/dev/idmc** and will log each line in that file as a message with the tag 'HOSTIDM' at priority **notice** to be treated by **syslogd** as other messages to the facility **local0** are.

SEE ALSO

syslog(3), syslogd(1M)

NAME

   login – sign on

SYNOPSIS

   login [-d *device*] [*name* [*environ* . . .]]

DESCRIPTION

   The **login** command is used at the beginning of each terminal session and allows
   you to identify yourself to the system. It may be invoked as a command or by
   the system when a connection is first established. It is invoked by the system
   when a previous user has terminated the initial shell by typing a CTRL-d to indicate an end-of-file.

   If **login** is invoked as a command it must replace the initial command interpreter. This is accomplished by typing

   exec login

   from the initial shell.

   login asks for your user name (if it is not supplied as an argument), and if
   appropriate, your password. Echoing is turned off (where possible) during the
   typing of your password, so it will not appear on the written record of the session.

   If there are no lower-case characters in the first line of input processed, **login**
   assumes the connecting TTY is an upper-case-only terminal and sets the port's
   termio(7) options to reflect this.

   login accepts a device option, *device*. *device* is taken to be the path name of the
   TTY port **login** is to operate on. The use of the device option can be expected to
   improve **login** performance, since **login** will not need to call **ttyname**(3).

   If you make any mistake in the login procedure, the message

   Login incorrect

   is printed and a new login prompt will appear. If you make five incorrect login
   attempts, all five may be logged in **/var/adm/loginlog** (if it exists) and the TTY
   line will be dropped.

   If you do not complete the login successfully within a certain period of time (e.g.,
   one minute), you are likely to be silently disconnected.

   After a successful login, accounting files are updated, the **/etc/profile** script is
   executed, the time you last logged in is printed, **/etc/motd** is printed, the user-
   ID, group-ID, supplementary group list, working directory, and command interpreter (usually **sh**) are initialized, and the file **.profile** in the working directory
   is executed, if it exists. The name of the command interpreter is – followed by
   the last component of the interpreter's path name (e.g., **-sh**). If this field in the
   password file is empty, then the default command interpreter, **/usr/bin/sh** is
   used. If this field is *, then the named directory becomes the root directory, the
   starting point for path searches for path names beginning with a /. At that point
   login is re-executed at the new level which must have its own root structure,
   including **/var/adm/login** and **/etc/passwd**.

The basic *environment* is initialized to:

HOME=*your-login-directory*
LOGNAME=*your-login-name*
PATH=`/usr/bin`
SHELL=*last-field-of-passwd-entry*
MAIL=`/var/mail/`*your-login-name*
TZ=*timezone-specification*

The environment may be expanded or modified by supplying additional arguments to **login**, either at execution time or when **login** requests your login name. The arguments may take either the form *xxx* or *xxx=yyy*. Arguments without an equal sign are placed in the environment as

L*n*=xxx

where *n* is a number starting at 0 and is incremented each time a new variable name is required. Variables containing an = are placed in the environment without modification. If they already appear in the environment, then they replace the older value. There are two exceptions. The variables PATH and SHELL cannot be changed. This prevents people, logging into restricted shell environments, from spawning secondary shells which are not restricted. **login** understands simple single-character quoting conventions. Typing a backslash in front of a character quotes it and allows the inclusion of such characters as spaces and tabs.

FILES

`/var/adm/utmp`	accounting
`/var/adm/wtmp`	accounting
`/var/mail/`*your-name*	mailbox for user *your-name*
`/var/adm/loginlog`	record of failed login attempts
`/etc/motd`	message-of-the-day
`/etc/passwd`	password file
`/etc/profile`	system profile
`.profile`	user's login profile
`/var/adm/lastlog`	time of last login

SEE ALSO

mail(1), newgrp(1M), sh(1), su(1M)
loginlog(4), passwd(4), profile(4), environ(5) in the *Programmer's Reference Manual*
Files and Directories in the *System Administrator's Guide*

DIAGNOSTICS

login incorrect if the user name or the password cannot be matched.
No shell, cannot open password file, or **no directory: consult a system engineer.**
No utmp entry. You must exec "login" from the lowest level "sh" if you attempted to execute **login** as a command without using the shell's **exec** internal command or from a shell other than the initial shell.

NAME

logins – list user and system login information

SYNOPSIS

logins [-dmopstuxa] [-g groups] [-l *logins*]

DESCRIPTION

This command displays information on user and system logins. Contents of the output is controlled by the command options and can include the following: user or system login, user id number, /etc/passwd account field value (user name or other information), primary group name, primary group id, multiple group names, multiple group ids, home directory, login shell, and four password aging parameters. The default information is the following: login id, user id, primary group name, primary group id and the account field value from /etc/passwd. Output is sorted by user id, displaying system logins followed by user logins.

-d   Selects logins with duplicate uids.

-m   Displays multiple group membership information.

-o   Formats output into one line of colon-separated fields.

-p   Selects logins with no passwords.

-s   Selects all system logins.

-t   Sorts output by login instead of by uid.

-u   Selects all user logins.

-x   Prints an extended set of information about each selected user. The extended information includes home directory, login shell and password aging information, each displayed on a separate line. The password information consists of password status (PS for passworded, NP for no password or LK for locked). If the login is passworded, status is followed by the date the password was last changed, the number of days required between changes, and the number of days allowed before a change is required. The password aging information shows the time interval that the user will receive a password expiration warning message (when logging on) before the password expires.

-a   Adds two password expiration fields to the display. The fields show how many days a password can remain unused before it automatically becomes inactive and the date that the password will expire.

-g   Selects all users belonging to **group**, sorted by login. Multiple groups can be specified as a comma-separated list.

-l   Selects the requested login. Multiple logins can be specified as a comma-separated list.

NOTES

Options may be used together. If so, any login matching any criteria will be displayed. When the -l and -g options are combined, a user will only be listed once, even if they belong to more than one of the selected groups.

NAME

logname – get login name

SYNOPSIS

logname

DESCRIPTION

logname returns the name of the user running the process.

FILES

/etc/profile

SEE ALSO

env(1), login(1)

cuserid(3C) in the *Programmer's Reference Manual*

environ(5) in the *System Administrator's Reference Manual*

NAME

look – find words in the system dictionary or lines in a sorted list

SYNOPSIS

/usr/ucb/look [–d] [–f] [–t*c*] *string* [*filename*]

DESCRIPTION

The **look** command consults a sorted *filename* and prints all lines that begin with *string*.

If no *filename* is specified, **look** uses **/usr/ucblib/dict/words** with collating sequence **–df**.

The following options are available:

–d   Dictionary order. Only letters, digits, TAB and SPACE characters are used in comparisons.

–f   Fold case. Upper case letters are not distinguished from lower case in comparisons.

–t*c*   Set termination character. All characters to the right of *c* in *string* are ignored.

FILES

/usr/ucblib/dict/words

SEE ALSO

grep(1), **sort**(1) in the *User's Reference Manual*

NAME

lookbib – find references in a bibliographic database

SYNOPSIS

/usr/ucb/lookbib *database*

DESCRIPTION

A bibliographic reference is a set of lines, constituting fields of bibliographic information. Each field starts on a line beginning with a '%', followed by a key-letter, then a blank, and finally the contents of the field, which may continue until the next line starting with '%'. See **addbib**.

lookbib uses an inverted index made by **indxbib** to find sets of bibliographic references. It reads keywords typed after the '>' prompt on the terminal, and retrieves records containing all these keywords. If nothing matches, nothing is returned except another '>' prompt.

It is possible to search multiple databases, as long as they have a common index made by **indxbib**. In that case, only the first argument given to **indxbib** is specified to **lookbib**.

If **lookbib** does not find the index files (the **.i[abc]** files), it looks for a reference file with the same name as the argument, without the suffixes. It creates a file with a **.ig** suffix, suitable for use with **fgrep** (see **grep**). **lookbib** then uses this **fgrep** file to find references. This method is simpler to use, but the **.ig** file is slower to use than the **.i[abc]** files, and does not allow the use of multiple reference files.

FILES

```
*.ia
*.ib        index files
*.ic

*.ig        reference file
```

SEE ALSO

addbib(1), indxbib(1), refer(1), roffbib(1), sortbib(1)

grep(1) in the *User's Reference Manual*

NOTES

Probably all dates should be indexed, since many disciplines refer to literature written in the 1800s or earlier.

NAME
lorder – find ordering relation for an object library

SYNOPSIS
lorder *file* . . .

DESCRIPTION
The input is one or more object or library archive *files* [see **ar**(1)]. The standard output is a list of pairs of object file or archive member names; the first file of the pair refers to external identifiers defined in the second. The output may be processed by **tsort**(1) to find an ordering of a library suitable for one-pass access by **ld**. Note that the link editor **ld** is capable of multiple passes over an archive in the portable archive format [see **ar**(4)] and does not require that **lorder** be used when building an archive. The usage of the **lorder** command may, however, allow for a more efficient access of the archive during the link edit process.

The following example builds a new library from existing .o files.

```
ar -cr library 'lorder *.o | tsort'
```

FILES
TMPDIR/∗**symref**	temporary files
TMPDIR/∗**symdef**	temporary files
TMPDIR	usually **/var/tmp** but can be redefined by setting the environment variable **TMPDIR** [see **tempnam** in **tmpnam**(3S)].

SEE ALSO
ar(1), **ld**(1), **tsort**(1), **tempnam**(3S), **tmpname**(3S), **ar**(4)

NOTES
lorder will accept as input any object or archive file, regardless of its suffix, provided there is more than one input file. If there is but a single input file, its suffix must be **.o**.

NAME

lp, cancel – send/cancel requests to an LP print service

SYNOPSIS

lp [*printing-options*] [*files*]
lp -i *request-IDs printing-options*
cancel [*request-IDs*] [*printers*]
cancel -u *login-ID-list* [*printers*]

DESCRIPTION

The first form of the **lp** command arranges for the named *files* and associated information (collectively called a *request*) to be printed. If no file names are specified on the command line, the standard input is assumed. The standard input may be specified along with named *files* on the command line by listing the file name(s) and specifying – for the standard input. The *files* will be printed in the order in which they appear on the shell command line.

The LP print service associates a unique *request-ID* with each request and displays it on the standard output. This *request-ID* can be used later when canceling or changing a request, or when determining its status. [See the section on **cancel** for details about canceling a request, and **lpstat**(1) for information about checking the status of a print request.]

The second form of **lp** is used to change the options for a request. The print request identified by the *request-ID* is changed according to the printing options specified with this shell command. The printing options available are the same as those with the first form of the **lp** shell command. If the request has finished printing, the change is rejected. If the request is already printing, it will be stopped and restarted from the beginning (unless the -**P** option has been given).

The **cancel** command allows users to cancel print requests previously sent with the **lp** command. The first form of **cancel** permits cancellation of requests based on their *request-ID*. The second form of cancel permits cancellation of requests based on the *login-ID* of their owner.

Sending a Print Request

The first form of the **lp** command is used to send a print request to a particular printer or group of printers.

Options to **lp** must always precede file names, but may be specified in any order. The following options are available for **lp**:

-c   Make copies of the *files* before printing. Normally, *files* will not be copied, but will be linked whenever possible. If the -**c** option is not given, then the user should be careful not to remove any of the *files* before the request has been printed in its entirety. It should also be noted that if the -**c** option is not specified, any changes made to the named *files* after the request is made but before it is printed will be reflected in the printed output.

-d *dest*   Choose *dest* as the printer or class of printers that is to do the printing. If *dest* is a printer, then the request will be printed only on that specific printer. If *dest* is a class of printers, then the request will be printed on the first available printer that is a member of the class. If *dest* is **any**, then the request will be printed on any printer which can handle it. Under certain conditions (unavailability of printers, file space limitations, and so on) requests for specific destinations may not be accepted [see **lpstat**(1)]. By default, *dest* is taken from the environment variable LPDEST (if it is set). Otherwise, a default destination (if one exists) for the computer system is used. Destination names vary between systems [see **lpstat**(1)].

−f *form-name* [**−d any**]

Print the request on the form *form-name*. The LP print service ensures that the form is mounted on the printer. If *form-name* is requested with a printer destination that cannot support the form, the request is rejected. If *form-name* has not been defined for the system, or if the user is not allowed to use the form, the request is rejected [see **lpforms**(1M)]. When the **−d any** option is given, the request is printed on any printer that has the requested form mounted and can handle all other needs of the print request.

−H *special-handling*

Print the request according to the value of *special-handling*. Acceptable values for *special-handling* are defined below:

     hold   Don't print the request until notified. If printing has already begun, stop it. Other print requests will go ahead of a held request until it is resumed.

     resume   Resume a held request. If it had been printing when held, it will be the next request printed, unless subsequently bumped by an **immediate** request. The **−i** option (followed by a *request-ID*) must be used whenever this argument is specified.

     immediate   (Available only to LP administrators) Print the request next. If more than one request is assigned **immediate**, the requests are printed in the reverse order queued. If a request is currently printing on the desired printer, you have to put it on hold to allow the immediate request to print.

−m   Send mail [see **mail**(1)] after the files have been printed. By default, no mail is sent upon normal completion of the print request.

−n *number*   Print *number* copies (default is 1) of the output.

−o *option*   Specify printer-dependent *options*. Several such *options* may be collected by specifying the −o keyletter more than once (−o *option*$_1$ −o *option*$_2$ . . . −o *option*$_n$), or by specifying a list of options with one −o keyletter enclosed in double quotes (that is, −o "*option*$_1$ *option*$_2$ ... *option*$_n$"). The standard interface recognizes the following options:

     nobanner   Do not print a banner page with this request. (The administrator can disallow this option at any time.)

nofilebreak
> Do not insert a form feed between the files given, if submitting a job to print more than one file.

length=*scaled-decimal-number*
> Print this request with pages *scaled-decimal-number* lines long. A *scaled-decimal-number* is an optionally scaled decimal number that gives a size in lines, columns, inches, or centimeters, as appropriate. The scale is indicated by appending the letter "i" for inches, or the letter "c" for centimeters. For length or width settings, an unscaled number indicates lines or columns; for line pitch or character pitch settings, an unscaled number indicates lines per inch or characters per inch (the same as a number scaled with "i"). For example, **length=66** indicates a page length of 66 lines, **length=11i** indicates a page length of 11 inches, and **length=27.94c** indicates a page length of 27.94 centimeters.
>
> This option may not be used with the **-f** option.

width=*scaled-decimal-number*
> Print this request with page-width set to *scaled-decimal-number* columns wide. (See the explanation of *scaled-decimal-numbers* in the discussion of **length**, above.) This option may not be used with the **-f** option.

lpi=*scaled-decimal-number*
> Print this request with the line pitch set to *scaled-decimal-number* lines per inch. This option may not be used with the **-f** option.

cpi=*scaled-decimal-number*
> Print this request with the character pitch set to *scaled-decimal-number* characters per inch. Character pitch can also be set to **pica** (representing 10 characters per inch) or **elite** (representing 12 characters per inch), or it can be **compressed** (representing as many characters as a printer can handle). There is no standard number of characters per inch for all printers; see the Terminfo database [**terminfo**(4)] for the default character pitch for your printer.
>
> This option may not be used with the **-f** option.

stty='*stty-option-list*'
> A list of options valid for the **stty** command; enclose the list with single quotes if it contains blanks.

-P *page-list*   Print the pages specified in *page-list*. This option can be used only if there is a filter available to handle it; otherwise, the print request will be rejected.

The *page-list* may consist of range(s) of numbers, single page numbers, or a combination of both. The pages will be printed in ascending order.

-q *priority-level*
Assign this request *priority-level* in the printing queue. The values of *priority-level* range from 0, the highest priority, to 39, the lowest priority. If a priority is not specified, the default for the print service is used, as assigned by the system administrator. A priority limit may be assigned to individual users by the system administrator.

-s   Suppress messages from **lp** such as those that begin with **request id is**.

-S *character-set* [**-d any**]
-S *print-wheel* [**-d any**]
Print this request using the specified *character-set* or *print-wheel*. If a form was requested and it requires a character set or print wheel other than the one specified with the **-S** option, the request is rejected.

For printers that take print wheels: if the print wheel specified is not one listed by the administrator as acceptable for the printer specified in this request, the request is rejected unless the print wheel is already mounted on the printer.

For printers that use selectable or programmable character sets: if the *character-set* specified is not one defined in the Terminfo database for the printer [see **terminfo**(4)], or is not an alias defined by the administrator, the request is rejected.

When the **-d any** option is used, the request is printed on any printer that has the print wheel mounted or any printer that can select the character set, and that can handle any other needs of the request.

-t *title*   Print *title* on the banner page of the output. The default is no title. Enclose *title* in quotes if it contains blanks.

-T *content-type* [**-r**]
Print the request on a printer that can support the specified *content-type*. If no printer accepts this type directly, a filter will be used to convert the content into an acceptable type. If the **-r** option is specified, a filter will not be used. If **-r** is specified, and no printer accepts the *content-type* directly, the request is rejected. If the *content-type* is not acceptable to any printer, either directly or with a filter, the request is rejected.

In addition to ensuring that no filters will be used, the **-r** option will force the equivalent of the **-o 'stty=-opost' option.**

-w   Write a message on the user's terminal after the *files* have been printed. If the user is not logged in, then mail will be sent instead.

　　　　　-y *mode-list*　Print this request according to the printing modes listed in *mode-list*. The allowed values for *mode-list* are locally defined. This option may be used only if there is a filter available to handle it; otherwise, the print request will be rejected.

Canceling a Print Request

The **cancel** command cancels requests for print jobs made with the **lp** command. The first form allows a user to specify one or more *request-IDs* of print jobs to be canceled. Alternatively, the user can specify one or more *printers,* on which only the currently printing job will be canceled.

The second form of **cancel** permits a user to cancel all of his or her own jobs on all printers. In this form the *printers* option can be used to restrict the printers on which the user's jobs will be canceled. Note that in this form, when the *printers* option is used, all jobs queued for those printers will be canceled. A printer class is not a valid argument.

Users without special privileges can cancel only requests associated with their own login IDs. The system administrator can cancel jobs submitted by any user. The *login-ID-list* must be enclosed in quotes if it contains blanks.

NOTES

Printers for which requests are not being accepted will not be considered when the **lp** command is run and the destination is **any**. (Use the **lpstat -a** command to see which printers are accepting requests.) On the other hand, if (1) a request is destined for a class of printers and (2) the class itself is accepting requests, then *all* printers in the class will be considered, regardless of their acceptance status.

For printers that take mountable print wheels or font cartridges, if you do not specify a particular print wheel or font with the -S option, whichever one happens to be mounted at the time your request is printed will be used. Use the **lpstat -p** *printer* -1 command to see which print wheels are available on a particular printer, or the **lpstat -S -1** command to find out what print wheels are available and on which printers. For printers that have selectable character sets, you will get the standard character set if you don't use the -S option.

FILES

　　　　　/var/spool/lp/∗

SEE ALSO

　　　　　enable(1), **lpstat**(1), **mail**(1).
　　　　　accept(1M),　　**lpadmin**(1M),　　**lpfilter**(1M),　　**lpforms**(1M),　　**lpsched**(1M),
　　　　　lpsystem(1M), **lpusers**(1M) in the *System Administrator's Reference Manual.*
　　　　　terminfo(4) in the *Programmer's Reference Manual.*

NAME

lpadmin – configure the LP print service

SYNOPSIS

lpadmin **-p** *printer options*
lpadmin **-x** *dest*
lpadmin **-d** [*dest*]
lpadmin **-S** *print-wheel* **-A** *alert-type* [**-W** *minutes*] [**-Q** *requests*]

DESCRIPTION

lpadmin configures the LP print service by defining printers and devices. It is used to add and change printers, to remove printers from the service, to set or change the system default destination, to define alerts for printer faults, and to mount print wheels.

Adding or Changing a Printer

The first form of the **lpadmin** command (**lpadmin -p** *printer options*) is used to configure a new printer or to change the configuration of an existing printer. The following *options* may appear in any order.

-A *alert-type* [**-W** *minutes*]

The **-A** option is used to define an alert to inform the administrator when a printer fault is detected, and periodically thereafter, until the printer fault is cleared by the administrator. The *alert-types* are:

mail   Send the alert message via mail [see **mail**(1)] to the administrator.

write   Write the message to the terminal on which the administrator is logged in. If the administrator is logged in on several terminals, one is chosen arbitrarily.

quiet   Do not send messages for the current condition. An administrator can use this option to temporarily stop receiving further messages about a known problem. Once the fault has been cleared and printing resumes, messages will again be sent when another fault occurs with the printer.

none   Do not send messages; any existing alert definition for the printer will be removed. No alert will be sent when the printer faults until a different alert-type (except **quiet**) is used.

shell-command

Run the *shell-command* each time the alert needs to be sent. The shell command should expect the message in standard input. If there are blanks embedded in the command, enclose the command in quotes. Note that the **mail** and **write** values for this option are equivalent to the values **mail** *user-name* and **write** *user-name* respectively, where *user-name* is the current name for the administrator. This will be the login name of the person submitting this command unless he or she has used the **su** command to change to another user ID. If the **su** command has been used to change the user ID, then the *user-name* for the new ID is used.

list   Display the type of the alert for the printer fault. No change is made to the alert.

The message sent appears as follows:

```
The printer printer has stopped printing for the reason given below.
Fix the problem and bring the printer back on line.  Printing has
stopped, but will be restarted in a few minutes; issue an enable
command if you want to restart sooner.  Unless someone issues a
change request
```

> lp -i *request-id* -P ...

```
to change the page list to print, the current request will be
reprinted from the beginning.

The reason(s) it stopped (multiple reasons indicate reprinted
attempts):
```

> *reason*

The LP print service can detect printer faults only through an adequate fast filter and only when the standard interface program or a suitable customized interface program is used. Furthermore, the level of recovery after a fault depends on the capabilities of the filter.

If the *printer* is **all**, the alerting defined in this command applies to all existing printers.

If the **-W** option is not used to arrange fault alerting for *printer*, the default procedure is to mail one message to the administrator of *printer* per fault. This is equivalent to specifying **-W once** or **-W 0**. If *minutes* is a number greater than zero, an alert will be sent at intervals specified by *minutes*.

-c *class*
> Insert *printer* into the specified *class*. *Class* will be created if it does not already exist.

-D *comment*
> Save this *comment* for display whenever a user asks for a full description of *printer* [see **lpstat**(1)]. The LP print service does not interpret this comment.

-e *printer1*
> Copy the interface program of an existing *printer1* to be the interface program for *printer*. (Options **-i** and **-m** may not be specified with this option.)

-F *fault-recovery*
> This option specifies the recovery to be used for any print request that is stopped because of a printer fault, according to the value of *fault-recovery*:

continue
> > Continue printing on the top of the page where printing stopped. This requires a filter to wait for the fault to clear before automatically continuing.

`beginning`
Start printing the request again from the beginning.

`wait` Disable printing on *printer* and wait for the administrator or a user to enable printing again.

During the wait the administrator or the user who submitted the stopped print request can issue a change request that specifies where printing should resume. (See the **-i** option of the **lp** command.) If no change request is made before printing is enabled, printing will resume at the top of the page where stopped, if the filter allows; otherwise, the request will be printed from the beginning.

-f allow:*form-list*
-f deny:*form-list*
Allow or deny the forms in *form-list* to be printed on *printer*. By default no forms are allowed on a new printer.

For each printer, the LP print service keeps two lists of forms: an "allow-list" of forms that may be used with the printer, and a "deny-list" of forms that may not be used with the printer. With the **-f allow** option, the forms listed are added to the allow-list and removed from the deny-list. With the **-f deny** option, the forms listed are added to the deny-list and removed from the allow-list.

If the allow-list is not empty, only the forms in the list may be used on the printer, regardless of the contents of the deny-list. If the allow-list is empty, but the deny-list is not, the forms in the deny-list may not be used with the printer. All forms can be excluded from a printer by specifying **-f deny:all**. All forms can be used on a printer (provided the printer can handle all the characteristics of each form) by specifying **-f allow:all**.

The LP print service uses this information as a set of guidelines for determining where a form can be mounted. Administrators, however, are not restricted from mounting a form on any printer. If mounting a form on a particular printer is in disagreement with the information in the allow-list or deny-list, the administrator is warned but the mount is accepted. Nonetheless, if a user attempts to issue a print or change request for a form and printer combination that is in disagreement with the information, the request is accepted only if the form is currently mounted on the printer. If the form is later unmounted before the request can print, the request is canceled and the user is notified by mail.

If the administrator tries to specify a form as acceptable for use on a printer that doesn't have the capabilities needed by the form, the command is rejected.

Note the other use of **-f**, with the **-M** option, below.

-h Indicate that the device associated with the printer is hardwired. If neither of the mutually exclusive options, **-h** and **-l**, is specified, this option is assumed.

-I *content-type-list*
> Allow *printer* to handle print requests with the content types listed in a *content-type-list*. If the list includes names of more than one type, the names must be separated by commas or blank spaces. (If they are separated by blank spaces, the entire list must be enclosed in double quotes.)

> The type **simple** is recognized as the default content type for files in the UNIX system. A **simple** type of file is a data stream containing only printable ASCII characters and the following control characters.

Control Character	Octal Value	Meaning
backspace	10_8	move back one character, except at beginning of line
tab	11_8	move to next tab stop
linefeed (newline)	12_8	move to beginning of next line
form feed	14_8	move to beginning of next page
carriage return	15_8	move to beginning of current line

> To prevent the print service from considering **simple** a valid type for the printer, specify either an explicit value (such as the printer type) in the *content-type-list*, or an empty list. If you do want **simple** included along with other types, you must include **simple** in the *content-type-list*.

> Except for **simple**, each *content-type* name is freely determined by the administrator. If the printer type is specified by the **-T** option, then the printer type is implicitly considered to be also a valid content type.

-i *interface*
> Establish a new interface program for *printer*. *Interface* is the pathname of the new program. (The **-e** and **-m** options may not be specified with this option.)

-l
> Indicate that the device associated with *printer* is a login terminal. The LP scheduler (**lpsched**) disables all login terminals automatically each time it is started. (The **-h** option may not be specified with this option.)

-M -f *form-name* [-a [-o filebreak]]
> Mount the form *form-name* on *printer*. Print requests that need the pre-printed form *form-name* will be printed on *printer*. If more than one printer has the form mounted and the user has specified **any** (with the **-d** option of the **lp** command) as the printer destination, then the print request will be printed on the one printer that also meets the other needs of the request.

> The page length and width, and character and line pitches needed by the form are compared with those allowed for the printer, by checking the capabilities in the **terminfo** database for the type of printer. If the form requires attributes that are not available with the printer, the administrator is warned but the mount is accepted. If the form lists a print wheel as mandatory, but the print wheel mounted on the printer is different, the administrator is also warned but the mount is accepted.

If the **-a** option is given, an alignment pattern is printed, preceded by the same initialization of the physical printer that precedes a normal print request, with one exception: no banner page is printed. Printing is assumed to start at the top of the first page of the form. After the pattern is printed, the administrator can adjust the mounted form in the printer and press return for another alignment pattern (no initialization this time), and can continue printing as many alignment patterns as desired. The administrator can quit the printing of alignment patterns by typing **q**.

If the **-o filebreak** option is given, a formfeed is inserted between each copy of the alignment pattern. By default, the alignment pattern is assumed to correctly fill a form, so no formfeed is added.

A form is "unmounted" either by mounting a new form in its place or by using the **-f none** option. By default, a new printer has no form mounted.

Note the other use of **-f** without the **-M** option above.

-M -S *print-wheel*
> Mount the *print-wheel* on *printer*. Print requests that need the *print-wheel* will be printed on *printer*. If more than one printer has *print-wheel* mounted and the user has specified **any** (with the **-d** option of the **lp** command) as the printer destination, then the print request will be printed on the one printer that also meets the other needs of the request.
>
> If the *print-wheel* is not listed as acceptable for the printer, the administrator is warned but the mount is accepted. If the printer does not take print wheels, the command is rejected.
>
> A print wheel is "unmounted" either by mounting a new print wheel in its place or by using the option **-S none**. By default, a new printer has no print wheel mounted.
>
> Note the other uses of the **-S** option without the **-M** option described below.

-m *model*
> Select *model* interface program, provided with the LP print service, for the printer. (Options **-e** and **-i** may not be specified with this option.)

-o *printing-option*
> Each **-o** option in the list below is the default given to an interface program if the option is not taken from a preprinted form description or is not explicitly given by the user submitting a request [see **lp**(1)]. The only **-o** options that can have defaults defined are listed below.
>
> > **length**=*scaled-decimal-number*
> > **width**=*scaled-decimal-number*
> > **cpi**=*scaled-decimal-number*
> > **lpi**=*scaled-decimal-number*
> > **stty**='*stty-option-list*'

The term "scaled-decimal-number" refers to a non-negative number used to indicate a unit of size. The type of unit is shown by a "trailing" letter attached to the number. Three types of scaled decimal numbers can be used with the LP print service: numbers that show sizes in centimeters (marked with a trailing **c**); numbers that show sizes in inches (marked with a trailing i); and numbers that show sizes in units appropriate to use (without a trailing letter), that is, lines, characters, lines per inch, or characters per inch.

The first four default option values must agree with the capabilities of the type of physical printer, as defined in the **terminfo** database for the printer type. If they do not, the command is rejected.

The *stty-option-list* is not checked for allowed values, but is passed directly to the **stty** program by the standard interface program. Any error messages produced by **stty** when a request is processed (by the standard interface program) are mailed to the user submitting the request.

For each printing option not specified, the defaults for the following attributes are defined in the **terminfo** entry for the specified printer type.

```
length
width
cpi
lpi
```

The default for **stty** is

```
stty='9600 cs8 -cstopb -parenb ixon
        -ixany opost -olcuc onlcr -ocrnl -onocr
        -onlret -ofill nl0 cr0 tab0 bs0 vt0 ff0'
```

You can set any of the **-o** options to the default values (which vary for different types of printers), by typing them without assigned values, as follows:

```
length=
width=
cpi=
lpi=
stty=
```

-o nobanner
Allow a user to submit a print request specifying that no banner page be printed.

-o banner
Force a banner page to be printed with every print request, even when a user asks for no banner page. This is the default; you must specify **-o nobanner** if you want to allow users to be able to specify **-o nobanner** with the **lp** command.

-r *class*
Remove *printer* from the specified *class*. If *printer* is the last member of *class*, then *class* will be removed.

-s *list*
Allow either the print wheels or aliases for character sets named in *list* to be used on the printer.

If the printer is a type that takes print wheels, then *list* is a comma or space separated list of print wheel names. (Enclose the list with quotes if it contains blanks.) These will be the only print wheels considered mountable on the printer. (You can always force a different print wheel to be mounted, however.) Until the option is used to specify a list, no print wheels will be considered mountable on the printer, and print requests that ask for a particular print wheel with this printer will be rejected.

If the printer is a type that has selectable character sets, then *list* is a comma or blank separated list of character set name "mappings" or aliases. (Enclose the list with quotes if it contains blanks.) Each "mapping" is of the form

> *known-name=alias*

The *known-name* is a character set number preceded by **cs** (such as **cs3** for character set three) or a character set name from the **Terminfo** database entry **csnm**. [See **terminfo**(4) in the *Programmer's Reference Manual*.] If this option is not used to specify a list, only the names already known from the Terminfo database or numbers with a prefix of **cs** will be acceptable for the printer.

If *list* is the word **none**, any existing print wheel lists or character set aliases will be removed.

Note the other uses of the **-S** with the **-M** option described above.

-s *system-name*[!*printer-name*]

Make a remote printer (one that must be accessed through another system) accessible to users on your system. *System-name* is the name of the remote system on which the remote printer is located; it must be listed in the systems table (**/etc/lp/Systems**). *Printer-name* is the name used on the remote system for that printer. For example, if you want to access *printer1* on *system1* and you want it called *printer2* on your system, enter **-p** *printer2* **-s** *system1*!*printer1*

-T *printer-type-list*

Identify the printer as being of one or more *printer-type*s. Each *printer-type* is used to extract data from the **terminfo** database; this information is used to initialize the printer before printing each user's request. Some filters may also use a *printer-type* to convert content for the printer. If this option is not used, the default *printer-type* will be **unknown**; no information will be extracted from **terminfo** so each user request will be printed without first initializing the printer. Also, this option must be used if the following are to work: **-o cpi**, **-o lpi**, **-o width**, and **-o length** options of the **lpadmin** and **lp** commands, and the **-S** and **-f** options of the **lpadmin** command.

If the *printer-type-list* contains more than one type, then the *content-type-list* of the **-I** option must either be specified as **simple**, as empty (**-I ""**), or not specified at all.

−u allow:*login-ID-list*
−u deny:*login-ID-list*

> Allow or deny the users in *login-ID-list* access to the printer. By default all users are allowed on a new printer. The *login-ID-list* argument may include any or all of the following constructs:

login-ID	a user on the local system
system-name!*login-ID*	a user on system *system-name*
system-name!all	all users on system *system-name*
all!*login-ID*	a user on all systems
all	all users on the local system
all!all	all users on all systems

> For each printer the LP print service keeps two lists of users: an "allow-list" of people allowed to use the printer, and a "deny-list" of people denied access to the printer. With the −u allow option, the users listed are added to the allow-list and removed from the deny-list. With the −u deny option, the users listed are added to the deny-list and removed from the allow-list.

> If the allow-list is not empty, only the users in the list may use the printer, regardless of the contents of the deny-list. If the allow-list is empty, but the deny-list is not, the users in the deny-list may not use the printer. All users can be denied access to the printer by specifying −u deny:all. All users may use the printer by specifying −u allow:all.

−U *dial-info*

> The −U option allows your print service to access a remote printer. (It does not enable your print service to access a remote printer service.) Specifically, −U assigns the "dialing" information *dial-info* to the printer. *Dial-info* is used with the dial routine to call the printer. Any network connection supported by the Basic Networking Utilities will work. *Dial-info* can be either a phone number for a modem connection, or a system name for other kinds of connections. Or, if −U direct is given, no dialing will take place, because the name direct is reserved for a printer that is directly connected. If a system name is given, it is used to search for connection details from the file /etc/uucp/Systems or related files. The Basic Networking Utilities are required to support this option. By default, −U direct is assumed.

−v *device*

> Associate a *device* with *printer*. *Device* is the path name of a file that is writable by lp. Note that the same *device* can be associated with more than one printer.

Restrictions

When creating a new printer, one of three options (−v, −U, or −s) must be supplied. In addition, only one of the following may be supplied: −e, −i, or −m; if none of these three options is supplied, the model standard is used. The −h and −l options are mutually exclusive. Printer and class names may be no longer than 14 characters and must consist entirely of the characters A-Z, a-z, 0-9 and

_ (underscore). If −s is specified, the following options are invalid: −A, −e, −F, −h, −i, −l, −M, −m, −o, −U, −v, and −W.

Removing a Printer Destination

The −x *dest* option removes the destination *dest* (a printer or a class), from the LP print service. If *dest* is a printer and is the only member of a class, then the class will be deleted, too. If *dest* is **all**, all printers and classes are removed. No other *options* are allowed with −x.

Setting/Changing the System Default Destination

The −d [*dest*] option makes *dest*, an existing printer or class, the new system default destination. If *dest* is not supplied, then there is no system default destination. No other *options* are allowed with −d.

Setting an Alert for a Print Wheel

−S *print-wheel* −A *alert-type* [−W *minutes*] [−Q *requests*]

The −S *print-wheel* option is used with the −A *alert-type* option to define an alert to mount the print wheel when there are jobs queued for it. If this command is not used to arrange alerting for a print wheel, no alert will be sent for the print wheel. Note the other use of −A, with the −p option, above.

The *alert-types* are:

mail   Send the alert message via the **mail** command to the administrator.

write   Write the message, via the **write** command, to the terminal on which the administrator is logged in. If the administrator is logged in on several terminals, one is arbitrarily chosen.

quiet   Do not send messages for the current condition. An administrator can use this option to temporarily stop receiving further messages about a known problem. Once the *print-wheel* has been mounted and subsequently unmounted, messages will again be sent when the number of print requests reaches the threshold specified by the −Q option.

none   Do not send messages until the −A option is given again with a different *alert-type* (other than **quiet**).

shell-command

Run the *shell-command* each time the alert needs to be sent. The shell command should expect the message in standard input. If there are blanks embedded in the command, enclose the command in quotes. Note that the **mail** and **write** values for this option are equivalent to the values **mail** *user-name* and **write** *user-name* respectively, where *user-name* is the current name for the administrator. This will be the login name of the person submitting this command unless he or she has used the **su** command to change to another user ID. If the **su** command has been used to change the user ID, then the *user-name* for the new ID is used.

list   Display the type of the alert for the print wheel on standard output. No change is made to the alert.

The message sent appears as follows:

The print wheel *print-wheel* **needs to be mounted**
on the printer(s):
printer (*integer1* **requests**)
integer2 **print requests await this print wheel.**

The printers listed are those that the administrator had earlier specified were candidates for this print wheel. The number $integer_1$ listed next to each printer is the number of requests eligible for the printer. The number $integer_2$ shown after the printer list is the total number of requests awaiting the print wheel. It will be less than the sum of the other numbers if some requests can be handled by more than one printer.

If the *print-wheel* is **all**, the alerting defined in this command applies to all print wheels already defined to have an alert.

If the **-W** option is not given, the default procedure is that only one message will be sent per need to mount the print wheel. Not specifying the **-W** option is equivalent to specifying **-W once** or **-W 0**. If *minutes* is a number greater than zero, an alert will be sent at intervals specified by *minutes*.

If the **-Q** option is also given, the alert will be sent when a certain number (specified by the argument *requests*) of print requests that need the print wheel are waiting. If the **-Q** option is not given, or *requests* is 1 or the word **any** (which are both the default), a message is sent as soon as anyone submits a print request for the print wheel when it is not mounted.

FILES
/var/spool/lp/*
/etc/lp

SEE ALSO
accept(1M), lpsched(1M), and lpsystem(1M)
enable(1), lp(1), lpstat(1), and stty(1) in the *User's Reference Manual*
dial(3C), terminfo(4) in the *Programmer's Reference Manual*

NAME

lpc – line printer control program

SYNOPSIS

/usr/ucb/lpc [*command* [*parameter...*]]

DESCRIPTION

lpc controls the operation of the printer, or of multiple printers. lpc commands
can be used to start or stop a printer, disable or enable a printer's spooling
queue, rearrange the order of jobs in a queue, or display the status of each
printer—along with its spooling queue and printer daemon.

With no arguments, lpc runs interactively, prompting with 'lpc>'. If arguments
are supplied, lpc interprets the first as a *command* to execute; each subsequent
argument is taken as a *parameter* for that command. The standard input can be
redirected so that lpc reads commands from a file.

Commands may be abbreviated to an unambiguous substring. Note: the *printer*
parameter is specified just by the name of the printer (as **lw**), not as you would
specify it to lpr(1) or lpq(1) (not as **–Plw**).

? [*command*]...

help [*command*]...

Display a short description of each command specified in the argument
list, or, if no arguments are given, a list of the recognized commands.

abort [**all**| [*printer...*]]

Terminate an active spooling daemon on the local host immediately and
then disable printing (preventing new daemons from being started by
lpr(1)) for the specified printers. The **abort** command can only be used
by the privileged user.

clean [**all**| [*printer...*]]

Remove all files created in the spool directory by the daemon from the
specified printer queue(s) on the local machine. The **clean** command can
only be used by the privileged user.

disable [**all**| [*printer...*]]

Turn the specified printer queues off. This prevents new printer jobs from
being entered into the queue by lpr(1). The **disable** command can only
be used by the privileged user.

down [**all**| [*printer...*]] [*message*]

Turn the specified printer queue off, disable printing and put *message* in
the printer status file. The message does not need to be quoted, the
remaining arguments are treated like echo(1). This is normally used to
take a printer down and let others know why (lpq(1) indicates that the
printer is down, as does the **status** command).

enable [**all**| [*printer...*]]

Enable spooling on the local queue for the listed printers, so that lpr(1)
can put new jobs in the spool queue. The **enable** command can only be
used by the privileged user.

exit

quit   Exit from **lpc**.

restart [**all**| [*printer* ...]]

> Attempt to start a new printer daemon. This is useful when some abnormal condition causes the daemon to die unexpectedly leaving jobs in the queue. This command can be run by any user.

start [**all**| [*printer* ...]]

> Enable printing and start a spooling daemon for the listed printers. The **start** command can only be used by the privileged user.

status [**all**| [*printer* ...]]

> Display the status of daemons and queues on the local machine. This command can be run by any user.

stop [**all**| [*printer* ...]]

> Stop a spooling daemon after the current job completes and disable printing. The **stop** command can only be used by the privileged user.

topq *printer* [*job#* ...] [*user* ...]

> Move the print job(s) specified by *job#* or those job(s) belonging to *user* to the top (head) of the printer queue. The **topq** command can only be used by the privileged user.

up [**all**| [*printer* ...]] Enable everything and start a new printer daemon. Undoes the effects of **down**.

FILES

/var/spool/lp/*
/var/spool/lp/system/pstatus

SEE ALSO

lpq(1), lpr(1), lprm(1)

echo(1) in the *User's Reference Manual*
lpsched(1M) in the *System Administrator's Reference Manual*

DIAGNOSTICS

?Ambiguous command

> The abbreviation you typed matches more than one command.

?Invalid command

> You typed a command or abbreviation that was not recognized.

?Privileged command

> You used a command can be executed only by the privileged user.

lpc: *printer* : **unknown printer to the print service**

> The **printer** was not found in the System V LP database. Usually this is a typing mistake; however, it may indicate that the printer does not exist on the system. Use 'lptstat -p' to find the reason.

lpc: error on opening queue to spooler

> The connection to **lpsched** on the local machine failed. This usually means the printer server started at boot time has died or is hung. Check if the printer spooler daemon /usr/lib/lp/lpsched is running.

lpc: Can't send message to LP print service

lpc: Can't receive message from LP print service
>   These indicate that the LP print service has been stopped. Get help from
>   the system administrator.

lpc: Received unexpected message from LP print service
>   It is likely there is an error in this software. Get help from system
>   administrator.

NAME
> lpfilter – administer filters used with the LP print service

SYNOPSIS
> lpfilter -f *filter-name* -F *path-name*
> lpfilter -f *filter-name* –
> lpfilter -f *filter-name* -i
> lpfilter -f *filter-name* -x
> lpfilter -f *filter-name* -l

DESCRIPTION
> The lpfilter command is used to add, change, delete, and list a filter used with the LP print service. These filters are used to convert the content type of a file to a content type acceptable to a printer. One of the following options must be used with the lpfilter command: -F *path-name* (or – for standard input) to add or change a filter; -i to reset an original filter to its factory setting; -x to delete a filter; or -l to list a filter description.
>
> The argument all can be used instead of a *filter-name* with any of these options. When all is specified with the -F or – option, the requested change is made to all filters. Using all with the -i option has the effect of restoring to their original settings all filters for which predefined settings were initially available. Using the all argument with the -x option results in all filters being deleted, and using it with the -l option produces a list of all filters.

Adding or Changing a Filter
> The filter named in the -f option is added to the filter table. If the filter already exists, its description is changed to reflect the new information in the input.
>
> The filter description is taken from the *path-name* if the -F option is given, or from the standard input if the – option is given. One of the two must be given to define or change a filter. If the filter named is one originally delivered with the LP print service, the -i option will restore the original filter description.
>
> When an existing filter is changed with the -F or – option, items that are not specified in the new information are left as they were. When a new filter is added with this command, unspecified items are given default values. (See below.)
>
> Filters are used to convert the content of a request into a data stream acceptable to a printer. For a given print request, the LP print service will know the following: the type of content in the request, the name of the printer, the type of the printer, the types of content acceptable to the printer, and the modes of printing asked for by the originator of the request. It will use this information to find a filter or a pipeline of filters that will convert the content into a type acceptable to the printer.
>
> Below is a list of items that provide input to this command, and a description of each item. All lists are comma or space separated.
>
> > Input types: *content-type-list*
> > Output types: *content-type-list*
> > Printer types: *printer-type-list*
> > Printers: *printer-list*
> > Filter type: *filter-type*

        Command: *shell-command*
        Options: *template-list*

Input types This gives the types of content that can be accepted by the filter. (The default is **any**.)

Output types

        This gives the types of content that the filter can produce from any of the input content types. (The default is **any**.)

Printer types

        This gives the type of printers for which the filter can be used. The LP print service will restrict the use of the filter to these types of printers. (The default is **any**.)

Printers This gives the names of the printers for which the filter can be used. The LP print service will restrict the use of the filter to just the printers named. (The default is **any**.)

Filter type This marks the filter as a **slow** filter or a **fast** filter. Slow filters are generally those that take a long time to convert their input. They are run unconnected to a printer, to keep the printers from being tied up while the filter is running. If a listed printer is on a remote system, the filter type for it must have the value **slow**. Fast filters are generally those that convert their input quickly, or those that must be connected to the printer when run. These will be given to the interface program to run connected to the physical printer.

Command This specifies the program to run to invoke the filter. The full program pathname as well as fixed options must be included in the *shell-command*; additional options are constructed, based on the characteristics of each print request and on the **Options** field. A command must be given for each filter.

        The command must accept a data stream as standard input and produce the converted data stream on its standard output. This allows filter pipelines to be constructed to convert data not handled by a single filter.

Options This is a comma separated list of templates used by the LP print service to construct options to the filter from the characteristics of each print request listed in the table later.

        In general, each template is of the following form:

          keyword pattern = replacement

        The *keyword* names the characteristic that the template attempts to map into a filter specific option; each valid *keyword* is listed in the table below. A *pattern* is one of the following: a literal pattern of one of the forms listed in the table, a single asterisk (*), or a regular expression. If *pattern* matches the value of the characteristic, the template fits and is used to generate a filter specific option. The *replacement* is what will be used as the option.

Regular expressions are the same as those found in the **ed**(1) or **vi**(1) commands. This includes the \ (...\) and \n constructions, which can be used to extract portions of the *pattern* for copying into the *replacement*, and the **&**, which can be used to copy the entire *pattern* into the *replacement*.

The *replacement* can also contain a *****; it too, is replaced with the entire *pattern*, just like the **&** of **ed**(1).

lp Option	Characteristic	*keyword*	Possible *patterns*
-T	Content type (input)	INPUT	*content-type*
N/A	Content type (output)	OUTPUT	*content-type*
N/A	Printer type	TERM	*printer-type*
-d	Printer name	PRINTER	*printer-name*
-f, -o cpi=	Character pitch	CPI	*integer*
-f, -o lpi=	Line pitch	LPI	*integer*
-f, -o length=	Page length	LENGTH	*integer*
-f, -o width=	Page width	WIDTH	*integer*
-P	Pages to print	PAGES	*page-list*
-S	Character set	CHARSET	*character-set-name*
	Print wheel	CHARSET	*print-wheel-name*
-f	Form name	FORM	*form-name*
-y	Modes	MODES	*mode*
-n	Number of copies	COPIES	*integer*

For example, the template

        MODES landscape = -1

shows that if a print request is submitted with the **-y landscape** option, the filter will be given the option **-1**. As another example, the template

        TERM * = -T *

shows that the filter will be given the option **-T** *printer-type* for whichever *printer-type* is associated with a print request using the filter.

As a last example, consider the template

        MODES prwidth\=\(.*\) = -w\1

Suppose a user gives the command

        lp -y prwidth=10

From the table above, the LP print service determines that the **-y** option is handled by a **MODES** template. The **MODES** template here works because the *pattern* **prwidth\=\(.*\)** matches the **prwidth=10** given by the user. The *replacement* **-w\1** causes the LP print service to generate the filter option **-w10**.

If necessary, the LP print service will construct a filter pipeline by concatenating several filters to handle the user's file and all the print options. (See **sh**(1) for a description of a pipeline.) If the print service constructs a filter pipeline, the

INPUT and OUTPUT values used for each filter in the pipeline are the types of the input and output for that filter, not for the entire pipeline.

Deleting a Filter

The **−x** option is used to delete the filter specified in *filter-name* from the LP filter table.

Listing a Filter Description

The **−1** option is used to list the description of the filter named in *filter-name*. If the command is successful, the following message is sent to standard output:

> **Input types:** *content-type-list*
> **Output types:** *content-type-list*
> **Printer types:** *printer-type-list*
> **Printers:** *printer-list*
> **Filter type:** *filter-type*
> **Command:** *shell-command*
> **Options:** *template-list*

If the command fails, an error message is sent to standard error.

SEE ALSO

lpadmin(1M)
lp(1) in the *User's Reference Manual*

NAME

lpforms – administer forms used with the LP print service

SYNOPSIS

lpforms **-f** *form-name options*

lpforms **-f** *form-name* **-A** *alert-type* [**-Q** *minutes*] [**-W** *requests*]

DESCRIPTION

The **lpforms** command is used to administer the use of preprinted forms, such as company letterhead paper, with the LP print service. A form is specified by its *form-name*. Users may specify a form when submitting a print request [see **lp**(1)]. The argument **all** can be used instead of *form-name* with either of the command lines shown above. The first command line allows the administrator to add, change, and delete forms, to list the attributes of an existing form, and to allow and deny users access to particular forms. The second command line is used to establish the method by which the administrator is alerted that the form *form-name* must be mounted on a printer.

With the first **lpforms** command line, one of the following options must be used:

-F *pathname*   To add or change form *form-name*, as specified by the information in *pathname*

-   To add or change form *form-name*, as specified by the information from standard input

-x   To delete form *form-name* (this option must be used separately; it may not be used with any other option)

-l   To list the attributes of form *form-name*

Adding or Changing a Form

The **-F** *pathname* option is used to add a new form, *form-name*, to the LP print service, or to change the attributes of an existing form. The form description is taken from *pathname* if the **-F** option is given, or from the standard input if the **-** option is used. One of these two options must be used to define or change a form. *Pathname* is the path name of a file that contains all or any subset of the following information about the form.

> **Page length**: *scaled-decimal-number1*
> **Page width**: *scaled-decimal-number2*
> **Number of pages**: *integer*
> **Line pitch**: *scaled-decimal-number3*
> **Character pitch**: *scaled-decimal-number4*
> **Character set choice**: *character-set/print-wheel* [**mandatory**]
> **Ribbon color**: *ribbon-color*
> **Comment**:
> *comment*
> **Alignment pattern**: [*content-type*]
> *content*

The term "scaled-decimal-number" refers to a non-negative number used to indicate a unit of size. The type of unit is shown by a "trailing" letter attached to the number. Three types of scaled decimal numbers can be used with the LP print service: numbers that show sizes in centimeters (marked with a trailing c); numbers that show sizes in inches (marked with a trailing i); and numbers that show sizes in units appropriate to use (without a trailing letter), that is, lines, characters, lines per inch, or characters per inch.

Except for the last two lines, the above lines may appear in any order. The **Comment:** and *comment* items must appear in consecutive order but may appear before the other items, and the **Alignment pattern:** and the *content* items must appear in consecutive order at the end of the file. Also, the *comment* item may not contain a line that begins with any of the key phrases above, unless the key phrase is preceded with a > sign. Any leading > sign found in the *comment* will be removed when the comment is displayed. Case distinctions in the key phrases are ignored.

When this command is issued, the form specified by *form-name* is added to the list of forms. If the form already exists, its description is changed to reflect the new information. Once added, a form is available for use in a print request, except where access to the form has been restricted, as described under the –u option. A form may also be allowed to be used on certain printers only.

A description of each form attribute is below:

Page length and Page Width
> Before printing the content of a print request needing this form, the generic interface program provided with the LP print service will initialize the physical printer to handle pages *scaled-decimal-number1* long, and *scaled-decimal-number2* wide using the printer type as a key into the **terminfo** database.

The page length and page width will also be passed, if possible, to each filter used in a request needing this form.

Number of pages
> Each time the alignment pattern is printed, the LP print service will attempt to truncate the *content* to a single form by, if possible, passing to each filter the page subset of 1-*integer*.

Line pitch and Character pitch
> Before printing the content of a print request needing this form, the interface programs provided with the LP print service will initialize the physical printer to handle these pitches, using the printer type as a key into the **terminfo** database. Also, the pitches will be passed, if possible, to each filter used in a request needing this form. *scaled-decimal-number3* is in lines per centimeter if a c is appended, and lines per inch otherwise; similarly, *scaled-decimal-number4* is in characters per centimeter if a c is appended, and characters per inch otherwise. The character pitch can also be given as **elite** (12 characters per inch), **pica** (10 characters per inch), or **compressed** (as many characters per inch as possible).

Character set choice

When the LP print service alerts an administrator to mount this form, it will also mention that the print wheel *print-wheel* should be used on those printers that take print wheels. If printing with this form is to be done on a printer that has selectable or loadable character sets instead of print wheels, the interface programs provided with the LP print service will automatically select or load the correct character set. If **mandatory** is appended, a user is not allowed to select a different character set for use with the form; otherwise, the character set or print wheel named is a suggestion and a default only.

Ribbon color

When the LP print service alerts an administrator to mount this form, it will also mention that the color of the ribbon should be *ribbon-color*.

Comment

The LP print service will display the *comment* unaltered when a user asks about this form [see **lpstat**(1)].

Alignment pattern

When mounting this form an administrator can ask for the *content* to be printed repeatedly, as an aid in correctly positioning the preprinted form. The optional *content-type* defines the type of printer for which *content* had been generated. If *content-type* is not given, **simple** is assumed. Note that the *content* is stored as given, and will be readable only by the user **lp**.

When an existing form is changed with this command, items missing in the new information are left as they were. When a new form is added with this command, missing items will get the following defaults:

Page Length: **66**
Page Width: **80**
Number of Pages: **1**
Line Pitch: **6**
Character Pitch: **10**
Character Set Choice: **any**
Ribbon Color: **any**

Deleting a Form

The **-x** option is used to delete the form *form-name* from the LP print service.

Listing Form Attributes

The **-1** option is used to list the attributes of the existing form *form-name*. The attributes listed are those described under **Adding and Changing a Form,** above. Because of the potentially sensitive nature of the alignment pattern, only the administrator can examine the form with this command. Other people may use the **lpstat** command to examine the non-sensitive part of the form description.

Allowing and Denying Access to a Form

The **-u** option, followed by the argument **allow:***login-ID-list* or **-u deny:***login-ID-list* lets you determine which users will be allowed to specify a particular form with a print request. This option can be used with the **-F** or **-** option, each of which is described above under **Adding or Changing a Form.**

The *login-ID-list* argument may include any or all of the following constructs:

login-ID	A user on any system
system_name!*login-ID*	A user on system *system_name*
system_name!**all**	All users on system *system_name*
all!*login-ID*	A user on all systems
all	All users on all systems

The LP print service keeps two lists of users for each form: an "allow-list" of people allowed to use the form, and a "deny-list" of people that may not use the form. With the **-u allow** option, the users listed are added to the allow-list and removed from the deny-list. With the **-u deny** option, the users listed are added to the deny-list and removed from the allow-list. (Both forms of the **-u** option can be run together with the **-F** or the **-** option.)

If the allow-list is not empty, only the users in the list are allowed access to the form, regardless of the contents of the deny-list. If the allow-list is empty but the deny-list is not, the users in the deny-list may not use the form, (but all others may use it). All users can be denied access to a form by specifying **-f deny:all**. All users can be allowed access to a form by specifying **-f allow:all**. (This is the default.)

Setting an Alert to Mount a Form

The **-f** *form-name* option is used with the **-A** *alert-type* option to define an alert to mount the form when there are queued jobs which need it. If this option is not used to arrange alerting for a form, no alert will be sent for that form.

The method by which the alert is sent depends on the value of the *alert-type* argument specified with the **-A** option. The *alert-types* are:

mail Send the alert message via the **mail** command to the administrator.

write Write the message, via the **write** command, to the terminal on which the administrator is logged in. If the administrator is logged in on several terminals, one is arbitrarily chosen.

quiet Do not send messages for the current condition. An administrator can use this option to temporarily stop receiving further messages about a known problem. Once the form *form-name* has been mounted and subsequently unmounted, messages will again be sent when the number of print requests reaches the threshold specified by the **-Q** option.

none Do not send messages until the **-A** option is given again with a different *alert-type* (other than **quiet**).

shell-command
Run the *shell-command* each time the alert needs to be sent. The shell command should expect the message in standard input. If there are blanks embedded in the command, enclose the command in quotes. Note that the **mail** and **write** values for this option are equivalent to the values **mail** *login-ID* and **write** *login-ID* respectively, where *login-ID* is the current name for the administrator. This will be the login name of the person submitting this command

unless he or she has used the **su** command to change to another login-ID. If the **su** command has been used to change the user ID, then the *user-name* for the new ID is used.

list   Display the type of the alert for the form on standard output. No change is made to the alert.

The message sent appears as follows:

> **The form** *form-name* **needs to be mounted**
> **on the printer(s):**
> *printer* (*integer1* **requests**).
> *integer2* print requests await this form.
> Use the *ribbon-color* **ribbon.**
> **Use the** *print-wheel* **print wheel, if appropriate.**

The printers listed are those that the administrator had earlier specified were candidates for this form. The number $integer sub 1$ listed next to each printer is the number of requests eligible for the printer. The number $integer sub 2$ shown after the list of printers is the total number of requests awaiting the form. It will be less than the sum of the other numbers if some requests can be handled by more than one printer. The *ribbon-color* and *print-wheel* are those specified in the form description. The last line in the message is always sent, even if none of the printers listed use print wheels, because the administrator may choose to mount the form on a printer that does use a print wheel.

Where any color ribbon or any print wheel can be used, the statements above will read:

> **Use any ribbon.**
> **Use any print-wheel.**

If *form-name* is **any**, the alerting defined in this command applies to any form for which an alert has not yet been defined. If *form-name* is **all**, the alerting defined in this command applies to all forms.

If the **-W** option is not given, the default procedure is that only one message will be sent per need to mount the form. Not specifying the **-W** option is equivalent to specifying **-W once** or **-W 0**. If *minutes* is a number greater than 0, an alert will be sent at intervals specified by *minutes*.

If the **-Q** option is also given, the alert will be sent when a certain number (specified by the argument *requests*) of print requests that need the form are waiting. If the **-Q** option is not given, or the value of *requests* is **1** or **any** (which are both the default), a message is sent as soon as anyone submits a print request for the form when it is not mounted.

Listing the Current Alert

The **-f** option, followed by the **-A** option and the argument **list** is used to list the type of alert that has been defined for the specified form *form-name*. No change is made to the alert. If *form-name* is recognized by the LP print service, one of the following lines is sent to the standard output, depending on the type of alert for the form.

> When *requests* requests are queued:
> alert with *shell-command* every *minutes* minutes
>
> When *requests* requests are queued:
> write to *user-name* every *minutes* minutes
>
> When *requests* requests are queued:
> mail to *user-name* every *minutes* minutes
>
> No alert

The phrase **every** *minutes* **minutes** is replaced with **once** if *minutes* (*-W minutes*) is 0.

Terminating an Active Alert

The **-A quiet** option is used to stop messages for the current condition. An administrator can use this option to temporarily stop receiving further messages about a known problem. Once the form has been mounted and then unmounted, messages will again be sent when the number of print requests reaches the threshold *requests*.

Removing an Alert Definition

No messages will be sent after the **-A none** option is used until the **-A** option is given again with a different *alert-type*. This can be used to permanently stop further messages from being sent as any existing alert definition for the form will be removed.

SEE ALSO

lpadmin(1M), terminfo(4)

lp(1) in the *User's Reference Manual*

NAME

lpq – display the queue of printer jobs

SYNOPSIS

/usr/ucb/lpq [-P*printer*] [-l] [+ [*interval*]] [*job#* . . .] [*username* . . .]

DESCRIPTION

lpq displays the contents of a printer queue. It reports the status of jobs specified by *job#*, or all jobs owned by the user specified by *username*. lpq reports on all jobs in the default printer queue when invoked with no arguments.

For each print job in the queue, lpq reports the user's name, current position, the names of input files comprising the job, the job number (by which it is referred to when using lprm(1)) and the total size in bytes. Normally, only as much information as will fit on one line is displayed. Jobs are normally queued on a first-in-first-out basis. Filenames comprising a job may be unavailable, such as when lpr is used at the end of a pipeline; in such cases the filename field indicates the standard input.

If lpq warns that there is no daemon present (that is, due to some malfunction), the lpc(1M) command can be used to restart a printer daemon.

OPTIONS

-P *printer*   Display information about the queue for the specified *printer*. In the absence of the -P option, the queue to the printer specified by the **PRINTER** variable in the environment is used. If the **PRINTER** variable is not set, the queue for the default printer is used.

-l   Display queue information in long format; includes the name of the host from which the job originated.

+[*interval*]   Display the spool queue periodically until it empties. This option clears the terminal screen before reporting on the queue. If an *interval* is supplied, lpq sleeps that number of seconds in between reports.

FILES

/var/spool/lp   spooling directory.
/var/spool/lp/tmp/*system_name*/*-0   request files specifying jobs

DIAGNOSTICS

printer **is printing**
    The lpq program queries the spooler **LPSCHED** about the status of the printer. If the printer is disabled, the superuser can restart the spooler using lpc(1M).

printer **waiting for auto-retry (offline ?)**
    The daemon could not open the printer device. The printer may be turned off-line. This message can also occur if a printer is out of paper, the paper is jammed, and so on. Another possible cause is that a process, such as an output filter, has exclusive use of the device. The only recourse in this case is to kill the offending process and restart the printer with lpc.

waiting for *host* **to come up**
> A daemon is trying to connect to the remote machine named *host*, in order to send the files in the local queue. If the remote machine is up, **lpd** on the remote machine is probably dead or hung and should be restarted using **lpc**.

sending to *host*
> The files are being transferred to the remote *host*, or else the local daemon has hung while trying to transfer the files.

printer disabled reason:
> The printer has been marked as being unavailable with **lpc**.

lpq: The LP print service isn't running or can't be reached.
> The **lpsched** process overseeing the spooling queue does not exist. This normally occurs only when the daemon has unexpectedly died. You can restart the printer daemon with **lpc**.

lpr: *printer* **: unknown printer**
> The **printer** was not found in the System V LP database. Usually this is a typing mistake; however, it may indicate that the printer does not exist on the system. Use 'lptstat -p' to find the reason.

lpr: error on opening queue to spooler
> The connection to **lpsched** on the local machine failed. This usually means the printer server started at boot time has died or is hung. Check if the printer spooler daemon **/usr/lib/lpsched** is running.

lpr: Can't send message to LP print service

lpr: Can't receive message from LP print service
> These indicate that the LP print service has been stopped. Get help from the system administrator.

lpr: Received unexpected message from LP print service
> It is likely there is an error in this software. Get help from system administrator.

SEE ALSO
lpc(1M), **lpr**(1), **lprm**(1)

lpsched(1M) in the *System Administrator's Reference Manual*
lp(1) in the *User's Reference Manual*

NOTES
Output formatting is sensitive to the line length of the terminal; this can result in widely-spaced columns.

NAME

lpr – send a job to the printer

SYNOPSIS

/usr/ucb/lpr [-P *printer*] [-# *copies*] [-C *class*] [-J *job*] [-T *title*]
    [-i [*indent*]] [-w *cols*] [-B] [-r] [-m] [-h] [-s]
    [-*filter_option*] [*filename* . . .]

DESCRIPTION

lpr forwards printer jobs to a spooling area for subsequent printing as facilities become available. Each printer job consists of copies of, or, with -s , complete pathnames of each *filename* you specify. The spool area is managed by the line printer spooler, lpsched. lpr reads from the standard input if no files are specified.

OPTIONS

-P *printer*
Send output to the named *printer*. Otherwise send output to the printer named in the **PRINTER** environment variable, or to the default printer, lp.

-# *copies*
Produce the number of *copies* indicated for each named file. For example:

    lpr -#3 index.c lookup.c

produces three copies of **index.c**, followed by three copies of **lookup.c**. On the other hand,

    cat index.c lookup.c | lpr -#3

generates three copies of the concatenation of the files.

-C *class*
Print *class* as the job classification on the burst page. For example,

    lpr -C Operations new.index.c

replaces the system name (the name returned by *hostname*) with **Operations** on the burst page, and prints the file **new.index.c**.

-J *job*
Print *job* as the job name on the burst page. Normally, lpr uses the first file's name.

-T *title*
Use *title* instead of the file name for the title used by **pr**(1).

-i[*indent*]
Indent output *indent* SPACE characters. Eight SPACE characters is the default.

-w *cols*
Use *cols* as the page width for **pr**.

-r
Remove the file upon completion of spooling, or upon completion of printing with the -s option. This is not supported in the SunOS compatibility package. However if the job is submitted to a remote SunOS system, these options will be sent to the remote system for processing.

-m	Send mail upon completion.
-h	Suppress printing the burst page.
-s	Use the full pathnames (not symbolic links) of the files to be printed rather than trying to copy them. This means the data files should not be modified or removed until they have been printed. -s only prevents copies of local files from being made. Jobs from remote hosts are copied anyway. -s only works with named data files; if the lpr command is at the end of a pipeline, the data is copied to the spool.
filter_option	The following single letter options notify the line printer spooler that the files are not standard text files. The spooling daemon will use the appropriate filters to print the data accordingly.

-p	Use pr to format the files (lpr -p is very much like pr | lpr).
-l	Print control characters and suppress page breaks.
-t	The files contain troff(1) (cat phototypesetter) binary data.
-n	The files contain data from ditroff (device independent troff).
-d	The files contain data from tex (DVI format from Stanford).
-g	The files contain standard plot data as produced by the plot(3X) routines (see also plot(1G) for the filters used by the printer spooler).
-v	The files contain a raster image. The printer must support an appropriate imaging model such as PostScript® in order to print the image.
-c	The files contain data produced by *cifplot*.
-f	Interpret the first character of each line as a standard FORTRAN carriage control character.

If no *filter_option* is given (and the printer can interpret PostScript), the string '%!' as the first two characters of a file indicates that it contains PostScript commands.

These filter options offer a standard user interface, and all options may not be available for, nor applicable to, all printers.

FILES

/etc/passwd	personal identification
/usr/lib/lp/lpsched	System V line printer spooler
/var/spool/lp/tmp/*	directories used for spooling
/var/spool/lp/tmp/*system*/*-0	spooler control files
/var/spool/lp/tmp/*system*/*-N	(*N* is an integer and > 0) data files specified in '*-0' files

DIAGNOSTICS

> lpr: *printer* : **unknown printer**
>> The **printer** was not found in the LP database. Usually this is a typing mistake; however, it may indicate that the printer does not exist on the system. Use 'lptstat -p' to find the reason.

> lpr: **error on opening queue to spooler**
>> The connection to **lpsched** on the local machine failed. This usually means the printer server started at boot time has died or is hung. Check if the printer spooler daemon **/usr/lib/lpsched** is running.

> lpr: *printer* : **printer queue is disabled**
>> This means the queue was turned off with

>>> **/usr/etc/lpc disable** *printer*

>> to prevent **lpr** from putting files in the queue. This is normally done by the system manager when a printer is going to be down for a long time. The printer can be turned back on by a privileged user with **lpc**.

> lpr: **Can't send message to the LP print service**

> lpr: **Can't receive message from the LP print service**
>> These indicate that the LP print service has been stopped. Get help from the system administrator.

> lpr: **Received unexpected message from LP print service**
>> It is likely there is an error in this software. Get help from system administrator.

> lpr: **There is no filter to convert the file content**
>> Use the 'lpstat -p   -l' command to find a printer that can handle the file type directly, or consult with your system administrator.

> lpr: **cannot access the file**
>> Make sure file names are valid.

SEE ALSO

lpc(8), lpq(1), lprm(1), plot(1G), troff(1)

plot(3X) in the *Programmer's Reference Manual*
lpsched(1) in the *System Administrator's Reference Manual*
lp(1), pr(1) in the *User's Reference Manual*

NOTES

lp is the preferred interface.

Command-line options cannot be combined into a single argument as with some other commands. The command:

> lpr -fs

is not equivalent to

> lpr -f -s

Placing the **−s** flag first, or writing each option as a separate argument, makes a link as expected.

lpr −p is not precisely equivalent to **pr | lpr**. **lpr −p** puts the current date at the top of each page, rather than the date last modified.

Fonts for **troff**(1) and T$_E$X® reside on the printer host. It is currently not possible to use local font libraries.

lpr objects to printing binary files.

The **−s** option, intended to use symbolic links in SunOS, does not use symbolic links in the compatibility package. Instead, the complete path names are used. Also, the copying is avoided only for print jobs that are run from the printer host itself. Jobs added to the queue from a remote host are always copied into the spool area. That is, if the printer does not reside on the host that **lpr** is run from, the spooling system makes a copy the file to print, and places it in the spool area of the printer host, regardless of **−s**.

NAME

lprm – remove jobs from the printer queue

SYNOPSIS

/usr/ucb/lprm [-P*printer*] [-] [*job #* . . .] [*username* . . .]

DESCRIPTION

lprm removes a job or jobs from a printer's spooling queue. Since the spool directory is protected from users, using lprm is normally the only method by which a user can remove a job.

Without any arguments, lprm deletes the job that is currently active, provided that the user who invoked lprm owns that job.

When the privileged user specifies a *username*, lprm removes all jobs belonging to that user.

You can remove a specific job by supplying its job number as an argument, which you can obtain using lpq(1). For example:

```
lpq  -Phost
host is ready and printing
Rank Owner    Job     Files    Total Size
active        wendy   385      standard input   35501 bytes
lprm -Phost 385
```

lprm reports the names of any files it removes, and is silent if there are no applicable jobs to remove.

lprm Sends the request to cancel a job to the print spooler, LPSCHED.

OPTIONS

-P*printer*   Specify the queue associated with a specific printer. Otherwise the value of the PRINTER variable in the environment is used. If this variable is unset, the queue for the default printer is used.

-            Remove all jobs owned by you. If invoked by the privileged user, all jobs in the spool are removed. Job ownership is determined by the user's login name and host name on the machine where the lpr command was executed.

FILES

/var/spool/lp/*   spooling directories

SEE ALSO

lpq(1), lpr(1)

lpsched(1M) in the *System Administrator's Reference Manual*
cancel(1), lp(1) in the *User's Reference Manual*

DIAGNOSTICS

lprm: *printer* : unknown printer
       The printer was not found in the System V LP database. Usually this is a typing mistake; however, it may indicate that the printer does not exist on the system. Use 'lptstat -p' to find the reason.

lprm: error on opening queue to spooler
> The connection to **lpsched** on the local machine failed. This usually means the printer server started at boot time has died or is hung. Check if the printer spooler daemon **/usr/lib/lpsched** is running.

lprm: Can't send message to the LP print service

lprm: Can't receive message from the LP print service
> These indicate that the LP print service has been stopped. Get help from the system administrator.

lprm: Received unexpected message from the LP print service
> It is likely there is an error in this software. Get help from system administrator.

lprm: Can't cancel request
> You are not allowed to remove another's request.

NOTES

An active job may be incorrectly identified for removal by an **lprm** command issued with no arguments. During the interval between an **lpq**(1) command and the execution of **lprm**, the next job in queue may have become active; that job may be removed unintentionally if it is owned by you. To avoid this, supply **lprm** with the job number to remove when a critical job that you own is next in line.

Only the privileged user can remove print jobs submitted from another host.

lp is the preferred interface.

NAME

lprof – display line-by-line execution count profile data

SYNOPSIS

lprof [-p] [-s] [-x] [-I *incdir*] [-r *srcfile*] [-c *cntfile*] [-o *prog*] [-V]

lprof -m *file1*.cnt *file2*.cnt *filen*.cnt [-T] -d *destfile*.cnt

DESCRIPTION

lprof reports the execution characteristics of a program on a (source) line by line basis. This is useful as a means to determine which and how often portions of the code were executed.

lprof interprets a profile file (*prog*.cnt by default) produced by the profiled program *prog* (a.out by default). *prog* creates a profile file if it has been loaded with the -ql option of cc. The profile information is computed for functions in a source file if the -ql option was used when the source file was compiled.

A shared object may also be profiled by specifying -ql when the shared object is created. When a dynamically linked executable is run, one profile file is produced for each profiled shared object linked to the executable. This feature is useful in building a single report covering multiple and disparate executions of a common library. For example, if programs prog1 and prog2 both use library libx.a, running these profiled programs will produce two profile files, prog1.cnt and prog2.cnt, which cannot be combined. However, if libx is built as a profiled shared object, libx.so, and prog1 and prog2 are built as profiled dynamically linked executables, then running these programs with the merge option will produce three profile files; one of them, libx.so.cnt, will contain the libx profile information from both runs.

By default, lprof prints a listing of source files (the names of which are stored in the symbol table of the executable file), with each line preceded by its line number (in the source file) and the number of times the line was executed.

The following options may appear singly or be combined in any order:

-p
Print listing, each line preceded by the line number and the number of times it was executed (default). This option can be used together with the -s option to print both the source listing and summary information.

-s
Print summary information of percentage of lines of code executed per function.

-x
Instead of printing the execution count numbers for each line, print each line preceded by its line number and a [U] if the line was not executed. If the line was executed, print only the line number.

-I *incdir*
Look for source or header files in the directory *incdir* in addition to the current directory and the standard place for #include files (usually /usr/include). The user can specify more than one directory by using multiple -I options.

-r *srcfile*   Instead of printing all source files, print only those files named in
                  -r options (to be used with the -p option only). The user can
                  specify multiple files with a single -r option.

-c *cntfile*   Use the file *cntfile* instead of *prog*.cnt as the input profile file.

-o *prog*   Use the name of the program *prog* instead of the name used
                  when creating the profile file. Because the program name stored
                  in the profile file contains the relative path, this option is neces-
                  sary if the executable file or profile file has been moved.

-V   Print, on standard error, the version number of lprof.

Merging Data Files

lprof can also be used to merge profile files. The -m option must be accom-
panied by the -d option:

-m *file1*.cnt *file2*.cnt *filen*.cnt -d *destfile*.cnt
                  Merge the data files *file1*.cnt through *filen*.cnt by summing the
                  execution counts per line, so that data from several runs can be
                  accumulated. The result is written to *destfile*.cnt. The data files
                  must contain profiling data for the same *prog* (see the -T option
                  below).

-T   Time stamp override. Normally, the time stamps of the execut-
                  able files being profiled are checked, and data files will not be
                  merged if the time stamps do not match. If -T is specified, this
                  check is skipped.

CONTROLLING THE RUN-TIME PROFILING ENVIRONMENT

The environment variable PROFOPTS provides run-time control over profiling.
When a profiled program (or shared object) is about to terminate, it examines the
value of PROFOPTS to determine how the profiling data are to be handled. A terminating shared object will honor every PROFOPTS option except file=*filename*.

The environment variable PROFOPTS is a comma-separated list of options interpreted by the program being profiled. If PROFOPTS is not defined in the environment, then the default action is taken: The profiling data are saved in a file (with
the default name, *prog*.cnt) in the current directory. If PROFOPTS is set to the
null string, no profiling data are saved. The following are the available options:

msg=[y| n]   If msg=y is specified, a message stating that profile data are being
                 saved is printed to stderr. If msg=n is specified, only the
                 profiling error messages are printed. The default is msg=y.

merge=[y| n]   If merge=y is specified, the data files will be merged after succes-
                 sive runs. If merge=n is specified, the data files are not merged
                 after successive runs, and the data file is overwritten after each
                 execution. The merge will fail if the program has been recom-
                 piled, and the data file will be left in TMPDIR. The default is
                 merge=n.

pid=[y| n]   If pid=y is specified, the name of the data file will include the
                 process ID of the profiled program. Inclusion of the process ID
                 allows for the creation of different data files for programs calling
                 fork. If pid=n is specified, the default name is used. The

default is **pid=n**. For **lprof** to generate its profiling report, the
−c option must be specified with **lprof** otherwise the default will
fail.

dir=*dirname*   The data file is placed in the directory *dirname* if this option is
specified. Otherwise, the data file is created in the directory that
is current at the end of execution.

file=*filename*   *filename* is used as the name of the data file in *dir* created by the
profiled program if this option is specified. Otherwise, the
default name is used. For **lprof** to generate its profiling report,
the −c option must be specified with **lprof** if the file option has
been used at execution time; otherwise the default will fail.

FILES

prog.**cnt**   profile data
TMPDIR   usually **/var/tmp** but can be redefined by setting the environment variable **TMPDIR** [see **tempnam** in **tmpnam**(3S)].

SEE ALSO

cc(1), **prof**(1), **fork**(2), **tmpnam**(3S)
The "**lprof**" chapter in the *Programmer's Guide: ANSI C and Programming Support
Tools*

NOTES

For the −**m** option, if *destfile*.**cnt** exists, its previous contents are destroyed.

Optimized code cannot be profiled; if both optimization and line profiling are
requested, profiling has precedence.

Including header files that contain code (such as **stat.h** or **utsname.h**) will
cause erroneous data.

Different parts of one line of a source file may be executed different numbers of
times (for example, the **for** loop below); the count corresponds to the first part of
the line.

For example, in the following **for** loop

```
                    main()
    1    [2]        {
                        int j;

    1    [5]         for (j = 0; j < 5; j++)
    5    [6]          sub(j);

    1    [8]         }

                    sub(a)
                    int a;
    5    [12]        {
    5    [13]         printf("a is %d\n", a);
    5    [14]        }
```

line 5 consists of three parts. The line count listed, however, is for the initialization part, that is, **j** = 0.

NAME

lpsched, lpshut, lpmove – start/stop the LP print service and move requests

SYNOPSIS

`/usr/lib/lp/lpsched`
`lpshut`
`lpmove` *requests dest*
`lpmove` *dest1 dest2*

DESCRIPTION

lpsched starts the LP print service; this can be done only by **root** or **lp**.

lpshut shuts down the print service. All printers that are printing at the time lpshut is invoked will stop printing. When lpsched is started again, requests that were printing at the time a printer was shut down will be reprinted from the beginning.

lpmove moves requests that were queued by **lp** between LP destinations. The first form of the lpmove command shown above (under **SYNOPSIS**) moves the named *requests* to the LP destination *dest*. *Requests* are request-IDs as returned by **lp**. The second form of the lpmove command will attempt to move all requests for destination *dest1* to destination *dest2*; **lp** will then reject any new requests for *dest1*.

Note that when moving requests, lpmove never checks the acceptance status [see **accept**(1M)] of the new destination. Also, the request-IDs of the moved request are not changed, so that users can still find their requests. The lpmove command will not move requests that have options (content type, form required, and so on) that cannot be handled by the new destination.

If a request was originally queued for a class or the special destination **any**, and the first form of lpmove was used, the destination of the request will be changed to *new-destination*. A request thus affected will be printable only on *new-destination* and not on other members of the **class** or other acceptable printers if the original destination was **any**.

FILES

`/var/spool/lp/*`

SEE ALSO

accept(1M), lpadmin(1M)
enable(1), lp(1), lpstat(1) in the *User's Reference Manual*

NAME

lpstat – print information about the status of the LP print service

SYNOPSIS

lpstat [*options*]

DESCRIPTION

The lpstat command prints information about the current status of the LP print service.

If no options are given, then lpstat prints the status of all the user's print requests made by lp [see lp(1)]. Any arguments that are not *options* are assumed to be *request-IDs* as returned by lp. The lpstat command prints the status of such requests. The *options* may appear in any order and may be repeated and intermixed with other arguments. Some of the keyletters below may be followed by an optional *list* that can be in one of two forms: a list of items separated from one another by a comma, or a list of items separated from one another by spaces enclosed in quotes. For example:

    -u "user1, user2, user3"

Specifying **all** after any keyletter that takes *list* as an argument causes all information relevant to the keyletter to be printed. For example, the command

    lpstat -o all

prints the status of all output requests.

The omission of a *list* following such key letters causes all information relevant to the key letter to be printed. For example, the command

    lpstat -o

prints the status of all output requests.

-a [*list*] Reports whether print destinations are accepting requests. *list* is a list of intermixed printer names and class names.

-c [*list*] Reports name of all classes and their members. *list* is a list of class names.

-d Reports the system default destination for output requests.

-f [*list*] [-l]
    Prints a verification that the forms in *list* are recognized by the LP print service. *list* is a list of forms; the default is **all**. The -l option will list the form descriptions.

-o [*list*] Reports the status of output requests: *list* is a list of intermixed printer names, class names, and *request-IDs*. The keyletter -o may be omitted.

-p [*list*] [-D] [-l]
    Reports the status of printers. *list* is a list of printer names. If the -D option is given, a brief description is printed for each printer in *list*. If the -l option is given, and the printer is on the local machine, a full description of each printer's configuration is given, including the form mounted, the acceptable content and printer types, a printer description, the interface used, and so on. If the -l option is given and the printer is remote, the only information given is the remote machine and printer

names, and the shell-commands used for file transfer and remote execution.

-r   Reports whether the LP request scheduler is on or off.

-R   Reports a number showing the position of the job in the print queue.

-s   Displays a status summary, including the status of the LP scheduler, the
            system default destination, a list of class names and their members, a list
            of printers and their associated devices, a list of the machines sharing
            print services, a list of all forms currently mounted, and a list of all
            recognized character sets and print wheels.

-S [*list*] [-1]
            Prints a verification that the character sets or the print wheels specified
            in *list* are recognized by the LP print service. Items in *list* can be charac-
            ter sets or print wheels; the default for the list is **all**. If the -1 option is
            given, each line is appended by a list of printers that can handle the
            print wheel or character set. The list also shows whether the print wheel
            or character set is mounted or specifies the built-in character set into
            which it maps.

-t   Displays all status information: all the information obtained with the -s
            option, plus the acceptance and idle/busy status of all printers.

-u [*login-ID-list*]
            Displays the status of output requests for users. The *login-ID-list* argu-
            ment may include any or all of the following constructs:

login-ID	a user on any system
system_name!*login-ID*	a user on system *system_name*
system_name!**all**	all users on system *system_name*
all!*login-ID*	a user on all systems
all	all users on all systems

-v [*list*] Reports the names of printers and the pathnames of the devices associ-
            ated with them or remote system names for network printers: *list* is a list
            of printer names.

FILES
        /var/spool/lp/*
        /etc/lp/*

SEE ALSO
        enable(1), lp(1)

NAME

lpsystem – register remote systems with the print service

SYNOPSIS

lpsystem [-t *type*] [-T *timeout*] [-R *retry*] [-y "*comment*"] *system-name*.br
  [*system-name* . . .]
lpsystem -l [*system-name* . . .]
lpsystem -r *system-name* [*system-name* . . .]
lpsystem -A

DESCRIPTION

The **lpsystem** command is used to define parameters for the LP print service, with respect to communication (via a high-speed network such as STARLAN or TCP/IP) with remote systems. Only a privileged user (that is, the owner of the login **root**) may execute the **lpsystem** command.

Specifically, the **lpsystem** command is used to define remote systems with which the local LP print service can exchange print requests. These remote systems are described to the local LP print service in terms of several parameters that control communication: type, retry and timeout. These parameters are defined in **/etc/lp/Systems**. You can edit this file with a text editor (such as **vi**) but editing is not recommended.

The *type* parameter defines the remote system as one of two types: **s5** (System V Release 4) or **bsd** (SunOS). The default type is **s5**.

The *timeout* parameter specifies the length of time (in minutes) that the print service should allow a network connection to be idle. If the connection to the remote system is idle (that is, there is no network traffic) for N minutes, then drop the connection. (When there is more work the connection will be reestablished.) Legal values are **n**, **0**, and N, where N is an integer greater than 0. The value **n** means "never time out"; **0** means "as soon as the connection is idle, drop it." The default is **n**.

The *retry* parameter specifies the length of time to wait before trying to reestablish a connection to the remote system, when the connection was dropped abnormally (that is, a network error). Legal values are **n**, **0**, and N, where N is an integer greater than 0 and it means "wait N minutes before trying to reconnect. (The default is 10 minutes.) The value **n** means "do not retry dropped connections until there is more work"; **0** means "try to reconnect immediately."

The *comment* argument allows you to associate a free form comment with the system entry. This is visible when **lpsystem -l** is used.

System-name is the name of the remote system from which you want to be able to receive jobs, and to which you want to be able to send jobs.

The command **lpsystem -l** [*system-name*] will print out a description of the parameters associated with *system-name* (if a system has been specified), or with all the systems in its database (if *system-name* has not been specified).

The command **lpsystem -r** *system-name* will remove the entry associated with *system-name*. The print service will no longer accept jobs from that system or send jobs to it, even if the remote printer is still defined on the local system.

The command **lpsystem -A** will print out the TCP/IP address of the local machine in a format to be used when configuring the local port monitor to accept requests from a SunOS system.

NOTES:

With respect to **/etc/lp/Systems**, this information is relatively minimal with respect to controlling network communications. Network addresses and services are handled by the **Netconfig** and **Netdir** facilities (see the "Network Services" chapter in the *System Administrator's Guide* for a discussion of network addresses and services.) Port monitors handle listening for remote service requests and routing the connection to the print service (see the "Service Access" chapter in the *System Administrator's Guide* for a discussion of port monitors.)

If the **Netconfig** and **Netdir** facilities are not set up properly, out-bound remote print service probably will not work. Similarly, if the local port monitors are not set up to route remote print requests to the print service, then service for remote systems will not be provided. (See "Allowing Remote Systems to Access Local Printers" and "Configuring a Local Port Monitor" in the "Print Service" chapter of the *System Administrator's Guide* to find out how to do this.)

With respect to the semantics of the *timeout* and *retry* values, the print service uses one process for each remote system with which it communicates, and it communicates with a remote system only when there is work to be done on that system or work being sent from that system.

The system initiating the connection is the "master" process and the system accepting the connection is the "slave" process. This designation serves only to determine which process dies (the slave) when a connection is dropped. This helps prevent there from being more than one process communicating with a remote system. Furthermore, all connections are bi-directional, regardless of the master/slave designation. You cannot control a system's master/slave designation. Now, keeping all this information in mind, if a master process times out, then both the slave and master will exit. If a slave times out, then it is possible that the master may still live and retry the connection after the retry interval. Therefore, one system's resource management strategy can effect another system's strategy.

With respect to **lpsystem -A**: a SunOS system (described with **-t bsd**) can be connected to your system only via TCP/IP, and print requests from a SunOS system can come in to your machine only via a special port (515). The address given to you from **lpsystem** will be the address of your system and port 515. This address is used by your TCP/IP port monitor (see **sacadm**(1M) and **nlsadmin**(1M)) to "listen" on that address and port, and to route connections to the print service. (This procedure is discussed in the "Service Access" chapter of the *System Administrator's Guide*.) The important point here is that this is where you get the address referred to in that procedure.

The command **lpsystem -A** will not work if your system name and IP address are not listed in **/etc/inet/hosts** and the printer service is not listed in **/etc/inet/services**.

FILES

/var/spool/lp/* /etc/lp/*

SEE ALSO

netconfig(4)

Network Programmer's Guide

System Administrator's Guide

NAME

`lptest` – generate lineprinter ripple pattern

SYNOPSIS

`/usr/ucb/lptest` [*length* [*count*]]

DESCRIPTION

`lptest` writes the traditional "ripple test" pattern on standard output. In 96 lines, this pattern will print all 96 printable ASCII characters in each position. While originally created to test printers, it is quite useful for testing terminals, driving terminal ports for debugging purposes, or any other task where a quick supply of random data is needed.

The *length* argument specifies the output line length if the the default length of 79 is inappropriate.

The *count* argument specifies the number of output lines to be generated if the default count of 200 is inappropriate.

NOTES

If *count* is to be specified, *length* must be also be specified.

This command is obsolescent.

NAME
>   lpusers – set printing queue priorities

SYNOPSIS
>   lpusers −d *priority-level*
>   lpusers −q *priority-level* −u *login-ID-list*
>   lpusers −u *login-ID-list*
>   lpusers −q *priority-level*
>   lpusers −l

DESCRIPTION
>   The **lpusers** command is used to set limits to the queue priority level that can be
>   assigned to jobs submitted by users of the LP print service.
>
>   The first form of the command (with −**d**) sets the system-wide priority default to
>   *priority-level*, where *priority-level* is a value of 0 to 39, with 0 being the highest
>   priority. If a user does not specify a priority level with a print request [see
>   **lp**(1)], the default priority is used. Initially, the default priority level is 20.
>
>   The second form of the command (with −**q** and −**u**) sets the default highest
>   *priority-level* (0-39) that the users in *login-ID-list* can request when submitting a
>   print request. The *login-ID-list* argument may include any or all of the following
>   constructs:
>
> | | |
> |---|---|
> | *login-ID* | A user on any system |
> | *system_name*!*login-ID* | A user on the system *system_name* |
> | *system_name*!**all** | All users on system *system_name* |
> | **all**!*login-ID* | A user on all systems |
> | **all** | All users on all systems |
>
>   Users that have been given a limit cannot submit a print request with a higher
>   priority level than the one assigned, nor can they change a request already
>   submitted to have a higher priority. Any print requests submitted with priority
>   levels higher than allowed will be given the highest priority allowed.
>
>   The third form of the command (with −**u**) removes any explicit priority level for
>   the specified users.
>
>   The fourth form of the command (with −**q**) sets the default highest priority level
>   for all users not explicitly covered by the use of the second form of this com-
>   mand.
>
>   The last form of the command (with −**l**) lists the default priority level and the
>   priority limits assigned to users.

SEE ALSO
>   **lp**(1) in the *User's Reference Manual*

NAME

ls – list contents of directory

SYNOPSIS

ls [–RadLCxmlnogrtucpFbqisf1] [*file . . .*]

DESCRIPTION

For each directory argument, ls lists the contents of the directory; for each *file* argument, ls repeats its name and any other information requested. The output is sorted alphabetically by default. When no argument is given, the current directory is listed. When several arguments are given, the arguments are first sorted appropriately, but file arguments appear before directories and their contents.

There are three major listing formats. The default format for output directed to a terminal is multi–column with entries sorted down the columns. The –1 option allows single column output and –m enables stream output format. In order to determine output formats for the –C, –x, and –m options, ls uses an environment variable, COLUMNS, to determine the number of character positions available on one output line. If this variable is not set, the terminfo(4) database is used to determine the number of columns, based on the environment variable TERM. If this information cannot be obtained, 80 columns are assumed.

The ls command has the following options:

–R   Recursively list subdirectories encountered.

–a   List all entries, including those that begin with a dot (.), which are normally not listed.

–d   If an argument is a directory, list only its name (not its contents); often used with –1 to get the status of a directory.

–L   When listing status, if an argument is a symbolic link, list the status of the file or directory referenced by the link rather than that of the link itself.

–C   Multi-column output with entries sorted down the columns. This is the default output format.

–x   Multi-column output with entries sorted across rather than down the page.

–m   Stream output format; files are listed across the page, separated by commas.

–1   List in long format, giving mode, number of links, owner, group, size in bytes, and time of last modification for each file (see below). If the file is a special file, the size field instead contains the major and minor device numbers rather than a size. If the file is a symbolic link, the filename is printed followed by ''->'' and the pathname of the referenced file.

–n   The same as –1, except that the owner's UID and group's GID numbers are printed, rather than the associated character strings.

–o   The same as –1, except that the group is not printed.

-g   The same as -l, except that the owner is not printed.

-r   Reverse the order of sort to get reverse alphabetic or oldest first as appropriate.

-t   Sort by time stamp (latest first) instead of by name. The default is the last modification time. (See -n and -c.)

-u   Use time of last access instead of last modification for sorting (with the -t option) or printing (with the -l option).

-c   Use time of last modification of the i-node (file created, mode changed, etc.) for sorting (-t) or printing (-l).

-p   Put a slash (/) after each filename if the file is a directory.

-F   Put a slash (/) after each filename if the file is a directory, an asterisk (*) if the file is an executable, and an ampersand (@) if the file is a symbolic link.

-b   Force printing of non-printable characters to be in the octal \ddd notation.

-q   Force printing of non-printable characters in file names as the character question mark (?).

-i   For each file, print the i-node number in the first column of the report.

-s   Give size in blocks, including indirect blocks, for each entry.

-f   Force each argument to be interpreted as a directory and list the name found in each slot. This option turns off -l, -t, -s, and -r, and turns on -a; the order is the order in which entries appear in the directory.

-1   Print one entry per line of output.

The mode printed under the -l option consists of ten characters. The first character may be one of the following:

d   the entry is a directory;
l   the entry is a symbolic link;
b   the entry is a block special file;
c   the entry is a character special file;
m   the entry is XENIX shared data (memory) file;
p   the entry is a fifo (a.k.a. "named pipe") special file;
s   the entry is a XENIX semaphore;
–   the entry is an ordinary file.

The next 9 characters are interpreted as three sets of three bits each. The first set refers to the owner's permissions; the next to permissions of others in the user-group of the file; and the last to all others. Within each set, the three characters indicate permission to read, to write, and to execute the file as a program, respectively. For a directory, "execute" permission is interpreted to mean permission to search the directory for a specified file.

ls -l (the long list) prints its output as follows:

```
-rwxrwxrwx  1 smith  dev    10876  May 16 9:42 part2
```

Reading from right to left, you see that the current directory holds one file, named **part2**. Next, the last time that file's contents were modified was 9:42 A.M. on May 16. The file contains 10,876 characters, or bytes. The owner of the file, or the user, belongs to the group **dev** (perhaps indicating "development"), and his or her login name is **smith**. The number, in this case **1**, indicates the number of links to file **part2**; see **cp**(1). Finally, the dash and letters tell you that user, group, and others have permissions to read, write, and execute **part2**.

The execute (**x**) symbol here occupies the third position of the three-character sequence. A − in the third position would have indicated a denial of execution permissions.

The permissions are indicated as follows:

r	the file is readable
w	the file is writable
x	the file is executable
−	the indicated permission is *not* granted
l	mandatory locking occurs during access (the set-group-ID bit is on and the group execution bit is off)
s	the **set-user-ID** or **set-group-ID** bit is on, and the corresponding user or group execution bit is also on
S	undefined bit-state (the set-user-ID bit is on and the user execution bit is off)
t	the 1000 (octal) bit, or sticky bit, is on [see **chmod**(1)], and execution is on
T	the 1000 bit is turned on, and execution is off (undefined bit-state)

For user and group permissions, the third position is sometimes occupied by a character other than **x** or −. **s** also may occupy this position, referring to the state of the **set**-ID bit, whether it be the user's or the group's. The ability to assume the same ID as the user during execution is, for example, used during login when you begin as root but need to assume the identity of the user you login as.

In the case of the sequence of group permissions, **l** may occupy the third position. **l** refers to mandatory file and record **l**ocking. This permission describes a file's ability to allow other files to lock its reading or writing permissions during access.

For others permissions, the third position may be occupied by **t** or **T**. These refer to the state of the sticky bit and execution permissions.

EXAMPLES

An example of a file's permissions is:

    −rwxr--r--

This describes a file that is readable, writable, and executable by the user and readable by the group and others.

Another example of a file's permissions is:

    −rwsr-xr-x

This describes a file that is readable, writable, and executable by the user, readable and executable by the group and others, and allows its user-ID to be assumed, during execution, by the user presently executing it.

Another example of a file's permissions is:

        -rw-rwl---

This describes a file that is readable and writable only by the user and the group and can be locked during access.

An example of a command line:

        ls -a

This command prints the names of all files in the current directory, including those that begin with a dot (`.`), which normally do not print.

Another example of a command line:

        ls -aisn

This command provides information on all files, including those that begin with a dot (**a**), the **i**-number—the memory address of the i-node associated with the file—printed in the left-hand column (**i**); the **s**ize (in blocks) of the files, printed in the column to the right of the i-numbers (**s**); finally, the report is displayed in the **n**umeric version of the long list, printing the UID (instead of user name) and GID (instead of group name) numbers associated with the files.

When the sizes of the files in a directory are listed, a total count of blocks, including indirect blocks, is printed.

FILES

/etc/passwd	user IDs for `ls -l` and `ls -o`
/etc/group	group IDs for `ls -l` and `ls -g`
/usr/share/lib/terminfo/?/*	terminal information database

SEE ALSO

chmod(1), find(1)

NOTES

In a Remote File Sharing environment, you may not have the permissions that the output of the `ls -l` command leads you to believe. For more information see the *System Administrator's Guide*.

Unprintable characters in file names may confuse the columnar output options.

The total block count will be incorrect if if there are hard links among the files.

NAME

ls – list the contents of a directory

SYNOPSIS

/usr/ucb/ls [–aAcCdfFgilLqrRstu1] *filename* . . .

DESCRIPTION

For each *filename* which is a directory, ls lists the contents of the directory; for each *filename* which is a file, ls repeats its name and any other information requested. By default, the output is sorted alphabetically. When no argument is given, the current directory is listed. When several arguments are given, the arguments are first sorted appropriately, but file arguments are processed before directories and their contents.

Permissions Field

The mode printed under the –l option contains 10 characters interpreted as follows. If the first character is:

d   entry is a directory;
b   entry is a block-type special file;
c   entry is a character-type special file;
l   entry is a symbolic link;
p   entry is a FIFO (also known as named pipe) special file;
s   entry is an **AF_UNIX** address family socket, or
–   entry is a plain file.

The next 9 characters are interpreted as three sets of three bits each. The first set refers to owner permissions; the next refers to permissions to others in the same user-group; and the last refers to all others. Within each set the three characters indicate permission respectively to read, to write, or to execute the file as a program. For a directory, execute permission is interpreted to mean permission to search the directory. The permissions are indicated as follows:

r   the file is readable;
w   the file is writable;
x   the file is executable;
–   the indicated permission is not granted.

The group-execute permission character is given as **s** if the file has the set-group-id bit set; likewise the owner-execute permission character is given as **s** if the file has the set-user-id bit set.

The last character of the mode (normally **x** or '–') is **true** if the 1000 bit of the mode is on. See **chmod**(1) for the meaning of this mode. The indications of set-ID and 1000 bits of the mode are capitalized (**S** and **T** respectively) if the corresponding execute permission is *not* set.

When the sizes of the files in a directory are listed, a total count of blocks, including indirect blocks is printed. The following options are available:

–a   List all entries; in the absence of this option, entries whose names begin with a '.' are *not* listed (except for the privileged user, for whom ls normally prints even files that begin with a '.').

-A   Same as −a, except that '.' and '..' are not listed.

-c   Use time of last edit (or last mode change) for sorting or printing.

-C   Force multi-column output, with entries sorted down the columns; for **ls**, this is the default when output is to a terminal.

-d   If argument is a directory, list only its name (not its contents); often used with −l to get the status of a directory.

-f   Force each argument to be interpreted as a directory and list the name found in each slot. This option turns off −l, −t, −s, and −r, and turns on −a; the order is the order in which entries appear in the directory.

-F   Mark directories with a trailing slash ('/'), executable files with a trailing asterisk ('*'), symbolic links with a trailing at-sign ('@'), and **AF_UNIX** address family sockets with a trailing equals sign ('=').

-g   For **ls**, show the group ownership of the file in a long output.

-i   For each file, print the i-node number in the first column of the report.

-l   List in long format, giving mode, number of links, owner, size in bytes, and time of last modification for each file. If the file is a special file the size field will instead contain the major and minor device numbers. If the time of last modification is greater than six months ago, it is shown in the format '*month date year*'; files modified within six months show '*month date time*'. If the file is a symbolic link the pathname of the linked-to file is printed preceded by '−>'.

-L   If argument is a symbolic link, list the file or directory the link references rather than the link itself.

-q   Display non-graphic characters in filenames as the character **?**; for **ls**, this is the default when output is to a terminal.

-r   Reverse the order of sort to get reverse alphabetic or oldest first as appropriate.

-R   Recursively list subdirectories encountered.

-s   Give size of each file, including any indirect blocks used to map the file, in kilobytes.

-t   Sort by time modified (latest first) instead of by name.

-u   Use time of last access instead of last modification for sorting (with the −t option) and/or printing (with the −l option).

-1   Force one entry per line output format; this is the default when output is not to a terminal.

FILES

/etc/passwd	to get user ID's for 'ls −l' and 'ls −o'.
/etc/group	to get group ID for 'ls −g'

NOTES

NEWLINE and TAB are considered printing characters in filenames.

The output device is assumed to be 80 columns wide.

The option setting based on whether the output is a teletype is undesirable as 'ls −s' is much different than 'ls −s | lpr'. On the other hand, not doing this setting would make old shell scripts which used ls almost certain losers.

Unprintable characters in file names may confuse the columnar output options.

NAME

ls, lc – list contents of directory

SYNOPSIS

ls [-RadLCxmlnogrtucpFbqisf1] [*names*]

lc [-1CFLRabcfgilmnopqrstux] [*name. . .*]

DESCRIPTION

For each directory argument, ls lists the contents of the directory for each file argument. lc functions the same as ls except that the lc default output format is columnar, even if the output is redirected. ls repeats its name and any other information requested. The output is sorted alphabetically by default. When no argument is given, the current directory is listed. When several arguments are given, the arguments are first sorted appropriately, but file arguments appear before directories and their contents.

There are three major listing formats. The default format for output directed to a terminal is multi–column with entries sorted down the columns. The –1 option allows single column output and –m enables stream output format. In order to determine output formats for the –C, –x, and –m options, ls uses an environment variable, **COLUMNS**, to determine the number of character positions available on one output line. If this variable is not set, the **terminfo**(4) database is used to determine the number of columns, based on the environment variable **TERM**. If this information cannot be obtained, 80 columns are assumed.

The ls command has the following options:

-R   Recursively list subdirectories encountered.

-a   List all entries, including those that begin with a dot (.), which are normally not listed.

-d   If an argument is a directory, list only its name (not its contents); often used with –1 to get the status of a directory.

-L   If an argument is a symbolic link, list the file or directory the link references rather than the link itself.

-C   Multi-column output with entries sorted down the columns. This is the default output format.

-x   Multi-column output with entries sorted across rather than down the page.

-m   Stream output format; files are listed across the page, separated by commas.

-1   List in long format, giving mode, number of links, owner, group, size in bytes, and time of last modification for each file (see below). If the file is a special file, the size field instead contains the major and minor device numbers rather than a size. If the file is a symbolic link, the filename is printed followed by "->" and the pathname of the referenced file.

-n   The same as –1, except that the owner's **UID** and group's **GID** numbers are printed, rather than the associated character strings.

-o   The same as –l, except that the group is not printed.

-g   The same as –l, except that the owner is not printed.

-r   Reverse the order of sort to get reverse alphabetic or oldest first as appropriate.

-t   Sort by time stamp (latest first) instead of by name. The default is the last modification time. (See –n and –c.)

-u   Use time of last access instead of last modification for sorting (with the –t option) or printing (with the –l option).

-c   Use time of last modification of the i-node (file created, mode changed, etc.) for sorting (–t) or printing (–l).

-p   Put a slash (/) after each filename if the file is a directory.

-F   Put a slash (/) after each filename if the file is a directory, an asterisk (*) if the file is an executable, and an ampersand (@) if the file is a symbolic link.

-b   Force printing of non-printable characters to be in the octal \ddd notation.

-q   Force printing of non-printable characters in file names as the character question mark (?).

-i   For each file, print the i-number in the first column of the report.

-s   Give size in blocks, including indirect blocks, for each entry.

-f   Force each argument to be interpreted as a directory and list the name found in each slot. This option turns off –l, –t, –s, and –r, and turns on –a; the order is the order in which entries appear in the directory.

-1   Print one entry per line of output.

The mode printed under the –l option consists of ten characters. The first character may be one of the following:

    d   the entry is a directory;
    l   the entry is a symbolic link;
    b   the entry is a block special file;
    c   the entry is a character special file;
    p   the entry is a fifo (named pipe) special file;
    –   the entry is an ordinary file.
    s   the entry is a **XENIX** semaphore.
    m   the entry is a **XENIX** shared data (memory).

The next 9 characters are interpreted as three sets of three bits each. The first set refers to the owner's permissions; the next to permissions of others in the user-group of the file; and the last to all others. Within each set, the three characters indicate permission to read, to write, and to execute the file as a program, respectively. For a directory, "execute" permission is interpreted to mean permission to search the directory for a specified file.

ls -l (the long list) prints its output as follows:

```
-rwxrwxrwx  1 smith  dev     10876  May 16 9:42 part2
```

Reading from right to left, you see that the current directory holds one file, named **part2**. Next, the last time that file's contents were modified was 9:42 A.M. on May 16. The file contains 10,876 characters, or bytes. The owner of the file, or the user, belongs to the group **dev** (perhaps indicating "development"), and his or her login name is **smith**. The number, in this case 1, indicates the number of links to file **part2**; see **cp**(1). Finally, the dash and letters tell you that user, group, and others have permissions to read, write, and execute **part2**.

The execute (**x**) symbol here occupies the third position of the three-character sequence. A – in the third position would have indicated a denial of execution permissions.

The permissions are indicated as follows:

r   the file is readable
w   the file is writable
x   the file is executable
–   the indicated permission is *not* granted
l   mandatory locking occurs during access (the set-group-ID bit is on and the group execution bit is off)
s   the set-user-ID or set-group-ID bit is on, and the corresponding user or group execution bit is also on
S   undefined bit-state (the set-user-ID bit is on and the user execution bit is off)
t   the 1000 (octal) bit, or sticky bit, is on [see **chmod**(1)], and execution is on
T   the 1000 bit is turned on, and execution is off (undefined bit-state)

For user and group permissions, the third position is sometimes occupied by a character other than **x** or –. **s** also may occupy this position, referring to the state of the **set**-ID bit, whether it be the user's or the group's. The ability to assume the same ID as the user during execution is, for example, used during login when you begin as root but need to assume the identity of the user you login as.

In the case of the sequence of group permissions, **l** may occupy the third position. **l** refers to mandatory file and record **locking**. This permission describes a file's ability to allow other files to lock its reading or writing permissions during access.

For others permissions, the third position may be occupied by **t** or **T**. These refer to the state of the sticky bit and execution permissions.

EXAMPLES

An example of a file's permissions is:

```
-rwxr--r--
```

This describes a file that is readable, writable, and executable by the user and readable by the group and others.

Another example of a file's permissions is:

    -rwsr-xr-x

This describes a file that is readable, writable, and executable by the user, readable and executable by the group and others, and allows its user-ID to be assumed, during execution, by the user presently executing it.

Another example of a file's permissions is:

    -rw-rwl---

This describes a file that is readable and writable only by the user and the group and can be locked during access.

An example of a command line:

    ls -a

This command prints the names of all files in the current directory, including those that begin with a dot (.), which normally do not print.

Another example of a command line:

    ls -aisn

This command provides information on all files, including those that begin with a dot (**a**), the i-number—the memory address of the i-node associated with the file—printed in the left-hand column (**i**); the size (in blocks) of the files, printed in the column to the right of the i-numbers (**s**); finally, the report is displayed in the numeric version of the long list, printing the UID (instead of user name) and GID (instead of group name) numbers associated with the files.

When the sizes of the files in a directory are listed, a total count of blocks, including indirect blocks, is printed.

FILES

/etc/passwd	user IDs for **ls -l** and **ls -o**
/etc/group	group IDs for **ls -l** and **ls -g**
/usr/share/lib/terminfo/?/*	terminal information database

SEE ALSO

    chmod(1), **find**(1)

NOTES

In a Remote File Sharing environment, you may not have the permissions that the output of the **ls -l** command leads you to believe. For more information see the *System Administrator's Guide*.

Unprintable characters in file names may confuse the columnar output options.

Section 4 − File Formats

SECTION 4 - FILE FORMATS

Where To Find Section 4 Manual Pages

NOTE	The Section 4 manual pages have been moved to another manual in this reference set. They are now located in the *System Files and Devices Reference Manual*.

Section 5 – Miscellaneous Facilities

Where To Find Section 5 Manual Pages

NOTE The Section 5 manual pages have been moved to another manual in this reference set. They are now located in the *System Files and Devices Reference Manual*.

1

Section 7 – Special Files

User's Reference Manual/System Administrator's Reference Manual

Where To Find Section 7 Manual Pages

NOTE	The Section 7 manual pages have been moved to another manual in this reference set. They are now located in the *System Files and Devices Reference Manual*.

Permuted Index

script rfuadmin Remote	File Sharing notification shell	rfuadmin(1M)
rumountall mount, unmount Remote	File Sharing resources rmountall,	rmountall(1M)
rfstart start Remote	File Sharing	rfstart(1M)
idload Remote	File Sharing user and group mapping	idload(1M)
number information from an object	file /table, debugging and line	strip(1)
identify processes using a file or	file structure fuser	fuser(1M)
sum calculate a checksum for a	file	sum(1)
print checksum and block count of a	file sum	sum(1)
fdp create, or restore from, a full	file system archive	fdp(1M)
create, or restore from, a full	file system archive ffile	ffile(1M)
ckbupscd check	file system backup schedule	ckbupscd(1M)
fsba	file system block analyzer	fsba(1M)
checkfsys check a	file system	checkfsys(1M)
interactive repair fsck (ufs)	file system consistency check and	fsck(1M)
fsdb (generic)	file system debugger	fsdb(1M)
fsdb (s5) s5	file system debugger	fsdb(1M)
fsdb (ufs) ufs	file system debugger	fsdb(1M)
ufsdump incremental	file system dump	ufsdump(1M)
file names and statistics for a	file system ff (generic) list	ff(1M)
file names and statistics for a ufs	file system ff (ufs) list	ff(1M)
makefsys create a	file system	makefsys(1M)
mkfs (bfs) construct a boot	file system	mkfs(1M)
mkfs (generic) construct a	file system	mkfs(1M)
mkfs (s5) construct an s5	file system	mkfs(1M)
mkfs (ufs) construct a ufs	file system	mkfs(1M)
mount (s5) mount an s5	file system	mount(1M)
umountfsys mount, unmount a	file system mountfsys,	mountfsys(1M)
quot summarize	file system ownership	quot(1M)
checker quotacheck	file system quota consistency	quotacheck(1M)
quotaon, quotaoff turn	file system quotas on and off	quotaon(1M)
repquota summarize quotas for a	file system	repquota(1M)
ufsrestore incremental	file system restore	ufsrestore(1M)
nfsstat Network	File System statistics	nfsstat(1M)
tunefs tune up an existing	file system	tunefs(1M)
fstyp (generic) determine	file system type	fstyp(1M)
(generic) make literal copy of	file system volcopy	volcopy(1M)
(s5) make a literal copy of an s5	file system volcopy	volcopy(1M)
(ufs) make a literal copy of a ufs	file system volcopy	volcopy(1M)
/umount (generic) mount or unmount	file systems and remote resources	mount(1M)
automount automatically mount NFS	file systems	automount(1M)
df report free disk space on	file systems	df(1)
free disk blocks and i-nodes for s5	file systems /(s5) report number of	df(1M)
(ufs) report free disk space on ufs	file systems df	df(1M)
time dcopy (generic) copy	file systems for optimal access	dcopy(1M)
time dcopy (s5) copy s5	file systems for optimal access	dcopy(1M)
fsck (bfs) check and repair bfs	file systems	fsck(1M)
fsck (generic) check and repair	file systems	fsck(1M)